Data Analysis Exercises

Up-to-date macro data is a great way to engage in and understand the usefulness of macro variables and their impact on the economy. Data Analysis exercises communicate directly with the Federal Reserve Bank of St. Louis's FRED site, so every time FRED posts new data, students see new data.

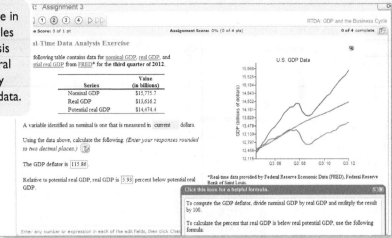

Current News Exercises

Posted weekly, we find the latest microeconomic and macroeconomic news stories, post them, and write auto-graded multi-part exercises that illustrate the economic way of thinking about the news.

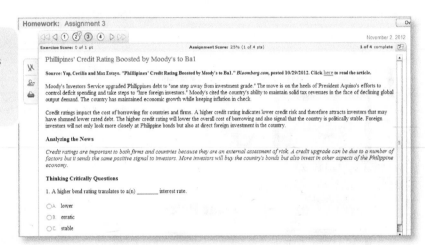

Interactive Homework Exercises

Participate in a fun and engaging activity that helps promote active learning and mastery of important economic concepts.

Pearson's experiments program is flexible and easy for instructors and students to use. For a complete list of available experiments, visit *www.myeconlab.com.*

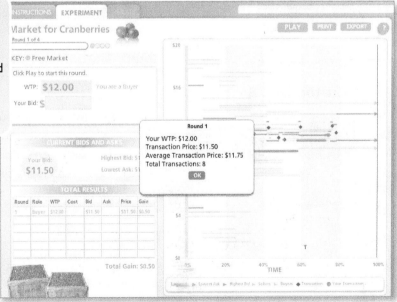

Digital

Complete **Digital** Experience

=

Allow your students to save by purchasing a stand-alone MyEconLab directly from Pearson at **www.myeconlab.com**. Pearson's industry-leading learning solution features a **full Pearson eText** and course management functionality. Most importantly, MyEconLab helps you hold students accountable for class preparation and supports more active learning styles. Visit **www.myeconlab.com** to find out more.

Instant eText Access

=

The **VitalSource CourseSmart eBookstore** provides instant, online access to the textbook and course materials students need at a lower price. VitalSource CourseSmart's eTextbooks are fully searchable and offer the same paging and appearance as the printed texts. You can preview eTextbooks online anytime at **www.coursesmart.com**.

Digital + Print

Great Content + Great **Value**

=

Package our premium bound textbook with a MyEconLab access code for the most enduring student experience. Find out more at **www.myeconlab.com**.

Great Content + Great **Price**

=

Save your students money and promote an active learning environment by offering a Student Value Edition—a three-hole-punched, full-color version of the premium textbook that's available at a 35% discount—packaged with a MyEconLab access code at your bookstore.

Custom

Customized Solutions

=

Customize your textbook to match your syllabus. Trim your text to include just the chapters you need or add chapters from multiple books. With no unused material or unnecessary expense, Pearson Learning Solutions provides the right content you need for a course that's entirely your own. **www.pearsonlearningsolutions.com**

Contact your Pearson representative for more information on Pearson Choices.

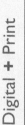

Macroeconomics

Canadian Edition

R. Glenn Hubbard
Columbia University

Anthony Patrick O'Brien
Lehigh University

Matthew Rafferty
Quinnipiac University

Jerzy (Jurek) Konieczny
Wilfrid Laurier University

Toronto

Dedication

For Constance, Raph, and Will
—R. Glenn Hubbard

For Lucy
—Anthony Patrick O'Brien

For Sacha
—Matthew Rafferty

For Joanna, Magda, Matt, and Adam
—Jerzy (Jurek) Konieczny

Editorial Director: Claudine O'Donnell
Marketing Manager: Loula March
Program Manager: Laura Pratt
Project Manager: Kimberley Blakey
Developmental Editors: Mary Wat/Martina van de Velde
Production Services: Cenveo® Publisher Services

Permissions Project Manager: Joanne Tang
Photo and Permissions Research: Lumina Datamatics
Text Permissions Research: Lumina Datamatics
Cover Design: Anthony Leung
Interior Design: Anthony Leung
Cover Image: © Martin Sundberg/Corbis

Credits and acknowledgments of material borrowed from other sources and reproduced, with permission, in this textbook appear on the pages with the respective material.

Original edition published by Pearson Education, Inc., Upper Saddle River, New Jersey, USA. Copyright © 2014 by Pearson Education, Inc. This edition is authorized for sale only in Canada.

FRED® is a registered trademark and the FRED® logo and ST. LOUIS FED are trademarks of the Federal Reserve Bank of St. Louis, **http://research.stlouisfed.org/fred2/**

Library and Archives Canada Cataloguing in Publication

Hubbard, R. Glenn, author
      Macroeconomics / R. Glenn Hubbard, Columbia University, Anthony Patrick O'Brien, Lehigh University, Matthew Rafferty, Quinnipiac University, Jerzy Konieczny, Wilfrid Laurier University.—First edition.

Includes bibliographical references and index.
ISBN 978-0-13-334919-1 (bound)

      1. Macroeconomics—Textbooks. I. O'Brien, Anthony Patrick, author
II. Rafferty, Matthew, author   III. Konieczny, Jerzy D., author   IV. Title.

HB172.5.H82 2014   339   C2014-904802-5

ISBN 13: 978-0-13-334919-1

About the Authors

Glenn Hubbard, Professor, Researcher, and Policymaker

R. Glenn Hubbard is the dean and Russell L. Carson Professor of Finance and Economics in the Graduate School of Business at Columbia University and professor of economics in Columbia's Faculty of Arts and Sciences. He is also a research associate of the National Bureau of Economic Research and a director of Automatic Data Processing, Black Rock Closed-End Funds, KKR Financial Corporation, and MetLife. Professor Hubbard received his Ph.D. in economics from Harvard University in 1983. From 2001 to 2003 he served as chair of the White House Council of Economic Advisers and chair of the OECD Economy Policy Committee, and from 1991 to 1993 he was deputy assistant secretary of the U.S. Treasury Department. He currently serves as co-chair of the nonpartisan Committee on Capital Markets Regulation and the Corporate Boards Study Group. Professor Hubbard is the author of more than 100 articles in leading journals, including *American Economic Review*; *Brookings Papers on Economic Activity*; *Journal of Finance*; *Journal of Financial Economics*; *Journal of Money, Credit, and Banking*; *Journal of Political Economy*; *Journal of Public Economics*; *Quarterly Journal of Economics*; *RAND Journal of Economics*; and *Review of Economics and Statistics*.

Tony O'Brien, Award-Winning Professor and Researcher

Anthony Patrick O'Brien is a professor of economics at Lehigh University. He received a Ph.D. from the University of California, Berkeley, in 1987. He has taught principles of economics, money and banking, and intermediate macroeconomics for more than 20 years, in both large sections and small honours classes. He received the Lehigh University Award for Distinguished Teaching. He was formerly the director of the Diamond Center for Economic Education and was named a Dana Foundation Faculty Fellow and Lehigh Class of 1961 Professor of Economics. He has been a visiting professor at the University of California, Santa Barbara, and at Carnegie Mellon University. Professor O'Brien's research has dealt with such issues as the evolution of the U.S. automobile industry, sources of U.S. economic competitiveness, the development of U.S. trade policy, the causes of the Great Depression, and the causes of black–white income differences. His research has been published in leading journals, including *American Economic Review*; *Quarterly Journal of Economics*; *Journal of Money, Credit, and Banking*; *Industrial Relations*; *Journal of Economic History*; *Explorations in Economic History*; and *Journal of Policy History*.

Matthew Rafferty, Professor and Researcher

Matthew Christopher Rafferty is a professor of economics and department chairperson at Quinnipiac University. He has also been a visiting professor at Union College. He received a Ph.D. from the University of California, Davis, in 1997 and has taught intermediate macroeconomics for 15 years, in both large and small sections. Professor Rafferty's research has focused on university and firm-financed research and development activities. In particular, he is interested in understanding how corporate governance and equity compensation influence firm research and development. His research has been published in leading journals, including the *Journal of Financial and Quantitative Analysis, Journal of Corporate Finance, Research Policy*, and the *Southern Economic Journal*. He has worked as a consultant for the Connecticut Petroleum Council on issues before the Connecticut state legislature. He has also written op-ed pieces that have appeared in several newspapers, including the *New York Times*.

Jerzy (Jurek) Konieczny, Professor and Researcher

Jerzy (Jurek) Konieczny is a professor of economics at Wilfrid Laurier University. He received a Ph.D. in 1987 from the University of Western Ontario (now Western University) in London, Ontario. He has taught macroeconomics at the intermediate and other levels, for the past 25 years. He was a visiting professor at the University of Bologna, Université libre de Bruxelles, University of Sydney, and University of Warsaw. Professor Konieczny's research has focused on price rigidities, costly price adjustment, and inflation. In particular, he is interested in the determinants of the frequency of price adjustment and why many firms change prices at regular intervals and charge round prices or prices ending in a nine. His research has been published in leading journals, including *American Economic Review; Journal of Monetary Economics; Journal of Money, Credit, and Banking; Canadian Journal of Economics; Economica;* and *Economic Inquiry.* He is the founding editor of the *Review of Economic Analysis,* an open access, general interest economic journal. He is also the director of the Rimini Centre for Economic Analysis *in Canada,* a private, non-profit organization dedicated to independent research in Applied Economics, Theoretical Economics, and related fields.

Brief Contents

Contents

Chapter 3   The Canadian Financial System   69

Chapter 4   Money and Inflation   102

Chapter 6 The Labour Market 180

Chapter 7 The Standard of Living over Time
and across Countries 204

Chapter 10   Explaining Aggregate Demand: The *IS–MP* Model   293

Chapter 11   The *IS–MP* Model: Adding Inflation and the Open Economy   333

Chapter 12   Monetary Policy in the Short Run   365

Chapter 13   Fiscal Policy in the Short Run   407

Preface

The students enrolled in today's intermediate macroeconomics courses are likely to become entrepreneurs, managers, bankers, stock brokers, accountants, lawyers, or government officials. Few of these students will pursue a Ph.D. in economics. Given this student profile, we believe it is important for the course to move from emphasizing models for their own sake to using theory to understand real-world, relevant examples and current policies that are in today's news headlines.

We believe that short-run macroeconomic policy plays too small a role in current texts. There was a time when it seemed self-evident that policy should be the focus of a course in intermediate macroeconomics. The extraordinary macroeconomic events surrounding the Great Depression, World War II, and the immediate postwar era naturally focused the attention of economists on short-run policy measures. But by the 1970s, the conventional Keynesian–neoclassical synthesis of Samuelson, Hansen, and Hicks had come to be viewed as inadequately grounded in microeconomic foundations and as paying insufficient attention to long-run considerations.

Although macroeconomic theory evolved rapidly in 1970s and 1980s, only in the 1990s did the first generation of modern intermediate textbooks appear. These new texts dramatically refocused the intermediate course. The result was a welcome emphasis on the long run and on microfoundations. The Solow growth model, rather than the Keynesian *IS–LM* model, became the linchpin of these texts.

Our Approach to Intermediate Macroeconomics

While in many ways we agree with the focus on the long run and on microfoundations, we have found ourselves in our own courses increasingly obliged to supplement existing texts with additional material, especially when discussing short-term macroeconomic policy, and especially since the Great Recession and the global financial crisis.

The Great Recession has changed how economists, students, and policymakers think about the economy. Many economists view the Great Recession and its aftermath as a watershed in macroeconomics, second only to the Great Depression. The financial crisis that precipitated the recession showed the importance of the financial system and financial regulation to macroeconomic theory and policy. The global nature of the crisis demonstrated that countries have become more connected economically and financially. The Canadian experience underscored the importance, at a time of crisis, of a well-regulated banking system and sound fiscal and monetary policies. While these features of the Canadian economy could not prevent the transmission of the recession, they helped make it milder and shorter than it was in the United States. Going into 2015, the world economy is still feeling the aftermath of the Great Recession: Unemployment in Europe is at near record high levels; several European countries as well as Japan are on the brink of another recession; interest rates in developed countries are at record lows; many countries struggle with ballooning debts; and the Canadian economy, after a relatively quick recovery from the recession, is sluggish.

The events of the past few years required a new approach to teaching macroeconomics. The main lessons are as follows:

1. The financial crisis makes it critical for students to receive more background on the financial system.
2. There should be greater emphasis on short-term macroeconomic analysis and short-term policy.
3. Students will be interested in macroeconomic models when they see them applied to understanding real-world events and current policies that are in today's news headlines.

It is important to note that our aim is certainly not to revolutionize the teaching of the intermediate macroeconomics course. Rather, we would like to shift its emphasis. We elaborate on our approach in the next sections.

Features of the Canadian Edition

The Canadian edition of the book benefits from the enthusiastic response of students and instructors who used the U.S. editions. The response confirmed our view that the market needed a text that provided more coverage of the financial system and presented a modern short-run model. The Canadian edition retains the key approach of the U.S. text while making several changes to address feedback from instructors and students and also to reflect our own classroom experiences.

The Great Recession and the Role of Current Events in the Study of Macroeconomics (Chapter 1)

The Great Recession plays a central role in the book. The first chapter contains a concise, detailed description of the developments in financial markets that led to the Great Recession, the international transmission of the recession, and its effect on Canada. We link the discussion of the Great Recession to the content in the book by adding brief summaries of book chapters. For example, the discussion of monetary policy actions in the Great Recession is followed by a brief summary of Chapter 12, "Monetary Policy in the Short Run." The discussion of the behaviour of GDP and its components during the Great Recession is followed by a brief summary of Chapter 16, "Consumption and Investment." In our experience, discussing the Great Recession at the beginning of the course increases student interest and helps students' understanding of the material. In addition, throughout the book, we focus on recent economic events. We provide numerous examples, both in the text and in special features.

A Modern Short-Run Model That Is Appropriate for the Intermediate Course (Chapters 10–13)

In many intermediate texts, the *IS—LM* model holds centre stage. The *IS—LM* model provides a useful way for instructors to present the major points of the Keynesian model of how short-run GDP is determined. By the start of this decade, however, three pedagogical shortcomings of the *IS—LM* model have become evident:

- Most importantly, the assumption of a constant money supply used in constructing the LM curve no longer describes the policy approach of the Bank of Canada or central banks from many other developed countries. Central banks target interest rates rather than the money supply, and so the LM curve is no longer as useful as it once was in discussing monetary policy.
- The LM curve is based on the trade-off between holding money and interest-earning assets. With interest rates as low as they have been in recent years, motivating the LM curve is difficult. Students do not find compelling the trade-off between cash that yields zero interest and assets that earn 1%–2% per year.
- The Keynesians versus Monetarists debates, while substantively important, are now a part of the history of macroeconomics.

In place of the *IS–LM* model, we introduce the *IS–MP* model. It replaces the LM curve with the MP curve, which represents the monetary policy of a central bank using interest rates to conduct monetary policy. The result is similar to the *IS–MP* model first suggested by David Romer. The *IS–MP* model shifts the focus from the central bank's targeting the money supply to the central bank's targeting interest rates. This change results in a more realistic approach that allows students to tie what they learn in class to the discussions they hear on the news. Many students reading texts that use the traditional *IS–LM* model are surprised to learn that the Bank of Canada has no targets for M1 or M2 and that articles in the financial press rarely discuss the money supply. At some time during the course, the Bank of Canada will make a policy announcement and students will read that the decision was whether to change the interest rate, rather than adjust the money supply. They will find it easier to understand with the *IS–MP* model and its focus on interest rates than with the LM model and its focus on the money supply.

We cover the *IS–MP* model in Chapter 10, "*IS–MP*: A Short-Run Macroeconomic Model." We include a full appendix on the *IS–LM* model at the end of the chapter for those who wish to cover that model. In Chapter 11, "The *IS–MP* Model: Adding Inflation and the Open Economy" we extend the model to include inflation and open economy considerations. We use the *IS–MP* model to analyze monetary policy in Chapter 12,"Monetary Policy in the Short Run," and fiscal policy in Chapter 13, "Fiscal Policy in the Short Run."

Significant Coverage of Financial Markets, Beginning with Chapter 3

One of the fundamental observations about conventional monetary policy is that, while the Bank of Canada has substantial influence over short-term nominal interest rates, long-term real interest rates have a much larger impact on the spending decisions of households and firms. To understand the link between nominal short-term rates and real long-term rates, students need to be introduced to the role of expectations and the term structure of interest rates. We provide a careful, but concise, discussion of the term structure in Chapter 3, "The Canadian Financial System," and follow up this discussion in Chapter 10, "Explaining Aggregate Demand: The *IS–MP* Model," and Chapter 12, "Monetary Policy in the Short Run," by analyzing why the Bank of Canada's interest rate targeting may sometimes fail to attain its goals.

Integration of International Topics (Chapters 5, 11, 12, 13)

When the crisis in subprime mortgages began in the United States, many policymakers thought it was not going to have major effects on the world economy. As it turned out, the U.S. subprime crisis devastated the economies of most of the developed world. That a problem in one part of one sector of one economy could cause a worldwide crisis is an indication that a textbook on macroeconomics must take seriously international economic linkages. We cover these linkages throughout the text, using data not just for Canada but for many other countries. We explore such issues as the dependence of the Canadian economy on the U.S. economy, the European sovereign debt crisis, and the increased coordination of monetary policy among central banks. We introduce international issues in Chapter 5, "The Global Financial System and Exchange Rates," which stresses the importance of international linkages for the economy.

Unlike in most texts, which treat the open economy separately from the closed economy, we integrate the discussion of the open economy into the relevant chapters. In Chapter 11, "The *IS–MP* Model: Adding Inflation and the Open Economy," we show how the equilibrium is determined in an open economy. In Chapter 12, "Monetary Policy in the Short Run," and in Chapter 13, "Fiscal Policy in the Short Run," we show how monetary and fiscal policies operate in the open economy. We also provide numerous international examples throughout the text, including the following:

- Hyperinflation in Zimbabwe (Chapter 4)
- Preventing Appreciation in China and Depreciation in Mexico (Chapter 5)
- Unemployment Rates around the World (Chapter 6)
- Comparison of GDP in China and Japan since 1952 (Chapter 7)
- What Explains Recent Economic Growth in India? (Chapter 8)
- Business Cycles around the World (Chapter 9)
- Deficits in G7 countries (Chapter 13)
- The European Debt Crisis: PIGS and FANGs (Chapter 15)
- Consumption and Investment around the world (Chapter 16)

Early Discussion of Long-Run Growth (Chapters 7 and 8)

Students need to be able to distinguish the macroeconomic forest—long-run growth—from the macroeconomic trees—short-run fluctuations in real GDP, employment, and the rate of inflation. Because many macroeconomic principles texts put a heavy emphasis on the short run, many students enter the intermediate macro course thinking that macroeconomics is exclusively concerned with short-run fluctuations. The extraordinary success of the market system in raising the standard of living of the average person in Canada and other developed economies comes as surprising news to many students. Students know where we are today, but the economic explanation of how we got here is unfamiliar to many of them.

In addition, it makes sense to us for students to first understand both a basic model of long-run growth and the determination of GDP in a flexible-price model before moving on to the discussion of short-run fluctuations and short-run policy. In Chapter 7, "The Standard of Living over Time and across Countries," we show the determination of GDP in a classical model and also discuss the difference between flexible-price models and fixed price models. We place this discussion in a broader context of the reallocation of resources. Chapter 8, "Long-Run Economic Growth," provides a concise step-by-step introduction to the Solow growth model and to endogenous growth models, including the AK growth models. The chapter explains how policy affects the growth rate of the standard of living. Both chapters integrate information about China, India, and other developing countries to illustrate applications of the models we discuss.

Modern Monetary Policy and Its Broadened Emphasis beyond Interest Rate Targeting (Chapters 4, 12, and 14)

The developments of the Great Recession have demonstrated the need to move monetary policy beyond the focus on interest rates, which had dominated policy since 1980s. To understand the broader reach of monetary policy, students need to be introduced to material that is largely missing from competing texts, in particular the increased importance of investment banking and role of securitization in modern financial markets. In addition, monetary policy decisions during the Great Recession require extended discussion of issues of moral hazard. While these discussions are common in money and banking texts, they have been largely ignored in intermediate macro texts. We cover these topics in Chapter 4, "Money and Inflation," Chapter 12,"Monetary Policy in the Short Run," and Chapter 14, "Aggregate Demand, Aggregate Supply, and Monetary Policy."

Flexible Chapter Organization

We have written the text to provide instructors with considerable flexibility. Instructors who wish to emphasize the short run can begin by covering Chapters 1–5 (Part 1, "Introduction" and Part 2, "The Financial System"), and perhaps Chapter 6, "The Labour Market", and then jump to Chapters 9–15 (Part 4, "Macroeconomics in the Short Run: Theory and Policy"), before covering Chapters 6–8 (Part 3, "Macroeconomics in the Long Run"). We have arranged content so that Chapters 9–15 can be taught without Chapters 6–8. If time is insufficient, the last two chapters can also be skipped.

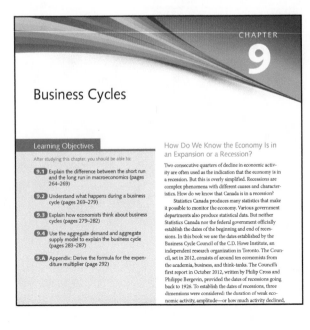

Special Features

We have developed a number of special features. Some are similar to the features that have proven popular and effective aids to learning in both Hubbard, O'Brien, Serletis, and Childs *Principles of Economics* and Hubbard and O'Brien *Money, Banking, and the Financial System*, while others were developed specifically for this book.

Contemporary Opening Cases

A common complaint among students is that economics is too dry and abstract. At the intermediate level, students will inevitably have to learn a greater amount of model building and algebra than they encountered in their first-year course. Nevertheless, a real-world approach can keep students interested. We open each chapter with a real-world example—drawn from either policy issues in the news or the business world—to help students begin the chapter with a greater understanding that the material to be covered is directly relevant. We revisit the examples within chapters to reinforce the link between macroeconomics and the real world. The introductory stories are

- "How Do We Know When We Are in a Recession?" (Chapter 2, "Measuring the Macroeconomy")
- "Why Is the Canadian Banking System the Best in the World?" (Chapter 3, "The Canadian Financial System")
- "Working for Peanuts?" (Chapter 4, "Money and Inflation")
- "Why Are Prices Higher in Canada than in the United States?" (Chapter 5, "The Global Financial System and Exchange Rates")
- "Firms Have Trouble Finding Workers; So Why Is the Unemployment Rate so High?" (Chapter 6, "The Labour Market")
- "Who Is Number One?" (Chapter 7, "The Standard of Living over Time and across Countries")
- "The Surprising Economic Rise of India" (Chapter 8, "Long-Run Economic Growth")
- "How Do We Know the Economy Is in an Expansion or a Recession?" (Chapter 9, "Business Cycles")
- "The Great Recession and the Policy Response" (Chapter 10, "Explaining Aggregate Demand: The *IS–MP* Model")
- "Where's the Inflation?" (Chapter 11, "The *IS–MP* Model: Adding Inflation and the Open Economy")
- "Why Didn't the Federal Reserve and the Bank of Canada Avoid the Great Recession?" (Chapter 12, "Monetary Policy in the Short Run")
- "How Canada Eliminated the Deficit" (Chapter 13, "Fiscal Policy in the Short Run")
- "Did Central Banks Create and Kill the Great Moderation?" (Chapter 14, "Aggregate Demand, Aggregate Supply, and Monetary Policy")
- "Drowning in a Sea of Debt?" (Chapter 15, "Fiscal Policy and the Government Budget in the Long Run")
- "Are All Tax Cuts Created Equal?" (Chapter 16, "Consumption and Investment")

Making the Connection Feature

Each chapter includes *Making the Connection* features that provide real-world reinforcement of key concepts and help students learn how to interpret what they read on the web and in newspapers. *Making the Connection* features use relevant, stimulating, and provocative news stories, many focused on pressing policy issues. Here are some examples:

- Why Should Canada Worry about the "Euro Crisis"? (Chapter 1)
- Is the Inflation Rate around the World Going to Increase in the Near Future? (Chapter 4)
- Will China's Standard of Living Ever Exceed that of Canada? (Chapter 8)
- Can There Be Too Much R&D? (Chapter 8)
- How Big Is the Multiplier? Is it the Same in Recessions and Expansions? (Chapter 9)
- Can Nominal Interest Rates Be Negative? (Chapter 12)
- Bank Crises and the Severity of the Great Recession (Chapter 13)
- The European Debt Crisis: PIGS and FANGS (Chapter 15)
- Record Household Debt in Canada (Chapter 16)

Making the Connection

How Expensive Gold Really Is

Gold has been used as money for a long time. The main reason is that it is very valuable. Indeed, it is so valuable that to describe something that is very expensive (or metaphorically invaluable), we can say it is "worth its weight in gold."

Just how valuable is gold? Disregarding antiques and jewellery, at the mid-2014 average price of US$1300 per troy ounce (31.1 grams), few things are literally worth their weight in gold. The most expensive iPhone 6 (129 grams, US$849) costs about 1/6th, and Google Glass (50 grams, $1500) costs 3/4 of its weight in gold.

The value of gold is, however, often exaggerated. In the 1995 movie *Die Hard with Vengeance*, the bad guys steal $140 billion dollars worth of gold from the vault of the Federal Reserve Bank of New York. There is, indeed, a lot of gold in the vault of the Federal Reserve Bank of New York. The bank belongs to the Federal Reserve System, the U.S. central bank. On behalf of the Fed it provides custodial services for gold owned by other central banks. In 2012 it held 6700 tonnes of gold. So far so good: If you are wondering where a huge amount of gold can be stolen from, the Federal Reserve Bank of New York is a prime candidate. (Note, however, that breaking into their vault may be difficult. Their security is described here: www.newyorkfed.org/aboutthefed/goldvault.html.)

In the movie the bad guys steal US$140 billion worth of gold and transport the gold in 14 dump trucks. Would that be possible, or is it a Hollywood exaggeration? Let us check. In 1995 the average price of gold was about US$385[4] per troy ounce or US$12 380 per kilogram. (An ounce equals 31.1 grams or 0.0311 kg; a kilogram of gold cost US$385/0.0311 = US$12 380.) The amount of gold stolen would have weighed approximately 11 309 tonnes (i.e., US$140 billion/(US$12 380/kg) = 11 309 091 kg = 11 309 tonnes). If it was divided equally among 14 trucks, each would have to transport over 800 tonnes. This is three times more than the capacity of the biggest truck in the world and about 50 times as much as a standard dump truck can carry. Gold is valuable but not *that* valuable.

See related problem 1.6 at the end of the chapter.

Solved Problem 5.3

Making a Financial Killing by Buying Chilean Bonds?

In September 2013 the interest rate on Canadian 1-year bonds was 1.09%; the interest rate on Chilean 1-year bonds was 4.93%. Could you make money by borrowing in Canada and putting the proceeds in Chilean bonds? Evaluate this investment strategy.

Solving the Problem

Step 1 Review the chapter material. This problem is about the role exchange rates play in explaining differences in interest rates across countries, so you may want to review the section "The Interest Parity Condition," which begins on page 126.

Step 2 Answer the question by using the interest parity condition to explain the relationship between expected changes in exchange rates and differences in interest rates across countries. If the interest parity condition holds, then a 3.84-percentage-point gap between the interest rate on a Canadian and Chilean government bond means that investors must be expecting that the value of the Canadian dollar will appreciate against the peso by 3.84%.

We can also mention a few real-world complications: Although the Canadian government can borrow money for one year at 1.09%, a private investor would have to pay a significantly higher interest rate to compensate lenders for the investor's higher default risk. Similarly, the interest parity condition holds only when investors see the two bonds being compared as having the same characteristics. In fact, investors will see the Chilean bond as having higher default risk and lower liquidity than Canadian bonds. So, a part of the gap between the two interest rates represents compensation for these characteristics of the Chilean bond rather than expectations of future changes in the exchange rate. In addition, by investing in Chile, a Canadian investor will be taking on exchange rate risk because the Canadian dollar could appreciate by more than the 3.84%, which would cause the investor to earn a lower return on Chilean bonds than on Canadian bonds.

So the short answer to the question is that, while the interest rate on Chilean bonds is higher than on Canadian bonds, the difference reflects expectations of changes in the exchange rate as well as other factors so that you are unlikely to make a killing by borrowing in Canada and putting the proceeds in Chilean bonds.

See related problems 3.8 at the end of the chapter.

Macro Data: Is the Decline of Industries that Produce Goods a Recent Phenomenon?

Industries that produce goods, such as cars, computers, and appliances, have become less important over time as a share of both GDP and total employment in Canada as well as in other high-income countries. At the same time, the share of services, such as haircuts or investment advice, has become more important.

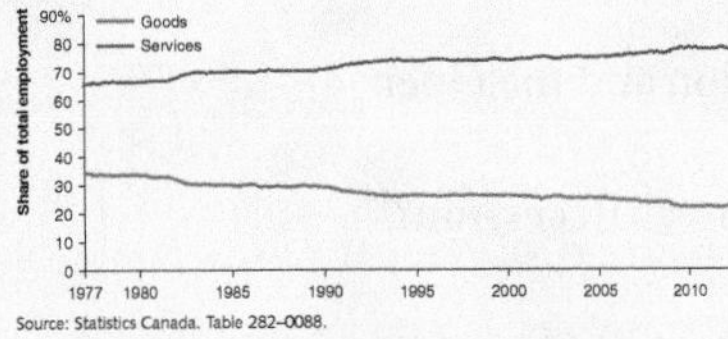

The figure shows that in Canada the percentage of workers in goods-producing industries decreased from 35% of total employment in April 1976 to 22% in August 2013. Goods-producing industries have been in relative decline since the end of World War II in 1945, a trend that seems unlikely to be reversed. Although the *relative* share of employment in goods-producing industries has declined, the *absolute number* of workers employed in these industries has increased. Employment in goods-producing industries increased from 3.37 million workers in April 1976 to 3.92 million workers in August 2013. This increase, though, is much smaller than the increase in employment in services-producing industries, which grew from 6.36 million workers in April 1976 to 13.84 million workers in August 2013.

What explains the decline in the share of employment in goods-producing industries? Given that the decline dates back at least as far as the 1940s, recent developments, such as competition from China or other effects of globalization,

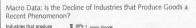

Source: Statistics Canada. Table 282–0088.

cannot be the main cause. Instead, many economists believe that the decreasing importance of the goods-producing sector is likely due to productivity growth being much faster in goods-producing industries than in service-producing industries. For example, it still takes just as many members of an orchestra to play Beethoven's Ninth Symphony in 2013 as it did in 1945. However, each manufacturing worker is much more productive today than 40 years ago. As a result, the need for manufacturing workers has not grown as rapidly as the need for service workers.

The figure illustrates another important point: using employment as the measure, Canada has been a service economy for a long time. In fact, services employment in 1976 was actually greater than goods employment in 2013, despite the growth in the economy and the population over the intervening 37 years.

See related problem D6.1 at the end of the chapter.

Avoiding a Common Mistake: a Movement along or a Shift in the Curve

Sometimes, when analyzing a model, students find it difficult to determine whether a change in a variable involves a movement along a curve, or a shift in the curve. This is actually easy to figure out as long as you remember what is on the axes. The rule is simple:

• If the variable that changes is on either axis, it is a movement along the curve.
• If the variable that changes is not on either axis, it is a shift of the curve

We can use the rule to look at the money demand curve. A change in the nominal interest rate, or in the quantity of money, involves a movement along a given money demand curve. A change in any other variable, for example in income or the price level, involves a shift of the curve.

The reason students have problems is that sometimes we draw a similar curve with another variable on the axis. For example, we can draw the money demand curve to show quantity demanded as a function of income. It will be a positively sloped curve: The higher the level of income, the higher the quantity of money demanded. It is illustrated in the figure below. To avoid confusion, we denote the money demand curve drawn as a function of income as MD(Y).

With the money demand curve drawn this way, a change in income, or in the quantity of money, involve a movement along the curve; a change in the nominal interest rate or a change in the price level involves a shift in the curve, as illustrated in the figure.

So whether a change in a variable leads to a movement along a curve or a shift of the curve depends on the context, whether the variable is on the axis or not. As long as you remember the variables on the axes, you will not make a mistake!

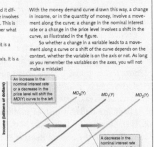

An increase in the nominal interest rate or a decrease in the price level will shift the MD(Y) curve to the left

A decrease in the nominal interest rate or an increase in the price level will shift the MD(Y) curve to the right

Income (billions of dollars)

Quantity of Money, M (billions of dollars)

Useful Math 4.2
Calculating the percentage change of a product or a ratio

There are simple and easy-to-remember formulas that relate variables to their percentage changes. We denote percentage change in variable X as %ΔX.

1. The percentage change of the product of two variables is equal to the sum of their percentage changes:

$$\%\Delta(XY) = \%\Delta X + \%\Delta Y.$$

2. The percentage change of a ratio is equal to the difference of percentage changes:

$$\%\Delta\left(\frac{X}{Y}\right) = \%\Delta X - \%\Delta Y.$$

These simple equations are often useful in assessing economic or business performance. For example, in 2012 nominal GDP in Canada grew by 3.1% [%Δ(P · Y) = 3.1%] while prices (GDP deflator) increased by 1.3% (%ΔP = 1.3%). Nominal GDP = P · Y so, using the first formula, %Δ(Nominal GDP) = %ΔP + %ΔY. Substituting the values, we obtain 3.1% = 1.3% + %ΔY and so %ΔY = 1.8%; real GDP increased 1.8%.

For another example consider Tim Hortons. It is a multi-franchise company that can grow by increasing the sales per franchise or by increasing the number of franchises. Increasing sales per franchise (called intensive

growth) is preferred to increasing the number of franchises (extensive growth). Last year total sales increased by 2%. Is it a good result? It depends on what happened with the number of franchises. The number of franchises increased by 3%. Denote the average sales per franchise by S, total sales by T, and the number of franchises by N. Since S = T/N, so, using the second equation, %ΔS = %ΔT − %ΔN = 2% − 3% = −1%. While total sales grew by 2%, this was the result of extensive growth. Sales per franchise fell by 1%, not a good thing.

Practice Question
As we will see in Chapter 5, the real exchange rate is equal to the nominal exchange rate multiplied by the domestic price level and divided by the foreign price level. We denote the nominal exchange rate as E. Using symbols:

$$\text{real exchange rate} = E \cdot \text{domestic}/\text{foreign}$$

(a) Calculate the rate of change of the real exchange rate.

(b) If the real exchange rate is constant, the nominal exchange rate appreciates 2% per year and domestic inflation is 2% per year, what is foreign inflation?

Solved Problem Feature

Including solved problems in the text of each chapter may be the most popular pedagogical innovation in the book. Students have fully learned the concepts and theories only when they are capable of applying them in solving problems. Certainly, most instructors expect students to solve problems on examinations. Our *Solved Problems* highlight one or two important concepts in each chapter and provide students with step-by-step guidance in solving them. Each *Solved Problem* is reinforced by a related problem at the end of the chapter. Students can complete related *Solved Problems* on MyEconLab and receive tutorial help. Here are examples of the *Solved Problems* in the book:

• 1.1, "Do Rising Imports Lead to a Permanent Reduction in Canadian Employment?"
• 2.1, "Calculating Real GDP"
• 3.1, "Interest Rates and Bond Prices"
• 6.2, "How Many Jobs Does the Canadian Economy Create Every Month?"
• 7.1, "Calculating the Marginal Product of Labour and the Marginal Product of Capital"
• 8.1, "Finding the Steady-State Levels of the Capital, Output, Consumption, Investment, and Depreciation per Person"
• 10.2, "Using the *IS–MP* Model to Analyze the GST Tax Cut"
• 16.1, "Effects of a Temporary Tax Cut on Consumption"

Macro Data Feature

Some chapters include a *Macro Data* feature that explains the sources of macroeconomic data and often cites recent studies using data. This feature helps students apply data to a recent event. An exercise related to each feature appears at the end of the chapter so instructors can test students' understanding. Examples include the following:

• Is the Decline of Industries that Produce Goods a Recent Phenomenon? (Chapter 6)
• Do High Rates of Saving and Investment Lead to High Levels of Income? (Chapter 8)
• Does the Bank of Canada Manage to Keep the Overnight Rate near the Target? (Chapter 12)
• Are Oil Supply Shocks Really That Important? (Chapter 14)
• Do Government Deficits Increase Real Interest Rates? (Chapter 15)

Avoiding a Common Mistake and Useful Math Features

After many years of teaching economics, we can identify some common mistakes that students make. There are different reasons for the mistakes: difficulty of economic concepts, misunderstanding of relationships between variables, or the fact that economic terms are not consistently used in popular media sources. While most students have few problems, alerting students to potential errors improves learning outcomes. We also added a few *Useful Math* features that help with understanding formula derivations. Examples of these features include the following:

• Interest Rates and Bond Prices Once Again (Chapter 3)
• A Movement along or a Shift in the Curve (Chapter 3)
• Calculating the Percentage Change of a Product or a Ratio (Chapter 4)
• Changes in the Actual Inflation Rate and the Fisher Effect (Chapter 4)
• Overvaluation, Devaluation, and Depreciation (Chapter 5)
• Calculating Bond Returns in Different Currencies (Chapter 5)

End-of-Chapter Problems, Data Exercises, Learning Objectives, and the Award-Winning MyEconLab

Each chapter ends with a *Key Terms* list, *Review Questions*, *Problems and Applications*, and *Data Exercises*. The problems are written to be fully compatible with MyEconLab, an online course management, testing, and tutorial resource. Using MyEconLab, students can complete select end-of-chapter problems online, get tutorial help, and receive instant feedback and assistance on the exercises they answer incorrectly. Instructors can access sample tests, study plan exercises, tutorial resources, and an online Gradebook to keep track of student performance and time spent on the exercises. MyEconLab has been a successful component of the Hubbard and O'Brien *Economics* and *Money, Banking, and the Financial System* texts because it helps students improve their grades and helps instructors manage class time.

The *Review Questions* and *Problems and Applications* are grouped under learning objectives. The goals of this organization are to make it easier for instructors to assign problems based on learning objectives, both in the book and in MyEconLab, and to help students efficiently review material that they find difficult. If students have difficulty with a particular learning objective, an instructor can easily identify which end-of-chapter questions and problems support that objective and assign them as homework or discuss them in class.

End-of-chapter problems test students' understanding of the content presented in each *Solved Problem*, *Making the Connection*, *Macro Data*, and chapter opener. Instructors can cover a feature in class and assign the corresponding problem for homework. The Test Item File also includes test questions that pertain to these special features.

Each chapter ends with several data exercises which involve collecting and analyzing macroeconomic data. The exercises direct students to macroeconomic data sources from Statistics Canada, other statistical offices, and international organizations, including the International Monetary Fund, the OECD, and the World Bank. By doing data exercises students will become familiar with these data sources, providing a useful base for their future empirical courses.

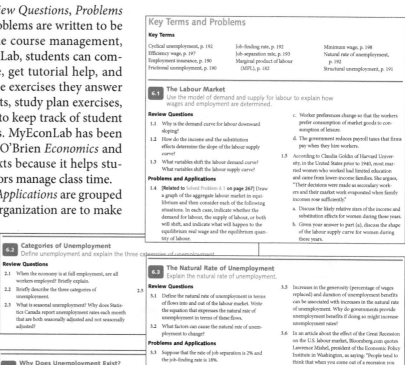

Supplements

The authors and Pearson Education have worked together to integrate the text, print, and media resources to make teaching and learning easier.

MyEconLab

MyEconLab is a powerful assessment and tutorial system that works hand in hand with *Macroeconomics*. MyEconLab includes comprehensive homework, quiz, test, and tutorial options, allowing instructors to manage all assessment needs in one program. Key innovations in the MyEconLab course for *Macroeconomics*, Canadian edition, include the following:

- *Data Analysis Exercises* allow students and instructors to use the very latest data from FRED®, the online macroeconomic data bank from the Federal Reserve Bank of St. Louis.

By completing the exercises, students become familiar with a key data source, learn how to locate data, and develop skills to interpret data.

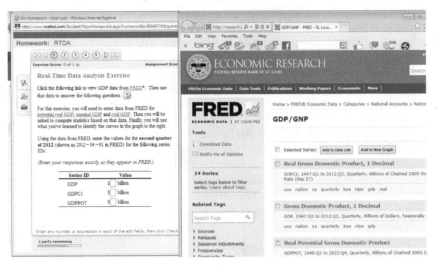

- In the eText available in MyEconLab, select figures are labelled.

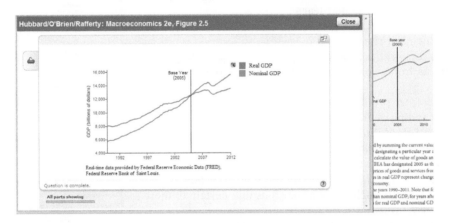

- Current News Exercises, new to this edition of the MyEconLab course, provide a turnkey way to assign gradable news-based exercises in MyEconLab. Every week, Pearson scours the news, finds a current article appropriate for the macroeconomics course, creates an exercise around this news article, and then automatically adds it to MyEconLab. Assigning and grading current news-based exercises that deal with the latest macro events and policy issues has never been more convenient.

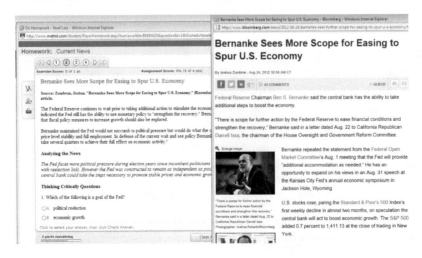

Other features of MyEconLab include the following:

- All end-of-chapter Questions and Problems, including algorithmic, graphing, and numerical questions and problems, are available for student practice or instructor assignment. Test Item File multiple-choice questions are available for assignment as homework.
- The Custom Exercise Builder allows instructors the flexibility of creating their own problems or modifying existing problems for assignment.
- The powerful Gradebook records each student's performance and time spent on the Tests and Study Plan, and generates reports by student or chapter.

A more detailed walk-through of the student benefits and features of MyEconLab can be found on the inside front cover of this book. Visit **www.pearsonmylabandmastering.com** for more information on and an online demonstration of instructor and student features.

Access to MyEconLab can be bundled with your printed text or purchased directly with or without the full eText at **www.pearsonmylabandmastering.com**.

Instructor's Manual

The *Instructor's Manual* includes chapter-by-chapter summaries, key term definitions, teaching outlines with teaching tips, and solutions to all review questions and problems in the book. The *Instructor's Manual* is available for download from **www.pearsonmylabandmastering.com**.

Test Item File

The Test Item File includes more than 1000 multiple-choice, short-answer, and essay questions. Test questions are annotated with the following information:

- **Difficulty:** 1 for straight recall, 2 for some analysis, and 3 for complex analysis
- **Type:** Multiple-choice, short-answer, and essay
- **Topic:** The term or concept that the question supports
- **Learning objective:** The major sections of the main text and its end-of-chapter questions and problems are organized by learning objective. The Test Item File questions continue with this organization to make it easy for instructors to assign questions based on the objective they wish to emphasize.
- **The Association to Advance Collegiate Schools of Business (AACSB) Assurance of Learning Standards:** Following the AACSB's learning objectives, these standards emphasize Communication; Ethical Reasoning; Analytic Skills; Use of Information Technology; Multicultural and Diversity; and Reflective Thinking.
- **Page number:** The page in the main text where the answer appears allows instructors to direct students to where supporting content appears.
- **Special feature in the main book:** Select questions support the chapter-opening vignette, the *Solved Problem*, *Making the Connection*, and *Macro Data*.

The Test Item File is available for download from **www.pearsonmylabandmastering.com**.

The multiple-choice questions in the Test Item File are also available in TestGen software for both Windows and Mac computers, and questions can be assigned via MyEconLab. The computerized TestGen package allows instructors to customize, save, and generate classroom tests. The TestGen program permits instructors to edit, add, or delete questions from the Test Item Files; analyze test results; and organize a database of tests and student results. This software allows for extensive flexibility and ease of use. It provides many options for organizing and displaying tests, along with search and sort features. The software and the Test Item Files can be downloaded from **www.pearsonmylabandmastering.com**.

PowerPoint Lecture Presentation

Instructors can use the PowerPoint slides for class presentations, and students can use them for lecture preview or review. These slides include all the graphs, tables, and equations from the textbook.

Student versions of the PowerPoint slides are available as PDF files in MyEconLab. These files allow students to print the slides and bring them to class for note taking. Instructors can download these PowerPoint presentations from **www.pearsonmylabandmastering.com**.

Instructors CourseSmart goes beyond traditional expectations—providing instant, online access to the textbooks and course materials you need at a lower cost for students. And even as students save money, you can save time and hassle with a digital eTextbook that allows you to search for the most relevant content at the very moment you need it. Whether it's evaluating textbooks or creating lecture notes to help students with difficult concepts, CourseSmart can make life a little easier. See how when you visit **www.coursesmart.com/instructors**.

Students CourseSmart goes beyond traditional expectations—providing instant, online access to the textbooks and course materials you need at an average savings of 50%. With instant access from any computer and the ability to search your text, you'll find the content you need quickly, no matter where you are. And with online tools like highlighting and note-taking, you can save time and study efficiently. See all the benefits at **www.coursesmart.com/students**.

Reviewers and Other Contributors

The guidance and recommendations of the following instructors helped us to revise the content and organization of this text:

Iris Au, University of Toronto

Kenneth I. Carlaw, University of British Columbia

Patrick Coe, Carleton University

Mehmet Dalkir, University of New Brunswick

Joseph DeJuan, University of Waterloo

Daniel DeMunnik, Dalhousie University

Mustapha Ibn Boamah, University of New Brunswick

Laura Lamb, Thompson Rivers University

Mykhaylo Oystrakh, University of Waterloo

Charlene Richter, British Columbia Institute of Technology

Gabriela Sabau, Memorial University

Greg Tkacz, St. Francis Xavier University

Andrew Wong, University of Alberta

While we could not incorporate every suggestion from every reviewer, we carefully considered each piece of advice we received. We are grateful for the hard work that went into their reviews and truly believe that their feedback was indispensable in revising this text. We appreciate their assistance in making this the best text it could be; they have helped teach a new generation of students about the exciting world of macroeconomics.

A Word of Thanks

We benefited greatly from the dedication and professionalism of the Pearson Economics team. Editorial Director Claudine O'Donnell is an enthusiastic proponent of modernizing the intermediate course. Claudine's energy was contagious and she provided support and encouragement at every stage of the process. Developmental Editors Maurice Esses, Mary Wat, and Martina van de Velde provided excellent help in organization and coordination. Program Manager Joel Gladstone and Project Manager Kimberley Blakey complemented the outstanding Pearson Economics team. Freelance editor Cat Haggert worked tirelessly to improve the clarity and eliminate errors. Ioan Ilea provided excellent and efficient research assistance. Finally, a good part of the burden of a project of this magnitude is borne by our families, and we appreciate their patience, support, and encouragement.

PART ONE: INTRODUCTION

Introduction to Macroeconomics and the Great Recession

Learning Objectives

After studying this chapter, you will:

1.1 Become familiar with the focus of macroeconomics and basic facts about the Canadian and other economies (pages 2–13).

1.2 Be able to explain how economists approach macroeconomic questions (pages 13–18).

1.3 Become familiar with the Great Recession and link the analysis of the Great Recession to the material covered in the book (pages 18–37).

When You Enter the Job Market Can Matter a Lot

If you could choose a year to be born, 1985 or 1986 would have been pretty good choices because you might have graduated college and entered the job market in 2007. You would have entered the labour force when the economy was expanding. The stock market was booming, and unemployment was low and declining. The unemployment rate for people with bachelor's degrees was 3.8%. As stock prices soared, many people felt wealthier than ever before.

If you were born in 1988 or 1989, you would be less lucky. You would have graduated and entered the job market in 2010, when unemployment was high and stock prices fell. While the **Great Recession** in Canada was relatively short, finding a job in 2010 was much harder than a few years earlier. The unemployment rate for people with bachelor's degrees was 5.5%. So, even if you had planned to work after graduation, you may have ended up going to graduate school to improve your job prospects.

The Canadian economy endured a brief but serious recession in 2008–2009, with substantial decline in income, numerous company closings, and a reduction in employment of almost 3% between October 2008 and August 2009. Sales of houses and cars fell significantly. Share prices were well below their levels of a few years earlier, which meant that hundreds of billions of dollars of wealth had been wiped out. Clearly, this was not the best of times to enter the labour force.

The Canadian economy has its ups and downs, and the consequences of the ups and downs can significantly affect people's lives. For instance, a recent study found that college students who graduate during an economic recession have to search longer to find a job, and end up

Continued on next page

accepting jobs that, on average, pay 9% less than the jobs accepted by students who graduate during economic expansions. What is more, students who graduate during recessions will continue to earn less for 8 to 10 years after they graduate. On the other hand, strong expansions result in rising income, profits, and employment. Searching for a job or starting a new business is a lot easier during a strong expansion than during a recession or a weak expansion. Clearly, understanding why the economy experiences periods of recession and expansion is important.

See related problem 1.8 at the end of the chapter.

Sources: Philip Oreopoulos, Till von Wachter, and Andrew Heisz, "The Short- and Long-Term Career Effects of Graduating in a Recession," *American Economic Journal: Applied Economic*s, 4, no. 1(2012): 1–29; and Statistics Canada, CANSIM Tables 281–0047 and 282–0004.

Introduction

Great Recession
The recession that started in the United States in 2007 and spread around the world. Also called the **Global Financial Crisis**. The most severe recession in many countries since the Great Depression (1929–33).

How can we understand these fluctuations in the economy? By learning *macroeconomics*. Economics is traditionally divided into the fields of microeconomics and macroeconomics. **Microeconomics** is the study of how households and firms make choices, how they interact in markets, and how the government attempts to influence their choices. **Macroeconomics** is the study of the economy as a whole, including topics such as inflation, unemployment, and economic growth. Both microeconomics and macroeconomics study important issues, but the Great Recession made macroeconomic issues seem particularly pressing. Although economic theory has the reputation for being dull, there was nothing dull about the Great Recession, which had a major impact on millions of families and thousands of firms.

Microeconomics The study of how households and firms make choices, how they interact in markets, and how the government attempts to influence their choices.

Macroeconomics The study of the economy as a whole, including topics such as inflation, unemployment, and economic growth.

Many students open an economics textbook and think, "Do I have to memorize all these graphs and equations? How am I going to use this stuff?" Once the final exam is over (at last!) everything learned is quickly forgotten. And it should be forgotten, because economics as an undigested lump of graphs and equations has no value. Graphs and equations are tools; if they are not used for their intended purpose, then they have no more value than a blunt pair of scissors forgotten in the back of a drawer. We have to admit that this textbook has its share of graphs you should know and equations you should understand. But no more than are necessary. When we present you with a tool, we use it, and we show you how to use it. Our intention is for you to remember these tools long after the final exam, even if this is the last economics course you ever take. With these tools, you can make sense of things that will have a huge effect on your life. Studying macroeconomics will be less of a chore if you keep in mind that *by learning this material you will come to understand how and why economic events affect you, your family, and the well-being of people around the world.*

What Macroeconomics Is About

1.1

Learning Objective
Become familiar with the focus of macroeconomics and the basic facts about the Canadian and other economies.

In this text, we will analyze the macroeconomics of the Canadian and world economies. This section provides you with an overview of some of the important ideas about macroeconomics. We will discuss these ideas in more detail in the following chapters.

Macroeconomics in the Short Run and in the Long Run

The key macroeconomic issue of the short run—a period of a few years—is different from the key macroeconomic issue of the long run—a period of decades or more. In the short run, macroeconomic analysis focuses on the **business cycle**, which refers to alternating periods of *economic expansion* and *economic recession* experienced by the Canadian and other economies. The Canadian economy has experienced periods of expanding production and employment, followed by periods of recession during which production and employment decline. The business cycle is not uniform: Each period of expansion is not the same length, nor is each period of recession.

Business cycle Alternating periods of economic expansion and economic recession.

For the long run, the focus of macroeconomics switches from the business cycle to **long-run economic growth**, which is the process by which increasing productivity and capital stock raises the average standard of living. A successful economy is capable of increasing production of goods and services faster than the growth in population. Increasing production faster than population growth is the only lasting way that the standard of living of the average person in a country can rise. Achieving this outcome is possible only through increases in *labour productivity*. **Labour productivity** is the quantity of goods and services that can be produced by one worker or by one hour of work.

Unfortunately, many economies around the world are not growing at all or are growing very slowly. In some countries in sub-Saharan Africa, living standards are barely higher, or are even lower, than they were 50 years ago. Many people in these countries live in the same grinding poverty as their ancestors did. In Canada, other developed countries, and many developing countries, however, living standards are much higher than they were 50 or 100 years ago. An important macroeconomic topic is why some countries grow much faster than others.

As we will see, one determinant of economic growth is the ability of firms to expand their operations, buy additional equipment, train workers, and adopt new technologies. To carry out these activities, firms must acquire funds from households, either directly through financial markets—such as the stock and bond markets—or indirectly through financial intermediaries—such as banks. Financial markets and financial intermediaries together comprise the *financial system*. As we will see in later chapters, the financial system has become an increasingly important part of the study of macroeconomics. Indeed, the well-functioning Canadian financial system helped make the Great Recession moderate compared to other countries. On the other hand, problems in the financial system caused the Great Recession to be severe in the United States and some European countries.

The focus of this book is the exploration of these two key aspects of macroeconomics: the long-run growth that has steadily raised living standards in Canada and some other countries and the short-run fluctuations of the business cycle.

Long-run economic growth The process by which increasing productivity raises the average standard of living.

Labour productivity The quantity of goods and services that can be produced by one worker or by one hour of work.

Long-Run Growth in Canada

By current standards, nearly everyone in the world was poor not very long ago. For instance, in 1900, although Canada was already enjoying one of the highest standards of living in the world, the typical Canadian was quite poor by today's standards. In 1900, few homes had electricity, indoor flush toilets, or running water. The lack of running water meant that before people could cook or bathe, they had to pump water from wells and haul it to their homes in buckets—on average about 40 000 litres per year per family. The result was that people washed themselves and their clothing only infrequently. A majority of families living in cities had to use outdoor toilets, which they shared with other families. Few families had electric lights, relying instead on candles or lamps that burned kerosene or coal. Most homes were heated in the winter by burning coal, which was also used as fuel in stoves. Many families saved on winter fuel costs by heating only the kitchen, abandoning their living rooms and relying on clothing and blankets for warmth in their bedrooms. Burning so much coal contributed to the severe pollution that fouled the air of most large cities. Poor sanitation and high levels of pollution, along with ineffective medical care, resulted in high rates of illness and premature death. Many Canadians became ill or died from diseases such as smallpox, typhus, dysentery, measles, and cholera that are now uncommon in developed nations. Life expectancy in 1900 was 50 years for men and 51 years for women, compared with 78 years for men and 82.5 years for women in 2012. And there were, of course, no modern conveniences like air conditioners, washing machines, dishwashers, or

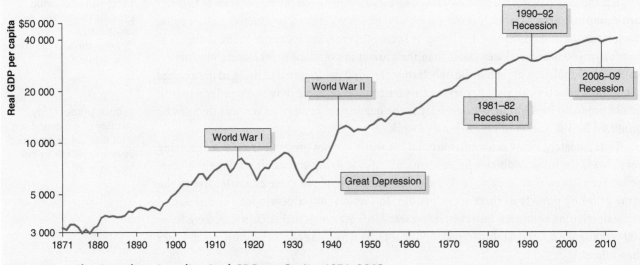

Figure 1.1 The Growth in Canadian Real GDP per Capita, 1871–2013

Measured in 2007 dollars, real GDP per capita in Canada grew from about $3000 in 1871 to over $45 000 in 2013. The average Canadian in the year 2013 could buy nearly six times as many goods and services as the average Canadian a hundred years earlier.

Note: The values in this graph are plotted on a logarithmic scale so that equal distances represent equal percentage increases. For example, the 100% increase from $10 000 to $20 000 is the same distance as the 100% increase from $20 000 to $40 000.

Sources: 1872–1986: R. Marvin McInnis, *Historical Canadian Macroeconomic Dataset 1871–1994*, Queen's University; 1987–2013: Statistics Canada, CANSIM Tables 380-0064 and 051-0005.

refrigerators. Without modern appliances, most women worked inside the home at least 80 hours per week.[1]

How did Canada get from the relative poverty of 1900 to the relative affluence of today? Will these increases in living standards continue? Will people living in Canada in 2100 look back on the people of 2014 as having lived in relative poverty? The answer to these questions is that changes in living standards depend on the rate of long-run economic growth. Most people in Canada, the United States, Western Europe, Japan, and other developed countries expect that over time, their standard of living will improve. They expect that year after year, firms will introduce new and improved products, new prescription drugs and better surgical techniques will overcome more diseases, and their ability to afford these goods and services will increase. For most people, these are reasonable expectations.

The process of long-run economic growth brought the typical Canadian from the standard of living of 1900 to the standard of living of today and has the potential to bring the typical Canadian of 100 years from now to a standard of living that people today can only imagine. **Real gross domestic product (GDP)**, which is the value of final goods and services produced during one year, adjusted for changes in the price level, provides a measure of the total level of income in the economy. Accordingly, we measure of the standard of living with real GDP per person, which is usually referred to as *real GDP per capita*. We typically measure long-run economic growth by increases in real GDP per capita over long periods of time, generally decades or more. Figure 1.1 shows real GDP per capita in Canada from 1871

Real gross domestic product (GDP) The value of final goods and services produced during one year, adjusted for changes in the price level.

---

[1]Office of the Superintendent of Financial Institutions, Office of the Chief Actuary, *Canadian Mortality Experience*, June 29, 2010.

to 2013. The figure shows that the long-run trend in real GDP per capita is strongly upward. The figure also shows that real GDP per capita fluctuates in the short run. For instance, real GDP per capita declined dramatically during the Great Depression of the 1930s and by smaller amounts during later recessions, including the recessions of 1990–92 and 2008–09. But it is the upward trend in real GDP per capita that we focus on when discussing long-run economic growth.

In Chapters 7 and 8, we will explore in detail why the Canadian economy has experienced strong growth over the long run, including the role of the financial system in facilitating this growth.

Some Countries Have Not Experienced Significant Long-Run Growth

One of the key macroeconomic puzzles that we will examine is why rates of economic growth have varied so widely across countries. Because countries have experienced such different rates of economic growth, their current levels of GDP per capita are also very different, as Figure 1.2 shows. GDP per capita is higher in Canada than in most other countries because, in the past, the Canadian economy has grown faster than have most other countries. Figure 1.2 shows that the gap between Canadian GDP per capita and GDP per capita in other high-income countries, such as the United States and Japan, is relatively small, but the gap between the high-income countries and the low-income countries is quite large. Although China has recently been experiencing rapid economic growth, this rapid growth began only in the late 1970s, when the Chinese government introduced economic reforms. As a result, GDP per capita in Canada is four and a half times greater than GDP per capita in China; current GDP per capita in China is similar to that in Canada in 1940. The gap between Canada and the poorest countries is larger still: Our GDP per capita is 30 times greater than GDP per capita in Uganda and a staggering 100 times greater than GDP per capita in the poorest country in the world, the Democratic Republic of Congo (DRC).

Why is average income in Canada so much higher than that in Uganda and China? Why is China closing the gap with developed countries, while DRC falls further behind? What explains the stark differences in income levels across countries? Why has it been so difficult to raise the incomes of the very poorest countries? In Chapters 7 and 8, we will address these important questions.

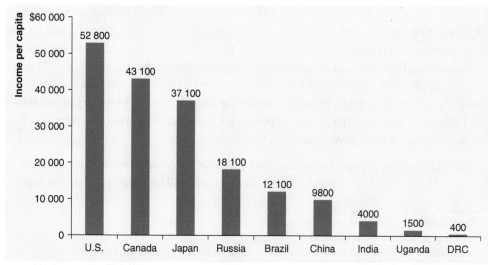

Figure 1.2

Differing Levels of GDP per Capita, 2013

Differing levels of long-run economic growth have resulted in countries today having very different levels of GDP per capita.

Note: Values are GDP per capita, measured in 2013 U.S. dollars corrected for differences in price levels across countries.

Source: U.S. Central Intelligence Agency, *The World Factbook 2014*, Washington, DC: Central Intelligence Agency, 2014.

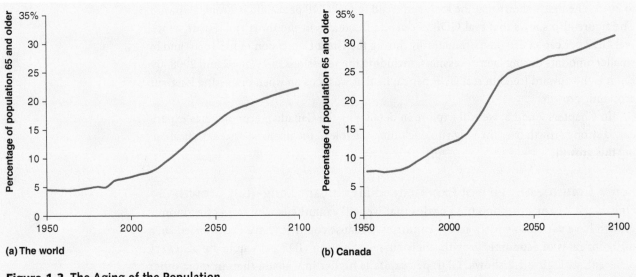

(a) The world

(b) Canada

Figure 1.3 The Aging of the Population

Panel (a) shows that low birthrates and increases in life span have resulted in an increasing percentage of people 65 and older in the world. Panel (b) shows that this trend also holds for Canada.

Source: United Nations, Department of Economic and Social Affairs, *World Population Prospects, the 2010 Revision.*

Aging Populations Pose a Challenge to Governments Around the World

Figure 1.3 panel (a) shows that the percentage of the world population over age 65 has been continually expanding. Since 1950, the percentage increased by two-thirds and is expected to almost triple by the end of the twenty-first century. Panel (b) shows the same pattern for Canada. In 2013, more than 14% of the Canadian population was older than 65. This percentage is expected to more than double by the end of the century and reach 31% in 2100. The aging of the population is the result of lower birthrates and of people living longer.

Some economists and policymakers fear that aging populations may pose a threat to long-run economic growth. A key part of the problem is that governments have programs to make payments to retired workers and to cover their healthcare costs. For instance, Canada has three programs that fill these roles:

1. *Old Age Security* (*OAS*) and *Guaranteed Income Supplement* (*GIS*), providing a monthly pension to most Canadians aged 65 and over. They are financed from general revenue.
2. *Canada Pension Plan* and *Quebec Pension Plan*, established in 1965 to provide basic income replacement to retired people. The plans are financed by contributions from workers and employers. Contributions are set at such a level that the program is, for at least 75 years, sustainable, i.e., it has sufficient funds to cover payments over the next 75 years.[2]
3. *Universal health care system*, established at the national level in 1960s to provide public health care coverage. Health care expenses are financed from general revenue of provinces and the federal government.[3]

Public spending on health care was 8% of GDP in 2012 and is projected to increase to 13% of GDP by 2031.[4] In other words, health care costs will increase significantly, leading

---

[2]Federal Budget 2012, *Job, Growth and Prosperity,* p. 200.

[3]Canadian Institute for Health Information.

[4]Public health care spending is assumed to remain 70% of total health care spending. OAS and GIS spending, which was 2.5% of GDP in 2013, is expected to remain below 2.9% of GDP until at least 2050. Sources: David A. Dodge and Richard Dion, *Chronic Healthcare Spending Disease,* C.D. Howe Institute (2011); Office of the Superintendent of Financial Institutions, *11th Actuarial Report on Old Age Security,* July 12, 2012.

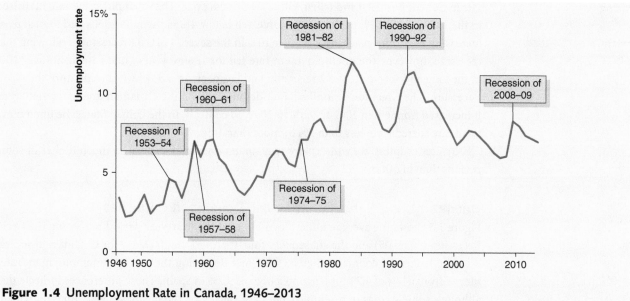

Figure 1.4 Unemployment Rate in Canada, 1946–2013

Unemployment rises and falls with the business cycle.

Sources: 1946–1975: Statistics Canada Archive, Series D491–497; 1976-2013: Statistics Canada, CANSIM Table 282-0085.

either to tax increases or to reduction in other spending. Most of the money for health care and OAS comes from taxes paid by people currently working. As the population ages, there are fewer workers paying taxes relative to the number of retired people receiving government payments. In the 1970s, there were seven workers for each person over the age of 65. By now, there are four, and by 2032 there will be only two workers for each person over the age 65.[5] The result is a funding crisis that can be solved only by either reducing government payments to retired workers, reducing spending on all other programs, or by raising the taxes paid by current workers.

In some European countries and Japan, birthrates have fallen so low that the total population has already begun to decline, which will make the funding crisis for government retirement programs even worse. How countries deal with the consequences of aging populations will be one of the most important macroeconomic issues of the coming decades.

Unemployment in Canada

The three topics we have just discussed concern the macroeconomic long run. As we already noted, the key macroeconomic issue of the short run is the business cycle. Figure 1.1 on page 4 shows the tremendous increase during the past century in the standard of living of the average Canadian. But close inspection of the figure reveals that real GDP per capita did not increase every year. For example, during the first half of the 1930s, real GDP per capita fell for several years in a row as Canada and many other countries experienced a severe economic downturn called the Great Depression. The fluctuations in real GDP per capita shown in Figure 1.1 reflect the underlying fluctuations in real GDP caused by the business cycle. Because real GDP is our best measure of economic activity, the business cycle is usually illustrated using movements in real GDP.

Most people experience the business cycle in the job market. The **labour force** is the sum of employed and unemployed workers in the economy, and the **unemployment rate** is the percentage of the labour force that is unemployed. As Figure 1.4 shows, the unemployment

Labour force The sum of employed and unemployed workers in the economy.

Unemployment rate The percentage of the labour force that is unemployed.

---

[5]Federal Budget 2012, *Job, Growth and Prosperity*, p. 194.

rate in Canada has risen and fallen with the business cycle. The unemployment rate increased in the 1950s to over 7% of the labour force, fell below 4% in the mid-1960s and then started increasing over time, reaching well over 10% in the severe 1981–82 recession. Following that recession, however, the unemployment rate fell for several years, then rose again over 10% in the long and severe 1990–92 recession and has been on a downward trend until the Great Recession. The Great Recession had a moderate effect on the Canadian unemployment rate: It increased from 6% in 2007 to 9.3% in 2009. In contrast, in the United States the unemployment rate soared from less than 5% to more than 10%.

In later chapters, we will explore why unemployment has been so much higher in some periods than in others.

Unemployment Rates Differ across Developed Countries

Figure 1.5 shows the average unemployment over the four-year period preceding the Great Recession (2005–08) and the subsequent four-year period (2009–12) for Canada and several other high-income countries. Before the Great Recession the average unemployment rates ranged from a low of 4.2% in Japan to a high of 9.7% in Spain. These differences indicate that although some swings in unemployment are caused by the business cycle, unemployment has been persistently higher in some countries than in others for reasons not connected to the business cycle. What explains these differences? The varying labour-market policies governments have pursued seem to be the key to explaining these differences in unemployment rates. As we will see, though, economists have not yet reached consensus on which policy differences are the most important.

The effect of the Great Recession on unemployment can be seen in Figure 1.5 by comparing the unemployment rates before the recession, in 2005–08, with the unemployment rates in 2009–12. The effect varied greatly across countries. The average unemployment rate in Canada increased by 1.5%, from 6.3% in 2005–08 to 7.8% in 2009–12; in the United States it increased by 3.9% from 5.1% to 9%. Unemployment changed little in the two low-unemployment countries: Japan and the Netherlands. The effect on the three big Eurozone countries varied a lot. Before the Great Recession, the unemployment rates in

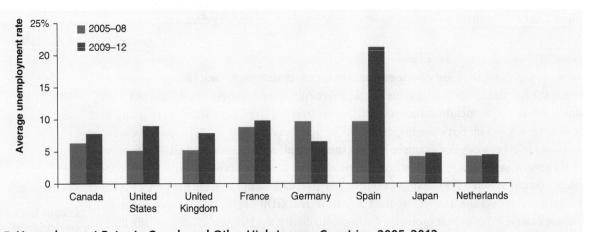

Figure 1.5 Unemployment Rates in Canada and Other High-Income Countries, 2005–2012

The average unemployment rate differs significantly across high-income countries. Differences in labour-market policies are the most likely explanation for these differences in unemployment rates. The effect of the Great Recession on unemployment varied greatly across countries. In Germany the unemployment rate fell by one third, in Spain it more than doubled. The increase in the average unemployment rate in the United States was more than twice Canada's.

Source: International Monetary Fund.

France, Germany, and Spain were similar. Subsequently, the unemployment rate fell by 3.1% in Germany, increased by 1% in France, and increased by an astounding 11.6% in Spain. The contrast between labour-market performance in Germany and Spain is striking. While in 2007 the unemployment rate in Spain was lower than in Germany, in 2012 it was 20 percentage points higher. Clearly, the Great Recession had different effects on unemployment across countries.

Inflation Rates Fluctuate over Time and across Countries

Just as the unemployment rate varies over time, and differs between Canada and other countries, so does the *inflation rate*. Figure 1.6 shows the **inflation rate** in Canada as measured by the percentage change in the average level of prices (here measured by the GDP deflator until 1914 and by CPI later; we discuss these price measures in Chapter 2) from one year to the next. The data in Figure 1.6 stretch back to 1872 to provide a long-run view of how the inflation rate in Canada has varied over time. There are several points to notice about inflation data:

Inflation rate The percentage increase in the price level from one year to the next.

1. Wars affect the inflation rate. Inflation was high during the World War I and immediately afterwards, and it was high following World War II.
2. The period between 1973 and 1982 stands out. Inflation was high: it was above 7% in every year; in five of those years it exceeded 10%. This was the longest period of high inflation, and the longest peacetime inflation, since 1872.
3. Periods of falling prices, or **deflation**, were relatively common until mid-1930s, but, since then, prices fell only in 1939 and 1953.
4. The period since 1993 also stands out. The inflation rate during the past 20 years has been around 2% and has not varied much. It is the longest period of low and stable inflation since 1872.

Deflation A sustained decrease in the price level.

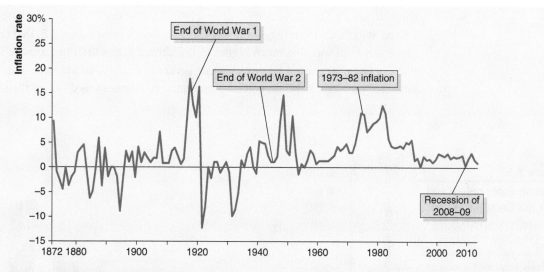

Figure 1.6 Inflation in Canada, 1872–2013

With the exception of the 1973–82 period, inflation in Canada has generally been high only during or after wars. Since 1954, prices have been increasing every year. The inflation rate during the past 20 years has generally been around 2%.

Sources: 1872–1914: R. Marvin McInnis, *Historical Canadian Macroeconomic Dataset 1871–1994*, Queens University; 1915–2013: Statistics Canada, CANSIM Table 326-0020.

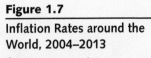

Figure 1.7

Inflation Rates around the World, 2004–2013

Countries can experience very different inflation rates.

Source: International Monetary Fund.

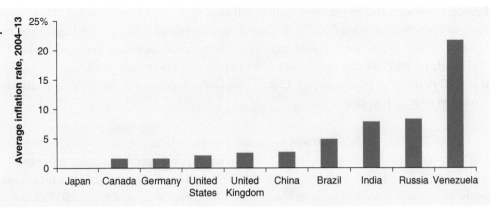

In later chapters, we will discuss what determines the inflation rate, why Canada has not experienced deflation during the past 50 years, and why inflation has been relatively low during recent years.

Figure 1.7 shows the average inflation rate for several countries around the world over 2004–2013. Some countries, including Japan, Canada, Germany, and the United States, experienced mild inflation. (The figure for Japan is essentially zero, so it is not showing in the graph.) Many other countries, though, experienced significantly higher inflation rates, as shown by the values in the figure for India, Russia, and Venezuela. In fact, the figure understates how much inflation rates can differ across countries. For instance, the inflation rate in Zimbabwe, not shown in the figure, was an extraordinary 15 billion percent in 2008! By exploring the reasons for the differences in inflation rates across countries, we will gain better insight into what makes prices increase over time.

Figure 1.8 shows the effect of the Great Recession on inflation. The average inflation rate over 2009–13 is lower than over 2004–08 in all developed countries in the figure, except for the United Kingdom. In Japan, where the inflation rate before the Great Recession was close to zero, prices have been falling. Note that the decline in the inflation rate in the United States was much bigger than in Canada. Recall from Figure 1.5, that the increase in unemployment was also much bigger in the United States than in Canada. This indicates that the Great Recession was much more severe in the United States than in Canada. The impact of the Great Recession on large emerging economies was different than on developed

Figure 1.8

Inflation Rates before and after the Great Recession

The average inflation rate over 2009–13 was lower than over 2004–08 in all developed countries except for the United Kingdom. The decline in inflation in the United States was much bigger than in Canada. Among large emerging economies, the inflation rate fell only in Russia.

Source: International Monetary Fund.

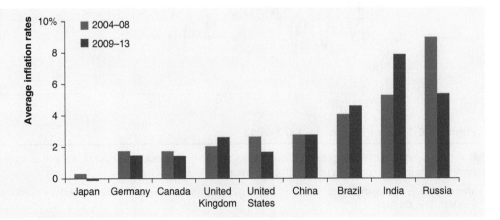

countries: the average inflation rate increased in Brazil and India, remained unchanged in China and fell only in Russia.

In later chapters we will discuss why a recession leads to a decline in the inflation rate.

Economic Policy Can Help Stabilize the Economy

A basic measure of economic stability is how much real GDP fluctuates from one year to the next. The more GDP fluctuates, the more erratic firms' sales are, and the more likely workers are to experience bouts of unemployment. Figure 1.9 shows the annual growth rate, i.e., year-over-year percentage change, of real GDP in Canada since 1872. Notice that, before 1950, real GDP went through much greater year-to-year fluctuations than it has since that time. In particular, during the past 60 years, the Canadian economy has not experienced anything similar to the sharp fluctuations in real GDP that occurred during the 1930s. The increased stability of the economy since 1950 is also indicated by the increased length of business cycle expansions and decreased length of recessions during these years. Since 1950, the Canadian economy has experienced long business cycle expansions, occasionally interrupted by brief recessions. Most other high-income countries have experienced similar increases in economic stability since 1950.

In later chapters, we will discuss at length the business cycle moderation that took place after 1950 and the role of macroeconomic policy.

Although there are a number of reasons the economies of most high-income countries became more stable after 1950, many economists believe that the *monetary policies* and *fiscal policies* governments have pursued played an important role. **Monetary policy** refers to the actions central banks take to manage the money supply and interest rates to pursue macroeconomic policy objectives. **Fiscal policy** refers to changes in government taxes and purchases that are intended to achieve macroeconomic policy objectives. A major focus of this textbook is exploring how macroeconomic policy can be used to stabilize the economy.

The severity of the Great Recession in the United States and in many other countries was due to the severity of the accompanying financial crisis. A **financial crisis** involves a significant disruption in the flow of funds from lenders to borrowers. As we will discuss in later chapters, recessions accompanied by financial crises are particularly deep and prolonged and provide challenges to government policymakers. Canada avoided the prolonged crisis as Canadian banks weathered the recession without major problems.

Monetary policy The actions that central banks take to manage the money supply and interest rates that are intended to achieve macroeconomic policy objectives.

Fiscal policy Changes in government taxes and purchases that are intended to achieve macroeconomic policy objectives.

Financial crisis A significant disruption in the flow of funds from lenders to borrowers.

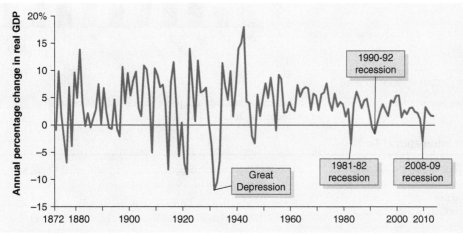

Figure 1.9

Fluctuations in Canadian Real GDP, 1872–2013

Real GDP had much more severe swings in the first half of the twentieth century than in the second half. The recessions in 1981–82, 1990–92, and in 2008–09 interrupted a long period of relative economic stability.

Sources: 1871–1994: R. Marvin McInnis, *Historical Canadian Macroeconomic Dataset 1871–1994*, Queens University; 1995–2013: Statistics Canada, CANSIM Table 380–0084.

International Factors Have Become Increasingly Important in Explaining Macroeconomic Events

The past 30 years have been a period of fast globalization. Links between countries, particularly capital flows, intensified as many countries reduced restrictions on the movement of capital. Advances in information technology and massive reductions in transportation and communication costs boosted globalization. In recent years savings greatly increased in several Asian countries, including China. Ben Bernanke, the former head of the U.S. central bank, the Federal Reserve (Fed), spoke of a "global savings glut" that had driven down interest rates in the United States and, given our close links with the U.S. economy, also in Canada. International trade has been increasing rapidly. In 1994 Canada signed a free trade agreement (NAFTA, the North American Free Trade Agreement) with the United States and Mexico; in 2014 Canada signed a free trade agreement with the European Union (CETA, Comprehensive Economic and Trade Agreement).

International Trade Economists measure the "openness" of an economy in terms of how much it trades with other economies. Figure 1.10 panel (a) shows that for Canada, both imports and exports have been growing as a percentage of GDP. Panel (b) shows the degree of openness in several countries. Some small countries, such as Belgium, export and import more than 80% of GDP because many firms based in those countries concentrate on exporting rather than on producing for the domestic market. Countries such as South Korea and Germany are heavily dependent on international trade, with exports and imports making up more than 50% of GDP. In Canada, the United Kingdom, India, China, and France exports and imports are around 30% of GDP. Japan and the United States are much less dependent on foreign trade, with exports and imports of around 15% of GDP.

As you probably know, the United States is our main trading partner. Three quarters of Canadian exports go to the United States and half of our imports are from the United States. Our second largest trading partner is China, with 4% of our exports and 11% of our imports. Because of our strong trade and financial links with the United States, many comparisons in the book are with the U.S. economy.

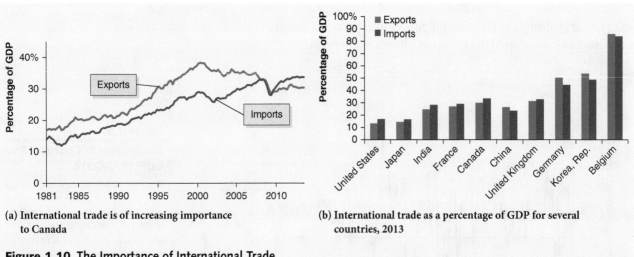

(a) International trade is of increasing importance to Canada

(b) International trade as a percentage of GDP for several countries, 2013

Figure 1.10 The Importance of International Trade

Panel (a) shows that since 1981, both imports and exports have been steadily rising as a fraction of Canadian GDP. Panel (b) shows that the importance of international trade differs across countries. Exports and imports, as a fraction of GDP, are similar in Canada, India, France, and the United Kingdom, with imports exceeding exports, and in China, with exports exceeding imports.

Sources: Statistics Canada, CANSIM Table 380-0084; World Bank (data for Japan – 2012).

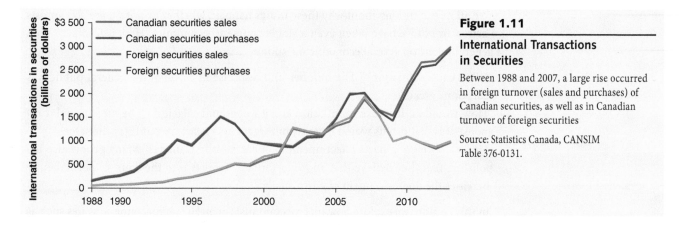

Figure 1.11

International Transactions in Securities

Between 1988 and 2007, a large rise occurred in foreign turnover (sales and purchases) of Canadian securities, as well as in Canadian turnover of foreign securities

Source: Statistics Canada, CANSIM Table 376-0131.

Panel (b) of Figure 1.10 indicates that the Canadian economy is much more open than the U.S. economy. But the reason for the openness is solely our trade with the United States. Canadian exports to countries other than the United States are only 7.5% of Canada's GDP, while U.S. exports to countries other than Canada are 11% of U.S. GDP (the corresponding numbers for imports are 17% and 15%). So, excluding bilateral trade, the Canadian economy is actually less open than the U.S. economy! This may change with Canada's new trade agreements negotiated with the European Union and with emerging markets in Asia and Latin America.

Global Financial Markets As markets in goods and services have become more open to international trade, so have the financial markets that help match savers and investors around the world. Over the past 20 years, there has been an explosion in the buying and selling of financial assets, such as stocks and bonds, as well as in the making of loans across national borders. A *stock* is a financial security that represents part ownership in a firm, while a *bond* is a financial security that represents a promise to repay a fixed amount of funds. Figure 1.11 shows the increased openness of Canadian capital markets. Between 1988 and 2007, a large rise occurred in foreign turnover (sales and purchases) of Canadian securities, as well as in Canadian turnover of foreign securities. The Great Recession led to a significant decline in turnover. Subsequently, while foreign turnover of Canadian securities quickly recovered, Canadian turnover of foreign securities continued to fall.

The increased openness of the Canadian and other economies has raised incomes and improved economic efficiency around the world. But increased openness also means that macroeconomic problems in one economy can have consequences for other economies. For example, the Great Recession reduced the demand for China's exports, and the Greek debt crisis that started in 2010 caused stock prices to decline around the world. Openness can also complicate the attempts of policymakers to stabilize the economy. In this textbook, we explore the macroeconomic implications of increasing trade and investment among countries, as well as the role of the international financial system.

How Economists Think about Macroeconomics

Macroeconomics happens to us all: over the course of your life, you may be laid off from your job during a recession or you will have friends or relatives who are. You are likely to see a stock market investment soar or collapse, find getting a loan to buy a house or car to be easy or difficult, and experience periods when prices of goods and services rise rapidly or slowly.

1.2

Learning Objective

Explain how economists approach macroeconomic questions.

We all have opinions about why these things happen, whether or not we are economists or whether or not we have taken even a single course in economics. Here is feedback from the general public on several economic questions:

- "What causes inflation?" The number-one response in a poll of the general public was "corporate greed."
- "How would an increase in inflation affect wages and salaries?" The most popular response was that profits would increase but wages and salaries would stay the same.
- "How do foreign imports affect unemployment rates in Canada?" Many people also tell pollsters that they believe that allowing foreign imports into the country permanently increases the unemployment rate in Canada.

In this section, we explore how macroeconomists analyze macroeconomic issues such as the causes of inflation and the effect of imports.

What Is the Best Way to Analyze Macroeconomic Issues?

Because you have already taken a course in principles of economics, you are probably skeptical of the validity of the poll responses mentioned in the previous paragraphs. What accounts for the differences that exist between the opinions of economists and non-economists? The key difference is that economists study economic problems systematically by gathering relevant data and then building a *model* capable of analyzing the data. For instance, suppose we want to look systematically at the claim that inflation is caused by corporate greed. A first step is to look at the data on inflation. Figure 1.6 on page 9 shows the inflation rate for each year since 1872. It is evident from the figure that the inflation rate has varied a lot over this long period. For instance, in the past 60 years, inflation varied from below 3% in the 1950s and 1960s to well above 10% in the late 1970s and early 1980s, and then it returned to relatively low rates around 2% for most of the years after the early 1990s.

By themselves, these data make the corporate greed explanation of inflation unlikely. If corporate greed were the cause of inflation, then greed would have to fluctuate as well, with corporate managers having been comparatively less greedy in the 1950s and 1960s, more greedy in the late 1970s and early 1980s, and then less greedy again beginning in the mid-1990s. This simple look at the data is, however, not systematic enough, for two reasons. First, just inspecting the data can give misleading results. Second, it is more useful to provide an alternative explanation rather than merely reject one. That is, we need to build a *macroeconomic model* that will allow us to explain inflation.

Macroeconomic Models

Economists rely on economic theories, or models, to analyze real-world issues, such as the causes of inflation. (We use the words *theory* and *model* interchangeably.) Economic models are simplified versions of reality. By simplifying, it is possible to move beyond the overwhelming complexity of everyday life to focus on the underlying causes of the issue being studied. For instance, rather than use a model, we could analyze inflation by looking at the details of how every firm in the country decides what price to charge. The problem with that approach is that even if we had the time and money to carry it out, we would end up with a huge amount of detailed information that would be impossible to interpret. And we would end up no closer to understanding why inflation has fluctuated over the years. In contrast, by building an economic model of inflation that simplifies reality by focusing on a few key variables, we would be more likely to increase our understanding of inflation. In particular, we would be better able to predict which factors are likely to make inflation higher or lower in the future. (Remember from your principles of economics class that an *economic variable* is something measurable that can have different values, such as the rate of inflation in a particular year.)

Sometimes economists use an existing model to analyze an issue, but in other cases they need to develop a new model. To develop a model, economists generally follow these steps:

1. Decide on the assumptions to be used in developing the model and decide which variables will be explained by the model and which variables will be taken as given.
2. Formulate a testable hypothesis.
3. Use economic data to test the hypothesis.
4. Revise the model if it fails to explain the economic data well.
5. Retain the revised model to help answer similar economic questions in the future.

In each chapter of this textbook, you will see the special feature *Solved Problem*. This feature will increase your understanding of the material by leading you through the steps of solving an applied macroeconomic problem. After reading the problem, you can test your understanding by working the related problem that appears at the end of the chapter. You can also complete related Solved Problems on www.myeconlab.com, which also allows you to access tutorial help.

Solved Problem 1.1

Do Rising Imports Lead to a Permanent Reduction in Canadian Employment?

Opinion polls show that many people believe that imports of foreign goods lead to a reduction in employment in Canada. On the surface, this claim may seem plausible: If Canadian automobile firms use more imported parts, the production at Canadian car parts firms declines, and they will lay off workers. Briefly describe how you might evaluate the claim that employment in Canada has been reduced as a result of imports.

Solving the Problem

Step 1 Review the chapter material. This problem is about how economists evaluate explanations of macroeconomic events, so you may want to review the section "What Is the Best Way to Analyze Macroeconomic Issues?" which begins on page 14.

Step 2 Discuss what data you might use in evaluating this claim. The relevant data are for imports and employment over the years. The data can be found at the Statistics Canada website.

Step 3 Draw a graph that shows (a) total employment and (b) imports as a percentage of GDP. One way of inspecting whether the data support the claim is to plot the data on a graph. Your graph should look like the one shown here, which shows for the years 1981 to 2012 imports as a percentage of GDP measured on the left vertical axis and a measure of total employment on the right vertical axis.

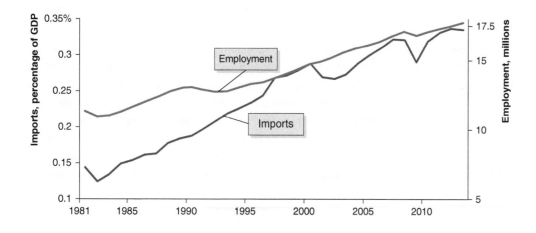

The graph shows that imports and employment have both increased over time, which makes it unlikely that imports have permanently reduced employment.

Step 4 **Discuss what else you might do to evaluate this claim.** Most economists see inspecting the data as only the first step in evaluating a claim about a macroeconomic event. Economists use models to provide systematic explanations. In this case, although the fact that imports and employment have both risen over the past 40 years makes it seem unlikely that rising imports have reduced employment, we cannot be entirely sure. It is possible that employment would have risen even more than it did if imports had increased less. In Chapter 6, we will study a model of the labour market to better understand what determines the level of employment in the long run. At that point, it will become more evident that the level of a country's imports has no effect on its level of employment in the long run.

Sources: Statistics Canada, CANSIM Tables 282-0002 and 380-0084.

See related problem 2.5 at the end of the chapter.

Assumptions, Endogenous Variables, and Exogenous Variables in Economic Models

Any model is based on making assumptions because models have to be simplified versions of reality in order to be useful. We cannot analyze an economic issue unless we reduce its complexity. For example, economic models make behavioural assumptions about the motives of consumers and firms. Economists assume that consumers will buy the goods and services that will maximize their well-being, or *utility*. Similarly, economists assume that firms act to maximize their profits. These assumptions are simplifications because they do not describe the motives of every consumer and every firm. How can we know if the assumptions in a model are too simplified or too limiting? We discover the validity of assumptions when we form hypotheses based on these assumptions and test the hypotheses using real-world data.

Exogenous variable A variable that is taken as given and is not explained by an economic model.

Endogenous variable A variable that is explained by an economic model.

In building a model, we must decide which variables we will attempt to explain with the model and which variables we will take as given. Economists refer to variables that are taken as given as **exogenous variables** and variables that will be explained by the model as **endogenous variables**. For example, suppose we build a macroeconomic model that explores the effect of changes in the money supply on the inflation rate. If we assume that the Bank of Canada determines changes in the money supply, then the money supply is an exogenous variable because we are not using the model to try to explain it. The inflation rate, though, would be an endogenous variable because we are attempting to explain it using the model.

Forming and Testing Hypotheses in Economic Models

A *hypothesis* in an economic model is a testable statement about an economic variable that may be either correct or incorrect. An example is the statement that the higher the level of income per person in a country, the higher the country's consumption per person will be. An economic hypothesis is usually about a *causal relationship*. In this case, the hypothesis states that increases in income per person *cause*, or lead to, higher consumption per person.

To evaluate a hypothesis, we need to test it. To test a hypothesis, we need to analyze statistics on the relevant economic variables. In our example, we might gather statistics on the level of income per person and consumption per person for different countries. Testing a hypothesis can be tricky. For example, showing that countries with higher income per person have higher consumption per person would not be enough to demonstrate that the higher income *caused* the higher consumption. Just because two things are *correlated*—that is, they happen at the same time—does not mean that one caused the other. For example, suppose that many of the countries with high levels of income per person also devote a small portion of their income to investment. The high level of consumption per person may then be just the effect of the fact that most of the income is consumed. Over a period of time, many economic variables change, which complicates testing hypotheses even further. In fact, when economists disagree about a hypothesis, it is often because of disagreements over interpreting the statistical analysis used to test the hypothesis.

Note that hypotheses must be statements that could, in principle, turn out to be incorrect. Statements such as "High taxes are good" or "High taxes are bad" are value judgments rather than hypotheses because it is not possible to disprove them. Economists accept and use an economic model if it leads to hypotheses that can be analyzed by statistical analysis. In many cases, the acceptance is tentative, however, pending new data or further statistical analysis. In fact, economists often refer to a hypothesis having been "not rejected" rather than having been "accepted" by statistical analysis. But what if statistical analysis clearly rejects a hypothesis? Then we need to consider why the hypothesis was rejected. Throughout this textbook, as we build economic models and use them to answer questions, you need to bear in mind the distinction between *positive analysis* and *normative analysis*. **Positive analysis** is concerned with *what is*, and **normative analysis** is concerned with *what ought to be*. Positive analysis leads to testable hypotheses, while normative analysis does not. For example, a statement that economic inequality ought to be reduced is not one that can be tested. Economics is concerned primarily with positive analysis, which measures the costs and benefits of different courses of action.

Positive analysis Analysis concerned with what is.

Normative analysis Analysis concerned with what ought to be.

In each chapter, the *Making the Connection* feature discusses a news story or another application related to the chapter material. The following *Making the Connection* discusses why it is important to understand macroeconomic issues.

Making the Connection

Why Should Canada Worry about the "Euro Crisis"?

The Eurozone includes 18 member states of the European Union that adopted the euro as their currency, starting in 1999. Monetary policy for the Eurozone is the responsibility of the European Central Bank (ECB). To be granted permission for their states to join the Eurozone, government officials agree to limits on their budget deficits and debt. The Great Recession worsened the debt problems of several Eurozone members as government spending increased and tax receipts fell. Ireland, Portugal, Greece, and Spain petitioned fellow Eurozone members and the International Monetary Fund (IMF) to approve loans that would allow them to avoid defaulting on their government-issued debt.

To secure the loans, government officials had to agree to economic reforms, spending cuts, and tax increases—so-called *austerity policies*. By the spring of 2012, voters in these countries began to resist the austerity policies, and it seemed possible that Greece and perhaps other countries might abandon the euro and resume using their previous currencies. In 2013 the economic situation in Italy deteriorated. Given the size of the Italian economy, the other Eurozone countries did not have sufficient funds to provide loans if Italy had been unable to borrow in private markets.

Although the "euro crisis" threatened Europe's economies, many people in Canada wondered if the crisis would affect them. Exports from Canada could suffer if European consumers reduced spending but, with three quarters of our exports going to the United States and only 10% going to the Eurozone, the effect would be small. But the euro crisis could threaten the supply chains of many Canadian manufacturers who rely on European companies for components such as engines and machinery. The crisis could also affect Canadian banks, but their holdings of euro-denominated debt are limited.

The Canadian economy could also suffer from the euro crisis for reasons that are difficult to measure. Some economists believe Europe's debt problems have contributed to a lack of confidence among business leaders in Canada and in the United States. A reduction in business confidence in the United States reduces U.S. imports from Canada. This lack of confidence and slower U.S. imports may be one reason for sluggish economic growth in Canada. However the euro crisis is resolved, it is one of many macroeconomic issues that have important implications for consumers, workers, and firms. The purpose of this textbook is to help you better understand these issues.

Sources: Emmanuel Samoglou, "Canadian Exposure to European Sovereign Debt," *Canadian Business*, July 11, 2011; "Canadian Bank Exposure to European Debt 'Limited'," *CBC News,* June 14, 2012; "How Europe's Contagion May Hit the U.S. Economy," *Bloomberg Business Week*, June 7, 2012; Holly Ellyatt, "Fears Rise that Italy's 2014 Budget Could Spark Further Trouble," *CNBC*, October 15, 2013.

See related problem 2.9 at the end of the chapter.

<table>
<tr><td>**1.3**</td></tr>
<tr><td>**Learning Objective**</td></tr>
<tr><td>Become familiar with the Great Recession and link the analysis of the Great Recession to the material covered in the book</td></tr>
</table>

The Great Recession and an Overview of the Book

We now turn to a description of the Great Recession—the most important economic event in the past 75 years. We briefly describe the events that led to this unprecedented crisis, and the policy responses. The analysis of the Great Recession is linked to the material covered in the book, with a brief summary of the relevant book chapters. The economic events of the Great Recession raised issues applicable to all areas of macroeconomics. Throughout the book, we will return many times to the events and lessons from the Great Recession. It will allow us to use recent events to illustrate macroeconomic concepts, reasoning, and policies.

Lehman Brothers Bankruptcy

The Great Recession started around 1 a.m. Eastern Standard Time on September 15, 2008. This is when Lehman Brothers, at the time the fourth-largest investment bank in the United States, filed for Chapter 11 bankruptcy protection, effectively going bankrupt.

Lehman Brothers had been in trouble for some time. Caught in the fall of real estate prices, it was losing large amounts of money as the value of its real estate and other asset holdings rapidly deteriorated. By September 2008 it became clear it was not going to survive on its own. During the September 13–14 weekend a high-level meeting took place in New York. The participants included Henry Paulson, then the Treasury Secretary, Ben Bernanke, then the chairman of the Federal Reserve(the U.S. central bank), and Timothy Geithner, then the president of the Federal Reserve Bank of New York. The general expectation was that the government and the Federal Reserve would step in and find a buyer who would save the firm from bankruptcy.

This expectation was based on Federal Reserve's actions six months earlier, when another investment bank, Bear Stearns, was failing. In that case the Federal Reserve arranged a purchase of Bear Stearns by JPMorgan Chase. To induce the purchase, it provided JPMorgan with a loan of $30 billion, secured by risky assets of Bear Stearns. In effect, the Federal Reserve limited potential losses JPMorgan Chase could suffer to $1 billion, making the purchase attractive. At that time, Ben Bernanke, the Federal Reserve chairman said: "I hope this is a rare event, I hope this is something we never have to do again." He was wrong. The next rescue, on September 8, was of Fannie Mae and Freddie Mac[6]—private companies created by the U.S. government to improve the liquidity in the housing market and the availability of mortgages. A week later it was Lehman's turn.

Why Was Lehman Brothers Allowed to Fail? Two potential buyers were interested in taking over Lehman: Bank of America—at that time the second largest financial institution in the United States—and Barclays—one of the largest British banks. But they demanded that the government provide guarantees limiting potential losses, just as it did in the Bear Stearns case. The Federal Reserve and the government officials decided against providing such guarantees. Their concern was what economists call **moral hazard.** Moral hazard is a situation when, after entering into a transaction, one party takes actions that make the other party to the transaction worse off. It arises when a company (or an individual) does not have to bear all consequences of its actions. If a bank knows it will be saved by government intervention when needed, it will engage in excessively risky activities. The reason is simple. The more risky the activity, the greater is the chance of a large profit, which goes to the bank. There is also a greater chance of a large loss, but in this case the government bailout would limit the losses. In other words, riskier activities increase the possibility of large gains but not the consequences of large losses.

Moral hazard A situation when, after entering into a transaction, one party takes actions that make the other party to the transaction worse off.

In Chapter 3 we study the financial system and its role in the economy. We describe banks and other financial intermediaries. We analyze the role central banks have in stabilizing the economy. We also discuss the term structure of interest rates—the relationship between short-term and long-term interest rates which is crucial for the understanding of monetary policy.

Treasury and Federal Reserve officials were concerned that, if they saved another failing investment bank, the pattern of government intervention would be established. So, to show financial companies that they cannot count on Federal Reserve support, U.S. Treasury and Federal Reserve officials decided to let Lehman Brothers fail.

Markets were caught unprepared. While there was a lot of talk about moral hazard, they did not believe that such a large institution will be allowed to fail. The bankruptcy of Lehman Brothers was by far the largest bankruptcy in the world. The company had almost $700 billion in assets. The largest previous bankruptcy was WorldCom, a telecommunication company, which failed in 2002 with $100 billion in assets.

Investment banks like Lehman Brothers are quite different from other firms. They borrow large amounts of money in short-term markets to acquire assets they hope will provide higher returns. They do have some capital, but it is very small compared to the size of their assets. Lehman, at time of bankruptcy, owed others well over $650 billion. Under normal circumstances, a bankruptcy of such a large financial firm would lead to substantial losses to its lenders. Some lenders, as a result, may run into financial problems. Sound institutions, ones that had large capital and/or little exposure to the failing company would, however, not be greatly affected apart from the decline in profits.

Credit Panic

But these were not normal circumstances. Since late 2006, house prices had been falling and borrowers were defaulting on their mortgages in unprecedented numbers. Many financial institutions held securities whose price depended on house prices (more on this later in this

---

[6]These names are commonly used. The actual names are Federal National Mortgage Association and Federal Home Loan Mortgage Corporation, respectively.

chapter). Their situation was precarious as the value of those securities declined. The biggest problem was that it was not clear who owed money to whom. Financial innovations had allowed firms to sell their mortgage loans to others. The transactions were complicated, with many loans combined into a big loan pool that was then sold to many buyers. Some financial institutions sold *credit-default swaps*. Credit-default swaps are contracts that act like insurance: They shift the risk of an asset from the swap buyer to the seller. The buyer pays the seller a fee related to the riskiness of the asset. If the value of the asset declines, the seller covers the loss. Credit-default swaps were not traded on organized exchanges and there was no central record of transactions. So it was difficult, if not impossible, to assess the effect of mortgage default on individual firms.

Now put yourselves in the shoes of a bank manager who is considering lending money. The economic situation is deteriorating. A large, venerable institution has just gone bankrupt. This raises the fear that many financial institutions and firms may be in difficult situation. You do not know whether your potential borrower will suffer from the collapse of Lehman Brothers. He may be exposed to Lehman Brothers directly (for example, if he bought credit-default swaps) or indirectly (through lending to others who in turn lent to Lehman). The danger to the borrower from the Lehman bankruptcy is difficult to assess. So you are not sure whether the potential borrower will be able to repay the loan.

It gets worse. It is also difficult to assess the ability of your existing customers to service their loans. With the collapse of Lehman Brothers, huge funds were frozen due to the bankruptcy process. If your existing customer lent money to Lehman, or lent money to an institution that lent money to Lehman, etc., they may not be able to repay the loan. So not only don't you know the financial situation of the potential borrower, but you do not really know even the financial prospects of your bank! What would you do in such situation? Most likely you would refuse the loan and keep the funds in cash as protection against possible problems. And that is what happened. With the complex web of relationship among financial institutions no one was sure what the financial position of other firms was; even their own position was in doubt. Financial markets went into panic and it became very difficult to obtain credit. Essentially, credit markets stopped operating. As the financier George Soros said, "the economy fell off the cliff."

According to the National Bureau of Economic Research, the private research institute that establishes the dates for U.S. recessions, the recession started in December 2007. In September 2008 people still hoped it would be a regular recession, but the financial turmoil made it much worse. Credit is the lifeblood of the economy. Firms borrow to invest, to maintain inventory, and to obtain operating funds. As the financial market panicked, credit became much more difficult to obtain than before. Investment fell as firms postponed every project they could. Production declined as suppliers stopped extending the customary credit and demanded immediate payment. As production fell, unemployment increased rapidly. The recession became much more severe and the term the Great Recession was born. The crisis was called the Great Recession to distinguish it from other, regular recessions. People were actually concerned about a repeat of the Great Depression—the most severe recession in modern history.

How bad did the recession appear to be? In January 2011 the Financial Crisis Inquiry Commission reported to the U.S. Congress on the causes of the crisis. It revealed a statement made in November 2009 by Ben Bernanke identifying the recession as "the worst financial crisis in global history, including the Great Depression."[7] He said all but one of the largest U.S. financial institutions were a week or two from collapse. Bernanke's comparison to the Great Depression was not made lightly. Few people know more about the Great Depression

---

[7]"Crisis Panel's Report Parsed Far and Wide," *New York Times*, January 27, 2011.

than he does. Before he joined the Federal Reserve, Bernanke was a professor of economics at Princeton and was one of the best known macroeconomists in the world. A large part of his academic career was devoted to studying the causes and lessons from the Great Depression.

In Chapter 9 we begin our study of business cycles. We discuss the difference between the short run and the long run in macroeconomics. We analyze what happens during a business cycle with output, unemployment, consumption, investment, and other macro-economic variables and what role slow adjustment of prices plays. We explain how economists think about business cycles. Finally, we use a simple aggregate supply–aggregate demand model to explain economy's behaviour over the business cycle.

Making the Connection

Federal Policy During Panics, Then and Now: The Collapse of the Bank of United States in 1930 and the Collapse of Lehman Brothers in 2008

The major Canadian banks are national banks, so they can handle regional crises. If a bank has high default rates in, say, Alberta, it can offset them with profits earned in the rest of the country. Canadian banks are also quite conservative. As a result, there have been no banking panics in Canada in the past 100 years. The situation in the United States is different. Banks, especially in the past, were local and often had a fairly homogenous customer base. So, for example, a crop failure in Iowa could lead to collapse of banks there as a large portion of their customers were unable to repay the loans. Following several panics in the nineteenth century and at the beginning of the twentieth century, in 1913 the Federal Reserve was established to stop bank panics. But, in fact, the worst bank panic in U.S. history occurred during the early 1930s, and the Federal Reserve did little to stop it. The panic occurred during the Great Depression, which began in August 1929. By the fall of 1930, many commercial banks found that their assets had declined significantly in value, as both households and firms had difficulty repaying loans. In October 1930, the Bank of United States, a private commercial bank in New York City, experienced a bank run. It appealed to the Fed for loans that would allow it to survive the liquidity crisis caused by deposit withdrawals. The term moral hazard had not yet been coined, but Federal Reserve officials were clearly familiar with the concept because they declined to save the Bank of United States on the grounds that the bank's managers had made risky mortgage loans to borrowers investing in apartment houses and other commercial property in New York City. The Federal Reserve believed that saving the Bank of United States would reward the poor business decisions of the bank's managers. They also doubted that, if the bank's assets were sold, the amount raised would be sufficient to pay off depositors.

Although the Federal Reserve's reasons for failing to save the Bank of United States were legitimate, they had adverse financial consequences for the entire economy. When the bank failed, the faith of depositors in the commercial banking system was shaken. Because deposit insurance did not yet exist, depositors were afraid that, if they delayed withdrawing their money and their bank failed, they would receive only part of their money back—and only after a delay. Further waves of bank failures took place over the next few years, culminating in the "bank holiday" of 1933, when President Franklin Roosevelt ordered every bank in the country shut down for a week so that emergency measures could be taken to restore the banking system. Although the Federal Reserve's actions during the bank panic had avoided the moral hazard problem, they resulted in a catastrophic meltdown of the U.S. financial system, which most economists believe significantly worsened and lengthened the Great Depression.

The following figure shows the number of banks that were forced to temporarily or permanently suspend depositor withdrawals, for each year from 1920 through 1939. The figure reveals that bank runs in the United States went from being fairly common in the 1920s, to reaching very high levels in the early 1930s, to practically disappearing after deposit insurance was established in 1934. In fact, the Federal Reserve acted as a lender of last resort infrequently over the next 75 years. It is worth noting that in Canada there were no bank failures, even though the decline in economic activity during the Great Depression was similar to that in the United States.

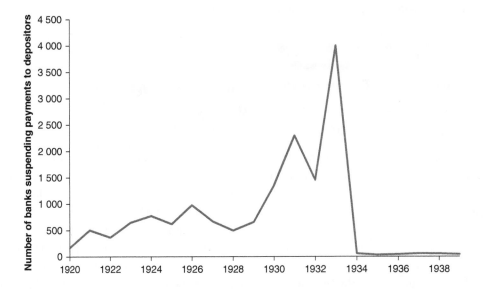

In 2008, the Federal Reserve was once again confronted with the dilemma of how to deal with the failure of a large financial firm. In the spring, Bear Stearns, a large investment bank, ran into difficulty because the declining prices for many of the mortgage-backed securities it held made other financial firms reluctant to lend it money. The Federal Reserve and the U.S. Treasury responded by arranging for JPMorgan Chase, a commercial bank, to purchase Bear Stearns for a very low price. That fall, though, fear of increasing moral hazard led the Federal Reserve and the Treasury to allow Lehman Brothers, also a large investment bank, to declare bankruptcy.

The Lehman Brothers bankruptcy had an immediate negative effect on financial markets, as the following graphs illustrate. Panel (a) shows the difference between the three-month London Interbank Offered Rate (LIBOR), which is the interest rate at which banks can borrow from each other, and the interest rate on three-month Treasury bills. The difference in these two interest rates is called the TED spread. It provides a measure of how much more risky are loans to banks than to the U.S. government. (Note that when a bank buys government bonds, it is equivalent to the bank lending money to the government.) After fluctuating in a narrow range around 0.5 percentage point during 2005, 2006, and the first half of 2007, the TED spread rose as problems in financial markets began in the second half of 2007, and then it soared to record levels immediately following the failure of Lehman Brothers. Panel (b) shows the decline in issuing of securities backed by credit-card debt. Issuance of these securities plummeted to zero in the last quarter of 2008. Because banks could not sell new credit-card loans, they became reluctant to issue new credit cards or increase credit limits on existing accounts. These measures made it more difficult for households to finance their spending. Many on Wall Street saw the bankruptcy of Lehman Brothers as such a watershed in the financial crisis that they began to refer to events as having happened either "before Lehman" (declared bankruptcy) or "after Lehman."

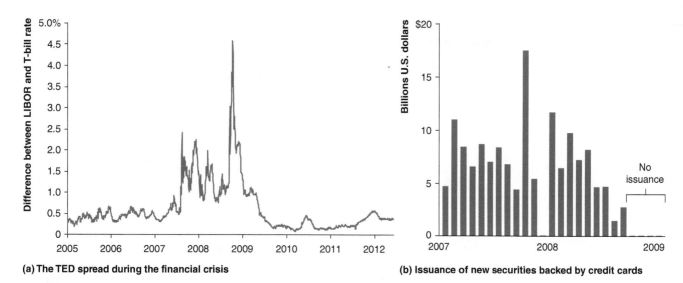

(a) The TED spread during the financial crisis

(b) Issuance of new securities backed by credit cards

Having failed to intervene to save Lehman Brothers from bankruptcy, the U.S. Treasury and the Federal Reserve reversed course later that same week to provide aid to AIG—the largest U.S. insurance company—that saved the firm from bankruptcy. For the remainder of 2008 and into 2009, the Treasury and the Federal Reserve appeared to have set aside concerns about moral hazard as they gave no indication that they would allow another large financial firm to fail. It remains to be seen whether the failure of Lehman Brothers will be viewed as being as significant an event in the 2007–09 financial crisis as the failure of the Bank of United States was in the 1929–33 crisis.

Sources: TED spread: Authors' calculations from British Bankers' Association data and Federal Reserve data; credit card securitization: Peter Eavis, "The Fed Goes for Brokerage," *Wall Street Journal*, March 4, 2009; and U.S. Federal Reserve System, Board of Governors, "Bank Suspensions, 1921–1936," *Federal Reserve Bulletin*, Vol. 23, September 1937, p. 907.

See related problem 2.10 at the end of the chapter.

The Policy Response (in brief)

We now describe briefly the policy response to the Great Recession; we provide a detailed analysis in Chapters 12 and 13. In the end, the recession was not as severe as feared. During the Great Depression, output fell around the world and unemployment reached 20% in Canada and 25% in the United States. The Great Recession was much milder. Several countries, in particular China, India, and Australia, were largely unaffected by the events. The unemployment rate stayed below 9% in Canada and 10% in the United States.

Monetary and fiscal authorities around the world reacted forcefully to stimulate economies, in part taking advantage from the lessons from the Great Depression. To fight the recession both monetary and fiscal policies were employed. The traditional monetary policy is to reduce short-term nominal interest rates. The central bank exerts direct control over the short-term interest rates by buying and selling short-term government bonds. Long-term real interest rates, which matter for investment, are set by market forces. But by affecting short-term interest rates the central bank affects the cost of funds to the banking sector and so, indirectly, influences long-term rates. If the cost of short-term funds goes down, financing costs for banks are lower and banks may (but do not have to) lower their long-term rates.

In Chapter 10 we develop our main macroeconomic model, the IS-MP model. It consists of three basic parts. In the first part, we look at the relationship between the real interest rate and aggregate expenditure. The second part describes the monetary policy—the setting of short-run nominal interest rates by the central bank. The third part describes the relationship between the short-run nominal interest rates that the central bank controls and the long-run real interest rates that affect aggregate expenditure.

In Chapter 11 we extend the IS-MP model to include inflation and the open economy. We use the extended model to study the Great Recession, as well as the effects of the oil shock. After the Great Recession, central banks greatly increased the quantity of money in the economy. We ask why this has not caused runaway inflation. We also look at the Eurozone, where some countries accumulated excessive debts, and ask whether the Eurozone will survive.

The problem with the traditional approach was that it has a limit. The nominal interest rate cannot be negative, since a negative nominal interest rate means that someone who, for example, deposits $100 for a year receives only $99 a year later.[8] So once the nominal interest rate is near zero, the central bank cannot lower it any further. During the Great Recession central banks had to resort to new approaches, called quantitative easing and forward guidance. Quantitative easing involves the purchases (or sales) of long-term assets, thus affecting long-term interest rates directly. Forward guidance is an announcement by the central bank that the interest rates will remain low for extended period of time.

In Chapter 12 we study monetary policy in the short run. We discuss the organization and the operation of the Bank of Canada and describe the goals and tools of monetary policy. We explain the limits to monetary policy and new tools introduced during the Great Recession. We also analyze why the central bank should, or should not, be independent and how monetary policy operates in an open economy.

In Chapter 14 we analyze the implications of expectations for macroeconomic policy. We describe simple rules in monetary policy and discuss the pros and cons of the central bank operating under policy rules rather than using discretionary policy. We also describe Canada's experience of reducing inflation and the policy of inflation targeting.

Fiscal policy involves changes in government spending and tax cuts. Higher government spending directly raises demand for goods and services. Lower taxes raise demand indirectly: They increase disposable income and may raise consumption. Deliberate changes in government spending and in taxes constitute the active part of fiscal policy. In addition, in a recession the fiscal situation is affected by automatic stabilizers—mechanisms built into the economy that affect taxes and spending when the economy goes into a recession. When income falls, taxes fall as well and the decrease in disposable income is smaller than the total fall in income. When people lose jobs, unemployment and welfare payments rise, offsetting in part the drop in income due to job loss.

In Chapter 13 we study fiscal policy in the short run. We describe the goals and tools of fiscal policy and distinguish between automatic stabilizers and discretionary fiscal policy. We use the IS-MP model to study the effects of fiscal policy in the short run, the challenges of using fiscal policy effectively and analyze how fiscal policy operates in an open economy.

Both active and automatic fiscal policies raise government deficit and debt. Indeed, in the Great Recession the debt of many countries exploded. National debt of some countries in

---

[8]In 2014, however, the European Central Bank did introduce an effective negative nominal interest rate on bank reserves, by imposing a penalty on bank reserves. As we will see later, under extraordinary circumstances the nominal interest rate has, sometimes, been negative.

the Eurozone increased so much that it raised concerns about their ability to repay the debt. The concerns that current policies are not sustainable led many countries to reduce spending, prolonging the recovery from the Great Recession.

In Chapter 15 we discuss basic facts about Canada's fiscal situation and analyze when fiscal policy is sustainable and when it is not. We look at how fiscal policy affects the economy in the long run. A comparison of the increase in national debt during the Great Recession shows large differences across countries. We return to the crisis in the Eurozone and compare PIGS—Portugal, Ireland, Greece, and Spain—countries that did poorly and required external help, with FANGs—Finland, Austria, Germany, and the Netherlands—countries where the economies went through the Great Recession without fundamental problems.

The Causes of the Great Recession

To understand what happened we have to backtrack a few years. In 2001 the U.S. economy went through a brief recession. The collapse of the tech stock market bubble (S&P fell by almost 30% and the tech-heavy NASDAQ market fell by 70% from their peaks in 2000) reduced the wealth of stock owners and, consequently, their consumption. The terrorist attacks on September 11, 2001, scared people into staying at home, and retail sales fell. The combined effect was a reduction in consumption large enough to put the U.S. economy into a recession. The Federal Reserve reacted to the 2001 recession by reducing interest rates, using the standard approach to monetary policy.

Many central banks, including the Bank of Canada, have explicit inflation targets. The Bank of Canada's target is to keep inflation between 1% and 3% per year; it is not tasked with affecting the level of output: "The cornerstone of the Bank's monetary policy framework is its inflation-control system, the goal of which is to keep inflation near 2 per cent—the midpoint of a 1 to 3 per cent target range."[9] But the Federal Reserve's goal is to "to promote effectively the goals of maximum employment, stable prices, and moderate long-term interest rates."[10] Unlike the Bank of Canada, the Federal Reserve has a *dual mandate*: it is concerned with both unemployment and the rate of inflation. So the U.S. central bank is more willing than the Bank of Canada to reduce interest rates when the economy is weak.

In Chapter 4 we focus on money and its role in the economy. We define what money is and explain its functions. We describe how the Bank of Canada changes the quantity of money in the economy, and how those changes affect the inflation rate. We discuss the relationships among the growth rate of money, inflation, and nominal interest rates. The chapter concludes with a description of costs of inflation and an explanation of the causes of hyperinflation.

Even after the recession ended and the economy started growing again, the Federal Reserve did not raise interest rates. Low interest rates and new developments in the financial sector increased the availability of credit to house buyers, allowing many households to buy housing for the first time, or buy a more expensive house. The low interest rates facilitated the house-price boom.

Developments in the Financial Sector

Three developments in the financial sector played a major role in the Great Recession:

- loan securitization
- subprime loans
- high leverage

---

[9]See http://www.bankofcanada.ca/en/monetary/monetary.html.
[10]Federal Reserve Act, section 2a.

Loan securitization is the practice of selling pools of mortgages to investors. It reduced the perceived riskiness of mortgage lending and allowed investors around the world to participate in the U.S. housing boom. The growth of subprime mortgage lending provided affordable mortgage financing to people who were considered risky borrowers. In the past they would not have been able to obtain loans or would have had to pay very high interest rates on these loans. Leverage, which relies on borrowed money to raise bank profits, increased the demand for securities but made the financial system fragile. We discuss them in turn.

Loan Securitization In the past, the bank that gave out a mortgage (the loan originator) would keep the mortgage on its books as an asset until maturity. If the mortgage was non-performing (i.e., when the borrower missed payments or defaulted on the loan) the value of the asset would be reduced and the bank that originated the loan would incur a loss.

Securitization The process of converting loans, and other financial assets that are not tradeable, into securities.

Financial innovations, through a process of loan **securitization**, changed this. Loan securitization is a financial operation in which various assets are pooled and used as collateral to issue securities. These assets can be mortgages, car loans, credit-card debt, etc. The operation uses a specially created company, the so-called *special purpose vehicle (SPV)*. Mortgages are transferred from the bank to the SPV, creating a mortgage pool. The pool contains many mortgages (sometimes thousands) and is perceived as less risky than individual mortgages since risks are diversified. The SPV issues securities backed by the pool, called mortgage-backed securities (MBS). Interest and principal payment on the underlying mortgages are used to pay interest on the securities. The mortgaged property is the collateral.

Before being sold, securities backed by the mortgage pool were evaluated by rating agencies. The securities often received AAA rating. This is the highest rating, the same as, for example, Canadian or German government bonds and higher than Japanese or U.S. government bonds. The reason for the high rating was that mortgage-backed securities were believed to have very little risk. In the past, house prices throughout the United States rarely, if ever, fell. They would fall in one region but increase in another. So people believed default risk was uncorrelated across regions. A single mortgage is risky, but when only a few mortgages in a pool are non-performing, the total cash flow from the pool is stable. Default rates may increase in one region but not in other regions, ensuring low overall default risk and steady cash flow. Another reason for the high ratings was that the rating agencies were paid by the issuers of securities they rated. The issuer wants the best rating possible as this would facilitate selling the securities: Many financial institutions (for example, insurance companies) can only buy highly rated securities. The rating agencies believed, not incorrectly, that better ratings will lead to more business. In the end many ratings turned out to be very wrong.

The securities created by pooling mortgages were sold to investors around the world. The interest they paid was based on the interest rates of the underlying mortgages. As the securities received high ratings and paid high interest, they were easily sold. As a result, the process of securitization was a very profitable one. The creators of mortgage pools (usually investment banks) received fees; investors who bought them received high interest payments; and originating banks sold the risky assets and were able to issue more mortgage loans.

The problem with securitization is that the loan originator no longer suffers a loss if the loan turns out to be non-performing. The bank makes money not when the loan is repaid, but when the loan is provided and sold. By selling mortgages the bank replenishes its funds and is able to provide more mortgages, increasing its profits. This creates moral hazard. The loan originator gets the full benefit from providing mortgages, but does not suffer much when they default. So it focuses on providing as many mortgages as possible and may not pay sufficient attention to evaluating borrowers.

Subprime Mortgages The demand for mortgage-backed securities was high. There was a huge inflow of funds from high savings in booming Asian countries as well as from oil producing countries. Owners of these funds were looking for relatively safe investments. U.S. government bonds were the preferred instrument, but their interest rates were low. So funds flowed into mortgage-backed securities, which had higher returns and good credit ratings. Demand for high-quality mortgages exceeded supply. A consequence was a rapid increase in **subprime mortgages**. A subprime mortgage is a mortgage provided to borrowers with poor credit rating, who cannot get a regular (prime) mortgage. They may have had credit problems in the past, a short employment history, or have declared personal bankruptcy. Such borrowers have a higher risk of default and are charged higher interest, to compensate the lender for higher risk. Securities backed by subprime mortgages had a high yield (paid high interest). Pooling subprime mortgages with prime mortgages created securities with high yields that appeared relatively safe: The risk was diversified and the loans were supported by property that could be repossessed in case of non-payment.

To expand the market for mortgages, lenders provided the so-called **adjustable rate mortgages (ARM)**. In these mortgages the initial interest rate, called a teaser rate, is low. After a few years (usually two or three) the interest rate is raised to a higher level. The bank may charge a 3% interest rate for two years and then increase the rate to 7%, doubling the required repayments. Also, lenders relaxed their demands for down payment. In 2005 almost 30% of buyers financed the entire purchase.

Subprime loans made buying housing a possibility for many Americans who, in the past, had problems obtaining mortgage credit. Low down payments and low initial interest rates made the purchases affordable. Even people with limited funds could buy housing: The initial payment could be zero, and mortgage payments for the first two or three years were low. So, in the end, mortgage credit became available to risky borrowers at favourable terms, encouraging them to buy housing.

Leverage **Leverage** is based on the concept of using borrowed money to acquire assets. There are many definitions; a simple one we will use below is that leverage is equal to the ratio of assets to the difference between assets and liabilities (excluding capital).[11]

To understand leverage we consider Myron's Investment Management to illustrate a risky investment and the use of leverage. The investment is a purchase of mortgage-based securities. There are two sources of financial return. The securities pay an interest rate of 6%. In addition, there is a possibility of a capital gain, if the securities increase in price, or a loss if they fall in price. So Myron's Investment Management bets on the future price of the securities. Let us assume that, if the bet is good, they will increase in price by 6%, for a total return of 12%; if the bet is bad, they will fall in price 6%, for a total return of zero.

Myron's Investment Management has $100. It considers two investments. In the first, it buys securities for $100. Its assets (securities) are $100, its capital (own funds) is $100, liabilities (excluding capital) are zero, and the leverage (assets divided by the difference between assets and liabilities) is $100/($100 − $0) = 1. Myron's Investment Management company also contemplates a leveraged investment. It would borrow $1900 and purchase $2000 of securities. In that case total assets would be $2000 (securities), liabilities (excluding capital) would be $1900, and the leverage would be $2000/($2000 − $1900) = 20. The interest rate on borrowed funds is 5%. If Myron's Investment Management makes the leveraged bet and the bet is good, it will make 12% of $2000, i.e., $240, and will pay $95 in interest (5% of the $1900 borrowed) for a total return of $145. Since its own funds are $100, its return on capital will be 145%. If the bet is bad, the return on holding the securities will be zero: (6% interest minus 6% capital loss) but they will still have to pay $95 interest for the borrowed funds. So the total return will be −$95 or −95%. These calculations are summarized in Table 1.1.[12]

Subprime mortgage A mortgage provided to a borrower with poor credit rating due to past credit problems, short employment history, or personal bankruptcy.

Adjustable rate mortgage (ARM) A mortgage in which the initial interest rate (called the teaser rate) is low. After a few years the rate is increased upwards, to a significantly higher level.

Leverage A measure of how much debt an investor takes on when making an investment.

---

[11]In accounting, capital is the firm's liability; it is an asset for company owners, or for shareholders.

[12]You may wonder why Myron's Investment Management makes $145 when times are good and loses only $95 when times are bad. This is because it took on risk. The securities are riskier than a loan and so they pay an interest of 6% while the interest on the loan is only 5%.

Table 1.1 Leverage Multiplies Gains and Losses

	Leverage	%change in asset price	Interest on loan	Interest received	Capital gain/loss	Total return	% return
Good bet	1	+6%	$0	$6	$6	$12	12%
	20	+6%	$95	$120	$120	$145	145%
Bad bet	1	−6%	$0	$6	−$6	$0	0%
	20	−$6	$95	$120	−$120	−$95	−95%

As you can see from this example, gains and losses are multiplied by leverage. In addition, when the leverage is high, a relatively small decline in the value of bank assets can wipe out its equity and make it insolvent. As it turned out, financial institutions around the world were very heavily leveraged. (Lehman's leverage increased from 24 in 2005 to 31 in 2007.) Leverage of 33 was not uncommon; some institutions had leverage of 50. Such high leverage greatly increased the risk of collapse. But while everyone knew financial firms were highly leveraged, the exact extent was not known: through various accounting tricks some institutions, including Lehman, reduced the level of leverage they reported.

Rising House Prices

Subprime and ARM mortgages make sense in a rising market. When the value of the house increases, the borrower can refinance the house, taking on a bigger loan. The proceeds from refinancing are expected to be used to make mortgage payments, so even borrowers with weak credit history should be able to service their mortgage. Buyers who took out ARM mortgages were expected to refinance when the teaser interest rate expired. These expectations were based on the fact that, before the Great Recession, house prices were increasing in the United States. Figure 1.12 shows the increase, and subsequent decline, in U.S. house prices.

Rising house prices provided a feeling of security to both borrowers and lenders. It seemed that the risk of default was limited. Even if the house owner ran into financial difficulties, she could borrow against the increasing value of the house and use the loan to make mortgage payments. New buyers flocked to the market as mortgages were easily available at favourable terms. With house prices rising, households were concerned that delaying purchase would lead to a higher expense in the future, or even that prices would increase beyond their reach.

Figure 1.12

U.S. House Prices

Between July 2003 and July 2006 U.S. house prices increased by 50%; between July 2006 and March 2012 they fell back to the level in July 2003, i.e., by a third.

Source: S&P/Case-Shiller National Home Price Index, 10 cities, seasonally adjusted, nominal, January 2000=100

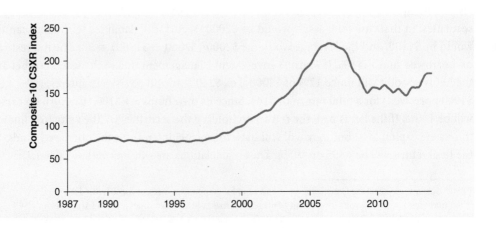

Other factors contributed to the increase in house prices. There was a significant amount of speculation, with a large proportion of housing bought for investment purposes, and not as personal residences. Properties were bought at early stages of construction and resold at a profit without even taking possession.

The decline in lending standards played an important role in the process. As already mentioned, securitization allows the bank providing the mortgage to eliminate default risk. The incentive then became to provide as many mortgages as possible. So borrowers were not adequately checked, and loans were made without sufficient attention to the ability to repay. As lending increased, more households bought housing, pushing prices up.

Wealth Effect of Higher House Prices The increase in house prices made homeowners feel wealthier. When households feel wealthier, they increase spending. The result of the increase in house prices was a rapid rise in consumption and a decline in savings. American households took on an unprecedented level of debt. The ratio of debt to disposable income increased by two-thirds, from 77% in 1990 to 127% in 2007. As long as interest rates remained low, the burden of the debt was bearable: The debt service ratio (the ratio of debt repayment to disposable income) increased from 12% in 1990 to only 14% in 2007. Investment also increased rapidly. With demand for housing high, residential construction, which is counted in national income accounts as investment, grew rapidly. With rising consumption all other types of investment were increasing as well. The economy grew fast, leading to higher incomes, more house purchases, and so on.

To summarize, the housing boom created favourable economic conditions. The economy was expanding fast, stimulated by the demand for housing. Many new buyers entered the housing market, taking on large amounts of debt. As long as house prices were increasing and interest rates were low, households were able to service the debt. There was a consumption boom, financed by home refinancing. At the same time, the financial system was becoming fragile, with high levels of bank leverage, complex links among financial institutions and large volume of loans to weak borrowers.

The Financial Crash

The Decline in House Prices The boom in the housing market, the increase in household debt, and the financial developments, in particular the expansion of risky, subprime lending, created a fragile financial system. As long as house prices were increasing and interest rates were low, the boom continued. Two developments ended the boom: Rising house prices led to overbuilding and a surplus of new homes, and mortgage rates increased. In July 2004 the Federal Reserve started increasing interest rates; by July 2006 they increased by 4%. As a result, mortgage interest rates rose as well, reducing demand for housing. With large supply and decreasing demand, house prices started falling in the second half of 2006.

Mortgage Defaults The fall in house prices led to mortgage defaults. Recall that ARMs were based on the assumption that, when the interest resets to a higher level, the borrower will refinance the home, taking on a larger mortgage, and use the proceeds to fund the higher mortgage payments. With house prices falling, this was no longer possible. Many borrowers found themselves unable to afford the higher interest rates and began to default on their mortgages. In addition, people who bought houses near the peak of the boom with little down payment ended up with negative equity: Their house was worth less than the amount of the mortgage debt. Houses with mortgage exceeding their value are called *under water*. Many owners gave up and walked away from their under-water houses, defaulting on their mortgages.

Why More Defaults in the United States? Non-recourse Loans Defaults were facilitated by the nature of mortgage loans in many U.S. states. Unlike in most countries, they are non-recourse loans. *Non-recourse loan* means that the mortgage loan is secured with property but the borrower is not personally responsible for the loan. So, in the case of loan default, the lender can take over (foreclose) the mortgaged property but has no claims against other assets of the borrower. A person walking away from their house loses it and suffers a deterioration of credit rating, making borrowing in the future difficult. But he can keep other assets and has no other obligations to the lender. A non-recourse loan allows the defaulting debtor to have a new start, without outstanding debts.

Default is much more costly for the borrower in the case of a recourse loan. In a recourse loan the borrower remains liable for the losses of the lender. When the bank forecloses and sells the property for less than the value of the mortgage, the former owner has to cover the difference. What is worse, the bank has limited incentive to get the best price possible since the borrower is responsible for the losses. So the former owner often ends up with a large debt. That is why people with recourse loans make extraordinary efforts not to fall behind in their payments and defaults are less common.

This difference in responsibilities in case of default is the reason why defaults were a much bigger problem in the United States than in other countries, even though house prices in several countries (South Africa, Spain, the United Kingdom, and Ireland) increased much more rapidly. With fewer defaults, the decline in house prices in these countries was less dramatic than in the United States.

Foreclosures and Further Decrease in House Prices The combination of higher interest rates, in particular on ARM mortgages, and the large number of properties that were under water led to a rapid increase in the number of defaults. Properties were foreclosed and put up for sale. This raised the supply of housing and led to a bigger decline in the price of housing, resulting in more defaults and foreclosures, further depressing housing prices. A vicious circle was created: as house prices fell, defaults and foreclosures increased, raising housing supply and leading to further price declines and more defaults.

Financial Institution Losses The value of mortgage-based securities depends on the number of non-performing mortgages. The pricing of such securities includes the possibility that a small proportion of mortgages will be defaulted on. The crisis led to much higher rate of default than expected, and the value of the securities fell. Financial institutions around the world incurred large losses. Some of the losses were covered by credit-default swaps, but these just moved losses from one institution to another.

As discussed before, the complex web of relationships between financial institutions made it difficult to assess the situation of potential borrowers. Banks were reluctant to lend money. Many institutions, in particular investment banks, found themselves unable to borrow. Investment banks typically borrow money in the short-term market and use the funds to buy less liquid assets, like real estate or mortgage-backed securities. They were now unable to borrow in the short-term market and had to resort to selling securities to repay maturing loans. This further depressed security prices and exacerbated financial markets problems. Another vicious circle was created: As the value of mortgage-based securities fell, many institutions sold them, further decreasing their price.

In the end, total losses of financial institutions were enormous; they were estimated by the IMF to be as high as $1.5 trillion. These losses wiped out a large portion of banking capital, leaving banks seriously undercapitalized.

Effect on the U.S. Economy

The problems described above were mostly of financial nature. But finance and the banking system are central to the economy. The role of the banking system is to take savings from people and institutions with excess funds and put them to the most effective use, providing credit to firms and consumers. Finance is like the blood system: When funds flow smoothly, everything works fine; when funds stop flowing, the economy stops. When the crisis started, two factors reduced the amount of available credit. As discussed before, banks found it difficult to assess the creditworthiness of potential borrowers. Also, banks started **deleveraging** (reducing their leverage) by decreasing their lending activity.

Deleveraging The reduction of leverage. For financial institutions it is achieved by reducing lending; for households it is achieved by reducing spending and repaying loans.

The effect on the U.S. economy was a decline in consumption, investment, and imports (with imports affecting other countries, in particular Canada).

Consumption fell for several reasons:

- lower household wealth
- reduced availability of credit
- unemployment concerns
- deleveraging

Household wealth declined as both house prices and stock markets fell. Just as rising wealth increases consumption, declining wealth reduces it. Households were no longer able to finance additional consumption by refinancing their homes. Consumer credit became much more difficult to obtain, and demand for cars and various large-ticket items, typically bought on credit, fell dramatically. As production fell, unemployment increased. Households concerned with the possibility of losing a job cut expenses, leading to a further decline in consumption. According to one report, the proportion of workers in the United States who were concerned about losing a job increased from 27% in February 2008 to 47% in February 2009. Over 70% of people knew someone who had lost a job in the previous six months.[13] Finally, to address their high debt levels households started deleveraging (which for households means reducing debt) by cutting their spending and repaying their loans.

Investment fell for three reasons:

- firms became less confident about the future
- firms reduced inventories
- housing starts declined

In national income statistics, there are three types of investment: business fixed investment, inventories, and residential construction. All three fell due to reduced availability of credit. Business fixed investment (building new factories, buying machinery etc.) is, by its very nature, forward looking. When an economy's prospects look bad, firms postpone investment projects. Firms reduced inventories to cut operational costs. And, as we already discussed, residential construction fell dramatically.

In Chapter 16 we analyze factors affecting consumption and investment. We discuss the macroeconomic implications of decision making by households and firms. The analysis of the determinants of personal consumption allows us to explain consumption smoothing: the tendency to consume constant amounts over time. We analyze government policies aimed at encouraging saving. We then turn to investment and study the determinants of private investment and the effects of government policies on private investment.

The Crisis Spreads Abroad

The U.S. economy constitutes about 20% of the world economy and is the world's biggest importer. The typical effect on other countries of a recession in the United States is through international trade. When output in the United States falls, so do U.S. imports from the rest of the world. But a recession in the United States need not, in general, cause a recession in

---

[13]*People Fear Losing Job the Most: Poll*, CNBC News February 19, 2009; http://www.cnbc.com/id/29275784

other countries. For example, in 2001 the recession in the United States did not spread even to Canada, even though our economy is far more dependent on exports to the United States than the economy of any other country.

Three Channels of Transmission   In the Great Recession the business cycle transmission went beyond the fall in U.S. imports. There were three channels:

- financial markets
- international trade and interconnected supply chains
- the effect of the U.S. crash on business and consumer attitudes in other countries

The most important channel was the effect through financial markets. Recall that mortgage-based securities were sold around the world. German banks, Spanish pension funds, Argentinean insurance companies, and other financial firms around the world bought securities that subsequently rapidly declined in value. As in the United States, the quality of assets on financial institutions' balance sheets was unknown. Apart from holding securities backed by subprime mortgages, many institutions sold credit-default swaps. They were not traded on organized exchanges and so there was no record on who owned money to whom and how a given institution was affected by the crisis.

One of the first banks to run into trouble was Northern Rock, a mid-size British bank that suffered a bank run in September 2007 and was nationalized (taken over by the government) a few months later. Many banks, especially in Europe, incurred large losses as they were even more leveraged than U.S. banks. The decline in the price of securities they held led them, just as U.S. banks, to reduce their lending activity. Credit became difficult to get, reducing investment and consumption.

The second channel was through international trade. As recession took hold, U.S. imports from the rest of the world declined. As the recession spread, other countries reduced their imports, and international trade declined rapidly. The decline was unprecedented: World trade fell by over 20%; Taiwan's trade fell by 40%. The decline in international trade was, initially, much more rapid than during the Great Depression (Figure 1.13).[14]

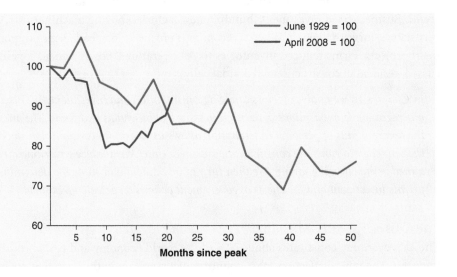

Figure 1.13

Decline in International Trade in the Great Depression and in the Great Recession

During the Great Recession, international trade fell faster than during the Great Depression, but started recovering much sooner.

Source: Based on Eichengreen and O'Rourke (2012).

---

[14]Barry Eichengreen and Kevin Hjortshøj O'Rourke, "A tale of two depressions redux", Voxeu.org, March 6, 2012.

Why did international trade collapse? In modern economies, complex goods are rarely produced in a single country. In recent years international, interconnected supply chains have been playing increasing role. Production is organized through these chains. Components are made in many different countries and the product assembled in another. The value of exports is then higher than the contribution of the products to GDP. This is because the value of exports is equal to the price of the product, and the contribution to GDP is equal to the value added: the difference between the price of the product, and the costs of supplies. A good example is the iPhone. According to information company IHS-iSuppli, materials in an iPhone 5s with 16 GB of memory cost $191, and manufacturing in China costs $8.[15] When, because of a recession, China assembles one fewer phone, its exports fall by $199 but output falls by only $8. During the Great Recession, trade in complex manufactured products was particularly affected, and so foreign trade declined much more rapidly than GDP.

The third channel of transmission was through the crisis' effect on consumer and business confidence in other countries. With the U.S. economy in recession, and banks everywhere in trouble, businesses reduced new investments and consumers cut their spending, in particular on durable goods. This led to an increase in unemployment and further declines in investment and consumption.

The Recession in Canada

Unlike in 2001, the U.S. recession did spread to Canada. When the Great Recession started, the Canadian economy was in good shape. Unemployment was low, the economy was growing fast, and the federal as well as many provincial governments had been running surpluses for a long time. The banking system was in good shape. Yet the Canadian economy still followed the U.S. economy into recession. It was transmitted to Canada through the other two channels: a decline in exports and a drop in business and consumer confidence.

The Canadian banking system weathered the Great Recession relatively well. Banks did not need government support and remained profitable. This was thanks to a tight regulatory regime and the prudent nature of Canadian banks, which had lower leverage and higher capital ratios. In fact, in a survey of executives from over 130 countries conducted by the World Economic Forum prior to Lehman collapse, Canadian banks were considered the soundest in the world. The housing boom in Canada was more modest than in the United States, and declines in house prices were limited. Canadian banks tend to keep mortgages rather than securitize them. This means they incur losses from mortgage default and so loan standards did not decline. While it is possible in Canada to buy a house almost entirely with borrowed money, such mortgages must be insured. As a result, there were relatively few mortgage defaults in Canada and mortgage insurance covered a large portion of the losses.

The export channel of transmission of a recession is particularly strong between Canada and the United States. The U.S. economy is by far our largest trading partner, and the Canadian economy depends crucially on exports to the United States. Three quarters of Canadian exports go to the United States; for comparison, our second largest trading partner is China, with 4% of Canadian exports. The severity of the U.S. recession resulted in a large decrease in demand for Canadian goods and services. The car industry was particularly affected. The Canadian car industry is a part of integrated North-American production process, with components and partially assembled vehicles moving, sometimes many times, across the border. Canadian automobile exports fell by 40%.

---

[15]Groundbreaking iPhone 5s Carries $199 BOM and Manufacturing Cost, IHS Teardown Reveals, HIS Pressroom, September 25, 2013.

Figure 1.14

Real GDP in Canada and the US, Q4 2008 = 100

The Great Recession in Canada started later than in the United States.

Sources: Statistics Canada, CANSIM Table 380–0084; Bureau of Economic Analysis, National Income and Product Accounts Tables, Table 1.1.6.

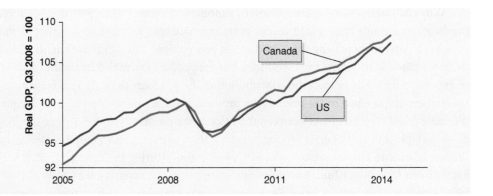

The last channel of transmission was also important. Canadian households became concerned about the severe recession in the United States and reduced spending. Investment fell as firms took a "wait and see" approach and delayed projects.

We will now briefly compare the Canadian experience with that in the United States. We will do a more detailed comparison later in the course, using your newly acquired macroeconomic knowledge.

Output   There is a popular saying that, if the United States sneezes, Canada catches a cold. In the Great Recession both countries caught a cold. Canada caught it from its neighbour but ours did not last as long. Output in the Great Recession in Canada and in the United States is compared in Figure 1.14. The scale on the horizontal axis is quarters. If you look carefully you may make the following observations: The rapid decline in output started in Canada one quarter later than in the United States, in the fourth quarter of 2008 versus the third quarter of 2008. (The recession in the United States actually started in December 2007 but, initially, output did not decline rapidly.) In the following three quarters output fell rapidly in both countries. Recovery in Canada started sooner and was stronger than in the United States.

Economists often compare business cycles by aligning data. This makes the similarities and differences more apparent. In our case we align the peaks before the start of the rapid decline of output. We set the value of U.S. GDP to 100 for the second quarter (Q2) of 2008; and the value of Canada's GDP to 100 for the third quarter (Q3) of 2008. Essentially we are moving Canadian data back a quarter to align the start of the rapid output decline in the two countries. The resulting data are in Figure 1.15. The numbers on the horizontal axis show the number of quarters before and after the beginning of the rapid drop in output.

Figure 1.15

Real GDP in Canada (Q3 2008 = 100) and in the U.S. (Q2 2008 = 100)

A better picture of the Great Recession in Canada and in the United States is obtained by delaying U.S. data by one quarter. The decline of output in Canada was as fast, but the recession was shorter and the economy recovered faster.

Sources: Statistics Canada, CANSIM Table 380–0084; Bureau of Economic Analysis, National Income and Product Accounts Tables, Table 1.1.6.

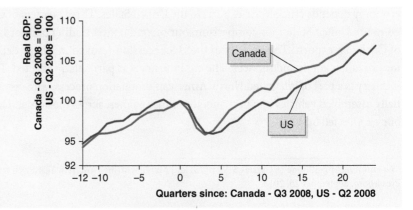

Now you can easily compare the behaviour of output in the Great Recession in Canada and in the United States. Prior to the crisis, output in both countries grew at similar rates. The first three quarters of rapid output decline were very similar. Afterward, Canadian output started increasing while, in the United States, output continued to fall, but at a slower rate. Once recovery started, Canadian GDP rose much faster than U.S. GDP. It reached its pre-crisis level 8 quarters after the beginning of the crisis (in Q3 2010) while U.S. GDP reached pre-crisis levels only after 12 quarters (in Q2 2011).

Why did Canada do better? There were three main reasons. First, Canadian banks were in better shape than U.S. banks, and the disruption in the banking system was smaller and shorter. Second, house prices in Canada did not crash, so the fall in consumption and investment were not driven by a decline in wealth. Third, as we show next, the Canadian dollar depreciated significantly, improving Canada's competitive position.

Unemployment Perhaps the biggest difference between the performance of the U.S. and Canadian economies was in unemployment. Traditionally, unemployment in the United States has been lower than in Canada, for reasons that we discuss in Chapter 6. Figure 1.16 shows the unemployment rates in Canada, the United States, and the European Union since 2005. The data are from OECD, which uses a common methodology to calculate unemployment rates, facilitating comparisons. Note that these rates, called by the OECD *harmonized unemployment rates*, differ slightly from the rates calculated by national statistical offices.

As you can see, in Figure 1.16, between 2005 and 2007 the unemployment rate in Canada was about 2% higher than in the United States. The unemployment rate in the United States started increasing earlier and, just prior to the Great Recession, the unemployment rates in both countries were similar: in Q3 2008 it was 6.1% in Canada and 6.0% in the United States. During the Great Recession the unemployment rates increased significantly in both countries, reaching a peak of 8.5% in Q3 2009 in Canada and 9.9% in Q4 2009 in the United States. The unemployment rates in both countries started declining in 2009, with the rates falling earlier in Canada. The improvement in Canada stalled in 2013 and, by Q1 2014, the unemployment rate in the United States fell below the level in Canada.

For comparison, Figure 1.16 shows the unemployment rate in the European Union. It increased almost continuously between 2008 and 2012 and started declining only in the second half of 2013, but has not fallen below 10% by 2014. Clearly, the unemployment situation in Canada and in the United States is much better than in the European Union.

In Chapter 6 we study unemployment. We begin by analyzing the determination of employment and real wages. Then we discuss the three categories of unemployment: frictional, which is related to job search; structural, which arises when workers' qualifications

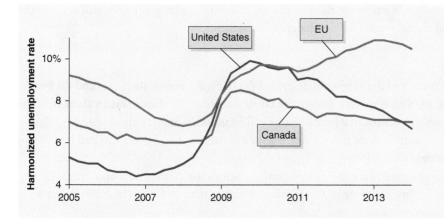

Figure 1.16

The Unemployment Rate in Canada, the United States, and the European Union (EU).

Before the Great Recession the unemployment rate in the United States was significantly lower than in Canada. During the recession it increased more and, by 2014, fell below the rate in Canada. The unemployment rate in the EU increased almost continuously between 2008 and 2012; it started to decline only in the second half of 2013 and remained much higher than in Canada or in the United States.

Source: OECD. Statsextracts

Figure 1.17

$US/$CAN Exchange Rate

In 2007 the Canadian dollar appreciated significantly. During the financial crisis it depreciated by 20% (or $US appreciated by 25%). It reached its pre-crisis level in January 2011.

Source: Bank of Canada.

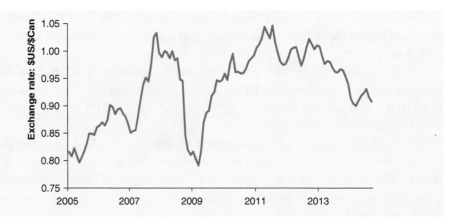

do not match employers' needs; and cyclical unemployment. We discuss the reasons for differences in the unemployment rates across countries, and in particular for the high unemployment rate in Europe. We conclude by analyzing government policies aimed at reducing unemployment.

The Exchange Rate An important factor in Canadian economic performance was the exchange rate, shown in Figure 1.17. In October 2007 the Canadian dollar reached parity with the U.S. dollar. (Parity means the exchange rate of one U.S. dollar for one Canadian dollar.) This was the consequence of a weak U.S. economy and high resource prices. The exchange rate stayed close to parity until the beginning of the Great Recession. During the financial panic that followed Lehman Brothers collapse, the Canadian dollar depreciated by 20% (from parity to $US0.8/$CAN); equivalently, the U.S. dollar appreciated by 25% (from parity to $CAN1.25/$US). This may strike you as surprising; after all, the economic problems were created in the United States. The reason for the appreciation of the U.S. dollar was that, when markets become very volatile, there is a "flight to quality": Many money managers switch to safe and liquid assets. The market for U.S. bonds is the largest and the most liquid in the world, and so offered a safe place to park funds temporarily until the financial situation cleared up. Since March 2009, after the panic subsided, the Canadian dollar started appreciating and remained at or above parity since March 2010. The depreciation of the Canadian dollar in 2008-09 lowered the price of Canadian exports to the United States and made the Great Recession in Canada less severe.

In Chapter 5 we focus on exchange rates. We analyze the advantages and disadvantages of fixed, flexible, and mixed exchange rate policies. We describe what happens when, with fixed exchange rates, there is pressure on the currency to appreciate or depreciate. We study the determination of exchange rates in the short and in the long run. We also analyze the international capital market and the balance of payments.

Summary

In this introduction to the course we described the Great Recession: its causes and the behaviour of the Canadian economy during the Great Recession. The goal was to show how the macroeconomic topics covered in the course will be useful to analyze current events. Macroeconomics matters. To show this we finish with a few examples of good and bad macroeconomic outcomes.

The first example is about unemployment. Before the Great Recession, from 2005 to 2007, the unemployment rate in Germany was higher than in Spain (in 2007, it was 8.7%

Martin Shields/Alamy

in Germany and 8.3% in Spain). By October 2013, the unemployment rate in Germany fell to 5.2% and increased to 26.7% in Spain. Youth unemployment (population aged 15–24) in 2006 was similar in both countries: 14% in Germany and 18% in Spain. By 2013 it fell to 8% in Germany and increased to 56% in Spain. In other words, in 2006 the unemployment rates in both countries were moderately high; seven years later they were very low in Germany and extraordinarily high (even higher than during the Great Depression) in Spain.

The second example is about public debt. In 2007, the debt-to-GDP ratio was 49.7% in Sweden and 28.6% in Ireland. In 2012, it was 48.8% in Sweden and increased to 127.5% in Ireland. In 2007 debt was low in both countries; by 2012 it fell in Sweden but it increased to unsustainable levels in Ireland.

The third example is about inflation. For the past 20 years, the inflation rate in Canada was stable at around 2% per year. In Zimbabwe, inflation got out of hand so that at the end of 2008, the central bank was printing banknotes with denomination of $100 trillion Zimbabwean dollars (100 followed by 12 zeroes); a facsimile of the note is shown above. You can imagine the damage inflation did to the Zimbabwean economy. With the value of domestic currency driven to zero it was abandoned, and the country switched to using U.S. dollars.

Key Terms and Problems

Key Terms

Adjustable rate mortgage (ARM), p. 27

Business cycle, p. 2

Deflation, p. 9

Deleveraging p. 31

Endogenous variable, p. 16

Exogenous variable, p. 16

Financial crisis, p. 11

Fiscal policy, p. 11

Great Recession, p. 1

Inflation rate, p. 9

Labour force, p. 7

Labour productivity, p. 3

Leverage, p. 27

Long-run economic growth, p. 3

Macroeconomics, p. 2

Microeconomics, p. 2

Monetary policy, p. 11

Moral hazard, p. 19

Normative analysis, p. 17

Positive analysis, p. 17

Real gross domestic product (GDP), p. 4

Securitization, p. 26

Subprime mortgages, p. 27

Unemployment rate, p. 7

What Macroeconomics Is About
Become familiar with the focus of macroeconomics.

Review Questions

1.1 What is long-run economic growth, and how is it measured? Have all countries experienced about the same amount of long-run economic growth? Briefly explain.

1.2 What is a business cycle? What has happened to the severity of the Canadian business cycle since 1950?

1.3 Describe the inflation rate in Canada over the past 40 years. When has Canada experienced high inflation? When has Canada experienced deflation? Are inflation rates roughly the same in countries around the world? Briefly explain.

1.4 Why is spending on health care and government retirement programs increasing in Canada and other high-income countries? What problems might this increased spending pose to the economy?

Problems and Applications

1.5 The average rate of growth of Canadian real GDP is approximately 3%, as measured over long periods of time. China has been averaging growth rates that are considerably higher than 3% for much of the past two decades, while some sub-Saharan African countries have experienced growth rates that are considerably lower than 3% or even negative.

    a. What is happening to the ratio of income in Canada to income in China?

    b. What is happening to the ratio of income between Canada and to income in these African countries?

    c. In general, for countries to "catch up" to higher-income countries, what must happen in terms of growth rates?

1.6 Consider the following statement: "A country like China is more open than a country like Belgium because it is larger and has a higher total value of imports and exports."

    a. How do economists define openness?

    b. Do you agree with this statement? Explain.

1.7 During the last recession and financial crisis, each of the programs listed below was implemented. Identify whether each of these programs represents monetary policy or fiscal policy.

    a. The Bank of Canada decreased interest rates.

    b. The federal government of Canada increased spending.

    c. The Chinese government increased spending on infrastructure, such as roads and high-speed trains.

    d. The U.S. Federal Reserve took actions that greatly increased the money supply.

1.8 [Related to the Chapter Opener **on page 1**] According to an economic study, "Increasing evidence suggests that even short [recessions] can have substantial ... effects on workers' careers." Why might graduating when there is a weak labour market have a substantial effect on a college graduate's career even after the economy has recovered and the job market has improved?

Source: Philip Oreopoulos, Till von Wachter, and Andrew Heisz, "The Short- and Long-Term Career Effects of Graduating in a Recession: Hysteresis and Heterogeneity in the Market for College Graduates," IZA Discussion Paper No. 3578, June 2008.

How Economists Think About Macroeconomics
Explain how economists approach macroeconomic questions.

Review Questions

2.1 Why do economists build models? Explain the steps generally used in building an economic model.

2.2 Explain the difference between an endogenous variable and an exogenous variable.

2.3 Why is it customary to say that a hypothesis has "not been rejected" rather than "accepted"?

2.4 What is the difference between normative analysis and positive analysis? Is economics concerned primarily with normative analysis or with positive analysis?

Problems and Applications

2.5 [Related to Solved Problem 1.1 **on page 15**] Many people believe that significant numbers of Canadian jobs have been "outsourced"—that is, firms have relocated operations to countries in which labour is cheaper, so the jobs have moved overseas. This happened, for example, with the steel industry. Briefly describe how you would analyze the following question: "Has the amount of outsourcing by Canadian companies been significant relative to the size of the Canadian labour market?" What problems might you expect to encounter in carrying out your analysis?

2.6 Explain which of the following statements would make a reasonable hypothesis to test. Use the concepts of normative and positive statements in your answers.

a. Increases in the duration of unemployment benefits lead to higher rates of unemployment.

b. Immigration is bad for society.

c. Increases in the labour force cause output to rise.

d. Welfare programs make workers lazy.

e. Higher rates of taxation increase work effort.

2.7 If you were studying the following relationships, which variable would be exogenous and which would be endogenous?

a. The effect of investment growth on the growth rate of GDP

b. The relationship between the amount of sunshine and plant growth

c. The relationship between hours of studying and a student's GPA

2.8 Consider the following statement: "Economic models use many simplifying assumptions. Therefore, they do not apply to the more complex events in the real world." Do you agree or disagree with this statement? Explain your answer.

2.9 **[Related to the** Making the Connection **on page 17]** Assume that you overheard a student make the following statement in your macroeconomics class:

The so-called European debt crisis may be important to people who live in Greece or Italy but it has little effect on the economy of Canada. Our economy does not depend on foreign trade as much as the economies of these countries do. And if we can't sell our exports in Europe, we can always sell them in the United States, South America, or Asia.

Write a response to this student that explains how debt crises in Europe can affect the Canadian economy.

2.10 **[Related to the** Making the Connection **on page 21]** Why did the U.S. Federal Reserve allow the Bank of United States to fail in 1930? Why did the U.S. Federal Reserve allow Lehman Brothers to fail in 2008? Contrast the Fed's actions following the failure of the Bank of United States with its actions following the failure of Lehman Brothers.

1.3 The Great Recession and an Overview of the Book
Become familiar with the Great Recession

Review Questions

3.1 What event started the Great Recession?

3.2 What is moral hazard? Why was it a problem during the Great Recession?

3.3 Which developments in the financial sector in the United States contributed to the Great Recession? Which one, in your view, was the most important?

3.4 How did the Great Recession get transmitted from the United States to Canada?

Problems and Applications

3.5 There is a saying that if the United States sneezes, Canada catches a cold. In common understanding it means that a recession in the United States causes a recession (perhaps a more severe recession) in Canada. Why would the Canadian

economy follow the U.S. economy into a recession? Is it always the case?

Source: Jean Boivin, "The 'Great' Recession in Canada: Perception vs. Reality," Bank of Canada, March 28, 2011.

3.6 During the Great Recession the U.S. government and the Federal Reserve helped several large financial institutions (except for Lehman Brothers) to survive while many manufacturing firms went bankrupt. Why is the bankruptcy of a financial firm a bigger problem than the bankruptcy of a manufacturing firm?

3.7 A purchase of a house is a leveraged transaction. The buyer puts up some of her own funds and borrows the rest.

a. Assume that the buyer borrows 80% of the value of the house. What is the leverage?

b. Before the Great Recession, some home buyers borrowed 100% of the value of the house. What is the leverage in this case?

3.8   A high-ratio mortgage is a mortgage that exceeds 80% of the value of the house, and the borrower's down payment is less than 20%. In Canada, such mortgages must be insured with the Canada Mortgage and Housing Corporation (CMHC).

a. What is, in your opinion, the reason for this requirement?

b. What is the effect of mandatory insurance of high-ratio mortgages on the likelihood of a financial crisis?

Data Exercises

D1.1: [Spreadsheet exercise] Statistics Canada offers a wide range of economic data at its website, (http://www5.statcan.gc.ca/cansim/home-accueil?lang=eng). Use these data to examine inflation for Canada from 1914 to the present.

a. Download annual data on the CPI (Table 326-0020) from 1914 to the present. Use the Add/Remove data tab to select 1914 as the starting year. Use the Manipulate tab to select Frequency of output data as Annual (average). Calculate the annual inflation rate. Are there years in which the CPI decreased?

b. Calculate the average CPI inflation rate for the period from 1970 to 1990 and from 1991 to the most recent year available. How does the inflation rate compare between the two periods?

D1.2: The Federal Reserve Bank of St. Louis offers a wide range of economic data collected from many sources at its website, called FRED (research.stlouisfed.org/fred2/), including data for Canada. We can use these data to compare the behaviour of real GDP per capita in Canada and the United States.

a. Download the annual data on real GDP per capita in Canada (CANRGDPC) and for the United States (USARGDPC) from 1960 to the present. Chart the two data series on the same graph. How does real GDP per capita in Canada compare to real GDP per capita in the United States? Have there been any changes in the relationship over time? Briefly explain.

b. Calculate and chart the ratio of real GDP per capita in Canada and the United States. Describe the trends in the ratio. When was the GDP per capita increasing faster in Canada than in the United States? When it was increasing slower?

c. The United States had a mild recession in 2001; there was no recession in Canada. Does the recession in the United States show in U.S. GDP data as a decline in GDP? Explain.

d. What happened with the ratio of GDP per capita in Canada and in the United States in 2002, compared to 2001?

D1.3: Download, from the Federal Reserve Bank of St. Louis FRED database (research.stlouisfed.org/fred2/), the annual data on the Consumer Price Index for Canada (CANCPIBLS) and the United States (USACPIBLS) from 1955 to the present. For both Canada and the United States calculate the inflation rate as the annual growth rate of the Consumer Price Index. Chart the two data series on the same graph. How does the inflation rate in Canada compare to the inflation rate in the United States? In particular, how do the inflation rates in the two countries compare since 1995? Has either country ever experienced negative inflation rates?

D1.4: [Spreadsheet exercise] Use the *Measuring Worth* data to practise the following spreadsheet skills, which you will need to use in later other chapters:

a. Import the data on inflation rates in Japan from 1990 to 2012 into a spreadsheet.

b. Chart the two series on the same graph. How do they compare with each other?

c. Find the average wage change and the average inflation rate. What is the standard deviation of each series?

d. What is the correlation coefficient for the two series? What does it mean?

Measuring the Macroeconomy

Learning Objectives

After studying this chapter, you should be able to:

2.1 Explain how economists use gross domestic product (GDP) to measure total production and total income (pages 43–49)

2.2 Discuss the difference between real GDP and nominal GDP (pages 50–53)

2.3 Explain how the inflation rate is measured, and distinguish between real and nominal interest rates (pages 54–60)

2.4 Understand how to calculate the unemployment rate (pages 61–62)

How Do We Know When We Are in a Recession?

The U.S. president Harry Truman famously remarked, "A recession is when your neighbour loses his job; a depression is when you lose yours." The typical description of a recession among non-economists is that it starts when there are two consecutive quarters of declining output. Such a description provides a simple, easily understandable, and precise criterion. In general, however, this simple definition is insufficient. Recessions differ greatly and cannot be summarized by the behaviour of output alone. Economists look at the behaviour of several macroeconomic variables: the employment rate (the proportion of adults who are working for pay), the unemployment rate (the ratio of unemployed to the sum of employed and unemployed), vacancies, factory orders, the proportion of industries that are contracting, and other measures.

Governments typically do not formally announce when the economy is in recession, in part because such announcement may not be credible. For example the government in power may be tempted to declare, before an election, that the economy is booming. Instead, the dating of recessions is left to independent economists. In Canada, the C.D. Howe Institute, an independent research organization, has recently undertaken the task of systematically dating Canadian recessions. The C.D. Howe Business Cycle Council determined, for example, that there was an expansion from April 1992 to October 2008 (the longest since the beginning of the data, in 1926), and a recession from October 2008 to May 2009 (one of the shortest). In the United States, most economists accept the dates for business cycle recessions and expansions determined by

Continued on next page

the National Bureau of Economic Research (NBER). For example, NBER determined that a business-cycle expansion began in November 2001 and ended in December 2007, and it determined that the following recession ended in June 2009, when the next expansion began.

How does the C.D. Howe Institute's Business Cycle Council determine when a recession begins and ends? There are no simple, clear rules. The Council defines a recession as a pronounced, pervasive, and persistent decline in aggregate economic activity. The Council looks both at the length and size of the decline in output and employment and the sectors of the economy that are affected. To call a recession, the Council requires that output falls for at least one quarter. The decline in output needs not be large, but it has to be persistent: A 0.1% drop in GDP in one quarter when in adjacent quarters the economy is growing strongly would not be considered a recession. The Council also looks at the proportion of sectors with falling output, particularly in manufacturing and construction. These two sectors vary the most over the business cycle. A general decline accompanied by robust growth in manufacturing and construction is unlikely to be a recession.

The recession timing as determined by the C.D. Howe's Business Cycle Council is as follows:

C.D. Howe Recession dates	
Beginning, quarter	End, quarter
1929:Q2	1933:Q1
1937:Q3	1938:Q2
1947:Q2	1948:Q1
1951:Q1	1951:Q4
1953:Q2	1954:Q2
1960:Q1	1961:Q1
1974:Q4	1975:Q1
1979:Q4	1980:Q2
1981:Q2	1982:Q4
1990:Q1	1992:Q2
2008:Q3	2009:Q2

The economic data used by the C.D. Howe are collected by Statistics Canada, the Canadian federal statistical agency. Statistics Canada is generally considered to be one of the best statistical offices in the world. It provides estimates of macroeconomic variables fairly quickly and the estimates are quite accurate: subsequent revisions are small. Nonetheless, the information is retrospective: first, the data measure economic activity during a period that has already passed; second, the collection and processing of data takes time. As a result, the start of a recession is determined several months after the recession has begun. The C.D. Howe Business Cycle Council list of recessions was published more than two years after the end of the last recession, and we do not know how long its delay in announcing future recessions and expansions will be. In the United States the delays are substantial. For example, the announcement that the most recent recession began in December 2007 was made by NBER twelve months later, in December 2008.

The Federal Government and the Bank of Canada are typically unwilling to wait a year or more to take action when they believe a recession may have begun. Newly issued macroeconomic data—whatever their flaws—guide the actions of policymakers. Businesses, investors, and households are in a similar position. Businesses often have to make decisions—such as whether to open new stores or factories or introduce new products—that will turn out to be good ideas if the economy is in an expansion and poor ideas if the economy heads into a recession. For example, in 2010–13 there was a condominium building boom in Toronto. When the demand for new condominiums fell, several developers had projects in development and were unable to sell them. Households are in a similar situation. When they buy houses, cars, or furniture, they may regret the decision if the economy unexpectedly falls into a recession and businesses start laying off workers.

We can conclude that knowledge of key macroeconomic data, including how they are constructed and their possible shortcomings, is very important to the study of macroeconomics.

Sources: Philip Cross and Philippe Bergevin, "Turning Points: Business Cycles in Canada since 1926," C.D. Howe Institute Commentary number 366, October 24, 2012, and National Bureau of Economic Research, "Statement of the NBER Business Cycle Dating Committee on the Determination of the Dates of Turning Points in the U.S. Economy," www.nber.org.

Introduction

In many countries, the Great Recession was one of the worst since the Great Depression of the 1930. How do we know that? How do we know how many people lost their jobs during the recession or what happened to the inflation rate? The answer is that economists, consumers, firms, and policymakers all rely on economic data gathered by statistical agencies. These data allow us to measure key aspects of the economy, including total production, total employment, and the price level. Economists rely on these data not just to measure the economy but also to test hypotheses derived from macroeconomic models of the economy.

In this chapter, we will focus on the data used in calculating three important measures of the macroeconomic performance of the economy:

1. Gross domestic product (GDP)
2. The inflation rate
3. The unemployment rate

We first discuss why GDP is chosen as a measure of economic activity. Then we explain how the numbers are calculated and which economic activity is included in the calculation of GDP. In Section 2.2 we discuss the calculation of price indices and the differences between the two most often used indices: the GDP deflator and the Consumer Price Index (CPI). In the last section we describe how Statistics Canada collects unemployment information.

GDP: Measuring Total Production and Total Income

2.1

Learning Objective

Explain how economists use gross domestic product (GDP) to measure total production and total income.

The rules used in calculating the gross domestic product (GDP) are called **national income accounting**. Nearly all countries around the world use similar rules to produce *national income accounts*, which is the name given to GDP and other related measures of total production and total income. To make data comparable across countries, and to have uniform methodology of calculating output, countries use the United Nation's System of National Accounts (SNA). In Canada the system is called the Canadian System of National Economic Accounts (CSNEA). The data are collected and compiled by Statistics Canada. Because these reports provide important information on the state of the economy, economists, business managers, policymakers, and financial analysts watch them closely.

CSNEA emphasizes the **gross domestic product (GDP)** and so it is the most commonly used measure of output in Canada. GDP is the market value of all **final goods and services** produced in a country during a period of time, typically a year. Final goods and services are produced for the purchase by the ultimate user and not to be used as input for the production of other goods. We count only final goods and services to avoid double counting. If goods and services that are produced for further processing (called *intermediate* goods and services) were included, they would be counted twice: once when they are produced, and again when the final product is produced. For example an engine installed in a car would have been counted once when it was produced and the second time when the car was produced.

National income accounting The rules used in calculating GDP and related measures of total production and total income.

Gross domestic product (GDP) The market value of all final goods and services produced in a country during a period of time, usually a year.

Final goods and services Goods and services that are produced for purchase by the ultimate user and not used as input for the production of other goods.

What Does "GDP" Mean?

- **Gross** means that depreciation of capital is not excluded. The alternative is *Net*, which means that depreciation is excluded.
- **Domestic** means produced in Canada by anyone, a Canadian or a foreigner. The alternative is *National*, which means produced by Canadians anywhere.
- **Product** means we are measuring production. The alternatives are to measure *Expenditure* or *Income*.

As you can see, there are some arbitrary decisions in the definition of GDP. We will first discuss why GDP is chosen as a measure of economic activity. Then we will explain how the numbers are calculated and which economic activity is included in the calculation of GDP.

Gross Production requires **capital goods**, machines, machine tools, factories, and office buildings that are used to produce other goods and services. During production capital

Capital goods Machines, machine tools, factories, and office buildings that are used to produce other goods and services.

goods get partially used up (depreciate). In addition, capital goods become obsolete. Due to depreciation and obsolescence the value of capital goods falls. Since depreciation is a cost of production, Statistics Canada should, in principle, subtract depreciation of capital from the calculation of GDP. For example, Simon's Pizza uses electricity, flour, and other supplies to make pizzas. Pizzas are baked in an oven that is worth $20 000 at the beginning of the year and $10 000 at the end of the year. During the year Simon's Pizza produces 10 000 pizzas. To account for the production of new goods and services, Statistics Canada should subtract the decrease in the value of the oven, $10 000, or $1 per each pizza, from the value of the company output. But, in practice, evaluating the amount of depreciation with a reasonable precision is difficult, and often impossible. Statisticians have only limited information about how much capital gets used up in the production process. There are three reasons for the difficulty. First, there are many types of capital goods that depreciate at different rates. Second, even identical capital goods may be used with different intensity. Third, capital goods may be used for a shorter or a longer period of time than their expected lifetime. For example, the chair on which you are sitting in the lecture hall may have an expected lifespan of 10 years. If the hall is renovated after 8 years the chair may be replaced earlier than expected. On the other hand, if university funding does not keep up with costs, the university may end up using the chair for a longer period of time than expected. Because of those problems, Statistics Canada is not able to calculate with much precision the amount of depreciation. Therefore, the preferred measure of output is gross output.

Domestic In the calculation of GDP, Statistics Canada takes into account goods and services produced in Canada, regardless of who produced them. GDP is closely related to employment, industrial production, and other economic variables that do not take the nationality of the firm into account. You may think of GDP as a measure of economic activity in Canada. To understand the concept of measuring *domestic* output, consider, for example, Toyota and TD Bank. Toyota is a Japanese company that produces cars in Canada. Canadian GDP includes the value of those cars. The TD Bank, which is a Canadian company, has a large presence in the United States. The value of its services provided abroad is not included in Canadian GDP. They are included in U.S. GDP.

Gross national product (GNP) The value of final goods and services produced by residents of a country, even if the production takes place outside that country.

Factors of production Capital, labour, and land used to produce goods and services.

In the past, gross *national* product was often used to measure the level of output. **Gross national product (GNP)** is the value of final goods and services produced by residents of a country, even if the production takes place outside that country. GNP measures the production of goods and services by **factors of production** (capital, labour, and land used to produce goods and services), owned by the country's residents. For example, Toyota owns a factory in Cambridge, Ontario. Output of the factory is included in our GDP, but GNP includes only income (wages, bonuses, etc.) of Canadians working at the factory. The return of Toyota's capital employed in Cambridge (i.e., profits earned by Toyota's Cambridge plant), is the output of foreign factors of production in Canada. It is included in our GDP but not in our GNP. In addition, there are some foreign employees at the Cambridge factory. Their income (wages, bonuses, etc.) is included in our GDP but not included in our GNP.

How about the TD Bank? The profits of its U.S. operations, as well as income of Canadians working at the bank in the United States, is the income of Canadian factors of production abroad and so it is included in Canadian GNP, but is not included in Canadian GDP.

We conclude that GDP equals GNP plus the earnings of foreign capital in Canada plus the earnings of foreigners working in Canada, minus the earnings of Canadian capital abroad minus the income of Canadians working abroad. We call the earnings of foreign capital in Canada plus the earnings of foreigners working in Canada the *income of foreign factors in*

Canada. We call the earnings of Canadian capital abroad and the income of Canadians working abroad the *income of Canadian factors abroad.* So

GDP = GNP + income of foreign factors in Canada − income of Canadian factors abroad.

We can further simplify this formula by defining *net factor payments* as income of foreign factors in Canada minus income of Canadian factors abroad. So GDP and GNP are related by the following identity:

$$GDP = GNP + \text{Net factor payments.} \tag{2.1}$$

Canadian GDP exceeds Canadian GNP by about 2%. The difference is mostly due to net capital earnings, as net labour earnings are close to zero. There is more foreign capital in Canada than Canadian capital abroad. This is not surprising: like Australia (where GDP exceeds GNP by 3%), Canada is a large country, with relatively small population and so is a net recipient of capital. Among developed countries the difference between GDP and GNP is the biggest in Ireland, where GDP exceeds GNP by 20%. This is because, with low profit taxes, a well-educated, English speaking population and access to the European Union, Ireland attracted large inflows of foreign capital, in particular from the United States. Conversely, GNP exceeds GDP by 7% in Switzerland and by 3% in Japan; both countries have large capital holdings abroad. One of the largest exporters of labour is the Philippines, where GNP exceeds GDP by about 10%. In the United States and in China net factor payments are small and the difference between GDP and GNP is less than 1%.

How Statistics Canada Calculates GDP

We will now describe some important rules about the definition of GDP and how the Statistics Canada calculates it.

GDP Is Measured Using Market Values When looking at individual firms or industries, we typically measure their output in terms of quantities, such as the number of cars produced by Toyota, the number of subscribers to Bell's internet service, or the number of cellphones produced worldwide. But in measuring total production, we can't just add the number of cars to the number of subscribers and so on because the result would be a meaningless number. Instead, we use market prices and calculate the *value* in dollar terms of all the goods and services produced. In addition to being convenient, market prices also tell us how much consumers value a particular good or service. If pears sell for $0.50 each and plums sell for $1.00 each, then the market prices tell us that consumers value a plum twice as much as a pear.

Calculating Value Added To avoid double counting, we include only **value added**: the difference between the value of output of a firm minus the cost of supplies. So if McDonald's buys a bun for $0.10 and sells a hamburger in the bun for $0.99, we count the output of McDonalds as $0.99 – $0.10 = $0.89. The value of the bun is included in the output of the bakery. Similarly, if the bakery buys flour from a mill for $0.04, the value of the output of the bakery is $0.10 – $0.04 = $0.06, and the value of the output of the mill is $0.04.

Value added The difference between the value of production and costs of supplies.

Imputed Values Statistics Canada uses the market values for goods and services in computing GDP, but in some cases, when there is no market for the good or service, the value has to be *imputed*, or estimated. The two important categories are the imputed rent for owner-occupied housing and the imputed value of government services provided at no charge or at partial cost. Housing provides a stream of housing services. For rental accommodation, the rent is the value of housing services. But many households own their houses or apartments and pay no rent. For owner-occupied housing, Statistics Canada calculates the rent of similar rental accommodation; this is the imputed value of housing services. Various government services, such as police, fire, elementary, and high school education, are provided free of charge. Other services, such as university education, require a partial payment by the user. These services do not have market prices. Statistics Canada imputes the value of these services as being equal to the cost of providing them.

Home Production and Underground Economy In the calculation of GDP, home production and the underground economy are not included. *Home production* includes all services produced outside the market, such as the services a homemaker provides to the homemaker's family. In principle the value of these services could be imputed, but the estimate would not be precise. Although home production is useful, usefulness is a value judgment and Statistics Canada cannot use value judgments in its calculations. The *underground economy* refers to the production and sale of goods and services that are not recorded, either to avoid tax payments or because they are illegal. Clearly, these are market transactions that are part of the economy. As with home production, the value of these goods and services could be estimated, but information on the underground economy is imperfect and the estimate would be very imprecise. In fact, in 2014 the Eurostat, the European Union statistical office, instructed European Union countries to include some underground economy activities in the calculation of the GDP but some countries decided not to do it.[1]

Note that neither the legality nor the usefulness of the good or service are reasons to exclude them from GDP. For example, alcohol or cigarettes illegally sold to under-age customers are counted. If something is produced, it is counted. Economists Friedrich Schneider of Johannes Kepler University and Dominik Enste of the University of Cologne have surveyed studies estimating the size of the underground economy in countries around the world.[2] They find the underground economy in Canada is around 10% of GDP, or about $150 billion. In contrast, the underground economy may be as high as 76% of GDP in Nigeria and 40% in Russia.

Most economists believe that the Statistics Canada's decision not to include some goods and services does not present a problem in using GDP data. Typically, we are the most interested in using GDP to measure *changes* in total production over a relatively brief period of time—say, a few years. It is unlikely that the total value of goods and services that are not counted by Statistics Canada (such as the services of homemakers or goods and services sold in the underground economy) changes much relative to the size of the economy over a short period. So, our measures of the *changes* in total production would not be much different, even if Statistics Canada were able to impute values for every good and service.

Existing Goods GDP includes only current production during the given time period. For example, the sale of a used car is not included because the production of the car has already been counted in an earlier period, when it was first sold. If we counted the sale of a used car, we would be double counting the car: first when it was initially produced and again when it was resold. When a used car is sold directly by the owner to the final user, GDP does not change. Note that when the car is sold through a used car dealer, GDP increases by the difference between what the dealer sells the car for and what he paid for it. This difference is the value of services provided by the dealer.

Production and Income

National income accounting reveals that *the value of total production in an economy is equal to the value of total income.* To see why, think about what happens to the money you

---

[1]"France refuses EU order to include drugs, prostitution in GDP figures," RFI, June 18, 2014.
[2]Friedrich Schneider and Dominik H. Enste, "Shadow Economies: Size, Causes, and Consequences," *Journal of Economic Literature*, Vol. 38, No. 1, March 2000, pp. 77–114.

spend on a single product. For example, if you purchase an ice cream at a local store for $6, all of the $6 must end up as someone's income. The store will use the proceeds to pay the producer for the ice cream, pay other suppliers (for electricity, store equipment, etc.), pay wages and bonuses to its employees, and pay rent for the property it leases. The rest becomes the store's profits, which can be negative. Similarly, the ice cream producer will pay for its supplies, wage costs, and rent, with the rest becoming a profit or a loss. The same will be the case with the suppliers of milk used in the production and so on, all the way to the breeder of the livestock. Every dollar will end up as someone's income in the form of wages, rents, or profits. Therefore, if we add up the total value of every good and service sold in the economy, we must get a total that is exactly equal to the value of all the income in the economy.

An Example of Measuring GDP   Consider a very simple economy in which only two goods are produced: Roots shirts and Tim Horton's donuts. The value of GDP can then be calculated as:

$$\text{GDP} = (\text{Quantity of Roots shirts} \times \text{Price per shirt})$$
$$+ (\text{Quantity of donuts} \times \text{Price per donut}).$$

If 10 000 Roots shirts are sold at a price of $60 per shirt, and 1 000 000 donuts are sold at a price of $0.99 per donut, then the value of GDP is:

$$\text{GDP} = (10\,000 \times \$60) + (1\,000\,000 \times \$0.99) = \$1\,590\,000.$$

By using this method for all final goods and services, Statistics Canada can calculate the value of *nominal* GDP. Nominal GDP means in terms of money. The alternative is *real* GDP, which means in terms of goods and services. We discuss the difference between nominal and real GDP later in the chapter.

National Income Identities and the Components of GDP

Statistics Canada divides its information on GDP into four major categories of expenditures:

1. Personal consumption expenditures, or "Consumption" (C)
2. Gross private domestic investment, or "Investment" (I)
3. Government consumption and government investment, or "Government purchases" (G)
4. Net exports of goods and services, or "Net exports" (NX)

We let Y represent GDP. The following equation is called the *national income identity*:

$$Y = C + I + G + NX. \tag{2.2}$$

This expression is an identity because Statistics Canada assigns all values of final goods and services produced in a given year into one of the four categories: consumption, investment, government purchases, or net exports. Table 2.1 shows the values, for 2013, of GDP and each of the major categories of expenditures, as well as their important subcategories.

We now briefly review some important points about the four categories of expenditures:

Consumption **Consumption** is the purchase of new goods and services by households, regardless of where the goods or services were originally produced. Consumption is divided into three categories. *Durable goods* are tangible goods with an average life of three years or more, such as cars, furniture, and televisions. *Nondurable goods* are shorter-lived goods, such as food and clothing. *Services* are consumed at the time and place of purchase, such as haircuts, healthcare, and education.

Consumption The purchase of new goods and services by households.

Table 2.1 GDP in Second Quarter 2014, at Annual Rates

Consumption	993.2	57%	
Goods	448.9		26%
Services	520.2		30%
Investment	336.5	19%	
Non-residential structures	102.7		6%
Machinery and equipment	78.6		5%
Intelectual property products	31.7		2%
Residential investment	114.1		7%
Changes in inventories	7.1		0%
Governments purchases	415.7	24%	
Exports	544.0	31%	
Goods	465.7		27%
Services	79.2		5%
Imports	566.4	33%	
Goods	462.4		27%
Services	103.6		6%
Statistical discrepancy	0.2	0%	
GDP	1729.3	100%	

Source: Statistics Canada, CANSIM, Table 380-0064. Some minor categories have been omitted.

As you can see, consumption is the main category of expenditure in Canada, amounting to over 55% of GDP. The share of consumption in GDP varies greatly across countries: In the United States it is 72%, in China only 34%. In Canada, as in most other high-income countries, the fraction of services in consumption has been rising over time relative to goods. As people's incomes rise, they tend to spend relatively less on food, clothing, and other goods and relatively more healthcare and other services.

Investment Spending by firms on new factories, office buildings, machinery, and net additions to inventories, plus spending by households and firms on new houses.

Investment **Investment** is divided into three categories. Fixed investment is spending by firms on new factories, office buildings, and machinery used to produce other goods. Residential investment is spending by households or firms on new single-family and multi-family homes. The third category is net changes in business inventories. Inventories are goods that have been produced in a given year but not sold. Statistics Canada adds net change in business inventories to obtain the value of production in a given year. In calculating net changes Statistics Canada counts with a plus the value of additions to inventories, and with a minus the value of subtractions from inventories. For example, if Toyota produces 100 000 Corollas in the Canada during 2013 but sells only 85 000, then the 15 000 unsold Corollas are included with a positive sign in the changes in business inventories and counted as investment spending by Toyota. In effect, Statistics Canada assumes that Toyota purchased the cars from itself. Conversely, if Gretzky Wines produces 100 000 bottles of wine during 2013 but sells 150 000, the extra 50 000 bottles are sold out of inventory and are counted as a negative inventory investment since they were produced before 2013.

Government purchases Spending by federal, provincial, and local governments on newly produced goods and services.

Government Purchases **Government purchases** includes spending by all levels of government (federal, provincial, and local), on newly produced goods and services. Some government purchases represent consumption spending, as when the government pays the salaries of teachers or RCMP personnel. Other government purchases represent investment spending, as when the government pays for new structures, such as bridges and school buildings, or equipment, such as rescue helicopters. Purchases of this type allow the government to provide services—such as transportation, education, or emergency rescue—in the future.

Economists often distinguish between government purchases and **government expenditures**. Government expenditures include government purchases, transfer payments, and interest payments on bonds. **Transfer payments**, which are one of the largest components of a government's budget, are payments by the government to individuals for which the government does not receive a new good or service in return. Examples of transfer payments include Old Age Security payments to people over 65, Employment Insurance payments to the unemployed, welfare payments to the poor and so on. Similarly, *equalization payments* (federal transfers to poorer provinces) or transfers between different levels of government are not included in government purchases.

Net Exports **Net exports** is the value of all exports of goods and services minus the value of all imports of goods and services. When exports are greater than imports, net exports are positive, and the country has a trade surplus. When exports are less than imports, net exports are negative, and the country has a trade deficit. When exports equal imports, net exports are zero, and foreign trade is in balance.

Statistics Canada adds net exports in order to obtain the value of production in a given year. Consumption, investment, and government purchases include goods sold in Canada. Exported goods and services are goods produced in Canada but not sold in Canada; they need to be added to the value of production. For example, a Roots sweatshirt that is exported to Brazil has been produced in Canada but not included in consumption, investment, or government purchases. Conversely, imported goods and services are not produced in Canada but are sold in Canada; they need to be subtracted from the value of production. For example if you purchase an iPhone made in China for $700 at an Apple store, Canadian consumption increases by $700. Statistics Canada records an increase in imports of $700, which means that net exports decline by $700. In the end, consumption increases by $700 and net exports decrease by $700 so that GDP does not change.[3]

Government expenditures The sum of government purchases, transfer payments an d interest payments on government debt.

Transfer payments Payments by the federal government to individuals for which the government does not receive a good or service in return.

Net exports The value of all exports minus the value of all imports.

Other Measures of Production and Income

Statistics Canada publishes data on several other measures of total income in addition to GDP and GNP. In producing goods and services, firms wear out some capital—such as machinery, equipment, and buildings—and have to replace it. *Depreciation* represents the value of worn-out or obsolete capital. If we subtract depreciation from GNP, we are left with *NNP: Net National Product*. Net national product is a better measure of output produced in Canada since depreciation is a cost of production. Depreciation, however, is difficult to measure. It depends on the type of equipment used, the intensity of its use, and many other factors. As Statistics Canada cannot compute depreciation precisely, the gross measure of output is more often used than the net measure of output.

Finally, Statistics Canada publishes data on disposable income. **Disposable income** is national income earned by households plus transfer payments minus personal tax payments. It is an important statistic since consumption depends on disposable income. As we have seen, consumption is the biggest part of GDP.

Disposable income National income plus transfer payments minus personal tax payments.

---

[3]This example is oversimplified as the store buys the phone in China for less than $700. Let the store purchase price be $500. This means imports increase by $500, causing net exports to decrease by $500. Because consumption increases by $700 and net exports decrease by $500, the change in expenditure is $200. GDP increases by $200, which is the value of retail services provided by the store in Canada.

Real GDP, Nominal GDP, and the GDP Deflator

2.2

Learning Objective
Discuss the difference between real GDP and nominal GDP.

The calculation discussed so far provides the value of *nominal GDP*. **Nominal GDP** is calculated by summing the current values of final goods and serves. It provides the value of total production calculated in terms of money. We can write the equation for nominal GDP, using the symbol Σ_{GDP} to denote that we add up the product of prices and quantities for all goods produced in Canada, as follows:

Nominal GDP The value of final goods and services calculated using current-year prices.

$$\text{Nominal GDP} = \Sigma_{GDP} \text{ (current-year quantities)} \times \text{(current-year prices).} \qquad (2.3)$$

Nominal GDP can increase either because the quantity of goods and services increases or because the prices used to value the quantities rise (or because some of both happens). Compare two cases: In the first, prices remain the same but output of all goods and services doubles; in the second, quantities of every good and service remain the same, but all prices double. In both cases the value of GDP will double but, of course, the outcomes are very different. Because we are primarily interested in GDP as a measure of production, we separate price changes from quantity changes by calculating a measure of production called *real GDP*. **Real GDP** is calculated by designating a particular year as the *base year* and then using prices in the base year to calculate the value of goods and services in all other years. For instance, let 2011 be the base year. So, real GDP for 2013 is calculated by using quantities of goods and services from 2013 and prices from 2011. We can write it as:

Real GDP The value of final goods and services calculated using base-year prices.

$$\text{Real GDP} = \Sigma_{GDP} \text{ (current-year quantities)} \times \text{(base-year prices).} \qquad (2.4)$$

Similarly, real GDP for 2014 is calculated using quantities from 2014 and prices from 2011. By keeping prices constant, we know that changes in real GDP between 2013 and 2014 represent changes in the quantity of goods and services produced in the economy.

Figure 2.1 shows nominal GDP and real GDP in Canada for the years 1980–2014. The data are from the International Monetary Fund, which uses 2007 as the base year. The lines for real GDP and nominal GDP intersect in the base year, since real and nominal GDP

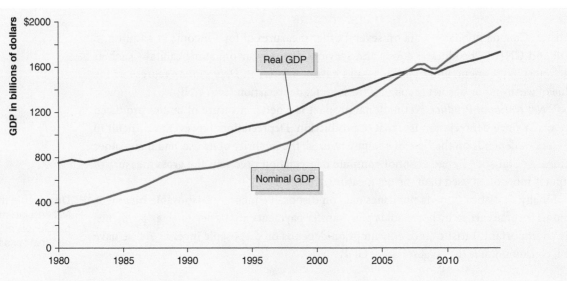

Figure 2.1 Nominal GDP and Real GDP, 1980–2014

Real GDP is calculated using prices from the base year. In years before the base year, real GDP is greater than nominal GDP. In years after the base year, nominal GDP is greater than real GDP.

Source: International Monetary Fund, World Economic Outlook database 2014. The numbers for 2014 are projections.

are equal in the base year. As prices were increasing throughout the period, nominal GDP increased faster than real GDP. So, in years before the base year of 2007, real GDP is greater than nominal GDP; in years after 2007, nominal GDP is greater than real GDP.

Solved Problem 2.1

Calculating Real GDP

Consider a very simple economy that produces only four final goods and services: apples, bagels, soap, and a cellphone contract. Assume that the base year is 2007. Use the information in the following table to calculate nominal and real GDP for 2013 and 2007, as well as the percentage change in real and in nominal GDP:

Product	2007		2013	
	Quantity	Price	Quantity	Price
Apples	300	$1.00	350	$1.50
Bagels	100	$0.50	90	$0.80
Soap	50	$7.00	50	$6.00
Cellphone contract	5	$60.00	7	$70.00

Solving the Problem

Step 1 **Review the chapter material.** This problem asks you to calculate real GDP, so you may want to review the section "Real GDP, Nominal GDP, and the GDP Deflator" which begins on page 50.

Step 2 **Calculate nominal GDP for the two years.** To calculate nominal GDP, we multiply the quantities produced during a year by the prices for that year to obtain the value of production for each good or service. Then, we add up the values.

For 2007:

Product	Quantity (2007)	Price (2007)	GDP, nominal, 2007$
Apples	300	$1.00	$300.00
Bagels	100	$0.50	$50.00
Soap	50	$7.00	$350.00
Cellphone contract	5	$60.00	$300.00
Nominal GDP in 2007			$1000.00

For 2013:

Product	Quantity (2013)	Price (2013)	GDP, nominal, 2013$
Apples	350	$1.50	$525.00
Bagels	90	$0.80	$72.00
Soap	50	$6.00	$300.00
Cellphone contract	7	$70.00	$490.00
Nominal GDP in 2013			$1387.00

Between 2007 and 2013 nominal GDP increased from $1000 to $1387, or by 38.7%: ($1387 − $1000) / $1000 = 38.7%. The increase was due to changes in both prices and quantities.

Step 3 **Calculate real GDP for 2013 and for 2007, using the prices for 2007.** To calculate real GDP for 2013, we need to multiply the quantities produced in 2013 by the prices for those goods and services in the base year 2007:

Product	Quantity (2013)	Price (2007)	Real GDP, 2013, 2007 prices
Apples	350	$1.00	$350.00
Bagels	90	$0.50	$45.00
Soap	50	$7.00	$350.00
Cellphone contract	7	$60.00	$420.00
Real GDP in 2013, prices from 2007			$1165.00

Notice that because the prices of three of the four products increased between 2007 and 2013, the value of real GDP is significantly less than the value of nominal GDP.

To calculate real GDP in 2007, we multiply quantities in 2007 by base-year prices. Because 2007 is the base year, our calculation of real GDP would be the same as our calculation of nominal GDP. *Nominal GDP is always equal to real GDP in the base year.*

Between 2007 and 2013 real GDP increased, in constant prices, from $1000 to $1165, or by 16.5%: ($1165 – $1000) / $1000 = 16.5%. This increase was due to changes in quantities.

See related problems 2.3, 2.4, and 2.5 at the end of the chapter.

Price Indices, the GDP Deflator, and the Inflation Rate

From year to year, prices of some goods and services, such as university tuition and wireless services, increase, while prices of other goods and services, such as computers and high-definition televisions, fall. To gauge what is happening to prices in the economy as a whole, economists need a measure of the prices of goods and services in the economy. Economists measure the price level with a *price index*, which is a measure of the average of the prices of goods and services in one year relative to a base year. In calculating the price index, prices of goods and services are weighted by their importance in expenditure. The weights are equal to quantities sold.

There are two commonly used price indices: the Consumer Price Index (CPI) and the GDP deflator. We now focus on the GDP deflator. (The CPI is analyzed in Section 2.3.) The **GDP deflator** is a measure of the price level calculated by dividing nominal GDP by real GDP and multiplying the result by 100:

GDP deflator A measure of the price level, calculated by dividing nominal GDP by real GDP and multiplying by 100.

$$\text{GDP deflator} = \frac{\text{Nominal GDP}}{\text{Real GDP}} \times 100. \tag{2.5}$$

Using the equations (2.3) and (2.4) for nominal GDP and real GDP, respectively, we can write the formula for the GDP deflator as

$$\text{GDP deflator} = \frac{\Sigma_{\text{GDP}}(\text{current-year quantities}) \times (\textit{current}\text{-year prices})}{\Sigma_{\text{GDP}}(\text{current-year quantities}) \times (\textit{base}\text{-year prices})} \times 100. \tag{2.6}$$

The differences between the numerator and denominator are indicated in italics in equation (2.6). In the numerator the sum is calculated using *current*-year prices and in the denominator the sum is calculated using the *base*-year prices. Because nominal GDP equals real GDP in the base year, the GDP deflator equals 100 in the base year.

Recall that the inflation rate is the percentage increase in the price level from one year to the next. The GDP deflator can be used to calculate the inflation rate. In symbols, if P_{t-1} is the price level last year, P_t is the price level this year, and π_t is this year's inflation rate, then

$$\text{Inflation rate} = \pi_t = \frac{P_t - P_{t-1}}{P_{t-1}} = \frac{P_t}{P_{t-1}} - 1. \tag{2.7}$$

Solved Problem 2.2

Calculating the Inflation Rate

Use the values for nominal GDP and real GDP given in the following table to calculate the inflation rate for 2012:

	2011	2012
Nominal GDP	$1720.75 billion	$1777.25 billion
Real GDP	$1356.87 billion	$1383.14 billion

Solving the Problem

Step 1 **Review the chapter material.** This problem asks you to calculate the inflation rate using values for the GDP deflator, so you may want to review the section "Price Indexes, the GDP Deflator, and the Inflation Rate," which begins on page 52.

Step 2 **Calculate the GDP deflator for each year.** To calculate the GDP deflator, you divide nominal GDP by real GDP and multiply by 100:

$$\text{GDP deflator for 2011} = \frac{\$1\,720.75 \text{ billion}}{\$1\,356.87 \text{ billion}} \times 100 = 126.8.$$

$$\text{GDP deflator for 2012} = \frac{\$1\,777.25 \text{ billion}}{\$1\,383.14 \text{ billion}} \times 100 = 128.5.$$

Step 3 **Calculate the inflation rate for 2012 and provide an interpretation of it.** You can calculate the inflation rate for 2012 as the percentage change in the GDP deflator between 2011 and 2012:

$$\frac{128.5 - 126.8}{126.8} = 1.3\%.$$

This calculation tells you that, on average, prices of final goods and services produced in Canada rose 1.3% in 2012.

See related problems 2.6 and 2.7 at the end of the chapter.

Avoiding a Common Mistake: GDP Deflator Change

Remember that the percentage change is equal to the difference between the new and the old value, divided by the old value. A common mistake is to forget to divide by the old value. In most cases the mistake is obvious to notice, but sometimes it is not. You are unlikely to make the mistake calculating, for example, the percentage change in the real GDP. The difference between GDP in 2012 ($1383.14 billion) and GDP in 2011 ($1356.87 billion) is $26.27 billion. This is obviously not a percentage change. The mistake can, however, be made when calculating the inflation rate. The difference between the GDP deflator in 2012 (128.5) and the GDP deflator in 2011 (126.8) is 1.7. Some students calculate the inflation rate as 1.7%. A person answering this way makes two mistakes. First, he has not divided by the old value. Second, the difference is equal to 1.7(i.e., 170%), not 1.7%. While the calculation is simple, this error is not uncommon.

2.3

Learning Objective

Explain how the inflation rate is measured, and distinguish between real and nominal interest rates.

Inflation Rates and Interest Rates

We have seen that inflation is measured by the percentage change in the price level from one year to the next. The GDP deflator provides a measure of the price level that allows us to calculate the inflation rate. But for many purposes, the GDP deflator is too broad a measure because it includes the prices of every good and service included in GDP. Economists and policymakers are usually interested in inflation as it affects the prices paid by the typical household. The typical household does not buy large electric generators or 40-story office buildings, which are among the goods whose prices are included in the GDP deflator. So, economists and policymakers often rely on the **Consumer Price Index (CPI)**, which includes only goods and services consumed by the typical household. The CPI does a better job than the GDP deflator at measuring changes in the *cost of living* as experienced by the typical household.

Consumer price index (CPI) An average of the prices of the goods and services purchased by consumers.

The Consumer Price Index (CPI)

The CPI is an average of the prices of the goods and services purchased by consumers. It is calculated by Statistics Canada to provide a measure of consumer prices paid by Canadian urban and rural households. The CPI is the most common measure of the rate of inflation faced by households. Bank of Canada uses the CPI to monitor economic conditions and the effects of monetary policy. Also, the CPI inflation rate is the basis for adjusting various payments. Pensions, wages, social support payments, tax brackets, and other dollar values are adjusted by the percentage equal to, or related to, the rate of inflation. Such adjusting is called **indexation**. Indexation protects the recipient against inflation. For example, the Canada Pension Plan is increased once a year to compensate CPP recipients for the increase in the price level in the previous year.

Indexation Increasing dollar values to protect their purchasing power against inflation.

The CPI is a weighted price index, with weights corresponding to the relative importance of goods and services in consumer expenditure. In calculating the weights, Statistics Canada uses its Survey of Household Spending. The prices are prices actually paid, including all discounts as well as taxes paid by consumers. Goods not sold in the market are excluded, so for example the CPI does not include the cost of medical services provided free of charge, but it does include medical supplies paid for by consumers. Every month CPI interviewers collect data by visiting retail outlets. For goods for which prices change infrequently, data are collected less often; for example train fares are collected twice a year and tuition fees are collected once a year. Prices of seasonal goods (for example winter coats) are collected only in months in which there are sufficient supplies of these goods. Almost two-thirds of the CPI basket falls into the categories of housing, transportation, and food.

Statistics Canada chooses one year as the base year, and the value of the CPI is usually set equal to 100 for that year. In any year other than the base year, the CPI is equal to the ratio of the dollar amount necessary to buy the market basket of goods in that year divided by the dollar amount necessary to buy the same market basket of goods in the base year, multiplied by 100. Figure 2.2 shows the CPI with the 2011 market basket of consumer goods and services (in which the quantities of goods and services are from 2011) and the value in 2002 set equal to 100. The rate shown is the year-on-year rate. This means that, for example, the inflation rate in December 2013 is equal to the value of the CPI index in December 2013 divided by the value of the CPI index in December 2012, minus 1 (see equation (2.7)), The value of CPI in 2013 was 122.7, i.e., the 2011 market basket of consumer goods and services was 22.7% more expensive in 2013 than in 2002.

Figure 2.2 shows that the inflation rate was unusually high in 1970s and early 1980s. Otherwise it was almost always below 5%. In most years since 1992 the inflation rate has been between 1% and 3%. During the Great Recession prices were lower than a year earlier

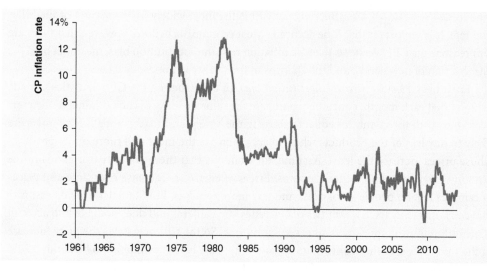

Figure 2.2

The Consumer Price Index (CPI) Inflation Rate

Between 1961 and 2013 the CPI inflation rate in Canada varied between − 0.9% in July 2009 and in September 2009, and 12.9% in July 1981. In most years since 1992 the CPI inflation rate has been between 1% and 3%.

Source: Statistics Canada. CANSIM Table 326-0020.

for four months (June–September 2009). The inflation rate also fell below zero in 1994, for an unusual reason. To deter cigarette smuggling caused by the large price difference between Canada and the United States, cigarette taxes were cut, reducing the prices of cigarettes by up to 50%. As cigarette expenditures constituted around 2% of the CPI basket, the tax reduction lowered the inflation rate by about 1%.

Differences between the GDP Deflator and the CPI

The GDP deflator and the Consumer Price Index are the most commonly used price indices. They are constructed for a different purpose and so differ with respect to

- the goods and services included in the index;
- the treatment of imported goods and services;
- the choice of weights.

The GDP deflator includes all domestically produced goods and services. This means it includes both consumer and investment goods but does not include imported goods and services. For example, it includes Canadian-built train engines but does not include iPads. The CPI is used to obtain a measure of prices and the rate of inflation for consumers. This means it includes only goods and services purchased by consumers. For example, it excludes train engines or computers purchased by businesses but includes iPads bought by consumers.

The third difference, the choice of weights, is more subtle. In the calculation of the GDP deflator, Statistics Canada uses *current-year weights*. It multiplies prices by quantities of the goods purchased in the current year. Recall that the GDP deflator is the ratio of nominal to real GDP. Consider, for example, GDP deflator for 2013 using, as base year, prices in 2011. It is the ratio of nominal GDP in 2013 to real GDP in 2013, using 2011 prices. In the numerator, nominal GDP is calculated by multiplying *quantities in 2013* by prices in 2013 and adding up. In the denominator, real GDP is calculated by multiplying *quantities in 2013* by prices in 2011, the base year, and adding up. In the calculation of the GDP deflator the *quantities are from the current year*.

Unlike with the GDP deflator, in the calculation of the CPI, the *quantities are from the base y*ear. CPI in 2013, using 2011 as the base year, is obtained by multiplying *quantities in 2011* by prices in 2013 and adding up. CPI in 2011 is obtained by multiplying *quantities in 2011* by prices in 2011 and adding up. The weights are the quantities of goods and services in 2011, the base year.

Bias in CPI Inflation Rate   Because the CPI is the most widely used measure of the inflation rate, it is important that it be accurate. Most economists believe, however, that there are four reasons the CPI *overstates* the true inflation rate: the substitution bias, the outlet bias, the introduction of new goods, and the changes in the quality of goods.

First, the CPI suffers from *substitution bias*. In constructing the CPI, Statistics Canada assumes that each month, consumers purchase the same quantity of each product in the market basket, with the quantities equal to those in the base year. In fact, though, consumers are likely to buy less of the products whose prices increase the most and more of the products whose prices increase the least. Assume, for example, that there are only two goods in the economy: cigarettes and digital cameras. Prices of cigarettes increase over time and prices of cameras fall. So people smoke less and buy more cameras. But Statistics Canada assumes that consumers buy fixed quantities of cigarettes and cameras and does not take into account substitution toward goods with lower inflation rate. So the CPI overstates the price increase in the market basket that consumers actually buy. This bias is estimated to be about 0.22% per year. That is, in the absence of the substitution bias, the CPI inflation rate would be, on the average, 0.22% lower than the reported yearly values.

Second, there is an *outlet bias* in the CPI data. Statistics Canada collects price data primarily from traditional retail outlets such as supermarkets and department stores. However, many households shop at large discount stores, such as Costco, or on the internet, and these sources are underrepresented in the sample of prices collected by Statistics Canada. This bias is estimated to be around 0.04% per year.

Third, the CPI suffers from a bias due to the *introduction of new goods*. The market basket is updated only every few years. The prices of many new goods, such as smart phones, Blu-ray players, and high-definition televisions, decrease significantly in the months after these goods are introduced, but these price decreases will not be reflected in the CPI if the goods are not included in the market basket. This bias is estimated to be around 0.2% per year

Fourth, the *quality of goods and services* changes over time, and these changes are not completely reflected in the CPI. For example, if you spend $2000 on a high-definition television in 2013, you will get a much better television than if you had spent $2000 on a high-definition television in 2010. It means that, in effect, the price of a television of constant quality has decreased. Statistics Canada attempts to make adjustments for changes in the quality of products, but doing so is difficult. In general, improvements in the quality of goods and services are not sufficiently reflected in the adjustment. The failure to fully adjust prices for changes in the quality of products results in an upward bias in the CPI. This bias is estimated to be no more than 0.05% per year.[4]

Overall, economists believe that the CPI inflation rate overestimates the actual inflation rate by around 0.5% per year. Is it important? The calculation of CPI inflation is used for two purposes: monetary policy and indexation. For the purpose of monetary policy, the bias is not critical, as long as it does not change over time. On the other hand, the bias makes a big difference for indexation over long periods of time. This is because the effects of the bias accumulate over time. For example, suppose that a CPP payment starts out at $40 000 in 2013. If, over the following 20 years, prices are increasing by 1.5% per year, the payment would grow to $53 874 ($40 000 $\times$ $(1.015)^{20}$ = $53 874) by 2033. Because of the bias, the official rate of inflation is 2% instead of 1.5% and so the adjustment will be 2% per year. After 20 years, the payment indexed at 2% per year will increase to $59 438, or 10% more than it

[4]For details, see Patrick Sabourin (2012), "Measurement Bias in the Canadian Consumer Price Index: An Update," *Bank of Canada Review*, Summer.

should. Excessive indexation has not been an important policy issue in Canada but it has been discussed extensively in the United States where the bias is about 1%. Several politicians proposed cutting indexation to limit the effects of future payments on government budget.

How the Bank of Canada Measures Inflation: Core Inflation

The CPI inflation is the main policy variable used by the Bank of Canada. Under the inflation targeting framework, introduced in 1991, the Bank of Canada aims to maintain the CPI inflation between 1% and 3%, and as close to 2% as possible. This means that the Bank of Canada pays very close attention to the behaviour of CPI inflation, and is not too concerned about the GDP deflator.

When the CPI inflation rate moves away from the target range, the Bank of Canada needs to decide whether to take action. The decision depends on the reason the inflation rate changes. If the Bank of Canada believes the change is temporary, it may decide to wait until the temporary reasons disappear and inflation returns to the target range. Changes in the CPI inflation rate are usually caused by changes in the most volatile subcomponents of CPI: the prices of energy, food, and mortgage costs. These changes are often temporary— for example, if the price of oil increases because of a war affecting a major oil producer. To distinguish between temporary and persistent changes, the Bank of Canada uses a second measure of inflation, called **core inflation**. It excludes a number of items from its calculations, such as fruits and vegetables, gasoline, fuel oil, natural gas, mortgage interest costs, intercity transportation, tobacco products, and changes in indirect taxes (for example, the HST). These components of expenditure have the most volatile inflation rates. By excluding them the core inflation measure is much more stable than CPI inflation. The comparison of core inflation with the CPI inflation rate provides the Bank of Canada with a more complete picture of inflation pressures and allows it to assess better the need for policy intervention.

Core inflation A measure of consumer price inflation used by the Bank of Canada, which excludes the most volatile CPI components.

Figure 2.3 shows the CPI and the core CPI inflation rates since 1995, using year-on-year monthly data. During the 1995–2013 period, CPI inflation varied between –0.9% in July 2009 and in September 2009 and 4.7% in February 2003; it was outside the Bank of Canada's target range of 1% to 3% numerous times, by as much as 2%, and for as long as six months. As you can see in Figure 2.3, core CPI inflation was indeed much more stable than CPI inflation. It varied between 0.9% in February 2011 and 3.3% in 2003 and has stayed outside of the range for no longer than one month, indicating that the changes in inflation were due

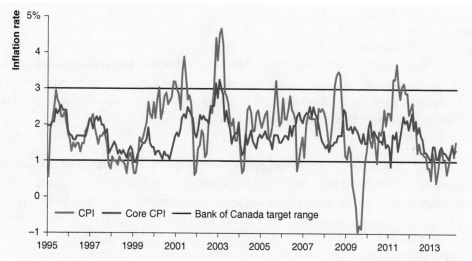

Figure 2.3

The Measures of the Inflation Rate, January 1995–March 2014

The CPI inflation rate is much more variable than the core inflation rate.

Source: Statistics Canada. CANSIM Table 326-0020.

to temporary factors. All departures above 3% and below 1% were temporary, with inflation quickly returning to the target range.

Interest Rates

The financial crisis and severe Great Recession showed that what happens in the financial system can affect the rest of the economy. A key economic variable in understanding the financial system is the interest rate. The **interest rate** is the cost of borrowing funds, usually expressed as a percentage of the amount borrowed. For example, if you borrow $1000 and have to pay back $1050 in one year, then you have paid $50 in interest, and the interest rate on the loan is 5%: ($1050 – $1000) / $1000 = 5%. Similarly, if you deposit money in a savings account or a certificate of deposit in a bank, the interest rate you earn is the return on your savings.

The **nominal interest rate** is the interest rate in terms of money: When the nominal interest rate is 5%, if you deposit 100 units of a currency, a year later you get 105 units of the same currency. Banks and other financial institutions almost exclusively quote nominal interest rates. These are the interest rates you pay on a loan or receive on your savings. Borrowers and lenders, however, base their decisions not on the nominal interest rate but on the **real interest rate,** which is the interest rate in terms of goods and services. This is because the decision to save involves postponing consumption: When you save, you decide not to consume today but postpone consumption into the future. The decision to borrow by a consumer, similarly, involves accelerating consumption: When you borrow, you can make the purchase earlier. In both cases, what matters is the return in term of goods and services. The decision to borrow by an investor involves doing the investment earlier. For example, borrowing to go to university to invest in your human capital allows you not to wait until you accumulated sufficient funds to afford tuition. What matters for the investor (and a student) is the amount of goods and services she needs to give up in the future to repay the loan.

Why are nominal and real interest rates different? Because of inflation. Inflation increases prices of goods and services over time. Consider, for example, Franco, who decides to postpone consumption of 100 kg of pasta. Pasta costs $10/kg, and the nominal interest rate is 5% per year. So Franco saves $1000 and a year from now he receives back the principal ($1000) plus the interest payment, 5% $\times$ $1 000 = $50. The total amount he receives is $1050. But this amount is not meaningful since the price of pasta may have changed. When the price of pasta increases due to inflation, $1050 buys less than 105 kg of pasta and so his real return, in terms of pasta, is less than 5%. For example, if the inflation rate is 2% per year, next year pasta costs $10.20/kg and he can buy approximately 103 kg of pasta. So his return *in terms of pasta* is, approximately, 3%. It is approximately equal to the difference between the nominal interest rate (5% in our example) and the inflation rate (2%).

Note that, at the time of saving, Franco knows he will receive $1050 in a year but he does not know the price of pasta a year from now. He knows the nominal interest rate but has to form expectations of the inflation rate, which in turn allow him to calculate the *expected* real interest rate. The approximate formula for the real interest rate is

$$r = i - \pi^e. \tag{2.8}$$

The *expected* real interest rate is approximately equal to the difference between the nominal interest rate and the expected rate of inflation. Why is it the *expected* real interest rate? Because borrowers and lenders do not know with certainty what the inflation rate will be during the period of a loan and so they do not know what the *actual* real interest rate will be. They must make borrowing or investing decisions on the basis of what they *expect* the inflation rate to be.

Interest rate The cost of borrowing funds, usually expressed as a percentage of the amount borrowed.

Nominal interest rate The interest rate in terms of money.

Real interest rate The interest rate in terms of goods and services; the nominal interest rate adjusted for the effects of inflation.

Expected and Actual Real Interest Rate We can generalize by noting that the *actual* real interest rate equals the nominal interest rate minus the *actual* inflation rate. If the actual inflation rate is greater than the expected inflation rate, the actual real interest rate will be lower than the expected real interest rate. In this case, borrowers will gain and lenders will lose. If the actual inflation rate is less than the expected inflation rate, the actual real interest rate will be greater than the expected real interest rate. In this case, borrowers will lose, and lenders will gain. To see this, assume that Franco and the bank both expect the inflation rate to be 2% per year. To postpone consumption he wants his real return to be 3%, and the bank is willing to pay 3% in real terms. Franco and the bank agree, therefore, to a nominal interest rate of 5%. What happens if the actual inflation rate turns out to be higher than they had expected, for example 4%? In that case, the actual real interest rate that Franco receives (and the bank ends up paying) equals 5% − 4% = 1%, which is less than the expected real interest rate of 3%. When the inflation rate turns out to be higher than Franco and the bank expected, Franco, who is the lender, loses by receiving a lower real interest rate than he expected. The bank, which in this case is the borrower, gains by paying a lower real interest rate than it was willing to pay.

Approximate and Exact Relationship between the nominal and the Real Interest Rate Why is equation (2.8) approximate? To see this, we need to do the actual calculation. (We will calculate the expected real interest rate; the actual real interest rate can be calculated in the same manner.) In our example pasta is $10/kg; Franco saves $1000 (i.e., the amount that buys 100 kg of pasta); the nominal interest rate is 5%; and he expects the inflation rate to be 2%. In a year Franco receives $1050 and he expects pasta will cost $10.20. This means that he expects to be able to buy

$$\frac{\$1050}{\$10.20 \text{ per kilogram}} = 102.94 \text{ kilograms of pasta.}$$

So the expected real interest rate is 2.94%:

$$\frac{102.94 \text{ kg} - 100 \text{ kg}}{100 \text{ kg}} = 2.94\%.$$

We can do the same calculation using symbols. Denote the expected real interest rate as r, the nominal interest rate as i, and the expected rate of inflation as π^e. In the calculations above we used $i = 5\%$ and $\pi^e = 2\%$.

In real terms, Franco saves 100 kg of pasta and expects to be able to buy

$$102.94 \text{ kg} = (1 + r)100 \text{ kg.}$$

Franco saves $1000 and, in a year, receives the principal plus 5%:

$$\$1050 = (1 + 5\%)\$1000 = (1 + i)\$1000.$$

A kilogram of pasta costs $10.00; he expects in a year it will cost, per kilogram:

$$\$10.20 = (1 + 2\%)\$10 = (1 + \pi^e)\$10.$$

So Franco expects to be able to buy

$$\frac{\$1050}{\$10.20/\text{kg}} = \frac{(1 + i)\$1000}{(1 + \pi^e)\$10/\text{kg}} = \frac{1 + i}{1 + \pi^e} 100 \text{ kg}$$

$$= (1 + r) \, 100 \text{ kg} = 102.94 \text{ kg.}$$

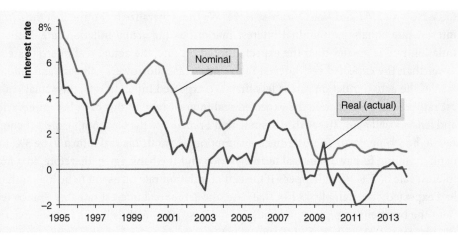

Figure 2.4

Nominal and Real Interest Rates, 1995–2013

Nominal and real interest rates tend to move together. The real interest rate can be negative. If the inflation rate is negative, the real interest rate is higher than the nominal interest rate.

Source: Statistics Canada, CANSIM Tables 176-0078 and 326-0020. The nominal interest rate is the rate on Treasury Bills, 1 year.

So the exact formula linking the expected real interest rate, the nominal interest rate, and expected inflation says that *one plus the expected real interest rate is equal to one plus the nominal interest rate divided by one plus the expected rate of inflation*:

$$1 + r = \frac{1 + i}{1 + \pi^e}. \tag{2.9}$$

How big is the difference between the approximate and the exact formula? Rearranging the last equation we obtain:[5]

$$r = i - \pi^e - r\pi^e.$$

The difference between the exact and the approximate formula is $r\pi^e$. As long as both the real interest rate and the expected inflation rate are small, $r\pi^e$ is a small number. In our example, the real interest rate calculating using the exact formula is 2.94%. Using the approximate formula it is 3%. The difference is 0.06%, or 60 grams of pasta. Franco probably does not care very much about such a small amount. The difference between the exact and the approximate amount matters when the inflation rate (and the expected inflation rate) is very high. It also matters when the amount saved is very large. In Canada you can use the approximate formula as long as the amount saved is not very large.

Figure 2.4 shows the nominal interest rate and the actual real interest rate for the period from 1992 to 2013. To calculate the actual real interest rate, we used the actual inflation rate as measured by year-on-year percentage changes in the CPI. Figure 2.4 shows that the nominal interest rate (we show the interest rate on Treasury Bills, 1 year) and the real interest rate tend to rise and fall together. Note that while the nominal interest rate on government bonds is always positive, the real interest rate has sometimes been negative. In particular, the (actual) real interest rate was negative for several years following the Great Recession. Note also that it is possible for the nominal interest rate to be lower than the real interest rate, as happened in the third quarter of 2009. For this outcome to occur, the inflation rate has to be

---

[5]Multiplying both sides by $1 + \pi^e$ we get $(1 + r)(1 + \pi^e) = 1 + i$. Multiplying out the brackets we get $1 + r + \pi^e + r\pi^e = 1 + i$. To obtain the exact formula subtract 1 from both sides and move $\pi^e + r\pi^e$ to the right side.

negative, since the actual real interest rate is approximately equal to the nominal interest rate minus the inflation rate.

Measuring Employment and Unemployment

We now turn to the description of how the rate of unemployment is measured. When most people think about an economic recession, they do not think about declines in GDP as much as they think about problems with finding and keeping a job. In fact, the unemployment rate can have important political implications. In most elections, unemployment is the main economic variable voters concentrate on.

To calculate the rate of unemployment, Statistics Canada conducts a monthly labour market survey. Around 50 thousand households are surveyed. Households stay in the sample for six months and, every month, one-sixth of the sample is replaced. The survey establishes whether the respondent worked or looked for a job. People are considered *employed* if they worked during the week before the survey or if they were temporarily away from their jobs because they were ill, on vacation, on strike, or for other reasons. People are considered *unemployed* if they did not work in the previous week but were available for work and had actively looked for work at some time during the previous four weeks.

Using the results of the survey, Statistics Canada estimates the numbers of employed and unemployed people in the entire Canadian population. The population is divided on the basis of several definitions. People can be out of the labour force, in the labour force, unemployed, and employed. People who neither worked nor looked for a job (for example students) are considered *out of the labour force*. The **labour force** is the sum of employed and unemployed workers. The **labour force participation rate** is the proportion of people 15 years old and over who are in the labour force. The **unemployment rate** is the percentage of the labour force that is unemployed:

Labour force = number of employed plus the number of unemployed.

$$\text{Labour force participation rate} = \left(\frac{\text{Labour force}}{\text{Number of people 15 years and over}}\right).$$

$$\text{Unemployment rate} = \left(\frac{\text{Number of unemployed}}{\text{Labour force}}\right).$$

For example, in September 2014 the number of people 15 and over was 29 126 800, the number of people working was 17 925 500, and the number of people unemployed was 1 297 700.[6] So the labour force was 17 925 500 + 1 297 700 = 19 223 200. The labour force participation rate was (17 925 500 + 1 297 700)/ 29 126 800 = 66% and the unemployment rate was 1 297 700/ (17 925 500 + 1 297 700) = 6.8%.

The official rate of unemployment may not provide an accurate assessment of the unemployment situation as it is sometimes difficult to distinguish between unemployed workers and people who are not in the labour force. The official unemployment rate includes just those workers who have looked for work in the past four weeks. But some *discouraged workers* might prefer to have a job but have given up looking because they

---

2.4

Learning Objective
Understand how to calculate the unemployment rate.

Labour force The sum of employed and unemployed workers in the economy.

Labour force participation rate The proportion of people 15 years old and over who are in the labour force.

Unemployment rate The percentage of the labour force that is unemployed.

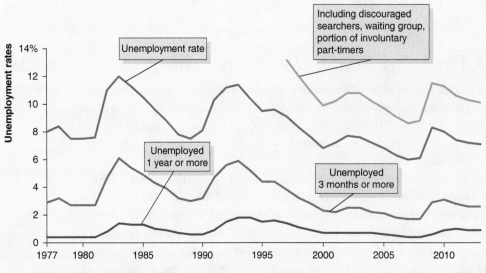

Figure 2.5 Alternative Measures of the Unemployment Rate, 1977–2013

Long-term unemployment in Canada increased during the Great Recession, but was lower than in the previous two recessions. It started declining in 2011. The comprehensive measure of unemployment, which includes discouraged workers, the waiting group, and involuntary part-timers, moves together with the unemployment rate.

Source: Statistics Canada, CANSIM Table 282-0086. Data which include discouraged searchers, the waiting group, and some of involuntary part-timers are only available from 1997.

believe finding a job is too difficult. These workers are not actively looking for a job and so they are not considered to be in the labour force and are not counted as unemployed. For example, in a recession some people choose to stay at home with kids as the chance of finding a job is low. Others choose to go to school to improve their qualifications. In addition, people with part-time jobs are counted as being employed, even if they would prefer to hold full-time jobs. Such workers are considered *underemployed* but are not counted as unemployed. Counting as employed a part-time worker who wants to work full time tends to understate the degree of joblessness in the economy and makes the employment situation appear better than it is. On the other hand, some respondents may declare themselves looking for a job while, in fact, they were not. Overall, the unemployment rate does provide only a partial picture of the level of unemployment and underemployment.

Since the unemployment rate does not provide a complete picture of the unemployment situation, Statistics Canada publishes supplementary measures of the unemployment. Figure 2.5 shows several of these measures. The long-term unemployment rate in the figure shows the percentage of the labour force that has been unemployed for one year or more. We also show the percentage of the labour force that has been unemployed for three months or more. Long-term unemployment is a particularly serious problem as job skills deteriorate among people who have been out of work for an extended time and it is difficult for them to find new employment. The long-term unemployment rate in Canada increased during the Great Recession, but the increase was not large and the rate started falling after 2011. In addition, the figure shows the unemployment rate plus discouraged searchers, the waiting group, and involuntary part-timers. As you can see, this comprehensive measure, available from 1997, moves together with the unemployment rate. We will return to the discussion of unemployment in Chapter 6.

Key Terms and Problems

Key Terms

Capital goods, p. 43

Consumer price index (CPI), p. 54

Consumption, p. 47

Core inflation, p. 57

Disposable income, p. 49

Factor of production, p. 44

Final goods and services, p. 43

GDP deflator, p. 52

Government expenditures, p. 49

Government purchases, p. 48

Gross domestic product (GDP), p. 43

Gross national product (GNP),
   p. 44

Indexation, p. 54

Interest rate, p. 58

Investment, p. 48

Labour force, p. 61

Labour force participation rate, p. 61

National income accounting, p. 43

Net exports, p. 49

Nominal GDP, p. 50

Nominal interest rate, p. 58

Real GDP, p. 50

Real interest rate, p. 58

Transfer payments, p. 49

Unemployment rate, p. 61

Value added, p. 45

 2.1

GDP: Measuring Total Production and Total Income

Explain how economists use gross domestic product (GDP) to measure total production and total income.

Review Questions

1.1   In what sense is GDP both a measure of total production and a measure of total income?

1.2   What is the difference between GDP and GNP? Is the difference between GDP and GNP large in Canada?

Problems and Applications

1.3   How would each of the following events change measured GDP?

   a. There is an increase in illegal drug sales.

   b. A train carrying Alberta crude derails, polluting a large river.

   c. There is a surge in sales of used cars, and there is a decline in sales of new cars.

1.4   By the 1960s, a larger percentage of women were entering the labour force. Because more women were working, their production of services within the home, such as cooking and cleaning, may have fallen. In addition, they may have employed others to do some tasks that they had previously done themselves, including caring for their children.

   a. How did these changes affect GDP as measured by Statistics Canada?

   b. If we define "actual GDP" as GDP measured with the inclusion of such things as household production, illegal goods and services, and other typically excluded variables, how would actual GDP have changed?

1.5   Which of the following goods and services are included in GDP? If the good or service is included in GDP, in which expenditure category is it included? If the good or service is not included in GDP, explain why not.

   a. Cynthia buys some house paint.

   b. Cynthia uses the paint that she purchased to paint her own house.

   c. Bruce hires a painter to paint his house.

   d. Randy sells the house that he bought 10 years ago and uses the proceeds to purchase a newly constructed condominium.

   e. Kishore buys a new Toyota Prius.

   f. Jane buys a 2005 Dodge truck to drive on the weekends.

   g. Adam, as a retiree, receives government pension.

1.6   Suppose that a simple economy produces pizza, video games, and candy. The following table gives quantities and prices for each good in three successive years:

	2011		2012		2013	
	Quantity	Price	Quantity	Price	Quantity	Price
Pizza	100	$0.50	125	$0.50	125	$0.60
Video games	75	$1.00	85	$1.00	85	$1.25
Candy	20	$5.00	30	$5.00	30	$6.00

a. Calculate nominal GDP in 2011, 2012, and 2013.

b. What is the growth rate of nominal GDP between 2011 and 2012? What is the growth rate of nominal GDP between 2012 and 2013?

c. Do the growth rates you calculated in part (b) measure the changes in the quantity of goods produced during these years? Briefly explain.

2.2 Real GDP, Nominal GDP, and the GDP Deflator
Discuss the difference between real GDP and nominal GDP.

Review Questions

2.1 What is the difference between nominal GDP and real GDP? Why do changes in nominal GDP usually overstate changes in total production in the economy? How can values for nominal GDP and real GDP be used to calculate a price index?

Problems and Applications

2.2 A worker produces car parts. The value of the parts he produces in an hour is $26.50 in January 2013 and $35.20 in January 2014.

a. Given this information, can you conclude that his output per hour has increased significantly in 2013?

b. The price per unit was $0.75 in January 2013 and $0.91 in January 2014. By what percentage did his output per hour increase?

2.3 [Related to Solved Problem 2.1 on page 51] Use the information in the following table to answer the questions. Assume that 2011 is the base year.

	2011		2012		2013	
Product	Quantity	Price	Quantity	Price	Quantity	Price
Grapes	100	$0.50	125	$0.50	125	$0.60
Raisins	75	1.00	85	$1.00	85	1.25
Oranges	20	5.00	30	$5.00	30	6.00

a. Calculate real GDP in 2011, 2012, and 2013.

b. Did real GDP grow by more in percentage terms between 2011 and 2012 or between 2012 and 2013? Briefly explain.

2.4 [Related to Solved Problem 2.1 on page 51] Use the information in the following table to calculate nominal and real GDP for 2005 and 2013. Assume that 2005 is the base year.

	2005		2013	
Product	Quantity	Price	Quantity	Price
Oranges	400	$0.50	440	$0.75
Plums	90	$0.50	85	$0.60
Haircuts	7	$30.00	10	$32.00
Pizza	60	$8.00	70	$8.25

2.5 [Related to Solved Problem 2.1 on page 51] The answer to Solved Problem 2.1 includes the following statement: "Notice that because the prices of three of the four products increased between 2005 and 2013, for 2013 the value of real GDP is significantly less than the value of nominal GDP."

Construct an example similar to the one in Solved Problem 2.1 for an economy with only four products. Show that it is possible to choose prices in 2013 so that although only one price increases, nominal GDP in 2013 is still greater than real GDP.

2.6 [Related to Solved Problem 2.2 on page 53] If the nominal GDP is 1.5 trillion, and the real GDP is 1.4 trillion, what is the GDP deflator?

2.7 [Related to Solved Problem 2.2 on page 53] Use the values for nominal GDP and real GDP given in the following table to calculate the inflation rate during 1930.

	1929	1930
Nominal GDP	$10 billion	$9 billion
Real GDP	$9.7 billion	$8.9 billion

2.8 The text states, "For years before the base year, real GDP is greater than nominal GDP. For years after the base year, nominal GDP is greater than real GDP." Suppose that the economy experiences *deflation*, with the price level falling. In this case, will the relationship between real GDP and nominal GDP for years before and after the base year still hold? Briefly explain.

2.3 Inflation Rates and Interest Rates

Explain how the inflation rate is measured, and distinguish between real and nominal interest rates.

Review Questions

3.1 What biases in the way the CPI is calculated may cause it to overstate the actual inflation rate?

3.2 How is the CPI inflation calculated? What is the difference between the CPI and the GDP deflator?

3.3 If the actual inflation rate is greater than the expected inflation rate, do borrowers gain or lose? Briefly explain.

Problems and Applications

3.4 Explain the major difference between the CPI and the core inflation. Why does the Bank of Canada prefer to use the core inflation to measure the inflation rate?

3.5 Suppose that a virus wipes out half the apple crop, causing the quantity produced to go down and the price to increase. Other fruits can be substituted for apples in many cases, so some consumers will switch to other items. What would be the effect of this on the CPI? On the core inflation?

3.6 During the 2008–2009 recession and financial crisis, nominal interest rates fell to nearly 0%, while the rate of inflation remained positive.

a. What happened to the real interest rate?

b. How would this movement in the real interest rate affect savers and borrowers?

c. If *nominal* interest rates were negative, what would happen if you put money in a savings account at a bank?

2.4 Measuring Employment and Unemployment

Understand how to calculate the unemployment rate.

Review Questions

4.1 How is the unemployment rate calculated?

4.2 What do economists mean by *discouraged workers*? Explain the effect discouraged workers have on the measured unemployment rate and the degree of joblessness in the economy. Why might the unemployment rate understate the extent of unemployment?

Problems and Applications

4.3 For each of the following, state whether the individual is included or not included in the labour force and, if included, whether that person is counted as employed or unemployed.

a. Soma is employed as a chef at a restaurant in Timmins.

b. Randy is working part time but is looking for a full-time job.

c. Bruce would like a job but has stopped looking.

d. Jessie won the lottery and quit her job. She is not seeking a new job.

e. José is in college.

f. Christina just graduated from college and is applying for jobs.

4.4 During recessions, industries such as construction often cut back on employees. The newly unemployed workers may seek jobs for a while and then become discouraged if they do not find new jobs.

a. If workers are seeking jobs, how does the Statistics Canada count those workers?

b. If workers have stopped seeking jobs, how does the Statistics Canada count those workers?

c. Use this information to explain why, when the economy begins to recover from a recession, the unemployment rate may initially increase.

4.5 Suppose that all workers in the economy are currently working 40 hours a week.

a. If all employers cut worker hours so that each employee is working 20 hours a week, what would happen to the unemployment rate?

b. What would happen to real GDP?

c. The unemployment rate is sometimes used as a measure of the slack in the economy or how far the economy is below potential GDP. How do

parts (a) and (b) of this question suggest that this might be misleading?

Data Exercises

D2.1: Using data from Statistics Canada (http://www5. statcan.gc.ca/cansim/a01?lang=eng), Table 380-0084 and 383-0008 analyze the recent movements in real GDP and inflation.

a. How has real GDP at market prices changed over the past year?

b. Is the economy currently in a recession or a recovery? (Hint: See the C.D. Howe Institute for official definitions of business cycle turning points.) Is your answer a surprise given your answer to part (a)?

c. Using the implicit price deflator, calculate the inflation rate over the past year.

D2.2: Using data from Statistics Canada (http://www5 .statcan.gc.ca/cansim/a01?lang=eng), Table 380-0084, and from St. Louis Federal Reserve database (FRED) (http://research.stlouisfed.org/ fred2/) series (GDPC1), analyze the composition of GDP.

a. Search for Income and Expenditure Accounts. What percentage of GDP is accounted for by each of the major GDP subcategories in Canada? How do those percentages compare to the percentages for the United States?

b. Because Canada is closely tied to the United States in terms of trade and proximity, business cycles in Canada are often very similar to those in the United States. How does the trend in Canada's GDP compare with that in the United States?

D2.3: Using data from Statistics Canada (http://www5 .statcan.gc.ca/cansim/a01?lang=eng), Table 380-0084 analyze personal consumption expenditures.

a. Find the most recent values for the household final consumption expenditure: (1) total, (2) on goods, and (3) on services. What percentage of household expenditure is spent on goods?

b. Download historical data for household final consumption expenditure: (1) total, (2) on goods, and (3) on services. Is there a

trend in the share of services in household expenditure?

D2.4: Using data from Statistics Canada (http://www5 .statcan.gc.ca/cansim/a01?lang=eng), Table 380-0084, analyze aggregate investment expenditures.

a. Find the most recent values for these three variables: (1) Gross Fixed Capital Formation, (2) Non-residential structures, machinery and equipment, and (3) residential structures.

b. Using the most recent values, compute the difference between gross fixed capital formation and Business gross fixed capital formation. What does the computed value represent?

D2.5: Using data from Statistics Canada (http://www5 .statcan.gc.ca/cansim/a01?lang=eng), Table 380-0084, analyze real exports and real imports.

a. Find the values for the most recent two years for Exports of goods and services and Imports of goods and services.

b. Compute the value of net exports for each of the two most recent years.

c. Calculate the ratio of exports of goods to exports of services. Why are exports of services so low?

D2.6: Using data from Statistics Canada (http://www5 .statcan.gc.ca/cansim/a01?lang=eng), Table 380-0030, analyze the difference between gross domestic product and gross national product

a. Find the most recent values for Gross domestic product and Gross national product.

b. Given the values found above, explain whether or not foreign factor income of Canadians exceeds Canadian factor income of foreigners.

c. If countries have a significant fraction of domestic production occurring in foreign-owned facilities, explain whether GDP will be larger or smaller than GNP.

D2.7: Using data from Statistics Canada (http://www5. statcan.gc.ca/cansim/a01?lang=eng), Table 380-0084, analyze income data.

---

a. Find the most recent values for these three variables: (1) Primary household income, (2) Household disposable income, and (3) Household final consumption expenditures.

b. Using the most recent values, compute the difference between household income and household disposable income. What does the difference represent?

c. Compute the ratio of consumption to disposable income. Use this ratio and the fact that disposable income increases dollar-for-dollar with a tax reduction to forecast the effect of a tax cut on spending by households.

D2.8: Using data from Statistics Canada (http://www5 .statcan.gc.ca/cansim/a01?lang=eng), Table 326-0020 analyze CPI (the Consumer Price Index) and inflation.

a. Find the most recent values and values from one year earlier for the CPI.

b. Using the CPI data for the two periods, calculate the year-over-year inflation rate.

D2.9: [Spreadsheet exercise] Using data from Statistics Canada (http://www5.statcan.gc.ca/cansim/ a01?lang=eng), Table 326-0020, and then performing calculations using Excel or some other compatible spreadsheet program such as Open Office, analyze CPI (the Consumer Price Index) and inflation.

a. Find the data for the All Items CPI. Use the "Add/Remove data," to change the beginning date to January 1960. You can leave the ending date as it is. Then click on the "save" button and then on the "download" button to download the data and save it to your computer. Finally, open the spreadsheet file.

b. Calculate the percentage change in CPI from a year ago for each of the observations, beginning with the observation one year later than the first observation.

c. Create a time series graph of the percentage change from 12 months earlier.

d. Using the spreadsheet information, which period experienced the highest inflation rate and what was the inflation rate equal to at the time?

D2.10: [Spreadsheet exercise] Using data from Statistics Canada (http://www5.statcan.gc.ca/can-sim/a01?lang=eng), Table 326-0020, and then

performing calculations using Excel or some other compatible spreadsheet program such as Open Office, analyze different price indexes and inflation.

a. Find the data for the "All-items CPI" and the "All-items CPI excluding food and energy." Use the "Add/Remove data" button to change the beginning date to 2006. You can leave the ending date as it is. Then click on the "save" button and then on the "download" button to download the data and save it to your computer. Finally, open the spreadsheet file.

b. Calculate the percentage change in each CPI index from a year ago for each of the observation, beginning with the observation 2007–07–01.

c. Create a time series graph of the percentage change from a year ago for both indexes. Make sure both data lines are on the same graph.

d. Using the spreadsheet information, identify any months when inflation was significantly different between the two measures. Briefly discuss what must have been true during this month or months.

D2.11: Using data from Statistics Canada (http://www5 .statcan.gc.ca/cansim/a01?lang=eng), Table 326-0020, analyze different categories of the CPI (the Consumer Price Index) and inflation.

a. Find the most recent values and values from the same month in 2010 for the following categories of the CPI: Food, clothing, footwear, and CPI Transportation.

b. Compute the percentage change in prices over the period from 2010 to the present period for each of the four CPI categories.

c. According to your calculations, which category had the lowest inflation and which category had the highest inflation?

D2.12: Using data from Statistics Canada (http://www5 .statcan.gc.ca/cansim/a01?lang=eng), Table 282-0047, analyze the labour force and unemployment.

a. Find the most recent values for these three variables: (1) Labour force (15 and over), (2) Total unemployed), and (3) Total unemployed – 27 weeks or more. Are the data reported annually, quarterly, or monthly?

What units are the values for these variables reported in?

b. Using the most recent values, compute the unemployment rate and the long-term (27 weeks or more) unemployment rate.

D2.13: Using data from Statistics Canada (http://www5 .statcan.gc.ca/cansim/a01?lang=eng), Table 176-0043, analyze nominal interest rates.

a. Find the most recent values the following four variables: (1) Treasury bills—3 month, (2) Selected government of Canada benchmark bond yields—long term, (3) Real return bonds—long term.

b. Calculate the difference between long and short rates between January 2008 and January 2012.

c. The difference between (2) Selected government of Canada benchmark bond yields—long term and (3) Real return bonds—long term is approximately equal to the expected inflation rate. The Bank of Canada target for inflation rate is to keep inflation in the 1%–3% range, and close to 2%. How does the expected inflation rate compare with the target?

d. Suppose the actual inflation rate is greater than the expected inflation rate. Will borrowers or lenders be made better off? Briefly explain.

The Canadian Financial System

Learning Objectives

After studying this chapter, you should be able to:

3.1 Describe the financial system and explain the role it plays in the economy (pages 71–80)

3.2 Understand the role of the central bank in stabilizing the financial system (pages 80–85)

3.3 Explain how interest rates are determined in the money market, and understand the risk structure and term structure of interest rates (pages 85–96)

3.A Online appendix: More on the term structure of interest rates

Why Is the Canadian Banking System the Best in the World?

If you use Google to search for : "The Canadian banking system," the top entry is the Wikipedia article "Banking in Canada," which starts as follows: "Banking in Canada is widely considered one of the safest banking systems in the world, ranking as the world's soundest banking system."

As we mentioned in Chapter 1, Canadian financial system survived the Great Recession without many problems. It is perhaps not surprising: On October 9, 2008, the World Economic Forum, an independent research organization, ranked Canadian banks to be the soundest in the world. They were ranked highest in 2009 and every year since. Not all rich countries do well in the ranking: In 2013 the United States was ranked 58th, Germany 64th, and the United Kingdom 105th.

What features contribute to the soundness of Canadian banks? They are large, strictly regulated, and managed by Canadian bankers who tend to be conservative.

Canadian banks are national banks, with a large branch network. They serve customers around the country and are not vulnerable to problems in one region. If, for example, the economic situation is poor in Alberta, bank losses there are offset by profits in the rest of the country. Canada has a strong regulatory system for financial institutions. The primary regulator is the Office of the Superintendent of Financial Institutions (OFSI). A unique feature of the Canadian banking system is the closeness between the regulators and banks. With only five large banks (Royal Bank of Canada, Bank of Montreal, Canadian Imperial Bank of Commerce, Bank of Nova Scotia, and Toronto-Dominion Bank) the regulators know chief

Continued on next page

executives personally. When OFSI is concerned about potential problems, it can deal with banks directly and informally. This makes it possible for the regulator to address problems quickly, before they become serious.

Investment banking in Canada is done mostly by subsidiaries of commercial banks. The banks, however, did not come to rely heavily on investment banking, which is riskier than commercial banking. As part of commercial banks, investment banking is tightly regulated, while in many other countries investment banks are subject to much lighter regulation than commercial banks.

Mortgages in Canada are also less risky than elsewhere. Loans exceeding 80% of the house value must be insured with the Canada Mortgage and Housing Corporation, a federal agency. Securitization and subprime lending had not developed in Canada as much as in the United States. With a large portion of mortgages remaining on their books, Canadian banks were exposed to mortgage risks. So they monitored risks carefully, which limited losses during the Great Recession.

But of course there is another side of the coin. A banking system that is solid and conservative does well in bad times, but may not perform so well in good times. It can be likened to a heavy truck. It is safe in a snowstorm, but it is not going to win many races on a sunny day. Many economists consider the Canadian banking system to be an oligopoly. There is little competition, and banking services are more expensive than elsewhere. Banks are protected from large foreign entrants, reducing incentives to compete.

Much of the soundness of the Canadian banking system is owed to the conservative nature of Canadian bankers. It is possible that, over time, the culture of Canadian banking will become more competitive and banks will become less sound.

Sources: John Greenwood, "Canadian Banks Win Top Marks from World Economic Forum", *Financial Post*, September 4, 2013; "The Charms of Canada" and "The Goldilocks Recovery," *The Economist*, May 6, 2010; Andrew Coyne, "Our So-Called Genius Banks," *MacLean's*, April 6, 2009; Doug Alexander and Sean B. Pasternak, "Canadians Dominate World's 10 Strongest Banks," *Bloomberg*, May 2, 2012, and Erik Heinrich "Why Canada's Banks Don't Need Help," *Time,* Nov. 10, 2008.

Introduction

The financial system channels funds from those who want to save to those who want to borrow. Households borrow for many reasons, including buying cars and houses or attending university. Firms, such as the aircraft producer Bombardier, use the financial system to obtain funds to expand, modernize factories and meet payrolls, among other purposes. Most governments, including the federal, provincial, and local governments, use the financial system to obtain funds to build new roads and bridges and to finance gaps between the taxes they collect and their spending.

When the financial system operates well, funds move smoothly from savers to borrowers, enhancing economic activity. When the financial system does not operate well, the economy can experience a recession. In extreme cases, the recession can be severe, as the Great Depression of the 1930s and, in some countries but not in Canada, the Great Recession.

In this chapter we describe how the financial system operates and explore some of the problems that can occur if the flow of funds through the system is disrupted. Understanding how the financial system works will help you understand the material in later chapters on long-run economic growth, the business cycle, and fiscal and monetary policy. This chapter focuses on the Canadian financial system. (In chapter 5, we expand the focus to the global financial system.) We begin with an overview of the financial system. We discuss financial markets and financial intermediaries, various types of financial assets, and the services provided by the financial system: risk sharing, liquidity, and information. We discuss the problems arising from asymmetric information in financial markets, when one party in a transaction has better information than the other party. We analyze the principal-agent problem and its role in the financial crisis. In Section 3.2 we describe financial crises and discuss government policies to prevent the occurrence of crises, in particular deposit insurance. We also study the role of the central bank in stabilizing the financial system. In the last section we discuss models and concepts that will help us to understand monetary policy: the money market, the calculation of the present value, and the relationship between interest rates for bonds of different maturities and from different issuers.

An Overview of the Financial System

The **financial system** is the network of banks, stock and bond markets, and other financial markets and institutions that make it possible for funds to flow from lenders to borrowers. Households and firms depend heavily on the financial system to attain their goals. For instance, consider how the financial system works for you. When you begin your career, you will probably want to save some of your income and take out a loan to buy a car or a house. Through the financial system, you can save in many ways, including putting funds in a savings account in a bank or buying stocks or bonds. You can get a loan from a bank, from the financial arm of a car company, or from a mortgage company.

At certain points in your life you are likely to be a borrower. You may have borrowed money to pay for university. If you need to buy a car without saving enough to pay for it completely, you are likely to borrow the funds from a bank or a car-finance company. If you start a business, you probably will not be able to finance the startup costs for the business out of your savings so, once again, you are likely to borrow funds from a bank. Large businesses are often in a similar situation. To find the money they need to expand and grow, large businesses either borrow from banks or sell stocks and bonds directly to savers. In fact, without a well-functioning financial system, economic growth is difficult because firms will be unable to expand and adopt new technologies. History shows that only countries with well-developed financial systems have been able to sustain high levels of economic growth.

Financial Markets and Financial Intermediaries

The financial system consists of *financial markets* and *financial intermediaries*. A **financial market** is a place or channel for buying or selling financial assets, that is, stocks, bonds, or other financial securities. An **asset** is anything of value owned by a person or a firm. If you own a laptop or a car, those are your assets. For a firm, the buildings and equipment it owns are assets. A **financial asset** is a financial claim, which means that if you own a financial asset, you have a claim on someone else to pay you money. For instance, a bank chequing account is a financial asset because it represents a claim you have against the bank to pay you an amount of money equal to the dollar value of your account.

Financial securities are *tradeable* financial assets, which means they can be bought and sold. Stocks, bonds, and other financial securities are bought and sold in financial markets, such as the Toronto or the New York Stock Exchange. **Stocks** are financial securities that represent partial ownership of a firm. If you buy 500 shares of stock in Rogers, you become the owner of about one millionth of the company, as Rogers has about 500 million shares. You have a legal claim to your portion of anything Rogers owns and to its profits. In practice, the decision to distribute profits depends on the management. Firms typically pay *dividends* to their shareholders in the form of a payment per share.

Bonds are financial securities that represent promised fixed payments in the future. When Rogers sells a bond, the firm promises to pay the holder of the bond an interest payment each year for the term of the bond as well as a final payment equal to the face value of the bond when the bond matures. For example, a three-year bond with a face value of $100 and an interest rate of 5% is a promise to pay $5 in a year and in two years, and $105 in three years. The interest payments that issuers of bonds pay to bondholders are called *coupon payments*. *Discount bonds*, for example Treasury bills issued by the Government of Canada, are a little different: They involve only a promise to pay a certain amount at maturity. Instead of paying interest, they are sold at a discount to the final payment, hence the name. For example,

3.1

Learning Objective

Describe the financial system and explain the role it plays in the economy.

Financial system The financial intermediaries and financial markets that together facilitate the flow of funds from lenders to borrowers.

Financial market A place or channel for buying or selling stocks, bonds, or other financial securities.

Asset Anything of value owned by a person or a firm.

Financial asset A financial claim on someone to pay you money.

Financial securities Tradeable financial assets that can be bought and sold.

Stock A financial security that represents a legal claim to a share in the profits and assets of a firm.

Bond A financial security issued by a corporation or government that represents a promise to make payments to the holder of the bond in the future.

Avoiding a Common Mistake: Calculating the Return on Investment

It is common for students to calculate the return in the discount bond example as 5%. The error is due to the fact that they divide the gain by $100. But remember that the rate of return is equal to the gain divided by the amount invested. The gain is the difference between the face value ($100) and the amount paid ($95). The amount invested is $95, the amount paid for the T-bill. So the return is $5/$95 = 5.26%

a $100, one-year Treasury bill is a promise to pay $100 in a year. If it sells for $95, the one-year return is ($100 − $95)/$95 = 5.26%.

Economists make a distinction between primary markets and secondary markets. A *primary market* is a financial market in which stocks, bonds, and other securities are sold for the first time. Such sale is called an *initial public offering* (IPO). For example one of the largest IPOs in Canada in 2013 was BRP Inc., the maker of Ski-doo and See-doo vehicles. Another example is Facebook Inc., which first sold stock in 2012. A *secondary market* is a financial market in which investors[1] buy and sell already existing securities. If you were to buy or sell shares of BRP or Facebook today, you would be doing so in the secondary market. Primary and secondary markets can be in the same physical—or virtual—location. For example, a firm may issue new shares of stock on the Toronto Stock Exchange, where shares of existing stock are being bought and sold. The primary market is relatively small: The value of shares sold in BRP IPO was $250 million; the value of shares sold in Facebook IPO, which was the 10th largest IPO ever, was $16 billion. For comparison, the total value of shares sold on the largest market, the New York Stock Exchange (NYSE), was $14 trillion in 2011; the total value of shares sold at the Toronto Stock Exchange was around $1.5 trillion.

Some financial assets—such as chequing or savings accounts, mortgages, car loans, and student loans—are not financial securities because they cannot be resold in a financial market. In other words, there is no secondary market for these assets. Some of these assets can be converted into securities through *securitization*, as we have discussed in Chapter 1. We return to securitization below.

Financial intermediary A firm, such as a commercial bank, that borrows funds from savers and lends them to borrowers.

A **financial intermediary** is a firm that borrows funds from savers and lends them to borrowers. The most important financial intermediaries are commercial banks. Other financial intermediaries include investment banks, mutual funds, hedge funds, pension funds, and insurance companies. Table 3.1 gives brief descriptions of several important financial intermediaries and provides Canadian and international examples. In effect, financial intermediaries act as go-betweens for borrowers and savers by borrowing funds from savers and lending them to borrowers. For example, suppose Carmen wants to open a café. Although you may be reluctant to lend money directly to Carmen, you may end up doing so indirectly: You deposit money in a bank, which then combines your deposit with money from other depositors to make a loan to Carmen. Financial intermediaries pool the funds of many small savers and lend the funds to many individual borrowers. The intermediaries earn a profit by paying savers less for the use of their funds than they charge borrowers. The profits they make are constitute the payment for intermediation services as well as compensation for risk. For example, a bank might pay you as a depositor a 2% interest rate, while it lends money to

---

[1]A brief note on terminology: In this chapter, when we refer to *investors*, we mean households and financial firms who buy stocks, bonds, and other securities as financial investments. It is important not to confuse financial investment with the macroeconomic term *investment*, which refers to spending by firms and households on *investment goods*, such as houses, factories, machinery, and equipment.

Table 3.1 Important Financial Intermediaries

Type of financial intermediary	Description	Examples
Commercial bank	A company that takes in deposits and makes loans to households and firms.	Royal Bank of Canada, HSBC
Investment bank	A company that provides advice to firms issuing new securities, underwrites the issuing of securities, and develops new securities.	RBC Capital Markets, TD Securities, Goldman Sachs
Mutual fund	A company that sells shares to investors and uses the funds to buy stocks, bonds, or other financial securities.	IGM Financial, Investors Group, Fidelity Investments
Hedge fund	A company that is similar to a mutual fund but one that obtains funds primarily from wealthy investors and uses the funds to make complicated—and often risky—investments.	Arrow Capital Management, Bridgewater Associates Management, Man Group
Pension fund	An institution that receives contributions from workers and uses the funds received to invest in financial securities to fund retirement benefits.	Ontario Teachers' Pension Plan, Federal Public Service Pension Plan
Insurance company	A company that sells insurance policies to households and firms and uses the funds received to invest in financial securities.	Manulife Financial, Aviva Canada, AIG, Allianz

Carmen's Café at a 6% interest rate. Carmen's Café pays the high rate as it is unable to borrow money directly from the savers and needs to buy intermediation services from the bank. Also, the bank needs to be compensated for the risk that Carmen's Café may not pay back (default on) the loan.

Some financial intermediaries, such as mutual funds, hedge funds, pension funds, and insurance companies, make investments in stocks and bonds on behalf of savers. For example, mutual funds sell shares to savers and then use the funds to buy a *portfolio* of stocks, bonds, mortgage loans, and other financial securities. Most mutual funds issue shares that the funds will buy back—or *redeem*—at a price that represents the underlying value of the financial securities owned by the fund. Large mutual fund companies, such as Investors Group or the U.S. company Fidelity Investments, offer many alternative stock and bond funds. Over the past 30 years, the role of mutual funds in the financial system has increased dramatically. Competition among hundreds of mutual fund firms gives investors thousands of funds from which to choose.

Financial intermediaries play a key role in the economy because they are the main source of loans to households and small businesses. Only the largest firms can borrow directly by issuing bonds. Households and small firms usually cannot issue bonds, so they have to borrow indirectly by getting loans from banks.[2] Therefore, when banks decide to tighten their requirements for loans, many consumers are unable to obtain the credit they need to buy cars and houses and small businesses have trouble financing their operations and investments.

---

[2]Other forms of credit, for example private borrowing or credit-based crowdfunding, exist but are much less important.

Making the Connection

The Controversial World of Subprime Lending

Subprime lending, which was one of the main triggers of the financial crisis and the Great Recession, had existed for a long time but became much more prevalent in the United States in the previous decade. A subprime loan is a loan given to a risky customer. When considering a loan, banks analyze the creditworthiness of potential borrowers. In Canada, information on individual credit history is kept by reporting agencies, for example Equifax Canada. In the United States, this information is often combined into a *credit score*, the so-called FICO score. Borrowers with high FICO scores are considered *prime* customers. These are customers with a good credit history of paying back loans in full and on time. Borrowers with lower scores are riskier. They often can get loans but, given the higher probability of default or delayed payments, they are charged a higher interest rate to compensate the lender for the extra risk. When you graduate and would like to take out a loan, you will likely have to pay a high interest rate since you will have limited credit history. After several years of paying your loans on time you will establish a credit history and will be charged lower interest rates.

Some borrowers with low credit scores have difficulty finding any lenders willing to make loans to them. Often referred to as *subprime borrowers*, these people typically have seriously flawed credit histories that may include failure to make payments on credit cards or on car loans, or they may have declared personal bankruptcy in the recent past. Prior to the mid-1990s, many banks and other lenders avoided making loans to subprime borrowers rather than charging them very high interest rates to compensate for the high default risk. The lenders reasoned that the only borrowers who would take out loans at very high rates were people almost certain to default on their loans. Analysts at some banks began to argue, however, that data on loans made to subprime borrowers showed that the higher interest rates these borrowers paid more than compensated for the higher default risk. In other words, subprime loans were actually more profitable than loans made to borrowers with higher credit scores. How does it work? Assume, for example, that the default rate for prime borrowers is 2%; and for subprime borrowers is 5%. If the interest rate charged to prime borrowers is 5% and to subprime borrowers is 11%, the lender is more than compensated for the higher default rate since it receives an additional 6% interest to compensate for the extra 3% risk of default.

Subprime borrowing, if conducted prudently, allows risky customers to buy housing. But during the house price boom in the United States, many loan issuers took on excessive risks, and were not sufficiently compensated by higher interest rates. Beginning in 2006, many of these subprime borrowers defaulted on their loans, causing lenders to suffer heavy losses and precipitating the financial crisis. As a result of this experience, most lenders tightened their lending standards and subprime borrowers found that once again they had difficulty obtaining loans.

By mid-2012, however, some lenders in the United States began to make loans to subprime borrowers. Although most lenders were still unwilling to make mortgage loans to subprime borrowers, lenders did believe they could profitably make other types of loans to these borrowers. For example, banks began increasing the number of prepaid debit cards, low-limit credit cards, and short-term loans they offered to subprime borrowers, many of whom have low incomes. Some policymakers and advocates for low-income people have been critical of these ways of extending credit to subprime borrowers. These critics argue that low-income borrowers often do not understand the terms of the borrowings, failing to realize, for example, how much they will be paying in fees. Banks and many economists argue, though, that subprime borrowers have high risks of default, so banks have to charge them high fees and high interest rates in order to make a profit. Restricting the fees and interest rates that banks charge would likely result in banks no longer being willing to provide credit to subprime borrowers. U.S. policymakers and financial regulators are faced with a difficult balancing act as they try to ensure that subprime borrowers retain access to credit.

Subprime mortgages have never become popular in Canada. Canadian banks are conservative and mortgages are regulated, for example by imposing a minimum down payment needed to obtain a mortgage or by requiring borrowers with an inadequate down payment to buy insurance that would compensate the lender in case of a default. In addition, securitization was not very common in Canada, and lending standards did not decline before the Great Recession. If anything, the subprime crisis in the United States made Canadian banks even more prudent.

Sources: "Chasing Fees, Banks Court Low-Income Customers," *New York Times*, April 25, 2012; Jessica Silver-Greenberg and Tara Siegel Bernard, "Lenders Again Dealing Credit to Risky Borrowers," *New York Times*, April 10, 2012; Meredith Whitney, "America's 'Unbanked' Masses," *Wall Street Journal*, February 24, 2012; Pete Evans, "Mortgage Market Tiptoes toward Subprime," *CBC News*, April 16, 2012; and "Comparing Canada and U.S. Housing Finance Systems," *Canada Mortgage and Housing Corporation*, http://www.cmhc-schl.gc.ca/en/corp/nero/jufa/jufa_018.cfm, accessed February 14, 2014.

See related problem 1.9 at the end of the chapter.

Stocks, Bonds, and Stock Market Indexes Buying shares gives you the opportunity to be a part owner of a firm. Granted, if you are buying a few shares in Rogers or Apple, you own only a very small piece of the firm. But that ownership allows you to participate in any of the growth and increased profits the firm may experience. For reasons we will discuss later in this chapter, only a relatively small number of Canadian firms are *publicly traded companies* that sell shares on one of the Canadian stock markets. Out of the hundreds of thousands of firms in Canada, about 6000 are traded on one of the Canadian stock markets; 1500 are traded on the largest stock market, the Toronto Stock Exchange. Shares of large companies are often cross-listed on other stock exchanges, usually in the United States. For example Rogers is listed on both the Toronto and the New York stock exchanges.

The performance of the stock market is often measured using stock market indexes. Like other indexes, stock market indexes are weighted averages of stock prices. Figure 3.1 shows movements from 1980 to 2014 in four stock indexes: the S&P TSX Composite (Toronto Stock Exchange), the U.S. Standard & Poor's (S&P) 500, the Japanese Nikkei 225, and (from 2000) the Chinese Shanghai Composite. The value of all indices in January 1, 2000 has been set equal to 100.

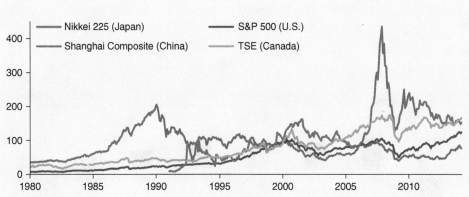

Figure 3.1

Stock Prices in Canada, the United States, Japan, and China, 1980–2014.
January 1, 2000 = 100.

Stock prices tend to rise and fall with the general economy. The Japanese stock market rose to high levels in the 1980s as a result of a strong economy. The Chinese stock market boomed during 2006 and 2007, before declining sharply during the financial crisis of 2007–09.

Source: finance.yahoo.com.

Stock prices usually mirror what is happening in the economy. When an economy is expanding, firms' profits and expected future profits rise, causing stock prices to increase. During an economic recession, the opposite occurs. Notice in Figure 3.1 that all four stock market indexes peaked at about the same time in 2000 and then again in 2007; all four indexes rebounded in 2009. These common movements in stock prices suggest that the forces affecting the business cycle and financial markets can be global in nature. In addition, factors specific to each economy can cause movements in stock prices. For example, during the 1980s, Japan experienced a surge in the value of real estate and stocks before both markets crashed. The increase in stock prices in China during 2006 and 2007 was particularly large, reflecting the optimism many investors had about the future growth of the Chinese economy.

Making the Connection

Investing in the Worldwide Stock Market

Suppose you decide to invest in stocks. How would you go about it? Traditionally, an investor would establish an account with a full service stockbroker, such as Cannacord Genuity Wealth Management, who would provide advice and purchase the shares in exchange for a payment or commission. Today, many investors who want to buy the shares of individual companies use online brokerage firms, such as TD Waterhouse, which typically charge much lower commissions than traditional brokerage firms but do not provide personal investment advice and other services offered by traditional brokers.

Investors can also purchase shares in mutual funds, which invest in a portfolio of stocks. For instance, the TD bank sells the TD European Growth Fund-I, which buys shares of European companies. Buying mutual funds allows savers with small amounts of money to reduce their risk by spreading their savings across the stocks of the many firms included in the fund. No-load mutual funds allow investors to avoid the commissions they would have to pay to buy individual stocks using brokers. In recent years, many investors have been purchasing *exchange-traded funds (ETFs)*. ETFs are very similar to mutual funds, except that, while mutual funds can be bought from or sold only to the investment firm that issues the funds, ETFs can be bought from and sold to other investors, just as if they were stocks.

The following figure lists world stock markets, by total value of the shares of the listed firms (in trillions of U.S. dollars) at the end of 2011.

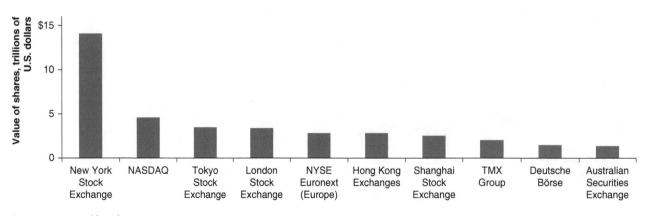

Source: www.world-exchanges.org

The New York Stock Exchange is the world's largest stock market, followed by NASDAQ, where many technology stocks are listed, and then the Tokyo and London markets. The Toronto Stock Exchange (TSX), operated with several smaller exchanges by the TMX group, is among the ten biggest stock markets in the world. Individuals, hedge funds, and some mutual funds invest in the stock of foreign firms. It is possible to buy individual stocks listed on foreign stock exchanges by setting up an account with a local brokerage firm in the foreign country. Although at one time only wealthy people invested directly in foreign stock markets, the internet has made it much easier for people of more moderate income to establish foreign brokerage accounts and to research foreign companies.

See related problem 1.10 at the end of the chapter.

Services Provided by the Financial System In addition to matching households that have funds to lend with households and firms that want to borrow funds, the financial system provides three key services to savers and borrowers:

1. Risk sharing
2. Liquidity
3. Collecting and distributing information

In financial markets, **risk** is the chance that the value of a financial security will change relative to what you expect. For example, you may have bought a share of stock in Blackberry in September 2007 to see it triple in value within a year, or in January 2011 to see it lose over 70% within a year. Of course such big changes in stock prices can, in general, be avoided by buying a diverse portfolio of shares. But this is still risky: In the year to March 2009, the TSX index lost 40%; it gained 40% in the following year.

Risk The chance that the value of a financial security will change relative to what you expect.

Most individual savers prefer to avoid risk and seek a steady return on their savings rather than erratic swings between high and low earnings. The financial system provides *risk sharing* by allowing savers to spread their money among many financial investments. For example, you can divide your money among a bank savings account, individual bonds, and a mutual fund to reduce the risk you face. Dividing your investment funds among different assets is called *diversification*, or, as the old saying has it, "Don't put all of your eggs in one basket."

Liquidity is the ease with which an asset can be exchanged for cash. The financial system provides the service of liquidity through markets in which savers can sell their stocks, bonds, and other financial securities. For example, savers can easily sell stocks and bonds issued by large corporations on the major stock and bond markets. Savers value liquidity because they want the reassurance that if they need money to buy goods and services they can easily convert their assets into cash. For instance, the retail stores and inventories of Canadian Tire are not very liquid because they cannot be easily converted into cash. The financial system, however, allows you to buy and sell the stock and bonds of the Canadian Tire Corporation, thereby making your savings much more liquid than if you directly owned physical stores. The need for liquidity explains why many financial institutions hold government bonds, in particular short-term government bonds called Treasury bills. While the return is very low, the market for Treasury bills is the most liquid market in Canada.

The financial system also provides savers with a third service by collecting and distributing *information*, including facts about borrowers and expectations about returns on financial securities. If you read a newspaper headline announcing that an automobile firm has invented a car with an engine that runs on water, how would you determine the effect of this discovery on the firm's profits? Financial markets do that job for you by incorporating information into the prices of stocks, bonds, and other financial securities. In this example, expectation of higher future profits would boost the prices of the automobile firm's stock and bonds.

Banking and Securitization

Typically, when we refer to "banks," we are thinking of *commercial banks*, which are financial firms that take in deposits and make loans to households and firms. Today, many financial firms engage not just in commercial banking but also in *investment banking*. The term "investment bank" is somewhat misleading. Traditionally, investment banks did not invest funds but were involved in two key activities: providing advice and management in mergers and acquisitions (M&A) and *underwriting* new issues of stocks (IPOs) and bonds. Mergers and acquisitions involve selling and buying companies, for example the purchase of YouTube by Google, or parts of companies, for example, the sale of Nokia's cellphone business to Microsoft, as well as combining companies, for example, the merger of Glencore and Xtrata. In underwriting, banks charge firms a fee to guarantee a certain price for the stocks and bonds the firm issues. For example, in the Facebook IPO in 2012, the underwriters guaranteed the price of $38. They actually had to buy shares in the stock market to prevent the price from falling below $38 as demand was lower than expected.

Investment banks are subject to less regulation in most countries than commercial banks, since they do not take deposits from individuals. They therefore have more freedom to move into new areas of finance. Beginning in the 1990s, investment banks, especially in the United States, became heavily involved in *securitization*. *Securitization* involves creating secondary markets for financial assets that previously could not be bought and sold and so were not considered financial securities. Most loans made by banks were financial assets to the banks, but they were not securities because they could not be sold in a market. For instance, when a bank granted a car loan, it would keep the loan and collect the payments until the loan *matured* when the borrower made the last payment. If the borrower failed to make payments on time or defaulted, the bank would suffer losses. Therefore the bank would carefully evaluate potential borrowers. Securitization bundles bank loans into securities that are then resold to investors. An investment bank would act as an intermediary, purchasing loans from banks, packaging them into securities, and selling the securities to investors. When loans are securitized, the banks that make the loans collect the payments from borrowers and send those payments to the investors who have bought securities based on the loans. This change in financial structure means that there is a good chance that when you take out a car loan at a local bank and write a cheque to the bank each month as payment on your loan, the money is ultimately received by someone who bought a security backed by your loan.

Securitization has been particularly important in the market for mortgage loans taken out by households to buy new and existing homes. Securitization has two important effects on the bank that provided the mortgage. It allows the bank to issue more loans. In addition, the mortgages are no longer the bank's assets. Once the bank sells the mortgage to an investment bank, it immediately receives funds that can be used to provide more loans. Perhaps more importantly, the bank that lent money is no longer affected when borrowers do not make payments on time or default on the loan. So, securitization makes it easier for banks to expand the volume of loans they make and reduces the risk of loan default to the bank providing the loan.

Asymmetric Information and the Principal–Agent Problems in Financial Markets

Securitization was at the heart of the financial crisis of 2007–09. In this section, we describe key difficulties that investors encounter in financial markets and how those difficulties led to the financial crisis.

Asymmetric Information   Many financial transactions, including loans, are subject to the problem of **asymmetric information**, a situation in which one party to an economic transaction has better information than does the other party. For example, households and firms that want to borrow money know more about their true financial condition than do lenders. A firm wanting to borrow money to avoid bankruptcy has a strong incentive to conceal its shaky financial condition from potential lenders. Similarly, an investment bank that wants to sell a security has an incentive to make the security appear less risky than it is.

Asymmetric information leads to two key problems: *adverse selection* and *moral hazard*. **Adverse selection** refers to a situation in which one party to a transaction takes advantage of knowing more than the other party before the transaction. Assume that the informational asymmetry is about the riskiness of investment project a potential borrower wants to undertake. While the borrower knows how risky the project is, the bank does not. Adverse selection results in the people and firms who most want to borrow money often being the riskiest borrowers. These borrowers have projects that bring in a high return if they are successful and a large loss if they are not. They are willing to pay high interest rates since, if the project is successful, they make a high return and, if the project fails, they can default on the loan. Consider, for example, a bank that charges 11% on loans. There are two customers, Michael and Joe. Both would like to undertake investment projects that have 50% chance of succeeding. Michael has a safe project with a return of 11% if things go well and 9% if they do not. Joe has a risky project: If things go well, he will make 30%; if they do not, he will lose 10%. Who will take the loan? Michael will not borrow since his return will be zero when things go well and minus 2% if they do not. On the other hand Joe will undertake the project since, if things go well, his return will be high (19%). If he is unlucky, he will default on the loan. For Joe, the chance of high return is worth the risk of default. But the bank should not lend to Joe since it will earn 11% when the project is successful and the loan is repaid, and lose 100% if Joe's project fails and he defaults on the loan. The problem is that both Michael and Joe promise to repay the loan and the bank, not knowing project characteristics, does not know which loan will be profitable.

What was the role of adverse selection in housing markets? Subprime borrowers would agree to high mortgage rates in the expectation that, when the price of the house increased, they would be able to borrow money against the higher value of the house and make interest payments. If house prices fell, they might default on their mortgages. This is indeed what happened. When house prices in the United States started falling in 2007, large numbers of subprime borrowers were unable to make interest payments and defaulted on their mortgages.

Moral hazard refers to actions people take after they have entered into a transaction that make the other party to the transaction worse off. For instance, once a firm or household has borrowed money, what will it do with the funds? The owner of a small firm may have told the bank that she would use a loan to upgrade computers, which is a low-risk project, but instead she may undertake a riskier project by opening a store in a new location.

Lenders encounter the adverse selection problem before a loan is made when they try to distinguish borrowers who are likely to pay back loans from borrowers who are unlikely to do so. Lenders encounter the moral hazard problem after they have made a loan when they deal with the possibility that borrowers will misuse borrowed funds.

Principal–Agent Problems   In many large corporations, moral hazard results in a *principal–agent problem*. Although the shareholders actually own a large corporation, top managers control the day-to-day operations of the firm. Because top managers do not own the firm, they may be more interested in increasing their own pay than in maximizing the profits of the firm. This separation of ownership of the firm from control of the firm can lead to a principal–agent problem because the agents—the firm's top management—pursue their own

> **Asymmetric information** A situation in which one party to an economic transaction has better information than does the other party.
>
> **Adverse selection** A situation in which one party to a transaction takes advantage of knowing more than the other party, before the transaction.
>
> **Moral hazard** A situation when, after entering into a transaction, one party takes actions that make the other party to the transaction worse off.

interests rather than the interests of the principals to whom they are ultimately responsible—the shareholders of the corporation.

Some economists believe that principal–agent problems were at the heart of the financial meltdown of 2007–09. Top managers of many financial firms, particularly investment banks, received large salaries and bonuses from creating, buying, and selling securities. Because these managers did not own the firms, they were less concerned with the degree of risk involved with securities backed by subprime mortgages. Similarly, the pay of bank employees who screened potential borrowers depended on the amount lent out. To maximize their income, they would relax lending standards and offer mortgages to people whose ability to pay was limited. The banks were less concerned about defaults than in the past because they would sell the mortgages to investment banks and so avoid losses when borrowers defaulted. In Canada, securitization was much less common than in the United States, and lending standards did not decline. As a result, the Canadian financial system did not suffer the problems affecting the United States, and the financial crisis in Canada was much less severe.

By 2008, increased awareness of principal–agent problems led many investors to realize that some securities were riskier than they had previously believed. As investors became more reluctant to invest in any but the safest securities, many financial firms found it difficult to raise the funds necessary to carry out their role of financial intermediation. As problems in the financial system increased during 2007–09, the attempts of the Federal Reserve (the Fed) to increase financial stability became the focus of economists and policymakers.

Financial Crises, Government Policy, and the Financial System

3.2

Learning Objective

Understand the role of the central bank in stabilizing the financial system.

Many economists believe that a central bank may be the most powerful organization in a country's economy. A central bank is an institution established by the government to operate as a "banker's bank," rather than as a bank for households and firms. Central banks, such as the Bank of Canada, the Federal Reserve in the United States, the Bank of Japan, and the European Central Bank, have the following policy responsibilities:

- regulating the money supply;
- acting as a lender of last resort to the banking system;
- acting as the government's bank by playing a role in the collection and disbursement of government funds;
- regulating the financial system; and
- facilitating the payment system by providing banks with cheque-clearing and other services.

This list refers to the routine, year-in, year-out policy responsibilities of a central bank. Sometimes, though, a central bank is faced with a *financial crisis* that requires it to take unusual policy actions. A financial crisis involves a significant disruption in the flow of funds from lenders to borrowers. Historically, most financial crises have involved the commercial banking system, but the 2007–09 crisis involved other types of financial intermediaries as well. To understand financial crises, we start by looking briefly at the operations of commercial banks and at the important economic concept of *leverage*.

Financial Intermediaries and Leverage

Consider the situation a typical commercial bank faces. Figure 3.2 shows the *balance sheet* of a commercial bank, such as the CIBC. A firm's balance sheet sums up its financial position on a particular day, usually the end of a quarter or a year. Assets are shown on the left side of its balance sheet and its liabilities are shown on the right side. In the simplified balance

Assets		Liabilities	
Reserves	$ 100	Deposits	$1000
Loans	$700		
Securities	$ 300	Net worth (capital)	$100
Total assets	$1100	Total liabilities + net worth (capital)	$1100

Figure 3.2

Simplified Balance Sheet of a Commercial Bank

The items of greatest economic importance on a bank's balance sheet are its reserves, loans, securities and deposits. Notice that the difference between the value of this bank's total assets and its total liabilities is equal to its net worth. Therefore, the left side of the balance sheet is always equal to the right side.

sheet shown in Figure 3.2, we include only a few of a typical bank's assets and liabilities and, for convenience, use very small dollar amounts. The bank's assets are its *reserves*, loans, and securities it holds, such as Treasury bills or securitized loans. A bank's reserves are the sum of the funds physically present in the bank (mostly notes) or funds on deposit with the Bank of Canada. The bank's liabilities are its deposits. You probably do not think of yourself as lending to a bank when you deposit money into your chequing account, but, in effect, you are. You give money to the bank and the bank pays you interest. You can withdraw your deposit at any time in some accounts (for example, in a chequing account that typically pays no interest) or by informing the bank in advance. So your deposit in a bank is the same as a loan that can be recalled at any time or a loan that can be recalled with a prior notice; in other words, it is a liability of the bank.

Banks make most of their loans and other investments using borrowed money in the form of deposits. Canada, like nearly all other countries, has a *fractional reserve banking system* where banks keep less than 100% of deposits as reserves. We will discuss reserves in more detail later in this section. When people deposit money in a bank, the bank uses most of the money to make loans or to invest in securities, holding relatively little as reserves. For example, in Figure 3.2, the bank has $1000 in deposits but only $100 in reserves.

Subtracting the value of a firm's liabilities from the value of its assets leaves its *net worth*, which is shown on the right side of the balance sheet. For a public firm, net worth is called shareholder's equity; for a bank, net worth is often referred to as the *bank's capital*.[3] The value of the assets on the left side of the balance sheet must always equal the sum of the value of the liabilities plus net worth shown on the right side. This equality holds because net worth is defined as the difference between the value of the firm's assets and the value of the firm's liabilities. Note that anything that reduces the value of a bank's assets without affecting the value of its liabilities will cause the bank's net worth to decline.

Leverage is a measure of how much debt an investor takes on in making an investment. There are several definitions of leverage in corporate finance and accounting. As before, we define leverage as the ratio of total assets to the difference between total assets and liabilities (excluding capital). We can write it simply as the ratio of total assets to capital:

$$Leverage = \frac{Total\ assets}{Capital}.$$

A bank's leverage is related to how much of its deposits it uses to lend out and to buy securities. We will first consider the concept of leverage with respect to a homeowner and then relate the concepts to bank leverage later in this section.

What difference does leverage make and what is the appeal of making leveraged investments? To answer these questions, consider the situation of a large group of leveraged

---

[3]Technically, under banking regulations, "Tier 1 capital" equals a bank's shareholder's equity, with some minor adjustments.

Table 3.2 Leverage in the Housing Market

Down payment	Leverage	Return on your investment from . . .	
		a 10% increase in the price of your house	a 10% decrease in the price of your house
100%	1	10%	−10%
20%	5	50%	−50%
10%	10	100%	−100%
5%	20	200%	−200%

investors: homeowners. Traditionally, most people taking out a mortgage loan to buy a house made a down payment equal to 20% of the price of the house and borrowed the other 80%, making their house a leveraged investment. In this case, leverage is 5; the value of the down payment, which is the homeowner's capital, is 1/5 of the value of the asset (the house).

To see how leverage works in the housing market, consider the following example, illustrated in Table 3.2: Suppose you buy a $200 000 house on January 1, 2014. We consider several scenarios that differ by the amount of down payment: a down payment of 100%, 20%, 10%, and 5%. In calculating your leverage, the house is your asset and the down payment is your capital. Leverage is shown in the second column in Table 3.2. For example, when you make the typical down payment of 20%, which in this case is $40 000, your leverage is calculated as follows: the asset is $200 000, the capital is $40 000 and the leverage is $200 000/$40 000 = 100% / 20% = 5. To continue the example, suppose that on January 1, 2015, the price of the house—if you decide to sell it—has risen to $220 000. The return you earned on the house depends on how much you invested when you bought it. For example:

- If you paid $200 000 in cash for the house, your return on that $200 000 investment is the $20 000 increase in the price of the house divided by your $200 000 investment, or 10%.
- If you made a down payment of 20%, or $40 000, and borrowed the rest by taking out a mortgage loan of $160 000, the return on your investment in the house is the $20 000 increase in the price of the house divided by your $40 000 investment, or 50%.
- If you made a down payment of 5%, or $10 000, the return on your investment is the $20 000 increase in the price of the house divided by your $10 000 investment, or 200%. In that case leverage allows you to triple your money even though the price of the house increases by only 10%.

The third column in Table 3.2 illustrates how the return on your investment increases as your down payment falls and leverage rises. As our example shows, the larger the fraction of an investment financed by borrowing, the greater the degree of leverage in the investment and the greater the potential return. But as the fourth column in the table shows, the reverse is also true: The greater the leverage, the greater the potential loss. To see why, consider once again that you buy a house for $200 000, except that in this case, after one year, the price of the house *falls* to $180 000. If you paid $200 000 in cash for the house—so your leverage was one—the $20 000 decline in the price of the house represents a loss of 10% of your investment. But if you made a down payment of only $10 000 and borrowed the remaining $190 000 (the leverage of 20), then the $20 000 decline in the price of the house represents a loss of 200% of your investment. In fact, the house is now worth $10 000 less than the amount of your mortgage loan. The *equity* in your house is the difference between the market price of the house and the amount you owe on a loan. If the amount you owe is greater than the price of the house, you have negative equity. A homeowner who has negative equity is also said to be "underwater" on his or her mortgage.

It is easy to see from Table 3.2 that the return on your investment is equal to the return on the asset times the leverage:

$$\text{Return on investment} = (\text{return on the asset}) \times (\text{leverage}).$$

We can conclude that *the more leveraged an investment, the greater the potential gain* and *the greater the potential loss*. Or, put another way, increased leverage results in increased risk.

Let's return to the discussion of commercial banks. Because banks finance most of their assets—loans and securities—with deposits, rather than capital, the more assets the banks have relative to their capital, the greater their leverage. If banks suffer losses on their assets—for instance, if the value of their security holdings declines—they can find themselves in the same position as the homeowner in our example. Just as a highly leveraged homeowner can have the equity in her house wiped out by a relatively small decline in the price of her house, a highly leveraged bank can have its net worth, or capital, wiped out by a relatively small decline in the prices of its assets.

In many countries, governments (or central banks) regulate bank leverage by requiring that banks keep sufficient capital. The amount of capital banks are required to hold, called *capital requirement* or *capital adequacy* ratio, depends on the riskiness of their liabilities. The more risky the liabilities are, the more capital a bank is required to hold. By imposing regulatory capital requirements, governments limit banks leverage. Regulators are concerned that, without capital requirements, a bank's managers may become highly leveraged in an attempt to earn high returns on the bank's investments. Bank managers are particularly likely to take on more risk than shareholders would prefer if the managers do not own significant stock in the bank and if the managers' salaries depend on how profitable the bank is. If the investments are profitable, managers get large bonuses; if they are not, the worst that can happen is that they will lose their jobs while shareholders bear the financial losses. As is often said, managers have unlimited upside and limited downside. In other words, banks and other financial intermediaries can experience significant principal–agent problems. Even in countries in which government regulations limit the leverage of commercial banks, other financial intermediaries are highly leveraged but often face less regulation. For instance, investment banks often borrow in the short term from other financial firms and use the funds to make investments. Like commercial banks, these financial intermediaries are subject to sharp declines in their net worth if the value of their investments falls.

Bank Panics

The financial crisis of 2007–09 was the most severe in many countries since the 1930s. The crisis of the 1930s and several financial crises that occurred prior to the 1930s involved the commercial banking system. To understand how problems in the commercial banking system can cause a financial crisis, we begin by noting that, when people deposit money in a bank, the bank uses most of the money to make loans or to invest in securities, holding relatively little as reserves. While the deposits may be withdrawn at any time, the loans are typically long term, with the bank having to wait months or years before being fully paid back. For example, car loans or mortgages typically have a term of several years. They are *illiquid*: The bank must wait years until the loans are repaid. If depositors want their money back, banks are faced with the problem of having loaned or invested most of the depositors' money without being able to easily get it back.

In practice, withdrawals are usually not a problem for banks because on a typical day about as much money is deposited as is withdrawn. Sometimes, though, depositors lose confidence in a bank if the bank's assets—such as loans and securities—lose value. When many depositors simultaneously decide to withdraw their money from a bank, there is a **bank run**.

Bank run A situation in which depositors who have lost confidence in a bank simultaneously withdraw their money.

Bank panic A situation in which many banks simultaneously experience rapid deposit withdrawals.

If many banks experience runs at the same time, the result is a **bank panic**. It is possible for one bank to handle a run by borrowing from other banks to pay off depositors, but if many banks simultaneously experience runs, the banking system may be in trouble. When banks experience a run, they face *liquidity problems* because their loans cannot be easily sold to provide funds to pay off depositors. In other words, the banks do not have enough liquid assets to pay off all the depositors who want their deposits back.

Before governments introduced policies to deal with bank failures, if depositors suspected that a bank had made bad loans or other investments, the depositors had a strong incentive to rush to the bank to withdraw their money. Depositors knew that the bank would have only enough cash and other liquid assets available to pay off a fraction of the bank's depositors. Once the bank's liquid assets were exhausted, the bank would have to shut its doors, at least temporarily, until it could raise additional funds. One way to raise funds for the bank would be to sell illiquid assets. In such forced sale the bank would have to accept sharply discounted prices and might become *insolvent* and permanently close its doors.

Insolvency The situation in which the value of a bank's or another firm's assets declines to less than the value of its liabilities, leaving it with negative net worth.

Insolvency is a situation in which the value of a bank's or another firm's assets declines to less than the value of its liabilities, with the result that the firm has negative net worth. Depositors of a failed bank were likely to receive only some of their money back and then usually only after a long delay.

Imagine being a depositor in a bank. If you suspected that your bank was having financial problems, you would want to be one of the first in line to withdraw your money. Even if you were convinced that your bank was well managed and its loans and investments were in good shape, if you believed that the bank's other depositors thought there was a problem, you would still want to withdraw your money before the other depositors arrived and forced the bank to close. In other words the stability of a bank depends on the confidence of its depositors. In such a situation, if bad news—or even false rumours—shake that confidence, a bank will experience a run.

Contagion The process of spreading the financial panic affecting a small number of institutions to other financial institutions and to the entire financial system.

Moreover, bad news about one bank can snowball and affect other banks in a process called **contagion**. Once one bank has experienced a run, depositors of other banks may become concerned that their banks might also have problems. These depositors have an incentive to withdraw their money from their banks to avoid losing it should their banks be forced to close. These other banks will be forced to sell loans and securities to raise money to pay off depositors. A key point is that if multiple banks have to sell the same assets—for example, securitized loans in the modern banking system—the prices of these assets are likely to decline. As asset prices fall, a process called *asset deflation*, the net worth of banks falls and some banks may even be pushed to insolvency. A bank panic feeds on a self-fulfilling perception: If depositors believe that their banks are in trouble, the banks are in trouble. Figure 3.3 illustrates the causes and consequences of bank panics and the feedback loops that cause a panic to become self-reinforcing. Ultimately, government intervention is needed to end the downward spiral illustrated in the figure.

Government Policies to Deal with Bank Panics

The failure of financially healthy banks due to liquidity problems hurts the ability of households and small- and medium-sized firms to obtain loans, which may reduce their spending and bring on an economic recession. A recession caused by a bank panic can lead to further problems for banks as households and firms default on loans and security values fall further. Additional bank failures make it even harder for households and firms to obtain loans, which further reduces spending and makes the decline in output even larger.

Governments have two main ways they can attempt to avoid bank panics: (1) the central bank can act as a *lender of last resort* and (2) the government can insure deposits. The Bank of Canada, established in 1935, and the Canada Deposit Insurance Corporation (CDIC),

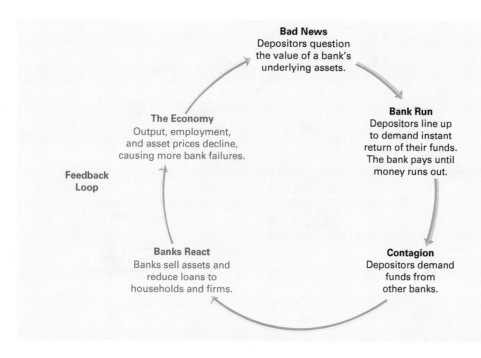

Figure 3.3

The Feedback Loop During a Bank Panic

Bank runs can cause good banks, as well as bad banks, to fail. Bank failures are costly because they reduce credit availability to households and firms. Once a panic starts, the fall in income, employment, and asset prices can cause more bank failures. This feedback loop can cause a panic to continue, unless the government intervenes.

established in 1967, play an important role in preventing bank panics. If a bank is short of liquidity, it can borrow funds from the Bank of Canada. This allows the bank to avoid a forced sale of its assets and consequent losses. Borrowing from the Bank of Canada prevents the collapse of financially viable banks when they face liquidity problems. Historically, the Bank of Canada has rarely had to play the role of the lender of last resort. The fact that emergency loans from the Bank of Canada are available reduces the risk of bank panics and the need to use the lender of last resort facility. CDIC insures individual bank deposits, up to $100 000 per institution (so if you have a $100 000 deposit at the CIBC and another at TD, both are insured). Knowing that their funds are safe, the rush to withdraw funds is avoided and bank panics are prevented. During the financial panic that followed Lehman Brothers bankruptcy, in many countries, including Canada, deposit insurance was increased preventing the situation from getting much worse.

The Money Market and the Risk Structure and Term Structure of Interest Rates

3.3

Learning Objective

Explain how interest rates are determined in the money market, and understand the risk structure and term structure of interest rates.

The interest rate is a key economic variable in the financial system. You encounter interest rates on your savings accounts, your credit card payments, and your student loans. In this section, we first look at interest rates using the *money market model* (which is also called the *liquidity preference model*). To better understand interest rates, we then look more closely at how to calculate one key set of interest rates: the interest rates on bonds.

The Demand and Supply of Money

The money market model focuses on how the interaction of the demand and supply for money determines the short-term nominal interest rate.[4] Recall that the *nominal interest*

---

[4]The money market model was first discussed by John Maynard Keynes in his book *The General Theory of Employment, Interest and Money*, which was published in 1936. Keynes referred to the model as the "liquidity preference model," a term that some economists still use. Note one possible source of confusion: Economists sometimes also use the phrase "money market" to refer to the market for bonds, such as Treasury bills, that mature in one year or less.

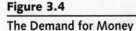

Figure 3.4

The Demand for Money

The money demand curve slopes downward because a lower nominal interest rate by reducing the opportunity cost of holding money, causes households and firms to switch from financial assets, such as T-bills, to money.

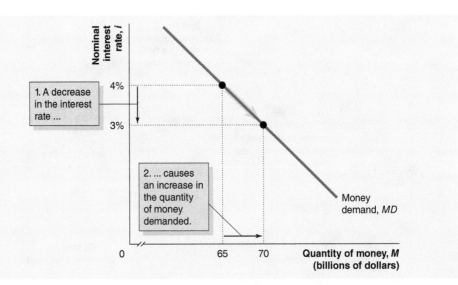

rate is the stated interest rate on a loan or bond, without correction for inflation. *Short-term* means that the loan or bond will mature, or be paid off, in one year or less. Figure 3.4 shows the demand curve for money. The nominal interest rate is on the vertical axis and the quantity of money is on the horizontal axis.

To understand why the demand curve for money in Figure 3.4 is downward sloping, consider that households and firms have a choice between holding money and holding other financial assets, such as Government of Canada Treasury bills (or T-bills). Money has a particularly desirable characteristic: it is perfectly liquid, so you can use it to buy goods, services, or financial assets. Money also has an undesirable characteristic: the currency in your wallet earns no interest. Alternatives to money, such as Government of Canada T-bills, pay interest, but you have to sell them if you want to use the funds to buy goods or services. By holding money, a household chooses higher liquidity at the cost of interest it could have earned if it held less liquid assets.

The interest rate that financial assets such as T-bills pay is the nominal interest rate: the interest rate in terms of money. When the nominal interest rate rises, the amount of interest that households and firms lose by holding money increases. When the nominal interest rate falls, the amount of interest households and firms lose by holding money decreases. Recall that the opportunity cost is what you have to forgo to engage in an activity. *The nominal interest rate is the opportunity cost of holding money.* We now have an explanation for why the demand curve for money slopes downward. When nominal interest rates on Treasury bills and other financial assets are low, the opportunity cost of holding money is low, so the quantity of money demanded by households and firms is high. When interest rates are high, the opportunity cost of holding money is high, so the quantity of money demanded is low. In Figure 3.4, a decrease in the nominal interest rate from 4% to 3% causes the quantity of money demanded by households and firms to rise from $65 billion to $70 billion.

Shifts in the Money Demand Curve

You know from the principles of economics course that the demand curve for a good is drawn holding constant all variables, other than the price, that affect the willingness of consumers to buy the good. Changes in variables other than the price cause the demand curve to shift. Similarly, the demand curve for money is drawn holding constant all variables,

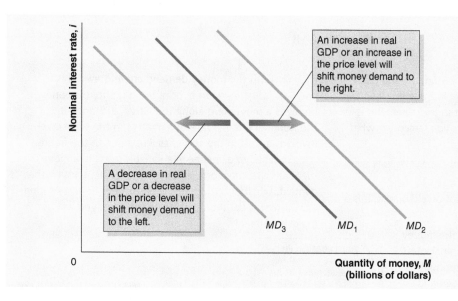

Figure 3.5

Shifts in the Money Demand Curve

Changes in real GDP or in the price level cause the money demand curve to shift. An increase in real GDP or an increase in the price level will cause the money demand curve to shift to the right, from MD_1 to MD_2. A decrease in real GDP or a decrease in the price level will cause the money demand curve to shift to the left, from MD_1 to MD_3.

other than the nominal interest rate, that affect the willingness of households and firms to hold money. Changes in variables other than the nominal interest rate cause the demand curve to shift. The two most important variables that cause the money demand curve to shift are

1. real GDP;
2. the price level.

An increase in real GDP means that the amount of buying and selling of goods and services will increase. Households and firms will need more money to conduct more transactions, so the quantity of money households and firms want to hold increases at each interest rate, shifting the money demand curve to the right. A decrease in real GDP decreases the quantity of money demanded at each interest rate, shifting the money demand curve to the left.

A higher price level increases the quantity of money required for a given amount of buying and selling. With a higher price level, more money (i.e., a larger number of dollars) is needed to pay for each transaction. For example, between 1914 and 2014, the price level in Canada increased over 20 times. This means that $20 is needed to buy something that could be bought for $1 a hundred years ago. An increase in the price level increases the quantity of money demanded at each interest rate, shifting the money demand curve to the right. A decrease in the price level decreases the quantity of money demanded at each interest rate, shifting the money demand curve to the left.

Figure 3.5 illustrates shifts in the money demand curve. An increase in real GDP or an increase in the price level will cause the money demand curve to shift to the right, from MD_1 to MD_2. A decrease in real GDP or a decrease in the price level will cause the money demand curve to shift to the left, from MD_1 to MD_3.

Equilibrium in the Money Market

In this chapter we assume for simplicity that the Bank of Canada is able to set the supply of money at whatever level it chooses. In fact, as we will discuss later, the Bank of Canada (and other central banks) does not have complete control of the money supply. At this point, however, the inability of the central bank to completely control the money supply is not important.

Avoiding a Common Mistake: a Movement along or a Shift in the Curve

Sometimes, when analyzing a model, students find it difficult to determine whether a change in a variable involves a movement along a curve or a shift in the curve. This is actually easy to figure out as long as you remember what is on the axes. The rule is simple:

- if the variable that changes is on either axis, it is a movement along the curve
- if the variable that changes is not on either axis, it is a shift of the curve

We can use the rule to look at the money demand curve. A change in the nominal interest rate, or in the quantity of money, involves a movement along a given money demand curve. A change in any other variable, for example in income or the price level, involves a shift of the curve.

The reason students have problems is that sometimes we draw a similar curve with another variable on the axis. For example, we can draw the money demand curve to show quantity demanded as a function of income. It will be a positively sloped curve: The higher the level of income, the higher the quantity of money demanded. It is illustrated in the figure shown here. To avoid confusion, we denote the money demand curve drawn as a function of income as MD(Y). With the money demand curve drawn this way, a change in income, or in the quantity of money, involves a movement along the curve; a change in the nominal interest rate or a change in the price level involves a shift in the curve, as illustrated in the figure.

So whether a change in a variable leads to a movement along a curve or a shift of the curve depends on the context, whether the variable is on the axis or not. As long as you remember the variables on the axes, you will not make a mistake!

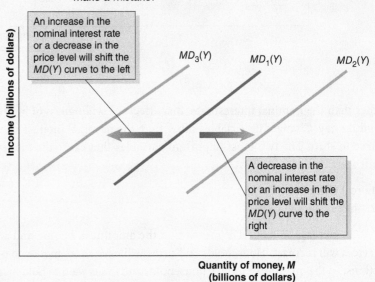

Assuming the Bank of Canada has full control of the money supply, the money supply curve, which shows the relationship between the amount of money in the economy and the nominal interest rate, is a vertical line. Changes in the interest rate do not affect the quantity of money supplied. The money supply curve depends on the decisions of the Bank of Canada. If the Bank increases the money supply, the money supply curve shifts right. If the Bank of Canada reduces the money supply, the money supply curve shifts to the left.

Figure 3.6 includes both the money demand and money supply curves to show how the equilibrium nominal interest rate is determined in the money market. Just as in other markets, equilibrium in the money market occurs where the money demand curve crosses the money supply curve. If the Bank of Canada increases the money supply, the money supply curve will shift to the right and the equilibrium interest rate will fall. Figure 3.6 shows that when the Bank of Canada increases the money supply from $65 billion to $70 billion, the money supply curve shifts to the right, from MS_1 to MS_2, and the equilibrium interest rate falls from 4% to 3%.

In the money market, the adjustment from one equilibrium to another equilibrium is a little different from the adjustment in the market for a good. In Figure 3.6, the money market is initially in equilibrium, with an interest rate of 4% and a money supply of $65 billion. Then the Bank of Canada increases the money supply by $5 billion by buying government bonds and increasing their prices. As we explain in the next section, an increase in the prices of

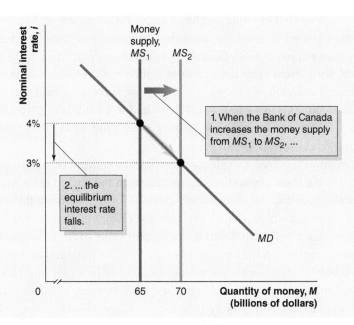

Figure 3.6

The Effect on the Interest Rate When the Bank of Canada Increases the Money Supply

When the Bank of Canada increases the money supply from $65 billion to $70 billion, the money supply curve shifts to the right from MS_1 to MS_2 and the equilibrium nominal interest rate falls from 4% to 3%.

financial assets means a decrease in their interest rates. Table 3.3 summarizes the key factors that cause shifts in the demand and the supply of money.

Calculating Bond Interest Rates and the Concept of Present Value

Interest rates on bonds are particularly important in the financial system. We now turn to the analysis of the relationship between bond prices and interest rates.

The relationship between bond prices and interest rates depends on the concept of **present value**. The present value is the value today of funds that will be received in the future. To calculate the present value, we ask how much money is needed today to generate the future payments. It is convenient to use simple examples to understand the concept of

Present value The value today of funds that will be received in the future.

Table 3.3 Summary of the Money Market Model

An increase in . . .	will shift the . . .	causing . . .	Graph of the effect on equilibrium in the money market
real GDP or an increase in the price level	money demand curve to the right	the nominal interest rate to increase.	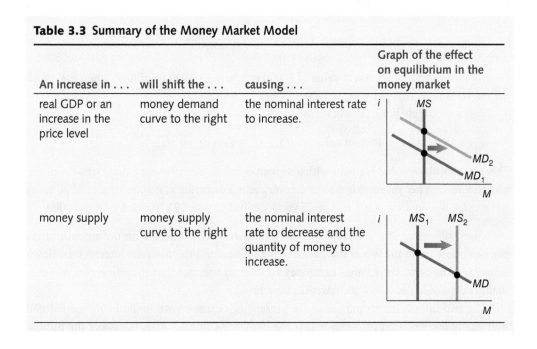
money supply	money supply curve to the right	the nominal interest rate to decrease and the quantity of money to increase.	

the present value. The first example involves a single future payment. Nancy's Consulting signs a one-year contract to provide accounting services to Bob's Construction Company. Bob's Construction will pay Nancy's Consulting $1100 in one year. What is the present value of the contract? The present value is the amount of money Bob's Construction needs to have today to generate a payment of $1100 a year from now. If the nominal interest rate is 10%, this amount is $1000. This is because $1000 deposited in a bank at a 10% nominal interest rate will grow to $1100 a year from now. So the present value of $1100 in a year, when the nominal interest rate is 10%, is $1000.

The first example involved a single payment, but the concept of present value can easily be extended to a stream of payments in the future. In the second example, assume that Nancy's Consulting contract for accounting services is for two years. At the end of the first year Nancy's Consulting will receive $1100 from Bob's Construction; and at the end of the second year it will receive $2420. What is the present value of the two-year contract? As in the previous example, it is the amount of money Bob's Construction needs today that, deposited in a bank, will generate the payment of $1100 in a year and of $2420 in two years. If the nominal interest rate is 10% per year, this amount is $3000. After a year the $3000 deposited in a bank will grow by 10%, to $3300. Bob's Construction will then make the $1100 payment and will have $2200 left. In the second year, it will receive 10% interest and will have $2420. This is the amount of the second payment. Notice that the present value of $1100 in a year is

$$\$1000 = \frac{\$1100}{(1 + 0.10)} = \frac{Future\ value_{+1}}{(1 + i)}.$$

Here, the subscript "+1" denotes that the future payment is received a year from now and i is the nominal interest rate. Similarly, the present value of $2420 two years from now is, denoting the payment received two years from now with the subscript "+2":

$$\$2000 = \frac{\$2420}{(1 + 0.10)^2} = \frac{Future\ value_{+2}}{(1 + i)^2}.$$

More generally, the present value of a single payment received n years from now, which we will denote $Present\ value_{+n}$, is

$$Present\ value_{+n} = \frac{Future\ value_{+n}}{(1 + i)^n}. \tag{3.1}$$

So, for example, the present value of $1000 received 25 years from now, when the nominal interest rate is 10% per year, is $1000/(1+i)^{25} = $92.30.

We can multiply both sides of equation (3.1) by $(1+i)^n$ to obtain

$$Present\ value_{+n} \cdot (1 + i)^n = Future\ value_{+n}. \tag{3.2}$$

This equation shows what happens with a deposit equal to $Present\ value_{+n}$ that earns the nominal interest rate i per year and is reinvested every year. For example, if you deposit $92.30 today and receive 10% interest every year, in 25 years you will receive $92.30 \cdot (1 + 0.1)^{25} = $1000.

Variables Affecting the Present Value The present value depends on the amount of the payment, how far in the future the payment is received, and the nominal interest rate. Economists use the term **time value of money** to refer to the fact that the value of a payment changes depending on when the payment is received.

The two important properties of the present value are shown in Table 3.4 on page 91, with examples. The first property is that the higher the interest rate, the lower the present

Time value of money
The way the value of a payment changes depending on when the payment is received.

Table 3.4 Properties of the Present Value

Properties of the present value	Interest rate	$1000 received in . . . years	Formula	Present value
	5%	1	$\dfrac{\$1000}{(1 + 0.05)}$	$952.38
The higher the interest rate, the lower the present value of a future payment,	10%	1	$\dfrac{\$1000}{(1 + 0.10)}$	$909.09
	15%	1	$\dfrac{\$1000}{(1 + 0.15)}$	$859.67
The further in the future the payment is received, the lower is its present value	10%	1	$\dfrac{\$1000}{(1 + 0.10)}$	$909.09
	10%	2	$\dfrac{\$1000}{(1 + 0.10)^2}$	$826.45

value of a future payment. The second property is that the further in the future the payment is received, the lower is its present value.

Anyone who buys a financial asset, such as a share or a bond, is really buying a promise to receive payments in the future. In case of a coupon bond, the holder receives the interest on a bond in the form of a *coupon*, which is a constant dollar amount that is paid each year, plus the face value at time of maturity. Similarly, investors receive a *dividend* payment from a firm when they buy a firm's stock. The price investors are willing to pay for a bond or a stock (or another financial asset) is (abstracting from risk) equal to the present value of the payments they will receive as a result of owning the bond or stock. In other words,

the price of a financial asset should equal the present value of the payments an investor expects to receive from owning that asset.

Take the case of a five-year coupon bond that pays an annual coupon of $60 and has a face value of $1000, which the owner of the bond will receive when the bond matures in five years. The expression for the price, P, of the bond is the sum of the present values of the six payments the investor will receive

$$P = \frac{\$60}{(1 + i)} + \frac{\$60}{(1 + i)^2} + \frac{\$60}{(1 + i)^3} + \frac{\$60}{(1 + i)^4} + \frac{\$60}{(1 + i)^5} + \frac{\$1000}{(1 + i)^5}.$$

We can use this reasoning to arrive at a general expression for the price of a bond that makes coupon payments, C, has a face value, FV, and matures in n years:

$$P = \frac{C}{(1 + i)} + \frac{C}{(1 + i)^2} + \frac{C}{(1 + i)^3} + \cdots + \frac{C}{(1 + i)^n} + \frac{FV}{(1 + i)^n}.$$

The dots indicate that we have omitted the terms representing the years between the third year and the nth year—which could be the tenth, twentieth, thirtieth, or another year.

The higher is the interest rate, the lower is the present value of a future stream of payments and so the lower is the price investors are willing to pay for the asset. So,

an increase in interest rates reduces the prices of existing financial assets, and a decrease in interest rates increases the prices of existing financial assets.

Avoiding a Common Mistake: Interest Rates and Bond Prices Once Again

Students often get confused by the inverse relationship between interest rates and prices of existing financial assets. The relationship is crucial to the understanding of many macroeconomic issues, in particular of how the monetary policy works, so it is important to remember how nominal interest rates are related to asset prices. The typical mistake is to think that, when the interest rate increases, lending money brings a higher return and so investors should be expected to pay more for the bonds. But this reasoning is not correct.

To avoid the confusion, you should think of a bond that has been sold as a stream of future payments. *Once the bond is sold, the price paid for the bond is irrelevant.* What matters is the stream of future payments: both the coupon payments and the face value paid when the bond is kept to maturity. The price of the bond is the present value of this stream of payments. When the interest rate increases, the present value of payments is lower and so the price of the bonds falls.

The easiest way to see that bond prices fall when the interest rate increases is to look at the pricing of a T-bill. Recall that a T-bill is a *discount bond*, (also called *zero-coupon bond*) which means it does not pay a coupon but is sold at a discount to its face value. Suppose, for instance, that you pay a price of $961.54 for a one-year T-bill with a face value of $1000. In exchange for your investment of $961.54 you will receive $1000 in one year. The interest rate, i, on the T-bill is equal to the difference between what you receive at the end of the year ($1000) minus what you paid for the bond ($961.54) divided by the price you paid ($961.54):

$$i = \left(\frac{\$1000 - \$961.54}{\$961.54} \right) = 4\%.$$

Suppose that right after you purchase the T-bill, the interest rate rises to 5%, How will that affect the price at which you could sell your Treasury bill to another investor? The potential buyer can now earn 5%, so the amount she would pay for the T-bill is one that makes the return on the T-bill equal to 5%. This amount is equal to the present value of a $1000 payment a year from now when the interest rate is 5%:

$$\text{Price} = \frac{\$1000}{(1 + 0.05)} = \$952.38.$$

As a result of the market interest rate for T-bills having risen from 4% to 5%, the price of your T-bill—should you decide to sell it—has fallen from $961.54 to $952.38. What is the intuition? Recall that a bond is a promise to make specific payments on specific dates in the future. Once the bond is sold, the price paid for it becomes irrelevant. The price of the bond is equal to the present value of its future payments. The present value depends, inversely, on the current interest rate. If the interest rate increases, the price falls; if the interest rate falls, the price increases. The present value does not depend on the amount originally paid for the bond.

When the price of an asset increases, the increase is a *capital gain*. When the price of an asset decreases, the decrease is a *capital loss*. In this case, you have suffered a capital loss of $9.16. So an increase in the interest rates leads to capital losses of bond holders. If, on the other hand, the market interest rate for T-bills falls, then the price of Treasury bills increases and the holder receives a capital gain.

Solved Problem 3.1

Interest Rates and Bond Prices

The federal government issues a variety of securities, including T-bills and bonds, which have maturities of up to 30 years. Suppose that a Government of Canada bond was issued 28 years ago, so it will mature in 2 years. If the bond pays a coupon of $45 per year and will make a final, face-value payment of $1000 at maturity, what is its price if the relevant market interest rate is 5%? What is its price if the relevant market interest rate is 10%?

Solving the Problem

Step 1 **Review the chapter material.** This problem is about the relationship between interest rates and bond prices, so you may want to review the section "Calculating Bond Interest Rates and the Concept of Present Value," which begins on page 89.

Step 2 **Explain what determines the price of a bond.** The price of a financial asset should equal the present value of the payments to be received from owning that asset. So, the price of the bond we are considering here should be equal to the present value of the two coupon payments of $45 received in one year and in two years and the face value payment of $1000 received in two years.

Step 3   **Determine the price of the bond if the interest rate is 5%.** To determine the price of the bond, calculate the sum of the present values of the three payments an owner of the bond would receive:

$$\text{Bond Price} = \frac{\$45}{(1 + 0.05)} + \frac{\$45}{(1 + 0.05)^2} + \frac{\$1000}{(1 + 0.05)^2} = \$990.70.$$

Step 4   **Determine the price of the bond if the interest rate is 10%.** Substituting 10% for 5% in the expression in step 3, we have

$$\text{Bond Price} = \frac{\$45}{(1 + 0.10)} + \frac{\$45}{(1 + 0.10)^2} + \frac{\$1000}{(1 + 0.10)^2} = \$904.55.$$

Notice that increasing the interest rate reduces the price of the bond. This result confirms the general point that an increase in interest rates reduces the prices of existing financial assets.

See related problem 3.7 at the end of the chapter.

The Economy's Many Interest Rates

For simplicity, economists refer to "the" interest rate in the economy, as if there were only one interest rate. In fact, of course, there are many interest rates. In the lobby of your local bank, you will probably find one poster showing the interest rate you will receive if you put money in a savings account and another poster showing the (higher) interest rate you will pay if you take out a car loan. We have already seen that the interest rates firms and governments pay (and investors receive) on bonds play an important role in the economy. In this section, we explore why the interest rates on some bonds are very different from the interest rates on other bonds.

Panel (a) of Figure 3.7 shows the interest rates that prevailed on February 16, 2014, for four bonds that all mature in about five years. They come from different issuers (borrowers). Economists refer to the relationship among interest rates on bonds that all mature at the same time, such as those shown in panel (a), as the **risk structure of interest rates**. Panel (b) of Figure 3.7 shows the interest rates on July 20, 2012, for Government of Canada bonds of different maturities. The relationship among interest rates on bonds that have the same characteristics except for having different maturities is called the **term structure of interest rates**. A common way to analyze the term structure is by looking at the **yield curve**, which is the relationship on a particular day among the interest rates on bonds that differ only with respect to their maturities.

We will now look more closely at the risk structure and the term structure of interest rates. As we will see in later chapters, they affect the operation of monetary policy: They link the interest rate the central bank controls—a short-term nominal interest rate, to the interest rate that affects the economy—the long-term real rate firms and households pay for borrowing.

The Risk Structure of Interest Rates Investors naturally prefer a higher rate of return on their investments to a lower rate of return. So, everything else being equal, when considering bonds with the same maturity, investors will prefer bonds with higher interest rates to bonds

Risk structure of interest rates The relationship among interest rates on bonds that have different characteristics but the same maturity.

Term structure of interest rates The relationship among the interest rates on bonds of different maturities that are otherwise similar.

Yield curve A curve that shows interest rate on bonds of different maturities that are otherwise similar.

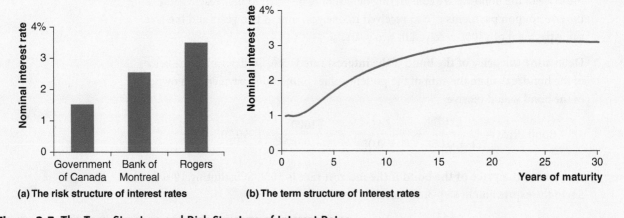

Figure 3.7 The Term Structure and Risk Structure of Interest Rates

Panel (a) shows an example of the risk structure of interest rates, which is the relationship among interest rates on bonds that all mature at the same time.

Panel (b) shows an example of the term structure of interest rates, which is the relationship among interest rates on bonds that have the same characteristics except for having different maturities.

Source: Bank of Canada

with lower interest rates. But everything else is usually not equal, because bonds differ in important characteristics. In general, bonds with unfavourable characteristics have higher interest rates to compensate investors for these unfavourable characteristics. Two important bond characteristics affecting the interest rate are default risk and liquidity.

Default risk The risk that the borrower will default on the bond.

- **Default risk.** Default risk refers to the chance that the firm or government issuing the bond will declare bankruptcy and stop paying interest on the bond at some time before it matures. Panel (a) of Figure 3.7 illustrates the risk structure of interest rates. Because the bond issued by Rogers shown in panel (a) of Figure 3.7 has a relatively high default risk, it also has a high interest rate. The Government of Canada bond shown in panel (a) has a low default risk, which is one reason it has a low interest rate. The bond issued by the Bank of Montreal has a lower default risk than the Rogers bond, but a higher default risk than the Government of Canada bond and so its interest rate is higher than for Government of Canada bonds but lower than for Rogers bonds.

Liquidity The ease of selling an asset without affecting its price.

- **Liquidity.** Liquidity is the ease of selling an asset without affecting its price. As we have seen, investors can buy and sell bonds in secondary markets. The more buyers and sellers there are in a market for a bond, the easier it is for an investor to sell the bond and the more liquid the bond is. Another reason federal government bonds have low interest rates is that they are very liquid. The market for these bonds is large and an investor who, for any reason, needs to sell or buy these bonds would not affect their price. On the other hand, the market for Rogers bonds is smaller and anyone selling or buying a significant quantity of these bonds may affect their price.

The Term Structure of Interest Rates Figure 3.7 panel (b) illustrates the term structure of interest rates by showing the interest rates on Government of Canada bonds for different maturities. It is showing the usual situation, when the yield curve is upward sloping. An upward-sloping term structure means that the longer the term of the bond, the higher is the interest rate. Most of the time the term structure looks like in Figure 3.7 panel (b), with long-term interest rates higher than short-term interest rates. To understand this, consider a simple example. Suppose you intend to invest $1000 for two years. You are weighing two options:

Option 1. Buying a bond that matures in two years—a two-year bond.
Option 2. Buying a one-year bond and, when it matures in one year, investing your money in another one-year bond.

Similar options exist for investing for a longer period of time. The investor can buy a long-term bond or a series of short-term bonds. Most of the time, but not always, the interest rate on the long-term bond will be higher than the interest rate on a one-year bond. The **term premium** is the additional interest investors require in order to be willing to buy a long-term bond rather than a comparable sequence of short-term bonds.

Why is the term premium usually positive? There are three reasons: *liquidity, default risk,* and *interest-rate risk.* The market for short-term bonds is usually more liquid than the market for long-term bonds. In addition, the plan to buy two one-year bonds provides the investor with flexibility to change plans after one year. You can decide after one year whether to buy a one-year bond or a longer-term bond or whether to invest in bonds at all. If you hold a two-year bond and your plans change, you must sell it. If the interest rates increased in the meantime, you will suffer a capital loss.

The longer is the term of the bond, the greater is default risk: the risk that the issuer will default on the bond. While you can assess the creditworthiness of the bond issuer quite precisely over a short period of time, market conditions can change over time and so, for a long-term bond, it is more difficult to evaluate the likelihood of a default. This makes long-term bonds riskier than short-term bonds. To compensate for higher risk, investors demand higher interest rates on long-term bonds.

The third reason long-term bonds are riskier than short-term bonds is the fact that changes in interest rates affect prices of long-term bonds more than they affect prices of short-term bonds. This risk is the **interest-rate risk.** Interest-rate risk refers to the risk that the price of a financial asset will fluctuate in response to changes in market interest rates. For instance, if you own a T-bill with an interest rate of 4% and new T-bills are issued with the same maturity but with an interest rate of 5%, the price at which you could sell your bond to other investors will fall. This fall in price would be necessary to compensate investors for buying a bond with a lower interest rate than the interest rate on newly issued bonds.

Although all bonds are subject to interest-rate risk, the longer the term of the bond, the greater the risk. The intuition is as follows: If the current interest rate on a 30-year bond is 4% and newly issued 30-year bonds have interest rates of 5%, then any investor who buys the bond which pays only 4% from you would be receiving a lower-than-market interest rate for 30 years. An investor would be willing to do this only if you offered to sell the bond at a significantly lower price. But if the interest rate increases for a one-year bond, the buyer would be receiving a lower-than-market interest rate for only one year and so would be willing to buy the bond with a smaller price cut. We can conclude that investors are exposed to greater interest-rate risk when they buy long-term bonds than when they buy short-term bonds. So, we expect that investors will be willing to buy long-term bonds issued by the Government of Canada—or anyone else—only if the interest rate is higher than on a short-term bond.

All three factors considered so far imply that the interest rate on long-term bonds should be higher than the interest rate on short-term bonds. While this is usually the case, sometimes the term structure is *inverted:* The short-term rates are higher than the long-term rates. The *expectations theory* of the term structure of interest rates provides an explanation of why and when this can happen. According to the *expectations theory*, the relationship between the interest rate on the one-year bond and the interest rate on the two-year bond should

Term premium The additional interest investors require in order to be willing to buy a long-term bond rather than a comparable sequence of short-term bonds.

Interest-rate risk The risk that the price of a financial asset will fluctuate in response to changes in market interest rates.

be such that the *average* of the interest rate on the current one-year bond and the interest *expected* on a one-year bond one year from now should equal the interest rate per year on the two-year bond. For example, the following situation, which produces an inverted term structure, would be consistent with the expectations theory:

1. Interest rate on the one-year bond today: 6%
2. Interest rate investors expect on the one-year bond one year from now: 4%
3. Interest rate (per year) on the two-year bond today:

$$5\% = \frac{6\% + 4\%}{2}.$$

As the short-term interest rate is expected to fall significantly, the two-year rate is lower than the one-year rate. The logic of the expectations theory is as follows: If an investor intends to invest over a period of years, the investor has the choice of buying one bond with a maturity equal to the desired period of investment or a sequence of shorter-term bonds. The expectations theory assumes that investors have no reason to prefer buying a long-term bond to buying a series of short-term bonds. Competition among investors will ensure that they receive the same expected return either way they invest. To see why the expected returns must be equal, consider what would happen if, for example, investors expected to receive a higher return from buying two one-year bonds. In that case, investors would increase their demand for one-year bonds. This increased demand would drive up the price of one-year bonds and—because bond prices and interest rates move in opposite directions—drive down their interest rate. Eventually, the interest rate on the one-year bond would fall to the point where investors would expect to receive the same return from pursuing either strategy.

The expectation theory can explain why the term structure is sometimes inverted. To result in an inverted term structure the expected decline in interest rates must be large enough to offset the term premium. For example, if the interest rate on a one-year bond is 6%, the expected interest rate on a two-year bond is 4% and the term premium is 0.5%, the interest rate on the two-year bond will be

$$5.5\% = \frac{6\% + 4\%}{2} + 0.5\%.$$

We now have a more complete explanation for the term structure of interest rates. Long-term interest rates are the average of expected short-term interest rates *plus* a term premium.

Interest rate on two-year bond

$$= \frac{\begin{array}{c}\text{Interest rate} \\ \text{on one-year bond today}\end{array} + \begin{array}{c}\text{Expected interest rate} \\ \text{on one-year bond next year}\end{array}}{2} + \text{Term premium.}$$

The term premium explains why the yield curve is typically upward sloping, like the one in Figure 3.7 panel (b). Because investors require a term premium to buy long-term bonds, the interest rates on long-term bonds will be above the interest rates on short-term bonds not only when investors expect future short-term rates to be higher, but also when investors expect future short-term rates to be constant or even when they expect them to be somewhat lower than current short-term rates. The yield curve will be downward sloping only when investors expect future short-term rates to be significantly lower than current short-term rates.

Both the term structure and the risk structure of interest rates play important roles in the effectiveness of Bank of Canada monetary policy, as we will discuss at length in Chapter 10.

Key Terms and Problems

Key Terms

Adverse selection, p. 79

Asset, p. 71

Asymmetric information, p. 79

Bank panic, p. 84

Bank run, p. 83

Bond, p. 71

Contagion, p. 84

Default risk, p. 94

Financial asset, p. 71

Financial intermediary, p. 72

Financial market, p. 71

Financial securities, p. 71

Financial system, p. 71

Insolvency, p. 84

Interest-rate risk, p. 95

Liquidity, p. 94

Moral hazard, p. 79

Present value, p. 89

Risk, p. 77

Risk structure of interest rates,
   p. 93

Stock, p. 71

Term premium, p. 95

Term structure of interest rates,
   p. 93

Time value of money, p. 90

Yield curve, p. 93

An Overview of the Financial System

Describe the financial system and explain the role it plays in the economy.

Review Questions

1.1 What purpose does the financial system serve?

1.2 What is a financial intermediary? Give three examples of financial intermediaries. What are the three key services that financial intermediaries perform for savers and borrowers?

1.3 Explain the process of securitization. What benefits does securitization of mortgage loans provide for banks? What benefits does securitization provide for people who want to buy a home?

1.4 What are adverse selection and moral hazard? What problems can they cause for the financial system?

Problems and Applications

1.5 For each of the following transactions, identify whether it occurs in a financial market, with or without a financial intermediary. If the transaction occurs in a financial market, state whether it occurs in a primary or secondary market:

   a. A bank makes a mortgage loan to a home buyer.

   b. A bank sells a mortgage loan to Canada Mortgage and Housing Corporation (CMHC).

   c. A startup company obtains financing by selling shares of stock to investors.

   d. One of the investors in a startup company resells her holding of the company's stock to someone else.

   e. The federal government sells Treasury bills at a weekly auction, where they are purchased by a pension fund.

   f. A pension fund resells some of its holdings of T-bills to a bank.

   g. An investor purchases 1000 shares of Rogers stock on the Toronto Stock Exchange (TSX).

   h. Rogers issues new stock, which it sells on the TSX.

1.6 An annual report for the Federal Reserve Bank of Dallas contained the following observation: "For the most part, we take the financial system's routine workings for granted—until the machinery blows a gasket. Then we scramble to fix it, so the economy can return to the fast lane." Why might most people, including most policymakers, tend to take the workings of the financial system for granted? Why can't the economy run in the "fast lane" if the financial system has "blown a gasket"?

   Source: Federal Reserve Bank of Dallas, *Annual Report, 2011*, p. 7.

1.7 Banks typically pay low interest rates on deposits and other savings accounts. Banks use the funds from deposits to make car loans and mortgage loans on which they charge much higher rates than they pay on chequing accounts. Why do people put their funds in chequing accounts rather than earning a higher interest rate by lending directly to people who want to buy houses or cars?

1.8 Some low-income countries have no stock market and only a few banks. What would you expect the effect to be on growth in these countries?

1.9 [Related to the Making the Connection on page 75] In 2013, two Canadian companies, Coinkite and Virtex, issued bitcoin debit cards that could be used like regular debit cards. At the time of writing the future of bitcoins was uncertain, but assume that the use of bitcoins becomes widespread. What would be the consequences for individuals and the economy as a whole of an innovation that improves access to banking services?

Source: David Mindich, "Canadian Companies Introduce Bitcoin Debit Card Services," *Paymentweek*, November 4, 2013.

1.10 Related to the Making the Connection **on page 77]** How does the globalization of financial markets improve the ability of the financial system to provide risk sharing, information, and liquidity?

3.2 **Financial Crises, Government Policy, and the Financial System**
Understand the role of the central bank in stabilizing the financial system.

Review Questions

2.1 What are the main functions performed by a central bank?

2.2 What is a bank run? Are only commercial banks subject to runs? Briefly explain a central bank's role as a lender of last resort in dealing with runs.

2.3 In what sense did the U.S. government "bail out" Bear Stearns in March 2008? How did the U.S. government's actions affect the extent of moral hazard in the financial system?

Problems and Applications

2.4 Suppose you purchase a new home for $150 000, making a down payment of 30% and taking out a mortgage on the balance.

  a. What is your leverage?

  b. What is the return on your investment in your home if one year later the price of the home increases by 20%?

  c. What is your return if the price of the home decreases by 20%?

  d. How would your answers to parts (a), (b), and (c) change if your down payment is only 15%? Explain why the return on your investment changes with the size of your down payment.

2.5 In 2011, Deutsche Bank AG, headquartered in Germany, became the largest bank in Europe by increasing its asset holdings at a time when other European banks were reducing their assets. As a result, Deutsche Bank's leverage increased. A *Bloomberg* article quoted a German banker as saying, "It's understandable: The higher your leverage, the higher the returns when times are good." But the article also noted, "The higher leverage also makes Deutsche Bank's earnings more volatile and dependent on market swings." Explain why higher

leverage results in higher returns "when times are good" and why it also makes "earnings more volatile and dependent on market swings."

Source: Aaron Kirchfeld, Elena Logutenkova, and Nicholas Comfort, "Deutsche Bank No. 1 in Europe as Leverage Hits Valuation," *Bloomberg*, March 27, 2012.

2.6 Chequing accounts and savings accounts at banks are insured by the CDIC, up to $100 000.

  a. Some economists argue that the existence of the CDIC increases the extent of moral hazard in the financial system. Briefly explain whether you agree with this argument.

  b. If the CDIC does increase moral hazard, why was it set up? How else might the government have dealt with the problem of bank panics?

2.7 Nassim Nicholas Taleb, an economist at New York University, argued that employees of financial firms that might be bailed out by the federal government during a financial crisis should not be allowed to receive bonuses. According to Taleb, bankers receive "a bonus if they make short-term profits and a bailout if they go bust." He argues that banning bonuses will reduce the principal–agent problem that affects large financial firms.

  a. What is the principal–agent problem?

  b. When considering the situation of a large financial firm that might be bailed out by the taxpayers, who is the principal and who is the agent?

  c. If Taleb's analysis is correct, how might banning paying bonuses reduce the principal–agent problem?

Source: Nassim Nicholas Taleb, "End Bonuses for Bankers," *New York Times*, November 7, 2011.

2.8 An article in the *New York Times* states,

  "In the last year and a half, the largest financial institutions have only grown bigger, mainly as a result of government-brokered mergers. They now enjoy borrowing at significantly lower rates than their smaller competitors, a result of the bond markets' implicit assumption that the giant banks are "too big to fail.""

a. Why are large banks able to borrow at lower rates than smaller banks?

b. Why does the bond market assume that these banks are too big to fail?

c. What are some of the possible consequences for the banking industry if the too-big-to-fail policy continues?

Source: David M. Herszenhorn and Sewell Chan, "Financial Debate Renews Scrutiny on Banks' Size," *New York Times*, April 21, 2010.

3.3 **The Money Market and the Risk Structure and Term Structure of Interest Rates**
Explain how interest rates are determined in the money market, and understand the risk structure and term structure of interest rates.

Review Questions

3.1 Why is the demand for money curve downward sloping? Draw a money demand and supply graph that shows how the central bank can decrease the short-run nominal interest rate.

3.2 Why is $100 you will receive in one year worth more to you than $100 you will receive in five years? What do economists mean by the "time value of money"?

3.3 What is the difference between the risk structure of interest rates and the term structure of interest rates?

Problems and Applications

3.4 Draw a graph of the money market. Show the effect on the money demand curve, the money supply curve, and the equilibrium nominal interest rate of each of the following:

a. The central bank decreases the money supply.

b. A recession causes real GDP to fall.

c. The price level increases.

d. The central bank increases the money supply at the same time as the price level falls.

3.5 Related to Avoiding a common mistake: **a movement along or a shift in the curve on page 88.**

a. Draw the money demand curve as a function of the price level (with the price level on the vertical axis).

Note that the curve should go through the origin: If the price level falls to zero, so does demand for money. (When the price level becomes very low, prices become low and little money is needed to buy goods and services; for example, a house may cost one dollar, and other goods proportionately less.)

b. A change in which variables means movement along the money demand curve you drew in part (a)?

c. Show the effect of a decrease in the nominal interest rate in the graph.

3.6 Assume that the interest rate is 10%. Would you prefer to receive: (a) $75 one year from now, (b) $85 two years from now, or (c) $90 three years from now? Would your answer change if the interest rate is 20%?

3.7 **Related to** Solved Problem 3.1 **on page 92** Suppose that a government bond was issued 27 years ago, so it will mature in three years. If the bond pays a coupon of $50 per year and will make a final face value payment of $1000 at maturity, what is its price if the relevant market interest rate is 5%? What is its price if the relevant market interest rate is 10%?

3.8 Bonds and loans have interest rates that vary according to how many years until they mature, their risk, their liquidity, and other factors. For each of the following pairs of loans and bonds, explain which would be likely to have the higher interest rate:

a. Credit card balance or a car loan

b. A 10-year government bond or a 10-year bond issued by Rogers

c. A 1-year or a 10-year government bond

d. A 1-year personal loan you make to a friend or a 1-year corporate bond

3.9 Assume that, in order to support resource exploration, the government reduces the tax rate paid on returns on bonds issued by resource companies. How would this lower tax rate affect the interest rate on resource companies bonds as investors buy and sell these bonds in the secondary market?

3.10 The following are data on the Government of Canada yield curve for October 31, 2013:

Time to maturity	Interest rate (%)
270 days	1.00%
1 year	0.99%
2 years	1.01%
5 years	1.74
10 years	2.50
30 years	3.01

a. Is the yield curve inverted for some maturities? What, in your opinion, is the reason for the inversion?

b. Given these data, why would an investor have been willing to buy a one-year Treasury bill with an interest rate of only 0.99% when the investor could have bought a 30-year Treasury bond with an interest rate of 3.01%?

Source: Bank of Canada

3.11 Suppose that today you observe the following interest rates on bonds with differing times to maturity:

Years to maturity	Interest rate
1 year	1.0%
2 years	3.0
3 years	3.5

a. Assume that the expectations theory is correct, so that there is no term premium for a two-year bond or a three-year bond. Use the information above to calculate the expected interest rate on a one-year bond one year from now and the expected interest rate on a one-year bond two years from now.

b. Now assume that the liquidity premium theory is correct and that the term premium on the two-year bond is 0.25% and the term premium on the three-year bond is 0.50%. Now calculate the interest rate on a one-year bond one year from now and the interest rate on a one-year bond two years from now.

3.12 Yield curves generally slope upward. A downward-sloping, or "inverted," yield curve is often thought to signal a future recession. Why might this observation be true?

3.13 With a zero-coupon bond, the buyer receives only the face value of the bond at maturity; the bond pays no coupons. Suppose that for a price of $675, you buy a 10-year, zero-coupon bond with a $1000 face value.

a. What interest rate will you receive over the life of the bond if you hold the bond to maturity?

b. Now suppose that the interest rate on equivalent bonds has risen to 10% after one year. If you decide to sell the bond, what price can you sell it for?

Data Exercises

D3.1: Go to the Bank of Canada website (http://www.bankofcanada.ca/). Search for "Yield Curves for Zero-Coupon Bonds." For the most recent date, graph the yield curve. Then explain how yield changes with the maturity of the bond.

D3.2: Go to www.bloomberg.com. In the Market Data menu toward the top of the page, under Rates and Bonds, find Government Bonds. This section gives yields and the yield curves for Australia, Germany, Japan, the United Kingdom, and the United States. How do the yield curves of the different countries vary?

D3.3: Go to the Bank of Canada website (http://www.bankofcanada.ca/). Search for Yield Curves for Zero-Coupon Bonds."

a. Download data for January 2, 1991. How do the rates in 1991 compare with the most recent data in question D3.1?

b. Plot the yield curve. Are there any inversions of the term structure?

c. Download data for January 2, 1992. Compare the following two strategies:

i. Buy a two-year bond on January 2, 1991

ii. Buy a one-year bond in January 2, 1991 and another one-year bond in January 2, 1992.

Which strategy yielded a higher return?

D3.4: Go to (http://www.bankofcanada.ca/). Search for "Selected Treasury Bill Yields: 10-year Lookup."

Download the monthly data for one-month and one-year Treasury bill rates for the past 10 years.

a. What is the average interest rate on each type of Treasury bill over this period?

b. What is the standard deviation? Which series is more volatile?

c. Graph the data. Do the rates move together?

d. Calculate the mean and standard deviation again, but end the series at 2007 rather than the current date. How does this change the mean and standard deviation? Briefly explain.

D3.5: Go to the Bank of Canada website (http://www. bankofcanada.ca/). Search for "Yield Curves for Zero-Coupon Bonds." Find the most recent values and the values 10 years earlier for 1-year, 5-year, and 30-year bonds. What happened with interest rates over this period?

D3.6: Go to the Bank of Canada website (http://www. bankofcanada.ca/). Search for "Yield Curves for Zero-Coupon Bonds." Download data for the period September 15, 2008, to December 15, 2008,

for bonds with maturity of 1 year, 5 years, and 30 years.

a. Graph the three rates over the three-month period. What happened with these interest rates in the three months after Lehman Brothers collapse?

b. Which rates fell the most over the three-month period?

c. What happened with the yield curve?

D3.7: Using data from the Bank of Canada (http://www. bankofcanada.ca/), analyze bond prices and interest rates.

a. Find the most recent values and the values from the same month one year and two years earlier for a one-year Government of Canada bond.

b. Suppose the bond has a face value of $2000. Using the interest rates found above, calculate the prices of the two bonds.

c. From the previous calculations, what can you determine about the relationship between bond yields and bond prices?

Money and Inflation

Working for Peanuts?

In Germany in 1923, people burned paper currency rather than wood or coal. In Zimbabwe in 2008, people were paying for health care with peanuts, not money. Burning paper money and using goods instead of money to pay for goods and services are signs that a country's money has become worthless.

People in most countries are used to some inflation. Even a moderate inflation rate of 2% or 3% per year gradually reduces the purchasing power of money. For example, if over the next 30 years the average rate of inflation in Canada is 2% (the mid-point of the current target inflation rate (see Chapter 12), a bundle of goods and services that costs $100 now will cost over $180 in 30 years. Germany and Zimbabwe experienced the much higher inflation rates known as *hyperinflation*, which is usually defined as a rate exceeding 50% per month (or 13 000% a year).

The inflation rates suffered by Germany and Zimbabwe were extreme, even by the standards of hyperinflations. In Germany a basket of goods and services that cost 100 marks in 1914 rose to 1 440 marks in January 1922, and then to 126 160 000 000 000 (i.e., 126 trillion) marks by December 1923. The German mark became nearly worthless. In Zimbabwe, the inflation rate reached 15 *trillion* percent by 2008. A tourist visiting the Victoria Falls Hotel in Zimbabwe during the summer of 2008 ordered dinner, two beers, and a mineral water. He received a bill for 1 243 255 000 Zimbabwean dollars. Subsequently, prices rose so much in Zimbabwe that you could have been a trillionaire in terms of the local currency and still be starving. By late 2008, Zimbabwe was printing banknotes with the value of $100 trillion Zimbabwe dollars. A facsimile of such banknote is on page 37.

Continued on next page

Countries suffer from hyperinflation when their governments allow the money supply to grow too rapidly. Between 1999 and 2008, the money supply in Zimbabwe rose over 7500% per year. In Germany, the money supply rose from 115 million marks in January 1922 to 1.3 billion in January 1923 and to 497 billion billion—or 497 000 000 000 000 000 000 (497×10^{18})—in December 1923.

Eventually hyperinflations are brought to an end, typically through a currency reform that introduces a new currency, places limits on money printing, and implements fiscal reforms. To make the reforms credible, budget deficit is usually eliminated so that the population can see there is no further reason for the government to print money. Credibility can also be established by making the central bank independent from the government. An independent central bank cannot be forced to print money to cover government deficit. In Germany, a new currency was issued and the government was committed to protecting the value of the currency. In contrast, the government of Zimbabwe was unable to make a credible commitment, and so it simply abandoned its own currency and began using the U.S. dollar instead.

But why would a government create so much money in the first place, especially when it knows that doing so will destroy the money's purchasing power? In this chapter, we will explore this question and other issues involving the relationship between money and prices.

Sources: Patrick McGroarty and Farai Mutsaka, "Hanging on to Dollars in Zimbabwe," *Wall Street Journal*, March 26, 2012; Steven D. Levitt and Stephen J. Dubner, "Freak Shots: $1 Billion Dinners and Other African Pricing Problems," *New York Times*, June 2, 2008; Federal Reserve Bank of Dallas, "Hyperinflation in Zimbabwe," *Globalization and Monetary Policy Institute, 2011 Annual Report*; Thomas Sargent, "The Ends of Four Big Inflations," in Robert E. Hall, ed., *Inflation: Causes and Effects* (Chicago: University of Chicago Press, 1982); "What Can You Do with a Zimbabwean Dollar?" *Economist*, July 26, 2010; "Zimbabwe Health Care, Paid with Peanuts," *New York Times*, December 18, 2010.

Introduction

In this chapter we analyze money, inflation and its costs, the role of the Bank of Canada in managing the money supply and inflation, and the relationship between the rate of inflation and nominal interest rates. We begin by looking at why modern societies use money and at the roles money plays in the economy. Money is used because it reduces the cost of exchange and allows for specialization, increasing the economy's efficiency. We look briefly at the history of money and describe its functions as a medium of exchange, a store of value, and a unit of account. In Section 4.3 we discuss how central banks change the monetary base

Useful Math 4.1: Constant Growth Rate

How do we calculate the increase in price over 30 years if inflation is constant at 2% per year, as discussed in the chapter opener? Let P_{2015} denote the price level in year 2015, P_{2016} denote the price level in 2016, and so on.

1. When the rate of inflation is 2% per year, the price level each year is equal to the price level in the previous year multiplied by 1.02. So, $P_{2016} = P_{2015} \cdot 1.02$; $P_{2017} = P_{2016} \cdot 1.02$; and so on.

2. Combining two consecutive years, we get $P_{2017} = P_{2016} \cdot 1.02 = (P_{2015} \cdot 1.02) \cdot 1.02 = P_{2015} \cdot 1.02^2$. The price level each year is equal to the price level two years prior multiplied by 1.02^2

3. Proceeding like this we get $P_{2045} = P_{2015} \cdot 1.02^{30} = P_{2015} \cdot 1.81$

Now let us calculate the increase in price over one year if the inflation rate is 50% per month.

1. After one month, prices increase by a factor of 1.5: $P_{Feb} = P_{Jan} \cdot 1.5$

2. After two months, prices increase by a factor of 1.5^2: $P_{Mar} = P_{Feb} \cdot 1.5 = P_{Jan} \cdot 1.5^2$ and so on.

3. After one year, the price level increases by the factor $1.5^{12} = 129.7$.

4. This means that the percentage increase in the price level over a year if the inflation rate is 50% per month is 12870%.

Avoiding a Common Mistake: Calculating Percentage Changes

Note that, when the price level increases by the factor 129.7, the percentage increase in price is 12 870%, *not* 12 970%. Why is that? The reason is that the percentage change is the percentage increase *above the previous level*. In other words, the percentage increase in price is the new price minus the old price divided by the old price. In the example above, denote the price at the beginning of the year as P. The price at the end of the year is $129.7P$. The percentage change in price is

$$\frac{129.7P - P}{P} = 128.7 = 12870\%.$$

An easy way to remember this is to recall that when the price doubles, it increases by 100%, not by 200%.

Practice question:

1. Calculate the number of years it takes for the price level to double when inflation is
   a. 1% per year (Hint: Use a spreadsheet program to multiply previous value by 1.01. Continue multiplying until the result is 2.)
   b. 2% per year
   c. 3% per year
2. Use the results to calculate X in the following approximate formula:

   Let inflation be k% per year and n denote the number of years it takes price level to double. Then $X = kn$

   Note that this useful formula holds well for small rates of inflation. The larger the rate of inflation, the less accurate the formula.

and influence the money supply through open market operations. In Section 4.4 we use the quantity theory of money to show that inflation is the result of fast growth of the money supply and analyze the Fisher effect, which shows how an increase in the inflation rate raises the nominal interest rate. In Section 4.5 we discuss the costs of expected and unexpected inflation, and of inflation uncertainty, as well as benefits of inflation. The chapter ends with a description of hyperinflation.

4.1

Learning Objective

Define money and explain its functions.

Real variables Variables measured in terms of goods and services.

Nominal variables Variables measured in terms of money.

Classical dichotomy The assertion that in the long run, *nominal* variables, such as the money supply or the price level, do not affect *real* variables, such as real GDP or the level of employment.

Money supply The quantity of assets available to households and firms to conduct transactions.

What Is Money, and Why Do We Need It?

In Chapter 2 we focused on real GDP and real GDP per worker. These are **real variables** because they are in terms of goods and services (i.e., they are adjusted for the effects of price changes). In this chapter, we focus on **nominal variables** such as the price level, the inflation rate, and the nominal interest rate.

In the long run, there is a separation between nominal and real variables. Economists call this separation the **classical dichotomy.** (In macroeconomics, "classical" refers to theories that were widely accepted before the Great Depression of the 1930s. Economists first discussed this dichotomy during that period.) According to the classical dichotomy, changes in nominal variables such as the price level or the **money supply** (that is, the quantity of assets available to households and firms to conduct transactions), affect only nominal variables such as nominal GDP, the nominal interest rate, or the nominal wage. Changes in nominal variables cannot cause changes in real variables such as real GDP or the level of employment. One implication of the classical dichotomy is *money neutrality*, or the assertion that in the long run, changes in the money supply have no effect on real variables. Today, most economists believe that the classical dichotomy is true in the long run, but not in the short run. In the short run, changes in the money supply can cause changes in real GDP.

In economics, the word *money* means any asset that is used to facilitate transactions. Various assets can play the role of money including, apart from cash, chequing accounts, saving accounts, and term deposits. As you will see later in the chapter, these assets are classified depending on how easily they can be used to pay for goods or services. The ease with which an asset can be used as payment is called the **liquidity of an asset.** This definition of liquidity is slightly different from the definition in the previous chapter, where we defined liquidity of financial assets as the ease of converting the asset into cash. In general, liquidity of an asset means the ease of converting the asset into its common use. So, for financial assets it is the ease of converting it into money, and for money it is an ease of using it in a transaction. Nowadays, when economists refer to *money*, they usually mean the most liquid assets: the total amount of notes and coins plus chequing account balances.

The meaning of *money* in economics is different from the common-language use of the word. When economists use the word *money*, they are not referring to wealth or income. In everyday conversation, we often describe people such as the American businessman and philanthropist Bill Gates (the richest person in the world in 2013) or the Canadian media magnate David Thompson (the richest person in Canada in 2013)[1] as "having a lot of money." In this case what we really mean is not the amount of currency they hold but the amount of resources they own—in other words, their wealth. Most of Mr. Gates's or Mr. Thompson's wealth is in the form of various financial and physical assets (shares and property); only a very small portion of their wealth is in cash. Similarly, we often describe people such as Gerard Schwartz, the CEO of Onex corporation, who was the best-paid executive in Canada in 2013, as someone who "makes a lot of money."[2] But income and money are not comparable. Income is a *flow*, measured in dollars *per unit of time*, for example a year or an hour. Money is a *stock*, measured in dollars *at a moment of time*.

So, when economists refer to money, they usually mean the total amount of paper currency, coins, and other assets available to households and firms to conduct transactions.

Barter, Money, and Transaction Costs

Simple economies can function without money. In the early stages of economic development, individuals often exchanged goods and services by trading output directly with each other. This type of exchange is called **barter.** For example, a trapper would exchange beaver pelts for food. In principle, people in a barter economy can obtain the goods and services they want. But it is complicated. The trapper needed to find someone who had food to sell and wanted to make himself a beaver coat. This requires a *double coincidence of wants*: The two parties to a transaction must need each other's goods or services. They also must need the right quantities. If the trapper had more beaver pelts than his food supplier needed, he would have to find people who were willing to exchange food for beaver pelts.

Exchange under barter required a lot of time and effort to find trading partners. The costs in time or other resources of making a trade or an exchange, called **transaction costs**, were very high. In other words a barter economy is inefficient, with a significant amount of resources devoted to conducting exchanges rather than to producing goods and services.

Barter became more and more difficult as economies developed. Transaction costs increased with the number of goods and services as it became more difficult to find a trading partner. There was thus an incentive to identify a specific good that most people would accept in exchange for goods and services. This good would be accepted in exchange not

Liquidity of an asset The ease of using the asset as payment in a transaction.

Barter Direct exchange of one good or service for another.

Transaction costs The costs in time or other resources of making a trade or an exchange.

---

[1]The richest Canadian citizen is actually the Hong-Kong business magnate, Li-Ka Shing, who holds dual Canadian and Hong-Kong citizenship.

[2]Adam Brown, "Forbes Billionaires: Full List Of The World's 500 Richest People," *Forbes,* March 3, 2014; Janet Mcfarland, "Executive compensation: Canada's 100 top-paid CEOs," *The Globe and Mail,* June 1, 2014.

because the seller needed it, but because of the expectation that it could be used in another exchange in the future. Economists consider any such good *money*.

Goods that played the role of money in the past include shells, beads, bottles of whisky, stone wheels, cigarettes, and precious metals. In Canada beaver pelts (as well as wheat and moose skins) were used by settlers as money in the first colonial settlement on the St. Laurence River at the beginning of the seventeenth century. Aboriginal people in Canada had long used "wampum": strings and belts made with beads of white and purple shells.[3]

Commodity Money

A common characteristic of the goods listed above is that, apart from facilitating transactions, they had another use. For example, shells, beads, and precious metals could be used to make jewellery; cigarettes could be smoked. We call such goods *intrinsically useful:* They have a use on their own. An intrinsically useful good (i.e., one that has value independent of its use as money) that plays the role of money is called **commodity money**.

Once money was invented—as it was many times and in many places around the world—transactions costs were greatly reduced. Money enabled producers to specialize. Under barter, a farmer had to grow a range of crops to make it easier to find a trading partner. With money, he could specialize in growing the crop in which he was the most productive. The high income levels in modern economies are based on the specialization that money makes possible. So, the answer to the question "Do we need money?" is "Yes, because money allows for specialization, reduces transaction costs, and raises productivity and incomes."

Not every physical good can be used as commodity money. To be useful in exchange, the good must be

- *acceptable* to most people;
- *valuable* relative to its weight;
- *standardized in terms of quality*, so that any two units are identical;
- *divisible*; and
- *durable*, so its value is not quickly lost due to wear and tear.

What distinguishes commodity money from other goods is that it is widely *acceptable* as a means of payment. Acceptability eliminates the need for double coincidence of wants. Money is a social convention: It is accepted in exchange for goods and services because of the expectation that other members of the society will accept it in turn. Thus commodity money differed from place to place. For example beaver pelts, which served as money in Northern Canada, were not very useful as payment in cities, where they were uncommon. Commodity money needs to be *valuable* relative to its weight so that the amount needed for a transaction can be transported relatively easily. This rules out, for example, rice. *Standardization* is important as it reduces the effort needed to assess the value of commodity money. Old paintings could, in principle, be used as money, but every transaction would require figuring out the value of the painting offered. Money should be *divisible* so that it can be used for large and small transactions—another reason to rule out old paintings or beaver pelts. Finally, commodity money needs to be *durable* so that the seller knows she will be able to use it in the future; this rules out, for example, fresh fish.

Commodity money A good used as money that has value independent of its use as money.

---

[3]The description in this paragraph of early money in Canada follows an excellent ebook by James Powell, *A History of the Canadian Dollar,* available at the Bank of Canada website: www.bankofcanada.ca/publications-research/books-and-monographs/history-canadian-dollar/ (Accessed May 5, 2013). See especially pp. 2 and 3.

There are many types of assets with these five characteristics. The most important are precious metals, in particular gold and silver. Because these metals are valuable, only relatively small amounts are needed in most transactions. People learned how to evaluate the purity of these metals and so could assess their value at a moderate cost. Once the purity was assessed, the value of a quantity of a precious metal could be easily established by weighing it. It is not difficult to divide gold and silver since both are relatively soft metals. Not surprisingly, in many societies, gold and silver have been a common form of commodity money.

Making the Connection

How Expensive Gold Really Is

Gold has been used as money for a long time. The main reason is that it is very valuable. Indeed, it is so valuable that to describe something that is very expensive (or metaphorically invaluable), we can say it is "worth its weight in gold."

Just how valuable is gold? Disregarding antiques and jewellery, at the mid-2014 average price of US$1300 per troy ounce (31.1 grams), few things are literally worth their weight in gold. The most expensive iPhone 6 (129 grams, US$849) costs about 1/6th, and Google Glass (50 grams, $1500) costs 3/4 of its weight in gold.

The value of gold is, however, often exaggerated. In the 1995 movie *Die Hard with Vengeance*, the bad guys steal $140 billion dollars worth of gold from the vault of the Federal Reserve Bank of New York. There is, indeed, a lot of gold in the vault of the Federal Reserve Bank of New York. The bank belongs to the Federal Reserve System, the U.S. central bank. On behalf of the Fed it provides custodial services for gold owned by other central banks. In 2012 it held 6700 tonnes of gold. So far so good: If you are wondering where a huge amount of gold can be stolen from, the Federal Reserve Bank of New York is a prime candidate. (Note, however, that breaking into their vault may be difficult. Their security is described here: www.newyorkfed.org/aboutthefed/goldvault.html.)

In the movie the bad guys steal US$140 billion worth of gold and transport the gold in 14 dump trucks. Would that be possible, or is it a Hollywood exaggeration? Let us check. In 1995 the average price of gold was about US$385[4] per troy ounce or US$12 380 per kilogram. (An ounce equals 31.1 grams or 0.0311 kg; a kilogram of gold cost US$385/0.0311 = US$12 380.) The amount of gold stolen would have weighed approximately 11 309 tonnes (i.e., US$140 billion/(US$12 380/kg) = 11 309 091 kg = 11 309 tonnes). If it was divided equally among 14 trucks, each would have to transport over 800 tonnes. This is three times more than the capacity of the biggest truck in the world and about 50 times as much as a standard dump truck can carry. Gold is valuable but not *that* valuable.

See related problem 1.6 at the end of the chapter.

The use of gold and silver as money has some disadvantages. Both are relatively soft metals. Consequently, during use, some of the metal rubs off and coins become lighter. In other words, an old coin would contain less precious metal than a new coin and thus be less valuable. In addition, the supply of gold and silver fluctuates with unpredictable discoveries and changes in mining technology. Gold also has the disadvantage that large quantities can be heavy and, therefore, difficult to transport.

---

[4]Lawrence H. Officer and Samuel H. Williamson, "The Price of Gold, 1257–Present," Measuring Worth, 2013, www.measuringworth.com/gold, accessed May 15, 2013.

A solution to some of these difficulties was the introduction of gold and silver certificates. A certificate was a claim on a specific quantity of gold or silver held in a vault. It allowed the holder to exchange the certificate for the precious metal on request. This type of money is called *representative money*: A claim on actual money that can be used in transactions. Gold and silver certificates became paper currency. The currency was *fully backed*: The value of certificates was equal to the value of precious metals held by the issuing institution, usually a bank.

A fully-backed currency is safe: A certificate holder can always exchange (redeem) it for precious metals, and there are enough precious metals for everyone to do it at the same time. Banks quickly found out, however, that few people bothered to redeem their certificates for gold and silver. The certificates were more convenient to use and the possibility of converting them into gold and silver was sufficient for them to be widely accepted. Banks therefore realized that the amount of certificates could exceed the amount of gold and silver they held. There was no problem as long as they were able meet current redemptions. They therefore issued more certificates and the currency became *partially backed*: The value of certificates exceeded the value of precious metals held by banks.

Seigniorage The profit from issuing money.

Seigniorage Issuing more certificates than the amount of precious metals is a profitable activity. The extra certificates can be lent to the public and earn interest. The issuer takes a piece of paper and converts it into an asset with a positive value. It is no wonder governments took over. While there exist privately issued currencies (for example, bitcoins or Salt Spring Island dollars), they depend on the willingness of the parties in the transaction to accept them. By their very nature, they are not widely accepted.

The Bank of Canada is the sole institution allowed to issue Canadian dollar banknotes. The Bank of Canada prints new notes and uses the proceeds to buy government bonds or interest-earning assets. The profit from issuing money is called **seigniorage**. The profit is the difference between interest earned and the cost of printing the notes. For example, the average $20 polymer banknote costs 19 cents to produce, 15 cents to distribute and is predicted to last, on average, around 7.5 years. The cost of maintaining the note is therefore around 4.5 cents per year. If the Bank of Canada uses it to buy government bonds yielding 2.5% per year, it earns 50 cents in interest, for a net yearly profit of 45.5 cents for each $20 dollar note.

Fiat money Money, such as paper currency, that has no value apart from its use as money.

Fiat Money What happens with the seigniorage? The Bank of Canada is wholly owned by the federal government. The profit becomes federal government revenue. In 2012, there was around $64 billion of notes in circulation. The Bank's interest earnings were $1.4 to 2.0 billion in recent years. The cost of issuing currency was $220 million.[5] The total amount of seigniorage was around 0.1% of Canadian GDP and 0.3% of federal government revenue. In some countries seigniorage is a much greater: For example in Italy and Greece, before they joined the Eurozone, it exceeded 5% of government revenue is some years.

The next step in the development of money was ending the convertibility of money into precious metals. The Canadian dollar was convertible into gold until 1914 and again between 1926 and 1931. Since 1931 the Canadian dollar is a **fiat money**: Canadian dollar banknotes have no value apart from their use as money.

Fiat money is *intrinsically useless*: It has no value apart from its use as money. (Fiat means "by order or by decree"; the value of money is assured by government order.) Why are people willing to exchange goods and services for pieces of intrinsically useless paper currency? The

---

[5]www.bankofcanada.ca/about/educational-resources/backgrounders (accessed May 11, 2013).

short answer is that money is a social convention. Households and firms have confidence that if they accept paper dollars in exchange for goods and services, they will be able to use the paper money to buy goods and services they want. Without this confidence, paper money could not serve as a medium of exchange.

Legal Tender If you look at a Canadian banknote, you will see the words "This note is legal tender." More precisely, legal tender in Canada includes notes issued by the Bank of Canada as well as coins issued by the Royal Canadian Mint. Most people think that "legal tender" means that Canadian dollars must be accepted in payment for transactions in Canada. But this is not the case. The payment method must be agreed upon by both the seller and the buyer; there is no legal requirement that the seller must accept Canadian dollars. According to the Bank of Canada website, "If bank notes are being offered as payment, they must have been issued by the Bank of Canada because no other bank notes are 'legal tender' in Canada." So a sign "we do not accept $100 bills" is perfectly legal, as is a sign "no cash payment accepted." The meaning of "legal tender" differs across countries. In the United States, cash must be accepted in private payments of debts; as in Canada, there is no legal obligation to accept dollars in exchange for goods and services. In the United Kingdom, legal tender "means that a debtor cannot successfully be sued for non-payment if he pays into court in legal tender."[6]

The Functions of Money

Money has three functions in the economy:

1. It acts as a medium of exchange
2. It is a store of value
3. It is a unit of account

Medium of Exchange If you are a teacher or an accountant, you are paid money for your services. You then use that money to buy goods and services. You essentially exchange your teaching or accounting services for food, clothing, rent, and other goods and services. But unlike with barter, where goods and services are exchanged directly for other goods and services, the exchanges you participate in involve money. Money acts as a **medium of exchange**. In other words, money is the medium through which exchange takes place. Because money is generally accepted as payment for goods and services or as payment for debts, you know that the money your employer pays you will be accepted at the stores where you purchase food, clothing, and other goods and services. Consequently, you can specialize in producing teaching or accounting services without having to worry about directly producing the other goods and services you require to meet your needs, as you would in a barter economy.

Medium of exchange Something that is generally accepted as payment for goods and services; a function of money.

Store of Value Money is a **store of value** as it allows the accumulation of wealth that can be used to buy goods and services in the future. For example, suppose you want to purchase an iPad next year that has a price of $500. If you have $500 in currency, you can put it aside and purchase the iPad in one year. Note, though, that if prices in an economy rise rapidly over time, as happened recently in Zimbabwe, the quantity of goods and services a given amount of money can purchase falls, and money's usefulness as a store of value is reduced. Of course, money is only one of many assets that can be used to store value. In fact, any asset—shares

Store of value The accumulation of wealth by holding dollars or other assets that can be used to buy goods and services in the future; a function of money.

---

[6]See www.bankofcanada.ca/banknotes/bank-note-series/past-series; www.treasury.gov/resource-center/faqs/Currency/Pages/legal-tender.aspx; www.royalmint.com/aboutus/policies-and-guidelines/legal-tender-guidelines (all accessed May 11, 2013).

of Apple stock, bitcoins, Government of Canada bonds, real estate, or Renoir paintings, for example—can be a store of value. There are two reasons money is used as a store of value. First, many of these assets are risky, while money is not. Second, money has the advantage of being perfectly liquid: It can be used in transaction without incurring additional costs.

In modern economies, the store of value role of money is not very important. For example, various bank accounts pay interest and are riskless, since they are insured by the Canada Deposit Insurance Corporation. Nowadays, few households hold significant portion of their wealth in cash.

Making the Connection

Money as a Store of Value in Cyprus

In March 2013 Cyprus became the fourth Eurozone country, after Greece, Ireland, and Portugal, to require a bailout of the banking system and prevent a default by Cypriot banks and the Cypriot government. In the previous 20 years Cyprus had become an off-shore banking centre, especially for wealthy Russians who wanted to hold their money out of the reach of the Russian tax office and other Russian institutions. The banking system became very large, with assets exceeding 800% of GDP. Cypriot banks held a lot of Greek government bonds and loans to private Greek borrowers. They incurred large losses when Greece de facto defaulted on loans from non-government lenders in 2011. Cyprus arranged an emergency loan from Russia, but by the spring of 2013 it was clear that the banking system was collapsing.

As in all Eurozone countries, the government guaranteed deposits up to €100 000. In case of a bank bankruptcy, the Cypriot government would have to cover all losses for deposits under €100 000. The government did not have adequate funds to meet the guarantees and asked the European Union for help. Cyprus needed €14.8 billion to fix the banking system and put national finances on a sustainable level. The so called "troika," the European Union, the International Monetary Fund, and the European Central Bank, agreed to provide Cyprus with a loan of only €10 billion, conditional on Cyprus contributing the remaining €4.8 billion. The reason for requiring Cypriot participation was concern about moral hazard. The troika was concerned that if it provided all the needed funds, Cyprus would return to previous, unsustainable policies and would run into trouble again.

The troika proposed that, to raise the €4.8 billion, uninsured deposits should be subject to a one-time tax of 15%. The Cypriot president, Nicos Anastasiades, did not agree. He insisted that no depositor should lose more than 9.9%. He did not want Cyprus to lose its role as an off-shore centre. Reducing tax on large depositors required a one-time tax on insured deposits of 6.75%. The troika agreed and the deal was announced on March 18, 2013. Banks were closed and Cypriots could withdraw only a limited amount of cash from bank machines.

The plan turned out to be very unpopular as it imposed costs on small depositors to reduce the tax on wealthy depositors, who were mostly foreigners. The deal was rejected by the parliament. In the final agreement, the guaranteed deposits were not taxed, but the damage was done. Depositors around the world realized that even government guarantees may be broken (with the result that even the governor of the Bank of Canada felt obliged to assure Canadians that their guaranteed deposits were safe). Further, unlike previous experience, it turned out that the return on bank deposits could be negative. This realization restored, at least for a time, the role of cash as a store of value.

Sources: James Mackintosh, "Bank Assets as Percentage of GDP," *Financial Times*, March 25, 2013; "What Went Wrong in Cyprus, *BBC News*, March 28, 2013; "Bank 'bail-in' plan shouldn't worry Canadians, Carney says," *The Canadian Press*, April 18, 2013.

Unit of Account Money serves as a **unit of account**, which means it is a way of measuring the value of goods and services in an economy. For example, when you purchase an iPad, the Apple store posts a price in terms of dollars rather than in terms of Apple shares or ounces of gold. Having an agreed-upon unit of account makes an economy more efficient because goods and services have a single price rather than many prices. A unit of account does not need to be the actual currency. The guinea was a gold coin that stopped circulating in Great Britain in 1816, when it was worth 21 shillings or 21/20 of a pound. It has remained a unit of account and some prices are still quoted in guineas. Note, however, that the value of the guinea was fixed in terms of the circulating currency.

> **Unit of account** A way of measuring value in an economy in terms of money; a function of money.

Making the Connection

When Money Is No Longer Money: Hyperinflation in Zimbabwe

At the time of its independence from Great Britain in 1980, Zimbabwe was relatively well off by the standards of sub-Saharan Africa. Zimbabwe's GDP per capita was 35% higher than that of Kenya and 20% higher than that of Nigeria. The following three decades were not good for Zimbabwe. Real GDP per capita declined by 45% while it tripled in Kenya and increased by 230% in Nigeria. As a result, in 2011 Zimbabwe was one of the poorest countries in the world, with income per capita 70% lower than in Kenya and 80% lower than in Nigeria.

What happened to Zimbabwe's economy? Zimbabwe has suffered from a long period of economic mismanagement and, in recent years, political strife as long-time president Robert Mugabe has attempted to maintain power in the face of widespread opposition. Beginning in 2005, high inflation made the country's problems much more acute. As noted in the chapter opener, between 1999 and 2008 the Zimbabwean central bank, the Reserve Bank of Zimbabwe (RBZ), caused the money supply to increase at an annual rate of 7500%. The inflation rate exceeded 100% per year in 2001 and exploded following a temporary stabilization in 2004. The inflation data below are for year-on-year inflation, i.e., the percentage change in the price level between a given month and the same month in the previous year. For example, the monthly inflation rate in October 2007 is the monthly average inflation between October 2006 and October 2007. Hyperinflation started in October 2007, when the inflation rate was almost 15 000% per year. It exceeded 2 000 000% per year in May 2008 and 230 000 000% in July 2008. After July 2008, price statistics were no longer collected. Steve Hanke and Alex Kwok estimated the inflation to be 3190% *per month* (over 9 billion % per year) in August, 690 000 000% per month (almost 4 billion billion percent, or 4×10^{18} % per year) in October and 79 600 000 000% per month (9×10^{22} % per year) in November 14, 2008.[7]

As the Zimbabwean dollar lost nearly all of its value, the economy reverted to barter or switched to using U.S. dollars and other foreign currencies. Because exchanging Zimbabwean dollars for foreign currency was difficult, imports plunged, and shortages of food and other basic goods became widespread. Reliable statistics on Zimbabwe's economy are difficult to find; but in 2008, one journalist described a situation bordering on economic collapse:

---

[7]As no official price statistics were collected after July 2008, Hanke and Kwok estimated the inflation rate on the basis of the stock of the insurance and investment company Old Mutual, which was listed on both the London Stock Exchange and the Zimbabwe Stock Exchange. A comparison of the prices of the stock at both exchanges provided an estimate of the exchange rate.

"Zimbabwe is in the midst of a dire economic crisis with unemployment at almost 80%, most manufacturing at a halt, and basic foods in short supply." Some estimates put the unemployment rate as high as 95%. Nearly the entire labour force had to scratch out a subsistence living as best they could. Many unemployed Zimbabweans were reported as surviving only by growing vegetables in vacant lots or along roads.

Why would the RBZ allow such high rates of growth in the money supply if the result was a ruinous hyperinflation? The answer is that the RBZ was not independent of the rest of the Zimbabwean government. When the Zimbabwean government decided in the early 2000s to greatly increase its spending, primarily to support the efforts of Robert Mugabe to retain power, it did so not by raising taxes or borrowing by selling government bonds to investors but by having the RBZ increase the money supply.

In November 2008 the economy abandoned the use of Zimbabwean dollars and switched to U.S. dollars. The use of U.S. dollars became legal in January 2009, legalizing the de facto abolition of domestic currency. By 2011 the economy was showing signs of recovery as the inflation rate declined to less than 3% per year. Real GDP rose by 4% in 2010 and 6% in 2011. Still, the country faced severe structural problems, the political situation remained uncertain, and many Zimbabweans did not trust the government to control the money supply responsibly.

Sources: "Zimbabwe's Independence: Thirty Years On," *Economist*, April 20, 2010; Angus Maddison, *Contours of the World Economy* (New York: Oxford University Press, 2007); "Zimbabwe Inflation Rockets Higher," August 19, 2008, news.bbc.co.uk; "What a Full-Fledged Economic Collapse Looks Like," *Economist*, May 6, 2009; Michael Hartnack, "Zimbabwe Inflation Tops 1000 Percent," Associated Press, May 13, 2006; International Monetary Fund, "Statement of the IMF's Mission to Zimbabwe," Press Release No. 10/420, November 8, 2010; "Move Over, Mugabe," *Economist*, April 14, 2012; Robertson Economic Information Services, "August 2007 Forecast Paper," 2007; Steve H. Hanke and Alex K. F. Kwok, "On the Measurement of Zimbabwe' Hyperinflation," *Cato Journal* 29, no. 2 (2009).

See related problem 1.7 at the end of the chapter.

How Is Money Supply Measured?

Recall that the money supply is the quantity of assets available to households and firms to conduct transactions. Changes in the money supply are associated with changes in nominal interest rates and prices. Information on the money supply is compiled by the Bank of Canada. The task of measuring money is complicated as many different assets are used in exchange. The crucial characteristic the Bank of Canada takes into account is the asset's liquidity: the ease with which it can be used in transactions. The most liquid assets are cash: notes and coins, as well as chequing account balances, which can be used to pay for transactions with cheques or debit cards. Less liquid assets include term deposits, demand and notice deposits, foreign exchange deposits, money market mutual funds, Canada Saving Bonds, and the like. These assets are less liquid since, in order to use them in transactions, their owner must convert them into cash at their bank (or transfer the funds over the internet), or first give a notice and wait a period of time to avoid a penalty.

Assets that can be used in transactions are classified into **monetary aggregates**. Monetary aggregates are broad measures combining, on the basis of liquidity, assets that can be used in exchange. The main monetary aggregates followed by the Bank of Canada are called **M1+** and **M2+.** They are shown in Figure 4.1. The M1+ aggregate is a narrow measure of the money supply. It consists of currency outside banks plus chequable deposits at chartered banks, trust and mortgage loan companies, credit unions, and caisses populaires. The M2+ aggregate is a broader measure of the money supply. It consists of currency outside banks plus bank personal deposits (including personal chequable deposits), bank

Monetary aggregates
Broad measures combining, on the basis of liquidity, assets that can be used in exchange.

M1+ A narrow measure of the money supply. Currency outside banks plus chequable deposits at chartered banks and other financial institutions.

M2+ A broad measure of the money supply. M1+ plus non-chequable and personal term deposits at chartered banks and other financial institutions.

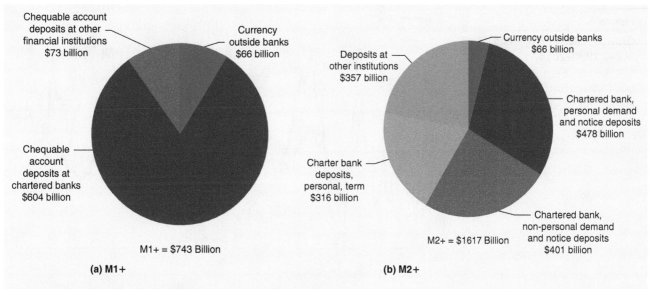

Figure 4.1 M1+ and M2+ and Their Components, March 2014

The Bank of Canada follows several monetary aggregates, of which M1+ and M2+ are the most important. M1+ is a narrow measure of the money supply. It includes currency outside banks and chequable deposits at chartered banks and other financial institutions. M2+ is a broad measure of the money supply. In addition to M1+ it includes non-chequable and personal term deposits at chartered banks and other financial institutions.

Source: Bank of Canada, Weekly Financial Statistics.

non-personal demand and notice deposits, and deposits at other financial institutions.[8] Households can easily convert these accounts into currency, although not as easily as the components of M1+.

Figure 4.2 shows the rates of growth of M1+ and M2+ in Canada between the years 1990 and 2014. M1+ and M2+ have similar growth rates over long periods of time but there are significant differences over short periods. The narrow aggregate (M1+) is more volatile. Note that, during the Great Recession, the rate of growth of M1+ increased in October 2008 and remained high until 2011. The rate of growth of the broad measure of the money supply (M2+) did not change much until November 2009 and then declined and remained below the pre-recession levels until 2014.

At one time fluctuations in the money supply were a major source of discussion among macroeconomists, investment analysts, and policymakers. This interest arose because, for most of the post–World War II period, there had been a stable short-run relationship between M1 and M2 (similar, respectively, to M1+ and M2+) and economic variables such as inflation, interest rates, and nominal GDP. Whether this relationship was stronger for M1 or for M2 was the subject of considerable debate. In Canada, monetary policy involved control of M1 between 1975 and 1981. The goal was to reduce the rate of inflation from the double-digit

---

[8]More precisely, M1+ (gross) consists of "currency outside banks plus all chequable deposits held at chartered banks, trust and mortgage loan companies, credit unions and caisses populaires (excluding deposits of these institutions); plus continuity adjustments (to 'smooth' a time series when there are structural breaks)." M2+ (gross) consists of "currency outside banks plus bank personal deposits, bank non-personal demand and notice deposits; less interbank deposits; plus continuity adjustments; plus deposits at trust and mortgage loan companies and at government savings institutions; deposits and shares at credit unions and caisses populaires; life insurance company individual annuities; money market mutual funds; plus continuity adjustments and other adjustments." Source: Bank of Canada backgrounder "Canada's Money Supply."

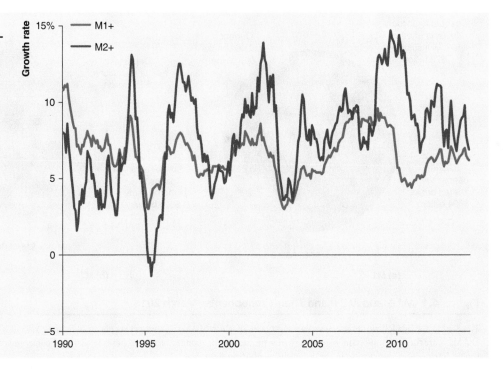

Figure 4.2

Growth Rates of M1+ and M2+, 1990–2014

M1+ and M2+ have similar growth rates over long periods of time but there are significant differences over short periods.

Source: Bank of Canada.

level that prevailed during that time. M1 was chosen because the link between inflation and the rate of growth of M1 was particularly strong. The Bank of Canada was successful in slowing down the growth of M1 between 1976 and 1981. Inflation, however, did not fall during that period. The reason was that banks increased liquidity by creating accounts that were not part of M1, and consequently the previously strong relationship between M1 and inflation broke down. This experience suggests that as banks and other financial firms respond to the demands of households and firms by developing new assets, the relationship between whatever we define as *money* and economic variables may change. Since late 1981 the Bank of Canada has therefore de-emphasized the significance of M1+ and M2+ in monetary policymaking.

The Bank of Canada and the Money Supply

4.2

Learning Objective

Explain how central banks change the money supply

We now describe how a central bank affects the money supply through open market operations. Open market operations discussed in this chapter are used by many central banks but are no longer the main tool of the Bank of Canada; we describe the way the Bank of Canada operates in Chapter 12. Here we focus on open market operations to stress that central banks do not have complete control of the money supply. The size of M1+ and M2+ depends not only on the central bank's actions, but also on the behaviour of the banking system and the nonbank public: household and firms.

We now develop a simple model of how the money supply is determined. It includes the behaviour of three actors:

1. The central bank, which is responsible for controlling the money supply and regulating the banking system.
2. The banking system, which creates the chequing accounts that are an important component of the M1+ measure of the money supply.

3. The nonbank public, (households and firms) that decides the form in which they wish to hold money (for instance, as currency or as chequing accounts).

The process of determining the money supply begins with the **monetary base** (also called **high-powered money**), which is equal to the amount of currency in circulation plus the reserves of the banking system:

$$\text{Monetary base} = \text{Currency in circulation} + \text{Reserves.}$$

Reserves are an asset to banks and consist of vault cash plus banks' deposits with the central bank. In the past the Bank of Canada required banks to hold a fraction of their chequing and other deposits as reserves. These reserves were called *required reserves*. Bank reserves often exceeded the required level; such reserves were called *excess reserves*. Since 1994 the Bank of Canada no longer requires banks to hold reserves. Nonetheless banks hold reserves to manage the regular cash flows: cash withdrawals (including ATMs) and cheque clearing. They also hold precautionary reserves for unexpected cash requirements. The reserves Canadian banks hold are called **desired reserves**. Desired reserves are simply the reserves a bank would like to hold. Note that, in countries with a reserve requirement, if a bank's reserves exceed required reserves, they are equal to the desired level. If a bank's reserves are equal to required reserves, desired reserves are likely lower than the required level.

Monetary base (or **high-powered money**) The sum of currency in circulation and bank reserves.

Desired reserves The reserves a bank would like to hold.

How a Central Bank Changes the Monetary Base

The main method many central banks use to control the monetary base is **open market operations.** Open market operations involve purchases and sales of securities, usually short-term government bonds, in financial markets (in the open market—hence the name). When a central bank buys bonds, it increases the monetary base; when the central bank sells bonds, it reduces the monetary base.

Open market operations Central bank's purchases and sales of securities, usually short-term government bonds, in financial markets.

To explain how open market operations affect the monetary base we consider two cases: a purchase from a bank and a purchase from nonbank public. If the central bank buys a government bond worth $1 million from a bank, it pays for the purchase by crediting the bank's account at the central bank with $1 million. Since the balance of the bank's account at the central bank is a part of the bank's reserves, the bank's reserves and the monetary base both increase by $1 million.

If the central bank buys the bond from nonbank public, it pays with a cheque. The seller will, typically, deposit the cheque into her account. Her bank will then send the cheque to the central bank, which would clear the cheque by adding funds to the bank's account at the central bank. If the entire cheque is deposited, the bank's reserves and the monetary base increase by $1 million. What happens if the seller of the bond takes part of the cheque in cash, for example $10 000? The bank deposits the entire cheque at the central bank and gives the depositor $10 000 in cash. The bank's deposits at the central bank increase by $1 million, and vault cash falls by $10 000. Reserves (the sum of deposits at the central bank and cash held by the banking system) increase by $990 000: the $1 million deposit at the central bank minus the $10 000 reduction in cash. The monetary base (reserves plus cash outside of the banking system) increases by $1 million: the $990 000 increase in reserves and the $10 000 increase in cash outside of the banking system.

Similarly, a sale of a government bond reduces bank reserves and the monetary base. When the central bank sells a bank a $1 million bond, it simply debits the bank's account at the central bank, reducing the bank's reserves and the monetary base by $1 million. If it sells the bond to nonbank public, the central bank receives a cheque that it clears by deducting the amount from the buyer's bank deposit and reducing the bank's reserves and the monetary base by $1 million.

Using open market operations the central bank has, essentially, full control of the monetary base. If it wants to buy bonds, it can always pay a high enough price to find the seller; if it wants to sell bonds, it can always accept a low enough price to find a buyer. This is because the central bank can create cash, on which it does not pay interest, and receives interests when it holds government bonds.

From the Monetary Base to the Money Supply: The Process of Money Creation

The monetary base is just a small portion of money supply. The central bank's control of the money supply depends on the behaviour of the other actors in the process of money creation: the banking system and the nonbanking public. The banking system affects the money supply by its choice of the level of desired reserves; the nonbank public affects the money supply by its choice of how much cash to hold.

Money multiplier A number that indicates how much the money supply increases when the monetary base increases by $1.

The link between the monetary base and money supply is called the **money multiplier**. The money multiplier tells us how much the money supply increases when the monetary base increases by $1. The multiplier can be calculated for different definitions of the money supply. Below we consider the multiplier for M1+. Similarly we could consider the multiplier for M2+ and for other monetary aggregates. We let M stand for the money supply, MB stand for the monetary base, m stand for the money multiplier and Δ stand for "change in". The multiplier is:

$$m = \frac{\Delta M}{\Delta MB}. \tag{4.1}$$

To know the effect of the open market purchase on the money supply, the central bank needs to know the value of the money multiplier. What follows is a brief description of how banks and the nonbank public also affect the money supply through the money multiplier. We provide a more detailed explanation of the money multiplier in the online appendix to this chapter. In the simple model below we use a linear equation, and so the multiplier is equal both to the ratio of the *change* in money supply to the *change* in reserves as well as to the ratio of the *level* of the money supply to the *level* of the monetary base:

$$m = \frac{\Delta M}{\Delta MB} = \frac{M}{MB}. \tag{4.2}$$

If we use the M1+ definition of the money supply, then M is the sum of currency in circulation, C, and chequing account deposits, D, while the monetary base is the sum of currency in circulation, and desired bank reserves, R.[9] So, we can expand the expression for the money multiplier to:

$$m = \frac{C + D}{C + R}. \tag{4.3}$$

It is convenient to express the equation for the multiplier in terms of the ratios of cash to deposits and reserves to deposits. The nonbank public—households and firms—determine how much currency they wish to hold relative to chequing account deposits; this ratio is equal C/D. Banks determine how much reserves they want to hold relative to chequing account deposits, which is equal R/D. The two ratios are *behavioural* parameters, which depend on how households and banks arrange their financial operations. To include these

---

[9]We ignore the possibility that desired reserves are lower than required reserves. It would make the analysis more complicated and would not affect results. It is not an issue in Canada since required reserves are zero.

ratios in the expression for the money multiplier, we multiply numerator and denominator by 1/D and simplify:

$$m = \left(\frac{C+D}{C+R}\right)\frac{(1/D)}{(1/D)} = \frac{(C/D)+1}{(C/D)+(R/D)}. \tag{4.4}$$

In March 2014 the money base was $71 billion, of which currency outside banks was $65 billion and bank reserves were 6 billion. The value of M1+ was 743 billion, so the multiplier was 743/71 = 10.5. This means the money supply M1+ is ten and a halftimes larger than the money base.

Since money supply = money multiplier times the monetary base, $M = m\ MB$, from equation (4.4), we obtain:

$$M = \left(\frac{C/D+1}{(C/D)+(R/D)}\right)\cdot MB. \tag{4.5}$$

As we have a linear equation, the multiplier also shows how much the money supply changes for a given change in the monetary base:

$$\Delta M = \left(\frac{C/D+1}{(C/D)+(R/D)}\right)\cdot \Delta MB. \tag{4.6}$$

Using the data from March 2014, since the multiplier equals 10.5, a $1 increase in the money base increases M1+ by $10.5. In other words, if the Bank of Canada buys $1 million of government bonds, M1+ increases by $10.5 million.

There are several important points to note about the expression linking the money supply to the monetary base:

1. The money supply will increase if either the monetary base or the money multiplier increases in value, and it will decrease if either the monetary base or the money multiplier decreases in value.
2. An increase in the currency-to-deposit ratio (C/D) causes the value of the money multiplier to decline and, if the monetary base is unchanged, it also causes the money supply to decline. This result makes economic sense: If households and firms increase their holdings of currency relative to their holdings of chequing account deposits, banks will have a relatively smaller amount of funds they can lend out, which reduces the money multiplier.
3. An increase in the reserves-to-deposit ratio (R/D) causes the value of the money multiplier to decline and, if the monetary base is unchanged, it also causes the value of the money supply to decline. This result also makes economic sense: An increase in R/D means that banks are holding relatively more reserves. They are not using these funds to make loans, which reduces the multiplier.

Figure 4.3 shows the money multiplier for M1+ in Canada since 1976. There has been a long-term upward trend in the multiplier. This is simply a reflection of the diminished use of cash in transactions. For any given amount of monetary base, more transactions are conducted using methods of payment other than cash. This is the result of financial innovations that make it easier to make non-cash payments. One such innovation is the use of debit cards, which provide direct access to chequing accounts. Canadians are among the heaviest users of debit cards in the world. Another is the use of credit cards, with the balances being paid for using chequing account balances.

As you can see from Figure 4.3, efforts by the Bank of Canada to slow down the rate of growth of M1+ led to a slight decline in the multiplier over the period 1976–81. Once the Bank of Canada abandoned the control of M1+, the multiplier started increasing rapidly.

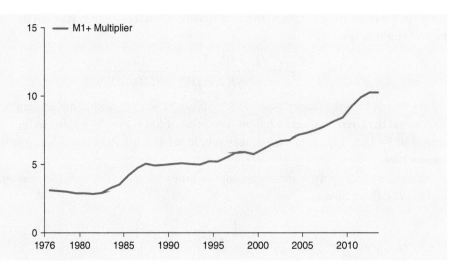

Figure 4.3

M1+ Multiplier in Canada

There has been a long-term upward trend in the size of the M1+ multiplier. This is because households and firms have been moving away from using cash for transactions. An important innovation was the introduction of debit cards, which provide direct access to chequing account balances.

Source: Statistics Canada, CANSIM Table 176-0025

4.3

Learning Objective

Describe the quantity theory of money, and use it to explain the connection between changes in the money supply and the inflation rate.

Quantity equation (or equation of exchange) An identity that states that the money supply multiplied by the velocity of money equals the price level multiplied by real GDP.

Velocity of money The average number of times that each dollar in the money supply is used to purchase goods or services in a given period.

The Quantity Theory of Money and Inflation

Writers dating back at least as far as the Greek philosopher Aristotle in the fourth century BC have discussed the connection between increases in the money supply and increases in the price level. During the sixteenth century, the Spanish conquest of Mexico and Peru resulted in huge quantities of gold and silver being exported to Europe, where they were minted into coins. The inflow of gold and silver into Europe was followed by the first prolonged period of inflation. Many writers noted that the sharp increase in the money supply led to an increase in inflation. In the early twentieth century, Yale economist Irving Fisher formalized the relationship between money and prices by proposing the **quantity equation** (also called the **equation of exchange**). The quantity equation is an identity that states that the money supply, M, multiplied by the *velocity of money*, V, equals the price level, P, multiplied by real GDP, Y:

$$MV = PY. \tag{4.7}$$

Why is it an identity? Because Fisher defined the **velocity of money**—or, simply, *velocity*—as the average number of times that each dollar in the money supply is used to purchase goods or services in a given period. So velocity is, by definition,

$$V = \frac{PY}{M}. \tag{4.8}$$

Since, by definition, V is always equal to $\frac{PY}{M}$ then, by multiplying both sides by M, we get $MV=PY$. Both sides of the quantity theory equation are always equal. The quantity equation is an identity. To see this, consider a simple example. Assume that the only good in the economy is pizza, and all transactions are paid in cash. A pizza costs $10 and during the year 100 pizzas are produced. The total amount of cash in the economy is $40. We can now calculate the velocity of cash:

$$V = \frac{\text{price of a pizza} \times \text{number of pizzas produced}}{\text{the amount of cash in the economy}} = \frac{\$10 \cdot 100}{\$40} = 25.$$

The quantity equation: $MV = PY$ becomes: $\$40 \cdot 25 = \$10 \cdot 100$. Both sides are equal because of the way velocity was calculated.

Unlike at the time of Fisher, there are now many different concepts of the money supply: the monetary base, M1+, M2+ etc. There are, therefore, many different velocities: the velocity of the monetary base, the velocity of M1+, the velocity of M2+, etc. The best way of thinking about the velocity of, for example, M1+, is as follows. Assume that the entire money supply consists solely of M1+ so that all transactions are conducted using components of M1+ (currency and chequing accounts). Velocity of M1+ is then *the average number of times each unit of M1+ is used during a year:*

$$V(M1+) = \frac{PY}{M1+}.$$

Since *PY* equals nominal GDP, the velocity of M1+ is simply nominal GDP divided by the value of M1+.

Similarly, the velocity of cash is calculated assuming all transactions are conducted using cash. The velocity of cash (the amount of notes and coins in circulation is then:

$$V(cash) = \frac{PY}{cash}.$$

In March 2014, Canadian nominal GDP was $1717 billion on annual basis, M1+ was $743 billion; and cash outside the banking system was $66 billion.[10] Using these data we can calculate the velocity of M1+ and of cash:

$$V(M1+) = \frac{\$1717\ billion}{\$743\ billion} = 2.3; \quad V(cash) = \frac{\$1717\ billion}{\$66\ billion} = 26.$$

The velocity of M1+ was 2.3. This means that, if all transactions in Canada in the first quarter 2014 had been paid for only with components of M1+, each unit of M1+ would have had to be used, on the average, 2.3 times. Similarly, the velocity of cash was 26; i.e., if all transactions had been paid in cash, each dollar would have had to be used on the average 26 times.

In fact, some transactions are done with cash, other with chequing accounts, other with credit cards, etc. This means that the numbers we obtained for velocity are not correct. For example, cash is used in only a small portion of transactions, and the actual number of times each dollar of cash circulates is much smaller. If we knew what amounts were paid using cash, using chequing accounts M2+, and in other ways we could, in principle, calculate the exact values of velocities for various monetary aggregates. We do not do so since, as we will see below, the variety and exact values of velocities are of secondary importance. What matters is *whether velocity is stable over time.* So from now on we will denote the amount of money as *M*, which may mean the monetary base or M1+ or some other monetary aggregate.

The quantity equation (4.7) tells us that the total amount of spending in the economy (*M V*) equals nominal GDP (*P Y*). Therefore, the money supply and the velocity of money together determine the level of nominal GDP. As we will see, the central bank determines the money supply in the long run, which means that as long as velocity is stable or changes in predictable ways, the central bank can also determine the level of nominal GDP in the long run.

The Quantity Theory of Money

A theory is a statement about the world that could be either true or false. The quantity equation (4.7) is always true, so it does not qualify as a theory. Irving Fisher turned the quantity

---

[10]Statistics Canada, CANSIM Tables 380-0064 and 176-0025.

Useful Math 4.2:
Calculating the percentage change of a product or a ratio

There are simple and easy-to-remember formulas that relate variables to their percentage changes. We denote percentage change in variable X as $\%\Delta X$.

1. The percentage change of the product of two variables is equal to the sum of their percentage changes:

$$\%\Delta(XY) = \%\Delta X + \%\Delta Y.$$

2. The percentage change of a ratio is equal to the difference of percentage changes:

$$\%\Delta\left(\frac{X}{Y}\right) = \%\Delta X - \%\Delta Y.$$

These simple equations are often useful in assessing economic or business performance. For example, in 2012 nominal GDP in Canada grew by 3.1% [$\%\Delta(P \cdot Y) = 3.1\%$] while prices (GDP deflator) increased by 1.3% ($\%\Delta P = 1.3\%$). Nominal GDP = $P \cdot Y$ so, using the first formula, $\%\Delta(\text{Nominal GDP}) = \%\Delta P + \%\Delta Y$. Substituting the values, we obtain 3.1% = 1.3% + $\%\Delta Y$ and so $\%\Delta Y$ = 1.8%: real GDP increased 1.8%.

For another example consider Tim Hortons. It is a multi-franchise company that can grow by increasing the sales per franchise or by increasing the number of franchises. Increasing sales per franchise (called intensive growth) is preferred to increasing the number of franchises (extensive growth). Last year total sales increased by 2%. Is it a good result? It depends on what happened with the number of franchises. The number of franchises increased by 3%. Denote the average sales per franchise by S, total sales by T, and the number of franchises by N. Since $S = T/N$, so, using the second equation, $\%\Delta S = \%\Delta T - \%\Delta N = 2\% - 3\% = -1\%$. While total sales grew by 2%, this was the result of extensive growth. Sales per franchise fell by 1%, not a good thing.

Practice Question

As we will see in Chapter 5, the real exchange rate is equal to the nominal exchange rate multiplied by the domestic price level and divided by the foreign price level. We denote the nominal exchange rate as E. Using symbols:

$$\text{real exchange rate} = E \cdot P^{\text{domestic}} / P^{\text{foreign}}.$$

(a) Calculate the rate of change of the real exchange rate.

(b) If the real exchange rate is constant, the nominal exchange rate appreciates 2% per year and domestic inflation is 2% per year, what is foreign inflation?

Quantity theory of money A theory about the connection between money and prices that assumes that the velocity of money is constant.

equation into the **quantity theory of money** by assuming that *velocity is constant*. Fisher argued that the average number of times a dollar is spent depends on factors that do not change very often, such as how often people get paid, how often they go grocery shopping, and how often businesses mail bills. Because this assertion that velocity is constant may be either true or false, the equation became a theory. As we will see, even if velocity is not constant, the quantity theory may still prove to be useful in predicting future inflation rates.

The Quantity Theory Explanation of Inflation

Applying the formula for the percentage change in the product to the quantity equation (4.7): $MV = PY$ we get:

$$\%\Delta M + \%\Delta V = \pi + \%\Delta Y. \tag{4.9}$$

The percentage change in the price level is the inflation rate, which we represent by $\pi = \%\Delta P$. According to the quantity equation, the percentage change in the money supply plus the percentage change in velocity equals the inflation rate plus the growth rate of real GDP.

The quantity theory assumes that velocity is constant, so the percentage change in V is 0. Inserting $\%\Delta V = 0$ into equation (4.9) we obtain:

$$\%\Delta M = \pi + \%\Delta Y.$$

So, this equation tells us that the growth rate of the money supply equals the inflation rate plus the growth rate of real GDP. Rewriting it, we have:

$$\pi = \%\Delta M - \%\Delta Y. \tag{4.10}$$

We now have an important conclusion from the quantity theory: *Inflation results from the money supply growing faster than real GDP.* For example, if the money supply grows by 5%, while real GDP grows by 3%, the inflation rate will be 2%. If the Bank of Canada were to increase the growth rate of the money supply from 5% to 6%, the quantity theory predicts that the inflation rate would increase from 2% to 3%. In other words, the quantity theory predicts that, holding the growth rate of real GDP constant, a 1 percentage point increase in the growth rate of the money supply will cause a 1 percentage point increase in the inflation rate.

Note that this conclusion about the source of inflation depends on the assumption that velocity is constant. Fluctuations in velocity, particularly in the short run, can break the link between changes in the rate of growth of the money supply and the inflation rate. In the long run, though, most economists believe that the quantity theory accurately predicts changes in the inflation rate. As a result, most economists agree that the central bank, by controlling the growth rate of the money supply, determines the inflation rate in the long run.

Solved Problem 4.1

The Effect of a Decrease in the Growth Rate of the Money Supply

The average annual growth rate of real GDP for Canada since World War II has been about 3%. Suppose that the growth rate of velocity is 0%. What happens to the inflation rate if the money supply growth rate decreases from 5% to 2%? Assume that the growth rate of velocity remains 0% and that changes in the growth rate of the money supply do not affect the growth rate of real GDP.

Solving the Problem

Step 1 **Review the chapter material.** The problem asks you to determine the effect of a decrease in the growth rate of the money supply on the inflation rate, so you may want to review the section "The Quantity Theory Explanation of Inflation," which begins on page 120.

Step 2 **Calculate the initial inflation rate.** The quantity equation tells us that:

$$\text{\% Change in } M + \text{\% Change in } V = \text{\% Change in } P + \text{\% Change in } Y,$$

so if the growth rate of velocity is 0%, we have:

$$\text{\% Change in } M = \pi_1 + \text{\% Change in } Y,$$

where π_1 = the initial inflation rate. We already know that the growth rate of real GDP is 3%, so the $\%\Delta Y = 3\%$. We also know that the growth rate of the money supply is initially 5%, so the $\%\Delta M = 5\%$. We can plug these two values into the above equation to get:

$$5\% = \pi_1 + 3\%$$

or

$$\pi_1 = 5\% - 3\% = 2\%.$$

Step 3 **Calculate the new inflation rate.** If the growth rate of the money supply decreases from 5% to 2%, then, given that velocity is unchanged, the inflation rate will also decrease. We assume that changing the growth rate of the money supply does not change the growth rate of real GDP, which, therefore, remains 3%. The quantity equation tells us:

$$\%\Delta M = \pi_2 + \%\Delta Y,$$

where the $\%\Delta M$ is now 2%, and π_2 is the new inflation rate.
We can solve for the new inflation rate:

$$2\% = \pi_2 + 3\%$$

$$\pi_2 = 2\% - 3\% = -1\%.$$

The 3 percentage point decrease in the growth rate of the money supply led to a 3 percentage point decrease in the inflation rate. In this case, the inflation rate is negative, so the price level is decreasing. In other words, deflation occurs. Note that there can be substantial changes in velocity in the short run, so the connection between changes in the rate of growth of the money supply and changes in the inflation rate are usually not as close as in this problem.

See related problem 3.7 at the end of the chapter.

Can the Quantity Theory Accurately Predict the Inflation Rate?

Velocity does not have to be constant in order for an increase in the growth rate of the money supply to cause an increase in the inflation rate. As long as velocity grows at a constant rate, there will be a close relationship between increases in the money supply and increases in the inflation rate. However, when the growth rate of velocity fluctuates, it is difficult for the central bank to predict how changes in the growth rate of the money supply will affect the inflation rate. For instance, an increase in the growth rate of the money supply might be offset by a decline in velocity, leaving the inflation rate unaffected. As described in the Making a Connection box on page 123, this indeed happened in the Eurozone and in the United States during the Great Recession: Despite huge increases in the monetary base, inflation did not rise because velocity fell.

What can we conclude, then, about the link between the growth rate of the money supply and the inflation rate? Because velocity sometimes moves erratically over short periods, we would not expect the quantity equation to provide good forecasts of inflation in the short run. Over the long run and across countries, however, there is evidence of a strong link between the growth rate of the money supply and the inflation rate. Figure 4.4 panel (a) shows the relationship between the growth rate of the M2 measure of the money supply and the inflation rate by decade in Canada. (We use M2 here because data for M2 are available for a longer period of time than for M1.) Because of variations in the rate of growth of real GDP and in velocity, there is not an exact relationship between the growth rate of M2 and the inflation rate. But there is a clear pattern: Decades with higher growth rates in the money supply were also decades with higher inflation rates. Both the inflation rate and the rate of growth of M2 were the highest in 1970s and the lowest in 1920s and 1930s. Except for the past 20 years, which were the period of rapid financial innovation, the relationship between the rate of inflation and the rate of growth of the money supply is very close. In other words, most of the variation in inflation rates across decades can be explained by variation in the rates of growth of the money supply.

Panel (b) provides further evidence consistent with the quantity theory by looking at rates of growth of the money supply and rates of inflation for 36 countries between 1995 and 2011. Although there is not an exact relationship between rates of growth of the money

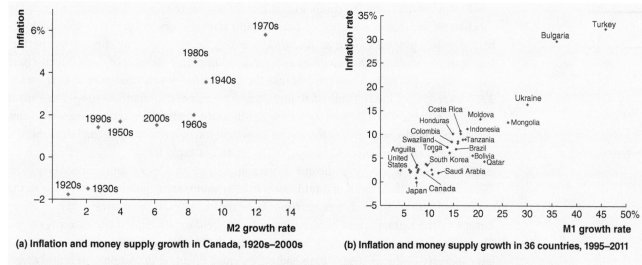

Figure 4.4 The Relationship between Money Growth and Inflation over Time and around the World

Panel (a) shows the relationship between the growth rate of M2 and the inflation rate for Canada from 1920s to the 2000s. Panel (b) shows the relationship between the growth rate of M1 and inflation for 36 countries during the 1995–2011 period. In both panels, high money growth rates are associated with higher inflation rates.

Sources: Panel (a): Inflation: Statistics Canada, CANSIM Table 326-0020. Money supply: for 1960s–2000s, Statistics Canada, CANSIM Table 176-0025; for 1920s–1950s, Cherie Metcalf, Angela Redish, and Ronald Shearer (1998) New Estimates of the Canadian Money Stock: 1871–1967, *Canadian Journal of Economics*. Panel (b): International Monetary Fund, *International Financial Statistics*.

supply and rates of inflation across countries, the figure shows that countries where the money supply grew rapidly tended to have high inflation rates, while countries where the money supply grew more slowly tended to have much lower inflation rates.

We can conclude that the basic prediction of the quantity theory is one of the most reliable relationships in macroeconomics:

> *If the central bank increases the growth rate of the money supply, then, in the long run, this increase will lead to a higher inflation rate.*

Making the Connection

Is the Inflation Rate around the World Going to Increase in the Near Future?

Through 2012, central banks increased bank reserves to help their economies recover from the Great Recession that started in 2008. In addition, the European Central Bank (ECB) bought bonds to support financial markets after governments in some European countries had difficulty selling bonds to private investors. The resulting increase in bank reserves increased the monetary base, which *can* lead to an increase in the money supply and higher prices, but not necessarily. The ECB's actions surprised some observers who had become accustomed to the central bank's anti-inflation stance. "The sovereign [debt] crisis has pushed the ECB into flooding the system with even more liquidity," wrote Morgan Stanley economist Joachim Fels. "Global excess liquidity should grow by even more, lifting the prices of commodities and other risky assets and adding to global inflation pressures." By mid-2012, the Eurozone inflation rate rose to 2.4%. Though this was above the ECB's target rate of 2%, some analysts predicted that weakness in Eurozone economies would reduce future inflation rates. Indeed, by late 2013, the problem of the Eurozone countries became the threat of deflation, with inflation declining below 0.5% in 2014 and prices falling in several countries.

In the United States, to combat the Great Recession the Federal Reserve reduced the short-term nominal interest rate to near 0% and started a new policy of purchasing long-term bonds, a process known as *quantitative easing*, in an attempt to improve the performance of the economy. Quantitative easing resulted in a large increase in the monetary base and could have been inflationary. Because the U.S. economy was slow to recover from the 2007–09 recession, the Fed embarked on two new rounds of quantitative easing. The United Kingdom also increased its monetary base significantly. Yet inflation did not increase. Why, despite the massive increases in the rate of growth of the money supply in the Eurozone, the United States and the United Kingdom, did inflation not explode?

The concept of money in the quantity equation is much wider than the monetary base. What matters is the amount of liquid assets held by nonbanking public. The increase in the monetary base did not lead to proportionally larger increases in the money supply in either Europe or the United States because many banks held on to most of their new reserves. Therefore, although the monetary base increased, the money multipliers decreased and the large increase in the monetary base had only a small effect on the amount of liquid assets held by the public. When the economies of Europe, the United States and the United Kingdom recover, however, banks will be more willing to lend out their new reserves, which will increase the possibility of a sudden rapid rise in the money supply. The quantity equation tells us that in the long run, a sustained increase in the money supply will cause an increase in the inflation rate. Many economists and policymakers, however, were more worried about slow growth than about inflation. John Williams, president of the Federal Reserve Bank of San Francisco, explained, "Some commentators have sounded an alarm that this massive expansion of the monetary base will inexorably lead to high inflation. . . . Despite these dire predictions, inflation in the United States has been the dog that didn't bark." The problem of how to avoid inflation when the economies recover remained one of the most pressing questions of macroeconomic policy.

Sources: Kevin Hall, "Bernanke Unveils Plan to Unwind Fed's Massive Asset Purchases," *McClatchy—Tribune Business News*, February 10, 2010; Neil Shah and Katie Martin, "Europe's Newest Risk: Inflation," *The Wall Street Journal*, May 14, 2010; Dave Kansas, "Whiffs of Inflation from Europe," *The Wall Street Journal*, January 4, 2011; John Hilsenrath, "Weak Report Lifts Chance of Fed Action," *The Wall Street Journal*, July 6, 2012; and Rahul Karunakar, "Euro Zone Price Pressures at 26-Month Low in May: ECRI," *Reuters*, July 6, 2012.

See related problem 3.6 at the end of chapter.

4.4

Learning Objective

Discuss the relationships among the growth rate of money, inflation, and nominal interest rates.

The Relationships among the Growth Rate of Money, Inflation, and the Nominal Interest Rate

As we have seen in Chapters 2 and 3, interest rates are critical for allocating resources in the economy. In this section, we discuss how the central bank can affect interest rates.

Real Interest Rates and Actual Real Interest Rates

In Chapter 2 we distinguished between the *expected real interest* rate and the *actual real interest rate*. The *expected real interest rate* is the real interest rate borrowers and lenders expect at the time that a financial decision is made. The actual real interest rate is determined by the actual rate of inflation over the life of the contract and is the real interest rate that borrowers end up paying and lenders actually receive. While the difference may be overlooked, it is crucial. Decisions of households and firms depend on the return (in case of lending or investing) or the cost (in case of borrowing) in terms of goods and services. The return and cost are not known at the time of the decision since they depend on the inflation rate over the life of the contract. So households and firms need to form expectations about the inflation rate. The actual real interest rate, while it is what borrowers end up paying and lenders actually receive, is not relevant for making economic decisions since it is not known when decisions are made.

From now on we will call the expected real interest rate simply *the real interest rate*, or sometimes, to stress that it depends on expectations, as the *(expected) real interest rate*.

You should remember this distinction when, for example, we are comparing the real interest rate with the actual interest rate. Such comparison usually involves an evaluation of whether the actual outcome was beneficial to the borrower or to the lender. If the actual inflation rate and the expected inflation rate are equal, the actual real interest rate and the (expected) real interest rate are also equal. When inflation turns out to be lower than expected, the actual real interest rate is higher than the (expected) real interest rate. So borrowers lose, since they pay more in real terms for the loan than they had originally expected. By the same token, lenders gain because they receive more than they originally expected.

For example, assume you are a pizza shop owner. You take out a one-year loan with a nominal interest rate of 6%. You and your bank both expect inflation rate to be 2%. This means that the real interest rate is 4%. You plan to increase the price of pizza in line with inflation (i.e., by 2% over the year), so you expect you will need to give up 4% of your output to pay the interest on the loan. If the inflation rate turns out to be 0%, and you are not able to change the price of pizza, then the actual real interest rate equals 6%. To pay the interest on the loan you will have to give up 6% of your output. You lose, because you have to give up more, and the bank benefits. However, if the inflation rate turns out to be 5%, then the actual real interest rate is 6% − 5% = 1%. You raise the price of pizza by 5% and, to pay the interest on the loan, you need to give up only 1% of your output. You gain and the bank loses because the actual real interest rate turned out to be lower than expected.

We can generalize by noting that if the inflation rate is greater than the expected inflation rate, the real interest rate will be less than the expected real interest rate; in this case, borrowers will gain, and lenders will lose. If the inflation rate is less than the expected inflation rate, the real interest rate will be greater than the expected real interest rate; in this case, borrowers will lose, and lenders will gain. Table 4.1 summarizes the important relationships between the nominal interest rate, the expected real interest rate, and the actual real interest rate.

The Fisher Effect

In the pizza shop example, the nominal interest rate was fixed, so we could see what happens to the real interest rate when the inflation rate rises above or falls below the expected inflation rate. However, the nominal interest rate, as with other interest rates, is fixed only when the borrower signs a loan contract. Before the borrower and lender agree on an interest rate, they are free to negotiate an interest rate based on their assessments of market conditions, including the expected inflation rate over the duration of the loan. To determine what nominal

Table 4.1 The Relationship between the Expected Real Interest Rate and the Actual Real Interest Rate

If the inflation rate …	then the actual real interest rate …	so …
is greater than the expected inflation rate	will be less than the (expected) real interest rate	borrowers will gain and lenders will lose.
is less than the expected inflation rate	will be greater than the (expected) real interest rate	borrowers will lose and lenders will gain.

interest rate will be acceptable to borrowers and lenders, we can rearrange the expression for the real interest rate, equation (2.8) on page 58, as follows:

$$i = r + \pi^e. \tag{4.11}$$

Fisher equation The equation stating that the nominal interest rate is the sum of the expected real interest rate and the expected inflation rate.

This equation states that the nominal interest rate is the sum of the expected real interest rate and the expected inflation rate. It is called the **Fisher equation**, after the same Irving Fisher who developed the quantity theory of money. The equation implies that the nominal interest rate changes when the expected real interest rate changes or when the expected inflation rate changes.

To understand the Fisher equation, let us return to the pizza shop example. Ask yourself what nominal interest rate you and the bank will agree on. The real interest rate is determined by real factors such as the willingness of households and firms to save and invest and the government's spending and taxing decisions. By the *classical dichotomy* discussed earlier in the chapter, the rate of inflation will not affect the real interest rate.

Fisher effect The assertion by Irving Fisher that the nominal interest rate rises or falls point-for-point with changes in the expected inflation rate.

With the expected real interest rate determined by real factors, the Fisher equation tells us that the nominal interest rate changes when the expected inflation rate changes. For example, assume that the real interest rate is 4%, and the expected inflation rate is 2%. In that case, the nominal interest rate on a loan is 4% + 2% = 6%. If the expected inflation rate rises from 2% to 3%, the nominal interest rate will also rise by 1%, to 7%. This adjustment of the nominal interest rate to changes in the expected inflation rate is called the *Fisher effect*. The **Fisher effect** holds that the nominal interest rate rises or falls point-for-point with changes in the expected inflation rate.

Do the data support the Fisher effect? Figure 4.5 shows the relationship between the inflation rate and the nominal interest rate for 56 countries over the period 1995–2011. There is a clear positive relationship between inflation and nominal interest rates, with nominal interest rates being higher in countries with higher inflation rates. Although the figure does not show nominal interest rates rising point-for-point with increases in inflation rates, the Fisher equation still provides a reasonable approximation of how inflation rates affect nominal interest rates around the world.

Figure 4.5

The Relationship between the Inflation Rate and the Nominal Interest Rate, 1995–2011

The figure shows a positive relationship between the inflation rate and the nominal interest rate for 56 countries. This relationship is consistent with the Fisher effect.

Source: International Monetary Fund, *International Financial Statistics.*

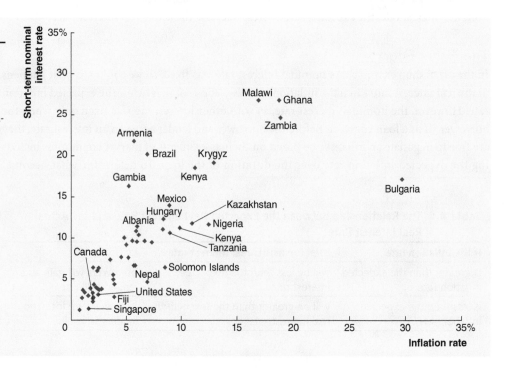

Avoiding a Common Mistake:
Changes in the Actual Inflation Rate and the Fisher Effect

We have just considered two situations which are often confused: (1) What happens when the inflation rate is different than expected, and (2) What happens when the expected inflation rate changes (i.e. the Fisher effect). In the first case, households and firms form expectations about the inflation rate and, on their basis, enter financial contracts. We then consider what happens when the actual inflation rate is different than expected *after* the contract has been signed. If, for example, the borrower and lender both expect the inflation rate to be 2% and want a 3% real return, they agree to an interest rate of 5%. If inflation turns out

different than expected, for example 4%, the actual real interest rate ends up being only 1% and the lender loses while the borrower gains.

In the second case, we consider what happens when the expected rate of inflation changes *before* the contract is signed. If, for example, the expected rate of inflation increases from 2% to 4% before the contract is signed, the Fisher effect tells us that the nominal interest rate on the contract will also increase, from 5% to 7%. The real interest rate will remain equal to 3% and both the borrower and lender will be, in real terms, unaffected.

Money Growth and the Nominal Interest Rate

If we combine the quantity theory of money with the Fisher effect we have an important relationship: In the long run, an increase in the growth rate of the money supply causes the inflation rate to increase, which then causes the nominal interest rate to increase. We can conclude that because the inflation rate varies across time and countries as a result of changes in the growth rate of the money supply, nominal interest rates will also vary across time and countries.

Solved Problem 4.2

Calculating the Nominal Interest Rate Using the Quantity Theory and Fisher Equations.

The money growth rate in Canada is 3% per year; the expected rate of change of velocity is 1% per year; real output growth is 2% per year; and the real interest rate is 3%. What is the nominal interest rate?

Solving the Problem

Step 1 **Review the chapter material.** You need to review the "Quantity Theory Explanation of Inflation" which begins on page 120 and the section: "The Relationships among the Growth rate of Money, Inflation, and and the Nominal Interest Rate" which begins on page 124.

Step 2 **Calculate the inflation rate.** In the presentation of the quantity theory equation we assumed the rates of growth of velocity, output, and the money supply were known with certainty. In general there is uncertainty about the value of these variables. Here we assume that the expected rates of change of velocity is uncertain. We denote it as $\%\Delta V^e$. Because of the uncertainty, the quantity equation (4.9) allows calculating the expected inflation rate, not the actual inflation rate: $\pi^e = \%\Delta M + \%\Delta V^e - \%\Delta Y$. So the expected inflation rate is $3\% + 1\% - 2\% = 2\%$.

Step 3 Calculate the nominal interest rate.

From the Fisher equation (4.11): $i = r + \pi^e$, so $i = 3\% + 2\% = 5\%$.

See related problem 4.4 at end of chapter.

4.5
Learning Objective
Explain the costs of a
monetary policy that
allows inflation to be
greater than zero.

The Costs of Inflation

In the previous sections we discussed the quantity theory of money, the inflation rate, and nominal interest rates. We now consider how inflation affects households and firms, and explore the benefits to society of reducing inflation. We discuss the costs of inflation, distinguishing between expected and unexpected inflation, the costs of deflation (decreasing price level), and the potential benefits of inflation.

Costs of Expected Inflation

There are four costs of expected inflation:

- Shoe-leather costs
- Menu costs
- Inflation tax
- Tax distortions

Shoe-leather costs The costs of inflation to households and firms from holding less money and making more frequent trips to the bank; costs related to expected inflation.

Shoe-Leather Costs Households and firms change their behaviour to avoid inflation by choosing to hold less of their wealth as cash. Other assets, such as savings accounts and bonds, have nominal interest rates greater than zero. Some of these assets: government bonds and insured bank deposits (up to $100 000) are riskless. But these other assets are less liquid than cash. When people want to use their wealth to purchase goods and services, they must first transfer funds from the less liquid interest-bearing assets into cash. This transfer takes time and effort, so it is costly. When deciding how much cash to hold, people face a tradeoff between losing potential interest earnings (which they would have earned if they kept bonds or other assets instead of cash) and gaining liquidity. By the Fisher equation a higher rate of inflation raises the nominal interest rate, and holding cash results in losing more interest and is less attractive. So, with higher inflation, people hold less cash and must transfer funds more often. Economists use the term **shoe-leather costs** to refer to the costs of inflation to households and firms from reducing cash holdings and making more frequent trips to the bank. The origin of the term is not difficult to guess: It was introduced at a time when the transfers required actual trips to the bank and shoes had leather soles. Nowadays, many transfers can be made on the internet, but the general principle is unaffected: The more interest is lost by holding cash instead of bonds, the less cash people hold and the more often they need to do the transfers.

Menu costs The costs to firms of changing prices due to reprinting price lists, informing customers, and angering customers; costs related to expected inflation.

Menu Costs When you go to a restaurant, you see the menu with prices printed on it. When you go to a retail store, you see prices on shelves or on individual items. **Menu costs** are the costs to firms of changing prices due to reprinting price lists, informing customers, or angering customers by frequent price changes. The higher the inflation rate, the more frequently firms change prices and the greater is the effort needed to change prices. In addition, inflation leads to larger changes in relative prices. Not all firms have the same menu costs, so when expected inflation occurs, some firms will change prices and others will not. Firms with low menu costs are likely to adjust their prices to the desired level quickly, but firms with high menu costs will not. For example, restaurants often have to pay to have new menus printed up, so the menu costs for restaurants are high, and restaurants therefore do not change prices frequently. But, the price of a litre of gas can change every day because it is relatively cheap and easy for gasoline stations to change posted prices. Therefore, gasoline prices often respond quickly to inflation, while prices at restaurants do not respond quickly. As a result, the relative prices of goods and services can change, making markets less efficient because the relative price changes do not reflect underlying changes in demand or in production costs.

Inflation Tax Inflation causes the purchasing power of money to decrease. Suppose you want to purchase an iPad next year. The current price of the iPad is $500, and you decide to keep $500 in your chequing account for one year and then purchase the device. If as a result of the central bank increasing the money supply, the inflation rate is 10% for the year, then the price of the iPad will rise to $550. Your $500 can no longer purchase the iPad because inflation reduced the purchasing power of your money. You are poorer: You are unable to buy as much as you could last year. This means that you lost a part of your wealth. Where did the wealth go? To the government. Recall that money is printed by the Bank of Canada, which is wholly owned by the federal government. When the Bank of Canada increases the money supply, it earns seigniorage, which it then passes on to the federal government. So as a result of the increase in the money supply the government received seigniorage, raising its wealth. In other words, inflation transferred wealth from individuals to the government, just as taxes do. The loss of purchasing power of cash due to inflation is called **inflation tax**.

> **Inflation tax** The loss of purchasing power of money due to inflation.

Inflation tax is, however, fundamentally different from other taxes. All other taxes are imposed by fiscal authorities (federal, provincial, and local). The inflation tax is imposed by the Bank of Canada. It is largely independent of the government and so fiscal needs do not determine the size of inflation tax. In other words, the federal government, while it receives the proceeds, does not determine the size of the tax. This is the consequence of central bank independence. As we discussed earlier, the situation in Zimbabwe was different. The central bank was not independent and was directed by the government. In Zimbabwe, inflation tax was similar to other taxes.

Tax Distortions Expected inflation also creates inefficiencies in the tax system by distorting the behaviour of households and firms. There are numerous distortions in the tax code that increase as the rate of inflation rises. The general problem is simple. The goal of economic activity is *real* consumption: the amount of goods and services you can buy. However, the basis of many taxes is the nominal value: property prices; the value of inventory, machinery, and other assets; nominal interest earned; etc. As these values rise with inflation, the tax that is paid on the increase in nominal, rather than real, values rises, distorting choices of households and firms. The most important distortions are related to capital gains and interest earnings.

A *capital gain* is the increase in the price of an asset. Assume that you buy shares of CIBC stock for $100 and sell them 10 years later for $200, and that the price level has doubled over the 10 years. The real price of the stock remained the same: the amount of goods and services you can buy when you sell it now for $200 is the same as the amount you could buy for $100 when you bought the share. Since there is no real gain, you should pay no tax. But you are taxed on the $100 gain. If inflation were zero over the 10 years and the price of the stock had not changed, you would have paid no tax. The failure to adjust the value of capital gains for inflation increases the tax burden on investors and may reduce the level of saving in the economy.

The tax code also fails to adjust for inflation the values of inventories and the tax allowances that businesses are allowed to take for the depreciation of buildings, machinery, and other assets. For example, assume that you buy a machine for your business for $100 000. The machine lasts 10 years, during which the price level doubles. The price of the machine also doubles and it now costs $200 000, which means that the real price has not changed. Clearly, the machine was a cost of production and you should be able to deduct from taxable profits the amount needed to replace the machine (i.e., $200 000). But you can deduct only the original cost of the machine, $100 000. This means your taxable profits are overstated and the profit tax you pay is too high. Taxing nominal capital gains makes the economy less efficient by increasing the real value of the tax payments corporations make, thereby reducing their real profits. This may lead firms to reduce investments in new factories and equipment. This tax burden is particularly large during periods of high inflation.

The second major reason expected inflation distorts financial decisions is due to the fact that lenders pay taxes on nominal rather than real returns. Suppose that expected inflation is 2% and that your marginal tax rate is 50%. You are making an investment with the real interest rate of 4%. Let us calculate nominal and real returns. Of course, what matters to you is your real after-tax return. Let us calculate it:

- The nominal interest rate, and the *nominal before-tax* return, are 2% + 4% = 6%.
- The *nominal after-tax* return is 6% · (1 − 50%) = 3%.
- The *real after-tax return*, obtained by subtracting the inflation rate from the before-tax return, is (1 − 0.50) · (6%) − 2% = 1%.

Suppose now that the expected inflation rate rises to 4% and that the real interest rate remains at 4%. The nominal interest rate, and the nominal before-tax return, are 4% + 4% = 8%. The nominal after-tax return is (1 − 0.50) · (8%) = 4% and the real after-tax return is (1 − 0.50) · (8%) − 4% = 0%. Even though the real interest rate remained unchanged, your real after-tax return fell because of inflation. Inflation reduces your after-tax return, discouraging saving.

There are, however, winners as well as losers during a period of high inflation. Borrowers such as corporations benefit from higher inflation because borrowers deduct nominal interest payments in calculating their income tax liabilities. Changes in expected inflation can change the real after-tax cost of borrowing. For example, with high expected inflation, corporations find selling bonds or taking out loans more attractive because nominal interest payments are deductible. Buying housing becomes more attractive relative to renting and investing in stocks because capital gains on the first property are not taxed. All these actions are undertaken only in order to reduce the tax bill and so create distortions in the economy.

Costs of Unexpected Inflation

When the inflation rate turns out to be higher or lower than expected, wealth is redistributed. For example, suppose you borrowed $500 to purchase an iPad instead of paying cash for it. You and the bank agreed on the real interest rate of 4%. You both expected the inflation rate to be 6% so that the nominal interest rate on the loan was set at 10%. After one year you repay the bank $550. What happens if the inflation rate turns out to be 8%? In that case, the actual real interest rate is 10% − 8% = 2%, less than you agreed on. You gain, and the bank loses. As we saw in Table 4.1 on page 125, when actual inflation is higher than expected, borrowers gain, and lenders lose.

In general, if inflation is higher than households and firms expected, there is a redistribution of wealth from lenders, such as banks, to borrowers. The total wealth in the economy does not change, but unexpected inflation can nevertheless generate true costs for the economy. To see this, we introduce the simple concept of *revealed preference*. It says that if, out of two equally costly alternatives you choose one, this means you prefer it to the one you have not chosen. In other words, you reveal preference for the alternative you chose. How can we apply it to the example above? You and the bank had the choice of many real interest rates. You could enter a contract with 2% real interest rate but instead you chose the real interest rate of 4%. By revealed preference, it means that a 4% real interest rate was preferred, or superior, to the inferior contract with the real interest rate of 2%. Because of unexpected inflation, however, you ended up with the inferior contract. While you gained and the bank lost, the concept of revealed preference implies that your gain was smaller than the bank's loss.

Inflation Uncertainty

Relative prices play an important role in allocating resources. The more the inflation rate changes from year to year, the more likely it is to distort relative prices. We can measure the volatility of inflation with the standard deviation of the inflation rate. Figure 4.6 shows

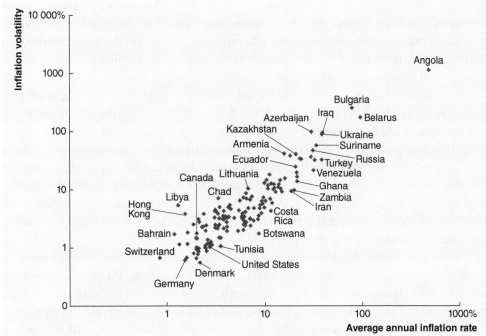

Figure 4.6

Inflation and Inflation Volatility around the World, 1996–2011

The volatility of inflation tends to increase as the average annual inflation rate increases. As the inflation rate increases, it becomes less predictable. The figure measures the volatility of inflation as the standard deviation of annual inflation rates. Note that the axes are in log base 10 scale.

Source: International Monetary Fund, *International Financial Statistics.*

the relationship between the average inflation rate and the volatility of the inflation rate for countries around the world. There is a clear tendency for the volatility of inflation to increase as the average inflation rate increases. Therefore, as the inflation rate increases, it becomes less predictable. In this situation, the ability of market prices to help households and firms allocate resources is reduced.

Inflation uncertainty is especially detrimental for long-term plans, in particular for investment decisions. Imagine you are considering building a bread factory with the help of a loan. We will make all the calculations in real terms. It takes five years for the factory to become operational. The cost of production will be 85% of the factory's output and, at current relative prices, you need, on the average, 10% of the factory output to pay off the loan. So, if nothing changes, you will earn an average profit equal to 5% of the factory's output. But over the five years the relative price of bread can change: If it goes up, you will benefit since less bread, and a smaller portion of output, will be needed to pay off the loan. If the relative price of bread goes down, you will lose since a larger portion of output is needed to pay off the loan.

When inflation is low, relative prices are fairly stable. Let us assume that you predict that there is a 50% chance you will need 8% of output to pay off the loan and a 50% chance that you would need 12% of output. So, after the production costs equal to 85% of output, you expect your profit will be between 3% and 7% of output. If the inflation rate is high, relative prices can change a lot. You now predict that you will need between 5% and 15% of output to pay off the loan, and so you expect your profit will be between 0% and 10% of output. Higher inflation, by allowing relative prices to change more, made the project riskier. You may not like the higher risk of the project and decide not to build the factory. We conclude that higher inflation uncertainty increases the riskiness of long-term projects and deters investment.

Benefits of Inflation

So far, we have emphasized the costs of inflation. However, many economists believe that there are some benefits to low inflation because it can allow for adjustments in relative prices in situations where nominal prices adjust slowly. Economists call such prices *sticky prices.*

Inflation Greasing the Wheels of the Labour Market The number of workers a firm employs depends on the real wage: the nominal wage divided by the price level. In a situation where the real wage needs to decrease to restore equilibrium in the labour market, this decrease can happen either by cutting the nominal wage or by keeping the nominal wage constant and letting inflation reduce the real wage.

Workers are often more reluctant to see their nominal wages cut than they are to see their real wages fall as a result of inflation, even when, in the end, the result is the same in real terms. For example, in 2012 the Government of Ontario, facing a large budget deficit, decided to reduce the real spending on teachers' wages. Rather than cutting the nominal wages, it froze nominal wages for two years. Clearly, it was concerned that cutting nominal wages would cause labour strife. With 2% inflation, after two years real wages have fallen by 4%. If, instead, inflation was zero, the same reduction would require cutting nominal wages. Economists sometimes refer to the situation where nominal wages are rigid but inflation allows the reduction of real wages as *inflation greasing the wheels of the labour market*.

There is no agreement among economists on how important "greasing the wheels" is. Compare two situations. In the first, nominal wages are frozen and the inflation rate is 4% per year. In the second, nominal wages decrease by 2% per year and the inflation rate is 2% per year. According to the "greasing the wheels" hypothesis, workers prefer the first situation. But in both cases the real wage falls by 4% per year. Workers who focus on nominal wages rather than on real wages exhibit *money illusion*: they attach importance to nominal values. That goes against the belief of most economists that people are rational and distinguish between nominal and real variables.

Zero Lower Bound During the Great Recession many central banks reduced the short-term nominal interest rates in order to reduce real interest rates and stimulate investment. But there is a limit to reducing the nominal interest rate: it cannot be negative. A negative nominal interest rate means that, if you buy a short-term government bond for $100, you will receive less than $100 when the bond matures. You would not buy such bond since you can put your cash in a safety deposit box or in a government-guaranteed bank account and not lose any of your money. [11] Recall that, by the Fisher equation, the real interest rate is equal to the nominal interest rate minus the inflation rate. With inflation of around 2% central banks were not able to lower the real interest rates below minus 2%. During the Great Recession this was insufficient and they had to resort to unconventional monetary policies that we will discuss in Chapter 12. This problem has become known as *zero lower bound on nominal interest rates*. Some economists argued that, to ameliorate the zero lower bound problem, central banks should target a higher inflation rate, for example 4%. With inflation of 4%, the real interest rate could have been lowered to minus 4%, providing a stronger stimulus for the economy. This suggestion has not been popular. There seems to be an agreement among central banks that the proper goal of monetary policy is an inflation rate of 2% or lower.

In May 2014 the European Central Bank found a novel way of overcoming the problem of zero lower bound and reducing the nominal interest rates below zero. It required banks to deposit a certain portion of their reserves at the ECB, and charged them a percentage fee on their deposits. This was, essentially, a tax on reserves, aimed at inducing banks to increase lending activity.

---

[11]During the Great Recession, nominal interest rates were actually, at times, very slightly negative in Germany, Switzerland, and the United States. Some financial institutions had large amounts of liquid funds (hundreds of millions of dollars) they wanted to put in riskless assets. Converting them for cash and stashing it in a safety deposit box was not practical. Bank accounts were risky since banks could fail and government insurance does not cover large deposits. The only way to safely store the funds was to buy government bonds, even if the nominal interest rate on these bonds was negative.

Hyperinflation and Its Causes

Hyperinflation occurs when the inflation rate is extremely high. At extremely high rates of inflation, the volatility of inflation is also typically high, making it difficult for households and firms to determine relative prices of goods and services, which can result in a severe misallocation of resources. When a country experiences hyperinflation, its currency will eventually cease to function as money, which is what happened in Germany in 1923 and more recently in Zimbabwe.

Prices rise rapidly during a hyperinflation, so households and firms try to minimize how much currency they hold, and firms must pay employees frequently. Employees must spend money quickly or convert it to more stable foreign currencies before prices increase further. Merchants raise prices as fast as possible. The ability of government to collect taxes diminishes significantly during a hyperinflation. Because tax bills typically are fixed in nominal terms, households and firms have an incentive to delay their payments to reduce their real tax burden.

Causes of Hyperinflation

Hyperinflations begin when governments rapidly increase the growth rate of the money supply, and hyperinflations end when governments reverse course and reduce the growth rate of the money supply in a credible manner. Hyperinflations are typically due to persistently large budget deficits. To understand why large budget deficits cause hyperinflations, we first look at the *government's budget constraint*. Governments purchase goods and services, G, and make transfer payments, TR. A government must raise the funds for these expenditures by collecting taxes, T, borrowing by selling more bonds, B, or printing money, M (for simplicity we do not consider interest on debt). So, in any given year

$$G + TR = T + \Delta B + \Delta M.$$

The government's budget deficit is the difference between its expenditure and its tax revenue, T. We can therefore rewrite the above equation with the government's budget deficit on the left side as

$$G + TR - T = \Delta B + \Delta M.$$

A government can finance a budget deficit either by issuing bonds (borrowing) or by printing money. Some governments, however, may have trouble selling bonds because investors believe that the government may not pay them back. If investors will not buy the government's bonds and the government is unable or unwilling to raise taxes or cut spending, the government can finance the budget deficit only by printing money. In these circumstances, to finance a large budget deficit, the growth rate of the money supply will have to increase dramatically, leading to higher inflation.

German Hyperinflation after World War I

At the end of World War I, the German government was unable to find the political support necessary to balance its budget by raising taxes or cutting expenditures. Once inflation began to accelerate, the structure of the tax system made the government's budget deficit worse. Taxes were levied in nominal terms, and there were lags between when the government levied a tax and when it collected the tax revenue. For example consider tax collection in October 1923. Inflation was at its peak and reached almost 29 500% *per month*.[12] Consider someone who earned 1000 papiermarks (the currency of the day) in September 1923 and paid a 30% tax on his earnings in October 1923. The government got 300 papiermarks in October 1923. With inflation of 29 500% the price level was 300.5 times higher in October

---

[12]All numbers in this section are from Steve H. Hanke and Nicholas Krus (2012), "World Hyperinflations," Cato Institute Working Paper, August.

than in September and the 300 papiermarks in tax revenue the government received in October had the same purchasing power as 1 papiermark in September. This revenue was the tax on 1000 papiermarks and so the effective tax rate was 0.1% (1 out of 1000). Clearly, tax revenues could not finance government expenditure. As a result, the government was forced to print money to finance the budget deficit, until eventually it was financing nearly 100% of its expenditures by printing money.

By the time the hyperinflation ended in Germany, the price level was *50 billion* times higher than before the hyperinflation. The inflation rate reached 21% *per day* during October 1923, so prices doubled every four days. A similar hyperinflation today in Canada would cause the price of a pack of gum to increase from $1.50 to nearly $45 000 after one month and $1.5 *billion* in two months. Such rapid increases in the price level made the papiermark essentially worthless.

How do hyperinflations end? Lowering the rate of growth of the money supply is not sufficient. As long as the underlying problem of insufficient government revenues is not solved, households and firms will be concerned that the government may return to printing money. The reforms need to be credible. The government must eliminate the budget deficit and make institutional changes that will prevent it from using the printing press again. In Germany, the hyperinflation ended in November 1923, after the German government made major policy changes. It:

- Established a new central bank in October 1923 called the Rentenbank. It issued a new currency, the Rentenmark, which was worth 1 trillion of the old German marks.
- Limited the ability of the Rentenbank to issue new currency.
- Limited the ability of the Rentenbank to extend loans to the German government.
- Cut the number of its employees by 25% in October 1923 and by another 10% in January 1924.
- Negotiated relief from the reparation payments it was making to France and the United Kingdom as part of the treaty to end World War I.

Just a few months after the establishment of the Rentenbank, the German government stopped borrowing from the central bank, balanced its budget, and the hyperinflation ended.

These steps were enough to bring the hyperinflation to an end—but not before the savings of anyone holding the old German currency had been wiped out. Most middle-income Germans were extremely resentful of this outcome. Many historians believe that the hyperinflation greatly reduced the allegiance of many Germans to the Weimar Republic, the government at that time, and may have helped pave the way for Adolf Hitler and the Nazis to seize power 10 years later.

Hyperinflations around the World

Why do hyperinflations happen? Hanke and Krus[13] provide a comprehensive list of over 50 hyperinflations since the First World War (plus the French hyperinflation in the eighteenth century). The list indicates several reasons: wars, revolutions, and regime changes, the collapse of communism in the 1990s, and fiscal mismanagement in South America.

During wars, revolutions, and regime changes government expenditures are very high because of armed conflict and reconstruction, and revenues fall. (Germany, in addition, had to pay WW1 reparations.) Examples include:

- wars (Greece in 1941, China in 1943, Philippines in 1944) and their aftermath (for example Austria, Germany, and Poland in 1920s)
- revolutions (France in 1795, China and Taiwan in 1947)
- civil wars, coups, and regime changes (the Soviet Union in 1922, Chile 1973, Yugoslavia 1992, Congo 1991, 1993, 1998)

---

[13]Hanke and Krus, 2012, p. 16.

Under the communist form of government, prices were controlled and revenue collection was organized differently than in market economies. In some countries households did not pay income taxes directly. As private property was very limited, most people were employed by state-owned enterprises. Governments received the difference between revenue from sales and costs of production. This difference included what in a market economy would be profits and income tax. When communism ended, government revenues collapsed and price controls ended. Governments resorted to printing money and shopkeepers raised prices, leading to short periods of hyperinflation in many countries.

Many South American governments in 1980s and 1990s ran extensive government programs, resulting in high government expenditures. At the same time tax collection was not well developed and governments had problems raising sufficient revenue. Governments resorted to printing money, resulting in persistent high inflation which, sometimes, would reach hyperinflation levels.

As you can see from this summary, hyperinflations are unusual events. In the past two decades the number of wars and coups declined, former communist countries succeeded in transforming their economies, and many South American countries reduced government spending and improved tax collection so they no longer need to rely on money printing. As a result, the only hyperinflation after 2000 was in Zimbabwe. It was the second highest hyperinflation in history; the record belongs to Hungary where, in July 1946, inflation reached 40 million billion percent per month (four followed by16 zeros) and 207% per day.

Key Terms and Problems

Key Terms

Barter, p. 105
Classical dichotomy, p. 104
Commodity money, p. 106
Desired reserves, p. 115
Fiat money, p. 108
Fisher effect, p. 126
Fisher equation, p. 126
Inflation tax, p. 129
Liquidity of an asset, p. 105
M1+, p. 112

M2+, p. 112
Medium of exchange, p. 109
Menu costs, p. 128
Monetary aggregates, p. 112
Monetary base (or high-powered money), p. 115
Money multiplier, p. 116
Money supply, p. 104
Nominal variables, p. 104
Open market operations, p. 115

Quantity equation (or equation of exchange), p. 118
Quantity theory of money, p. 120
Real variables, p. 104
Seigniorage, p. 108
Shoe-leather costs, p. 128
Store of value, p. 109
Transaction costs, p. 105
Unit of account, p. 111
Velocity of money, p. 118

4.1 ## What Is Money, and Why Do We Need It?
Define money and explain its functions.

Review Questions

1.1 Briefly describe the four functions of money.

1.2 Describe the five characteristics needed for an asset to be used as a medium of exchange. Identify two types of assets that have these five characteristics.

1.3 Explain why the Bank of Canada publishes data on the M2+ monetary aggregate even though currency

and chequing account deposits, which are the most liquid of assets, are already measured in M1+.

Problems and Applications

1.4 Each of the following has been used as money at some time in the past. Briefly discuss how well each fulfills the four functions of money.

a. Gold or silver

MyEconLab Visit **www.myeconlab.com** to complete these exercises online and get instant feedback.

b. Cigarettes

c. Salt

d. First Nations beads

1.5 People living in Yap, an island group in the Pacific, at one time used as money large stone disks known as Rai. These disks can be up to 12 feet in diameter and were made of a stone that is not native to the islands, so they had to be transported by canoe with great difficulty and risk. The stones were valued both due to their scarcity and because of the history of their acquisition.

   a. How well do large stones fulfill the functions of money?

   b. In 1874, a Western immigrant to the islands used ships to transport more stones to Yap. While these stones were larger, they did not have the history of risk and hardship associated with them.

      i. What effect would the introduction of these new stones have on Yap's money supply and on the overall value of stones?

      ii. How does what happened to Yap's money illustrate a central problem of commodity monies?

      iii. How would you expect old stones to be valued relative to new stones? Briefly explain.

1.6 [Related to the Making the Connection on page 107.] In 2012 the New York Fed held 6700 tonnes of gold.

Find the value of the gold at the beginning of 2012 and at the beginning of 2013. (Hint: use www.gold .org/investment/statistics/gold_price_chart/.)

1.7 [**Related to the** Making the Connection **on page 112.**]

After the French Revolution in 1789, France experienced a hyperinflation similar to Zimbabwe's. At one point, the French currency was worth so little that people used it for fuel rather than to purchase goods and services.

   a. What function(s) of money did the French currency fail to fulfill during the hyperinflation?

   b. Eventually, France issued a new currency, backed by gold. Why might the French government have believed that it needed to back the new currency with gold?

1.8 On January 1, 2002, Germany officially adopted the euro as its currency, and the deutsche mark stopped being legal tender. According to an article in the *Wall Street Journal*, many Germans continued using the deutsche mark, and many stores in Germany continued to accept it. Briefly explain how it is possible for a currency to continue to be used when the government that issued it has replaced it with another currency.

Source: Vanessa Fuhrmans, "Who Needs the Euro When You Can Pay with Deutsche Marks?" *Wall Street Journal*, July 18, 2012.

4.2 | **The Bank of Canada and the Money Supply**
Explain how central banks change the money supply.

Review Questions

2.1 Why does the central bank have greater control over the monetary base than over the money supply?

2.2 What three actions by households and firms, banks, or the central bank will cause the value of the money multiplier to decline?

Problems and Applications

2.3 In July 2012, the money supply, as measured by M2+, was approximately $1524 billion. The monetary base was approximately $62 billion.

   a. What was the value of the money multiplier?

   b. Why is the value of the money multiplier typically greater than 1?

Source: Bank of Canada

2.4 As of mid-2014, U.S. and European banks continued to hold large amounts of reserves, leading to concern that potential increases in lending activity could increase the money supply and the inflation rate. Use the money multiplier to explain how a reduction in reserves could lead to an increase in the money supply.

2.5 Consider the following statement: "Only the central bank can print money. Therefore, the central bank has complete control over the money supply." Do you agree with this statement? Briefly explain.

2.6 Briefly explain why the monetary base is often called "high-powered money."

2.7 Suppose that the desired reserve ratio is 13%, and the currency-to-deposit ratio is 2.

   a. What is the value of the money multiplier?

b. If the central bank conducts open market operations and buys $100 million in government bonds from banks, what will happen to the money supply?

c. How would your answer to part (b) change if banks become concerned about the risk involved in making loans and now choose to hold 20% of chequing account deposits as reserves?

4.3 The Quantity Theory of Money and Inflation

Describe the quantity theory of money, and use it to explain the connection between changes in the money supply and the inflation rate.

Review Questions

3.1 What is the difference between the quantity equation and the quantity theory of money?

3.2 Explain why most economists agree that the Bank of Canada determines the inflation rate in the long run.

3.3 How accurate are the quantity theory's predictions of inflation? Briefly explain.

Problems and Applications

3.4 [Related to the Making the Connection on page 123.]

Would you expect that the quantity theory would do a better job of predicting inflation in high-income countries such as Canada and Germany or in less developed countries such as Kenya or Zimbabwe? Briefly explain.

3.5 In 2012, the money supply, M1+, was $668 billion and nominal GDP was $1658 billion.

a. What was the velocity of money measured using M1+?

b. In 2012, the monetary base was $60.4 billion. What was the velocity of money measured using the monetary base?

c. Briefly explain why these measures of velocity are different.

3.6 [Related to Making the Connection on page 123.] Following the stock market crash in 1989, Japan experienced periods *deflation*, or a falling price level. Explain using the quantity theory of money how deflation is possible. Is it necessary for the quantity of money to decline for deflation to occur?

3.7 [Related to Solved Problem 4.1 on page 121.] Assume that the growth rate of real GDP is 3%, the growth rate of velocity is 0%, the rate of growth of the money supply is 4%, and that changes in the rate of growth of the money supply do not affect real GDP.

a. What is the current rate of inflation?

b. What will happen to the inflation rate if the rate of growth of the money supply increases to 7%?

c. What will happen to the inflation rate if the rate of growth of the money supply increases to 7%, and, at the same time, the growth rate of velocity increases to 2%?

4.4 The Relationships among the Growth Rate of Money, Inflation, and the Nominal Interest Rate

Discuss the relationships among the growth rate of money, inflation, and nominal interest rates.

Review Questions

4.1 If the inflation rate turns out to be greater than the expected inflation rate, will the expected real interest rate be higher or lower than the actual real interest rate?

4.2 Explain under what circumstances lenders gain and borrowers lose if the inflation rate differs from the expected inflation rate.

4.3 According to the Fisher effect, what must occur for the nominal interest rate to increase by 5%? To decrease by 5%?

Problems and Applications

4.4 [Related to Solved Problem 4.2 on page 127.] The long-run growth rate of real GDP for Canada is about 3%, and the expected real interest rate on 10 year government bonds has averaged about 2.5%.

MyEconLab Visit **www.myeconlab.com** to complete these exercises online and get instant feedback.

a. If the growth rate of velocity is 0% and the rate of growth of the money supply is 6%, in the long run what is the nominal interest rate?

b. What will happen to the nominal interest rate in the long run if the rate of growth of the money supply falls to 3%?

c. What will happen to the nominal interest rate in the long run if the rate of growth of the money supply falls to 3% and the growth rate of real GDP falls to 2.5%?

4.5 Suppose that the inflation rate turns out to be higher than expected. Is this good news or bad news for investors who bought bonds issued when the inflation rate was expected to be lower? Briefly explain.

4.6 Suppose that inflation has been equal to 3% per year for several years and that the real interest rate that banks require on typical mortgage loans is 2%.

a. What nominal interest rate would banks currently be charging on 30-year home mortgages?

b. Suppose that the Bank of Canada unexpectedly decreases the rate of growth of the money supply by 1%, and this change is expected to be permanent. How are banks likely to change the nominal interest rate they charge on mortgages?

c. What effect is the Bank of Canada's action likely to have on the actual real interest rate that banks receive on mortgages made prior to the increase in the growth rate of the money supply?

4.7 In the summer of 2012, as worries about the possibility of the Spanish government defaulting on its sovereign debt rose, the nominal interest rate on the government's bonds increased sharply.

a. Why did the nominal interest rate increase?

b. Would you expect there to be a difference between the actual real interest rate and the expected real interest rate in this situation?

4.8 During the Great Depression, the price level fell during some years.

a. With a falling price level, what happens to the actual real interest rate? Does your answer depend on what happens to the nominal interest rate? Briefly explain.

b. In contrast, during the 2007–09 financial crisis, nominal interest rates on short-term government bonds were close to zero, and inflation remained positive for most of this period. What was the actual real interest rate on the bonds during this period?

c. Assume that savers expected inflation to be positive. Why would they be willing to hold government bonds with the real interest implied by positive inflation and the nominal interest rate of zero?

4.5 The Costs of Inflation
Explain the costs of a monetary policy that allows inflation to be greater than zero.

Review Questions

5.1 What is seigniorage? In what sense is it an inflation tax?

5.2 Explain how inflation can be costly to an economy, even if it is expected.

5.3 It is often said that inflation "greases the wheels of the labour market." Explain what this statement means.

Problems and Applications

5.4 Some central banks set an explicit inflation target, essentially committing themselves to keeping inflation within a certain range. How might an explicit inflation target affect the expected inflation rate?

5.5 Forty years ago, it was typical for grocery stores to post prices by labelling each individual can or box. When prices changed, an employee would have to relabel every item in the store so that the cashier could enter them correctly into the cash register. (Bar code scanners had not yet been invented.) Today, most prices are posted on shelf labels and scanned into cash registers using bar codes.

a. How has this change to pricing items in stores affected menu costs?

b. Are menu costs the same for all grocery store items? Briefly explain.

5.6 Suppose that consumer preferences are changing, so that more consumers want to buy chicken and fish and fewer want to buy beef and pork.

a. If inflation is low and fully anticipated, how would you expect the relative price of these goods to change, and how would that affect production of these goods?

b. Suppose now that inflation is volatile, so that it is difficult to tell the difference between an increase in the price of an individual good and an increase in the overall price level. How might volatile inflation lead to a misallocation of resources?

5.7 From 1939 until the early 1960s, the price of nearly all comic books was $0.10. In the late 1960s and early 1970s, as the inflation rate increased significantly, comic book publishers frequently increased their prices. Often, though, they would first sell comics at the higher price in only a few cities, selling at the old price elsewhere. Briefly explain why publishers would have expected that this strategy would increase their profits.

5.8 The idea of shoe-leather costs is that people wear out their shoes going back and forth to the bank. While people are unlikely to actually wear out their shoes in this way, what are some examples of actual costs that you might incur by trying to reduce the costs to you of inflation?

4.6 Hyperinflation and Its Causes
Explain the causes of hyperinflation.

Review Questions

6.1 What is hyperinflation, and why does it occur?

6.2 Why would a government risk experiencing hyperinflation by printing money rather than issuing bonds to finance a large budget deficit?

Problems and Applications

6.3 While hyperinflations are always caused by rapid growth in the money supply, they can be intensified by the actions of households and firms trying to protect themselves from inflation by spending money as soon as they receive it.

a. What is likely to happen to the velocity of money during a hyperinflation?

b. Use the quantity equation to show how the change in velocity affects the inflation rate.

6.4 Hyperinflation reduces economic growth, both through resource misallocation and by reducing saving and investment.

a. Why does hyperinflation cause misallocation of resources?

b. Why does hyperinflation reduce saving and investment?

c. What effects do the misallocation of resources and reduced saving and investment have on economic growth?

6.5 Hyperinflation occurred in U.S. South during the Civil War (1861–65). Unable to tax effectively in a largely agricultural economy, the Confederate government was forced to print money.

a. Explain how the rapid increase in the money supply combined with wartime scarcity of goods would cause prices to escalate.

b. In 1864, the Confederate government attempted to reduce inflation by reducing the money supply by approximately one-third. The Confederacy forced paper currency to be converted into bonds by a specific date (or converted at a penalty after that date). What do you expect the immediate effect of this policy would have been?

6.6 [Related to the Chapter Opener on page 102.]

The following table shows the approximate *daily* rates of inflation from some of the notable hyperinflation episodes in history:

Country	Month with Highest Inflation Rate	Daily Inflation Rate
Hungary	July 1946	207%
Zimbabwe	November 2008	98%
Germany	October 1923	20.9%
France	August 1796	4.77%
Russia	January 1992	4.22%
Argentina	July 1989	3.69%

For each of the hyperinflations shown in the table, calculate the amount of time it would take for prices to double. (Hint: Because these are daily rates, in some cases, prices will double in a matter of hours.)

A simple way of calculating the approximate amount of time it will take prices to double is to divide 70 by the growth rate; this is called the Rule of 70. It is an approximate formula; the higher is the inflation, the worse is the approximation. You can use it for the last three countries without a problem; for Germany it is only a rough approximation. For Zimbabwe and for Hungary you need to do the direct calculation.

Source: Steve H. Hanke and Nicholas Krus, "World Hyperinflations," *Cato Working Paper*, August 2012.

6.7 **[Related to the** Chapter Opener **on page 102.]** By the end of 2008, Zimbabwe was experiencing inflation that was estimated to be 80 billion percent per month. The peak daily inflation rate was 98% per day. Because of the rapidly falling value of paper money, the government was forced to issue currency in larger and larger denominations, including a $50 billion dollar note. (The highest denomination note was $100 trillion. You can buy it now on eBay for around $15). An economist in Zimbabwe was quoted as saying, "It is a waste of resources to print Zimbabwe dollar notes now. Who accepts a currency that loses value by almost 100 percent daily?"

a. The government of Zimbabwe authorized many stores to make transactions in foreign currencies. What difficulties would this cause stores and consumers?

b. If inflation is 98% per day, how much value does the currency lose in a day?

Source: "Zimbabwe Introduces $50 Billion Note," CNN.com, January 10, 2009.

Data Exercises

D4.1: Using data from Statistics Canada (www5.statcan.gc.ca/CANSIM/), Table 176-0025, analyze the money supply.

a. Download and graph monthly data for M1+ gross and M2+ gross for the period from 1990 to the present (use the add/remove data button). Calculate the growth rate as the percentage change from the same month in the previous year. Describe the relationship between the two measures of the money supply. Which is more volatile?

b. In general, what happens to M1+ and M2+ as the monetary base increases?

c. Is the relationship that you found in part (a) different after 2009?

D4.2: **[Related to the** Chapter Opener **on page 102].** Steve Hanke at the Cato Institute (www.cato.org/zimbabwe) has calculated a hyperinflation index for Zimbabwe and other countries suffering from hyperinflations.

a. Where does Zimbabwe rank in Hanke's index? How long did it take for prices to double at the peak of the hyperinflation?

b. Search media sources to find out what the current state of Zimbabwe's economy is. How did the government get to this point?

D4.3: The World Bank (www.worldbank.org) has data on money growth rates and inflation for different countries. These data are listed under "Money and Quasi-Money" growth, which is roughly the same as M2+ in Canada. Choose 10 countries to analyze.

a. Which countries have the most rapid rates of money growth? The slowest?

b. Compare the data on rate of money growth with the growth rate of consumer prices. Are the data consistent or inconsistent with the quantity theory?

D4.4: [Spreadsheet exercise] Use data from the World Bank (www.worldbank.org) to do the following:

a. Find the correlation coefficient for M2 growth and consumer price growth for each country in the group of 10 high-income countries.

b. Find the correlation coefficient for each country in the group of 10 low-income countries.

c. Now find the correlation coefficient for the entire group of twenty countries.

d. If you have had a statistics class covering regression analysis, run a regression using money growth as the independent variable and the average price growth as the dependent variable. Explain your results.

D4.5: Using data from Statistics Canada (www5.statcan.gc.ca/CANSIM/), Table 176-0025, analyze the money supply.

a. Find data for the M1+ (gross) and the M2+ (gross) from 1990 to the present.

b. Using the data found above, calculate M1+ as a proportion of M2+ for each of the years.

c. Explain whether this proportion has increased, decreased, or remained the same over time.

D4.6: Using data from Statistics Canada (www5.statcan.gc.ca/CANSIM/), Table 176-0025, analyze the relationship between the monetary base and the wider aggregates, M1+ and M2+.

a. Find data for the monetary base (*MB*), M1+ (gross) and the M2+ (gross) from 1990 to the present.

b. Calculate the ratios *MB*/M1+ and *MB*/M2+ and show them on a graph.

c. Was there any trend in the ratio of monetary base to wider aggregates?

d. What does the trend imply about the multiplier?

The Global Financial System and Exchange Rates

Why Are Prices Higher in Canada than in the United States?

The increase in the value of the Canadian dollar to parity with the U.S. dollar in 2007 and 2009 led to complaints that prices in Canada are higher than in the U.S. In particular, buyers of books complained loudly about high book prices in Canada. Unlike for most products, both the Canadian and U.S. prices are often printed on the cover, making price comparisons straightforward. One Canadian found an interesting solution: "Retired police officer Boyd Berman, of Brampton, was so enraged by the gap in book prices he brought in U.S. dollars and insisted on paying the U.S. price. The bookseller eventually agreed, he said." A *Toronto Star* article reported, in 2011, a study by BMO Nesbitt Burns Inc., which compared prices of several goods and found them to be around 20% higher on the average in Canada. For example, an iPod touch (8GB) cost $249.99 in Canada and $204.99 in the United States when the exchange rate was US$1.02 for Can$1, so that its U.S. price in Canadian dollars was $209.09. Price differences are not restricted to Canada versus the United States. It is a common complaint in the United Kingdom that tech goods are more expensive there than in the United States.

There are several reasons why Canadian prices are higher. Many firms price to market, varying markups across markets. The U.S. market is, in general, more competitive than markets in other countries, and so lower prices in the United States are not surprising. Retailers in Canada point to higher distribution and labour costs as well as tariffs and duties. As a large and sparsely populated country, Canada has high distribution costs. Minimum wages are higher, raising retailer costs. For some products,

Continued on next page

import tariffs and duties are higher in Canada. Perhaps more importantly, prices of goods are relatively stable, and when the Canadian dollar increases in value firms do not respond immediately by lowering Canadian dollar prices. Economists often analyze *exchange rate pass through*: the percentage change in prices of imported goods resulting from a 1% change in the exchange rate. Recent studies suggest that the pass through has been declining over time. The reason is greater competition among retailers. A change in the exchange rate affects the cost of imported goods. When the Canadian dollar falls (depreciates), the cost of imported goods increases but retailers reduce margins rather than raise prices in proportion to the change in the exchange rate. Similarly when the Canadian dollar rises (appreciates), retailers increase margins rather than reduce prices. The pass through has been declining over

time due to a slow shift toward more differentiated products, for which prices are less sensitive to costs.

Because of slow pass through, retail prices in Canada are lower than in the United States when the Canadian dollar is weak, and higher than in the United States when the Canadian dollar is strong. Between 2002 and 2007 the Canadian dollar appreciated from US$0.62 to parity, an appreciation of 60%. Even such a large appreciation takes time to be reflected in retail prices. Initially, firms may consider the appreciation to be temporary and refrain from reducing Canadian prices to avoid the need to increase them if the Canadian dollar reverses trend. It is comforting to Canadian consumers to know that prices tend to become more equal. In September 2013, the cheapest iPod touch (16GB) cost US$229 in the United States and Can$229 in Canada.

Sources: Dana Flavelle, "Why Are We Paying 20% More than Americans for the Same Goods?," *The Toronto Star*, April 14, 2011; Doug Porter, "Raging Loonie: What It Can and Can Not Do," BMO Capital Markets, April 14, 2011; Jeannine Bailliu, Wei Dong, and John Murray, "Has Exchange Rate Pass-Through Really Declined? Some Recent Insights from the Literature," *Bank of Canada Review*, Autumn 2010, pp. 1–8; "Who, What, Why: Are Tech Goods Cheaper in the United States than the UK?" BBC News, June 12, 2013.

Introduction

One of the most important economic developments of the past 40 years is that countries have become more connected through increased trade and increased investment. International trade has become increasingly important to most countries, including Canada. In addition, firms and governments now have a much greater ability to borrow from investors in other countries, and investors have the ability to spread their investments across bonds and other securities issued in many countries.

We begin our discussion of the global financial system with the balance of payments, which shows the links between the Canadian economy and foreign economies. We analyze both the current account, which records foreign trade, factor income, and transfers, and the financial account, which records asset purchases. In Section 5.2 we discuss exchange rates and exchange rate regimes: fixed, flexible, and managed exchange rates. We summarize their advantages and disadvantages. In Section 5.3 we describe factors affecting exchange rates. In the last section we consider the loanable funds model and the effects of changes in saving and investment in the presence of international capital markets. The chapter concludes with the analysis of a simple model that we use to analyze international capital markets.

5.1

Learning Objective

Explain how to calculate the balance of payments.

The Balance of Payments

Every household and every firm in Canada participates in the global economy. For example, many of the parts included in BlackBerry's phones are made outside of Canada, and some of the phones are assembled abroad. A local restaurant may seem to be far removed from the global economy, but it is likely to serve wine from France and fruits and vegetables grown in Latin American countries, and it probably uses tables, chairs, and plates manufactured in China or elsewhere.

When Chinese firms export goods to Canada, they usually receive Canadian dollars in exchange (sometimes the parties to the transaction agree to a payment in a third currency, most often the U.S. dollar). The Chinese recipients of these dollars have to do something with them. They can use the dollars to purchase Canadian goods and services, purchase Canadian financial assets such as stock or bonds, exchange them for other currencies, or simply hold on to the dollars. This flow of goods, services, currencies, and financial investments also occurs between many other countries.

Most people do not have trouble understanding the significance of data on the unemployment and inflation rates or on the growth rate of GDP. But data on the international economy are more difficult to understand. What does it mean if Canada runs a trade deficit? Is it always bad news? What is a current-account deficit? In this section, we explain how to measure the trade and financial flows among countries.

Consumers, firms, and investors in one country routinely interact with consumers, firms, and investors in other countries. A consumer in Canada may use a keyboard assembled in China; a consumer in Indonesia may use a BlackBerry cellphone designed by Black-Berry in Canada and produced in China; and a consumer in France may watch a television made in South Korea and wear a sweater made in Italy. A book publisher may hire a firm in India to set and print its books. A British financial firm may buy Canadian bonds on behalf of a Chilean pension fund. Nearly all economies are *open economies* and have extensive interactions in trade or finance with other countries. In an **open economy**, households, firms, and governments borrow, lend, and trade internationally. In a **closed economy**, households, firms, and governments do not borrow, lend, or trade internationally.

There are different ways to measure how open an economy is. One way is to measure the sum of exports and imports relative to GDP, as shown in Figure 5.1. Panel (a) shows the ratio

Open economy An economy in which households, firms, and governments borrow, lend, and trade internationally.

Closed economy An economy in which households, firms, and governments do not borrow, lend, or trade internationally.

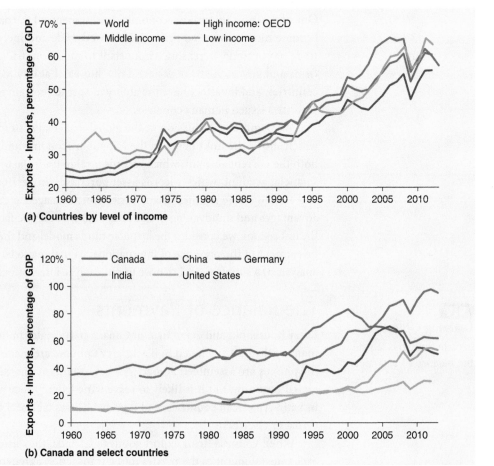

Figure 5.1

Trade as a Percentage of GDP, 1960–2013

Global trade has been growing in importance since 1960. Exports plus imports rose from 25% of world GDP in 1960 to 60% of world GDP in 2012. Exports plus imports are generally a greater percentage for smaller economies like Canada and a smaller percentage of GDP for large economies such as the United States.

Source: World Bank, *World Development Indicators.*

(a) Countries by level of income

(b) Canada and select countries

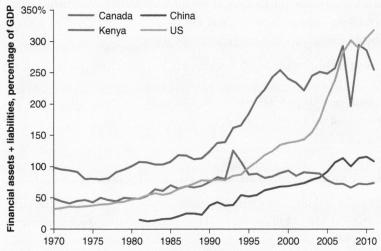

Figure 5.2

Financial Links as a Percentage of GDP, 1970–2011

Financial links among countries have increased substantially since 1970, particularly in high-income countries, such as Canada and the United States. The increase in financial links has been smaller in low-income countries, such as Kenya, that have been experiencing slow economic growth.

Note: Data for China are only available beginning in 1981.

Source: Philip R. Lane and Gian Maria Milesi-Ferretti, "The External Wealth of Nations Mark II: Revised and Extended Estimates of Foreign Assets and Liabilities, 1970–2004," *Journal of International Economics*, 73, November 2007, pp. 223–50, updated and extended version of dataset constructed, available at www.philiplane.org/ewn.html.

of the sum of exports and imports to GDP for the world and for countries classified into high, middle and low income. The ratio increased from around 25% of world GDP in 1960 to around 60% in 2012. The ratio does not seem to depend on income level: it is similar for low, middle, and high-income countries.[1] Figure 5.1 panel (a) shows the severe effect of the Great Recession on world trade: It reduced trade for all income levels. In panel (b) you can see the ratio for Canada and other countries. In Canada, the ratio was increasing until 2000 and fell afterwards. For China and India, as well as for Germany, it increased faster than for Canada and the United States. Of the countries shown in panel (b), China suffered the greatest decline in trade during the Great Recession. In general, the ratio of exports plus imports to GDP is lower for large countries but China is an exception, with a similar ratio to Canada.

In addition to international trade in goods and services, there are significant flows of financial assets, such as stocks and bonds, among countries. By being more open to financial flows, countries typically increase their opportunities for economic growth. Firms can borrow funds from investors in other countries, and investors have the opportunity to receive higher returns than if they were able to invest only in their own country. One measure of economic openness to financial flows is the sum of external financial assets and financial liabilities as a percentage of GDP. For most countries, this measure of openness to financial flows has increased significantly over the past 40 years. This is illustrated in Figure 5.2, which shows the sum of financial assets and liabilities as a percentage of GDP for several countries. Note that the increase in this measure has been particularly large for high-income countries, such as Canada and the United States. The increase has also been large for developing countries that have achieved rapid economic growth, such as China. Low-income countries, such as Kenya, where economic growth has been slow, have typically not experienced as large an increase in financial flows.

Just as economists have a system of accounting for measuring economic activity within a country, they also have a system of accounting for measuring economic interactions among

---

[1]Of course there are big differences between countries. For example, in 2012 the ratio of exports to imports varied between 27% for Brazil and 450% in Hong Kong. Exports and imports can exceed 100% of GDP since, when exports involve imported components, the entire value of is included in foreign trade but only the value added is included in GDP.

Balance of payments A record of a country's trade with other countries in goods, services, and assets.

Current account The part of the balance of payments that records a country's net exports, net factor payments, and net transfers.

Financial account The part of the balance of payments that records purchases of assets a country has made abroad and foreign purchases of assets in the country.

countries. Economists call this system the **balance of payments**, which is a record of a country's trade with other countries in goods, services, and assets.

As Table 5.1 illustrates, the balance of payments has two parts:

1. The **current account** records a country's net exports, net factor payments, and net transfers.
2. The **financial account** records purchases of assets a country has made abroad and foreign purchases of assets in the country.

The Current Account

The current account in the balance of payments records the following three items:

1. *Net exports*, which is the difference between exports and imports of goods and services. In 2013, Canada exported $565.7 billion worth of goods and services to other countries and imported $597.6 billion worth of goods and services from other countries—see Table 5.1. As a result, net exports were −$31.9 billion, which means that Canada ran a *trade deficit* of $31.9 billion. Until the Great Recession, Canada usually had a trade surplus; since 2009, Canada has had a trade deficit.
2. *Net factor payments*, which are the income Canadian firms and households receive from investments and employment in other countries, minus the income foreign firms and households receive from investments and employment in Canada. Many Canadian firms have subsidiaries abroad, and many foreign firms have Canadian subsidiaries. When subsidiaries of Canadian firms abroad (for example TD Bank in the United States) earn a profit or pay dividends, income flows from other countries to Canada. Conversely, when subsidiaries of foreign firms in Canada (for example Toyota Canada) earn a profit or pay dividends, income flows from Canada to other countries. Net factor payments also include employment income of Canadians abroad minus employment income of foreigners in Canada. In 2013 net factor payments were −$25.9 billion. This means that foreign factor income in Canada exceeded Canadian factor income abroad by $25.9 billion.

Table 5.1 Balance of Payments, 2013 (billions of Canadian dollars)

Current Account		
Exports of goods and services		565.7
Imports of goods and services		597.6
Net exports	−31.9	
Investment and employment income received		71.9
Investment and employment income paid		97.9
Net factor payments	25.9	
Net transfers	−2.9	
Current account	**−60.7**	
Financial account		
Increase in foreign holdings of Canadian assets		124.3
Increase in Canadian holdings of foreign assets		−65.9
Financial account	**58.3**	
Statistical discrepancy	**2.4**	

Source: Statistics Canada, CANSIM II Tables 376–0101 and 376–0102

This is the usual situation: As a large country with relatively small population, Canada imported a lot of capital in the past, and so profits of foreign companies in Canada exceed profits of Canadian companies abroad.

3. *Transfers*, which are the difference between transfer payments made by Canadian residents to residents of other countries and the transfer payments residents of other countries make to residents of Canada, including government transfers. For example, donations by Canadian residents to the victims of the 2010 earthquake in Haiti would count as transfers from Canada abroad. Typically, transfer payments are a small component of the current account.

If the current-account balance is negative, the country runs a *current-account deficit*. A current-account deficit indicates that a country is consuming more than its current income, which can happen only if the country borrows from residents of other countries or sells assets to them. A current-account surplus indicates that a country is consuming less than its current income, so it must be lending to the rest of the world or buying assets from the rest of the world. As you can see from Table 5.1, in 2013 Canada ran a current-account deficit of $60.7 billion. This means that the current-account transactions resulted in a net outflow of funds. An outflow of funds is the result of import of goods as well as factor payments and transfers to foreigners. The inflow of funds is the result of export of goods as well as factor payments and transfers received from foreigners.

The Financial Account

The financial account records the flow of funds into and out of a country. There is a *capital outflow* from Canada when a Canadian firm builds a factory in another country or when a Canadian investor purchases financial assets, such as bonds, of foreign firms or governments. For example, if Barrick Gold builds a mine in Peru or if Canadian households use their retirement accounts to purchase Peruvian stocks and bonds, there is a capital outflow from Canada to Peru. Conversely, there is a *capital inflow* into Canada when a foreign firm builds a factory in Canada or when a foreign investor purchases financial assets in Canada. For example, when Toyota builds a factory in Ontario, there is a financial inflow into Canada. In 2013 the capital inflow was $124.3 billion and the capital outflow was $65.9 billion so the financial account had a surplus equal to $58.3 billion = $124.3 billion − $65.9 billion.[2] The positive balance of the financial account means that financial account transactions resulted in a net inflow of funds into Canada.

Notice that we are using the word *capital* to refer not only to physical capital goods, such as factories, but also to financial assets, such as stocks and bonds. When firms build factories or buy physical capital goods in foreign countries, they are engaging in **foreign direct investment**. When investors buy stocks or bonds issued in another country, they are engaging in **foreign portfolio investment**.

Foreign direct investment Investment into production or firms by foreigners, either by setting up or expanding firms or by purchasing companies.

Foreign portfolio investment The purchase of financial assets, such as stocks or bonds, by foreigners.

The sum of the current account and the financial account is zero. To understand this, imagine that the only transaction is the export of a product to Chile, worth $1. Imports, factor payments, and transfers are all zero. So there is a current-account surplus of $1. The Canadian exporter receives Chilean pesos worth $1 that he can lend abroad to earn a return. This is a capital outflow of $1 and a financial account of −$1 so that the sum of the current and financial accounts is zero.

In practice not all transactions are correctly recorded and the sum of the current and financial accounts differs from zero by an item called *the statistical discrepancy*. In 2003, the

---

[2]The value of inflows minus outflows ($124.3 billion − $65.9 billion = $58.4 billion) differs from the financial account balance ($58.3 billion) because of rounding.

sum of current account (−$60.7 billion), and the capital account ($58.3 billion) was −$2.4 billion so that the statistical discrepancy was $2.4 billion. In our discussion we omitted the third component of the balance of payments: the capital account. The capital account records generally minor transactions such as (1) migrants' transfers, which consist of goods and financial assets people take with them when they enter or leave the country, and (2) sales and purchases of non-produced, non-financial assets, which include copyright, patents, trademarks, or rights to natural resources. The definitions of the financial account and the capital account are sometimes misunderstood because, prior to 1999, the capital account recorded all the transactions included now in both the financial account and the capital account. In other words, capital account transactions went from being a very important part of the balance of payments to being a relatively unimportant part. Because the balance on what is now called the capital account is very small (in 2013 Canada had a deficit of $53 million), for simplicity we ignored it in Table 5.1 and the remainder of the chapter.

Exchange Rates and Exchange Rate Policy

5.2

Learning Objective

Understand the advantages and disadvantages of different exchange rate policies.

A firm that operates entirely within Canada, such as a local restaurant or hardware store, will price its products in Canadian dollars and will use Canadian dollars to pay its suppliers' invoices, wages and salaries to its workers, interest to its bondholders, and dividends to its shareholders. A multinational corporation such as Bombardier, in contrast, may sell its products in many different countries and receive payments in many different currencies. Its suppliers and workers may also be spread around the world and may have to be paid in local currencies. Corporations may also use the international financial system to borrow in a foreign currency. For example, in 2012, many Brazilian firms received large loans from foreign banks or sold bonds to foreign investors. Many of these loans and bonds were denominated in U.S. dollars. When firms make extensive use of foreign currencies, they must deal with fluctuations in the exchange rate.

In this section, we explore exchange rates, how they affect imports and exports, and the exchange rate policies of different countries.

Nominal Exchange Rates

Nominal exchange rate
The price of one country's currency in terms of another country's currency.

The **nominal exchange rate** (also called simply the exchange rate) is the price of one currency in terms of another country's currency. By convention, we typically express the nominal exchange rate as units of foreign currency per unit of domestic currency, as in 80 Japanese yen per Canadian dollar. This means that the price of one Canadian dollar is 80 yen. In Japan, of course, we would express the exchange rate as the price of a yen in Canadian dollars, as in $0.0125 per yen, which means that the price of one yen is 0.0125 Canadian dollars.

Avoiding a Common Mistake: How the Exchange Rate Is Defined

Perhaps more accurately, this box should be titled "Avoiding a Common Confusion." There are two ways of defining the exchange rate: 1. as the price of domestic currency in terms of foreign currency and 2. as a price of foreign currency in terms of domestic currency. Their use is often inconsistent. For example, in a newspaper the exchange rate of the Canadian dollar may be quoted as follows: Yen: 80; Euro: 1.25. The first is the price of the Canadian dollar in yen, but the second is the price of one euro in Canadian dollars.

More confusing is the fact that you may have used the second definition of the exchange rate in an earlier course. In this book we use the first definition: The exchange of the Canadian dollar in terms of a foreign currency is the price of the Canadian dollar in the foreign currency. So the exchange rate of the Canadian dollar in terms of the euro is 0.8: It costs 0.8 euro to buy one Canadian dollar. The advantage of the definition we use is that, when the Canadian dollar becomes more valuable, its exchange rate increases.

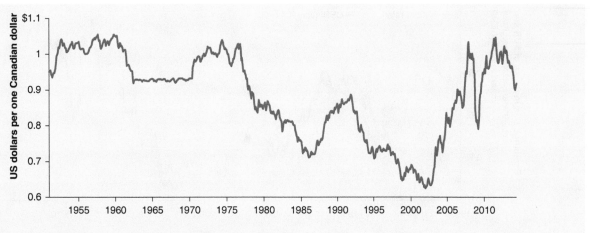

Figure 5.3 The Canadian Dollar Spot Exchange Rate against the U.S. Dollar, 1951–2014

Over the past 60 years the exchange rate fluctuated widely, between 0.625 (January 2002) and 1.055 (October 1959).

Source: Statistics Canada, CANSIM Table 176-0064

An immediate exchange of one currency for another currency is carried out at the current exchange rate, or **spot exchange rate**. Figure 5.3 shows the exchange rate of the Canadian dollar in terms of the U.S. dollar since 1951. The exchange rate fluctuated widely. Until 1961 Canada maintained flexible exchange rates. From 1952 to 1961 the Canadian dollar traded above *parity* (i.e., it cost more than the U.S. dollar). A dispute between monetary and fiscal authorities in 1961 led to a rapid **currency depreciation,** that is, a decrease in the value of the Canadian dollar. The exchange rate was fixed between May 1962 and June 1970 at the level of 0.925, plus or minus 1%.[3] You can see this period clearly in Figure 5.3. After the return to a flexible exchange rate, the Canadian dollar experienced rapid **currency appreciation**, that is, an increase in its value, and remained near parity for the next five years. From 1976 until 2002, except for the period 1986–91, the Canadian dollar depreciated, reaching the lowest-ever level of 0.625 in January 2002. The Canadian dollar then slowly returned to parity with the U.S. dollar (in October 2007). It remained near parity except for the Great Recession, when, as we discussed in Chapter 1, the flight to quality led to appreciation of the U.S. dollar and depreciation of the Canadian dollar. In the second half of 2013 the Canadian dollar started depreciating again and, at the time of writing, the exchange rate in terms of the U.S. dollar was around 0.9.

The exchange rate used to exchange currencies in the future is called a **forward exchange rate**. There are two types of contracts involving exchanging currencies in the future: *forward exchange contracts* and *future exchange contracts*. Forward contracts are usually negotiated between two financial firms—typically, commercial banks. For example, CIBC might agree today with Deutsche Bank that in 90 days, they will exchange $100 million for euros, at an exchange rate of $1 = 0.75 euro. Unlike forward contracts, futures contracts are financial products which, like stocks and bonds, are publicly traded on financial exchanges, such as the Chicago Board of Trade or the New York Mercantile Exchange. The details of futures contracts, such as the amounts of currency involved per contract and the dates on which the contract will expire, are established by the exchange.

Spot exchange rate The current price of one country's currency for another currency, for immediate exchange.

Currency depreciation A decrease in the market value of one country's currency relative to another country's currency, when the exchange rate is flexible.

Currency appreciation An increase in the market value of one country's currency relative to another country's currency when the exchange rate is flexible.

Forward exchange rate The exchange rate used to exchange currencies in the future.

[3]More details are in the e-book *A History of the Canadian Dollar* by James Powell, available at the Bank of Canada website: http://www.bankofcanada.ca/2005/12/a-history-of-the-canadian-dollar-by-james-powell/

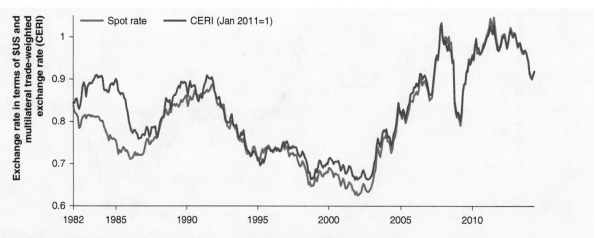

Figure 5.4 The Multilateral, Trade-Weighted Exchange Rate of the Canadian Dollar against Six Largest Trading Partners (CERI) and the Bilateral Exchange Rate against the U.S. dollar 1982–2014

The multilateral exchange rate of the Canadian dollar follows closely the exchange rate against the U.S. dollar, since the United States is our biggest trading partner by far and the U.S. dollar has a weight of 0.76 in the CERI index. To make the data comparable in the graph, the value of CERI in January 2011 has been set equal to 1.

Source: Statistics Canada, CANSIM Table 176-0064

The existence of forward contracts and futures contracts allows firms to *hedge* against exchange rate fluctuation. Hedging involves entering in contracts designed to reduce the risk of a loss. For example, Brazilian private jet maker Embraer may suffer losses if the value of the Brazilian currency, the real, increases against the euro. Suppose, for example, that Embraer has sold a jet to Air France for €50 million, which the French firm will pay in six months, when the plane is delivered. Embraer faces the risk, known as *exchange rate risk*, that in the six months between when it sells the plane and when it receives the payment, the value of the real will rise against the euro. If the value of the real rises, Embraer will receive fewer reals in exchange for the €50 million payment made by Air France. By entering into a forward contract at the time it sells the jet, Embraer can fix the exchange rate at which it will exchange euros for reals in six months, thereby reducing its exchange rate risk. Typically, firms do not buy and sell forward contracts themselves; instead, they rely on banks to provide them with this service.

Multilateral exchange rate An index in which the value of the currency is measured against the average of the country's main trading partners.

Each currency has a spot exchange rate versus every other individual currency, sometimes called a *bilateral exchange rate*. Economists and policymakers also find it useful to look at a country's **multilateral exchange rate**, an index in which the value of the currency is measured against the average of the country's main trading partners, with the weights equal to the partners' share of foreign trade. Figure 5.4 shows the multilateral exchange rate of the Canadian dollar (called the Canadian Dollar Effective Exchange Rate Index, CERI) as well as the exchange rate in terms of the U.S. dollar. CERI measures the value of the Canadian dollar against a basket of currencies of our six biggest trading partners, As you can see, CERI and the U.S. dollar exchange rate move very closely together. This is because the U.S. dollar has a weight of just over 75% in the CERI index, reflecting the importance of United States in Canadian foreign trade.[4]

Real Exchange Rates

The nominal exchange rate tells us how much foreign currency we can receive in exchange for one unit of domestic currency—such as how many Brazilian reals we receive for one

---

[4]The currencies and their weights are United States dollar: 0.7618; Euro: 0.0931; Japanese yen: 0.0527; Chinese yuan: 0.0329; Mexican peso: 0.0324; U.K. pound: 0.0271. The weights are based on 1999–2001 trade data. See www.bankofcanada.ca/rates/exchange/ceri/.

Canadian dollar. The nominal exchange rate is important for financial transactions, where the goal is to earn a return, or hedge a payment. The **real exchange rate** is the rate at which goods and services in one country can be exchanged for goods and services in another country. The real exchange rate is important for trade in goods and services. Just as real GDP gives a better measure of the growth of an economy than does nominal GDP, the real exchange rate gives a better measure of prices of Canadian goods relative to the prices of foreign goods than does the nominal exchange rate. So when economists and policymakers want to gauge the effect of a change in exchange rates on Canadian exports and imports, they rely on the real exchange rate rather than on the nominal exchange rate.

Real exchange rate The rate at which goods and services in one country can be exchanged for goods and services in another country.

Measuring the Real Exchange Rate with a Single Good: The McDonald's Big Mac Index We can use the McDonald's Big Mac to illustrate calculating the real exchange rate. The real exchange rate in terms of Big Macs is the number of Big Macs we can receive in the United States in exchange for what we would pay for one Big Mac in Canada. The *Economist* magazine keeps track of the prices of Big Macs around the world. In July 2013, the *Economist* reported that the price of a Big Mac was $5.53 Canadian dollars in Canada and US$4.56 in the United States. At that time, the nominal exchange rate was US$0.952 for one Canadian dollar. We can carry out this calculation in two steps:

We use the nominal exchange rate to convert the price of a Big Mac in Canada into U.S. dollars:

$$(US\$0.952/Can\$1.00) \times Can\$5.53 = US\$5.27.$$

Then we divide the result by the price of a Big Mac in the United States:

$$Real\ exchange\ rate = \frac{(US\$0.952/Can\$1.00) \times Can\$5.53}{US\$4.56} = \frac{US\$5.27}{US\$4.56} = 1.155.$$

So the real exchange rate = 1.155 Big Macs in the United States per Big Mac in Canada. Note that the real exchange rate is in terms of goods rather than in terms of currency.

Measuring the Real Exchange Rate Using Price Levels Of course we do not measure the real exchange rate in terms of the price of a single good, such as the Big Mac. We measure the real exchange rate in terms of average prices, or the price level, in each country. Recall that we can measure the price level by using a price index, such as the Consumer Price Index or the GDP deflator. If we let E stand for the nominal exchange rate, e stand for the real exchange rate, P stand for the domestic price level, and P^* stand for the foreign price level, we have the following general expression for the real exchange rate:

$$e = E\frac{P}{P^*}. \tag{5.1}$$

For example, if the real exchange rate between the Canadian dollar and the U.S. dollar were 1.15, then this value would indicate that, on the average, prices in Canada are 15% higher than in the U.S.

Equation (5.1) shows that the real exchange rate can change for any of three reasons: when the nominal exchange rate changes, when the domestic price level changes, and when the foreign price level changes. Usually, the real exchange rate changes when the nominal exchange rate changes, since price levels change slowly over time. Figure 5.5 shows movements in the real exchange rate of the Canadian dollar against the U.S. dollar, over the period 1951–2013. As you can see, movements in the real exchange rate are mostly due to changes in the nominal exchange rate.

Changes in the Real and in the Nominal Exchange Rate It is important not to confuse the real and the nominal exchange rates. Real means *in terms of goods and services*. If the real

Figure 5.5

The Real Exchange Rate and the Nominal Exchange Rate against the U.S. Dollar, 1951–2013 (2005=1)

Changes in the real exchange rate follow changes in the nominal exchange rate closely since prices adjust slowly over time.

Sources: Statistics Canada, CANSIM Tables 176-0064, 326-0020 and U.S. Department of Labor

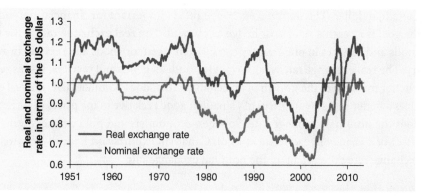

exchange rate is 1.2, it means that, for a given amount of money you can (after exchanging currency) get 20% more goods and services in the foreign country. Nominal means in terms of money. If the nominal exchange rate is 1.2, it means that if you exchange a $100 note, you will get the amount of 120 in the foreign currency. The confusion may come from the fact that, as you can see in Figure 5.5, changes in the real exchange rate closely follow changes in the nominal exchange rate. This is because the ratio of Canadian to U.S. prices has been relatively stable.

What is the significance of the real exchange equal to one, marked with a solid line in Figure 5.5? The real exchange rate tells you how much of goods and services abroad you can buy for one unit in Canada. When the real exchange rate is equal to one, the price levels in Canada and abroad (taking into account the exchange rate) are equal. This means that a bundle of goods and services in Canada can buy one bundle abroad. When the real exchange rate is greater than one, goods and services in Canada are, on the average, more expensive, and when the real exchange rate is less than one, goods and services in Canada are, on the average, cheaper. As you can see in Figure 5.5, between 1993 and 2005 goods and services in Canada were cheaper than in the United States. Since mid-2005 they were almost continually more expensive. Note that the price of the Big Mac is not a bad indicator of relative prices. In July 2013 the Big Mac was 15.5% more expensive in Canada than in the United States, while overall the price level was 12% higher. We will return to the significance of the real exchange rate being equal to one when we discuss theories of exchange rate determination later in the chapter.

The Foreign Exchange Market

To finance international trade and international financial transactions, banks and other financial firms around the world trade over US$5 trillion worth of currency each day on the foreign exchange market. That amount represents nearly $600 for every person in the world each day. The value of currency traded in a week is about equal to the value of all foreign trade in a year. Clearly, most transactions on the foreign exchange market are unrelated to the trade in goods and services.

The foreign exchange market is global, and trades occur 24 hours a day.[5] Typically, rather than actual physical currency, banks trade bank deposits. So, a U.S.-based bank might trade a bank account denominated in U.S. dollars to a German bank in exchange for a bank account denominated in euros. The foreign exchange market is, in effect, virtual, in that most

---

[5]For a description of the foreign exchange market see: William Barker, "The Global Foreign Exchange Market: Growth and Transformation," *Bank of Canada Review*, 2007, p. 3–12.

trading takes place between large banks that are linked by computer, rather than on a physical exchange. Although the volume of transactions is large, transactions are concentrated in just a few locations and among just a small number of currencies. More than half of all foreign exchange transactions involve financial firms in the United States or the United Kingdom. The U.S. dollar is used in 85% of foreign exchange trades, followed by the euro (39%), the yen (19%), and the British pound (13%). Note that each transaction involves two currencies.[6]

Exchange Rate Policy

Countries follow different exchange rate policies. When countries choose an exchange rate policy, economists say that there is an **exchange rate system**, or an *exchange rate regime*. Countries have typically used three major types of exchange rate systems:

Exchange rate system An arrangement among countries about how exchange rates should be determined.

- A fixed exchange rate system
- A floating exchange rate system
- A managed exchange rate system

In a **fixed exchange rate system**, exchange rates are set at levels determined and maintained by central banks. Historically, the two most important fixed exchange rate systems were the *gold standard* and the *Bretton Woods system*. Under the gold standard, which lasted from the nineteenth century to the 1930s, a country's currency consisted of gold coins and of paper currency that the government was committed to redeem for gold. The gold standard was a fixed exchange rate system because exchange rates were determined by the amount of gold in each country's currency. Under the gold standard, the size of a country's money supply depended on the amount of gold available. To expand its money supply rapidly during a war or an economic depression, a country had to abandon the gold standard.

Fixed exchange rate system A system in which exchange rates are set at levels determined and maintained by government or central bank.

During the Great Depression of the 1930s, many countries, including Canada, decided to abandon the gold standard in order to increase the flexibility of their exchange rates and gain greater control of their money supplies. Near the end of World War II, many economists and policymakers argued that a return to a fixed exchange rate system would help the world economy recover from more than 15 years of depression and war. The result was a conference held in Bretton Woods, New Hampshire, in 1944 that set up an exchange rate system where the United States pledged to buy or sell gold at a fixed rate of $35 per ounce. The central banks of all other countries that joined the Bretton Woods system pledged to buy and sell their countries' currencies at a fixed rate against the U.S. dollar. By fixing their exchange rates against the U.S. dollar, these counties were fixing the exchange rates among their currencies as well. Unlike under the gold standard, neither the United States nor any other country was willing to redeem its paper currency for gold domestically. The United States would redeem dollars for gold only if the dollars were presented by a foreign central bank. The Bretton Woods system worked well for many years until the Vietnam War, and the associated U.S. monetary expansion, led to a large increase in U.S. dollar holdings by foreign central banks. Redemptions of the dollars for gold reduced U.S. reserves, and in 1973 the Bretton Woods system collapsed.

Following the collapse of the Bretton Woods system, most countries switched to a **floating exchange rate system**, with exchange rates determined by the buying and selling of currencies in the foreign exchange market. The Canadian dollar was actually floated earlier, in 1970.

Floating exchange rate system A system in which the foreign exchange value of currency is determined in the foreign exchange market.

Some countries found that the floating exchange rate system led to too much instability in their exchange rates. As a result, some central banks intervened occasionally to influence

---

[6]Bank for International Settlements, "Triennial Central Bank Survey," September 2010.

their exchange rates by buying and selling currencies in the foreign exchange market. Until 1998, the Bank of Canada would intervene to slow down rapid depreciation or appreciation. For example if a disruption in oil supply from the Middle East was expected to lead to an appreciation of the Canadian dollar by a large amount over a period of two days, the Bank of Canada would intervene in the foreign exchange market so that the change would take longer. The Bank of Canada would not try to set the level of an exchange rate, but only stretch the period over which the exchange rate would reach a new level. Since 1998 the Bank of Canada does not intervene in the foreign exchange market, except in extraordinary circumstances. Some central banks, however, actively manipulate the level of their currency exchange rate. Such system is called a *managed floating exchange rate system*. Under a **managed floating exchange rate system**, private buyers and sellers in the foreign exchange market determine the value of currencies most of the time, with occasional government intervention. Some governments (for example China) impose limits on capital flows to help in the foreign exchange intervention. These limits may be necessary for the management of the exchange rate. With free flows of capital, central bank intervention is often insufficient to affect the exchange rate for a longer period of time. For example, the Bank of Japan can attempt to affect the exchange rate between the U.S. dollar and yen by buying or selling the two currencies. But the Bank of Japan's purchases or sales will be very small relative to the total amount of buying and selling of U.S. dollars and yen in the foreign exchange market. So it is unlikely that a central bank intervention can affect the exchange rate of a widely traded currency for more than a brief period.

> **Managed floating exchange rate system**
> A system in which private buyers and sellers in the foreign exchange market determine the value of currencies most of the time, with occasional central bank intervention.

Policy Choices and the Current Exchange Rate Systems

The current exchange rate system reflects three key policy choices:

- Canada, like most developed countries, allows the dollar to float against other currencies.
- Eighteen countries in Europe have adopted the euro as their common currency.
- Some developing countries have pegged their exchange rates against a single country's currency (usually the U.S. dollar) or against a basket of currencies.

Determination of the Exchange Rate under Flexible Exchange Rates

Under a pure flexible exchange rate system, the central bank does not undertake transactions on the foreign exchange market and allows the exchange rate to be determined by the supply and demand for the country's currency. When demand exceeds supply, the currency becomes more valuable (appreciates). When supply exceeds demand, the currency becomes less valuable (depreciates). Let's consider how this works with the Canadian dollar. Below, we will use a simple demand-supply graph and draw both demand and supply of the Canadian dollar as functions of the nominal exchange rate, E.

Demand for Canadian Dollars Demand for Canadian dollars comes from many sources. The three most important are foreign demand for Canadian goods and services, foreign demand for Canadian physical assets (companies, land), and foreign demand for Canadian paper assets: bonds, Treasury bills, etc. The higher is the demand for Canadian goods, services, and assets (both physical and financial), the higher is the demand for Canadian dollars. This is because, to buy Canadian goods, services, or assets, you usually need Canadian dollars. Of course, if you want to buy Canadian maple syrup, you may find someone who will sell you it to you and accept payment in U.S. dollars or Indonesian Rupiahs; similarly if you want to buy property, shares, bonds, etc., you can do the transaction in a foreign currency. But most such transactions require Canadian dollars. Most shares in Canadian companies are listed on Canadian stock exchanges; most Canadian land and firms are domestically owned, etc.

To draw the demand curve in terms of the nominal exchange rate, we need to explain how changes in the nominal exchange rate affect these three sources of demand.

Foreign demand for Canadian goods and services depends negatively on the real exchange rate. The lower is the real exchange rate, $e = EP/P^*$, the cheaper are Canadian goods and services relative to foreign goods and services, which increases foreign demand for Canadian goods and services. As we have seen in Figure 5.5, changes in the real exchange rate closely follow changes in the nominal exchange rate. This is because the ratio of Canadian to foreign prices, P/P^*, is relatively stable. So the lower the nominal exchange rate, the lower is the real exchange rate, and foreign demand for Canadian goods and services and Canadian dollars is higher.

Foreign demand for Canadian physical assets or claims on physical assets depends negatively on the real exchange rate in the same way as foreign demand for goods and services. When, for example, a South African farmer wants to buy land or a processing plant in Canada, the real exchange rate affects his costs. So a lower nominal exchange rate means a lower real exchange rate and cheaper Canadian physical assets. Foreign demand for Canadian physical assets increases, resulting in higher demand for Canadian dollars.

Foreign demand for Canadian paper assets depends negatively on the nominal exchange rate. To see this, we will use an example; *Useful Math 5.1* on this page will help you understand the example. A pension fund from Chile considers buying Canadian government bonds and hold them for a year. The nominal interest rate in Canada (which is the foreign country here, since we analyze the investment from the point of view of a Chilean fund) is $i^* = 1.2\%$; the nominal interest rate in Chile is 6.5% and the exchange rate is $E = 500$ Chilean pesos per dollar. The pension fund is assumed to care only about the expected return and ignore differences in default risk and exchange rate risk. The pension fund expects the exchange rate in a year to be $E^e_{+1} = 525$ pesos to a Canadian dollar. If they buy one Canadian dollar now for 500 pesos, a year from now they receive \$1.012, for which they expect to buy $1.012 \times 525 = 531.3$ pesos. Their expected return in pesos is $6.26\% = (531.3 - 500)/500$. The return on Chilean bonds is 6.5%, so the pension fund does not buy Canadian bonds.

Useful Math 5.1:
Calculating Bond Returns in Different Currencies

We need to learn how to calculate the return on bonds in a foreign currency. In order to earn interest on foreign currency bonds, you need to convert your money into the foreign currency, earn interest on the foreign bond, and then convert the total back to your money. So the return on foreign bonds will depend on their interest rate and on the current and future exchange rates. Future exchange rates are not known, so you need to form expectations of the future exchange rate. Therefore the return you will calculate will be the expected return.

Let us consider a simple example. You are a manager of a Chilean pension fund and you would like to calculate the expected return on Canadian bonds. The data are as follows:

- Current exchange rate = 500 pesos/Canadian dollar.

- Interest rate on Canadian bonds = 1.2% per year.

- Expected exchange rate a year from now = 525 pesos/ Canadian dollar.

We will do the calculation for 500 pesos. For 500 pesos you can buy \$1 today. If you invest \$1 and earn interest of 1.2%, in one year you will have \$1.012. As you expect the exchange rate to be 525 pesos/Canadian dollar, you expect this to be worth $\$1.012 \times 525$ pesos/\$ = 531.3 pesos. Your expected return in Chilean peso is, therefore

$$\frac{531.3 - 500}{500} = 6.26\%.$$

Let us denote the foreign (in this case Canadian, since we are analyzing the investment from the point of view of a Chilean fund) interest rate as i^*, the nominal exchange rate as E and the expected nominal exchange rate one year from now as E^e_{+1} (the superscript e stands for *expected*, the subscript +1 stands for *in a year*). We can rewrite this equation as

$$\% \ return \ on \ foreign \ bonds = \frac{E^e_{+1}(1 + i^*) - E}{E}. \quad (5.2)$$

Now let us assume that, just before they execute the transaction, the exchange rate falls to 495 pesos to a Canadian dollar. In general such depreciation will not affect expectations of the exchange rate a year from now, which will remain equal to 525. So we use equation (5.2) with $E_{+1}^e = 525$, $E = 495$, and $i^* = 1.2\%$. The expected return in Canada is now 7.33% = $(525 \times 1.012 - 495)/495$. It exceeds the 6.5% return on Chilean bonds and so, as the nominal exchange rate falls, demand for Canadian bonds increases. Higher demand for Canadian bonds means higher demand for Canadian dollars.

Supply of Canadian Dollars Supply of Canadian dollars on the foreign exchange market is determined by similar factors as demand. It depends on the Canadian demand for foreign goods and services, foreign physical assets, and foreign paper assets. The lower the Canadian demand for foreign goods, services, and assets, the lower the supply of Canadian dollars on the foreign exchange market. A lower nominal exchange rate means a lower real exchange rate, making foreign goods and services more expensive and reducing Canadian imports. A lower nominal exchange rate makes foreign assets more expensive, so Canadians buy less foreign assets. Finally, consider a Canadian pension fund that thinks of buying Chilean bonds. Let us use the previous numbers (the interest rate in Canada is 1.2%, the interest rate in Chile is 6.5%, and the expected exchange rate in a year is 525 pesos to one Canadian dollar). When the exchange rate falls from 500 to 495, the expected return on Canadian bonds increases above the return on Chilean bonds, and so demand for Chilean bonds falls. In all cases, less foreign currency is needed to buy imported goods and services and foreign assets and so the supply of Canadian dollars on the foreign exchange market falls.

We conclude that the lower the nominal exchange rate, the higher the demand for Canadian dollars and the lower is the supply of Canadian dollars on the foreign exchange market. So we can draw the demand and supply for Canadian dollars as a function of the nominal exchange rate. Figure 5.6 shows the determination of the nominal exchange rate under flexible exchange rates. Equilibrium is at E^* where the supply and demand for the Canadian dollar on the foreign exchange market are equal. When the exchange rate is higher than the equilibrium value, for example when it is equal to E_1, the supply of the Canadian dollar exceeds demand. Just as with anything else, when supply exceeds demand the price falls. In this case the price of the Canadian dollar is the exchange rate. The exchange rate falls; that is, the Canadian dollar depreciates. Conversely when the exchange rate is below the equilibrium value, for example, when it is equal to E_2, there is excess demand for Canadian dollars and the exchange rate increases; that is, the Canadian dollar appreciates.

Figure 5.6

Determination of the Exchange Rate when the Rate Is Flexible

Equilibrium is at E^* where demand and supply for Canadian dollars are equal. If the exchange rate exceeds E^* there is excess supply and the Canadian dollar becomes less valuable; that is, it depreciates. If the exchange rate is below E^* there is excess demand for Canadian dollars and the Canadian dollar becomes more valuable; that is, it appreciates.

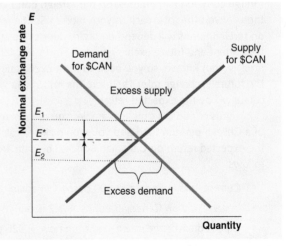

Factors Shifting the Demand and Supply Curves of the Canadian Dollar

We now consider factors affecting the position of the supply and demand curves. To do this we look at any given nominal exchange rate and ask what changes affect the demand and supply at that particular value of the nominal exchange rate. So we hold the nominal exchange rate constant and look at the effect of changes in other variables on demand and supply of Canadian dollars. The rule is simple: Anything that makes Canadian goods, services, or assets more attractive relative to foreign ones shifts the demand curve to the right and the supply curve to the left. There are three important factors:

- the ratio of Canadian to foreign prices
- the difference between domestic and foreign interest rates (the *interest rate spread*)
- a shift in demand toward Canadian goods and services

The ratio of Canadian to foreign prices matters since the demand and supply of Canadian dollars related to goods, services, and real assets depend on the real, not the nominal, exchange rate. For a given nominal exchange rate, the lower are Canadian prices relative to foreign prices, the lower is the real exchange rate, since $e = EP/P^*$. This makes Canadian goods, services, and real assets more attractive relative to foreign ones. So demand for Canadian dollars rises, shifting the demand curve right, and supply falls, shifting the supply curve left.

The *interest rate spread* is the difference between Canadian and foreign interest rates. It affects the profitability of investments in Canada versus investments abroad. A higher interest spread (a higher Canadian interest rate or a lower foreign interest rate) makes Canadian assets relatively more attractive to both Canadians and foreigners. The demand for Canadian assets increases, raising the demand for Canadian dollars at the given nominal exchange rate, so the demand curve shifts right. We study the effect of prices and the interest rate differential in more detail later in the chapter.

If, for some reason, demand in Canada or around the world shifts toward Canadian goods, services, and assets and away from foreign goods, services, and assets, the demand curve for Canadian dollars shifts right and the supply curve shifts left. A good example is the sovereign debt crisis in Europe. Bonds of many European countries became perceived as risky, and financial institutions moved their funds to countries perceived as safe, including Canada. At the given nominal exchange rate the increased risk of European assets raised demand for Canadian dollars and reduced supply, moving the demand curve right and supply curve left.

These changes are illustrated in Figure 5.7. An increase in demand and/or a reduction in supply of Canadian dollars leads to appreciation of the Canadian dollar. The equilibrium at which demand and supply are equal moves from point A to point B. The Canadian dollar appreciates from E_1^* to E_2^*.

In addition, Canada is perceived as a resource country. An increase in resource prices, in particular an increase in the price of oil, raises both the demand for and the supply of Canadian dollars. Higher resource prices reduce the demand for Canadian resources but, as resource demand is inelastic,[7] raise the amount spent on Canadian resources and so increase the demand for Canadian dollars. Higher resource prices raise Canadian income, raising imports and increasing the supply for Canadian dollars. To avoid confusion, the effect of higher resource prices is not shown in Figure 5.7.

---

[7]Demand is inelastic when a 1% increase in price lowers demand by less than 1%.

Figure 5.7

Factors Shifting the Canadian Dollar Demand and Supply Curves

A lower real exchange rate, a higher interest spread, a shift of demand toward Canadian goods and services, and expectations of these changes increase the demand for the Canadian dollar and reduce supply, leading to appreciation from E^*_1 to E^*_2.

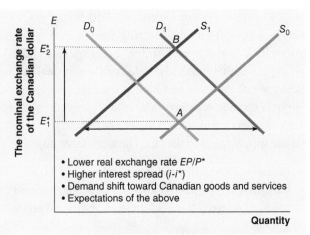

- Lower real exchange rate EP/P^*
- Higher interest spread $(i\text{-}i^*)$
- Demand shift toward Canadian goods and services
- Expectations of the above

Expectations and the Exchange Rate The demand and supply of Canadian dollars are affected by expectations of future changes. As soon as, for example, traders expect an increase in Canadian interest rates, they can predict that the exchange rate will rise, that is, that the Canadian dollar will appreciate. This means that buying Canadian dollars today and selling them in the future becomes profitable. Foreign currency traders immediately increase the demand for Canadian dollars while institutions that were planning to sell Canadian dollars delay the sales. As a result, there is an immediate increase in demand and a reduction in supply so that the demand curve shifts right and the supply curve shifts left, leading to an immediate appreciation of the dollar.

Managing a Fixed Exchange Rate

An exchange rate arrangement is called a fixed exchange rate system when the country sets the value of the exchange rate at a certain level relative to the value of some other currency or a basket of currencies and its central bank intervenes on the foreign exchange markets by buying or selling its currency so as to maintain the fixed value of the exchange rate. Having a fixed exchange rate can provide important advantages for a country that has extensive trade with another country. When the exchange rate is fixed, business planning becomes much easier. For instance, if the South Korean won increases in value relative to the Canadian dollar, Hyundai, a Korean car manufacturer, may have to choose between raising the dollar price of cars it exports to Canada, thereby reducing sales, or keeping prices constant, reducing profits. If the exchange rate between the Korean won and the Canadian dollar is fixed, Hyundai's planning is much easier.

An example of a fixed exchange rate system is that of Hong Kong. Since 1983 the exchange rate of the Hong Kong dollar in terms of the U.S. dollar has been fixed at 0.1282 (i.e., one Hong Kong dollar cost 12.82 U.S. cents), with small differences allowed from time to time. Between 1990 and 2012 the range was between 0.1295 and 0.1279; the difference between the maximum and minimum value was around 1%.[8]

The terminology for changes in the fixed exchange rate is different than for changes in the flexible exchange rate. Under fixed exchange rates, an increase in the value of the

---

[8]The exchange rate between the Hong Kong and the United States dollars is usually quoted as 7.8 Hong Kong dollars for one United States dollar. Using our definition, it is the exchange rate of the United States dollar in terms of the Hong Kong dollar.

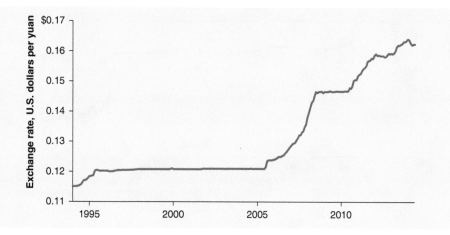

Figure 5.8

The Exchange Rate of Chinese Yuan in Terms of the U.S. Dollar, 1994–2014

Between 1995 and 2005 China maintained fixed exchange rate in terms of the U.S. dollar. After 2005 the yuan started appreciating.

Source: Oanda.com

currency is called a **currency revaluation**; a decrease in the value of the currency is called a **currency devaluation**.

How does the central bank control the exchange rate? By buying and selling the country's currency on the foreign exchange market, using or acquiring foreign currency reserves.

Preventing Appreciation Consider first the pressure for a currency to appreciate—which had often been the case with the Chinese yuan. Figure 5.8 shows the exchange rate of the yuan in terms of the U.S. dollar. Between May 1995 and June 2005, the exchange rate was fixed around 0.12 U.S. dollar per one yuan. Very small variations were allowed; the largest was 0.2% in a month. During this time there was a strong pressure for the Chinese yuan to appreciate. A pressure to appreciate means that, at the fixed exchange rate, there was excess demand for Chinese yuan. People were willing to pay, for example, 0.125 U.S. dollars per yuan.

Since the Chinese central bank had committed to a fixed exchange rate, it needed to prevent appreciation. It increased the supply of yuan on the foreign exchange market so that demand and supply intersected at the exchange rate of 0.12. To do this the Chinese central bank sold yuan on the foreign exchange market and bought foreign currencies. This is shown in Figure 5.9.

As a result of the intervention, the Bank of China's foreign currency reserves have increased. In principle, the Chinese central bank can prevent appreciation of the yuan indefinitely, since it issues (prints) the domestic currency. The down side is that an increase in the amount of currency leads to higher money supply and higher inflation, as we learned

Currency revaluation An increase in the market value of one country's currency relative to another country's currency when the exchange rate is fixed.

Currency devaluation A decrease in the market value of one country's currency relative to another country's currency when the exchange rate is fixed.

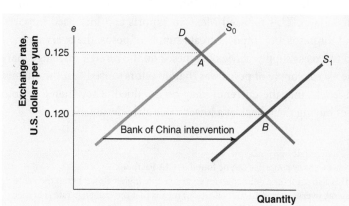

Figure 5.9

Preventing Appreciation

Without intervention, the high demand for yuan would have resulted in equilibrium at point A, with the yuan appreciating to US$0.125/yuan. To prevent appreciation, the Bank of China increases the supply of yuans so that equilibrium is at B and the exchange rate remains unchanged at US$0.12/yuan.

Figure 5.10

The Exchange Rate of the Mexican Peso, March 1, 1993–March 1, 1994

Until December 1994 Mexico maintained fixed exchange rate in terms of the U.S. dollar. As the central bank run out of reserves, Mexico switched to a flexible exchange rate.

Source: Oanda.com

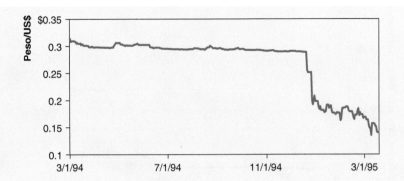

in Chapter 4. In fact, the scale of the foreign exchange intervention of the Chinese central bank has been huge.[9] At the end of 2013 China's reserves were US$3.8 trillion. (For comparison, the reserves of the United States, with a much larger economy, are only $150 billion.) In the end, under political pressure to let its currency appreciate, China abandoned the fixed exchange rate in 2005 and switched to a managed exchange system. The yuan is allowed to appreciate but China controls the speed of the appreciation. The huge foreign exchange reserves allow China to run a managed system.

Preventing Depreciation Consider now the pressure for the currency to depreciate—which was the case with the Mexican peso in 1994. Mexico went through several crises in 1980s, but in 1990s its economic situation looked good. The NAFTA agreement (the free trade agreement between Canada, Mexico, and the United States) was concluded in 1993, with the expectation that it would provide positive impetus to the economy. However, in 1994 there were several negative internal developments. At the beginning of the year a revolt started in the southern state of Chiapas. In March, the presidential candidate from the ruling party, Luis Donaldo Colosio, was assassinated and in September, the Secretary General of the ruling party, José Francisco Ruiz-Massieu, was assassinated. In November, his brother accused leading members of the ruling party of ordering the assassination and the Attorney General of a cover-up. These events created the impression of serious political instability. What do investors do when they are concerned with stability? They take their money elsewhere. The political events led to an increase in the supply of Mexican pesos on the foreign exchange market and a reduction in demand for the Mexican pesos (Figure 5.10). There was excess supply of Mexican pesos on the foreign exchange market. Another reason for the excess supply of pesos was that the peso had become **overvalued**: The real exchange rate was above one. The peso became overvalued because the inflation rate in Mexico was significantly higher than in the United States. High inflation and a fixed exchange rate meant that, over time, goods in Mexico became more expensive than in the United States. This reduced Mexican exports and increased imports. Since exports create demand for pesos and imports create supply of pesos, the overvaluation of the currency contributed to excess supply of Mexican pesos on the foreign exchange market. The third reason for the excess supply of pesos was that investors sensed that the current situation was not sustainable and that the currency may be devalued. They therefore sold pesos with the expectation of buying them back at a lower price after devaluation.

Currency overvaluation (undervaluation) Overvaluation (undervaluation) is a situation in which, at the current exchange rate, the real exchange rate is higher (lower) than one.[10]

---

[9]The value of the exchange reserves for many countries can be found at CIA Factbook.

[10]Overvaluation (undervaluation) is also sometime defined as an exchange rate higher (lower) than the value that induces trade balance. In general, overvaluation (undervaluation) means that the exchange rate is higher (lower) than the value implied by some model or criterion.

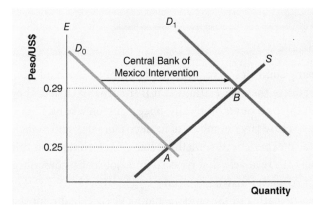

Figure 5.11

Preventing Depreciation

Without intervention, the peso would depreciate to US$0.25. The central bank of Mexico buys pesos on the foreign exchange market, increasing its demand from D_0 to D_1 and maintaining a fixed exchange rate of US$0.29, but it loses reserves.

For all three reasons mentioned above (political instability, the overvaluation of the peso, and investor sentiment that the currency was likely to be devalued), at the fixed exchange rate there was an excess supply of pesos and pressure for the peso to depreciate. The Mexican central bank (Banco de Mexico) was trying to maintain the exchange rate around US$0.29 per peso, but people were willing to pay, for example, only US$0.25. To maintain the high exchange rate Banco de Mexico had to intervene on the foreign exchange market. It did so by buying pesos, increasing the demand for pesos. This is illustrated in Figure 5.11. To buy pesos the central bank was selling its foreign exchange reserves. It was doing exactly the opposite of what the Chinese central bank did to prevent appreciation of the currency.

There is a fundamental difference between preventing appreciation and preventing depreciation. To intervene on the foreign exchange market, the Chinese central bank had to sell what it had, essentially, in infinite supply: Chinese currency. As long as the Chinese central bank, the People's Bank of China, had paper, ink, and electricity, it could print new currency at will. (In practice, all they needed was electricity as, nowadays, central banks can create money on a computer, without printing actual notes.) On the other hand, the Banco de Mexico had to sell assets it had in limited supply: foreign exchange reserves. These reserves fell from almost US$30 billion in February of 1994 to about US$10 billion in December of that year. The government gave up and devalued the peso by 15% on December 20. In the end, Banco de Mexico simply ran out of reserves. On December 21, trying to maintain the new exchange rate, the Banco de Mexico lost US$4.5 billion in reserves. With just US$6 billion left, on December 26 it switched to a flexible exchange rate.

Avoiding a Common Mistake: Overvaluation, Devaluation, and Depreciation.

You should not confuse overvaluation with devaluation or depreciation. Overvaluation means that the currency is expensive. Often, but not always, an overvalued currency eventually falls in value. Under a fixed exchange rate, this decrease in value is determined by the central bank and is called devaluation. Under a flexible exchange rate, the value of the currency is determined in the foreign exchange market and, when the value declines, it is called depreciation. Mexico had a fixed exchange rate and an overvalued currency. The central bank, as discussed above, did devalue the currency on December 20, 1994. But overvaluation does not necessarily lead to a decline in the value of the currency. For example, while most economists agree that the Swiss franc has been overvalued for a long time, it does not tend to depreciate.

Making the Connection

Greece Experiences a "Bank Jog"

In the past, commercial banks in many countries were subject to bank runs. In a bank run, depositors withdrew their funds because they were afraid that if their bank closed, they would not get back all the money in their accounts. Typically, once a run on a bank began, the bank was quickly forced to close because large numbers of its depositors demanded their money back. In 2012, Greek banks also experienced something like a bank run, but in this case, depositors withdrew their money at a relatively slow pace, so some journalists described Greek banks as undergoing a "bank jog" rather than a bank run.

After June 2002, all countries participating in the euro, including Greece, had removed their individual currencies from circulation. After that date, all deposits in Greek banks were in euros, rather than in drachmas, the previous Greek currency. The period from 2002 until the beginning of the global economic recession and financial crisis in 2007 was one of relative economic stability in most of Europe. With low interest rates, low inflation rates, and expanding employment and production, the advantages of the euro seemed obvious. The countries using the euro no longer had to deal with problems caused by fluctuating exchange rates. Having a common currency made it easier for consumers and firms to buy and sell across borders.

The recession and financial crisis resulted in falling real GDP and higher unemployment. A sovereign debt crisis that developed in 2010 made the problems worse. *Sovereign debt* refers to bonds issued by governments. The recession caused large increases in government spending and reductions in tax revenues as incomes and profits declined. Governments in a number of European countries, particularly Greece, Ireland, Spain, Portugal, and Italy, financed the resulting budget deficits by selling bonds. By the spring of 2010, many investors began to doubt the ability of some countries, particularly Greece, to make the interest payments on the bonds. If Greece defaulted, investors would be likely to stop buying bonds issued by several other European governments, and the continuation of the euro would be called into question.

The ECB helped Greece avoid a default by directly buying its bonds. The International Monetary Fund and the European Union put together aid packages meant to keep Greece and other countries from defaulting. In exchange for the aid, Greece was required to adopt an *austerity policy* of cutting government spending and raising taxes even though doing so resulted in significant protests from unions, students, and other groups.

In 2012, unhappiness over spending cuts and higher taxes, along with continuing high unemployment, led Greek voters to elect politicians who vowed to reverse the austerity policy. As a result, speculation increased that Greece would abandon the euro. Many Greeks were afraid that the government might decide to exchange their euro bank deposits for drachmas at a rate of one for one. If the drachma then depreciated—as was widely expected—bank depositors would suffer heavy losses. In response, beginning in May, Greek banks began to lose deposits. Depositors either held their withdrawals as cash or deposited them in foreign banks. Unlike with a normal bank run, however, Greek depositors believed that they had ample time to withdraw their money because the ECB was willing to provide euro currency to Greek banks to meet withdrawals and because it was unclear whether Greece actually would stop using the euro.

The Greek bank jog indicated a potential new source of instability in the global financial system: not only might depositors in euro countries lose faith in banks because of actions by the banks—for instance, making bad loans—depositors could also become concerned that their country might leave the euro or that the ECB would not be willing to supply an unlimited number of euros to local banks.

Sources: David Enrich, Sara Schaefer Muñoz, and Charles Forelle, "Europe Bank Fear Flight of Deposits," *Wall Street Journal*, May 20, 2012; Matthew O'Brien, "End of the Marathon: The Meaning of Greece's = 'Bank Jog,'" *Atlantic*, May 17, 2012; and Damien McElroy, "Greeks Withdraw Savings in National = 'Bank Jog,'" (UK) *Telegraph*, May 20, 2012.

See related problem 2.8 at the end of the chapter.

Table 5.2 summarizes the advantages and disadvantages of different exchange rate policies.

What Factors Determine Exchange Rates?

Our earlier discussion of the real exchange rate measured in terms of Big Macs raises an interesting question: Why isn't the real exchange rate always one? That is, why shouldn't you be able to exchange 1 Canadian Big Mac for 1 U.S. Big Mac and not for 1.155 Big Macs? According to the **law of one price**, identical products should sell for the same price everywhere, including in different countries, as long as they are freely tradeable. If the law of one price does not hold, then arbitrage should be possible. **Arbitrage** refers to buying a product in one market and reselling it in another market at a higher price. The profits received from engaging in arbitrage are called *arbitrage profits*.

Purchasing Power Parity

Consider applying arbitrage to the values in our Big Mac example from page 151. We will do the calculation in U.S. dollars. One Big Mac costs US$4.56 in the United States and Can$5.53 in Canada. At the exchange rate of 0.952 U.S. dollars for 1 Canadian dollar, Can$5.53 buys US$5.27. Therefore you could buy a Big Mac in the United States for US$4.56, sell it in Canada for Can$5.53 and exchange it for US$5.27, for a profit of US$0.71 or Can$0.74. If this process works for one Big Mac, why not try it for millions of Big Macs and become very wealthy? The problem is that if this path to easy riches is obvious to you, it will be obvious to many people. Many people will sell Canadian dollars for U.S. dollars to buy low-priced U.S. Big Macs.

5.3

Learning Objective
Discuss what factors determine exchange rates.

Law of one price The notion that identical products should sell for the same price everywhere, including in different countries, as long as they are freely tradeable.

Arbitrage Taking advantage of price differences across markets by buying a product in one market and reselling it in another market at a higher price.

Table 5.2 Advantages and Disadvantages of Various Exchange Rate Policies

Exchange rate system	Advantages	Disadvantages
Fixed exchange rate system	Easier for businesses to plan and to borrow in other currencies.	Difficult to maintain. Eliminates possibility of depreciation during a recession.
Floating exchange rate system	No need for government intervention. Allows exchange rate to reflect demand and supply in the market.	Can make business planning difficult.
Managed float exchange rate system	Allows greater exchange rate stability than in a floating system.	Central bank interventions are likely to be ineffective with a widely traded currency. Interventions are effective against short-run pressures but not against fundamental trends.

This increased supply should cause the Canadian dollar to depreciate until the exchange rate reaches US$0.825 per Canadian dollar. At that exchange rate, arbitrage profits are eliminated, and 1 U.S. Big Mac exchanges for 1 Canadian Big Mac, so the real exchange rate equals 1.

While our example is a bit absurd (Who would buy an old Big Mac from you for the same price they can get a fresh one from a McDonalds?), the reasoning we have just gone through leads to the theory of **purchasing power parity (PPP)**. It states that, in the long run, nominal exchange rates adjust to equalize the purchasing power of different currencies. That is, in the long run, *the real exchange rate should equal* 1. This theory should hold because, if it does not, then opportunities for arbitrage profits exist.

> **Purchasing power parity (PPP)** The theory that, in the long run, nominal exchange rates adjust to equalize the purchasing power of different currencies.

We can use the theory of purchasing power parity to analyze the effect on nominal exchange rates of differences in inflation rates among countries. The real exchange rate is $e = E \times (P/P^*)$. Using the formulas for the rate of change of a product and of a ratio (see *Useful Math 4.2* on page 120), and the fact that the percentage change in the price level is equal to the inflation rate: % change in $P = \pi$ and % change in $P^* = \pi^*$, we obtain:

$$\% \text{ change in } e = \% \text{ change in } E + \pi - \pi^*. \tag{5.3}$$

Assuming that the PPP holds, the real exchange rate is constant (and equal to 1), so its rate of change is zero. We therefore obtain the relationship between the percentage change in the nominal exchange rate and the inflation rates at home and abroad:

$$\% \text{ change in } E = \pi^* - \pi. \tag{5.4}$$

This last equation tells us that, if the purchasing power parity holds, the percentage change in the nominal exchange rate is equal to the difference between the foreign and domestic inflation rates. For example, if the inflation rate in Turkey is higher than the inflation rate in Canada, we would expect the nominal exchange rate to increase, that is, the value of the Canadian dollar to appreciate in terms of the Turkish lira.

Why Purchasing Power Parity Does Not Hold Exactly

The theory of purchasing power parity offers an explanation of movements in nominal exchange rates in the long run. Even in the long run, though, we would not expect purchasing power parity to hold exactly, for three main reasons.

First, not all goods and services are traded internationally. For example, a Big Mac is perishable, and so despite the assumptions in our earlier example, the search for arbitrage profits would not force the real exchange rate expressed in terms of Big Macs to equal 1. Similarly, housing and most services are not traded internationally. Non-tradeable goods and services are a large component of GDP. Second, countries impose barriers to trade such as *tariffs*, which are taxes on imports, and *quotas*, which are limits on the quantities of goods that can be imported. For example, Canada limits imports of dairy products so, even though milk is much cheaper in the United States, it cannot be imported. Third, arbitrage is hampered by transportation costs. Not all goods can be easily transported; Big Macs, being quite perishable, are not suitable for transport.

Of all these reasons for the failure of the purchasing power parity, the first is the most important. Retail services are not tradeable and so, even if a Gap sweater in Canada is cheaper than in Switzerland, profitable arbitrage is not possible since to sell the sweater in Switzerland, you need to incur the high retail cost there. In fact, companies make arbitrage difficult by branding, warranty rules, and other tricks. An iPhone is cheaper in Canada than in China, but you will not be able to sell it in an Apple store in China and the Canadian warranty may not be recognized.

Because of these problems, purchasing power parity gives a reasonable, but not exact, guide to movements in nominal exchange rates in the long run. In particular, countries that have relatively high inflation rates usually see the value of their currencies depreciate, and countries that have relatively low inflation rates usually see the value of their currencies appreciate. This is why, for example, the exchange rate of the Canadian dollar in terms of the Japanese yen is around 80 yen for a Canadian dollar. After World War II, Japan experienced a period of very rapid inflation, which led to a depreciation of the yen.

In the short run, though, purchasing power parity does a poor job in explaining movements in nominal exchange rates. A key reason is that purchasing power parity focuses on the demand for goods and services in different countries to explain movements in nominal exchange rates. As we noted in the chapter opener, however, in the short run most of the buying and selling of currency is not motivated by the need to finance international trade but by the desire to engage in international financial investments.

The Interest Parity Condition

The huge demand for foreign exchange for purposes of financial investment reflects the increase in *international capital mobility* in recent decades. Policymakers in many countries have removed regulations that once hindered financial investments across national borders. The internet allows investors in one country to easily access information about firms in other countries. The internet also makes it easier for investors to connect with financial firms, particularly brokerage firms, to make investments in foreign firms for them. In this section, we explore how international capital mobility affects exchange rates.

We can again use the example of the Chilean insurance company from page 155. Suppose that it intends to invest 500 million pesos in one-year government bonds. It is looking for the highest expected return on the investment, and it does not care which country it invests in. The Canadian bond interest rate is 1.2%, and the Chilean bond interest rate is 6.5%. To keep the example simple, assume that the company considers the two bonds to be identical except for their interest rates; also, we ignore the exchange rate risk. That is, it believes they have the same default risk, liquidity, information costs, and other characteristics. Which bonds should it purchase? The company wants the investment return to be in Chilean pesos since it pays out insurance claims in pesos. If it buys the Canadian bond, it first has to exchange pesos for Canadian dollars at the beginning of the year, and then at the end of the year it has to exchange Canadian dollars (plus interest earned) for pesos. It might receive more than the 1.2% return if, during the time its funds are invested in Canadian bonds, the Canadian dollar appreciates relative to the peso. For example, suppose that the current exchange rate is 495 pesos for a Canadian dollar and a year from now they expect the exchange rate to be 525 pesos to a Canadian dollar. After one year the company would receive a return of 1.2% in Canadian dollars and then exchange the dollars into pesos. The expected total return on a Canadian bond, using equation (5.2) (see *Useful Math* 5.1, on page 155) with $E^e_{+1} = 525$, $E = 495$, and $i^* = 1.2\%$, is $7.33\% = (525 \times 1.012 - 495)/495$. It exceeds the 6.5% return on Chilean bonds. Even though the interest rate in Canada is lower, the expected appreciation of the Canadian dollar more than compensates for it.

Since the expected return in Canada is higher, the insurance company will sell pesos on the foreign exchange market and buy Canadian dollars. Of course, other investors would do the same. The supply of pesos, and demand for Canadian dollars on the foreign exchange market both increase. So the Canadian dollar appreciates in terms of the Chilean peso, for example to 496. Since the appreciation has little effect on the expected exchange rate a year from now, the expected appreciation of the Canadian dollar becomes smaller. Before, the Canadian dollar was expected to appreciate from 495 to 525, but it has now already appreciated to 496 and so it is expected to appreciate only from 496 to 525. The expected return on Canadian bonds, using the equation (5.2), with $E^e_{+1} = 525$, $E = 496$ and $i^* = 1.2\%$, is now $7.12\% = (525 \times 1.012 - 496)/496$. The appreciation of the Canadian dollar today reduced expected appreciation and the expected return on Canadian bonds.

Interest parity condition
The proposition that differences in interest rates on similar bonds in different countries reflect investors' expectations of future changes in exchange rates.

This process will go on until the expected return on Canadian bonds falls to the same level as the return on Chilean bonds, that is, 6.5%. This will be the case when the expected appreciation of the Canadian dollar is equal to the difference between the Chilean and the Canadian interest rates. Economists call this result the **interest parity condition**.

If we denote, as before, the domestic interest rate as i, the foreign interest rate as i^*, the nominal interest rate as E, and the expected nominal interest rate one year from now as E^e_{+1} (the superscript e standing for *expected*), the interest parity condition is that the interest rate on a domestic bond is equal to the interest rate on a foreign bond minus the expected rate of appreciation of the domestic currency.

$$i = i^* - \frac{E^e_{+1} - E}{E}. \tag{5.5}$$

Solved Problem 5.1

Making a Financial Killing by Buying Chilean Bonds?

In September 2013 the interest rate on Canadian one-year bonds was 1.09%; the interest rate on Chilean one-year bonds was 4.93%. Could you make money by borrowing in Canada and putting the proceeds in Chilean bonds? Evaluate this investment strategy.

Solving the Problem

Step 1 **Review the chapter material.** This problem is about the role exchange rates play in explaining differences in interest rates across countries, so you may want to review the section "The Interest Parity Condition," which begins on page 165.

Step 2 **Answer the question by using the interest parity condition to explain the relationship between expected changes in exchange rates and differences in interest rates across countries.** If the interest parity condition holds, then a 3.84-percentage-point gap between the interest rate on a Canadian and Chilean government bond means that investors must be expecting that the value of the Canadian dollar will appreciate against the peso by 3.84%.

We can also mention a few real-world complications: Although the Canadian government can borrow money for one year at 1.09%, a private investor would have to pay a significantly higher interest rate to compensate lenders for the investor's higher default risk. Similarly, the interest parity condition holds only when investors see the two bonds being compared as having the same characteristics. In fact, investors will see the Chilean bond as having higher default risk and lower liquidity than Canadian bonds. So, a part of the gap between the two interest rates represents compensation for these characteristics of the Chilean bond rather than expectations of future changes in the exchange rate. In addition, by investing in Chile, a Canadian investor will be taking on exchange rate risk because the Canadian dollar could appreciate by more than the 3.84%, which would cause the investor to earn a lower return on Chilean bonds than on Canadian bonds.

So the short answer to the question is that, while the interest rate on Chilean bonds is higher than on Canadian bonds, the difference reflects expectations of changes in the exchange rate as well as other factors so that you are unlikely to make a killing by borrowing in Canada and putting the proceeds in Chilean bonds.

See related problem 3.8 at the end of the chapter.

Does the interest parity condition always hold? Although the interest parity condition provides important insight into movements in exchange rates, in practice, differences in interest rates on similar bonds depend on several factors. First, investors typically see even similar bonds as having important differences in default risk and liquidity. Second, typically, the costs of purchasing foreign financial assets—the *transactions costs*—are higher than for domestic assets. For instance, brokerage firms may charge an investor higher commissions to buy a foreign firm's bonds than they would charge to buy a domestic firm's bonds. Finally, the interest parity condition, as we have stated it, does not take into account the exchange rate risk from investing in a foreign asset.

The interest parity condition provides an insight into what happens with the exchange rate when a country's interest rate increases or decreases relative to interest rates in another country. For example, suppose that the interest rate on a one-year Canadian bond is currently 2%, the interest rate on a comparable French one-year government bond is 4%, and the Canadian dollar is expected to appreciate by 2% against the euro. If the Bank of Canada takes actions that lead the Canadian bond interest rate to fall to 1%, we would expect the demand for Canadian dollars to decrease since the expected return on Canadian bonds has fallen. As a result, investors exchange Canadian dollars for euros in order to invest in French bonds. An increase in the supply of Canadian dollars will cause the exchange rate to decrease. The Canadian dollar will depreciate and, in the new equilibrium, fewer euros will be required to buy one Canadian dollar. We conclude that a reduction in Canadian interest rates leads to a depreciation of the Canadian dollar.

We can check whether this is consistent with the interest parity condition. A change in the exchange rate today usually does not affect expectations of the exchange rate a year from now. With the expected exchange rate a year from now unchanged, a 1% depreciation of the Canadian dollar will indeed maintain the interest rate parity condition. The expected return on Canadian bonds will now consist of the 1% interest payment and 3% expected appreciation and will be equal to the return on French bonds.

The Loanable Funds Model and the International Capital Market

5.4

Learning Objective

Use the loanable funds model to analyze the international capital market.

The interest rate is a key economic variable in the financial system. We have used the money market model to show how the interaction of the demand and supply for money determines the *short-run nominal interest rate* (see Chapter 2). In this section, we will use the loanable funds model to analyze the determinants of the *long-run real interest rate*. Recall that the nominal interest rate is the stated interest rate on a loan, while the real interest rate is the nominal interest rate adjusted for the effects of inflation. The long-run real interest rate is most relevant to households and firms making decisions about whether to invest in long-lived assets, such as houses or factories. In addition, the loanable funds model is useful when looking at the flow of funds between financial markets.

We begin our discussion of the loanable funds model by noting that the financial system is composed of the many markets through which funds flow from lenders to borrowers: the market for stocks, the market for bonds, the market for mutual fund shares, and so on. For simplicity, we combine these markets into a single market for loanable funds. To analyze the market we need to determine factors influencing the supply and demand for loanable funds.

Saving and Supply in the Loanable Funds Market

Let's first focus on the loanable funds market in a single economy. The supply of loanable funds is equal to the total flow of funds into financial markets from all sources: household savings, government savings, and inflows of loanable funds from abroad that we will call, by analogy, foreign savings.

Saving from households ($S^{\text{Households}}$) equals the funds households have left from their incomes (including transfer payments received from the government) after buying goods and services and paying taxes to the government.

Saving from the government ($S^{\text{Government}}$) equals the difference between the government's tax receipts and its spending on goods and services and on transfer payments to households.

Saving from the foreign sector (S^{Foreign}) equals minus net exports (i.e., $-1 \times$ net exports). What we call "foreign savings" is the flow of funds from abroad. To see why it equals the negative of net exports, consider that, if Canada imports more than it exports, more Canadian dollars flow out of the country to purchase imports than flow back in as foreign firms and foreign households buy Canadian exports. These extra Canadian dollars held by households and firms outside Canada are available to be reinvested back into Canadian financial markets.[11] Saving from the foreign sector is referred to as a *net capital inflow*.

Using symbols for these sources of saving, we have

$$S = S^{\text{Households}} + S^{\text{Government}} + S^{\text{Foreign}}.$$

Let's look more closely at the components of saving. Recall that the basic national income identity is

$$Y = C + I + G + NX,$$

where

Y = national income
C = consumption expenditure
I = investment expenditure on capital goods, such as factories, houses, and machinery, and changes in business inventories
G = government purchases of goods and services
NX = net exports of goods and services.

Household income equals the amount of funds received by households from the sale of goods and services (Y), plus what is received from the government as transfer payments (TR) such as Canada Pension Plan (CPP) or Employment Insurance (EI) payments. Using these definitions and letting T stand for households' tax payments to government, we have the following expressions for the three sources of saving:

$$S^{\text{Households}} = (Y + TR - T) - C,$$

$$S^{\text{Government}} = T - (G + TR),$$

$$\text{and } S^{\text{Foreign}} = -NX.$$

In Figure 5.12, we draw the supply of loanable funds, or saving, as a function of the real interest rate. The line is upward sloping, implying that the higher is the real interest rate, the higher is the supply of loanable funds. To explain this relationship, we consider the three sources of saving separately. For households, an increase in the real interest rate has two effects, the substitution and the income effect, which we will discuss in detail in Chapter 16. For now we assume that a higher real interest rate increases household savings. Foreign savings, of net capital inflow, increase when the real interest rate increases. Keeping constant the expected inflation rate, a higher real interest rate means a higher nominal interest rate. As we discussed in the previous section, when the Canadian nominal interest rate rises, foreign

---

[11]We are simplifying here by ignoring items in the current account other than net exports, but this simplification does not significantly affect the main point.

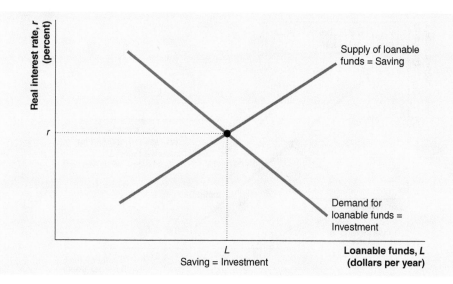

Figure 5.12

The Market for Loanable Funds

The supply of loanable funds is determined by (1) the willingness of households to save, (2) the extent of government saving, and (3) the extent of foreign saving that is invested in Canadian financial markets. The demand for loanable funds is determined by the willingness of firms to borrow money to engage in new investment projects. Equilibrium in the market for loanable funds determines the real interest rate and the quantity of loanable funds exchanged. At equilibrium in the loanable funds market, the total quantity of saving must equal the total quantity of investment.

investors increase their demand for Canadian dollars in order to buy Canadian financial assets. An increased demand for Canadian dollars increases the real exchange rate, reducing Canadian exports and increasing Canadian imports. Our net exports become more negative, which increases the net capital inflow. Finally, government savings are not affected by changes in the real interest rate as the government makes decisions about taxes and expenditures without paying a lot of attention to the level of market interest rates. Overall, the supply of loanable funds rises with the real interest rate.

Investment and the Demand for Loanable Funds

The demand for loanable funds is determined by the willingness of firms to borrow money to engage in new investment projects, such as building new factories or carrying out research and development of new products, and by the demand by households for new houses.[12] In determining whether to borrow funds, firms compare the real return (that is, the return adjusted for inflation) they expect to make on an investment with the real interest rate they must pay to borrow the necessary funds. For example, suppose that the Hudson Bay Company is considering opening several new stores and expects to earn a real return of 8% on its investment. That investment will be profitable if Hudson Bay can borrow the funds at a real interest rate of 6% but will not be profitable if the real interest rate is 10%. In Figure 5.12, we show the demand for loanable funds as downward sloping because the lower the real interest rate, the more investment projects firms can profitably undertake, and the greater the quantity of loanable funds they will demand.

Explaining Movements in Saving, Investment, and the Real Interest Rate

Equilibrium in the market for loanable funds determines the quantity of loanable funds that will flow from lenders to borrowers each period. Equilibrium also determines the real interest rate that lenders will receive and that borrowers must pay. Notice that because the supply of loanable funds represents saving, and the demand for loanable funds represents investment, in equilibrium, the value of saving equals the value of investment.

We draw the demand and supply curves for loanable funds by holding constant all factors, other than the real interest rate, that affect the willingness of borrowers to demand

---

[12]Once again, be alert to the important difference between *financial investment* in stock, bonds, and other securities and *investment expenditure* on houses, factories, machinery, equipment, and inventories.

Figure 5.13

An Increase in the Demand for Loanable Funds

An increase in the demand for loanable funds increases the equilibrium real interest rate from r_1 to r_2 and increases the equilibrium quantity of loanable funds from L_1 to L_2. As a result, saving and investment expenditure both increase.

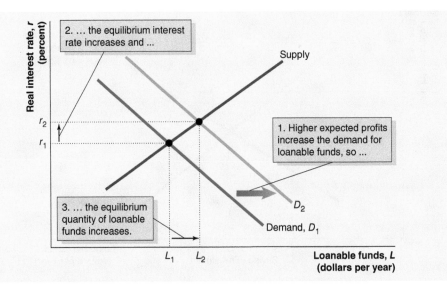

funds and lenders to supply funds. A change in a variable that affects the willingness to demand or supply funds will shift the demand or the supply curve, respectively. For example, Figure 5.13 shows that if firms expect higher profits in the future, the real interest rate, national saving, and the level of investment will all change. The higher expected profits shift the investment demand curve to the right, which increases the real interest rate from r_1 to r_2 and the equilibrium quantity of loanable funds from L_1 to L_2. Similarly, a reduction in corporate taxes increases investment profitability and shifts the investment demand curve to the right, raising the real interest rate and the equilibrium quantity of loanable funds. Notice that the increase in the quantity of loanable funds means that both the quantity of saving and the quantity of investment has increased.

We can also use the market for loanable funds to examine the effect of a government budget deficit or surplus. When the government's spending exceeds its tax receipts, the government's budget is in deficit, and the total amount of saving in the economy is decreased. Holding constant other factors that affect the demand and supply of loanable funds, Figure 5.14 shows the effects of a budget deficit as a shift to the left in the supply of loanable funds, from S_1 to S_2. In the new equilibrium, the real interest rate is higher and the equilibrium quantity of loanable funds is

Figure 5.14

The Effect of a Budget Deficit on the Market for Loanable Funds

When the government runs a budget deficit, the supply of loanable funds shifts to the left, from S_1 to S_2. The equilibrium real interest rate increases from r_1 to r_2 and the equilibrium quantity of loanable funds falls from L_1 to L_2. As a result, saving and investment both decline.

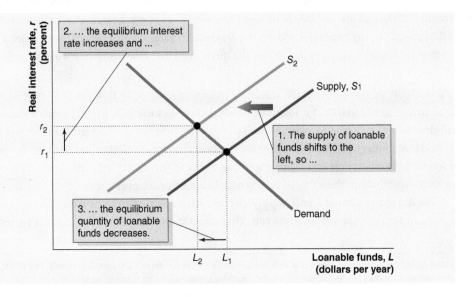

lower. A deficit has reduced the level of total saving in the economy and, by increasing the interest rate, it has also reduced the level of investment by firms. By borrowing to finance its budget deficit, the government will have crowded out some firms that would otherwise have been able to borrow to finance investment. **Crowding out** refers to the reduction in private investment that results from an increase in government purchases. Figure 5.14 shows the decline in investment due to crowding out by the movement from L_1 to L_2 on the demand for loanable funds curve.

Crowding out The reduction in private investment that results from an increase in government purchases.

Figure 5.14 shows that an increase in the budget deficit will reduce national saving, leading to higher real interest rates and lower investment. Similarly, an increase in net exports (which reduces foreign savings and net capital inflow), or a reduction in tax incentives for saving (for example a decrease in RRSP limits) will shift the supply curve to the left, raising the real interest rate and lowering the quantity of saving and investment.

The International Capital Market and the Interest Rate

The foreign sector affects the domestic interest rate and the quantity of funds available in the domestic economy. Foreign households, firms, and governments may lend funds to borrowers in Canada if the expected returns are higher than in other countries. Similarly, if opportunities are more profitable outside Canada, loanable funds will be drawn away from Canadian markets to investments abroad. In this section, we expand the loanable funds model to analyze the interaction between Canadian and foreign bond markets.

Borrowing and lending take place in the *international capital market*, where households, firms, and governments borrow and lend across national borders. The *world real interest rate*, r_w, is the interest rate that is determined in the international capital market. The quantity of loanable funds that is supplied in an open economy can be used to fund projects in the domestic economy or abroad. In thinking of the international economy, it is useful to make a distinction between *small open economies* and *large open economies*. Shifts in the supply or demand for loanable funds in small open economies, such as the economies of Canada or the Netherlands, do not have much effect on the world real interest rate as they are relatively small compared to the world market. However, changes in the behaviour of lenders and borrowers in large open economies, such as the economies of the United States, China, Japan, and Germany, do affect the world real interest rate. In the following sections, we consider interest rate determination in each case.

Small Open Economy

In a closed economy the equilibrium domestic real interest rate is determined by the intersection of the demand curve and supply curve for loanable funds in the country, and we ignore the world real interest rate. In an open economy, the world real interest rate is determined in the international capital market. To simplify matters, we will not include considerations related to default risk, liquidity, or the variability of exchange rates and inflation. In other words, we assume that domestic and foreign bonds have the same characteristics, and that uncertainty about the inflation rate is the same. We discuss what happens when these assumptions are not met at the end of this section.

In the case of a small open economy, the quantity of loanable funds supplied or demanded is too small to affect the world real interest rate. So, a small open economy's domestic real interest rate equals the world real interest rate, as determined in the international capital market. Why must the domestic interest rate in a small open economy equal the world interest rate? Suppose that the world real interest rate is 3%, but the domestic real interest rate in Canada is 2%. A lender in Canada would not accept an interest rate of less than 3% because we assume that the lender could easily buy foreign bonds with a 3% interest rate. So, domestic borrowers would have to pay the world real interest rate of 3%, or they would be unable to borrow.

Figure 5.15

Determining the Real Interest Rate in a Small Open Economy

The domestic real interest rate in a small open economy is the world real interest rate, r_w, which in this case is 3%. If the world real interest rate were greater than 3%, the country would lend internationally. If the world real interest rate were less than 3%, the country would borrow internationally.

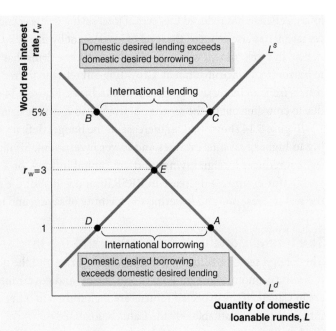

Figure 5.15 shows the supply and demand curves for loanable funds for a small open economy. As we focus on the analysis of capital flows, in Figure 5.15 we show domestic supply and demand. If the world real interest rate, r_w, is 3%, the quantity of loanable funds supplied and demanded domestically are equal (point *E*), and the country neither lends nor borrows funds in the international capital market. Suppose instead that the world real interest rate is 5%. In this case, the quantity of loanable funds supplied domestically (point *C*) is greater than the quantity of funds demanded domestically (point *B*). What happens to the excess supply of loanable funds? Those funds are loaned on the international capital market at the world real interest rate of 5%. Because the country is small, the amount of funds it has to lend is small relative to the world market, so lenders in the country have no trouble finding borrowers in other countries. As our earlier discussion of the balance of payments indicates, this international lending represents a current-account surplus.

Now suppose that the world real interest rate is 1%. As Figure 5.15 shows, the quantity of loanable funds demanded domestically (point *A*) now exceeds the quantity of funds supplied domestically (point *D*). How is this excess demand for funds satisfied? By borrowing on the international capital market. Because the country is small, the amount of funds it wants to borrow is small relative to the world market, so borrowers in the country have no trouble finding lenders in other countries. As our earlier discussion of the balance of payments indicates, this international borrowing represents a current-account deficit.

To summarize: The real interest rate in a small open economy is the same as the real interest rate in the international capital market. If, at that interest rate the quantity of loanable funds supplied domestically exceeds the quantity of funds demanded domestically, the country invests some of its loanable funds abroad. If, at that interest rate, the quantity of loanable funds demanded domestically exceeds the quantity of funds supplied domestically, the country finances some of its domestic borrowing needs with funds from abroad.

Large Open Economy

Shifts in the demand and supply of loanable funds in large countries—such as the United States, and, to a lesser extent China, Japan, and Germany—are sufficiently large that they affect the world real interest rate, so these countries are considered large open economies.

To simplify the discussion, suppose we think of the world as two large open economies: the economy of the United States and the economy of the rest of the world. Then the real interest rate in the international capital market equates desired international lending by the United States with desired international borrowing by the rest of the world. Using this assumption, Figure 5.16 illustrates how interest rates are determined in a large open economy. The figure presents a loanable funds graph for the United States in panel (a) and a loanable funds graph for the rest of the world in panel (b). In panel (a), if the world real interest rate is 3%, the quantity of loanable funds demanded and supplied in the United States are both equal to $300 billion. However, we can see in panel (b) that at an interest rate of 3%, the quantity of loanable funds demanded in the rest of the world is $800 billion, while the quantity of loanable funds supplied is only $700 billion. This tells us that foreign borrowers want to borrow $100 billion more from international capital markets than is available. Foreign borrowers therefore have an incentive to offer lenders in the United States an interest rate greater than 3%.

The interest rate will rise until the excess supply of loanable funds from the United States equals the excess demand for loanable funds in the rest of the world. Figure 5.16 shows that this equality is reached when the real interest rate has risen to 4% and the excess supply of loanable funds in the United States and the excess demand for loanable funds in the rest of the world both equal $50 billion. In other words, at a 4% real interest rate, desired international lending by the United States equals desired international borrowing by the rest of the world. Therefore, the international capital market is in equilibrium when the real interest rate in the United States and the rest of world equals 4%.

Our analysis implies that factors that cause the demand and supply of funds to shift in a large open economy will affect not just the interest rate in that economy but the world real interest rate as well. For example, the decline in investment demand in the United States, the Eurozone, and Japan during the Great Recession shifted the demand curve for loanable funds to the left, lowering the world real interest rate.

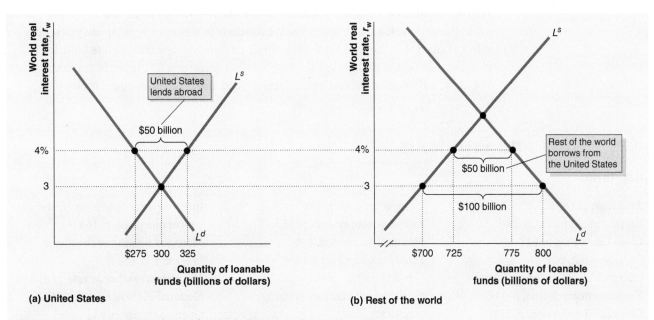

(a) United States

(b) Rest of the world

Figure 5.16 Determining the Real Interest Rate in a Large Open Economy

Saving and investment shifts in a large open economy can affect the world real interest rate. The world real interest rate adjusts to equalize desired international borrowing and desired international lending. At a world real interest rate of 4%, desired international lending by the domestic economy equals desired international borrowing by the rest of the world.

Finally, what happens when our assumptions are not met and bonds in different countries have different risk characteristics and liquidity, or the uncertainty about the inflation rate and the exchange rate differs across countries? The analysis is the same; but the differences between bonds introduce a wedge between real interest rates. To see this, we will look at the real interest rates on Argentinian bonds and on Canadian bonds. Let the world real interest rate be 3%. At the time of writing, Argentinian bonds were rated as CCC+ by the Standard and Poor's bond rating agency. Bond ratings are not like grades: While getting two C grades and a C+ is not terrible, the CCC+ rating was the second lowest bond rating given by Standard and Poor's (Only the tiny country of Grenada had a lower rating.) The low rating of Argentinian bonds is the consequence of Argentina's debt default in 2002. To buy Argentinian bonds, investors would require a very large risk premium over the world interest rate. Also, the market for Argentinian bonds is small, with limited liquidity. In addition, the real interest rate on Argentinian bonds was highly uncertain since the official inflation data were widely considered unreliable. (In other words, the government was perceived as cheating.) Finally, the exchange rate of the Argentinian peso was very volatile. Let us assume that investors required an extra 10% to compensate for the high risk premium, low liquidity of the bond market, and the uncertainty about the inflation and exchange rate in Argentina. To illustrate this in Figure 5.16, we could draw the demand and supply curves intersecting at the real interest rate of 13% when the world interest rate is 3%.

Let us now consider Canada. Government of Canada bonds are rated AAA. A student with straight A's is a very good student and, indeed, a triple A bond rating is the highest rating: Canadian government bonds have a very small default risk. The market for Canadian government bonds is relatively liquid. In the past 20 years the inflation rate in Canada has been very stable, reducing the uncertainty about the real interest rate. Finally, the exchange rate of the Canadian dollar is not terribly volatile. This means that investors will accept a lower real interest rate on Canadian bonds than the real-world interest rate. Let us assume that the low default risk, relatively liquid bond market and low uncertainty about the real interest rate and the exchange rate are worth 1% to investors, so that they will accept the real interest rate of 2% on Canadian bonds when the world real interest rate is 3%. To illustrate this in Figure 5.16, we could draw the demand and supply curves intersecting at the real interest rate of 2% when the world real interest rate is 3%. We conclude that our model adequately describes the effect of changes in the world real interest rate on domestic real interest rate (and, for a large country, the effect of changes in the domestic real interest rate on the world real interest rate) but the actual values of the real interest rate depend also on country characteristics.

Key Terms and Problems

Key Terms

Arbitrage, p. 163

Balance of payments, p. 146

Closed economy, p. 144

Crowding out, p. 171

Currency appreciation, p. 149

Currency depreciation, p. 149

Currency devaluation, p. 159

Currency overvaluation (undervaluation), p. 160

Currency revaluation, p. 159

Current account, p. 146

Exchange rate system, p. 153

Financial account, p. 146

Fixed exchange rate system, p. 153

Floating exchange rate system, p. 153

Foreign direct investment, p. 147

Foreign portfolio investment, p. 147

Forward exchange rate, p. 149

Interest parity condition, p. 166

Law of one price, p. 163

Managed floating exchange rate system, p. 154

Multilateral exchange rate, p. 150

Nominal exchange rate, p. 148

Open economy, p. 144

Purchasing power parity, p. 164

Real exchange rate, p. 151

Spot exchange rate, p. 149

5.1   The Balance of Payments
Explain how to calculate the balance of payments.

Review Questions

1.1 What is the difference between an open economy and a closed economy?

1.2 What is the purpose of the balance of payments? Briefly discuss the components of the current account and the financial account.

1.3 What are a trade deficit, a current-account deficit, and a financial account deficit? Is it possible for a country to run a balance of payments deficit?

Problems and Applications

1.4 Briefly explain in which of the three balance of payments accounts each of the following transactions would occur:

   a. An export of goods

   b. A purchase of bonds

   c. A gift to someone in another country

   d. A dividend paid on stock owned in another country

1.5 A political columnist makes the following assertion: "China has a huge balance of trade surplus with the rest of the world. In addition, the rest of the world is investing huge amounts in China, which is the main way that China is able to fund investments in new factories." Use your knowledge of the balance of payments accounts to analyze the columnist's argument.

1.6 An article in the *Economist* magazine states: "India aims to fund its current-account deficit mainly by attracting … flows of FDI [foreign direct investment]." What is foreign direct investment? In what sense can foreign direct investment fund a country's current-account deficit?

   Source: "Travelers Checked," *The Economist*, May 19, 2012.

1.7 Consider the following statement: "Because the percentage of Japanese and U.S. GDP accounted for by trade (34.2 and 30.7% respectively, for the sum of exports and imports) is much less than for many other countries (88% for the European Union countries, 62% for Canada), trade is not very important for the two countries." Briefly explain whether you agree with this statement.

   Source: CIA Factbook

1.8 The table below represents the balance of payments for a small nation in 2014. All values are in millions of dollars. Calculate the missing values in the table and briefly explain how you arrived at your answers.

Current Account		
Exports of goods and services	6525	
Imports of goods and services	____	
Net exports		1223
Income received on investments and labour compensation	1108	
Income payments on investments and labour compensation	−640	
Net factor payments		____
Net transfers		−303
Balance on current account		____
Financial Account		
Increase in foreign holdings of assets in the country	____	
Increase in the country's holdings of assets in foreign countries	−2469	
Net financial derivatives	17	
Balance on financial account		−1436
Capital Account		
Balance on capital account	−5	
Statistical discrepancy	____	
Balance of payments		____

5.2   Exchange Rates and Exchange Rate Policy
Understand the advantages and disadvantages of different exchange rate policies.

Review Questions

2.1 Most people in Canada rarely exchange Canadian dollars for another currency. So why do economists and policymakers worry about fluctuations in exchange rates?

2.2 Briefly explain the difference between each of the following:

   a. A nominal exchange rate and a real exchange rate

b. A bilateral exchange rate and a multilateral exchange rate

c. A currency appreciation and a currency depreciation

d. A fixed exchange rate system and a floating exchange rate system

2.3 Briefly explain the similarities and the differences between the gold standard and the Bretton Woods systems.

2.4 Briefly discuss the policy choices reflected in current exchange rate systems.

Problems and Applications

2.5 According to an article in *The Wall Street Journal*, "Japan's three largest auto makers are signaling plans to shift more production overseas to deal with the strong yen."

a. What does the article mean by a "strong yen"?

b. What problem does a strong yen cause for Japanese automobile companies?

c. How would moving production overseas help Japanese automobile companies deal with a strong yen?

Source: "Japan's Big Car Makers Grapple with Strong Yen," *The Wall Street Journal*, June 26, 2012.

2.6 In each of the following cases, calculate the real exchange rate:

a. A bottle of wine sells for $16 in Canada and €10 in France, and the nominal exchange rate is €1 = $1.3.

b. A book sells for $10 in Canada and ¥950 in Japan, and the nominal exchange rate is $1$1 = ¥100.

c. A shirt sells for $45 in Canada and £30 in the United Kingdom, and the nominal exchange rate is $1 = £0.67.

2.7 If you were a Canadian firm whose business mainly involves importing or exporting goods, why might you prefer an exchange rate system like Bretton Woods to the current system?

2.8 [Related to Making the Connection on page 162] In mid-2012, as Greece considered leaving the euro, *Canadian Business* published an article about mass bank withdrawals. Were bank depositors afraid that Greek banks were likely to fail? If not, what were they afraid of? Would depositors in Canadian banks be likely to have similar fears about Canadian banks? Briefly explain.

Source: Graham F. Scott, "Europeans Draining Bank Accounts," *Canadian Business*, June 12, 2012.

5.3 | **What Factors Determine Exchange Rates?**
Discuss what factors determine exchange rates.

Review Questions

3.1 What is purchasing power parity? Why doesn't purchasing power parity hold exactly?

3.2 Assuming that purchasing power parity holds, write an equation that expresses the relationship among the percentage change in the nominal exchange rate, the domestic inflation rate, and the foreign inflation rate. Briefly explain this equation.

3.3 What is the interest parity condition?

3.4 What problems can exchange rate fluctuations cause for firms?

Problems and Applications

3.5 If the euro appreciates, how will this affect your purchases of Canadian and German goods? Explain.

3.6 Suppose that you are planning to study abroad in Mexico for a semester. In planning for your trip, you calculate what you spend in a semester in Canada. Then you check to see what the current exchange rate is.

a. If you spend $2000 per semester on food, entertainment, and other incidental expenses in Mexico, and if the current exchange rate is $1 = 12 pesos, how many pesos do you need if your expenses are identical?

b. Assuming that you consume the same amount of food and other goods no matter where you are in Mexico, do you think that the method you used in part (a) will correctly calculate the number of pesos you need for your trip? Briefly explain.

3.7 Suppose that the inflation rate in Canada is 5%, and the inflation rate in the United Kingdom is 8%. Use purchasing power parity to predict what is likely to happen to the exchange rate between the pound and the Canadian dollar.

3.8 **[Related to** Solved Problem 5.1 **on page 166]** According to an article in the *Globe and Mail*, investors are borrowing money in yen, where interest rates are low, and exchanging it for currencies in countries where interest rates are higher, such as Canada and the United States. Is it certain that investors actually are profiting from this difference in interest rates? Explain.

Source: Scott Barlow, "The yen carry trade turns Japan's pain into our gain," *Globe and Mail*, December 27, 2012.

3.9 According to an article in *The Wall Street Journal* on the effects of fluctuations in the exchange value of the

real on Brazilian firms, "Companies most at risk are those with large amounts of foreign currency debt."

a. What is foreign currency debt?

b. Why would firms in Brazil have foreign currency debt?

c. Why would having foreign currency debt make firms in Brazil more vulnerable to fluctuations in the exchange value of the real? Would these firms be equally hurt by an appreciation of the real as by a depreciation of the real? Briefly explain.

Source: Luciana Magalhaes, "Currency Volatility Poses Risk for Brazilian Companies," *Wall Street Journal*, May 6, 2012.

5.4 The Loanable Funds Model and the International Capital Market
Use the loanable funds model to analyze the international capital market.

Review Questions

4.1 What determines the supply of loanable funds? What determines the demand for loanable funds?

4.2 In the loanable funds model, why is the demand curve downward sloping? Why is the supply curve upward sloping?

4.3 Briefly explain what happens to the world real interest rate if the government of Monaco runs a large government budget deficit.

Problems and Applications

4.4 Suppose this graph represents the demand and supply of loanable funds in Canada. Use the graph to answer the following questions.

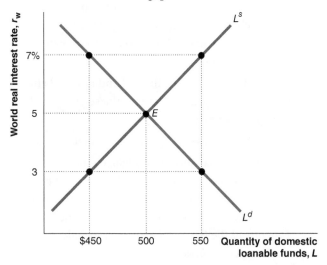

a. If the world real interest rate is 5%, explain what would give foreign borrowers an incentive to offer lenders in Canada an interest rate greater than 5%.

b. If the world real interest rate is 5%, explain what would give foreign lenders an incentive to offer borrowers in Canada an interest rate less than 5%.

4.5 Draw a graph of the market for loanable funds in a closed economy. Show the effect on the equilibrium real interest rate and quantity of funds loaned and borrowed of each of the following events:

a. Consumers decide to spend less.

b. The government decreases its spending.

c. Businesses become pessimistic about future profitability.

d. The government's budget deficit increases, and at the same time, investment in new capital goods becomes more profitable.

4.6 Suppose that in a small open economy, the domestic quantity of loanable funds supplied equals the domestic quantity of loanable funds demanded. In other words, there is no foreign lending or borrowing. If the government budget deficit increases, what will happen in the market for loanable funds? Will the country lend or borrow internationally? Briefly explain.

4.7 Suppose that in a large open economy, the quantity of loanable funds supplied domestically is initially equal to the quantity of funds demanded domestically. Then an increase in business taxes discourages investment. Draw a graph of the loanable funds market to show how this change affects the quantity of loanable funds and the world real interest rate. Does the economy now borrow or lend internationally?

4.8 In a small open economy, how would each of the following events affect the equilibrium interest rate and the amount of international lending or borrowing that the country engages in?

a. A natural disaster causes extensive damage to homes, bridges, and highways, leading to increased investment spending to repair the damaged infrastructure.

b. Taxes on businesses are expected to be increased in the future.

c. The World Cup soccer matches are being televised, and many people stay home to watch them, reducing consumption spending.

d. The government proposes a new tax on saving, based on the value of people's investments as of December 31 each year.

4.9 Repeat problem 4.8 for a large open economy.

4.10 An article in the *Economist* magazine refers to the United Kingdom as a "small open economy." If this statement is correct, will the U.K. economy experience crowding out if the government runs a budget deficit? Briefly explain.

Source: "Austerity Is Pain. So Is Tight Money," *Economist*, January 19, 2012.

Data Exercises

D5.1: Using data from Statistics Canada http://www5.statcan.gc.ca/cansim/a01?lang=eng, Table 176-0064, analyze the trade-weighted value of the Canadian dollar.

a. Download monthly data on the trade-weighted exchange rate for the Canadian dollar against major currencies (CERI) from 1991 to the present, as well as monthly data for the exchange rate of the U.S. dollar.

b. What has been the long-term trend in the trade-weighted exchange value of the Canadian dollar? How did they compare to the long-term trend in the U.S. dollar exchange rate?

c. What effect should changes in the exchange rate have had Canadian net exports to the United States and to the rest of the world? Briefly explain.

d. What has been the trend in the exchange value of the Canadian dollar over the last year?

D5.2: Using data from Statistics Canada (http://www5.statcan.gc.ca/cansim/a01?lang=eng), Table 176-0103, analyze the relationship between the exchange rate and the current account.

a. Download quarterly data on the current-account balance.

b. Download data on the trade-weighted exchange rate for the Canadian dollar (CERI-Table 176-0064). How do the current account movements correspond with exchange rate movements?

D5.3: Using data from Statistics Canada (http://www5.statcan.gc.ca/cansim/a01?lang=eng) Table 376-0102, download the data on net acquisitions of financial assets and liabilities.

a. Look at recent Net acquisition of financial assets. How has the value changed over the past five years?

b. Look at recent Net incurrence of liabilities. How has the value changed over the past five years?

D5.4: [Spreadsheet exercise] The Bank for International Settlements (BIS) publishes data on real effective exchange rates and indexes of nominal effective exchange rates (www.bis.org/statistics/eer/index.htm). These indexes attempt to measure competitiveness.

a. Find and download the real and nominal effective exchange rate for the Chinese yuan for the past five years.

b. Plot the two series against each other.

c. The nominal effective exchange rate of the yuan changes little because it has been a fixed rate. What accounts for the differences between the two exchange rates? (Hint: It may be helpful to read the BIS's explanation of its indexes of competitiveness.)

D5.5: Using data from Statistics Canada (http://www5 .statcan.gc.ca/cansim/a01?lang=eng) Table 176-0064, analyze foreign exchange rates.

  a. Find the most recent values for the U.S dollar/ Canadian dollar, British pound/Canadian dollar and the Japanese yen/Canadian dollar foreign exchange rates.

  b. Explain whether the exchange rates are quoted as Canadian dollars per unit of foreign currency or units of foreign currency per Canadian dollar.

  c. Given the way exchange rates are reported by Statistics Canada, what happens with the exchange rate when the Canadian dollar appreciates? What happens when it depreciates?

  d. Suppose an iPad sells for 500 Canadian dollars in Canada., 500 U.S. dollars in the United States, 400 pounds in the United Kingdom, and 40 000 yen in Japan. What is the price of an iPad in each country in terms of Canadian dollars.

  e. Assuming no transportation costs, explain in which county you would want to purchase an iPad and in which country you would want to sell the same iPad in order to make the highest profit possible.

D5.6: Using data from Statistics Canada (http://www5 .statcan.gc.ca/cansim/a01?lang=eng) Tables 176-0064 and 228-0058, analyze foreign exchange rates.

  a. Find two recent values, a year apart, for the yen/ Canadian dollar and pound/Canadian dollar foreign exchange rates as well as the values for exports to Japan and the United Kingdom.

  b. Given the change in the exchange rates between the two periods, explain whether Canadian exports to Japan and the United Kingdom changed in the direction that economic theory would predict.

  Note: You need to use Step 5 under the Add/Remove data button to show trade with Japan and the United Kingdom. In Step 3, select the customs basis.

D5.7: Using data from Statistics Canada (http://www5 .statcan.gc.ca/cansim/a01?lang=eng) Tables

176-0064 and 228-0058, analyze foreign exchange rates.

  a. Find two recent values, a year apart, for the yen/Canadian dollar and pound/dollar foreign exchange rates.

  b. Given the change in the exchange rate between the two periods, discuss whether Canadian imports to Japan and the United Kingdom changed in the direction that economic theory would predict.

  Note: You need to use Step 5 under the Add/Remove data button to show trade with Japan and the United Kingdom. In Step 3, select the customs basis.

D5.8: Using data from Statistics Canada (http://www5 .statcan.gc.ca/cansim/a01?lang=eng) Table 176-0064, analyze exchange rates.

  a. Find the most recent value and the value from the same month one year earlier for the euro exchange rate in terms of the Canadian dollar (i.e., the price of one euro in dollars).

  b. Using the values found above, compute the percentage change in the euro's value.

  c. Explain whether the Canadian dollar appreciated or depreciated against the euro.

D5.9: Using data from Statistics Canada (http://www5 .statcan.gc.ca/cansim/a01?lang=eng), Tables 380-0072, 380-0076, and 380-0079, analyze savings and investment.

  a. Find the most recent values and the values from the same quarter three years earlier for household net saving, corporation net saving, and net general government savings.

  b. Using the values found above, compute the total net saving in the economy for each period.

  c. Draw a graph to show the loanable funds market in equilibrium. Explain which curve represents total net saving.

  d. On the graph drawn in part (c), show the effect on the loanable funds market from the change in total net saving between the two periods in part (a).

The Labour Market

Learning Objectives

After studying this chapter, you should be able to:

6.1 Use the model of demand and supply for labour to explain how wages and employment are determined (pages 182–188)

6.2 Define unemployment and explain the three categories of unemployment (pages 188–192)

6.3 Explain the natural rate of unemployment (pages 192–197)

6.4 Understand factors that prevent real wage from adjusting to the equilibrium level (pages 197–199)

Firms Have Trouble Finding Workers; So Why Is the Unemployment Rate so High?

The Great Recession was the most severe the world economy had experienced since the Great Depression of the 1930s. In 2014, more than four years after the end of the recession, the unemployment rate was 6.9% in Canada, 6.7% in the United States, and 7.2% in the United Kingdom. The proportion of workers who were long-term unemployed (defined as over six months or over a year), increased dramatically in the United States, although the increase in Canada was much smaller. The situation was much worse in the European Union, where the unemployment rate was almost 12%. The unemployment rate was over 10% in France, 12% in Italy, and an astonishing 24% in Spain and 27% in Greece. What was worse, the unemployment rate in many European countries was increasing, reaching record levels month after month. Unemployment had been so high for so long that some economists had begun speaking of the "new normal," in which unemployment rates might be stuck at higher levels for many years.

But despite the severity of the recession and slow recovery, some firms continued to hire workers. Many firms were reporting shortages of skilled workers, even while millions remained unemployed. In Canada, in the first quarter of 2013 almost 300 000 jobs went unfilled. A report by the consulting firm Deloitte found that 600 000 manufacturing jobs were going unfilled in the United States because firms could not find skilled workers. In Italy, where youth unemployment exceeded 50%, Giovanni Pagotto, a plastics manufacturer, caused an uproar complaining he could not find workers. A study by Italy's chambers of commerce

Continued on next page

found pressing shortages of economists, managers, engineers, mathematicians, and salespeople.

The experiences of these firms reflected two aspects of the labour markets. First, economists agree that during recessions and expansions alike, millions of jobs are created and destroyed every month. This is just a normal churn in the labour market. Some firms close, others are created, some firms expand, others shrink. In a recession, the rate of job destruction increases, while the rate of job creation falls.

The second aspect of the labour market involves structural unemployment, which arises from a persistent mismatch between the skills of workers and the requirements of jobs. No one doubted that part of the high unemployment rates during and after the recession represented cyclical unemployment, or unemployment due to the recession. But was the level of structural unemployment unusually high? Some economists were skeptical that a rise in structural unemployment could account for more than a small percentage of the overall increase in unemployment. Economists and policymakers have debated the reasons why unemployment has remained persistently high since the end of the recession.

The disagreement among economists involves more than just how to categorize the unemployed. The types of economic policies to combat unemployment depend at least in part on what was causing the high rates of unemployment. If unemployment is due to temporary, recession-related causes, temporary solutions such as a fiscal stimulus may help. But unemployment could be caused by structural changes in the economy, accelerated by the recession. In that case, there is a mismatch between jobs and skills, and alleviating the mismatch requires long-term labour market policies.

Sources: Dario Thuburn, "Unfilled jobs in Italy spark heated debate," Agence France Presse, August 25, 2013; "Close to 300 000 jobs remain unfilled in Q1," *CNW*, May 16, 2013; David Jolly, "Unemployment in Euro Zone Reaches a Record High," *New York Times*, April 2, 2013; Ian Silvera, "Italy's Youth Unemployment at 42% as Jobless Rate Hits 37-Year High", " *International Business Times*, January 8, 2014.

Introduction

When most people think about how well the economy is doing, they focus on the state of the labour market. How easy is it for them, members of their family, and friends to find jobs? Are they receiving pay raises or pay cuts? By the spring of their senior year, most college students are face to face with the state of the economy as they consider their job prospects. As we saw in Chapter 1, entering the labour force when the job market is weak can mean not only a much longer job search but also possibly having to work for years in a relatively low-paying job or a job that is not career-related. Not surprisingly, the unemployment rate is probably the most closely watched macroeconomic statistic by the general public. When the government releases new statistics on the labour market, good news usually causes stock prices to rise, and bad news causes stock prices to fall.

Economists devote significant time and resources to analyzing the labour market. In this chapter, we discuss what economists mean by the phrase *full employment*. As it turns out, full employment does not mean that every worker who wants a job has one. Economists use a definition of full employment that reflects the fact that the labour market is dynamic and that workers are constantly entering and leaving employment.

We begin this chapter by analyzing a simple model of labour demand and labour supply with perfectly flexible wages. In the model, the real wage adjusts to equate labour demand with labour supply and the labour market is in equilibrium, with only voluntary unemployment so that the only people who are unemployed are those who are unwilling to work at the conditions they are offered. In Section 6.2 we look at unemployment data for Canada, the United States, and the European Union and conclude that some unemployment must be involuntary, in the sense that workers willing to work at current conditions are not able to find employment. We then look at the three types of unemployment: frictional (unemployment that is related to job search), structural (unemployment caused by a mismatch of qualifications), and cyclical (unemployment arising from cyclical fluctuations in the job market).

In Section 6.3 we define and analyze the factors affecting the natural rate of unemployment. Finally, we look at several reasons for unemployment arising when wages do not adjust to clear the labour market.

The Labour Market

6.1

Learning Objective
Use the model of demand and supply for labour to explain how wages and employment are determined.

Economists rely on the basic model of demand and supply to analyze the labour market. We now develop a simple model of demand and supply of labour. In the model we abstract from differences between jobs, qualifications, etc., and concentrate on the demand for and supply of labour.

Nominal and Real Wages

The price of labour is the wage. We will use the wage as a shortcut for the total cost of an employee and include "fringe benefits," such as retirement benefits and bonuses. The nominal wage (W) is how much workers are paid in dollars. The real wage, w, represents the purchasing power of the nominal wage and is calculated by dividing the nominal wage by the price level, P:

$$Real\ wage = w = \frac{W}{P}. \tag{6.1}$$

For example, if the nominal wage in 2013 is $40 per hour and the price level is $2 (i.e., a bundle of goods costs $2), then the real wage is 20 (bundles of goods). If the inflation rate is 3% while the nominal wage remains unchanged, the real wage will fall to 19.42. This is because a bundle of goods now costs $2.06 = $2 × (1 + 0.03) and so $40 buys only 19.42 bundles of goods: $40/$2.06 = 19.42.

The Demand for Labour Services

Firms employ workers and capital (buildings, machines, and other equipment) to produce goods and services. The demand for labour of an individual firm is equal to the number of workers that would maximize the firm's profits. The total demand for labour is the sum of individual firms' demands. In our simple model we look at changes in the number of workers when the amount of capital the firm employs is fixed. The **marginal product of labour (MPL)** is the extra output a firm receives from adding one more unit of labour, holding everything else constant. In general, as we discuss in more detail in the next chapter, the marginal product of labour decreases as the number of workers increases: Each additional worker produces less extra output than the last worker employed. An intuitive explanation is that as the number of workers increases while the amount of capital does not change, each worker has less capital to work with and so is less productive. The marginal product of labour curve is shown in Figure 6.1 as a downward sloping line, reflecting the inverse relationship between the number of workers and the marginal product of labour.

Marginal product of labour (MPL) The extra output a firm receives from adding one more unit of labour, holding everything else constant.

Consider a typical firm, called Dale's Café. It hires workers to maximize profits. We assume that the firm is small and so changes in its demand for labour do not affect wages. The value of an additional worker's output is $P \cdot MPL$, where P is the price of the firm's output, and the cost is the nominal wage, W. So the effect on profits of an extra worker is, in nominal terms

$$\Delta Profit = P \cdot MPL - W. \tag{6.2}$$

Dale's Café will hire labour as long as the change in profit is greater than zero. As its workforce increases, the marginal product of labour declines: Each additional worker makes

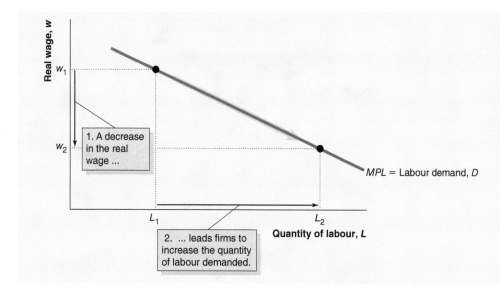

Figure 6.1

The Labour Demand Curve

The demand curve for labour is the marginal product of labour curve. It slopes downward because the marginal product of labour decreases as the number of workers rises. As the real wage decreases from w_1 to w_2, firms increase the quantity of labour demanded from L_1 to L_2. As firms hire more workers, the marginal product of labour decreases.

fewer coffees. The firm stops hiring when the additional profit from an extra worker falls to zero, i.e., when $P \cdot MPL - W = 0$. Dividing both sides by P and rearranging we obtain

$$MPL = (W/P). \tag{6.3}$$

Equation (6.3) shows that profits are maximized when the marginal product of labour equals the real wage. In case of Dale's Café, the marginal product of labour is the number of extra coffees made by an additional worker and the real wage is the number of coffees the additional worker's salary would buy. The number of workers that maximizes Dale's Café's profits is shown in Figure 6.1: When the real wage is w_1, the number of workers Dale's Café would like to employ is L_1. If the real wage decreases to w_2, the firm will hire additional workers until the marginal product of labour falls enough to restore the equality (6.3). The number of workers will increase from L_1 to L_2. Conversely, if the real wage increases, the firm will lay off workers until the marginal product of labour rises enough to restore the equality. The total demand for labour will be the sum of demands of firms like Dale's Café. All of them increase the number of workers they demand when the real wage falls, and reduce the number of workers they demand when the real wage increases. The demand curve for labour shows the relationship between the cost of labour: the real wage, $w = W/P$, and the number of workers the firm wants to employ. This number of workers can be read from the marginal product of labour curve. *Therefore, the marginal product of labour curve is the same as the demand for labour curve.* This is illustrated in Figure 6.1.

Shifting the Demand Curve

The demand curve for labour shows the relationship between the real wage rate and the quantity of labour demanded, holding everything else constant. For labour demand, "everything else" is any variable other than the real wage that affects the willingness of firms to hire workers. Because the labour demand curve is the marginal product of labour curve, "everything else" includes factors that affect the marginal product of labour, such as the amount of capital, the skill level of workers, and technology. Changes in these variables cause the demand curve to shift. To understand why the demand curve for labour shifts, think from the firm's point of view. Firms hire workers to produce goods and services. Anything that makes workers more productive will make the workers more valuable to the firm. The more productive workers become, the more workers the firm is willing to hire at the current real

Figure 6.2

Shifting the Labour Demand Curve

If technology improves, the marginal product of labour increases, which shifts the labour demand curve to the right, from D_1 to D_2. Similar reasoning shows that an increase in the capital stock or in the skill level of workers also shifts the labour demand curve to the right.

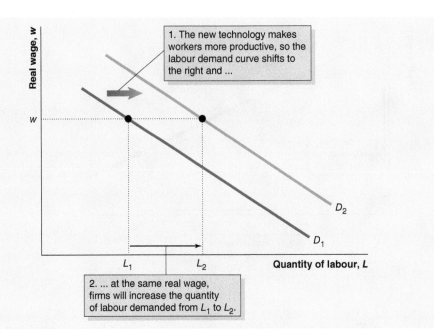

1. The new technology makes workers more productive, so the labour demand curve shifts to the right and ...

2. ... at the same real wage, firms will increase the quantity of labour demanded from L_1 to L_2.

wage, so the labour demand curve shifts to the right. This is illustrated in Figure 6.2, where the labour demand curve shifts from D_1 to D_2. If the real wage remains fixed at w, the quantity of labour demanded will increase from L_1 to L_2. By similar reasoning, an increase in the capital stock would also increase the quantity of labour demanded. For example consider an accounting firm. If it gives its auditors better hardware to work with, each worker can carry out more audits, so the marginal product of labour will increase, shifting the labour demand curve to the right.

The Supply of Labour Services

We turn now to considering how households decide the quantity of labour to supply. Of the many trade-offs each of us faces in life, one of the most important is how to divide up the 24 hours in a day between labour and leisure. Every hour spent working reduces the amount of time left for sleeping, reading, watching television, playing sports, or other forms of leisure. Because by working we lose leisure, *the wage is the opportunity cost of leisure*. In that sense, we can consider the real wage to be the price of leisure.

To understand the effect of an increase in the real wage on the quantity of labour supplied, imagine that you just received a real wage increase of 10%. Would you be willing to work more hours or fewer hours? Microeconomics tells us that there are two effects: a substitution effect and an income effect. The *substitution effect* is the effect of changing a relative price, in our case changing the relative price of leisure. When the real wage increases, leisure becomes more expensive relative to goods and services, in the sense that if you want to buy extra goods, you need to give up more leisure. As leisure becomes more expensive, you choose to have less leisure and work more. The substitution effect increases your labour supply. The *income effect* is the effect of the change in income on demand for goods. When the real wage increases permanently due to, for example, productivity improvements, you can buy more while working the same number of hours. Microeconomics tells us that, with higher income, we consume more of normal goods.[1] Empirical evidence shows that leisure

---

[1] A good is normal if an increase in income raises demand for it.

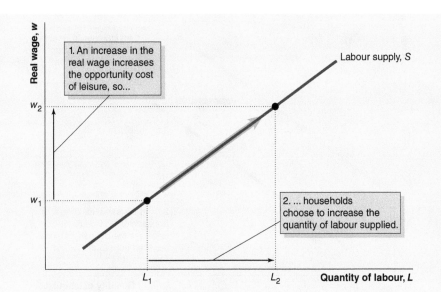

Figure 6.3

The Labour Supply Curve

Assuming the substitution effect is stronger than the income effect, an increase in the real wage from w_1 to w_2 causes the quantity of labour supplied to increase from L_1 to L_2 and the labour supply curve to slope upward.

is a normal good and so a higher income raises the demand for leisure and reduces the supply of hours of work. The two effects operate in the opposite direction: When the real wage increases, the substitution effect leads you to supply more hours of labour, while the income effect leads you to supply fewer hours of labour. Whether you would increase or decrease the quantity of hours you supply depends on which of these tendencies is stronger for you.[2] For the aggregate labour market, which includes all the workers in the country, evidence suggests that, in the short run, the substitution effect is stronger than the income effect, so an increase in the real wage leads to an increase in the quantity of labour supplied. In other words, the labour supply curve slopes upward, as shown in Figure 6.3. As the real wage increases from w_1 to w_2, the quantity of labour supplied increases from L_1 to L_2.

Factors That Shift the Labour Supply Curve

The labour supply curve shows the relationship between the real wage and the quantity of labour supplied, holding constant other factors that might affect the willingness of households to supply labour. These factors include households' wealth, preferences for leisure over labour, and income taxes. When these other factors change, the labour supply curve shifts. For example, households typically respond to an increase in wealth by "purchasing" more leisure time and supplying fewer hours of labour. The result is that when household wealth increases, the labour supply curve shifts to the left, as shown in Figure 6.4.

An increase in income tax rates reduces after-tax income, so the opportunity cost of leisure decreases. As a result, households purchase more leisure and decrease the quantity of labour supplied, so the labour supply curve shifts to the left. This explanation assumes, once again, that the substitution effect is stronger than the income effect. Similarly, an increased preference for leisure shifts the labour supply curve to the left.

Equilibrium in the Labour Market

We now consider equilibrium in the labour market under the assumption that real wages are completely flexible. (We analyze reasons for real wage rigidity later in the chapter.)

---

[2]It also depends on whether your employer allows you the flexibility to adjust the number of hours that you work.

Figure 6.4

Shifting the Labour Supply Curve

The labour supply curve shifts to the left, from S_1 to S_2, if wealth increases, income taxes increase, or there is a shift in preference toward leisure. As a result, the quantity of labour that households supply at the fixed real wage, w, falls from L_1 to L_2.

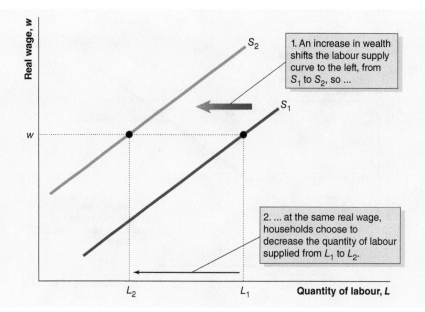

1. An increase in wealth shifts the labour supply curve to the left, from S_1 to S_2, so ...

2. ... at the same real wage, households choose to decrease the quantity of labour supplied from L_1 to L_2.

Figure 6.5 shows equilibrium in the aggregate labour market at point A, with equilibrium wage rate w^* and equilibrium quantity of labour L^*. If the real wage is below equilibrium, as at w_1, the quantity of labour demanded, L_2, is greater than the quantity of labour supplied, L_1. Competition among firms will drive up the real wage to w^*, where the quantity of labour demanded equals the quantity of labour supplied, and upward pressure on the real wage is eliminated. If the real wage started above the equilibrium real wage, the quantity of labour supplied would exceed the quantity of labour demanded. Some workers would offer to work for a lower real wage, which would eventually drive the real wage down to w^*, where the quantity of labour demanded equals the quantity of labour supplied, and downward pressure on the real wage is eliminated.

The Effect of Technological Change

A change in a variable, apart from the real wage, that affects the demand or supply of labour will cause the demand curve and/or the supply curve to shift. Consider a change in

Figure 6.5

Equilibrium in the Labour Market

If the real wage equals w^*, the labour market is in equilibrium. At the real wage w_1 the quantity of labour demanded, L_2, would exceed the quantity of labour supplied, L_1, resulting in a shortage of labour. The competition among firms will drive up the real wage to w^*.

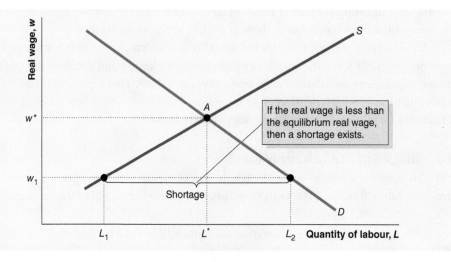

If the real wage is less than the equilibrium real wage, then a shortage exists.

Shortage

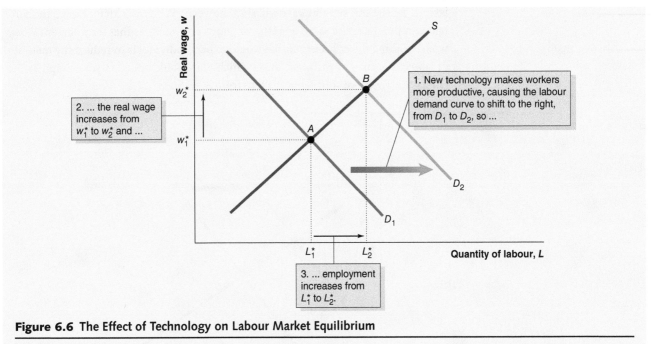

Figure 6.6 The Effect of Technology on Labour Market Equilibrium

When new technology makes workers more productive, the marginal product of labour increases, so the labour demand curve shifts to the right, from D_1 to D_2. As a result, the real wage increases to w_2^* and the quantity of labour increases to L_2^*.

technology that increases labour productivity, such as better hardware for accountants that allows them to do more audits. As shown in Figure 6.6, the labour demand curve shifts to the right and, at the original real wage, w_1^*, demand for labour exceeds supply. Competition among firms drives the real wage up until it increases to its new equilibrium value, w_2^*.

Solved Problem 6.1

Why Don't People Work as Much as They Did Decades Ago?

In the early twentieth century, it was common to work 48 to 50 hour per week. Steel workers at some firms worked 12-hour days into the 1920s. Today, 40 hours is the typical work week, and more people routinely work less than 40 hours than work more. In 1979, employed Canadians worked, on the average, 38.6 hours; in 2012 this fell to 36.6 hours. What explains the decline? The wealth of Canadian households has been increasing over time. Predict the effect this increase in wealth had on the equilibrium real wage and the level of employment. Use a graph to support your answer.

Solving the Problem

Step 1 **Review the chapter material.** This problem is about determining the effect of an increase in wealth on the aggregate labour market, so you may want to review the section "Equilibrium in the Labour Market," which begins on page 185.

Step 2 **Draw a graph that shows the effect of the increase in wealth on the labour demand and labour supply curves.** The labour demand curve shows the relationship between the real wage and the quantity of labour that firms want to hire, holding capital, technology, and the level of efficiency constant. The increase in wealth should not affect the marginal product of labour. The labour demand curve should not shift since the increase in wealth is unlikely to affect the marginal product of labour. The labour supply curve will shift, however. When wealth increases, individuals can purchase the same quantity of goods and services that they currently buy while working fewer hours. So, we would expect individuals to reduce the quantity of labour supplied at each real wage, which you should show on your graph as the labour supply curve shifting to the left, from S_1 to S_2.

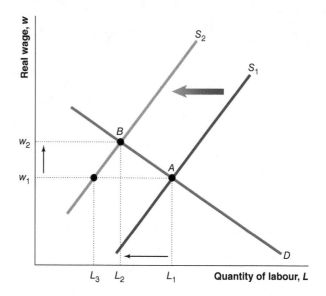

Step 3 **Use your graph to explain the effect on the real wage and quantity of labour.** The graph shows that at the original real wage of w_1 a shortage of labour exists because the quantity of labour supplied is L_3 and the quantity of labour demanded is L_1. As a result, the equilibrium real wage will rise, while the equilibrium quantity of labour will decrease, from L_1 to L_2.

Over the years, people in high-income countries such as Canada, France, Germany, and the Netherlands have spent fewer hours working and more time in leisure. This Solved Problem helps explain why: As wealth has increased, individuals have used the increase in wealth to "purchase" more leisure time, thereby decreasing the number of hours spent working.

Source: Work–Weekly Hours Worked, Human Resources and Skills Development Canada, http://www4 .hrsdc.gc.ca/.3ndic.1t.4r@-eng.jsp?iid=19

See related problem 1.4 at the end of the chapter.

6.2

Learning Objective

Define unemployment and explain the three categories of unemployment.

Categories of Unemployment

We begin this section with a brief review of unemployment data. Figure 6.7 shows unemployment rates for Canada, the United States, Japan, and the 28 countries of the European Union. As the way the unemployment rate is calculated varies across countries, we show the data from the OECD, which are calculated using common methodology. In all countries, the unemployment rate has fluctuated greatly over time. The unemployment rate for Canada varied from a high of 12% in 1983 to a low of 6% in 2007 (just before the Great Recession). The figure also shows that the average unemployment rate has varied substantially across countries. For example, since 1991, the unemployment rate has averaged 4% in Japan, 6% in the United States, 8% in Canada, and over 9% for countries of the European Union. Note that during the Great Recession the unemployment rate in the United States increased much more than in Canada but after the recession ended, it declined faster and by the end of 2013

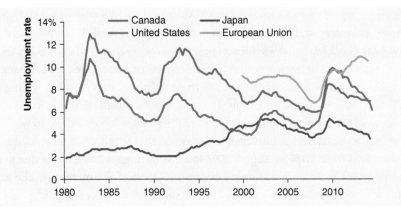

Figure 6.7

Unemployment Rates around the World, 1980–2014

The unemployment rate fluctuates over time for all countries, rising during recessions and falling during expansions. Data for the European Union are available starting in 1999.

Source: Organisation for Economic Co-operation and Development.

fell below the Canadian rate. Also, while the unemployment rate has been decreasing recently in Canada, Japan, and the United States, it has been rising in the European Union.

Duration of Unemployment

In addition to the variation in the average unemployment rates across countries, there is also variation in the average amount of time a worker is unemployed, or the *duration* of unemployment. Figure 6.8 shows the average duration of unemployment, measured in months, for Canada, the United States and the European Union (Data for the European Union start in 1995.) The average duration of unemployment has been much higher in Europe than in Canada and the United States throughout. The average duration was a little higher in Canada than in the United States until the Great Recession. The Great Recession had little effect on the duration of unemployment in Canada, but the duration of unemployment in the United States doubled.

Differences in the average duration of unemployment have important policy implications. Workers who are unemployed for long periods of time are more likely to be unemployed for structural reasons than for frictional or cyclical reasons. Policies designed to help the long-term unemployed are more likely to be effective if they involve retraining or other programs that help workers gain new skills and move from declining industries into expanding ones.

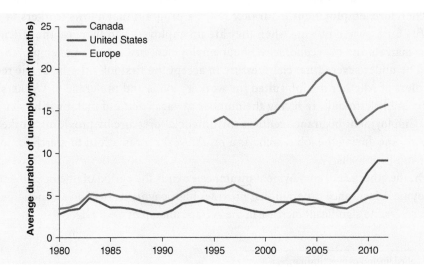

Figure 6.8

Unemployment Duration in Canada, Europe and the United States, 1980–2012

The average duration of unemployment is much higher in Europe than in Canada or the United States. Since the beginning of the Great Recession, the duration in the United States doubled while in Canada there was little change.

Source: Organisation for Economic Co-operation and Development.

Voluntary and Involuntary Unemployment When we analyze unemployment, the distinction between voluntary and involuntary unemployment is crucial. Unemployment is voluntary if a worker gets a job but does not accept it. The worker may find the job inadequate and continue to search for a better job or decide to enjoy leisure. This is the type of unemployment that exists in our demand and supply model. In equilibrium, every worker willing to accept the equilibrium real wage can find a job. This observation means that any worker who does not have a job must prefer to continue searching for a better job or leisure to working at the prevailing real wage. It seems implausible, however, that when the unemployment rate in Canada increased from 6.1% in August 2008 to 8.7% in August 2009, it was due to a sudden increase in people's preference for leisure over work. Most of the increase in the unemployment rate was almost certainly involuntary, which means that workers who wanted jobs at the current wage could not find them.

Categories of Unemployment To better understand unemployment, in this section we begin by discussing three categories of unemployment that economists have found useful in analyzing the labour market:

- Frictional unemployment
- Structural unemployment
- Cyclical unemployment

Frictional Unemployment and Job Search

Workers have different skills, interests, and abilities, and jobs have different skill requirements, working conditions, and wages. As a result, most workers spend at least some time engaging in *job search*, just as most firms spend time searching for new persons to fill job openings. **Frictional unemployment** is short-term unemployment that arises from the process of matching the job skills of workers to the requirements of jobs. It takes time for workers to search for jobs and for firms to search for new employees, so there will always be some workers who are frictionally unemployed because they are between jobs and in the process of searching for new ones.

Frictional unemployment Short-term unemployment that arises from the process of matching the job skills of workers to the requirements of jobs.

Would eliminating all frictional unemployment be good for the economy? No, because some frictional unemployment actually increases economic efficiency. Frictional unemployment occurs because workers and firms take the time necessary to ensure a good match between the skills of workers and the requirements of jobs. By devoting time to job search, workers end up with jobs they find satisfying and in which they can be productive. Of course, having more productive and more satisfied workers is also in the best interest of firms.

Employment insurance (EI) A government program that allows workers to receive benefits for a period of time when they are unemployed.

Therefore, **employment insurance (EI)**[3], a program that allows workers to receive benefits for a period of time when they are unemployed, can increase the efficiency of labour markets and the economy. Without employment insurance, an unemployed worker would be under severe financial pressure to accept the first job offer he or she received, regardless of whether the job suited the worker's skills and preferences. Workers would also be unlikely to quit, reducing the number of vacancies and making it harder to find a job. Employment insurance reduces this financial pressure by providing workers with some income during the job search. As a result, workers can afford to search for jobs that better suit their skills.

On the other hand, employment insurance extends the period of unemployment. So an employment insurance program that provides high payments over an extended period of time may lead to significant increase in the average unemployment rate.

---

[3]Often called unemployment insurance.

Structural Unemployment

Structural unemployment arises from a persistent mismatch between the job skills or attributes of workers and the requirements of jobs. While frictional unemployment is mostly short term, structural unemployment can last for longer periods because workers need time to learn new skills. In the past the biggest changes in employment in Canada were from agriculture to manufacturing, and later from manufacturing to services. The latter trend continues and, for example, between 2003 and 2013 employment in manufacturing fell by over 500 000 workers, or by almost a quarter. Many of the workers who lost jobs found themselves with qualifications that were no longer in demand. A steelworker cannot easily become a firefighter or a nurse. He is likely to be unemployed for a long period.

Technological change is another cause of structural unemployment. Technological change in Canada and other developed countries has tended to eliminate unskilled jobs while increasing the demand for skilled jobs. For example, computers and information technology have eliminated many unskilled jobs, such as typist positions, and reduced the demand for

Structural unemployment Unemployment that arises from a persistent mismatch between the job skills or attributes of workers and the requirements of jobs.

Macro Data: Is the Decline of Industries that Produce Goods a Recent Phenomenon?

Industries that produce goods, such as cars, computers, and appliances, have become less important over time as a share of both GDP and total employment in Canada as well as in other high-income countries. At the same time, the share of services, such as haircuts or investment advice, has become more important.

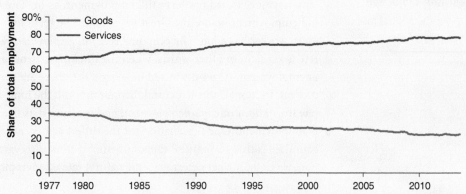

The figure on the right shows that in Canada the percentage of workers in goods-producing industries decreased from 35% of total employment in April 1976 to 22% in August 2013. Goods-producing industries have been in relative decline since the end of World War II in 1945, a trend that seems unlikely to be reversed. Although the *relative share* of employment in goods-producing industries has declined, the *absolute number* of workers employed in these industries has increased. Employment in goods-producing industries increased from 3.37 million workers in April 1976 to 3.92 million workers in August 2013. This increase, though, is much smaller than the increase in employment in services-producing industries, which grew from 6.36 million workers in April 1976 to 13.84 million workers in August 2013.

What explains the decline in the share of employment in goods-producing industries? Given that the decline dates back at least as far as the 1940s, recent developments, such as competition from China or other effects of globalization,

cannot be the main cause. Instead, many economists believe that the decreasing importance of the goods-producing sector is likely due to productivity growth being much faster in goods-producing industries than in service-producing industries. For example, it still takes just as many members of an orchestra to play Beethoven's Ninth Symphony in 2013 as it did in 1976. However, each manufacturing worker is much more productive today than 40 years ago. As a result, the need for manufacturing workers has not grown as rapidly as the need for service workers.

The figure illustrates another important point: Using employment as the measure, Canada has been a service economy for a long time. In fact, services employment in 1976 was actually greater than goods employment in 2013, despite the growth in the economy and the population over the intervening 37 years.

Source: Statistics Canada. Table 282–0088.

See related problem D6.1 at the end of the chapter.

clerical staff. At the same time, these innovations have increased the demand for workers who produce computers, computer software, and other related products. These latter jobs often require more skills than the jobs computers and information technology have eliminated. Low-skilled workers who are unable to acquire the skills necessary to find employment become structurally unemployed.

Cyclical Unemployment

Cyclical unemployment
Unemployment caused by the business cycle, measured as the difference between the actual rate of unemployment and the natural rate of unemployment.

When the economy enters a recession, many firms find their sales falling and cut back on production. As production falls, firms lay off workers. Workers who lose their jobs because of a recession experience *cyclical unemployment*. Economists define **cyclical unemployment** as the difference between the actual level of unemployment and the level of unemployment in normal times, when the economy is neither in a boom or in a recession. This rate of unemployment is called the **natural rate of unemployment** and it is discussed in the next section. It consists of frictional unemployment plus structural unemployment. So, when the unemployment rate equals the natural rate, cyclical unemployment is zero. Most economists believe that the natural rate of unemployment in Canada is equal to a measured unemployment rate of 6% to 7%.

Natural rate of unemployment The normal rate of unemployment, consisting of frictional unemployment plus structural unemployment.

The Natural Rate of Unemployment

Learning Objective

Explain the natural rate of unemployment.

You may have heard the term full employment, as in, The Canadian economy operated at full employment before the Great Recession. The term *full employment* does not mean that every worker has a job. The economy is at *full employment* when the cyclical unemployment rate is zero, or, in other words, when the unemployment rate is equal to the natural rate of unemployment. As we discussed in Section 6.2, there are three categories of unemployment: cyclical, frictional, and structural. Economists call the long-run equilibrium unemployment rate the *natural rate of unemployment* and measure it as the sum of structural and frictional unemployment. One explanation for the differences in average unemployment rates across countries is that the natural rate of unemployment also varies across countries. In this section, we explain what determines the natural rate of unemployment.

A Simple Model of the Natural Rate of Unemployment

Even in the best economic times, some workers leave one job for another or stop working to return to school or pursue other activities, while other workers lose jobs as their firms close or productivity improvements make their jobs unnecessary. As a result, there is a constant flow of workers from employment to unemployment and from unemployment to employment, even when cyclical unemployment is zero. One way to think of the natural rate of unemployment is as the rate of unemployment that exists in the long run when the economy is in a steady state and the flow of workers into employment equals the flow of workers into unemployment. Let's explore this point further. First, assume for simplicity that the labour force is constant. The labour force is the sum of employed and unemployed workers. Denote the size of the labour force as L, the number of employed workers as N and the number of unemployed workers as U. So:

$$L = N + U. \tag{6.4}$$

Job-finding rate The percentage of unemployed workers who find a job in a given period.

Every month, some unemployed workers find jobs. We call the percentage of unemployed workers who find a job in a given period the **job-finding rate**, and denote it f. The total number of workers finding jobs is equal fU. Every month, some employed workers leave, or separate from, their job either voluntarily or involuntarily. We call the percentage of employed workers who separate from a job (lose it or quit) in a given period the job-separation rate, and denote it s. The total number of job separations is sN. So the change in employment is

$$\Delta N = fU - sN. \tag{6.5}$$

Job-separation rate The percentage of employed workers who separate from a job (lose it or quit) in a given period.

When the labour market is in equilibrium and unemployment is at the natural rate, the number of workers finding jobs equals the number of workers separating from jobs. The natural rate of unemployment, denoted u^N, is equal to the ratio U/L when the flow into and out of employment are equal so that change in employment is zero : $\Delta N = 0$. In that case we have

$$fU = sN. \tag{6.6}$$

To calculate the natural rate of unemployment, substitute $N = L - U$ in the above equation to get $fU = s(L - U)$. Dividing both sides by L and rearranging we obtain

$$u^N = \frac{s}{s + f}. \tag{6.7}$$

This equation tells us that the natural rate of unemployment depends on the rate at which workers find jobs, f, and the rate at which workers separate from jobs, s. As the rate of workers finding jobs increases, the natural unemployment rate decreases. As the rate of workers separating from jobs increases, the natural unemployment rate increases.

The job-finding and separation rates fluctuate with economic conditions. When these rates are constant and the flows into and out of employment are equal, the unemployment rate equals the natural rate of unemployment. For example, suppose that, every month, 1.5% of the employed lose their jobs while 25% of the unemployed find a job. Therefore, $s = 0.015$ and $f = 0.250$. The natural rate of unemployment would then be

$$u^N = \frac{1.5\%}{1.5\% + 25\%} = 5.7\%.$$

This model of the natural rate of unemployment provides important guidance to policymakers. The model tells us that if policymakers want to lower the natural rate, they must find ways either to reduce the rate of job separation or increase the rate of job finding. We discuss government policies to reduce the natural rate of unemployment in Section 6.4.

Solved Problem 6.2

How Many Jobs Does the Canadian Economy Create Every Month?

The following data on employment in Canada is provided by Statistics Canada (in thousands):

July 2013	August 2013	Change
17 710	17 769	59.2

You may be tempted to conclude that the economy created 59.2 thousands of jobs in August 2013. Is this correct?

Solving the Problem

Step 1 **Review the chapter material.** This problem is about understanding employment flows in the Canadian labour market, so you may want to review the section "A Simple Model of the Natural Rate of Unemployment," which begins on page 192.

Step 2 **Answer the problem by explaining how to interpret the data.** Statistics Canada provides data on total employment each month. The change in total employment from one month to the next tells us the *net* change in employment: the difference between the change in the number of workers who found employment and the change in the number of workers who lost (or quit) employment. So, while it is correct to say that employment changed by just under 60 000, the data do not tell us anything about the number of new jobs created and jobs lost. The actual number of jobs created is 60 000 plus the number of jobs lost. Stephen Tapp collected data on job hires and separations in Canada during the period 1988–2006. The monthly average of hires was 245 000, and the monthly average of separations was 227 000, for the average monthly change of employment of 18 000. In other words, the change in employment was, during this period, less than 10% of the number of new job hires. Confusing the net change in employment with the total amount of job creation is a common mistake.

Source: Stephen Gordon "Big numbers behind a small gain in jobs," *Globe and Mail*, November 05, 2010.

The natural rate of unemployment changes when either the amount of structural or frictional unemployment changes. Structural and frictional unemployment vary over time and across countries based on the following factors:

- *Demographics*, including changes in the age, gender, and race of the population.
- *Public policy*, including changes in employment insurance, taxes, and laws governing the labour market.
- *Technological change*, including the introduction of new products that displace old products and increases in labour productivity.
- *Sectoral shifts*, including the growth and decline of different industries and changes in where industries locate.

Demographics Younger workers are less experienced and change jobs more frequently than do older workers. In addition, it often takes younger workers longer to find a job when entering the labour force. As the workforce ages, the average worker finds a job more easily, so frictional and structural unemployment decline. From April 1976 to August 2013 the unemployment rate for people aged 16 to 24 averaged 14.2% while for people 25 and older it averaged just 7.0%. Canada experienced high birthrates from the mid-1940s to the mid-1960s—the baby boom—and lower birthrates in the years since. The average age of the Canadian work force began to rise in the 1970s, and it has continued to increase. As workers became older, the job-finding rate increased and the job-separation rate fell, reducing the natural rate of unemployment.

The unemployment rate also varies by gender, so the percentage of men and women in the labour force also affects the natural rate of unemployment. This effect is actually modest because the unemployment rates for men and women are very similar: From April 1976 to August 2013 the average unemployment rate for males was 8.6% and for females 8.3%. While labour force participation of women increased over time, the effect on the natural rate of unemployment was small.

Public Policy Public policies that affect work incentives affect the natural rate of unemployment. For example, EI provides employed workers with payments for a period of time after losing their jobs. Suppose that you lose your job as an accountant at Ernst & Young and are receiving employment insurance (EI) payments. As long as you receive employment insurance (EI) payments, you are less likely to accept a sales job working at the Bay than you would be without EI. You stay unemployed longer. This means the higher is EI, or the longer is the period of eligibility, the higher is the average rate of unemployment.

Marginal tax rates can also affect how people decide to divide their time between work and leisure. The marginal tax rate is the fraction of each dollar earned that must be paid in taxes. The higher the marginal tax rate, the lower the after-tax wage from another hour of work. Countries in Western Europe not only have higher unemployment rates than in the United States, but workers in those countries work fewer hours per year. Nobel Laureate Edward Prescott of Arizona State University argues that differences in the natural rate of unemployment between the United States and Europe are mainly due to differences in marginal tax rates. For Prescott's explanation to be correct, however, changes in marginal tax rates need to have a large effect on households' labour supply decision. In other words, the *elasticity of labour supply* with respect to the after-tax wage would have to be large. Many estimates of the elasticity of labour supply indicate that it is very low. As a result, the observed increases in income tax rates in Western Europe do not appear to be large enough by themselves to explain the large increases in leisure taken by workers in those countries.

Some economists argue that the more restrictive labour market regulations in Europe provide a better explanation for higher unemployment rates and fewer hours worked. In most European countries, for example, it is difficult to fire workers, which makes firms more cautious about hiring them in the first place. Firms may also adopt more capital-intensive technology that reduces the need to hire workers, or they may be reluctant to expand operations. These actions may decrease the rate of job finding and therefore increase the natural rate of unemployment.

Making the Connection

Are Strict Labour Laws to Blame for Unemployment in France?

In July 2012, French carmaker Peugeot shocked the government of the new president of France, François Hollande, when it announced plans to close a factory outside Paris and lay off thousands of workers. Peugeot's decision followed a €700 million loss ($860 million) in the first half of 2012. Analysts place much of the blame for Peugeot's woes on its high unit labour costs, due in part to France's strict labour laws and high payroll taxes.

Peugeot is not the only French company to suffer from high labour costs. Unless employees steal or are extremely negligent, it is difficult for any firm in France to fire workers. Economist Elie Cohen, a former board member of France Télécom, a telecommunications company that has had difficulty competing with firms from countries with less restrictive labour laws, said, "In France, you can't fire people just because your industry or technology is changing." Another cost of doing business in France and other European countries is workers' guaranteed annual vacation leave, which can run from four to six weeks. The Court of Justice of the European Union ruled in 2012 that workers in European Union countries are entitled to extended time off if they become ill on their vacations. The extra time off is equal to the number of days workers are ill while on vacation.

Not surprisingly, many firms are reluctant to hire in the first place. This reluctance can reduce the rate of job finding and increase the natural rate of unemployment. Economists have offered a number of reasons for the differences between unemployment rates in Western Europe and North America, including different preferences among workers, differences in tax rates, long-term disability payments, and the influence of labour unions. Figure 6.7 shows that the unemployment rate in Europe has been higher than in Canada and in the United States for the past 20 years.

Sources: Lelia Abboud, "At France Télécom, Battle to Cut Jobs Breeds Odd Tactics," *Wall Street Journal*, August 14, 2006; "National Lampoon's European Vacation," *Wall Street Journal*, June 27, 2012; and Carol Matlack, "Layoffs at Peugeot Signal France's Deepening Problems," *Bloomberg Businessweek*, July 12, 2012.

See related problem 3.7 at the end of the chapter.

We can conclude that a generous employment insurance system, high tax rates, and restrictive labour regulations tend to increase the natural rate of unemployment, while a generous system of long-term government disability payments tends to decrease it. The last effect is due to the fact that, with a generous disability system, some long-term unemployed workers switch to disability payments. Of course, all these policies have effects beyond the natural rate of unemployment. For example, policymakers may believe that restrictive labour regulations provide important protections to workers. Policymakers often face a tradeoff between attempting to reduce the natural rate of unemployment while retaining policies that serve other purposes.

Technological Change Increases in productivity can reduce employment in the short run because new technology and other sources of improved productivity make some jobs obsolete. However, new technology can increase employment by creating demand for new products. For example, employment in the newspaper business has declined over the past two decades, as many people get their news online or from cable television channels. But the growth of online news and cable television has created new jobs. Workers who lose their jobs producing newspapers and who cannot make the transition to the new jobs online or on cable may become structurally unemployed, which would cause the natural rate of unemployment to increase. However, those who make the transition find better jobs with higher wages due to technological progress.

We can conclude that *technological change and increases in labour productivity ultimately make workers as a group better off*, even though some individual workers may be made worse off. The loss of jobs by workers at newspapers and the increase in jobs for workers in online and cable news is an example of what economists call *creative destruction*, a phrase first used by the Austrian economist Joseph Schumpeter. New technology destroys existing jobs but simultaneously creates jobs making new and better products elsewhere in the economy. Overall, technological change has a large effect on the mix of employment across industries, but it probably has a small effect on the natural rate of unemployment.

Sectoral Shifts Changes in the prices of key raw materials, such as oil, can cause employment to shift across sectors and increase structural unemployment. The price of a barrel of oil rose from US$2.00 in December 1973 to US$32.63 in July 1980. Canadian households responded to the large price increase by conserving energy, for example, by switching from large automobiles with low gas mileage to smaller automobiles—often imported from Japan—with high gas mileage. As a result, the demand for autoworkers in Canada decreased dramatically. Autoworkers who could not develop the new skills needed for another career became structurally unemployed.

Economists refer to the process of output and employment increasing in some industries while declining in other industries as *sectoral shifts*. As sectoral shifts occur, markets work to move labour from one industry to another. During the transition, some workers will have difficulty finding new jobs and may become structurally unemployed. The figure in the Macro Data box on page 191 showed a long-term movement of labour from the goods-producing sector to the service-producing sector in Canada. This trend is not unique to Canada: The decrease in the relative importance of the manufacturing sectors is particularly evident in high-income countries. For countries in the Organisation for Economic Co-operation and Development (OECD) such as Canada, France, Germany, and the United States, manufacturing as a percentage of GDP decreased from 20% in 1998 to 15% in 2009. In contrast, the manufacturing sector has been relatively constant in countries such as China and India. The Chinese manufacturing sector was 32% of GDP in 1998 and 32% in 2009, while the Indian manufacturing sector was 16% of GDP in 1998 and 15% of GDP in 2009. In high-income countries, labour has been flowing from the manufacturing sector to the service sector, while in many low-income countries, labour has been flowing from the agricultural sector to the manufacturing sector. As these reallocations take place, the natural rate of unemployment may temporarily increase.

Why Wages May Be Higher than Equilibrium Wages

6.4

Learning Objective
Understand factors that prevent real wage from adjusting to the equilibrium level.

In the equilibrium in the labour market model from Section 6.1, all workers who want jobs can find them. But why then is there unemployment? The answer is that, in reality, there are many types of *frictions* that prevent the real wage from adjusting to maintain the labour market continually at equilibrium.

Equilibrium Real Wages and Unemployment

Figure 6.9 shows a labour market with unemployment. At point A, the labour market is in equilibrium because the quantity of labour demanded is equal to the quantity of labour supplied. All the workers who want jobs can find them, so there is no unemployment. However, if the real wage, w_2, is above the equilibrium real wage, w^*_1, the quantity of labour supplied by households, L_3, is greater than the quantity of labour demanded by firms, L_2. Because the quantity of labour employed cannot be greater than the quantity of labour demanded, L_2 also represents employment in the economy. As a result, some workers would like to have a job at the prevailing wage, w_2, but cannot find one. In other words, there is unemployment equal to $L_3 - L_2$.

Why doesn't the real wage quickly decline to restore equilibrium in the labour market and eliminate unemployment? In this section, we provide three explanations for why the real wage may remain above the equilibrium real wage for a period of time: efficiency wages, labour unions, and minimum wage laws.

Efficiency Wages

In many cases, firms choose to pay higher-than-market wages. We call such a wage an **efficiency wage**. Efficiency wages make the workforce more productive and increase profits for three reasons: they motivate workers to work harder, they reduce labour turnover, and they increase the average quality of workers.

Some firms can ensure that workers work hard by supervising them. For example, a telemarketing firm can monitor workers electronically to ensure that they make the required

Efficiency wage A higher-than-market wage that a firm pays to motivate workers to be more productive and to increase profits.

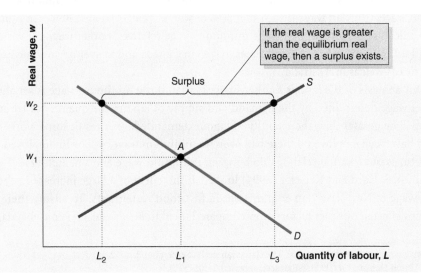

Figure 6.9

A Labour Market with Unemployment

If the real wage, w_2, is at a level above the equilibrium real wage, w^*_1, then the quantity of labour supplied is greater than the quantity of labour demanded. Some workers who would prefer to have a job at a real wage of w_2 cannot find one.

number of phone calls per hour. Most firms, however, must rely on workers being self-motivated to work hard. If you receive an efficiency wage that is more than you would earn at your next best alternative job, you are less likely to take actions that will get you fired. You are more likely to work harder, take only necessary sick days, etc. An efficiency wage also makes workers less likely to switch jobs when alternative jobs pay only the market wage. When a worker quits a job, the firm incurs the cost of finding and training a new worker. If that cost is high enough, the efficiency wage may increase profits by reducing quits and the need to hire new workers. Firms may also pay efficiency wages to improve the quality of their workers. High wages attract many job applicants and allow the firm to select the most qualified ones.

Labour Unions around the World

Labour unions are organizations of workers that bargain with employers over wages and working conditions for their members. In Canada, labour legislation requires firms to allow unions to organize and requires firms to negotiate with unions. Unions typically bargain for wages that are above the market level. The higher wages result in firms in unionized industries hiring fewer workers. According to the Canadian Labour Congress, over the working career a unionized worker earns half a million dollars more than a nonunionized worker. Note also that the presence of a union in an industry may raise wages in nonunionized firms as well, as management wants to avoid the workforce joining a union. For example, nonunionized car companies pay similar wages to unionized ones.

The importance of unions in the private sector has been declining slowly over time. The relative strength of unions has declined in recent years in many countries due to increased competition arising from globalization and the slow growth in the demand for labour in goods-producing industries, where unions tend to be concentrated. In Canada, fewer than 16% of workers in the private sector and 70% of public workers belong to a union.[4] Overall, around 30% of workers are unionized; the proportion varies from 24% in Alberta to 40% in Quebec. Unionization rates vary across countries, with around 70% of the labour force unionized in Scandinavian countries, 35% in Italy, 25% in the United Kingdom, 20% in Germany and Japan, and 10% in the United States and South Korea.[5]

Minimum Wage Laws

Minimum wage A legal minimum hourly wage rate that employers are required to pay employees.

A **minimum wage** is a legal minimum hourly wage rate that employers are required to pay employees. In April 2014 minimum wages in Canada varied from $9.95 an hour in Alberta to $11.00 in Nunavut and Ontario, with some exceptions for inexperienced workers and workers receiving gratuities. A more interesting statistic is the ratio of the minimum wage to the median wage. (Median wage is such that 50% of workers earn less and 50% earn more.) The ratio indicates how low or high is the minimum wage relative to other wages. It varies from around 0.4 in Japan and the United States to 0.45 in Canada and to over 0.5 in some European countries as well as in Australia.

Our analysis of the labour market suggests that, if the minimum wage is set above the market wage determined by the demand and supply of labour, the quantity of labour supplied will be greater than the quantity of labour demanded. As a result some workers, who would have been employed if there had been no minimum wage, will be unemployed.

It turns out that the relationship between minimum wage and unemployment is more complicated. Card and Krueger (1994) looked at the effect of a large increase in the minimum wage in New Jersey on employment in fast-food restaurants. To ensure their results were not affected by other factors, they compared them to neighbouring Pennsylvania, where

---

[4]"Unions on decline in private sector," The Canadian Press, September 2, 2012.
[5]Trade Union Density, OECD StatsExtracts, accessed 04/05/2014.

the minimum wage remained unchanged. They found that the increase in minimum wages did not reduce employment; if anything, employment actually increased.[6] How can this be? Our labour market analysis assumes that the labour market is competitive. But Card and Krueger argued that the fast-food job market is monopsonistic.[7] In a monopsonistic market the buyer can affect the price. Fast-food firms use their monopsonistic power to artificially reduce their wages and raise their profits. When forced to pay higher wages they do not reduce employment but earn lower profits. Fast-food firms may also raise prices to offset the effect of a higher minimum wage on profits. There is no agreement among economists on whether minimum wage laws increase or reduce unemployment, but regardless of the direction, the effect is not large.

---

[6]David Card and Alan B. Krueger, "Minimum Wages and Employment: A Case Study of the Fast-Food Industry in New Jersey and Pennsylvania," *American Economic Review* 84, no. 4 (1994): 772–793.

[7]Monopsony is a situation in which the purchaser has monopoly power. In our case the purchaser is the employer, who buys labour services.

Key Terms and Problems

Key Terms

Cyclical unemployment, p. 192

Efficiency wage, p. 197

Employment insurance, p. 190

Frictional unemployment, p. 190

Job-finding rate, p. 192

Job-separation rate, p. 193

Marginal product of labour (MPL), p. 182

Minimum wage, p. 198

Natural rate of unemployment, p. 192

Structural unemployment, p. 191

 6.1

The Labour Market

Use the model of demand and supply for labour to explain how wages and employment are determined.

Review Questions

1.1 Why is the demand curve for labour downward sloping?

1.2 How do the income and the substitution effects determine the slope of the labour supply curve?

1.3 What variables shift the labour demand curve? What variables shift the labour supply curve?

Problems and Applications

1.4 [Related to Solved Problem 6.1 **on page 187**] Draw a graph of the aggregate labour market in equilibrium and then consider each of the following situations. In each case, indicate whether the demand for labour, the supply of labour, or both will shift, and indicate what will happen to the equilibrium real wage and the equilibrium quantity of labour.

a. A technological change occurs that increases the productivity of all workers.

b. The government increases income tax rates.

c. Worker preferences change so that the workers prefer consumption of market goods to consumption of leisure.

d. The government reduces payroll taxes that firms pay when they hire workers.

1.5 According to Claudia Goldin of Harvard University, in the United States prior to 1940, most married women who worked had limited education and came from lower-income families. She argues, "Their decisions were made as secondary workers and their market work evaporated when family incomes rose sufficiently."

a. Discuss the likely relative sizes of the income and substitution effects for women during these years.

b. Given your answer to part (a), discuss the shape of the labour supply curve for women during these years.

Source: Claudia Goldin, "The Quiet Revolution That Transformed Women's Employment, Education, and Family," *American Economic Review, Papers and Proceedings* 96, no. 2, May 2006, pp. 1–21.

1.6 Suppose that workers become concerned about the future and therefore wish to increase their hours of work relative to leisure. At the same time, there is an increase in the capital stock, which makes workers more productive.

  a. Draw a graph of the labour market, showing the effect of these changes.

  b. Can you predict the effect on the equilibrium quantity of labour? On the real wage?

1.7 In countries with declining populations, governments have begun to offer income subsidies for families with children. What effect is such a subsidy likely to have on the labour market, all other things being equal? Support your answer with a graph.

1.8 During a recession, some people drop out of the labour force. On the other hand, some retired people re-enter the job market.

  a. Why might retired people re-enter the job market during a recession?

  b. Assume that retired people look for a job in the hospitality industry. Use a graph to explain what is happening in the labour market in the hospitality industry.

1.9 Consider the following statement: "Increases in the capital stock are harmful to workers because the increases are the result of firms substituting capital for labour, thus reducing overall employment." Do you agree with this statement? Briefly explain.

1.10 The graph below shows the labour market. The initial equilibrium is at point *A*. The new equilibrium is at point *B*.

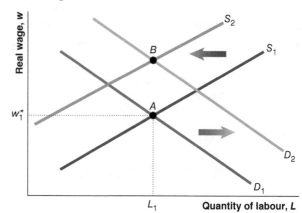

  a. What factors could have caused the shifts shown on the graph?

  b. Show the new equilibrium real wage and quantity of labour on the graph. Did the real wage and employment increase or decrease?

  c. How would your answer to part (b) change if the size of the labour demand shift had been greater than the size of the labour supply shift?

6.2 ## Categories of Unemployment
Define unemployment and explain the three categories of unemployment.

Review Questions

2.1 When the economy is at full employment, are all workers employed? Briefly explain.

2.2 Briefly describe the three categories of unemployment.

2.3 What is seasonal unemployment? Why does Statistics Canada report unemployment rates each month that are both seasonally adjusted and not seasonally adjusted?

Problems and Applications

2.4 Structural unemployment can result from the development of new products that replace old products. A classic example is typewriters being replaced by personal computers.

  a. How might technological change cause structural unemployment?

  b. Would you expect a similar effect on unemployment when companies develop new flavours of soft drinks or new styles of clothing?

2.5 For each of the following examples, identify the category of unemployment.

  a. Marty has been laid off from her job at an aircraft plant but expects to be recalled when the economy starts expanding.

  b. Raghuram has just graduated from university and has not found a job yet.

  c. Angelo works as a lobsterman in Nova Scotia in the summer, but the industry shuts down in the winter.

  d. Gregory worked in an automobile plant in Ontario, but the plant was shut down permanently.

2.6 Suppose that the government wants to reduce the rate of frictional unemployment.

　a. What types of measures might target frictional unemployment?

　b. There is some evidence that frictional unemployment has decreased over the past two decades. What might explain this decrease?

2.7 Suppose that the government wants to reduce the rate of structural unemployment.

　a. What types of measures might target structural unemployment?

　b. Do measures such as the extension of unemployment insurance in industries affected by technological change tend to increase or decrease structural unemployment? Briefly explain.

2.8 Consider the following statement: "Because there will always be frictional and structural unemployment, there is no reason for government policymakers to be concerned about them. They should only be concerned about cyclical unemployment." Do you agree with this statement? Briefly explain.

6.3 The Natural Rate of Unemployment
Explain the natural rate of unemployment.

Review Questions

3.1 Define the natural rate of unemployment in terms of flows into and out of the labour market. Write the equation that expresses the natural rate of unemployment in terms of these flows.

3.2 What factors can cause the natural rate of unemployment to change?

Problems and Applications

3.3 Suppose that the rate of job separation is 2% and the job-finding rate is 18%.

　a. What is the natural rate of unemployment?

　b. If the job-finding rate doubles, what is the new natural rate of unemployment?

　c. Return to the original scenario. If the rate of job separation is cut in half, what is the new natural rate of unemployment?

　d. Which has a larger effect: a doubling of the job-finding rate or a halving of the job-separation rate? Does your result have any implications for government policy? Briefly explain.

3.4 Briefly explain the effect of each of the following factors on the natural rate of unemployment:

　a. There is an increase in the rate of technological change.

　b. The percentage of wages replaced by unemployment benefits is increased.

　c. Improvements in information technology make it faster to match jobs and workers.

　d. There is a recession.

3.5 Increases in the generosity (percentage of wages replaced) and duration of unemployment benefits can be associated with increases in the natural rate of unemployment. Why do governments provide unemployment benefits if doing so might increase unemployment rates?

3.6 In an article about the effect of the Great Recession on the U.S. labour market, Bloomberg.com quotes Lawrence Mishel, president of the Economic Policy Institute in Washington, as saying: "People tend to think that when you come out of a recession you get the labour market you had when you entered it. This time you may get something quite different." Why might a prolonged recession cause changes in the natural rate of unemployment?

Source: Matthew Benjamin and Rich Miller, "'Great' Recession Will Redefine Unemployment as Jobs Vanish," Bloomberg.com, May 3, 2009.

3.7 [Related to the Making the Connection on page 195] Some European companies have U.S. subsidiaries, and the labour practices they employ in the United States may be very different from those they employ in Europe. *Bloomberg Businessweek* reports: "With more than 5 million Americans now employed by foreign-owned companies, U.S. labour unions are starting to export their grievances." If U.S. unions are successful in getting these companies to follow European practices, what would you expect to see happen to the natural rate of employment in the United States?

Source: Carol Matlack, "U.S. Labour Takes Its Case to European Bosses," *Bloomberg Businessweek*, January 22, 2010.

6.4 **Why Wages May be Higher than Equilibrium Wages.**

Examine factors that prevent real wage from adjusting to the equilibrium level.

Review Questions

4.1 How does a real wage above the equilibrium wage cause unemployment?

4.2 Briefly explain the reasons the real wage may remain above the equilibrium wage for a period of time.

Problems and Applications

4.3 Suppose the equations for the demand and supply of labour are given by

$$L_D = 100 - 2w$$
$$L_S = 10 + 3w,$$

where w is the real wage and L_D and L_S are the quantity of labour demanded and supplied, respectively.

a. Solve for the equilibrium wage and the quantity of employment and graph your results.

b. Assume that the government imposes a $10 minimum wage when the price level is $0.5. Find the new quantity of labour demanded and supplied.

c. How many people lose their jobs because of the new minimum wage? How many workers are now unemployed?

4.4 In 1914, Ford Motor Company doubled its wage to $5 per day, a rate that was considerably above the average wage at that time.

a. In terms of efficiency wages, explain why Ford would have had an incentive to use this wage policy.

b. What data would you need to determine whether Ford's wage increase was successful in achieving its goals?

4.5 Some craft unions, such as electricians, restrict the number of workers who can join the union and then negotiate with employers to hire only union workers. Use a demand and supply graph to illustrate the effect of a craft union on employment and wages in an industry.

4.6 Unemployment in the labour market is increased by forces that keep wages from falling to the equilibrium level. Other than efficiency wages, unionism, and minimum wages, what other factors might cause this wage stickiness?

Data Exercises

D6.1: [Related to Macro Data feature on page 191]

The CIA *World Factbook* (https://www.cia.gov/library/publications/the-world-factbook/) gives for most countries the sectoral composition of GDP, that is, how production is divided up among agriculture, industry, and services.

a. Examine the sectoral compositions for France, Japan, the United Kingdom, and the United States. Are they similar to or different from those of Canada?

b. Examine the sectoral compositions for China, India, Bangladesh, and Kenya. How do these sectoral compositions compare to those you found in part (a)?

c. What implications might the different sectoral compositions have for natural rates of unemployment?

D6.2: Under the World Bank's Labour and Social Protection data bank (see data.worldbank.org/topic/labor-and-social-protection), there is information on long-term unemployment by country.

a. In which of the following countries: Canada, the United States, France, Germany, Spain, and Italy, is the percentage of long-term unemployed individuals (as a percentage of total unemployed individuals) the highest? The lowest?

b. Can you relate the differences in the duration of unemployment to differences in labour markets in these countries?

D6.3: Using data from Statistics Canada (http://www5.statcan.gc.ca/cansim/a01?lang=eng), Table 282-0085, analyze unemployment rates.

a. Download monthly data on the official unemployment rate (R4) from 2002 to the present.

What was the average rate of unemployment for the 2002–06 period?

b. What has been the average rate of unemployment from 2007 to the present?

c. At this time, does it appear that the labour market has recovered from the Great Recession?

D6.4: Using data from Statistics Canada (http://www5 .statcan.gc.ca/cansim/a01?lang=eng), Table 282-0085, analyze the duration of unemployment.

a. For the period from 1977 to the present, download monthly data on the percent of unemployed who are unemployed for a year or more (R1), for three months or more (R2), and the official rate. Chart the data series on a graph.

b. The two most severe Canadian recessions since World War II occurred from June 1981 to October 1982 and from March 1990 to April 1992. Based on your graph, which of the two recessions was more severe? Briefly explain.

c. What was the effect, if any, of the most recent recession on the duration of unemployment?

D6.5: Using data from Statistics Canada (http://www5 .statcan.gc.ca/cansim/a01?lang=eng), Tables 326-0020 and 282-0069, analyze CPI (the consumer price index) and wages.

a. Find the most recent values and the values from one year earlier for the All-items CPI wages for Total employees, all occupations.

b. Using the CPI data and nominal wage data from above, compute the average hourly real wage for each year.

c. Over the one-year interval under examination, calculate the percentage change in the average hourly nominal wage and the average hourly real wage.

D6.6: Using data from Statistics Canada (http://www5 .statcan.gc.ca/cansim/a01?lang=eng), Table 282-0087 and data from the OECD (http://stats.oecd. org/Index.aspx?QueryId=36376) analyze the natural rate of unemployment.

a. Download annual data for the NAIRU—a concept related to the natural rate of unemployment from 1970 to the present. Chart the data series in a graph.

b. During 2008/2009, the unemployment rate increased from 6.1% in August 2008 to 8.7% a year later. How did the increase compare to the changes in the OECD estimate of the NAIRU?

c. Given your answer to part (b), should the government focus on policies to reduce cyclical unemployment or the NAIRU? Briefly explain.

D6.7: Using data from the OECD (http://stats.oecd.org/) find the information on the minimum wage as percentage of median wage for OECD countries (Search for "minimum wage".) From the same source, find data on youth unemployment (ages 15–24). (Search for "unemployment rates by age," click "labour force statistics," click "short-term statistics," and at the top of the page select "Unemployment rate, aged 15–24, all persons."

a. Calculate the correlation between minimum wage as percentage of median wage and youth unemployment. Is it consistent with theory?

b. Exclude data for Greece and Spain, where youth unemployment is very high, and calculate the correlation. Are the results different?

The Standard of Living over Time and across Countries

Learning Objectives

After studying this chapter, you should be able to:

7.1 Describe the aggregate production function (pages 205–212)

7.2 Explain how real GDP is determined in the long run (pages 212–217)

7.3 Understand why the standard of living varies across countries (pages 217–219)

7.4 Understand why total factor productivity varies across countries (pages 219–223)

Who Is Number One?

What is the leading economy in the world today? In ranking the economic performance of countries, economists generally use two related measures: GDP and GDP per capita. The following table shows the top 15 economies in 2013, based on these two measures:

Rank		GDP ($ trillion)	Rank		GDP per capita ($ thousand)
1	United States	16.7	7	Singapore	62.4
2	China	13.4	9	Norway	55.4
3	India	5.0	11	Switzerland	54.8
4	Japan	4.7	14	United States	52.8
5	Germany	3.2	15	Hong Kong	52.7
6	Russia	2.6	18	Netherlands	43.3
7	Brazil	2.4	19	Canada	43.1
8	United Kingdom	2.4	21	Australia	43.0
9	France	2.3	22	Austria	42.6
10	Mexico	1.8	26	Sweden	40.9
11	Italy	1.8	28	Taiwan	39.6
12	Korea, South	1.7	29	Germany	39.5
13	Canada	1.5	31	Belgium	37.8
14	Spain	1.4	32	Denmark	37.8
15	Indonesia	1.3	34	United Kingdom	37.3

Notes: Calculated using PPP exchange rates. The ranks in income per capita are for all countries; we list only countries with population over 5 million.
Source: CIA Factbook, 2014

Both of these measures have some merit. The sheer size of an economy, as measured by GDP, can help a country's firms achieve economies of scale, and a large economy may be better able to support a large military,

Continued on next page

thereby increasing the country's political influence in the world. From the point of view of the average person's standard of living, however, GDP per capita is a more important measure. GDP per capita measures the quantity of goods and services available to the average person in the country and, therefore, is a good measure of the standard of living of the typical person. A country can have a large economy as measured by GDP, but a low standard of living as measured by GDP per capita. Compare, for example, United States with China, and Canada with Indonesia. The Chinese economy is three-quarters of the size of the U.S. economy and, given the fast growth in China, is going to be larger than the U.S. economy within a few years. But GDP per capita in China is less than 20% of U.S. GDP per capita. The Canadian and Indonesian economies are of similar size, but the GDP per capita in Indonesia is 8 times lower.

Rank	GDP ($ trillion)		Rank	GDP per capita ($ thousand)	
1	United States	16.7	14	United States	52.8
3	China	13.4	121	China	9.8
14	Canada	1.5	19	Canada	43.1
16	Indonesia	1.3	158	Indonesia	5.2

The differences in GDP per capita actually understate the true difference in living standards between these countries. For example, the average person in Canada and the United States lives longer, has more years of education, is much less likely to die in infancy or during childbirth, experiences less corruption, and is much less likely to suffer serious medical problems because of pollution than is the average person in China or in Indonesia.

Sources: U.S. Central Intelligence Agency, *The World Factbook 2014*; United Nations Development Program, *Human Development Report, 2012* (New York: Palgrave Macmillan, 2010).

Introduction

Real GDP per capita is a key economic concept because it helps determine the standard of living of the average person in a country. Although Canada, the United States, Japan, Western Europe, and certain other countries have attained high standards of living, billions of people remain stuck in grinding poverty. In fact, the standard of living in some countries in Asia and Africa has increased relatively little in hundreds of years. Why are some countries rich and others poor? In this chapter, we begin building a model that can help answer that question. We start by introducing the aggregate production function, which links the level of output to the amount of capital and labour and to total factor productivity. We then describe a specific production function often used by economists: the Cobb–Douglas production function. In Section 7.2 we analyze firms' choice of the amount of capital and labour they employ. In Section 7.3 we discuss three factors affecting differences between countries in GDP per capita: total factor productivity, capital per worker, and the proportion of the population that is working. We conclude that differences in total factor productivity across countries are the main sources of the large differences in real GDP per capita. In the last section we describe factors that determine the differences in total factor productivity: human capital, government, social institutions, the rule of law, and geography.

7.1

Learning Objective

Describe the aggregate production function.

The Aggregate Production Function

When discussing the standard of living, we are most interested in real GDP *per capita* because that is the best measure of the quantity of goods and services available per person. We begin by developing a model to explain real GDP and then adjust the model to explain real GDP per capita.

To understand how real GDP gets produced, we can think first about how an individual firm combines land, labour, natural resources, and capital—such as machinery, equipment, factories, and office buildings—to produce goods and services. The relationship between the inputs employed by a firm and the maximum output it can produce with those inputs is called the firm's *production function*. A firm's *technology* is the process it uses to turn inputs into outputs of goods and services. The production function represents the firm's technology. The production function is a microeconomic concept when we apply it to an individual firm, but on a macroeconomic level, we can think about how an economy turns the total available inputs into goods and services. So, we can say that the **aggregate production function** is an equation that shows the relationship between the inputs employed by firms and the maximum output firms can produce with those inputs. At the macroeconomic level, we measure output as real GDP, and we include only labour and capital as inputs because land is a relatively minor component of production, even in a land-rich economy such as Canada.

We can write a general version of the aggregate production function as:

$$Y = A\,F(K, L), \tag{7.1}$$

where:

Y = real GDP

K = quantity of capital goods available to firms, or the *capital stock*

L = quantity of labour

A = efficiency index, which measures how efficiently the economy transforms capital and labour into real GDP.

For the sake of simplicity, in the rest of this textbook we will refer to the aggregate production function simply as the *production function*.

The efficiency index A plays an important role in this and the next chapter, where we analyze economic growth. It measures the efficiency of the economy. The higher it is, the more the economy produces with given capital and labour, and the higher is real GDP. Some of the factors that can affect the value of A include technology, government regulations and institutions, the quality of the labour force, and a nation's geography. In fact, A measures the effect of any factor that determines real GDP other than the quantities of capital and labour.

The Cobb–Douglas Production Function

The general form of the production function is used by economists to analyze economic growth and derive qualitative predictions, for example, that a higher level of capital or higher efficiency leads to higher level of output. But economics is, by its very nature, quantitative. When economic policy is considered, economists are asked to determine the policy's effects in dollars or in a percentage change in GDP. To answer these quantitative questions, economists often analyze the factors that determine real GDP by using a specific production function known as the **Cobb–Douglas production function**. The Cobb–Douglas production function is usually written as

$$Y = AK^{\alpha}L^{1-\alpha}. \tag{7.2}$$

In the Cobb–Douglas production function, output is the product of the efficiency index A and the level of capital and labour, which are raised to exponents that add up to one, as you can see in equation (7.2). Let's look at an example using values similar to those economists use for Canada: K = \$5.7 trillion, L = 18 million workers, A = 1.55, α = 1/3, $1 - \alpha$ = 2/3. Given these values, according to the Cobb–Douglas production function, the level of real GDP for the year will be

$$Y = 1.55(\$5\,700 \text{ billion})^{1/3} (0.019 \text{ billion workers})^{2/3} = \$1\,902 \text{ billion}.$$

The Cobb–Douglas production function is relatively simple, and economists have continued to use it for more than 90 years because it does a good job of explaining changes in real GDP over time within a country as well as the differences in the levels of real GDP among countries.

Aggregate production function An equation that shows the relationship between the inputs employed by firms and the maximum output firms can produce with those inputs.

Cobb–Douglas production function A widely used macroeconomic production function that takes the form $Y = AK^{\alpha}L^{1-\alpha}$.

There are several important characteristics of the Cobb–Douglas production function we are using here:

- The function exhibits *constant returns to scale*.
- The function exhibits *diminishing returns*.
- Capital and labour both earn shares of total income equal to the value of their exponents in the production function.

We consider the first two characteristics of the Cobb–Douglas production function here and the last one later in the chapter.

Constant Returns to Scale   A production function has **constant returns to scale** if increasing all inputs by the same percentage increases real GDP by that percentage.

We can write this property of the production function as:

$$A \, F(zK, zL) \; = \; zY. \tag{7.3}$$

For example if $z = 2$, doubling the amount of both capital and labour doubles the amount of output produced. The Cobb–Douglas production function we are using here has constant returns to scale because the exponents (α on the capital term and $1 - \alpha$ on the labour term) sum to 1. For example, if we double K and L, we have:

$$A(2K)^{1/3}(2L)^{2/3} \; = \; 2^{(1/3 + 2/3)} \, AK^{1/3} \, L^{2/3} \; = \; 2(AK^{1/3} \, L^{2/3}) \; = \; 2Y.$$

The idea behind the constant returns to scale assumption is straightforward. Consider, for example, Jan's Pizza Ltd. Jan's Pizza has one pizza shop, employs 20 people, and has two ovens. It produces 2000 pizzas a day. Under constant returns to scale, if Jan's Pizza doubled in size to two shops, four ovens, and 40 employees, it would be producing 4000 pizzas a day.

In many firms or industries, however, returns to scale are not constant. *Decreasing returns to scale* are when increasing all inputs by the same percentage raises output by a smaller percentage. As an example, consider Asli's Pizza Company. It has 10 shops, 20 ovens, and 200 employees. But the large company requires a head office. Ten employees work in the head office. The remaining 190 pizza workers make only 19 500 pizzas. Even though the capital and workforce of Asli's Pizza is 10 times the capital and employment of Jan's Pizza, its output is only 9.75 times larger. Decreasing returns to scale occur because of complications in running a large business.

In some industries, increasing returns to scale are common. *Increasing returns to scale* are when raising all inputs by the same percentage raises output by a bigger percentage. For example, a computer programmer may write five apps a year, but two computer programmers, by exchanging ideas and working together, may together write eleven apps a year.

Constant returns to scale A property of a production function such that if all inputs increase by the same percentage, real GDP increases by the same percentage.

Making the Connection

Increasing Returns to Scale in Sock Production

Increasing returns to scale explain the existence of industrial clusters, where firms in the same industry locate in the same area. For example, high-tech firms locate in Waterloo, Ontario, even though office and housing costs are higher than in nearby cities. This is because there are many such companies in Waterloo and locating near them raises the productivity of the new companies. Increasing returns generated in industrial clusters are not limited to high-tech places like Waterloo, Ottawa, or San Jose or major industries like car production in Detroit. The city of Datang in China, about 200 km from Shanghai, makes one-third of all socks in the world—around 10 billion pairs a year. To understand this concentration of one industry in a distant place, you need to think about production in wide terms—including design, ordering, and purchasing. Industry concentration in one place makes it easier to follow the latest industry trends and developments, not only in sock fashion but also in production technology and machinery. International wholesale buyers can get everything they want in one place and, as the *New York Times* points out, "...these days, buyers from New York to Tokyo want to be able to buy 500 000 pairs of socks all at once." An example of an earlier cluster is the island of Murano, near Venice, which has specialized in the production of glass since the thirteenth century.

Sources: David Barboza, "In Roaring China, Sweaters Are West of Socks City," *The New York Times*, December 24, 2004; Tania Branigan, "Sock City's decline may reveal an unraveling in China's economy," *The Observer*, September 9, 2012.

Marginal product of capital (*MPK*) The extra output a firm receives from adding one more unit of capital, holding all other inputs and efficiency constant.

Diminishing marginal product Each additional unit of input (capital or labour) raises output by less than the previous unit.

Diminishing Marginal Product We now turn to studying the effect on output of an increase in capital, while holding the efficiency index, *A*, and labour constant, and similarly the effect on output of an increase in labour, while holding the efficiency index, *A*, and capital constant. The amount by which output increases as a result of a one-unit increase in capital is called the **marginal product of capital (*MPK*)**. Similarly, the amount by which output increases as a result of a one-unit increase in labour is called the *marginal product of labour* (*MPL*). In symbols, we have

$$MPK = \frac{\Delta Y}{\Delta K}, \text{ and } MPL = \frac{\Delta Y}{\Delta L}. \tag{7.4}$$

We say that an input has **diminishing marginal product** if each additional unit raises output by less than the previous unit. Capital has diminishing marginal product because labour and efficiency are fixed; so as the economy adds more capital goods, there are fewer workers per machine. With fewer workers per machine, the machines are not used as efficiently, so the marginal product of capital decreases. Labour experiences diminishing marginal product for similar reasons. To illustrate diminishing marginal product of capital in a microeconomic context, consider a simple example of two equity analysts named Carmen and Kenneth, who manage funds for clients. Their contribution to GDP is equal to the management fees they earn. They monitor markets with the help of a Bloomberg terminal, a device that provides access to real time market data and analysis and allows placing electronic trades. If Carmen and Kenneth have only one Bloomberg terminal, they need to take turns. A second Bloomberg terminal allows them to work independently, raising the return on clients' funds and fees they earn. A third terminal can be used if one of the other two is out of service; this happens infrequently and so the extra fees, and additional output, are small. In other words, the marginal product of capital, while still positive, will be declining. In this example we keep the amount of labour fixed at two workers and vary the amount of capital. We can explain diminishing marginal product of labour with a similar example that fixes capital at one terminal and varies the amount of labour using the one terminal. If only Carmen is working, she has the Bloomberg terminal to herself and generates large fees. When Kenneth is hired, they have to share the terminal and so additional fees Kenneth generates are lower than those earned by Carmen when she worked alone.

Diminishing marginal products are shown in Figure 7.1, which graphs a Cobb–Douglas production function. The production functions in panels (a) and (b) show the relationship between a single input and output. Panel (a) shows a graph of the aggregate production function from equation (7.1), with the level of real GDP (*Y*) on the vertical axis and the amount of the capital stock (*K*) on the horizontal axis. In this panel, we hold *A* and *L* constant and illustrate how real GDP changes as the capital stock increases. The production function becomes flatter, which means that each additional unit of capital

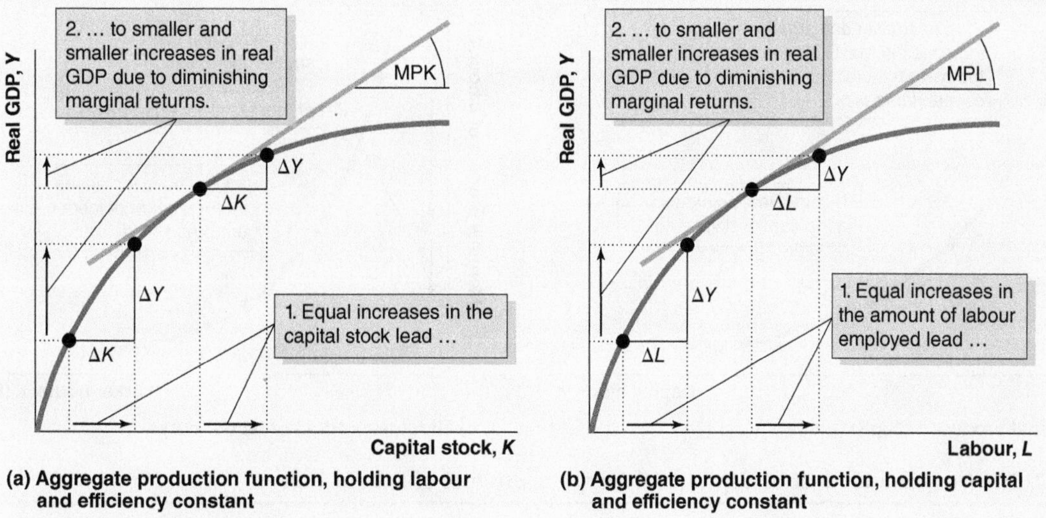

(a) Aggregate production function, holding labour and efficiency constant

(b) Aggregate production function, holding capital and efficiency constant

Figure 7.1 Aggregate Production Functions

Panel (a) shows the aggregate production function, holding labour and efficiency constant while allowing the capital stock to vary. Panel (b) shows the aggregate production function, holding the capital stock and efficiency constant while allowing labour to vary.

Both graphs look similar; they differ only with respect to the variable on the horizontal axis. In Chapter 3 we discussed a common mistake in determining whether there is a movement along the curve or a shift of the curve. Recall that this depends on whether the variable is on an axis.

So in panel (a), where capital stock is on the horizontal axis, a change in the amount of capital means movement along the production function. A change in the number of workers means a shift in the production function. In panel (b), with the amount of labour on the horizontal axis, a change in the quantity of labour means movement along the production function, but a change in the amount of capital means a shift of the production function.

increases output less than the previous unit. Similarly, Figure 7.1 panel (b) shows the graph of the aggregate production function from equation (7.1), with the level of real GDP (Y) on the vertical axis and the number of workers (L) on the horizontal axis. In this panel, we hold A and K constant and illustrate how real GDP changes as the number of workers increases. The production function becomes flatter, which means that each additional worker increases output less than the previous hire. The marginal product of capital, MPK, is the slope of the production function at a single point in panel (a); similarly, the marginal product of labour, MPL, is the slope of the production function at a single point in panel (b).

Constant Returns to Scale and Diminishing Marginal Product What is the difference between returns to scale and marginal products? When we talk about returns to scale, we ask *how much output increases when both inputs are increased by the same percentage.* When we talk about marginal returns, we ask *how much output rises when one input increases and the other input stays constant.* The Cobb–Douglas production function exhibits both constant returns to scale and diminishing marginal product.

The Demand for Labour and the Demand for Capital

Figure 7.2 shows the marginal product of capital [in panel (a)] and the marginal product of labour [in panel (b)] curves. At the level of the individual firm, marginal product of capital and labour may not be decreasing. For example, adding another machine may improve the workflow in the company. But at the level of the economy, the marginal product of capital decreases as the capital stock increases. Similarly, the

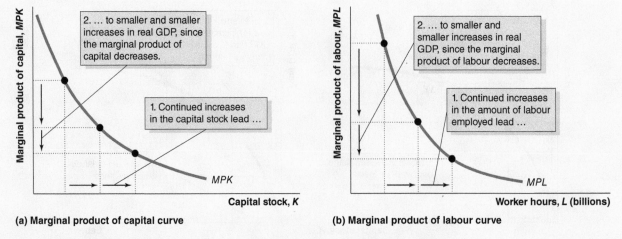

Figure 7.2 The Marginal Product of Capital and Marginal Product of Labour Curves

In panel (a), the marginal product of capital is always positive, but it decreases as the capital stock increases. Similarly, in panel (b), the marginal product of labour decreases as the quantity of labour increases. The downward slope for the marginal product of capital and marginal product of labour curves is the result of diminishing marginal product. All countries have similarly shaped marginal product of capital and marginal product of labour curves.

marginal product of labour decreases as the labour stock increases. All countries have downward-sloping marginal product of capital and marginal product of labour curves because diminishing returns apply to all types of capital and labour. Notice that these curves slope downward very much like demand curves do. In fact, the marginal product of capital *is* the demand curve for capital, and the marginal product of labour *is* the demand curve for labour. We explain why the marginal product curves are also demand curves in the next section.

Changes in Capital, Labour, and Total Factor Productivity

To this point, we have been referring to A in the Cobb–Douglas production function as "efficiency" or, more specifically, as an index of the overall level of efficiency of transforming capital and labour into real GDP. A is intended to capture increases in output that result from factors other than increases in the amount of capital and labour. Because these other factors raise output by increasing the ability of labour or capital to produce more output, A is also called **total factor productivity (TFP)**.

Total factor productivity (TFP) An index of the overall level of efficiency of transforming capital and labour into real GDP.

The production function in of Figure 7.1 panel (a) on page 209 shows the relationship between capital stock and output, holding labour and total factor productivity constant. Figure 7.3 shows what happens when labour or total factor productivity increase: The production function shifts up (since labour is not on either axis), and real GDP increases. Panel (a) shows that if labour increases from, say, 18 million workers to 19 million workers, real GDP will increase from Y_1 to Y_2, i.e., by $Y_2 - Y_1$. If labour increases from 19 million workers to 20 million workers, real GDP will increase from Y_2 to Y_3, i.e., by $Y_3 - Y_2$, which is less than $Y_2 - Y_1$ due to diminishing marginal product of labour. Figure 7.3 panel (b) shows that if total factor productivity (A) increases from, say, 1000 to 2000, real GDP will increase from Y_1 to Y_2. If total factor productivity increases from 2000 to 3000, real GDP will increase from Y_2 to Y_3, but in this case, the increases will be the same size. Total factor productivity is not subject to diminishing marginal product. This point is important because, as we will see, it helps explain why increases in total factor productivity, rather than increases in labour or capital, are the key to sustained economic growth.

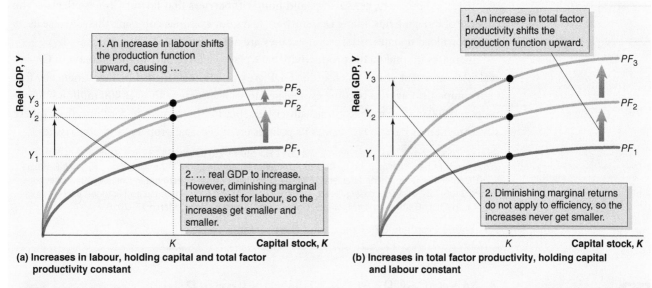

Figure 7.3 The Effect of an Increase in Labour and Total Factor Productivity in the Aggregate Production Function

In panel (a), an increase in the number of workers will shift the production function up and increase real GDP, but labour experiences diminishing marginal product. As a result, further increases in the number of workers will lead to smaller and smaller increases in real GDP. In panel (b), an increase in total factor productivity will shift the production function up and increase real GDP. In contrast to labour, total factor productivity does not experience diminishing marginal product, so the increases in real GDP do not get smaller.

Making the Connection

Foreign Direct Investment Increases Real GDP in China

In 2011, the purchase or building of capital goods by foreign firms in China—*foreign direct investment (FDI)*—reached $116 billion. This news was good for China because investment in manufacturing plants by foreign firms such as the Taiwanese company Hon Hai (Foxconn)—the world's largest electronics manufacturer that assembles Apple products, among others—increases China's stock of capital goods. The increase in the Chinese capital stock causes a movement along China's production function [drawn with capital on the horizontal axis, as in Figure 7.1 (a)]. Because new capital goods are subject to diminishing marginal product, however, we know that the rapid growth the Chinese economy has experienced in recent years must be due to more than the accumulation of capital goods. As panel (b) shows, increases in total factor productivity are not subject to diminishing marginal product. International companies such as Apple or Volkswagen have invested billions of dollars in China. Some of this investment has been used to establish modern research facilities that develop new technology. When these foreign firms build new factories in China, those factories typically employ new technology. Technology is an important component of total factor productivity, so the transfer of technology from other countries to China is an important means of increasing China's total factor productivity.

Despite the recent growth in FDI, there are signs that some foreign companies are reconsidering investing in China. Much of the increase in FDI in China in 2011 was from firms in Asian countries such as Hong Kong, Taiwan, and Japan. Sluggish economic growth in developed economies was one reason for the decline in spending. Another reason was restrictions the Chinese government imposed on FDI. China has pledged to protect the intellectual property rights of foreign companies, but executives of many firms, in particular of U.S. companies, have expressed frustration regarding the Chinese government's policies on the theft of intellectual property, censorship, and nontariff barriers that favour Chinese firms at the expense of foreign firms. Many U.S. software firms, for example, complain that Chinese users often download updates of software that they are not recorded as having purchased.

Increases in total factor productivity have played a large part in the increase in China's real GDP in recent years. Much of the GDP growth has been fuelled by investments by foreign companies eager to become established in an economy with over 400 million internet users and 700 million mobile phone subscribers. But for this growth to continue, the Chinese government may have to reconsider its policies on intellectual property and other issues.

Sources: Zhou Xin and Nick Edwards, "China 2011 FDI Stutters to Record $116 Bln," *Reuters*, January 18, 2012; Loretta Chao, "China Issued a Record Number of Patents in 2009," *The Wall Street Journal*, February 4, 2010; Chinmei Sung, Zheng Lifei, and Li Yanping, "Foreign Direct Investment in China in 2010 Rises to Record $105.7 Billion," *Bloomberg News*, January 17, 2011; and John Boudreau and Brandon Bailey, "Doing Business in China Getting Tougher for U.S. Companies," *Mercury News*, March 27, 2010.

See related Problem 1.7 at the end of the chapter.

7.2

Learning Objective

Explain how real GDP is determined in the long run.

Profit Total revenue minus total cost.

A Model of Real GDP in the Long Run

To fully explain how real GDP is determined, we need to explain how firms choose the quantity of capital goods to purchase and the quantity of labour to hire. To begin, we assume firms maximize **profit**, which equals the total revenue received by a firm minus the total cost a firm pays to produce output. The level of real GDP results from the profit-maximizing decisions of the many individual firms in the economy. In what follows, we make four assumptions:

1. Firms purchase capital and hire labour only if doing so maximizes profits.
2. Firms operate in *perfectly competitive markets*, so each firm is a *price taker*—that is, each firm is small relative to the market and takes the market price of the goods and services it sells as given, or fixed.
3. Firms take the prices of capital goods and labour as given.
4. Firms decide how much capital and labour to hire and how much output to produce using available technology, based on the prices of output and inputs.

For simplicity, we consider the behaviour of a single representative firm and assume that all firms behave the same as that representative firm. The firm produces output, Y, and sells it at the perfectly competitive price, P. In addition, the firm takes the *nominal wage rate*, W, and the *nominal rental cost of capital*, R, as given. We measure the cost of capital using the rental cost rather than the purchase price because the rental cost represents the use of capital services for a given period, just as the wage represents the cost of labour services. If firms do not own capital, they can rent it and *pay* the rental cost. If they currently own capital, they could have chosen to rent it out and *receive* the rental cost. So the rental cost is the opportunity cost to the firm of using its own capital.

The firm receives revenue by selling output, so total revenue is PY. To produce output, the firm hires labour at the wage rate, W, and rents capital at the rental rate, R. Profits are equal to revenue (PY) minus costs ($WL + RK$):

$$\text{Profits} = PY - (WL + RK) = PY - WL - RK. \tag{7.5}$$

The Markets for Capital and Labour

Firms hire capital and labour in markets, so we can use the model of demand and supply to explain the quantities of capital and labour firms hire. Unlike in the previous chapter, we assume that the supply of labour and capital at any given moment of time is fixed and does not respond to market prices. (Over time, of course, the quantities of capital and labour will change.) This assumption simplifies our analysis without affecting results. Because we are assuming that the firm is small relative to the market, it cannot influence the price of output, the wage, or the rental cost of capital. If the firm hires one more worker, it can produce more output, so the revenue from hiring one more worker equals the price of output multiplied by the extra output from hiring the worker, which is the marginal product of labour (*MPL*). To hire that worker, the firm must pay the nominal wage of *W*. Therefore, the change in profit from hiring one more worker is the difference between the additional revenue earned and the additional cost paid:

$$\Delta \text{Profit} = P \cdot MPL - W.$$

The firm maximizes profit, so it will hire labour as long as the change in profit is greater than zero. As it hires more workers, the marginal product declines. The firm stops hiring when the additional profit from an extra worker falls to zero: $P \cdot MPL - W = 0$. What matters to the firm, however, is the real wage, which we denote with the lower case, *w*. The real wage is equal to the nominal wage, *W*, divided by the price of output, *P*: $w = W/P$. Rearranging the previous equation, we find that the firm will hire additional workers until the marginal product of labour is just equal to the real wage:

$$MPL = (W/P). \tag{7.6}$$

If the real wage decreases, the firm will hire additional workers until the marginal product of labour falls to the level of the new real wage. Similarly, if the real wage increases, the firm will lay off workers until the marginal product of labour rises enough to restore the equality. The demand curve for labour shows the relationship between the cost of labour, i.e., the real wage ($w = W/P$), and the number of workers the firm wants to employ. This number of workers can be read from the marginal product of labour curve. *Therefore, the marginal product of labour curve is the same as the demand curve for labour curve.* This is illustrated in Figure 7.4, panel (b).

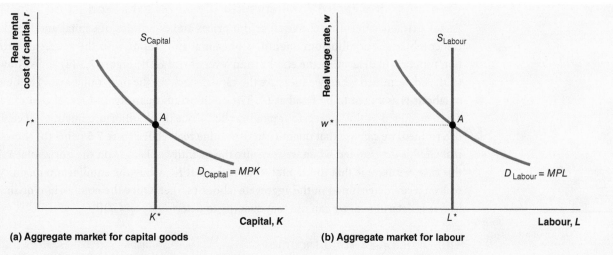

(a) Aggregate market for capital goods   (b) Aggregate market for labour

Figure 7.4 Aggregate Capital and Labour Markets

Panel (a) shows the aggregate market for capital goods, and panel (b) shows the aggregate market for labour. The demand curves slope downward, reflecting diminishing marginal product of capital and labour. The supply curves for capital and labour are vertical lines, reflecting the assumption that the quantity supplied does not respond to changes in prices. The intersections of the demand and supply curves determine the equilibrium quantities of capital and labour.

We can make a similar argument about a firm renting capital. The change in profit from adding one more unit of capital, holding the quantity of labour constant, is

$$\Delta \text{Profit} = P \cdot MPK - R.$$

The firm maximizes profit, so it will add capital goods as long as the change in profit is greater than zero. The *real rental price of capital*, r, is the nominal rental price, R, divided by the price of output, P: $r = R/P$. So the firm will add capital goods as long as the marginal product of capital exceeds the real rental cost of capital. Because of diminishing returns, the marginal product of capital declines as the firm adds more capital. Rearranging the previous equation we find that the firm will add capital until the marginal product of capital is just equal to the real rental price:

$$MPK = (R/P). \tag{7.7}$$

If the real rental cost of capital decreases, the firm will add more units of capital until the marginal product of capital falls enough to again equal the real rental cost, and if the real rental cost rises, the firm will sell capital or let its capital stock wear out, or depreciate, until the marginal product of capital rises enough to again equal the real rental cost. The demand curve for capital shows the relationship between the cost of capital, the real rental price ($r = R/P$), and the amount of capital the firm wants to employ. This amount of capital can be read from the marginal product of capital curve. *Therefore, the marginal product of capital curve is the demand curve for capital goods.* This is illustrated in panel (a).

We make the simplifying assumption that everything we have discussed so far about a single firm holds true for every firm in the economy. So we can refer to the *aggregate capital market* and the *aggregate labour market*. Figure 7.4 shows these two markets. The real rental cost of capital is r, and the real wage rate is w. The demand curves slope downward, reflecting diminishing marginal product of capital and labour. The supply curves for capital and labour are vertical lines, reflecting our assumption that at any particular time, the quantity of capital and labour supplied does not respond to changes in price. The intersections of the demand and supply curves determine the equilibrium quantities of capital and labour. In the next section, we substitute those quantities into the aggregate production function to determine real GDP.

Combining the Factor Markets with the Aggregate Production Function

Factor markets determine the equilibrium prices and quantities of capital and labour. We can combine the equilibrium quantities of capital and labour with the aggregate production function to determine the equilibrium level of real GDP. Figure 7.5 (a) shows how real GDP is determined when we measure the capital stock on the horizontal axis. The quantity of labour is assumed to be fixed at L^*. The equilibrium quantity and rental cost of capital are determined in the aggregate capital market. Once the equilibrium quantity of capital is determined, we can use that quantity to determine real GDP. Figure 7.5 panel (b) shows how real GDP is determined when we measure the quantity of labour on the horizontal axis. In this case, we assume that the capital stock is fixed at K^*, while the equilibrium quantity and real wage are determined in the aggregate labour market. Once the equilibrium quantity of labour is determined, we can use that quantity to determine real GDP.

The Division of Total Income

The Cobb–Douglas production function provides an interesting answer to the question, What determines how much of total income labour receives and how much capital receives? To understand the answer, consider first the total amount of income received by labour and by capital. We saw earlier that, in equilibrium, workers receive the real wage, w. Similarly, in equilibrium, owners of capital receive the real rental price of capital, r. Therefore, the *total*

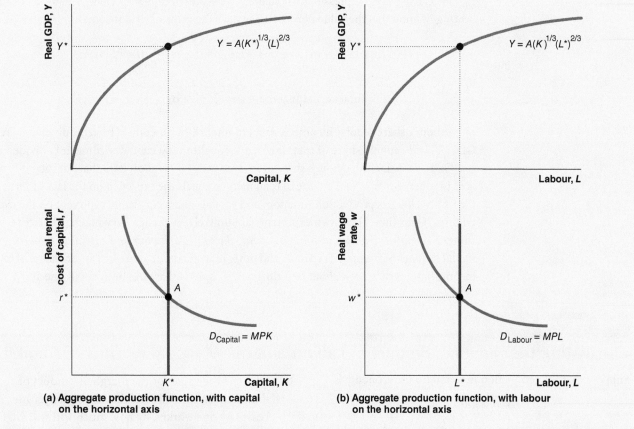

(a) Aggregate production function, with capital on the horizontal axis

(b) Aggregate production function, with labour on the horizontal axis

Figure 7.5 Determination of Real GDP

Panel (a) shows how potential real GDP is determined when we measure the capital stock on the horizontal axis. Panel (b) shows how potential real GDP is determined when we measure the quantity of labour on the horizontal axis. In the lower graph in each panel, we show how the equilibrium quantity (of capital or labour) is determined. The upper panels use the production function and the level of each input to determine the level of real GDP.

---

income received by labour equals wL and the *total* income received by capital equals rK. Because the real wage equals the marginal product of labour e and the real rental price of capital equals the marginal product of capital we can say that

$$\text{Total labour income} = MPL \cdot L,$$

and

$$\text{Total capital income} = MPK \cdot K.$$

With the Cobb–Douglas production function, the marginal product of labour and the marginal product of capital equal the following:[1]

$$MPL = (1 - \alpha)(Y/L),$$

and

$$MPK = \alpha(Y/K).$$

---

[1]We can derive these expressions using calculus. The marginal product of labour shows how output changes as a result of changes in labour, holding other determinants of output constant, or in symbols, $\dfrac{\partial Y}{\partial L}$. Calculating this partial derivative gives us $MPL = \dfrac{\partial Y}{\partial L} = \dfrac{\partial [AK^\alpha L^{(1-\alpha)}]}{\partial L} = (1 - \alpha)AK^\alpha L^{-\alpha} = (1 - \alpha)\dfrac{[AK^\alpha L^{(1-\alpha)}]}{L} = (1 - \alpha)\left(\dfrac{Y}{L}\right)$, and similarly for MPK.

We can use these expressions to calculate the shares of capital and labour in total income, bearing in mind that the value of real GDP equals the value of total income.

$$\text{Total labour income} = MPL \cdot L = (1-\alpha)\left(\frac{Y}{L}\right)L = (1-\alpha)Y.$$

$$\text{Total capital income} = MPK \cdot K = \alpha\left(\frac{Y}{K}\right)K = \alpha Y.$$

Labour's share of total income is equal to total labour income, $(1 - \alpha)Y$, divided by real GDP, Y, and capital's share of total income is equal to total capital income, αY, divided by real GDP, Y. So, indeed, labour's share of income is $(1 - \alpha)$ and capital's share of total income is α. In other words, labour's share of total income equals the exponent on the labour term in the Cobb–Douglas production function, and capital's share equals the exponent on the capital term. Over time, these two exponents are unlikely to change very much. Therefore, we come to the following conclusion: *Over time, the shares of labour and capital in total income should be roughly constant.* In Canada and other high-income countries, labour's share of total income has typically been about two-thirds, and capital's share has been about one-third.

Solved Problem 7.1

Calculating the Marginal Product of Labour and the Marginal Product of Capital

Suppose that the production function for the economy is

$$Y = AK^{1/2}L^{1/2}.$$

Assume that real GDP is $1000 billion, the capital stock is $4000 billion, and the labour supply is 15 million (or 0.015 billion) workers.

a. Calculate the value of the marginal product of capital. Given this value, if the capital stock increases by $1 billion, by how much will real GDP increase?

b. Calculate the value for the marginal product of labour. Given this value, if the labour supply increases by one worker, by how much will real GDP increase?

c. What fraction of total income is received by labour, and what fraction is received by capital?

Solving the Problem

Step 1 **Review the chapter material.** This problem is about calculating values for the marginal products of capital and labour, so you may want to review the section "The Division of Total Income," which begins on page 214.

Step 2 **Answer part (a) by calculating the value of the marginal product of capital, and use the value to determine how much real GDP will increase if the capital stock increases by $1 billion.** We know that the marginal product of capital for a Cobb–Douglas production function is equal to the exponent on the capital term multiplied by (Y/K). In this case:

$$MPK = (1/2)\,(Y/K).$$

Substituting the given values, we have:

$$MPK = (1/2)\,(\$1000 \text{ billion}/\$4000 \text{ billion})$$

$$= \$0.125 \text{ per dollar of capital.}$$

So, in this case, an increase of $1 billion in the capital stock would increase real GDP by $0.125 billion.

Step 3 **Answer part (b) by calculating the value of the marginal product of labour, and use the value to determine how much real GDP will increase if the labour supply increases by one worker.** We know that the marginal product of labour for a Cobb–Douglas production function is equal to the exponent on the labour term multiplied by (Y/L). Or, in this case:

$$MPL = (1/2)(Y/L).$$

Substituting the given values, we have

$$MPL = (1/2)(1000 \text{ billion}/0.015 \text{ billion workers})$$

$$= \$33\,333 \text{ per worker.}$$

So, in this case, one additional worker would increase real GDP by \$33 333.

Step 4 **Answer part (c) by determining labour and capital's shares of total income.** We can answer this part with an observation rather than a calculation. Because the production function in this problem is a Cobb–Douglas production function, the shares of labour and capital in total income both equal the value of their exponents, which is 1/2.

See related Problems 2.5 and 2.6 at the end of the chapter.

What Determines Levels of Real GDP per Capita across Countries?

7.3
Learning Objective
Understand why the standard of living varies across countries.

As we have seen in the chapter introduction, the level of real GDP per capita varies enormously across countries. Excluding oil-rich countries and banking centres, in 2013 it varied from \$62 400 in Singapore to \$400 in the Democratic Republic of Congo. Excluding Singapore and Norway, GDP per person in advanced economies varied between \$55 000 in Switzerland and \$23 000 in Portugal. It was \$9800 in China, \$4000 in India, and \$2800 in Africa's most populous country, Nigeria. What determines these differences? GDP per capita is affected by total factor productivity, by the amount of capital per worker, and by the proportion of the population working. In this section we discuss these three factors and conclude that differences in total factor productivity across countries are the main sources of the large differences in real GDP per capita.

To analyze the differences in levels of real GDP across countries, we rewrite the production function in per-worker terms. Recall that as the production function is constant returns to scale, multiplying both capital and labour by the same number multiplies output by that number. So let us multiply capital and labour by $1/L$, the inverse of the number of workers. We obtain

$$Y\frac{1}{L} = AF\left(K\frac{1}{L}, L\frac{1}{L}\right) = AF\left(\frac{K}{L}, \frac{L}{L}\right) = AF\left(\frac{K}{L}, 1\right).$$

When the production function is constant returns to scale, output per worker depends only on the level of capital per workers. (The second argument in the production function, L/L, is always equal to 1.) We will denote with lower case letters the amounts per worker. So $y = Y/L$ is output per worker and $k = K/L$ is the **capital–labour ratio**. Using this notation we can write the production function as $y = A F(k, 1)$. Since the last argument is always equal to 1 we can drop it. We use the lower case letter f to denote the *per worker production function*:

$$y = A f(k). \tag{7.8}$$

Capital–labour ratio
The dollar value of capital goods per unit of labour, measured as the dollar value of capital divided by the total number of workers.

Equation (7.8) tells us that output per worker, $y = Y/L$, depends on total factor productivity, A, and the capital–labour ratio, $k = K/L$. The per worker production function looks like the production function in Figure 7.1 (panel a) on page 209, except that the capital–labour ratio is on the horizontal axis, and real GDP per worker is on the vertical axis.

Diminishing Marginal Returns Figure 7.6 shows the per worker production function. Along the per worker production function, as the capital–labour ratio increases, the increases of output per worker become progressively smaller. This is similar to, but not the same as, diminishing marginal product of labour and capital. Recall that diminishing marginal product of capital means that, when we increase capital while keeping labour constant, the increases in output become progressively smaller. In the case of the per worker production function, the number of workers need not be constant. What matters is the capital-labour ratio. For example, in most countries, over time both capital and labour increase. When capital increases faster than labour, which has been the case in Canada and other developed countries, the capital–labour ratio increases. Figure 7.6 illustrates that, when the capital per worker increases, the increases in output per worker become progressively smaller. We call this property of the per worker production function *diminishing marginal returns*, to distinguish it from diminishing marginal product. The intuition for diminishing marginal returns should be familiar: As we increase the quantity of capital relatively to the number of workers, each worker has more capital to work with and the increase in output per worker becomes progressively smaller.

Increases in total factor productivity will shift the entire production function up, just as we saw with the production function in Figure 7.3 on page 211.

The per worker production function determines how much output, or real GDP, the economy can produce *per worker*. The standard of living, measured as the real GDP *per capita*, depends also on the proportion of workers in the population:

$$\frac{\text{Real GDP}}{\text{population}} = \left(\frac{\text{Real GDP}}{\text{number of workers}}\right)\left(\frac{\text{number of workers}}{\text{population}}\right).$$

Since the ratio of real GDP to the number of workers is equal to $A f(k)$, real GDP per capita depends on

- total factor productivity, A
- the capital–labour ratio, $k = K/L$
- the proportion of workers in population, number of workers/population

---

Figure 7.6

The per Worker Production Function

The per worker production function is very similar to the production function we used earlier except that the capital–labour ratio is on the horizontal axis, and real GDP per worker is on the vertical axis. Because the production function gets flatter and flatter as the capital–labour ratio increases, the per worker production function exhibits diminishing marginal returns.

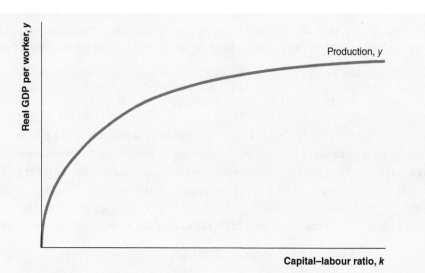

Which of those factors is the most important? Without a doubt, it is total factor productivity that matters most. The effect of differences in the capital–labour ratio is muted by diminishing marginal returns. The proportion of workers in the population depends on the unemployment rate as well as the proportion of people who are active in the labour force, in particular on the labour participation of women. But these differences are not nearly as large across countries as differences in total factor productivity.

What Explains Total Factor Productivity?

What determines total factor productivity? Although no single theory has emerged, economists have identified several important factors, which we discuss next.

7.4
Learning Objective
Understand why total factor productivity varies across countries.

Research and Development and the Level of Technology

Total factor productivity measures the overall efficiency of an economy in transforming inputs into real GDP. Two of the most important factors determining total factor productivity are the stock of knowledge that the world possesses and the associated level of technology. For example, the invention of computers made workers more productive by giving them new and better types of capital goods to work with. Word processing software allows one administrative assistant today to do work that would have required several typists in 1950. Assembly-line workers in automobile plants now operate and oversee robots rather than doing much of the manual labour themselves. As a result, one worker today can produce many more automobiles than could a team of workers in 1950. In all examples, new capital goods have made labour more productive.

Quality of Labour

The quality of labour, like the quality of capital goods, can change over time. Workers become more productive as they acquire **human capital**, which is the accumulated knowledge and skills that workers acquire from education and training or from life experiences. There are two basic ways for workers to acquire human capital: through education and through *learning by doing*.

First, a worker can attend school for formal training to gain skills that are useful in the workplace. Students learn science, math, English, and other subjects that make them more productive workers. According to the Organisation of Economic Co-operation and Development (OECD), among 25- to 64-year-olds, Canada had the highest proportion of people with tertiary education (i.e., post-secondary school) in 2010. Of Canadians in that age group, 24% completed college and 26% completed a university degree. Canada has the highest proportion of people with college degrees. The proportion of population with university degrees is higher in the United States (34%), Israel and Norway (30%), and a few other countries.

Figure 7.7, from the OECD, divides the population into two age groups: 25–34 years old and 55–64 years old. The first number, marked by an arrow, is the proportion of population that obtained tertiary degrees recently—these people are 25–34 years old. The second number, marked by a square, is the proportion of population that obtained tertiary degrees 30 years earlier—these people are 55–64. The length of the arrow indicates the change over the past 30 years in the proportion of people who get tertiary education. In Canada, the proportion for young people with tertiary degrees is third highest (after South Korea and Japan). Note that some of the countries that grew rapidly in the past 30 years: South Korea, Japan, and Ireland, are characterized by the biggest increase in the share of population with tertiary education. In contrast, in China the share of the population with tertiary education is very low and has changed little in the past 30 years.

Second, as Nobel Laureate Kenneth Arrow of Stanford University has argued, workers can accumulate skills through *learning by doing*.[2] Arrow noted that the more often workers perform a

Human capital
The accumulated knowledge and skills that workers acquire from education and training or from life experiences.

---

[2]Kenneth J. Arrow, "Economic Implications of Learning by Doing," *Review of Economic Studies* 29, no. 3 (1962): 155–173.

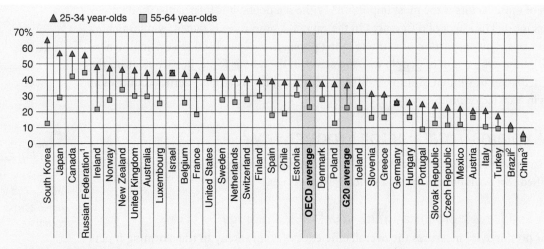

1. Year of reference 2002.
2. Year of reference 2009.
3. Year of reference 2000.
Countries are ranked in descending order of the percentage of 25- to 34-year-olds who have attained tertiary education.

Figure 7.7 Population with Tertiary Education, 2011

The proportion of population with tertiary education varies a lot across countries. It is the highest in South Korea, Japan, and Canada and the lowest in Brazil and China. Over the past 30 years the proportion increased the most in South Korea, Japan, Ireland, and Poland.

Source: OECD (2012), *Education at a Glance 2012: OECD Indicators*, OECD Publishing. http://dx.doi.org/10.1787/eag-2012-en

task, the more quickly they perform the task—thereby improving their productivity. Arrow cited evidence from engineering studies showing that the amount of time it takes to build an airplane decreases as workers build more airplanes. This relationship emerges because the workers have acquired knowledge and skills through building the previous airplanes, which makes them more productive.

Government and Social Institutions

Nobel Laureate Douglass North of the Hoover Institution and Robert Paul Thomas of the University of Washington have emphasized the importance of government and social institutions in explaining differences in labour productivity and the standard of living across countries.[3] North and Thomas, along with many other economists, believe that in addition to markets, secure property rights are necessary for sustained economic growth. Individuals and firms are unlikely to risk their own funds, and investors are unlikely to lend them funds, unless the profits from risky investment projects are safe from being seized by the government or by criminals. In other words, property rights must be secure to encourage investment and capital accumulation. In some countries, property rights are not secure, so individuals are reluctant to devote the resources required to develop new goods and services or expand existing businesses.

Economists Daron Acemoglu and Simon Johnson of Massachusetts Institute of Technology and James Robinson of Harvard University have analyzed the role of government and

---

[3]Douglass North and Robert Paul Thomas, *The Rise of the Western World: A New Economic History* (New York: Cambridge University Press, 1973).

social institutions in explaining differences in levels of real GDP per capita.[4] European countries colonized large regions of the world between the 1600s and the 1800s. In countries such as Canada, the United States, Australia, and New Zealand, Europeans came as settlers and established institutions that enforced the rule of law. These favourable institutions encouraged investment, which led to faster economic growth and higher real GDP per capita. In Africa and other areas, Europeans came primarily to extract natural resources and so did not establish government institutions that favoured investment. Acemoglu, Johnson, and Robinson find that the areas of the world in which the Europeans established strong property rights are generally rich today, while the regions in which Europeans did not establish strong property rights are generally poor.

The experiences of the former European colonies have reinforced the view of many economists that government institutions play a critical role in explaining differences among countries in real GDP per capita.

Making the Connection

How Important Were the Chinese Economic Reforms of 1978?

For much of its history, China was ruled by hereditary dynasties. The last of these, the Qing Dynasty, ended in 1911, at which time the Republic of China was established. The Republic of China had difficulty extending its authority over the whole of the country, and by the 1930s the government had become involved in a civil war with the Communist Party, led by Mao Zedong. The Communists eventually won the civil war and established the People's Republic of China in 1949. The government under Mao created a socialist economy based on state ownership of major industries. Without a system of secure property rights, markets in China were limited and unimportant. For example, rather than selling their crops in the market, farmers had to turn over their crops to the Chinese government. The Chinese government allowed few foreign firms or individuals to purchase financial or physical assets in the country. In 1958, Mao launched what he called the Great Leap Forward, which forced Chinese peasants to move from their farms into cities to build roads and other infrastructure projects. The result was a decline in agricultural output and widespread famine. Mao started another movement, the Cultural Revolution, in 1966 to further advance socialism and rid China, often by violent means, of those who were suspected of advocating free market capitalism.

After Mao's death in 1976, a power struggle resulted in Deng Xiaoping becoming the leader of the Communist Party in 1978. Under Deng's leadership, China instituted many economic reforms, including allowing private ownership of farms and businesses and the establishment of special economic zones that foreign investors could use to establish joint venture enterprises with Chinese firms. The standard of living in China increased rapidly after the country instituted major economic reforms, including opening the country to international trade and investment. This reform allowed foreign technology to flow into the country more easily. China also started allowing agricultural workers to sell some of their crops in markets and keep the proceeds from the sales. This reform provided agricultural workers with a financial incentive to work harder. The reforms accelerated in the 1980s and 1990s to allow a greater role for the market.

---

[4]Daron Acemoglu, Simon Johnson, and James Robinson, "The Colonial Origins of Comparative Development: An Empirical Investigation," *American Economic Review* 91, no. 5 (2001): 1369–1401.

To illustrate China's economic growth, in the figure below we show the ratio of China's GDP to Japan's GDP. The data are at purchasing power parity (PPP) exchange rates. The ratio is of total GDP; the picture for GDP per capita would be quite different since the population in China is over 10 times larger than in Japan (in 1960 it was 7 times larger). As is evident from the picture, until the 1978 reforms China grew more slowly than Japan. From the economic point of view the Great Leap Forward was in fact a great leap backward: While in 1958 the GDP of China was twice the GDP of Japan, in 1961 it was 10% lower. During the Cultural Revolution China's relative position deteriorated further: In 1966 China's GDP was 2% higher than Japan's GDP; in 1976 it was 40% lower. Note, however, that the deterioration of China's relative position was, in part, due to economic boom in Japan. After economic reforms in 1978, growth in China accelerated, raising the ratio of China's to Japan's GDP, in particular after the crash in Japan in 1990, which started a period of very slow economic growth there.

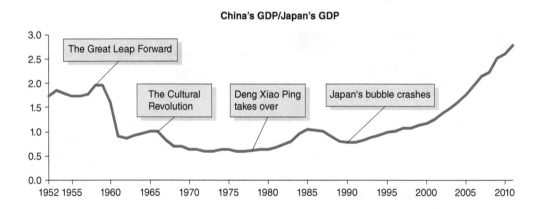

China's GDP/Japan's GDP

The reforms that began in the 1970s allowed total factor productivity and real GDP per capita to increase rapidly in China. Despite the strides it has made toward liberalizing its economy since the 1970s, China has a way to go in the area of economic freedom. An index published by the Fraser Institute in Vancouver measures the degree to which the policies and institutions of countries are supportive of economic freedom. The index uses 42 categories to measure economic freedom in five areas: government expenditures and taxes, property rights, soundness of the money supply, international trade, and government regulation. China ranked only 88th in 1980, the first year the index was published, but even lower—92nd—in 2011. While China has more economic freedom today than it had in 1978, its economic freedom appears to have decreased relative to other countries in recent years. A failure to move toward greater economic freedom could slow China's economic growth in the future.

Sources: Mark Williams, "Foreign Investment in China: Will the Anti-Monopoly Law Be a Barrier or a Facilitator?" *Texas International Law Journal* 45, no. 1 (2009): 127–155; "The Second Long March," *Economist*, December 11, 2008; Robert Lawson and Joshua Hall, *Economic Freedom of the World: 2011 Annual Report*, Fraser Institute, 2011, Vancouver; and Penn World Table Version 8.0.

See related Problem 4.9 at the end of the chapter.

Geography

Some economists argue that geography plays an important role in explaining living standards. In fact, since as long ago as Adam Smith's 1776 book, *An Inquiry into the Nature and Causes of the Wealth of Nations*, economists have pointed out that geography affects a country's potential to achieve a high standard of living. For example, access to navigable rivers and having a coastline makes trade easier and should increase labour productivity and the standard of living. Canada has access to the Atlantic and the Pacific oceans, and the main economic development was along large navigable lakes and rivers. Countries such as Bolivia and Niger are landlocked and mountainous, so transportation is difficult. Jeffrey Sachs of Columbia University argues that geography affects the standard of living for another reason. Sachs, along with economists Andrew Mellinger of Harvard and John Gallup of Portland State University, argues that tropical climates experience higher rates of infectious disease such as malaria.[5] Many countries that are poor today have had high rates of infectious disease in the past. Infectious disease affects health, especially that of infants and young children, and these health problems can affect labour productivity later in life. For example, children with serious illnesses often grow up to be shorter than healthy children. Workers who are shorter because they suffered from illness or malnutrition as children are often less productive in agricultural or manufacturing jobs that require strength. This adverse link between geography and health may explain why agricultural productivity is lower in tropical areas, such as Burundi, Malawi, Uganda, and Zambia. Low agricultural productivity increases the likelihood of famines and has a further negative effect on health, labour productivity, and the standard of living.

The Financial System

The financial system allocates resources by matching borrowers with lenders. When the financial system works well, households and firms that want to borrow to finance the accumulation of physical or human capital can find lenders. To the extent that firms and the government pay for R&D with funds obtained through the financial system, a well-functioning financial system can lead to more investment in R&D. The financial system can also affect total factor productivity by improving the efficiency of the economy. The financial system allocates funds to the firms that are willing to pay the most to obtain the funds. These firms are typically those whose investment projects have the best likelihood of success. Therefore, a good financial system ensures that resources flow to their most productive uses, and total factor productivity for the economy increases. As a consequence, labour productivity and the standard of living are higher.

Research by Thorsten Beck of the World Bank, Ross Levine of the University of Minnesota, and Norman Loayza of the Central Bank of Chile has shown that the financial system has a significant effect on total factor productivity.[6] It is not just banks that matter for economic growth; Ross Levine and Sara Zervos of the World Bank have found that stock market liquidity also affects productivity and capital accumulation.[7] The more liquid a stock market, the easier it is for investors to sell stocks. Investors are more likely to purchase stocks that they know are easy to sell. As a consequence, stock prices are higher, and it is less costly for firms to issue new stock to pay for investment projects. This research tells us that the development of financial markets plays an important role in improving the allocation of funds to those individuals and firms with the most productive investment opportunities. As a result, the economy has a larger capital stock, is more efficient, and has a higher level of labour productivity and a higher standard of living.

---

[5]Jeffrey Sachs, Andrew Mellinger, and John Gallup, "Climate, Coastal Proximity, and Development," in *Oxford Handbook of Economic Geography* (New York: Oxford University Press, 2000).

[6]Thorsten Beck, Ross Levine, and Norman Loayza, "Finance and the Sources of Growth," *Journal of Financial Economics* 58, no. 1–2 (2000): 261–300.

[7]Ross Levine and Sara Zervos, "Stock Markets, Banks, and Economic Growth," *American Economic Review* 88, no. 3 (1998): 537–558.

Key Terms and Problems

Key Terms

Aggregate production function, p. 206

Capital–labour ratio, p. 217

Cobb–Douglas production function, p. 206

Constant returns to scale, p. 207

Diminishing marginal product, p. 208

Human capital, p. 219

Marginal product of capital (MPK), p. 208

Profit, p. 212

Total factor productivity (TFP), p. 210

The Aggregate Production Function
Describe the aggregate production function.

Review Questions

1.1 What are the distinguishing characteristics of a Cobb–Douglass production function?

1.2 With the Cobb–Douglas production function, $Y = AK^{1/4}L^{3/4}$, if both capital and labour increase by 30%, what will happen to real GDP?

Problems and Applications

1.3 Briefly explain whether the following Cobb–Douglas production function exhibits constant returns to scale: $Y = AK^{1/2}L^{3/4}$.

1.4 Draw a graph of the aggregate production function with capital, K, on the horizontal axis.

   a. Why does the graph have the shape that you have drawn?

   b. Indicate on the graph the effect of an increase in the capital stock.

   c. Indicate on the graph the effect of an increase in the productivity of labour.

1.5 To answer the following questions, assume that the labour force is 14 million workers, the capital stock is $5000 billion, and real GDP is $1500 billion:

   a. If the production function is $Y = AK^{1/2}L^{1/2}$ what is total factor productivity?

   b. If the production function is $Y = AK^{1/4}L^{3/4}$ what is total factor productivity?

1.6 Assume that the labour force is 20 million workers, the capital stock is $2 500 billion, and total factor productivity is 5.

   a. If the production function is $Y = AK^{1/3}L^{2/3}$, what is real GDP?

   b. If the labour force increases to 22 million workers, what will happen to real GDP?

   c. If total factor productivity doubles, what will happen to real GDP?

1.7 [Related to the Making the Connection on page 211] In the 1950s, China had a very rapid population growth rate, which it was able to reduce dramatically over the next half century. During the past two decades, China has experienced rapid growth in both the overall level of economic efficiency and the capital stock.

   a. Draw a graph of China's aggregate production function. Put labour on the horizontal axis. Show the effect of increases in labour on real GDP.

   b. Draw a graph to show the effect of increases in total factor productivity on real GDP. Are increases in labour or increases in total factor productivity likely to result in larger increases in Chinese real GDP in the long run? Briefly explain.

A Model of Real GDP in the Long Run
Explain how real GDP is determined in the long run.

Review Questions

2.1 Explain how firms choose the profit-maximizing quantities of capital and labour.

2.2 How do individual markets for capital and labour relate to aggregate capital and labour markets?

2.3 What determines the shares of labour and capital in total income? How are these shares related to the Cobb–Douglas production function?

Problems and Applications

2.4 The graphs below show the production function and the labour market. Assume that the labour market is currently in equilibrium at point *A*.

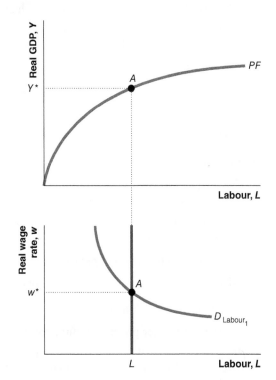

Suppose that total factor productivity decreases.

a. Use the graphs to show the effect on the real wage rate and on real GDP.

b. Now suppose that, at the same time, there is an increase in the labour force. Use the graphs to show the effects. Briefly explain your results.

c. Why is the effect on output different in these two cases?

2.5 [Related to Solved Problem 7.1 **on page 216**] Suppose that the production function is $Y = AK^{1/4} L^{3/4}$.

a. What is the marginal product of labour (*MPL*)?

b. What is the marginal product of capital (*MPK*)?

c. Graph the approximate shapes of the *MPL* and *MPK* curves.

d. What are the shares of labour and capital in total income?

2.6 [Related to Solved Problem 7.1 **on page 216**] Suppose that the production function is $Y = AK^{1/4} L^{3/4}$. Assume that A=1000, the current level of the capital stock is $5 000 billion, and the labour force is 20 million workers.

a. Find the marginal product of labour.

b. Graph the marginal product of labour.

c. Graph the production function, putting labour on the horizontal axis and assuming that capital is constant.

d. Now assume that the capital stock increases to $6000 billion. Show the effect of this increase on your graph of the production function. What effect did the increase in the capital stock have on the marginal product of labour?

2.7 Suppose that the production function is given by $Y = AK^{1/5} L^{4/5}$.

a. If $A = 2000$, $K = \$10\,000$ billion, and $L = 50$ million workers, what is real GDP?

b. Find the real wage.

c. Find the real rental cost of capital.

d. Graph the relationship between the production function and the labour and capital markets.

2.8 Consider the economy described in Problem 2.7. Briefly explain the likely changes in real GDP, the real wage, and the real rental cost of capital under each of the following scenarios. Include a graph with your answers.

a. There are breakthroughs in technology that improve the productivity of all factors of production, causing *A* to increase to 2100.

b. A devastating earthquake causes the capital stock to decrease to $5000 billion.

c. A wave of immigration causes the labour force to increase to 60 million workers.

2.9 The productivity of labour is usually a function of at least three factors: the technology available, the amount of capital available, and the human capital (skills) of the workforce. Compare the likely real wages in the following pairs of countries, assuming that all other factors are identical. Draw a graph to support your answer to each part.

a. Country A is more technologically advanced than Country B.

b. Country C has a larger labour force than Country D.

c. Country E has more skilled workers than Country F.

2.10 Some firms produce in both China and Canada. Assume that the labour and capital markets in the two countries are not currently in equilibrium. Suppose that the marginal product of capital in Canada is $100 per dollar of capital, and the real rental cost of capital is $50. Assume further that the marginal product of capital in China is

$20 per dollar of capital, and the real rental rate on capital is $5.

a. All other things being equal and assuming that labour cannot be moved from one country to another, should firms move production from Canada to China or vice versa? Explain your answer in terms of profit-maximizing employment decisions for firms.

b. What would happen to the marginal product of capital in each country if this reallocation occurred? What would happen to real wages?

 ## Why Real GDP per Worker Varies among Countries

7.3 Understand why the standard of living varies across countries.

Review Questions

3.1 What is the per worker production function? What is the equation for the per worker production function?

3.2 Which two factors determine labour productivity? Which of the two is more important? Briefly explain.

3.3 Why does the standard of living ultimately depend on labour productivity?

Problems and Applications

3.4 Suppose that $y = Ak^{1/4}$, the capital–labour ratio is $20 000 per worker, the level of total factor productivity is 500, 60% of the population works, and there are 60 million workers. What are real GDP per worker and real GDP per capita?

3.5 Assume that total factor productivity is constant.

a. Use the per worker production function to show the effect of a decrease in the capital–labour ratio. What happens to the marginal product of labour? Briefly explain.

b. What happens to real GDP per capita?

c. What happens to the marginal product of capital?

3.6 Assume that the capital–labour ratio is constant.

a. Use the per worker production function to show the effect of an increase in total factor productivity. What happens to the marginal product of labour? Briefly explain.

b. What happens to real GDP per capita?

c. What happens to the marginal product of capital?

 ## What Explains Total Factor Productivity?

7.4 Understand why total factor productivity varies across countries.

Review Questions

4.1 How do increases in total factor productivity increase the standard of living?

4.2 What factors cause total factor productivity to change?

4.3 What is human capital? How does the acquisition of human capital improve the quality of labour? What are the two basic ways in which workers can acquire human capital?

Problems and Applications

4.4 According to an article in the *New York Times*, "A recent study by the Battelle Memorial Institute, a research firm, predicts that China's spending [on research and development] will match ours around 2022." Why might China have an incentive to increase its spending on research and development? Is this increase in spending on research and development likely to raise real GDP per capita in China to the level of real GDP per capita in the United States? Briefly explain.

Source: Adam Davidson, "Will China Outsmart the United States?" *New York Times*, December 28, 2011.

4.5 Consider the following policies aimed at increasing economic growth: (1) increasing spending on health care in order to reduce communicable diseases; (2) increasing student loans to increase college enrollments; (3) providing tax subsidies to firms to increase spending on physical capital; and (4) providing tax breaks to increase spending on research and development. Briefly discuss which of these four policies would be most effective for each of the following countries: Canada, China, and Uganda.

4.6 **[Related to the** Chapter Opener **on page 204]**

A 2012 Gallup poll states that while Brazil, Russia, China, India, and South Africa are all experiencing economic growth, only Brazil and China have a majority of citizens who believe they are experiencing an improvement in their standard of living. The poll states, "It is uncertain how long high growth rates will last for emerging-market countries. To continue to spur high growth rates and allow gains across income levels, leaders must implement sustainable policies."

What is meant by "sustainable policies"? What are some examples of sustainable policies that policymakers could implement in these countries? How might the implementation of these policies help raise standards of living and continue current high growth rates?

Source: Krista Hoff, "Emerging Economies Struggle to Improve Standard of Living. In: Brazil, China Majorities See Their Standard of Living Improving," *GALLUP World*, April 9, 2012.

4.7 According to an article in *The Economist* magazine, the cost of eliminating deaths from malaria in sub-Saharan Africa would be about $6.7 billion for bed nets, diagnostic tests, medicines, and so on. The total economic benefit would be between $231 billion and $311 billion "in lives saved and malaria cases averted, if you factor in productivity gains and savings in the cost of treatment." The article refers to the required expenditure as "a brilliant investment." With the return so high relative to the cost, is it likely that private firms would make this investment in eliminating deaths from malaria? Briefly explain.

Source: "Net Benefit," *The Economist*, July 14, 2012.

4.8 Consider the following statement: "Without a well-functioning financial system, it is not possible for an economy to reach its full potential for real GDP per capita." Is it more likely that a strong banking system or strong stock and bond markets would be more important in facilitating economic growth in a developing economy? Briefly explain.

4.9 **[Related to the** Making the Connection **on page 221]**

Most countries that have high levels of real GDP per capita have economies that can roughly be characterized as free markets. China's economy is one of the most rapidly growing in the world, yet parts of that economy are state controlled.

a. How did the 1978 economic reforms change the structure of the Chinese economy?

b. What advantages might state control of some parts of the economy have in increasing real GDP per capita? Are these advantages likely to persist in the long run?

Data Exercises

D7.1: Using data from Statistics Canada (http://www5 .statcan.gc.ca/cansim/a01?lang=eng), Table 383-0012, analyze the relationship between labour productivity in the manufacturing sector and in the non-farm business sector as a whole.

a. Download data, from 1997 to the latest data, on (1) labour productivity, total economy; (2) business sector, goods; and (3) agriculture, forestry, fishing, and hunting. Use the add/remove data button to add labour productivity to the table.

b. Which has increased more since 1997, labour productivity in the business sector or in agriculture?

c. Download the data on labour productivity in wholesale trade and in retail trade. How does productivity growth in trade compare to growth in productivity in the business sector?

D7.2: Using data from the St. Louis Federal Reserve (FRED) (http://research.stlouisfed.org/fred2/), analyze differences in labour productivity among Canada, China, India, and the United States.

a. From 1952 to the present, download data for real GDP per worker for Canada (RGDPLWCAA627NUPN),

China (RGDPL2CNA627NUPN), India (RGDPLWINA627NUPN), and the United States (RGDPLWUnited StatesA627NUPN). Chart the series on a graph.

b. Calculate the relative productivity of workers in Canada and the United States, measured by Canadian labour productivity divided by U.S. labour productivity. Describe the change in this measure of relative productivity since 1950.

c. Repeat part (b) for Canada and China and Canada and India.

Long-Run Economic Growth

Learning Objectives

After studying this chapter, you should be able to:

8.1 Understand the effect of capital accumulation on labour productivity (pages 231–236)

8.2 Understand the effect of labour force growth on labour productivity (pages 236–241)

8.3 Understand the effect of technological change on labour productivity and the standard of living (pages 241–244)

8.4 Explain balanced growth path, convergence, and long-run equilibrium (pages 245–248)

8.5 Explain the determinants of technological change using the endogenous growth model (pages 248–255)

8.A Appendix: Discuss the contributions of capital, labour, and efficiency to the growth rate of real GDP (pages 260–262)

The Surprising Economic Rise of India

When you have a computer problem and need technical support, the person who takes your call may well be in India. This is one indication of how Indian information technology firms have been expanding relative to Canadian-based firms. The largest steel company in the world, ArcelorMittal, although now headquartered in Luxembourg, was founded in India by the Mittal family. Tata Motors, India's largest automobile company, made headlines when it introduced the Nano car, which it sold in India for only $2200. Tata also owns Jaguar and Land Rover. Increasingly, Canadian consumers find themselves buying Indian goods and services, and Canadian firms find themselves competing against Indian firms.

The rapid economic rise of India surprised people in many countries, including Canada. In 1950, India was desperately poor. India's real GDP per capita in 1950 was less than $1000 measured in 2013 dollars, or less than 10% of 1950 Canadian real GDP per capita. Twenty-five years later, India had fallen even further behind Canada, Recent years tell a much different story. Between 1993 and 2013, real GDP per capita in India grew at an average annual rate of 5.5%, well above the average growth rate of 2% experienced by Canada. After centuries of extreme poverty, India has finally begun to close the gap between its standard of living and the standard of living in high-income countries such as Canada and the countries of Western Europe. It is, however, going to be a long-term process. Over the 20 years of rapid growth between 1993 and 2013, India closed only a small portion of the GDP per capita gap: Indian GDP is now 9% of Canadian GDP while in 1993 it was just under 5% of Canadian GDP.

Continued on next page

India remains a very poor country. It has a population of 1.2 billion, more than half of whom are employed in agriculture and, in many cases, produce barely enough to feed themselves. Infant mortality remains high, and as many as half of all adult women and one-quarter of adult men are unable to read and write. Still, the rapid economic growth that began in the early 1990s provides hope for a better life for India's population.

What explains the higher growth rates in India during the past 20 years? Clearly, an increase in growth was not inevitable. Prior to 1947 India was part of the colony of British India, which also included the modern countries of Pakistan and Bangladesh. In 1950, real GDP per capita was about the same in all three countries. By 2013, however, as India experienced much faster economic growth, real GDP per capita in India was $4000, in Pakistan $3100, and in Bangladesh only $2100. So, countries that are geographically close and share the same colonial history can have very different experiences with economic growth. In this chapter, we begin explaining economic growth by focusing on a few key ideas that explain what determines the growth rate of real GDP per capita in the long run.

See related Problem 4.8 at the end of the chapter.

Sources: "Business in India," *The Economist*, September 30, 2010; Angus Maddison, *Contours of the World Economy* (New York: Oxford University Press, 2007); "GDP per Person Forecasts," *The Economist*, January 13, 2011; and www.cia.gov/library/publications/the-world-factbook/index.html.

Introduction

In Chapter 7, we saw that capital per worker and the level of efficiency, as measured by total factor productivity (TFP), are the key determinants of the *level* of labour productivity at a particular time. In this chapter, we focus on factors affecting *the rate of growth* of the economy. There are many factors affecting the rate of growth of real GDP per capita, such as the rate of investment in capital (which depends on the saving rate), the rate of population growth, and the efficiency with which resources and technology are used in production. We focus on capital accumulation and technological progress and consider both the rate of growth of total output, as well as the rate of growth of output per person.

We begin the chapter by analyzing the workhorse macroeconomic growth model: the Solow growth model. A central concept of the growth model is the steady state: a situation in which capital per person and output per person are constant. Changes in the saving rate have only temporary effects on the rate of growth of GDP: An increase in the saving rate leads to faster growth for a time, but in the long run growth returns to its previous rate. In Section 8.2 we analyze the effect of labour force growth in the Solow model. The higher is the growth rate of the labour force, the lower is the level of output per person in steady state. This explains why many countries with fast-growing populations like India, Nigeria, or Yemen are poor. In Section 8.3 we consider the effects of technological change, which in the Solow model is exogenous, i.e., it is not explained by the model. We conclude that technological change is the main force of growth of output per capita in the Solow model. This explains why technologically advanced countries like Canada, the United States, or Germany have high income per capita. In Section 8.4 we analyze the long-run growth equilibrium and *convergence*: the phenomenon that poorer countries grow faster than richer countries. Convergence does take place within countries; for example, poorer Canadian provinces grow faster than richer provinces. Similar convergence has been observed among U.S. states and Japanese prefectures. Across countries, however, evidence on convergence is limited. While many countries in Southeast Asia have been growing fast and catching up to developed countries, growth in many African countries has been slow. The Solow growth model implies that the main force of growth is technological progress, but treats it as an exogenous variable and does not explain how technological progress comes about. We conclude the chapter with a description of endogenous growth models in which market forces determine the rate of technological progress and the speed of economic growth.

The Solow Growth Model

Labour productivity is the key determinant of real GDP per capita and, therefore, of the standard of living in a country. In this section, we use a model first developed in the 1950s by Nobel Laureate Robert Solow of the Massachusetts Institute of Technology.[1] The **Solow growth model** has become the foundation for how economists think about economic growth. The model can help us understand the key factors that determine why some countries have experienced rapid economic growth while others have stagnated and remain desperately poor. It also indicates the type of policies that can be used to spur growth, raise incomes, and reduce the poverty and suffering experienced by hundreds of millions of people in low-income countries. In fact, Nobel Laureate Robert Lucas has remarked, "The consequences for human welfare involved in questions [about policies to increase economic growth] are simply staggering: once one starts to think about them, it is hard to think about anything else."[2]

The Solow model begins with the aggregate production function for real GDP per worker (see Chapter 7) where y is real GDP per worker, k is capital per worker, or the capital–labour ratio, and A measures the overall level of economic efficiency, or *total factor productivity*:

$$y = Af(k). \qquad (8.1)$$

Assumptions We make several simplifying assumptions that facilitate the analysis but do not affect our results. We assume that the capital–labour ratio is subject to diminishing marginal returns. The economy is closed, with no government sector so net exports, taxes, and government expenditures are zero and all output is either consumed or invested in new capital goods. Households save a constant portion of their income and, with the help of the financial system (which we do not discuss explicitly) savings are converted into investment. We also assume that the ratio of the number of workers (L) to the size of the population (which we will denote N) is constant, so that the size of the population and the number of workers grow at the same rate. So instead of calculating variables *per person*, for example capital per person, K/N, we will calculate them *per worker*, for example the capital–labour ratio, K/L.

We develop the model in three steps. In this section both the number of workers and total factor productivity are constant. In the next section we consider population growth, and in the following section we analyze the effect of changes in total factor productivity. In this and the next section total factor productivity is assumed to be one, $A = 1$, so the production function is $y = f(k)$. With no government and foreign trade, output is divided into consumption and investment:

$$y = c + i. \qquad (8.2)$$

A constant portion, s, of income is saved so that savings are sy. The rest, $(1 - s)y$ is consumed:

$$c = (1 - s)y. \qquad (8.3)$$

Capital Accumulation

Capital stock plays a key role in determining how real GDP grows over time in the Solow model. To analyze the level of capital stock we analyze **capital accumulation**, or the change

8.1

Learning Objective
Understand the effect of capital accumulation on labour productivity.

Solow growth model A model that explains how the long-run growth rate of the economy depends on saving, population growth, and technological change.

Capital accumulation
The change in the capital stock over time.

---

[1]Robert Solow, "A Contribution to the Theory of Economic Growth," *Quarterly Journal of Economics* 70, no. 1 (1956): 65–94.
[2]Robert E. Lucas, Jr., "On the Mechanics of Economic Development," *Journal of Monetary Economics* 22, no. 1 (1988): 3–42.

in the capital stock over time. Since we assumed that the number of workers are constant, the capital–labour ratio, $k = K/L$, changes whenever the level of the capital stock, K, changes.

At any given time the capital–labour ratio and the capital stock are affected by two factors: *investment* in new capital and *depreciation*. Investment in new capital increases the capital–labour ratio. Depreciation, which is the process of existing machinery, equipment, and other capital wearing out or becoming obsolete, reduces the capital–labour ratio. By comparing investment and depreciation we will be able to determine what happens with capital stock over time.

Investment Savings are assumed to be a constant portion of income: savings = sy. The loanable funds model in Chapter 5 shows that financial markets operate to ensure that saving equals investment. So investment is

$$i = sy. \tag{8.4}$$

Substituting the production function, $y = f(k)$, into equation (8.4), we have the following expression, called the *investment function*:

$$i = sf(k). \tag{8.5}$$

Depreciation refers to the reduction in the capital stock that occurs either because machinery, equipment, and other capital goods become worn out by use or because they become obsolete. For instance, a business may find its computers are obsolete if they are too slow or have too little memory to be used with new software programs. We assume that the **depreciation rate**, d, is a constant fraction of the capital–labour ratio between zero and one:

$$\text{Depreciation} = dk. \tag{8.6}$$

Depreciation rate The rate at which the capital stock declines due to either capital goods becoming worn out by use or becoming obsolete.

Investment and depreciation are shown in Figure 8.1. Panel (a) shows the relationship between the production function and the investment function. The figure shows how investment per worker increases as the capital–labour ratio, k, increases. Notice that the investment function has the same general shape as the production function. This occurs because we have assumed a constant saving rate for the economy. For example, if the saving rate is 0.3, the vertical distance from the horizontal axis to the investment function is 0.3 of the vertical distance to the production function. As the capital–labour ratio increases, investment increases but at a decreasing rate, just as output does. Panel (b) shows depreciation. It is a straight line with a positive slope, equal to d. The higher the depreciation rate, the steeper is the depreciation line.

Steady State in the Solow Growth Model

The only two factors affecting the capital–labour ratio are investment and depreciation, since there is no population growth or technological progress. Investment increases the capital–labour ratio and depreciation reduces it. Denoting the change in the capital–labour ratio as Δk and using equations (8.5) and (8.6) we get

$$\Delta k = i - dk = sf(k) - dk. \tag{8.7}$$

where the second equality has been obtained by using (8.5) to substitute $f(k)$ for investment, i. This equation is a key one for the Solow growth model because it tells us how the capital–labour ratio changes over time. If investment exceeds depreciation, the capital–labour ratio increases; if investment is smaller than depreciation, the capital–labour ratio decreases.

Steady state A long-run equilibrium in the Solow growth model.

Steady State We define a **steady state** as the long-run equilibrium of the economy. The steady state will depend on the specific assumptions of our model. In the current model, without population growth or technological progress, the steady state is a situation in which

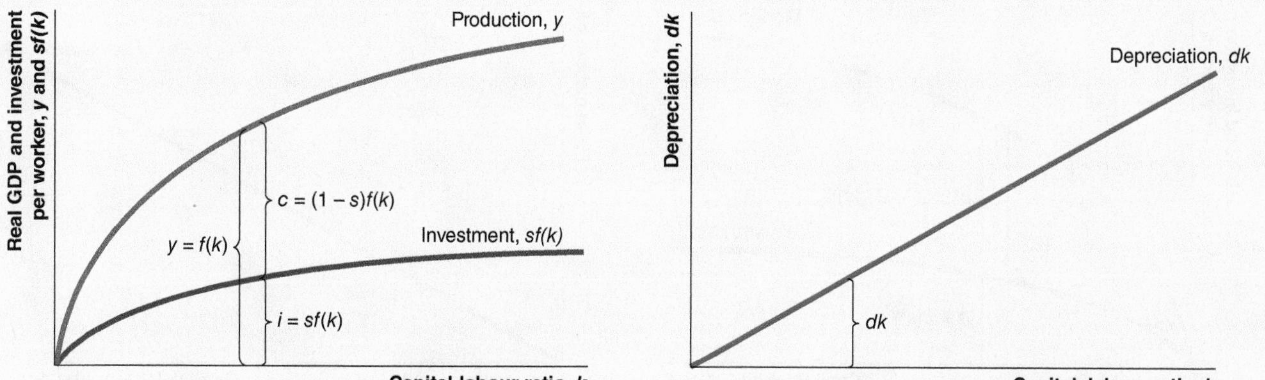

(a) Investment and real GDP per worker

(b) Depreciation

Figure 8.1 Production, Investment, and Depreciation

The production function shows that as the capital–labour ratio increases, real GDP per worker also increases, causing savings and investment per worker to increase. Because of diminishing marginal returns, the increase in investment per worker gets smaller and smaller as the capital–labour ratio increases. The slope of the depreciation line is constant and equal to the depreciation rate.

the capital–labour ratio is constant. In the steady state capital, labour, and real GDP are all growing *at the same rate*.[3] Since capital and real GDP grow at the same rate as labour, the capital–labour ratio, k, and real GDP per worker, y, are constant, hence the term steady state.

Our main task now is to determine the steady-state level of the capital–labour ratio, which we will denote as k^*. We will then ask what determines the level of k^*, and what happens when, initially, the capital–labour ratio is not equal to the steady-state level, k^*. Finally we will analyze factors that affect k^*.

When investment is exactly equal to depreciation, the capital–labour ratio does not change and the economy is in the steady state. This requires that the increase in the capital–labour ratio due to investment is exactly equal to the reduction in the capital–labour ratio due to depreciation. Then Δk in equation (8.7) is zero and the capital–labour ratio is constant. Since both investment and depreciation depend on the capital–labour ratio, the level of capital–labour ratio must be just right. We denote the steady-state values of variables with a "*". The steady-state capital–labour ratio, k^*, is obtained from equation (8.7) by setting $\Delta k = 0$ and rearranging terms:

$$sf(k^*) = dk^*. \tag{8.8}$$

The left side of the equation is equal to the level of investment in the steady state; the right hand side is equal to the level of depreciation in the steady state. When the capital–labour ratio is equal to its steady-state value, k^*, investment equals depreciation, and so the capital–labour ratio remains constant over time.

The steady state is shown in Figure 8.2. Panel (a) shows output and investment; panel (b) shows depreciation. To find the steady state we need to find such a level of capital–labour ratio that investment, which increases the capital–labour ratio, is equal to depreciation, which reduces it.

We now turn to the analysis of the existence and stability of the steady state. This is easiest to do graphically, by placing the investment function and the depreciation line together

---

[3]For now, we are assuming that population and the number of workers are constant, and the growth rate is zero. It will be positive in the next section when we consider population growth.

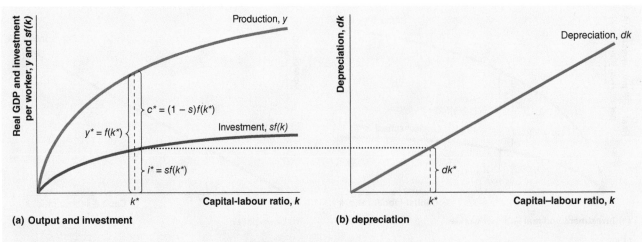

(a) Output and investment **(b) depreciation**

Figure 8.2 The Steady-State Level of the Capital–Labour Ratio

The steady state of the capital–labour ratio, k^*, is indicated with the dashed line. When investment is equal to depreciation, the economy is in the steady state with the capital–labour ratio equal k^*, output $y^* = f(k^*)$, consumption $c^* = (1-s)f(k^*)$ and investment $i^* = sf(k^*)$.

in one graph, as is done in Figure 8.3. For any given capital–labour ratio, the investment line shows additions to the capital–labour ratio, and the depreciation line shows deletions from the capital–labour ratio. Where the two lines intersect, additions (investment) are equal to deletions (depreciation). The intersection of the two lines determines the level of capital–labour ratio in the steady state, which we denote k^* in Figure 8.3.

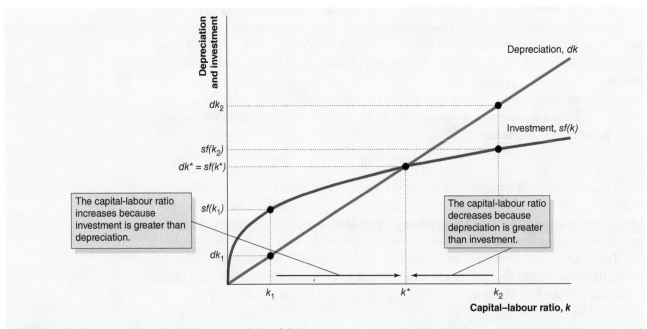

Figure 8.3 Steady State in the Solow Growth Model

In the steady state, the capital–labour ratio is constant, so the change in the capital–labour ratio is zero. The steady state occurs where the investment function intersects the depreciation line. If the capital–labour ratio is below the steady-state value, investment per worker, $sf(k_1)$, is greater than depreciation, dk_1, so the capital–labour ratio increases toward the steady-state capital–labour ratio, k^*. If the capital–labour ratio is above the steady-state value, investment per worker, $sf(k_2)$ is less than depreciation, dk_2, so the capital–labour ratio decreases toward the steady-state capital–labour ratio, k^*.

Existence of the Steady State The steady-state level of capital–labour ratio, k^*, is where the two lines intersect. Because of diminishing marginal returns, the investment line becomes flatter as the capital–labour ratio increases. It eventually has to intersect the depreciation line. More precisely, for the steady state to exist, the slope of the investment function must be initially higher than the slope of the depreciation line, and eventually smaller. So, for the steady state to exist, for very small levels of capital per person its marginal product should be large, and it should fall near zero as the capital–labour ratio becomes very large.[4]

Stability Stability here means that, if the economy is currently not at the steady state, it will move toward the steady state. To see whether the steady state is stable, we ask what happens when capital is not equal to the steady state level. For example, suppose that the initial capital–labour ratio is below the steady-state level and equals k_1 in Figure 8.3. At that ratio the level of investment, $sf(k_1)$, is greater than depreciation, dk_1, so $\Delta k > 0$, and the capital–labour ratio increases toward the steady-state capital–labour ratio, k^*. Similarly, suppose the initial capital–labour ratio is above the steady-state level; for example, it equals k_2 in Figure 8.3. In that case investment, $sf(k_2)$, is lower than depreciation, dk_2, and the capital–labour ratio falls toward the steady-state level. So, indeed, the steady state is stable: When the capital labour ratio is below k^* it increases over time, and when the ratio is above k^* it falls over time.

How fast is the adjustment to the steady state? As you can see from the graph, it is faster the further the economy is from the steady state. The increase in the capital–labour ratio is the vertical distance between the investment function and the depreciation line. As the economy adjusts to the steady state, the distance becomes smaller and so the adjustment slows down.

Solved Problem 8.1

Finding the Steady-State Levels of the Capital, Output, Consumption, Investment, and Depreciation per Person

Consider an economy in which the production function is Cobb–Douglas with total factor productivity equal 1, capital share of output of 1/3, the saving rate of 0.4, and the depreciation rate of 0.1. Find the steady-state level of capital–labour ratio. What is the level of output, consumption, savings, investment, and depreciation, all per person, in the steady state?

Solving the Problem

Step 1 **Review the material in Chapter 7 and in this chapter.** The Cobb–Douglas production function was analyzed in Chapter 7. The question asks about a situation when the capital share of output is 1/3. To determine the form of the Cobb–Douglas production function, you may want to review the sections: "The Cobb–Douglas Production Function" and "The Division of Total Income" in Chapter 7. The problem asks you to calculate the steady-state capital–labour ratio and the values of several variables, so you may also want to review the Solow model and the section "Steady State in the Solow Growth Model" in this chapter.

---

[4]Note also that there is another steady state, where capital per person is zero. In that steady state nothing ever happens: output, consumption, and investment are all zero.

Step 2 **Determine the form of the Cobb–Douglas production function.** As shown in Chapter 7, with the Cobb–Douglas production function, $Y = K^{\alpha} \cdot L^{1-\alpha}$, the capital share of output equals α. In our example, the capital share of output is 1/3 so the Cobb–Douglas production function is $Y = K^{1/3} \cdot L^{2/3}$. To obtain the capital–labour ratio, we need to convert this to the per-worker form. Dividing both sides by the number of workers, L, we obtain

$$\frac{Y}{L} = \frac{K^{1/3} \cdot L^{2/3}}{L} = \frac{K^{1/3}}{L^{1/3}} \cdot \frac{L^{2/3}}{L^{2/3}} = \frac{K^{1/3}}{L^{1/3}}.$$

Using the per-worker notation $y = Y/L$, $k = K/L$, the per-worker Cobb–Douglas production function is:

$$y = k^{1/3}.$$

Step 3 **Use the steady-state equation to calculate the steady-state capital–labour ratio, k^{*}.** The change in the capital–labour ratio is the difference between investment, i, and depreciation, dk. Recall that the operation of the financial markets assures that investment is equal to savings. We assumed that savings are a constant portion of output: savings $= sf(k)$. Therefore the change in capital–labour ratio is $\Delta k = sf(k) - dk$. In the steady state the capital–labour ratio is equal to k^{*} and is constant. This means $\Delta k = 0$ and $sf(k^{*}) = dk^{*}$ (see equation (8.8)). Rearranging and moving the terms involving k^{*} to the left side we obtain

$$\frac{k^{*}}{f(k^{*})} = \frac{s}{d}. \tag{8.9}$$

Equation (8.9) is a general equation, which holds for any form of the production function. It says that, in steady state, the ratio of capital to output (recall that $f(k^{*}) = y^{*}$) is equal to the ratio of the saving rate to the depreciation rate. We can use this equation with the Cobb–Douglas production function: $= f(k) = k^{1/3}$, so

$$\frac{k^{*}}{(k^{*})^{1/3}} = \frac{s}{d}.$$

Simplifying the left hand side and substituting the values of the saving and depreciation rates we assumed at the beginning: $s = 0.4$, $d = 0.1$ we get $(k^{*})^{2/3} = 4$, so $k^{*} = (4)^{3/2} = 8$.

Step 4 **Use the growth model equations to calculate output, consumption, savings, investment, and depreciation, all per person, in the steady state.**

We have

$$y^{*} = k^{*\frac{1}{3}} = 8^{\frac{1}{3}} = 2; \text{ savings} = \text{investment} = sy^{*} = 0.4 \cdot 2 = 0.8;$$
$$c = (1 - s)\, y^{*} = 0.6 \cdot 2 = 1.2; \text{ depreciation} = dk^{*} = 0.1 \cdot 8 = 0.8.$$

We can check that our calculations are correct by comparing investment with depreciation. They are both equal 0.8 so, indeed, the economy is in the steady state.

Labour Force Growth and the Solow Growth Model

8.2

Learning Objective

Understand the effect of labour force growth on labour productivity.

We now extend our model by considering population growth. Recall that we assume, for simplicity, that the number of workers grows at the same rate as population so that the proportion of population that is working is constant. When the number of workers is growing, the capital–labour ratio changes for three reasons. It is increased by investment and decreased by depreciation as well as by the increase in the number of workers.

We can think of the effect of the labour force increasing as *diluting* the capital stock over more workers. What is the amount of dilution? Capital stock per worker is $k = K/L$. Recall from *Useful Math 4.2* that the rate of growth of the ratio is equal to the difference in the rates of growth. Using this formula we find that the rate of growth of the capital stock per person is equal to the rate of growth of the capital stock *minus* the rate of growth of the number of workers. Denote the rate of growth of the number of workers as n. If the capital stock is constant, then capital stock per person is growing at the rate $(-n)$; i.e., it is being diluted at the rate n. So the effect of dilution due to increasing population equals the labour force growth rate, n, multiplied by the capital–labour ratio, k:

$$\text{Dilution} = nk. \tag{8.10}$$

Conceptually, dilution has the same effect on the capital–labour ratio as depreciation did in our previous discussion. For the capital stock to remain constant, taking into account dilution, investment must equal the sum of depreciation plus the dilution due to labour force growth: $i = dk + nk = (d + n)k$. We call this level of investment *break-even investment* because it represents the investment rate necessary to keep the capital–labour ratio constant. To see this, consider the following example. Trygve's Trucking Services has 50 trucks and 100 drivers. Its capital–labour ratio is ½ truck per driver. The depreciation rate is $d = 10$; a truck lasts, on the average, 10 years, so that each year the company has to replace 5 trucks. The workforce grows at $n = 2\%$ per year; each year the company hires two extra drivers. With depreciation equal to 10% and the workforce growing at 2%, during the course of the year the number of trucks falls to 45 and the number of workers increases to 102. To maintain the capital–labour ratio constant at ½ truck per driver, Trygve's Trucking Services needs to replace depreciated trucks and get trucks for new drivers. Depreciation is $d \cdot 50 = 10\% \cdot 50 = 5$ trucks; extra workers need $n \cdot 50 = 2\% \cdot 50 = 1$ truck. The break-even level of investment is $(d + n) \cdot 50 = 6$ trucks. If the company buys 6 trucks it will have 51 trucks and 102 drivers and so will maintain the capital–labour ratio of 1 truck per two drivers.

Our discussion implies that, with population growth, equation (8.7) needs to be modified to include the dilution due to population growth. The change in the capital–labour ratio now depends on the relationship between actual investment and break-even investment:

$$\Delta k = sf(k) - (d + n)k. \tag{8.11}$$

As you can see from equations (8.7) and (8.11), the model without population growth is a special case of the present model with $n = 0$. So the analysis is similar. Recall that steady state is the long-run equilibrium of the economy. With population growth, in the steady state the capital–labour ratio is constant. Figure 8.4 analyzes the steady state in the Solow growth model, taking growth in the labour force into account. Figure 8.4 is very similar to Figure 8.3 on page 234. The only difference is that the line labelled "Depreciation" in Figure 8.3 is now labelled "Break-Even Investment," and the slope of the line has changed from d to $d + n$. As before, k^* is the steady-state capital–labour ratio. If the economy is below this level, for example at k_1 investment is greater than break-even investment, and the capital–labour ratio increases until it reaches k^*. If the economy is above this level, for example at k_2, investment is less than break-even investment, and the capital–labour ratio decreases until it reaches k^*.

The Effect of an Increase in the Labour Force Growth Rate

Economists use the Solow growth model to help explain why the standard of living is higher in some countries than in others. Incorporating the growth rate of the labour force into the model brings us closer to this objective. Figure 8.5 shows what happens when the growth rate of the labour force increases. The break-even investment line becomes steeper, which causes the steady-state capital–labour ratio to decline from k_1^* to k_2^*. A lower capital–labour ratio

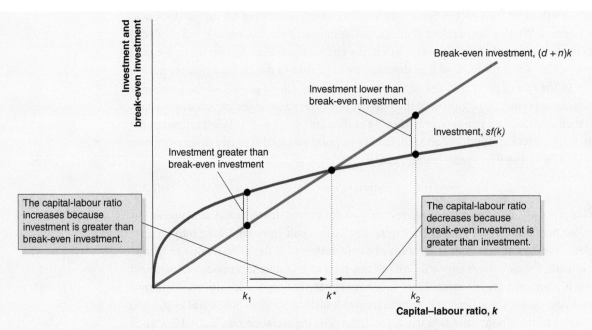

Figure 8.4 **Labour Force Growth in the Solow Model**

When labour force growth is not zero, the slope of the break-even investment line is $d + n$. To keep the capital–labour ratio constant, the economy must now invest enough to replace capital goods that wear out due to depreciation and to provide new workers with the steady-state amount of capital. The steady state occurs when investment equals the break-even level of investment, which keeps the capital–labour ratio constant.

results in a lower level of real GDP per worker and, therefore, a lower level of real GDP per capita. So, the Solow growth model predicts that a higher labour force growth rate will lead to a lower standard of living.

Notice that the growth rate of the labour force and the depreciation rate both affect the slope of the break-even investment line in the same way. Therefore, the Solow growth model predicts that a higher depreciation rate will also lead to a lower capital–labour ratio and a lower standard of living.

Figure 8.5

An Increase in the Labour Force Growth Rate

An increase in the labour force growth rate makes the slope of the break-even investment line steeper. The capital–labour ratio decreases because the level of investment is now less than the break-even level of investment. As a result, the capital–labour ratio decreases from the original steady-state value of k_1^* to the new steady-state value of k_2^*. A lower capital–labour ratio results in lower real GDP per worker.

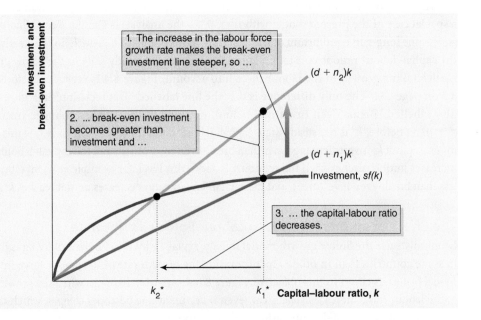

Growth in the Steady State with Growing Population We now need to keep track of both the values per person (or per worker), as well as totals in the steady state, since population and the number of workers are both growing at the rate n. The capital–labour ratio, k^*, is constant in the steady state. As a result, output per worker, $y^* = f(k^*)$, consumption per worker, $c^* = (1 - s)y^*$, and investment per worker, $i^* = sf(k^*)$, which all depend on k^*, are also constant. But population, N, and the number of workers, L, increase at the rate of n. This means that total values (not per worker) also grow at the rate n. These are capital, $K^* = Lk^*$; real GDP, $Y = Ly^*$, consumption, $C = Lc^*$, and investment, $I = Li^*$. The change in population growth rate from n_1 to n_2, shown in Figure 8.5, *does not affect* the steady-state growth rate of real GDP per worker. Once the economy reaches the new steady state, k_2^*, the values per person are again constant. The change in the population growth rate does affect the rate of growth of total values, which grow at the new population growth rate. So the Solow model with population growth can explain why the GDP of India is larger than the GDP of Nepal, or the GDP of the United States is larger than the GDP of Mexico. It can also explain why countries with fast population (and labour force) growth will be relatively poorer. For example, the population growth rate in Canada in 2013 was 0.75% per year while in Kenya it was 2.11% per year. The Solow model cannot, however, explain differences in steady-state growth rates per person across countries. We have to look elsewhere for an explanation of why Canada has experienced significant steady-state growth in real GDP per capita, while countries such as Bangladesh have not.

Solved Problem 8.2

The Effect of a Decrease in the Labour Force Growth Rate on Real GDP per Worker

According to the United Nations' Population Division, the world's population growth rate averaged 1.7% per year between 1950 and 2010. The following table shows the Population Division's forecasts for the population growth rates for different regions in the world:

Period	Africa	Asia	Europe	North America	South America	World
1950–2010	2.5	1.8	0.5	1.2	2.1	1.7
2010–2100	1.4	0.1	0.1	0.5	0.2	0.4
Change in the population growth rate	1.1%	1.7%	0.64%	0.7%	1.9%	1.3%

Sources: United Nations, Population Division; and calculations based on the median variant forecast.

In every region, the forecast is for slower population growth. The slower population growth should reduce the growth rate of the labour force. What effect does the Solow growth model predict this reduction will have on the standard of living in the world?

Solving the Problem

Step 1 **Review the chapter material.** The problem asks you to determine the effect of a decrease in the labour force growth rate on the standard of living, so you may want to review the section "The Effect of an Increase in the Labour Force Growth Rate," which begins on page 237.

Step 2 **Use a graph to determine the effects of a decrease in the labour force growth rate in the Solow model.** In Section 8.2, we saw that the break-even investment line is $(d + n)k$. So the slope of the break-even investment line depends on the depreciation rate and the labour force growth rate. When the labour force growth rate decreases, the slope of the break-even investment line will decrease so that it becomes less steep.

The labour force growth rate does not affect the investment function. Your graph showing the effect of the decrease in the labour force growth rate should look like this:

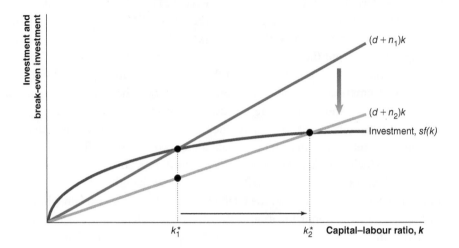

Step 3 **Determine the effect on the capital–labour ratio.** The break-even investment line becomes less steep, so at the initial capital–labour ratio, k_1^* the level of investment is now greater than the new level of break-even investment. As a result, the capital–labour ratio begins to increase toward the new steady-state capital–labour ratio, k_2^*. The change in the capital–labour ratio is the vertical distance between the investment curve and the new break-even investment line. The vertical distance gets smaller as the capital–labour ratio increases due to diminishing marginal returns to capital; the capital–labour ratio increases slower the closer the economy is to the new steady state. Growth stops when the economy reaches the new steady state, where the new capital–labour ratio is k_2^*.

Step 4 **Determine the effect of the capital–labour ratio on the standard of living.** With greater amount of capital per person, labour productivity has increased and so the effect of the decrease in the population growth rate is to increase the standard of living of the average person. The United Nations predicts that the population growth rate will decrease during the 2010–2100 period for all regions of the world, although the decrease in the population growth rate will vary across regions. The largest decrease is expected to occur in Asia and South America, so, all else being equal, you should expect that the increase in the standard of living that results from slower labour force growth rates will be highest on these continents.

See related Problem 2.3 at the end of the chapter.

Saving Rates and Growth Rates

Can differences in growth rates be explained by the differences in saving rates? Some Asian countries like Japan, Singapore, South Korea, and Taiwan grew rapidly when their saving rate increased. Among large countries, China has the highest saving rate and the highest growth rate. As we will see below, in the Solow growth model higher saving and investment rates have only *temporary* effects on growth. As the saving rate increases, the steady-state capital–labour ratio rises. The economy grows faster during the transition to the new steady state but, once the new steady state is reached, the growth rate is the same as before.

Figure 8.6 shows the effect of an increase in the saving rate. A higher saving rate leads to a proportional upward shift in the investment function. Saving is now higher than

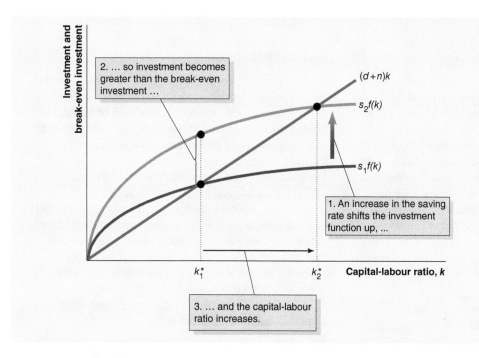

Figure 8.6

An Increase in the Saving Rate

An increase in the saving rate from s_1 to s_2 leads to a proportional upward shift of the investment function. At the old steady-state level of the capital–labour ratio, k_1^* the level of investment is now greater than the break-even level of investment. During the transition to the new steady state at k_2^*, the capital–labour ratio increases. But the increase is temporary.

break-even investment. The capital–labour ratio increases over time until the economy reaches the new steady state at k_2^*. What about the growth rate of output? In the initial steady state at k_1^* the capital–labour ratio is constant and output per worker and per person are constant. During the transition between the steady states the capital–labour ratio and output per person both increase. But this growth is only temporary. Once the new steady state is reached at k_2^*, the capital–labour ratio and output per person are again constant. So while an increase in the saving rate results in a period of faster growth and so increases the level of income per person, the growth rate eventually returns to the original value. We can conclude that, while the Solow growth model can explain differences in the level of income per person, it cannot explain the differences in growth rates. To understand these differences, we must consider other factors.

Technological Change and the Solow Growth Model

So far, we have seen that changes in the saving rate, the labour force growth rate, and the depreciation rate affect the steady-state *levels* of real GDP per worker and real GDP per capita but have only temporary effects on the growth rates. In this section, we will see that technological change causes real GDP per worker and real GDP per capita to grow in the steady state.

Technological Change

Up to now we have used total factor productivity—the A in the production function, $y = Af(k)$—to represent the overall level of efficiency in the economy. Changes in total factor productivity give us a way of measuring the effects of changes in technology. An increase in A will shift the production function at all levels of the capital–labour ratio, leading to a higher level of real GDP per worker and a higher standard of living.

But focusing just on changes in total factor productivity assumes that improvements in technology or efficiency affect capital and labour equally. Many changes in technology, however, are *labour augmenting*. **Labour-augmenting technological change** involves improvements in economic efficiency that increase the productivity of labour but that do not directly make capital goods more efficient. For example, when robots were introduced into

8.3

Learning Objective

Understand the effect of technological change on labour productivity and the standard of living.

Labour-augmenting technological change

Improvements in economic efficiency that increase the productivity of labour but that do not directly make capital goods more efficient.

Macro Data:
Do High Rates of Saving and Investment Lead to High Levels of Income?

The Solow growth model predicts that, in equilibrium, the higher the saving rate, the higher the level of real GDP per worker. This prediction seems reasonable because a high saving rate results in a high investment rate and a higher capital–labour ratio. A higher capital–labour ratio makes it possible to produce more output per worker. But how well does this prediction hold up when we look at real-world data? The figure below plots the level of real GDP per capita in 2009 and the rate of investment between 1971 and 2009 for 120 countries, with each point representing one country. (Real GDP data are per capita, rather than per worker, but recall that there is a close relationship between real GDP per worker and real GDP per capita.)

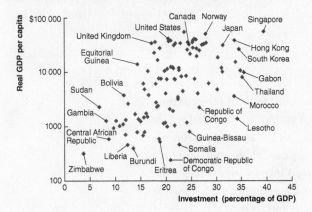

The graph shows that, although the relationship is not exact, the Solow model's prediction is confirmed; countries with high investment rates have higher levels of real GDP per capita than do countries with low investment rates. The fact that the Solow model does a reasonably good job of explaining the actual experiences of countries around the world is a key reason economists have widely accepted the model.

There are two important points to bear in mind, though: First, as we will discuss later, the basic Solow model explains some, but not all, of the key facts about economic growth. For this reason, the model needs to be extended. Second, when looking at data, we need to remember the important distinction between *correlation* and *causality*. The graph shows that investment rates and levels of real GDP per capita are correlated—that is, they tend to occur together—but the graph does not provide direct evidence that higher investment rates cause economies to have higher levels of real GDP per capita. It is possible that we are observing a case of *reverse causality*—that is, having a high level of real GDP per capita may cause high investment rates. Most economists, though, believe that the data in the graph confirm the prediction of the Solow model that high investment rates cause high levels of real GDP per capita.

Source: Penn World Tables version 7.0: http://pwt.econ.upenn.edu/.

See related Problem 1.4 at the end of the chapter.

automobile factories in the 1970s, they increased the number of automobiles that could be assembled by a given number of workers.

We begin our analysis of labour-augmenting technological change by using the production function expressed in terms of levels of variables (see Chapter 7) rather than the per-worker production function we have been using in this chapter. We make one change to the production function: We measure the labour input in *effective units, EL*, where E represents the efficiency of labour. So, the production function is

$$Y = F(K, EL). \qquad (8.12)$$

New technology, new methods of organizing production, and improvements in the skill level of the labour force make workers more productive and so increase the efficiency of labour. The labour input in the production function can increase if the number of workers increases or if the efficiency of the existing workers improves, so we can think of the term EL as measuring the number of *effective workers*. If better training or access to better technology makes workers on average 3% more productive this year than last year, then the effect on the production function is the same as if the economy had 3% more workers. For example, the population and labour force of Brazil are about the same size as the population and labour force of Pakistan. But workers in Brazil are more highly trained and have access to better technology on their jobs. If the E in Brazil is twice the level of E in Pakistan, then the effective labour supply in Brazil is double the effective labour supply in Pakistan.

A simple assumption is that labour-augmenting technological change grows at a constant rate, g. There are, then, two sources of growth in the effective labour force: Growth in the number of workers, n, and growth in the effectiveness of workers, g. Therefore, the growth rate of the effective labour force is $n + g$. To incorporate technological change into the model, we focus on capital per *effective* worker and output per *effective* worker. To distinguish between variables per effective worker and per worker we put a bar above the per-effective-worker variables. So $\bar{y} = Y/EL$ denotes output per effective worker and $\bar{k} = K/EL$ denotes capital per effective worker.

In the previous section, break-even investment consisted of the amount of investment necessary to replace depreciation plus the amount of dilution of the capital stock due to labour force growth. With labour-augmenting technological change, break-even investment now also has to include the dilution from the growth in the number of effective worker. Therefore, the break-even level of investment now equals $(d\bar{k} + n\bar{k} + g\bar{k}) = (d + n + g)\bar{k}$. To see this let us use our previous example of Trygve's Trucking Services. Assume that the better organization of drivers' work (for example, better scheduling with computers or monitoring traffic delays with a GPS system) improves their efficiency by 6% per year, in the sense that each driver, working the same hours, can transport 6% more goods. The initial effectiveness of workers is $E = 2$. The firm has 50 trucks. There are $L = 100$ drivers so the number of *effective* workers is $EL = 200$. The firm has 1/4 truck per *effective* driver. The depreciation rate is 10% so that a year later the firm has 45 trucks left. Drivers become $g = 6\%$ more effective: The efficiency is now $E = 2(1 + 0.06) = 2.12$ and the number of drivers increases by $n = 2\%$, to $L = 102$. Therefore the firm has now $EL = 2.12 \cdot 102 = 216.24$ *effective* drivers. To maintain the constant ratio of 1/4 truck per *effective* driver, it now needs 54.06 trucks. We round it down to 54 trucks.[5] the break-even level of investment is 9 trucks: 5 to replace depreciated trucks (10% × 50), 1 to equip new drivers (2% × 50), and 3 to cover increase in effectiveness (6% × 50). The break-even investment is $(10\% + 2\% + 6\%) \cdot 50 = 9$.

With technological change, the expression for the change in k becomes

$$\Delta\bar{k} = sf(\bar{k}) - (d + n + g)\bar{k}. \tag{8.13}$$

Equation (8.13) is similar to the equation (8.11), with two differences. The variables in (8.13) are *per effective worker* while in (8.11) they are per worker. The second difference is that the break-even level of investment now includes the term $g\bar{k}$.

Figure 8.7 shows equilibrium in the Solow growth model with labour-augmenting technological change.

Steady-State Growth Rates

While the Solow growth model in this section looks very similar to the model from the earlier sections, it is different in one very important way. In the previous sections, capital per worker was constant in the steady state, so real GDP per worker and, therefore, the standard of living were also constant in the steady state. As a result, the Solow growth model could not explain why the standard of living would grow in the steady state, as it has in Canada, the United States, France, Germany, Australia, and many other countries.

With technological change in the steady state (i.e., in the long-run equilibrium of the economy), capital, real GDP and consumption *per effective worker* are constant, so the growth rate of $\bar{k}$ and $\bar{y}$ is zero. Recall, from *Useful Math 4.2*, that the rate of growth of the product is the sum of the rates of growth. Capital per worker, $K/L = \bar{k}E$, is the product of $\bar{k}$ which

---

[5]We need to round the number of trucks as the calculation is, in fact, approximate. But as you can see the difference between the approximate number of trucks needed (9) and the exact number (9.06) is small.

Figure 8.7

Equilibrium with Technological Change

With labour-augmenting technological change increasing at rate g, the break-even rate of investment becomes $(d + n + g)\bar{k}$. The steady-state level of the ratio of capital to effective labour, $\bar{k}$, is determined by the intersection of the investment function and the break-even investment line.

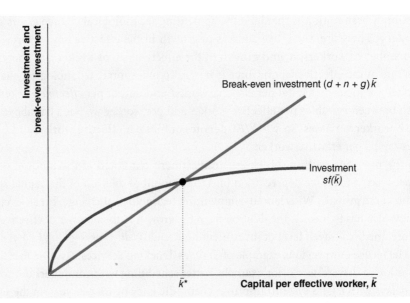

grows at the rate zero, and E, which grows at the rate g. So capital per worker grows at the rate g in the steady state. Similarly, real GDP per worker, $Y/L = \bar{y}E$, consumption per worker, and investment per worker all grow at the rate g in the steady state. Using the same formula, total capital, $K = \bar{k}EL$, grows at the rate $n + g$ in steady the state and so do real GDP and consumption. Table 8.1 summarizes the growth rates of important variables in the Solow growth model. With population growth and technological progress, the *values per effective worker are constant* in steady state. The values per worker grow at the rate g; total values grow at the rate $n + g$.

What about the standard of living, which we measure as real GDP per capita? The relationship between real GDP per capita and real GDP per worker is

$$(Y/\text{Population}) = (Y/L)(L/\text{Population}).$$

If we make the reasonable assumption that a constant share of the population is working, then in the steady state, both real GDP per worker and real GDP per capita grow at rate g. Changes in the saving rate, labour force growth rate, and depreciation rate will affect the steady-state level of real GDP per capita but not the steady-state growth rate. *Only changes in the underlying rate of labour-augmenting technological change will affect the steady-state growth rate of the standard of living.* The Solow growth model has allowed us to reach an important conclusion: Countries that have experienced sustained increases in their standard of living have achieved them because of sustained technological change, not because of other variables such as higher rates of saving and investment or higher rates of population growth.

Table 8.1 Steady-State Growth Rates of the Key Variables in the Solow Growth Model

Type of Variable	Examples			Rate of Growth in the Steady State
Values per effective worker	$\bar{k} = \dfrac{K}{EL}$	$\bar{y} = \dfrac{Y}{EL}$	$\bar{c} = \dfrac{C}{EL}$	Zero
Values per worker	$k = \dfrac{K}{L}$	$y = \dfrac{Y}{L}$	$c = \dfrac{C}{L}$	Rate of technological growth
Total values	Y	K	C	Rate of technological growth plus population growth

Steady State, Convergence, and Long-Run Equilibrium

In the previous section we determined that, when there is technological change, in the steady state the capital–labour ratio and real GDP per worker grow at the same rate. This steady state is often called **balanced growth**, and the economy is described as being on the *balanced growth path*. Balanced growth occurs when the capital–labour ratio and real GDP per worker grow at the same constant rate. Table 8.1 summarizes the steady-state growth rates of key variables in the Solow model on the balanced growth path.

8.4
Learning Objective
Explain balanced growth, convergence, and long-run equilibrium.

Balanced growth A situation in which the capital–labour ratio and real GDP per worker grow at the same constant rate.

Return to the Balanced Growth Path

The experiences of Germany and Japan after World War II provide good examples of how an economy that is off its balanced growth path eventually converges back to that path. By the end of World War II in 1945, both Germany and Japan had experienced large decreases in their capital–labour ratios as factories, bridges, and transportation networks in both countries were destroyed during the war. The decrease in the capital–labour ratio resulted in declines in real GDP per worker and real GDP per capita. Figure 8.8 shows real GDP per capita for Germany and Japan. The vertical axis is logarithmic. Recall from *Useful Math 4.1* that if a variable grows at a constant rate, the graph of its logarithm is a straight line with a slope equal to the rate of growth. Germany grew at roughly constant rate from around 1850 to the beginning of the World War I; Japan from around 1870 to the beginning of World War II. Both countries experienced a large decrease in real GDP per capita at the end of World War II, while in the years immediately after the war, both countries grew much more rapidly than they did before the war. Germany grew rapidly from the end of the war until about 1960, when it appears to have made up for the losses since 1914, returning to the original growth path; it has since grown at the same rate as it did prior to the war. Japan grew rapidly from the end of the war until the mid-1970s, more than making up for the losses since 1940. While its rate of growth returned to the pre-1940 level, it reached a higher balanced growth path.

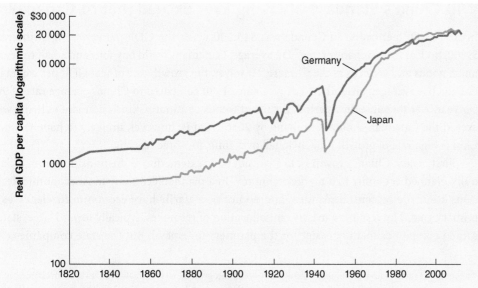

Figure 8.8

Post-World War II Growth in Germany and Japan

Germany and Japan experienced a large decrease in real GDP per capita at the end of World War II due to destruction of their capital stock. Germany grew rapidly from the end of the war until about 1960. After 1960, Germany appears to have grown at the same rate as it did prior to the war. Japan grew rapidly from the end of the war until the mid-1970s, but it appears to have moved to a higher balanced growth path compared to the one it was on before the war.

Sources: The Conference Board, *Total Economy Database*, www.conference-board.org/data/economy database/, Angus Maddison, Statistics on World Population, GDP and Per Capita GDP, 1–2008, http://www .ggdc.net/MADDISON/oriindex.htm.

Table 8.2 Summary of Adjustments to the Steady State

If. . .	the capital–labour ratio. . .	so growth from convergence is. . .	and the growth rate of the economy. . .
$\overline{k} = \overline{k}^*$	equals the steady-state value	zero	equals the balanced growth rate, and the economy remains on the balanced growth path.
$\overline{k} > \overline{k}^*$	is greater than the steady-state value	negative	is less than the balanced growth rate, so the economy converges to the balanced growth path.
$\overline{k} < \overline{k}^*$	is less than the steady-state value	positive	is greater than the balanced growth rate, so the economy converges to the balanced growth path.

What economic forces cause countries to return to their balanced growth path? We can use the Solow growth model, in particular Figure 8.3,[6] and the experience of Germany to explain the process. Assume that in 1939, before World War II, the German economy was in steady state and on its balanced growth path. In terms of Figure 8.3 the economy's level of capital per effective worker was k^* and, according to Table 8.1 on page 244, the capital–labour ratio and real GDP per worker were both growing at the rate g. By the end of the war, large portions of Germany's capital stock had been destroyed and capital per effective worker fell to the level k_1 in Figure 8.3. From 1945 to 1960, the capital–labour ratio in Germany increased for two reasons. First, labour-augmenting technological change was positive. Second, Germany was returning from the artificially low capital–labour ratio of 1945 to the steady-state capital–labour ratio, k^*. Because the growth rate of the capital–labour ratio helps determine the growth rate of real GDP per worker, the growth rate of real GDP per worker during these years was also the result of both labour-augmenting technological change and additional growth caused by the return to the balanced growth path. As real GDP per worker approached its steady-state value, real GDP per capita in Germany returned to the balanced growth path. Table 8.2 provides a summary of adjustments to the balanced growth path.

Making the Connection

Will China's Standard of Living Ever Exceed that of Canada?

In 2013, GDP per capita in Canada was $43 100 while the GDP per capita in China was $9800, both at PPP exchange rates.[7] On average, Canadians could buy four and a half times as much goods and services as the Chinese. However, the growth rate of real GDP per capita in Canada has averaged around 2% per year since 1980 compared to China's average rate of 9% per year over the same time period. If current trends continue, China's standard of living will exceed the Canadian standard of living by 2036. That is, however, unlikely to happen since China's high rate of growth is likely to fall over time, for three reasons.

First, recent China's growth is, to a considerable extent, due to the transition from a centrally planned economy to a market economy. In a planned economy most economic decisions are made by central planners and do not necessarily have economic efficiency as a primary goal. The result is a massive misallocation of resources, typically toward large, state-owned companies that are easier for the planners to control. But the state companies use

---

[6]In Figure 8.3 there is no technological change or population growth, so the break-even level of investment is dk. As an exercise, redraw Figure 8.3 with technological change and population growth. Put capital per affective worker on the horizontal axis. Convince yourself that the description of the adjustment process we describe here does not change.

[7]The data are from the CIA Factbook.

capital inefficiently. During the transition to a market economy these companies are replaced by private firms that respond to market forces and are more productive. We can think of the transition to a market economy as moving China's balanced growth path from the old growth path with inefficient firms to a new growth path that is higher because of improved efficiency. Once the transition is complete, China's growth rate will fall. Second, much of China's economic growth has been fuelled by shifting workers from the agricultural sector, where their productivity was low, to manufacturing jobs in the city, where their productivity was much higher. The large supply of agricultural workers helped keep manufacturing wages low and provided China with a cost advantage in manufacturing goods compared with Canada and other high-income countries. However, China has exhausted much of its supply of low-wage agricultural workers, so manufacturing wages have already begun to rise, eroding China's cost advantage. Third, the process of rapid economic growth led to drastic deterioration of the environment. In 2006 China became the world's largest emitter of CO_2; in 2012 its emissions per head passed those of the European Union. To combat pollution, the Chinese government introduced many policies aimed at reducing emissions. These policies, which include a carbon tax and a limit on emissions in energy production, will raise production costs in China and could slow growth.

There already is evidence that the factors that led to China's rapid growth rate are changing. The cost advantage that drove many foreign manufacturers to relocate production to China is diminishing and production is moving to other countries, for example the Philippines and Vietnam.

The experience of Japan in the past two decades offers a sobering lesson for China: Throughout the 1970s, Japan grew faster than Canada, and there was much discussion about when Japan would surpass Canada in real GDP per capita. But in the 1990s, Japan's average annual growth rate of per capita GDP was only 0.5%, well below the growth rate of Canada, and Japan experienced a decrease in the growth rate of total factor productivity. Although growth in Japan increased during the early 2000s, the country has never approached the growth rates of the years before 1990. Whether China will also suffer a rapid decline in growth rates remains to be seen.

From these arguments we could conclude that the standard of living in China is unlikely to exceed the standard of living in Canada by 2036. But could this ever happen? The short answer is, why not? In 1500 China was among the wealthiest countries in the world, with some of the most advanced technologies known. It was bypassed by Western Europe as a result of the Industrial Revolution. In 1500 income per capita in China was 90% of that in Germany; by 1913, it was only 10% of German income.[8] On the other hand, in the second half of the past century several Asian countries were able to raise their rate of economic growth. Of these countries, GDP per capita in Singapore and Hong Kong is currently higher than in Canada; in Taiwan it is only 10% lower and in South Korea it is 20% lower. An important factor in future growth of GDP per capita in China relative to Canada is going to be R&D spending. Chinese R&D spending has been rising rapidly and, as a proportion of GDP, has already exceeded Canadian spending. It is therefore possible that, eventually, the standard of living in China will exceed that in Canada.

Sources: Nicholas Eberstadt, Fumio Hayashi, and Edward C. Prescott, "The 1990s in Japan: A Lost Decade," www.minneapolisfed.org/research/wp/wp607.pdf; Chris Buckley, "Silver Lining in China's Smog as it Puts Focus on Emission," *New York Times*, September 1, 2013; Netherlands Environmental Assessment Agency, "China now no. 1 in CO_2 emissions; USA in second position," www.pbl.nl/en/dossiers/Climatechange/moreinfo/Chinanowno1inCO2emissionsUSAinsecondposition.

See related Problem 4.5 at the end of the chapter.

---

[8]Angus Maddison, *Contours of the World Economy, 1–2030 AD* (Oxford University Press, 2007).

Do All Countries Converge to the Same Steady State?

Our discussion so far suggests that countries eventually converge to their steady state. But does this mean that all countries converge to the *same* steady state and the same level of real GDP per capita? That seems unlikely because real GDP per capita varies dramatically across countries. In 2013, according to World Bank, average real GDP per capita was $12 000 and ranged from over $100 000 in Qatar to around $500 in the Democratic Republic of Congo (DRC). Economists have closely studied the extent to which poor countries such as the DRC or Bangladesh are closing the gap in the level of real GDP per capita between themselves and high-income countries such as the United States or Canada. The process of catching up to richer countries is called *convergence*. For convergence to take place, we should see an inverse relationship between current levels of real GDP per capita and future growth rates of real GDP per capita. In other words, low-income countries should have higher growth rates than high-income countries.

We do see some evidence of convergence within countries with similar economic systems. When looking at Western European countries we see that the countries with low real GDP per capita in 1960 have grown more rapidly, just as the Solow growth model would predict. Similarly, the Canadian provinces, the U.S. states, and the Japanese prefectures that had lower incomes per person 50 years ago have grown faster than the provinces, states, and prefectures, respectively, with higher incomes 50 years ago.[9] But as the huge gap between Canada and Bangladesh indicates, many low-income countries have not been converging to the levels of real GDP per capita of the high-income countries. In fact, many low-income countries have had growth rates that were lower, not higher, than the growth rates of high-income countries.

What explains the mixed evidence on whether convergence is taking place? The Solow growth model predicts that countries will converge *provided* that they have the same steady state. Steady states can differ among countries, however, as a result of differences in saving rates, labour force growth rates, or the rates of labour-augmenting technological change. Instead of convergence, countries exhibit *conditional convergence*, where each country converges to its own steady state. Research indicates that once we have taken into account differences in their steady states, countries do converge to the steady state at a rate of about 2% a year.[10] Moreover, if low-income countries do not raise their saving rates, increase human capital, or take other measures to increase total factor productivity, the gap in real GDP per capita between high-income and low-income countries is unlikely to disappear.

Endogenous Growth Theory

8.5
Learning Objective
Explain the determinants of technological change using the endogenous growth model.

Endogenous growth theory A theory of economic growth that tries to explain the growth rate of technological change.

As we have seen, in the Solow model technological change is the cause of sustained increases in real GDP per worker and in the standard of living. Given the importance of technological change in explaining economic growth, a major shortcoming of the Solow model is that it does not explain why the rate of technological change differs over time and across countries. Instead, the Solow model assumes that technological change is determined *exogenously*, or outside the model. (See Chapter 1 for the definitions of exogenous and endogenous.)

In recent years, some economists have addressed this limitation of the Solow model by developing new models that explain technological change. These models are known as **endogenous growth theories** because they explain technological change within the model,

[9]Robert Barro and Xavier Sala-i-Martin, "Convergence Across States and Regions," *Brookings Papers on Economic Activity* 1991, no. 1 (1991): 107–182.
[10]N. Gregory Marnkiw, David Romer, and David N. Weil, "A Contribution to the Empirics of Economic Growth," *Quarterly Journal of Economics* 107, no. 2 (1992): 407–437.

or *endogenously*. There are many different endogenous growth models, but in this section, we focus on two general approaches. The first approach is to argue that, contrary to what we have assumed to this point, capital is not subject to diminishing marginal returns. The second approach assumes that research firms produce new technology and ideas in much the same way that other firms produce automobiles or clothing.

AK Growth Models: Reconsidering Diminishing Returns

Is it possible that capital is not subject to diminishing returns? Earlier, we gave a strong argument that capital as conventionally thought of—machinery, computers, buildings, and other physical capital—*is* subject to diminishing returns. Increases in physical capital increase output, but by increasingly smaller amounts. Endogenous growth theory takes a broader view of capital and includes, apart from physical capital, both *human capital* and *knowledge*. Human capital and knowledge may not be subject to diminishing returns. If an economy accumulates physical and human capital at the same rate, the ratio of physical to human capital remains constant, and the marginal product of capital may not decline. As physical capital increases, a country becomes richer, and the country may invest more in education and devote more resources to on-the-job training. Increased education and on-the-job training, in turn, should both lead to more human capital. In addition, as an economy accumulates more capital goods of a given type, *learning by doing* occurs, so the existing workers become more proficient at using capital goods. These more highly skilled workers can keep the marginal product of capital from declining. Firms also have an incentive to increase on-the-job training as they install new capital. For example, as personal computers became widespread, firms invested in human capital by training office workers to use them. Similarly, when computer-aided robots became widely used in manufacturing, automobile firms and other manufacturers invested in retraining workers.

There are also good reasons to argue that knowledge is not subject to diminishing returns. As real GDP grows, firms may have both the resources—from the additional revenues they earn—and the incentive to increase their spending on *research and development (R&D)*. The additional R&D will produce additional knowledge that may further increase the productivity of capital. In fact, some economists have argued that knowledge is subject to *increasing* returns.

Most economists continue to believe that capital experiences diminishing marginal returns. Nevertheless, relaxing the assumption of diminishing marginal returns can provide useful insights into understanding economic growth. So, we now consider a model in which capital is not subject to diminishing returns. For simplicity, we assume that the value of the labour input is fixed so there is essentially no difference between real GDP, real GDP per worker, and real GDP per capita. Therefore, the model in this section determines real GDP but also the standard of living, as measured by real GDP per capita. The production function is

$$Y = AK. \tag{8.14}$$

As usual, Y equals real GDP, and A is a constant. The constant A is equal to Y/K, or output per unit of capital. Recall that the marginal product of capital is $\Delta Y/\Delta K$. In this model, the marginal product of capital is always equal to the constant A rather than declining as K increases, so capital is not subject to diminishing returns. A model of this type is called an *AK growth model*, after the form of the production function that it uses.

With the *AK* production function, investment equals

$$sY = sAK. \tag{8.15}$$

Depreciation, as before, equals dK. In the absence of population growth, the change in capital stock is the difference between investment and depreciation:

$$\Delta K = sAK - dK. \tag{8.16}$$

We can divide each side of the equation by the capital stock to find an expression for the growth rate of the capital stock:

$$\frac{\Delta K}{K} = sA - d. \tag{8.17a}$$

As the production function is $Y = AK$ and A is constant, the rate of growth of real GDP is equal to the rate of growth of capital stock. (Since population is constant, the rate of growth of GDP per worker and per person are also equal to the rate of growth of capital stock).

$$\frac{\Delta Y}{Y} = sA - d. \tag{8.17b}$$

This endogenous growth equation tells us that *the growth rate of real GDP per worker depends on the national saving rate*, so the national saving rate emerges as an important determinant of the growth rate of real GDP per worker and the standard of living. In contrast with the Solow model's conclusion that the saving rate is irrelevant in explaining long-run growth, this endogenous growth model indicates that countries with high saving rates experience high growth rates, and countries with low saving rates experience low growth rates.

The *AK* growth model depends on the assumption that capital does not experience diminishing marginal returns. As a result, economists have developed other types of endogenous growth models that still assume diminishing marginal returns to capital.

Two-Sector Growth Model: The Production of Knowledge

Many economists are not happy with the assumption of the *AK* model that capital has constant marginal returns. In the second endogenous growth model capital has diminishing returns. The model was pioneered by Paul Romer of New York University. It looks explicitly at the production of knowledge.[11] In Romer's model, the economy has two sectors. The first sector consists of manufacturing firms, such as Bombardier or BlackBerry, that use technology to produce both consumption and investment goods for households and other firms. The second sector consists of firms that produce ideas and new technology, *E*, that are useful in manufacturing. We call these firms *research firms* or *research universities*. In reality, many large firms such as Bombardier both produce goods and services and devote substantial resources to research. As a result, the distinction between manufacturing firms and research firms is a bit artificial, but it does provide important insights.

In this model, the labour supply, *L*, is divided between the manufacturing and research sectors. A constant fraction, *p*, of the labour force works in the research sector, so *pL* is the quantity of labour devoted to the research sector and the remaining quantity of labour, $(1 - p)L$, is devoted to the manufacturing sector. Therefore, we can write the production function for manufacturing goods as

$$Y = F[K, (1 - p)EL], \tag{8.18}$$

where $(1 - p)EL$ represents the effective quantity of labour in the manufacturing sector. Notice that this is the same production function we used with the Solow model when discussing labour-augmenting technological change except that we now allow for the fact that only $1 - p$ of the labour force is devoted to manufacturing goods. We assume that the production function in equation (8.18) has constant returns to scale, but capital has diminishing marginal returns.

---

[11]Paul Romer, "Endogenous Technological Change," *Journal of Political Economy* 98, no. 5, Part 2 (1990): S71–S102.

Because we are not using an *AK* production function, increased saving and capital accumulation do not cause long-run economic growth. In the two-sector growth models, endogenous growth arises from the research sector, where new ideas and technology are produced. We model the production of new ideas as

$$\Delta E = zpEL, \tag{8.19}$$

where pEL is the quantity of effective labour employed in the research sector and z measures the productivity of researchers in producing new ideas and technology.

The last equation for these two-sector growth models is the equation for capital accumulation, which is the same as equation (8.7) for the Solow growth model, discussed earlier in the chapter:

$$\Delta K = sY - dK. \tag{8.20}$$

The innovation with the two-sector growth models is that technological change is not exogenous; it is produced by the resources that society devotes to the discovery of new technology and ideas.

Technological progress can be expressed as the rate of change of labour efficiency, $g = \Delta E/E$. Using equation (8.19) the rate of change of labour efficiency is

$$\Delta E/E = g = zpL. \tag{8.21}$$

Equation (8.21) is the main result. It shows that the growth rate of labour-augmenting technological change depends on the size of the labour force, L, the proportion of the labour force devoted to research, p, and the productivity of researchers, z. Therefore, policies that make researchers more productive, that increase the proportion of the labour force devoted to research, or that increase the labour force, will lead to higher rates of labour-augmenting technological change.

Policies to Promote Economic Growth

The *AK* growth models and the two-sector models are important because they can give us further insight into policies that may increase living standards in the long run.

Increasing the National Saving Rate The *AK* growth model shows that the national saving rate is an important determinant of the steady-state growth rate. Therefore, if this model is accurate, government policies that affect the saving rate may be important determinants of the standard of living in the long run. For example, *budget deficits*, such as those Canada has run since the Great Recession, reduce the national saving rate and so may reduce the steady-state growth rate. In contrast, *budget surpluses*, such as those Canada ran between 1997 and 2007, increase the national saving rate and the steady-state growth rate. Apart from its budget, the government can affect the national saving rate in a variety of ways. The government allows households to save tax-free through retirement programs such as RRSP. These programs encourage households to save more and should increase the funds available to finance the capital accumulation that generates endogenous growth in the *AK* growth models.

Making the Connection

What Explains Recent Economic Growth in India?

Economists Barry Bosworth of the Brookings Institution and Susan Collins of the University of Michigan used a growth accounting procedure to explain recent economic growth in India. (See the appendix to this chapter for more on growth accounting.) They showed that the growth rate of real GDP per worker increased from 2.4% per year between 1978 and 1993 to 4.6% per year between 1993 and 2004. Bosworth and Collins report that total factor productivity growth increased from 1.4% per year before 1993 to 2.7% per year after 1993. This observation means that 1.3 percentage points of the increase in labour productivity (over half the increase) was due to faster total factor productivity growth. The rest came from an increase in the growth rate of the capital stock. Since 2004, total factor productivity growth has slowed. A report by The Conference Board, a business research firm, found that from 2005 to 2010, "India's transition to a higher growth path had been ... resource-consuming and ... constrained by a continuing need for reforms." Although Bosworth and Collins believe that the future prospects for India's economy are good, they point out that the country has devoted much of its high level of private saving to financing a large government debt. Bosworth and Collins also note that without an expansion of India's production of goods, rather than services, the country will have difficulty absorbing a large number of underemployed and undereducated workers. About one-third of the working-age population has no education at all.

Another obstacle to growth is the difficulty India has had investing in infrastructure, such as airports, highways, and the electrical system. Critics complain that approval for land acquisition and environmental clearances severely impedes spending on infrastructure investment, as do widespread corruption and government inefficiency. Approval for some projects, such as a new airport in Mumbai, has been delayed for years. In 2012, a weak monsoon season, which reduced the water necessary for hydroelectric power, combined with infrastructure problems and resulted in a blackout affecting over 600 million people. Coal has also been in short supply for India's power plants. Policymakers in India must meet these demographic and educational challenges if the country is to continue its high growth rates.

Sources: Barry Bosworth and Susan Collins, "Accounting for Growth: Comparing China and India," *Journal of Economic Perspectives* 22, no. 1 (2008): 45–66; Sudeshna Sen, "India, China, Top Global Labour Productivity," *Economic Times of India*, January 19, 2011; Prasenjit Bhattacharya, "Why Singh's Infrastructure Pitch May Fall on Deaf Ears," June 8, 2012, wsj.com/indiarealtime/; Jim Yardley, "In India, Dynamism Wrestles with Dysfunction," *New York Times*, June 8, 2011; and Biman Mukherji, Saurabh Chaturvedi, and Santanu Choudhury, *The Wall Street Journal Asia*, August 3, 2012 p. 3.

See related Problem 5.10 at the end of the chapter.

Promoting Research and Development In the two-sector growth model, the growth rate of technological change depends on the resources that an economy devotes to creating knowledge. Governments have adopted a number of policies to increase the resources devoted to research and development (R&D). For example:

- The Canadian government has provided special tax credits for R&D spending. Paul Romer has argued that without tax credits, firms will devote too few resources to R&D. The creation of knowledge has *spillover benefits* because firms cannot typically capture all the profits to be made from creating the knowledge. For instance, researchers at Texas Instruments (TI) developed the first integrated circuit, which was a necessary component in pocket calculators and other products on which TI earned substantial profits. But the profits TI earned from developing the integrated circuit were tiny compared with the total profits earned by the many firms selling products using integrated circuits. Tax credits help reduce the gap between the private return firms earn from R&D and the total *social return* to the economy.

- Governments also grant individuals and corporations *patents* on new technologies that give inventors the exclusive right to sell the new technology. Patents greatly increase the profitability of R&D. For example, if other firms had been free to copy and sell the Windows operating system software immediately after Microsoft introduced it, Microsoft would have been unlikely to incur the costs involved in developing it.

- Governments fund many research activities through grants to university and private researchers and also directly conduct some research. This research is often used by companies, increasing their productivity. For example, the forerunner to the internet was the Advanced Research Project Agency Network (ARPANET), developed by the U.S. Defense Department to help defence researchers at universities around the country.

We can think of these policies as increasing the proportion of the labour force devoted to research, p, in the production function for new ideas and technology.

Making the Connection

Can There Be Too Much R&D?

The motivation for government incentives for R&D is that the social benefits resulting from research activity can exceed private benefits. The social benefits could be higher because, even with a well-functioning patent system, the inventor is often unable to capture all of the benefits of the technology. For example, RIM, later renamed BlackBerry, developed a secure method of mobile communication. The encrypted communication provided by RIM allowed businesses to communicate using mobile technology without worry that the communications would be monitored. The benefits of increased business efficiency (the social benefits) vastly exceeded what RIM charged for the use of its networks (the private benefits). Governments hope to foster this type of result by investing in R&D.

On the other hand, Philippe Aghion from Harvard University and Peter Howitt from Brown University have pointed out that sometimes private benefits exceed the social benefits of an invention. Their work draws on an earlier analysis of *creative destruction* by an Austrian economist, Joseph Schumpeter. Schumpeter pointed out that, in the process of technological progress, new inventions replace old ones. An invention of a new, superior product (creation) eliminates from the market the older, now inferior, product (destruction). The inventor gains the entire market at the expense of the incumbent firm. The social benefit is the difference between the new and the old product, but the private benefit is the entire market. A good example is the smartphone. RIM used to be a market leader, selling more than half of all smartphones in 2010. The introduction of the iPhone allowed Apple not only to expand the smartphone market but also to capture RIM's portion of the market and its profits.

To link the ideas of social and private benefits and creative destruction, consider the following example. Karl's Mousetrap Manufacturing is a market leader. It produces 1000 units that cost $1.00 each to produce and sells them for $1.29. The benefit the mousetrap provides to the buyer is equivalent to $1.40. Now Rosa's Mousetrap Co. contemplates investing in the development of a better mousetrap. It estimates it would also cost $1.00 to produce but the buyer's benefit would be $1.50. Rosa's Mousetrap Co. would set the price at $1.30, sell 1000 units, and drive Karl's Mousetrap Manufacturing out of the market. What is the social benefit of the invention? It is equal to the difference between the benefit of the new and the old mousetrap, minus development costs. The new one provides a benefit of $1.50, the old one provides a benefit of $1.40, and the costs of production are the same. So the social benefit is $0.1 \times 1000 = $10 minus development costs. What is the private benefit to Rosa's Mousetrap Co. from developing a better mousetrap? It is the profit it expects to earn: $0.30 \times 1000 = $30 minus development costs. If the better mousetrap costs $15 to develop, its social benefit is negative: $10 − $15 so it should not be undertaken. But the private benefit is positive: $30 − $15 = $15 and so Rosa's Manufacturing will develop the better mousetrap. It *creates* a better product and *destroys* the previous market leader, hence the name creative destruction.

Patent races are a related example of potentially excessive inventive activity. When technological progress makes possible the development of a new product, many companies invest resources in R&D to be the first to patent the new product and capture the market. A recent example is a substance called graphene. It is a form of carbon, one atom thick, with unique physical properties. The possible uses are diverse and include, for example, foldable electronic newspapers, DNA sequencing, tires, and vodka distillation. It was developed in 2004 and a worldwide patent race quickly ensued, with the *Wall Street Journal* reporting that there were over 9000 published patents in May 2013. The paper cites James Tour, a graphene expert at Rice University, as saying, "As soon as I find something, boom! I file a patent for it." If Mr. Tour is the first to develop a new use of graphene and patents it, his private benefit will be the profit from the product minus his own development costs. The social benefit will be diminished by development costs of all companies that tried to develop the same use but lost the race.

Overall, many governments have the view that incentives for inventive activity are insufficient, and many countries devote significant resources and regulations to promote research and development.

Sources: Michael Lewis, "India demands full BlackBerry access," *The Toronto Star*, January 31, 2011; "The Ongoing Battle Between India and Research In Motion," Knowledge@Wharton, University of Pennsylvania, October 19, 2010; Philippe Aghion and Peter Howitt, "A Model of Growth Through Creative Destruction," *Econometrica* 60, no. 2 (1992): 323–351; and Gautam Naik, "Wonder Material Ignites Scientific Gold Rush. Atom-Thin Graphene Beats Steel, Silicon; A Patent 'Land Rush'," *Wall Street Journal*, August 24, 2013.

See related Problem 5.11 at the end of the chapter.

Increasing Human Capital Governments provide the majority of the primary school, high school, and college education in most countries. Education can provide workers with the knowledge and skills that make them more productive at either producing goods or new ideas and technology. By reducing the price of education, the government encourages households to accumulate more skills and become more productive. These policies increase K in the AK growth models or increase z in the production function for new ideas in the two-sector growth model. In either case, increases in human capital can increase the steady-state growth rate of real GDP per capita.

Reducing Income Tax Rates When people choose to devote more hours to leisure than to work, they are giving up the income that they could have earned had they chosen to work. So the wage rate is the opportunity cost of an hour of leisure. The higher the *after-tax* wage rate, the greater the opportunity cost of leisure, so the person may choose to work longer hours (recall, however, that the income effect works in the opposite direction). A higher tax rate reduces the after-tax wage and may reduce the hours that households will devote to working. We would expect, then, that a higher tax rate will decrease L and the growth rate of new ideas. We should note that the tax rate that maximizes economic growth is difficult to determine. In addition, a tax rate that is too low may make it difficult for governments to fund necessary activities, including building the infrastructure that is important for growth.

Reforming the Political Process and Establishing the Rule of Law In many developing countries, the political process is dominated by a small elite that is concerned primarily with its own financial interests. Not surprisingly, in these countries, policies that might spur economic growth are rarely implemented. Even in democratic countries, *property rights* and the *rule of law* may not be well enforced. For entrepreneurs in a market economy to succeed, the government must guarantee private property rights and enforce contracts. Unless entrepreneurs feel secure in their property, they will not risk starting a business. It is also difficult for businesses to operate successfully in a market economy unless they can use an independent court system to enforce contracts. The rule of law refers to the ability of a government to enforce the laws of the country, particularly with respect to protecting private property and enforcing contracts. The failure of many developing countries to guarantee private property rights and to enforce contracts has hindered their economic growth.

Key Terms and Problems

Key Terms

Balanced growth, p. 245

Capital accumulation p. 231

Depreciation rate, p. 232

Endogenous growth theory, p. 248

Labour-augmenting technological
    change, p. 241

Solow growth model, p. 231

Steady state, p. 232

The Solow Growth Model
Understand the effect of capital accumulation on labour productivity.

Review Questions

1.1 What does it mean to say that an economy is "accumulating capital"? Why does the marginal product of capital decrease as capital is accumulated?

1.2 What is the difference between a stock variable and a flow variable?

1.3 What is depreciation? Explain what happens to the depreciation line when the rate of depreciation increases and when it decreases.

Problems and Applications

1.4 [Related to the Macro Data feature **on page 241**] An article in *The Economist* argues, "As China's capital accumulates, its population ages and its villages empty, saving will grow less abundant and good investment opportunities will become scarcer."

   a. Why might an aging population lead to a lower saving rate? Why might China's saving rate fall as it accumulates more capital?

   b. Discuss the likely consequences of these trends for China's steady-state value of real GDP per capita.

   Source: "Beyond Growth," *The Economist*, May 26, 2012.

1.5 Use a graph to show the effect of an increase in the depreciation rate on the steady-state level of the capital–labour ratio and level of real GDP per worker.

1.6 Suppose that the production function for an economy is given by $y = k^{1/4}$. The depreciation rate is 10%, and the saving rate is 20%.

   a. Find the steady-state capital–labour ratio for this economy.

   b. Find the steady-state real GDP per worker for this economy.

   c. Find the steady-state levels of investment per worker and consumption per worker.

1.7 Suppose that the economy described in Problem 1.6 is at the steady-state capital–labour ratio. A change in preferences causes the saving rate to decrease to 10%.

   a. Describe the forces that will move the economy to the new steady state.

   b. Find the new steady-state capital–labour ratio, level of real GDP per worker, level of investment per worker, and level of consumption per worker.

1.8 The former Soviet Union, a planned economy, was able to maintain consistently high rates of investment for decades. Use the Solow growth model to explain the limitations of growth through high rates of saving and investment.

8.2 Labour Force Growth and the Solow Growth Model
Understand the effect of labour force growth on labour productivity.

Review Questions

2.1 What is break-even investment? What happens to the break-even level of investment when the growth rate of the labour force decreases?

2.2 Explain the effect on the steady-state level of the standard of living of an increase in the growth rate of the labour force and of a decrease in the growth rate of the labour force.

Problems and Applications

2.3 [Related to Solved Problem 8.2 on page 239] Following World War II, many countries, including Canada, experienced a baby boom—an increase in the growth rate of the population.

a. Use a Solow model graph to demonstrate the effect of a baby boom on the steady-state capital–labour ratio.

b. Explain the effect of the baby boom on real GDP and on the standard of living.

c. The Canadian economy experienced strong growth in real GDP per capita during the years of the baby boom. Reconcile this fact with your answer to part (b).

2.4 Some countries experiencing low birthrates are offering women incentives to have children, such as income subsidies and other benefits. Does the analysis in this section suggest that a decline in the birthrate is bad for the standard of living?

2.5 Suppose that the production function for an economy is given by $y = k^{1/3}$. The depreciation rate is 10%, the saving rate is 24%, and the growth rate of the labour force is 2%.

a. Find the steady-state capital–labour ratio for this economy.

b. Find the steady-state level of real GDP per worker for this economy.

2.6 Suppose that the economy described in Problem 2.5 is at the steady-state capital–labour ratio. A change in preferences causes the growth rate of the labour force to decrease to 1%.

a. Describe the forces that will move the economy to the new steady state.

b. Find the new steady-state capital–labour ratio and level of real GDP per worker.

8.3 Technological Change and the Solow Growth Model
Understand the effect of technological change on labour productivity and the standard of living.

Review Questions

3.1 What is labour-augmenting technological change, and how is it different from total factor productivity?

3.2 What is the difference between real GDP per worker and real GDP per effective worker?

3.3 Assume that the economy is currently in the steady state. How will each of the following affect the steady-state growth rate of the standard of living?

a. A decrease in the depreciation rate

b. An increase in the saving rate

c. A decrease in the growth rate of labour-augmenting technological change

Problems and Applications

3.4 Suppose that there is an increase in the growth rate of labour-augmenting technological change. The per-worker form of the production function for an economy is given by $y = 10k^{1/4}$. The depreciation rate is 10%, the investment rate is 0%, and the growth rate of the labour force is 2%.

a. What happens to the steady-state level of real GDP per effective worker?

b. What happens to the steady-state level of real GDP per worker?

c. Why are your answers to parts (a) and (b) different?

3.5   Suppose that the production function for an economy is given by $y = k^{1/3}$. The depreciation rate is 5%, the saving rate is 16%, the growth rate of the labour force is 2%, and the growth rate of labour-augmenting technological change is 1%.

  a. Find the steady-state level of capital per effective worker.

  b. Find the steady-state real GDP per effective worker.

3.6   Suppose that the labour force growth rate increases.

  a. What is the effect on the steady-state growth rate of real GDP per worker?

  b. What is the effect on the steady-state growth rate of real GDP?

  c. Why are your answers to parts (a) and (b) different?

3.7   A report on the differences in the labour force growth rate in the United States and Latin America contains the following statement: "A long-term slowing of labour force growth could reduce the pace of overall economic growth." Assuming no change in the capital stock, use the Solow growth model to explain whether you agree with this statement. Draw a graph to support your answer. Are there factors not taken into account in the Solow model that might change your assessment of the statement? Briefly explain.

Source: "U.S. Behind Latin America in Growth of Labour Force," www.metlife.com, May 24, 2012.

8.4   Steady State, Convergence, and Long-Run Equilibrium
Explain balanced growth path, convergence, and long-run equilibrium.

Review Questions

4.1   What is a balanced growth path?

4.2   Why did Germany diverge from a balanced growth path at the end of World War II? Why did it return?

4.3   What happens to growth from convergence and to the overall growth rate of the economy if the actual capital–labour ratio is

  a. greater than the steady-state capital–labour ratio.

  b. less than the steady-state capital–labour ratio.

  c. equal to the steady-state capital–labour ratio.

Problems and Applications

4.4   Consider the following statement: "If the economy is at the steady state, it must not be growing." Is this statement true, false, or uncertain? Briefly explain.

4.5   [Related to the Making the Connection **on page 246**] Suppose that all economies have the same value for capital's share of income. A developed country has a saving rate of 28% and a population growth rate of 1% per year. A less-developed country has a saving rate of 10% and a population growth rate of 4% per year. In both countries, the rate of labour-augmenting technological change is 2% per year, and capital depreciates at 4% per year. Use this information and the Solow model to answer the following:

  a. Are the countries likely to converge to the same *level* of real GDP per capita?

  b. Are the countries likely to converge to the same *growth rate* of real GDP per capita?

4.6   Suppose that an economy is growing at its steady-state rate of 4% per year when a natural disaster destroys one-quarter of its capital stock, leaving all other factors of production unchanged.

  a. What will be the immediate effect on the capital–labour ratio and real GDP per worker?

  b. After the disaster, will the economy grow at the same 4% rate in the short run? Explain.

  c. What will be the long-run growth rate of the economy?

4.7   How would your answer to Problem 4.6 change if, in addition to the loss of capital stock, the natural disaster also caused a permanent reduction in the rate of labour-augmenting technological change?

4.8   [Related to the Chapter Opener **on page 229**] In 2011, the growth rate of the Canada was about 1.6%, and real GDP per capita was about $43 100. The growth rate in India was 4.7%, and real GDP per capita was about $4000. The growth rate in Angola was 5.6%, and real GDP per capita was about $6300. Is it possible that the levels of real GDP per capita in these countries will converge to the Canadian level of real GDP per capita, given enough time? Explain.

Source: U.S. Central Intelligence Agency, *World Factbook*.

8.5	**Endogenous Growth Theory**

Explain the determinants of technological change using the endogenous growth model.

Review Questions

5.1 Why does growth occur in *AK* growth models?

5.2 Why does growth occur in two-sector growth models?

Problems and Applications

5.3 Suppose the government decides to impose a tax on consumption, which discourages consumption and encourages saving. Use the *AK* growth model to explain the likely effect on the balanced growth path.

5.4 The government allows households to save tax-free for retirement through RRSPs. Suppose that these plans increase the national saving rate. Use the *AK* growth model to answer the following questions:

   a. What effect would these plans have on the growth rate of the standard of living?

   b. Suppose that these plans also reduce government revenue and government saving. How would this assumption affect your answer to part (a)?

5.5 Which is more likely to increase the growth rate of the standard of living: a decrease in income tax rates or a tax cut targeted at corporate spending on research and development? Briefly explain.

5.6 The world's population growth rate is expected to decrease during the twenty-first century. Use the two-sector growth model to explain how this will affect the growth rate of the standard of living in the world.

5.7 An article in *The Economist* about economic growth in Africa contains the following statement:

   One [of the big drivers of Africa's growth] is the application of technology. Mobile phones have penetrated deep into the bush. More than 600m Africans have one; perhaps 10% of those have access to mobile-internet services. The phones make boons like savings accounts and information on crop prices ever more available.

   Use the *AK* growth model to explain how this technological change will affect the growth rate of real GDP per capita in Africa.

   Source: "The Sun Shines Bright: The Continent's Impressive Growth Looks Likely to Continue," *The Economist*, December 3, 2011.

5.8 Some studies have projected that Brazil's informal, or underground, economy may be as large as 40% of the country's GDP. An article about Brazil's informal economy states:

   Companies that operate outside the law save money by avoiding tax and welfare payments, allowing them to compete despite being inefficient, but informality also denies them the possibility of accessing markets for capital and technology that would improve their productivity.

   Use your knowledge of endogenous growth theory to explain the implications for economic growth in Brazil if these companies operating in the informal economy are denied access to capital and technology.

   Source: Brian Asher, "Study: Brazil's Informal Economy Stifling Productivity Growth," *Wall Street Journal*, July 5, 2012.

5.9 What effect would each of the following government actions have on the steady-state growth rate of the standard of living?

   a. A growing budget surplus

   b. A decreased incentive for individuals to save in RRSPs

   c. The elimination of the capital gains tax

   d. A cut in funding for research and development at universities

   e. An increase in income tax rates

5.10 [Related to the Making the Connection on page 251] The *AK* growth model highlights the importance of private capital accumulation in generating economic growth. India has devoted a substantial portion of its high level of private saving to finance government debt. Use the *AK* growth model to show the effect on India's growth rate of the standard of living if India's private saving were available to finance private investment. What type of private investment projects are likely to have the largest effect on economic growth.

5.11 [Related to the Making the Connection on page 253] The two-sector growth model developed by Paul Romer shows that the rate of labour-augmenting technological change depends on the proportion of the labour force devoted to research and development and on the productivity of researchers.

a. Suppose that government subsidies for green
energy lead to a larger fraction of the labour
force devoted to research and development.
Use the two-sector growth model to explain the
effect on the growth rates of labour-augmenting
technological change and the standard of living.

b. Now suppose that government subsidies for
green energy do not increase the fraction of the

labour force devoted to research and development. Instead, the subsidies simply cause existing researchers to move from other areas into
green energy. What would have to be true about
the productivity of researchers in green energy
for the subsidy to still increase the growth rates
of labour-augmenting technology and the standard of living?

Data Exercises

D8.1: The U.S. Central Intelligence Agency's *World Factbook* (https://www.cia.gov/library/publications/the-
world-factbook/) offers many comparative tables of
world data. Go to this site and find the following:

a. The countries with the highest and lowest real
GDPs

b. The countries with the highest and lowest per
capita real GDPs, adjusted for purchasing power

c. The countries with the most equal and least
equal income distributions

d. The countries with the highest and lowest real
GDP growth rates

Where does Canada rank in these categories?

D8.2: One determinant of the productivity of labour is
the human capital, or the skills and education of
the labour force. Use the CIA *World Factbook* Web
site (https://www.cia.gov/library/publications/
the-world-factbook/) to look up education expenditures as a percentage of GDP. Which countries
spend the most on education? The least? Is there a
correlation between education spending and real
GDP per capita?

D8.3: A 2007 World Bank development report titled
"Development and the Next Generation" suggests
that countries with rapidly growing populations
could achieve higher rates of economic growth by
investing in education and health care for their 15-
to 24-year-old populations.

a. Find the press release related to this report on
the World Bank's Web site (www.worldbank.org).

b. What does the report mean when it calls these
young populations a "development dividend"?
Is it also possible that these populations
could be a drag on economic growth? Briefly
explain.

D8.4: Go to the World Bank's Web site (www.worldbank
.org) and look up the most recent *World Development Report*. What are the current challenges for
global growth? At what rate is the world expected
to grow? How are growth rates different in different
regions?

D8.5: [Spreadsheet exercise] Using data from CANSIM
(http://www5.statcan.gc.ca/cansim/), Table 380-
0084, analyze the long-run growth rate in Canada.

a. Download quarterly data on real GDP from
1981 to the present. Calculate the growth rate
of real GDP as the percentage change from the
same quarter during the previous year. Graph
your results. Calculate the long-run growth
trend by calculating the average growth rate over
this time period.

b. What is the standard deviation of quarterly real
GDP growth?

c. Can you identify the 1990–92 and 2008–09
recessions?

d. What happened to the economy in 1990–92? Did
the economy return to its long-run growth trend
after this period?

e. Has the economy returned to its long-run
growth path since the latest recession?

Appendix

Growth Accounting

8.A

Learning Objective

Discuss the contributions of capital, labour, and efficiency to the growth rate of real GDP.

Technology, labour, and capital all contribute to the growth of real GDP. Nobel Laureate Robert Solow of MIT developed a procedure known as *growth accounting* that allows us to determine how much of the growth rate of real GDP is due to each of these three factors.[12] In this appendix, we use growth accounting to show that total factor productivity has been the most important determinant of economic growth.

The Growth Accounting Equation for Real GDP

Growth accounting starts with the Cobb-Douglas production function (see Chapter 7), where real GDP depends on capital, labour, and total factor productivity:

$$Y = AK^{\alpha}L^{1-\alpha}. \tag{A8.1}$$

Therefore, there are three sources of growth: capital accumulation, labour force growth, and growth in total factor productivity. We know that if labour and total factor productivity are constant, the extra output from an additional unit of capital is MPK. So

$$\Delta Y = MPK\Delta K. \tag{A8.2}$$

Because the marginal product of capital is $\alpha(Y/K)$, we can rewrite (A8.2) as

$$\Delta Y = \alpha(Y/K)\Delta K,$$

or

$$\Delta Y/Y = \alpha(\Delta K/K). \tag{A8.3}$$

This equation tells us that if the capital stock grows and all other inputs remain constant, the growth rate of real GDP equals capital's share of income multiplied by the growth rate of the capital stock.

Similarly, we can show that if the labour force grows and all other inputs remain constant, the growth rate of real GDP equals labour's share of income multiplied by the growth rate of the labour force:

$$\Delta Y/Y = (1 - \alpha)(\Delta L/L). \tag{A8.4}$$

If capital and labour both grow, we have

$$\Delta Y/Y = \alpha(\Delta K/K) + (1 - \alpha)(\Delta L/L).$$

Real GDP can also grow if total factor productivity grows. If capital and labour are constant, but total factor productivity grows, we have

$$\Delta Y/Y = \Delta A/A. \tag{A8.5}$$

where $\Delta A/A$ is the growth rate of total factor productivity. Putting all this together, we can write the growth rate of real GDP as

$$\Delta Y/Y = \alpha(\Delta K/K) + (1 - \alpha)(\Delta L/L) + (\Delta A/A). \tag{A8.6}$$

---

[12]Robert Solow, "Technical Change and the Aggregate Production Function," *Review of Economics and Statistics* 39, no. 3 (1957): 312–320.

Table 8A.1 Sources of Growth for Canada

Source of Growth	Symbol	Average Annual Growth Rate
Real GDP Growth	$\Delta Y/Y$	3%
Contribution of Capital	$\alpha(\Delta K/K)$	$(1/3) \times 3\% = 1\%$
Contribution of Labour	$(1 - \alpha)(\Delta L/L)$	$(2/3) \times 1\% = 2/3\%$
Contribution of Total Factor Productivity	$\Delta A/A$	$3\% - 1\% - 2/3\% = 4/3\%$

(Real GDP Growth) = (Contribution from capital) + (Contribution from labour) + (Contribution from total factor productivity).

We can observe everything in this equation except total factor productivity, so we measure the contribution of total factor productivity as the *residual* after all directly observable sources of growth have been accounted for. In fact, the growth rate of total factor productivity is also known as the *Solow residual*.

Growth Accounting for Canada

Below we provide approximate accounting for Canada over the past 50 years. Over that period, real GDP growth averaged 3% per year, labour force growth averaged 1%, and the capital stock average growth rate was 3%. Capital's share of income has averaged about one-third in Canada. We can use this information to determine the contributions of capital, labour, and total factor productivity to the growth rate of real GDP, which we do in Table 8A.1.

The table shows that capital, labour, and total factor productivity have contributed about equally to economic growth. However, capital and labour are both subject to diminishing marginal returns, so the ultimate source of economic growth is total factor productivity growth.

Total Factor Productivity as the Ultimate Source of Growth

Is it possible for a government to spur rapid economic growth by encouraging the accumulation of physical capital goods, such as factories and machines? Yes, but only for a period of time. Capital accumulation is subject to diminishing marginal returns, so growth driven by the addition of more factories and machines eventually diminishes to zero. For economic growth to be sustainable, it must be driven by increases in total factor productivity. We can illustrate this point with an important historical example: the Soviet Union.

Table 8A.2 uses data from Nicholas Crafts of the University of Warwick to show what growth accounting can tell us about one of the most striking events of the twentieth century: the economic collapse of the Soviet Union.[13] To obtain his results, Crafts used a growth accounting equation for real GDP per worker similar to

$$\Delta y/y = \alpha(\Delta k/k) + (\Delta A/A), \qquad (A8.7)$$

where y is real GDP per worker or labour productivity and k is the capital–labour ratio.

The Soviet Union was formed from the old Russian Empire following the Communist Revolution of 1917. Under Communism, the Soviet Union was a centrally planned economy where the government owned nearly every business and made all production and pricing decisions. In 1960, Nikita Khrushchev, the leader of the Soviet Union, addressed the United

---

[13]Nicholas Crafts, "Solow and Growth Accounting: A Perspective from Quantitative Economic History," *History of Political Economy* 41, Supplement 1 (2009): 200–220.

Table 8A.2 Accounting for Labour Productivity Growth in the Soviet Union, 1920–1985

	Labour Productivity Growth $\Delta Y/Y$	Contribution from Capital $\alpha(\Delta K/K)$	Contribution from Total Factor Productivity $\Delta A/A$
1928–1940	2.5%	2.0%	0.5%
1940–1950	1.5	–0.1	1.6
1950–1970	4.0	2.6	1.4
1970–1985	1.6	2.0	–0.4

Source: Nicholas Crafts, "Solow and Growth Accounting: A Perspective from Quantitative Economic History," *History of Political Economy* 41, Supplement 1 (2009): 200–220.

Nations in New York City. He declared to the United States and the other democracies, "We will bury you. Your grandchildren will live under Communism."

Many people at the time took Khrushchev's boast seriously. After all, labour productivity growth in the Soviet Union was extremely rapid following World War II, averaging 4.0% per year during the 1950–70 period when Khrushchev made his boast. This growth rate far exceeded that of Canada, the United States, and many other Western countries and caused some economists in the United States to predict incorrectly that the Soviet economy would someday surpass the U.S. economy. But if you look closely at the data in Table 8A.2, you can see that Soviet labour productivity growth was driven primarily by capital accumulation. The Soviet economic system was quite good at accumulating more and more capital goods, such as factories. Unfortunately for the Soviets, diminishing returns to capital meant that the additional factories the Soviet Union was building resulted in smaller and smaller increases in real GDP per worker. To keep labour productivity growth high, the Soviet Union had to devote more and more resources to accumulating capital goods, which meant diverting resources away from private consumption.

The Soviet Union did experience increases in total factor productivity, but for a 15-year period leading up to its collapse, total factor productivity *decreased* by 0.4% per year. Why did the Soviet Union fail the crucial requirement for growth: developing new ways to make the economy efficient? The key reason is that in a centrally planned economy, the persons in charge of running most businesses are government employees and not entrepreneurs or independent businesspeople, as is the case in market economies. Soviet managers had little incentive to adopt new ways of doing things. Their pay depended on producing the quantity of output specified in the government's economic plan, not on discovering new, better, and lower-cost ways to produce goods. In addition, these managers did not have to worry about competition from either domestic or foreign firms.

Entrepreneurs and managers of firms in Canada, by contrast, are under intense competitive pressure from other firms. They must constantly search for better ways of producing the goods and services they sell. Developing and using new technologies is an important way to gain a competitive edge and higher profits. The drive for profit provides an incentive for technological change that centrally planned economies are unable to duplicate. In market economies, entrepreneurs and managers who have their own money on the line are the ones who make decisions about which investments to make and which technologies to adopt. In the Soviet system, these decisions were usually made by salaried bureaucrats trying to fulfill a plan formulated in Moscow. Nothing concentrates the mind like having your own funds at risk.

In hindsight, it is clear that a centrally planned economy, such as the Soviet Union's, could not, over the long run, grow faster than a market economy. The Soviet Union collapsed in 1991, and contemporary Russia now has a more market-oriented system, although the government continues to play a much larger role in the economy than does the government in Canada.

PART FOUR: MACROECONOMICS IN
THE SHORT-RUN: THEORY AND POLICY

Business Cycles

How Do We Know the Economy Is in an Expansion or a Recession?

Two consecutive quarters of decline in economic activity are often used as the indication that the economy is in
a recession. But this is overly simplified. Recessions are
complex phenomena with different causes and characteristics. How do we know when Canada is in a recession?

Statistics Canada produces many statistics that make
it possible to monitor the economy. Various government
departments also produce statistical data. But neither
Statistics Canada nor the federal government officially
establish the dates of the beginning and end of recessions.
In this book we use the dates established by the Business
Cycle Council of the C.D. Howe Institute, an independent
research organization in Toronto. The Council, set in
2012, consists of around ten economists from academia,
business, and think-tanks. The Council's first report in
October 2012, written by Philip Cross and Philippe Bergevin, provided the dates of recessions going back to 1926.
To establish the dates of recessions, three dimensions were
considered: duration (how long was growth rate negative
or near zero), amplitude (how much activity declined),
and scope (how widespread the downturn was). A necessary condition was that economic activity declines for
at least one quarter, with weak economic activity in an
adjacent quarter so that output falls, or stagnates, over two
quarters. The scope is established by looking at industries
experiencing decline in economic activity. A decline in
manufacturing, construction, and related industries is
considered necessary for a recession.

The C.D. Howe Business Cycle Council criteria to
establish business cycle dates are similar to those of the

Continued on next page

Business Cycle Dating Committee created in 1978 by the National Bureau of Economic Research (NBER), a private research group located in Cambridge, Massachusetts. Nine economists on the NBER's Business Cycle Dating Committee determine the beginning and ending of recessions. The NBER defines a recession as a period during which "[...] a significant decline in economic activity spreads across the economy and [which] can last from a few months to more than a year." Like the C.D. Howe Council, the NBER does not use a hard definition of a recession: "In both recessions and expansions, brief reversals in economic activity may occur—a recession may include a short period of expansion followed by further decline; an expansion may include a short period of contraction followed by further growth. The committee applies its judgment based on the above definitions of recessions and expansions, and has no fixed rule to determine whether a contraction is only a short interruption of an expansion, or an expansion is only a short interruption of a contraction."

The NBER Business Cycle Dating Committee declares a recession when its members conclude that there is enough evidence that a recession has started. The committee looks at GDP data, monthly data on payroll employment, aggregate hours worked, and real personal income excluding transfer payments. As the official GDP data in the United States are available only quarterly, the committee also considers monthly estimates of real GDP constructed by Macroeconomic Advisers, a private, non-partisan economic research group, and a second monthly real GDP series constructed by James Stock of Harvard University and Mark Watson of Princeton University, two economists on the committee. Typically, a recession is identified with a substantial delay. The latest recession, which started in the United States in December 2007, was identified only in December 2008—a year later.

As you can see, the determination of a recession is in part science and in part art. There are no hard rules; rather, there are minimum conditions that need to be met for an economic slowdown to be considered a recession. To be called a recession, an economic slowdown must affect the wider economy negatively for more than a few months. We can conclude that dating recessions is a complex task, undertaken by committees of specialists who take many features of the economy into account.

Sources: Philip Cross and Philippe Bergevin, "Turning Points: Business Cycles in Canada since 1926," C.D. Howe Institute Commentary No. 366, October 2012; The NBER's Business Cycle Dating Committee, http://www.nber.org/cycles/recessions.html, accessed October 6, 2013.

Introduction

The analysis of long-run economic growth is a key part of modern macroeconomics. In this chapter, we begin to shift our focus from the long run to the short run. We discuss the Keynesian and classical approaches to the analysis of the business cycle. They differ with respect to the assumptions on how fast prices and wages adjust when real GDP is not equal to potential. The Keynesian approach focuses on the stickiness of prices and wages in the short run. We analyze the reasons for slow adjustment of prices and wages: the fact that markets are imperfectly competitive, price changing is costly, and wages are set in long-term contracts. In Section 9.2 we describe what happens during the business cycle. We discuss the reasons for the reduction in output variability after 1950, a period called the Great Moderation. We also describe the costs of the business cycle. In Section 9.3 we consider the effect of shocks and describe the multiplier effect of shocks on real GDP. In the last section we develop a simple model of aggregate demand–aggregate supply and use it to describe how the economy reacts to shocks in the short and in the long run.

9.1

Learning Objective

Explain the difference between the short run and the long run in macroeconomics.

The Short Run and the Long Run in Macroeconomics

In microeconomic analysis, economists rely heavily on the model of demand and supply. Economists usually assume that the markets they are analyzing are in equilibrium. For example, they assume that the quantity of oranges demanded equals the quantity of oranges supplied. Put another way, economists typically assume that markets *clear* because prices rise to eliminate shortages and fall to eliminate surpluses. We know that it is not literally true that all markets for goods are in equilibrium all the time. If you cannot find a popular toy during the holidays or cannot get a reservation at a favourite restaurant on a Saturday night or are waiting in line to buy Apple's latest electronic gadget, you know that prices do *not* adjust continuously to keep all markets cleared all the time. Still, these examples of *disequilibrium* are exceptions to typical market behaviour, and assuming that markets are in equilibrium does not distort in any significant way our usual microeconomic analysis.

We made the same assumption of market clearing in analyzing long-run economic growth when we ignored the fact that unemployment sometimes exists in labour markets and that the level of real GDP does not always equal *potential GDP*. **Potential GDP** is the level of real GDP attained when firms are producing at capacity and labour is fully employed. In the long run, nominal wages and prices are flexible, so capital and labour are fully employed. Our analysis of economic growth takes the long-run perspective, so we could safely ignore the possibility that labour might be unemployed and firms might be producing below capacity. In this chapter, we shift our focus to the short run, in which nominal wages and prices are not flexible enough to maintain full employment. We begin our discussion of the short run by considering the *business cycle*, or the alternating periods of **expansion** and **recession** that the Canadian economy has experienced for 150 years. Two key facts about the business cycle are

- Unemployment rises—and employment falls—during a recession, and unemployment falls—and employment rises—during an expansion.
- Real GDP declines during a recession, and real GDP increases during an expansion.

The Keynesian and Classical Approaches

Do the movements in employment and output during the business cycle represent equilibrium, market-clearing, behaviour? Or do these movements represent disequilibrium, non-market-clearing behaviour? Economists have debated these questions for many years. An early focal point in that debate was the 1936 publication of *The General Theory of Employment, Interest, and Money* by the British economist John Maynard Keynes. In that book, Keynes argued that the high levels of unemployment and low levels of output that the world economy was experiencing during the Great Depression represented disequilibrium. He labelled the perspective that the economy was always in equilibrium as *classical economics*. Economists continue to use these labels today. **Keynesian economics** refers to the perspective that business cycles represent disequilibrium, or non-market-clearing behaviour, and **classical economics** refers to the perspective that business cycles can be explained using equilibrium analysis.

If the Keynesian view is correct, then the increase in cyclical unemployment during a recession primarily represents *involuntary unemployment*, or workers who are unable to find jobs at the current wage rate. Similarly, the decline in real GDP occurs primarily because some firms would like to sell more goods or services at prevailing prices but are unable to do so. If the classical view is correct, the labour market and the markets for goods and services remain in equilibrium during the business cycle. Although employment and output decline during a recession, they do so because of the voluntary decisions of households to supply less labour and decisions of firms to supply fewer goods and services.

The majority of economists believe that the essentials of the Keynesian view of the business cycle are correct, although the details of their explanations of the business cycle are significantly different from those that Keynes offered in 1936. These views are often called the *new Keynesian economics*. Some economists, however, believe that the classical view is correct. The views of these economists are sometimes called the *new classical macroeconomics*. The word *new* is used to distinguish these views from the original Keynesian and classical approaches to macroeconomics.

Potential GDP The level of real GDP attained when firms are producing at capacity and labour is fully employed.

Expansion The period of a business cycle during which real GDP and employment are increasing.

Recession The period of a business cycle during which real GDP and employment are decreasing.

Keynesian economics The perspective that business cycles represent disequilibrium, or non-market-clearing behaviour.

Classical economics The perspective that business cycles can be explained using equilibrium analysis.

In this and the following chapters, although we will focus on the Keynesian view, we will also keep in mind the new classical view.

Macroeconomic Shocks and Price Flexibility

Macroeconomic shock An exogenous, positive or negative event that has a significant effect on an important sector of the economy or on the economy as a whole.

The word *cycle* in the phrase *business cycle* can be misleading because it suggests that the economy follows a regular pattern of recessions and expansions of the same length and intensity, in a self-perpetuating cycle. Although decades ago some economists thought of business cycles in more or less this way, today most do not. Instead, most economists—of both the Keynesian and classical schools—see the business cycle as resulting from the response of households and firms to *macroeconomic shocks*. A **macroeconomic shock** is an exogenous event that has a significant effect on an important sector of the economy or on the economy as a whole.[1] Examples of macroeconomic shocks are a financial crisis, the collapse of a housing bubble, a significant innovation in information technology, a significant increase in oil prices, or a change in monetary policy or fiscal policy. The event may be unexpected or expected. When the shock is expected, households and firms can sometimes prepare and reduce its effect, but it is difficult to reduce the effect completely. For example an increase in the price of raw materials because of rapid growth in China and strong conditions in advanced economies in 2006–08 was mostly expected, yet firms were not able to avoid the increase in costs. Because of the inability to prepare for unexpected events, however, they tend to have bigger effects on the economy than expected events.

Macroeconomic shocks require many households and firms to change their behaviour. For example, the Great Recession reduced the demand for cars. Workers at the Canadian car companies had to find other jobs; car companies had to learn how to survive in the new circumstances, with a much smaller volume of sales. Similarly, as use of smart phones and tablets is spreading, firms making computers have to switch production to these devices or move to other industries.

One of the benefits of the market system is its flexibility. Every month in Canada, new firms open and existing firms expand their operations, creating hundreds of thousands of jobs, while at the same time other firms close or contract their operations, destroying hundreds of thousands of jobs. Generally, a market system can handle the flow of resources—labour, capital, and raw materials—from declining industries to expanding industries. In fact, the two big transitions in the Canadian economy: from agriculture to manufacturing and from manufacturing to services, were accomplished without long-term increases in unemployment.

A macroeconomic shock, however, requires an economy to make these adjustments quickly, so the results can be disruptive. For example, at the height of the housing bubble in Ireland from 2005 to 2007, residential construction and related industries employed 12% of all workers in the economy. By 2009, residential construction employed only about 3% of workers. Workers formerly employed in the construction industry were not able to quickly change their qualifications and enter other fields, so the decline in construction led to high levels of unemployment. No wonder the Irish economy, which was one of the fastest-growing economies in Europe, experienced a severe recession.

We know from microeconomic analysis that markets adjust to changes in demand and supply through changes in prices. One reason an economy may have difficulty smoothly adjusting to a macroeconomic shock is that nominal prices and nominal wages may not fully adjust to the effects of the shock in the short run. In fact, many economists believe that a key

---

[1]Recall that economists refer to something that is taken as given as *exogenous* and something that will be explained by the model as *endogenous* (see Chapter 1).

difference between the short run and the long run is that *in the short run nominal prices and nominal wages are "sticky," while in the long run nominal prices and nominal wages are flexible.* By "sticky," economists mean that prices and wages do not fully adjust in the short run to changes in demand or supply, but adjust fully in the long run. Economists call the slow adjustment of nominal prices and wages to shocks *nominal price and wage rigidity* or *nominal price and wage stickiness.* Keynesian economists initially focused on nominal wage stickiness because that is what Keynes emphasized in *The General Theory.* In recent years, *new Keynesian economists* have shifted the focus to nominal price stickiness.

Why Are Nominal Prices Sticky in the Short Run?

The fact that prices are often sticky in the short run is a key reason macroeconomic shocks can result in fluctuations in total employment and total output. So, understanding why prices can be sticky is an important macroeconomic issue.

Several factors cause price stickiness. Many firms operate in *imperfectly competitive* markets. Unlike in a *perfectly competitive* market, firms in imperfectly competitive markets have some control over prices. Imagine a market in which several companies produce the same (or similar) products and charge the same price. Each firm will be concerned that, if it raises prices and other firms do not, its price will be higher than what competitors charge and it will lose customers. In addition, firms may be reluctant to upset repeat customers with frequent or large price changes. Repeat customers are the most valuable customers as they provide a stream of revenue for the firm. So, for example, a hairdresser, who has many repeat customers, may keep prices constant for a long time, while a highway hotel, where most customers stay once or twice, would change prices all the time. Customers and firms may also agree to long-term contracts. For instance, many households sign contracts fixing for a year, or longer period, the price for services like phone or cable connection, car insurance, or goods bought regularly, like electricity.

Another reason for price stickiness is costs to firms from changing prices. The costs are called *menu costs* because one of the original examples of the expense of changing prices was the cost of printing new restaurant menus. But the costs of changing prices are more complex than the name suggests. They include decision costs (the cost of figuring out the best price), communication costs (the costs of informing sales personnel and customers), as well as posting costs (the costs of attaching price labels, printing catalogues etc.). One study found that the decision and communication costs are 30 times larger than the costs of posting the price. [2] If changing prices is costly, firms face a trade-off when demand or supply curves shift. A firm will lower its price following a decline in demand if the benefit to doing so would be greater than the cost. The firm will not lower its prices if the benefit would be less than the cost. The same is true following an increase in demand: If the benefit from raising the price does not exceed the cost, the firm will hold its price constant.

Customers may also be angered if a firm raises prices, as might happen, for instance, if a hardware store raised the price of snow shovels after a winter storm. For example, the mobile app company Uber, which connects customers with drivers and with ridesharing services, uses "surge" pricing. Whenever demand exceeds supply, as is the case during holidays or, indeed, during a snowstorm, Uber raises prices (as much as sevenfold) to reflect the surge of demand. This attracts more drivers to provide services and reduces demand. While this policy assures that cars are available, customers do not like it and the firm's pricing policy is very unpopular.

---

[2]Mark J. Zbaracki, Mark Ritson, Daniel Levy, Shantanu Dutta, and Mark Bergen, "Managerial and Customer Costs of Price Adjustment: Direct Evidence from Industrial Markets," *Review of Economics and Statistics* 86, no. 2 (2004): 514–533.

In addition, before firms adjust their prices, they must determine how much demand and supply have shifted in their individual markets and how long-lived these shifts might be. For example, the manager of a hotel may realize that the economy has moved into a recession and may expect that demand for rooms in the hotel has declined. But rather than lower prices right away—and run the risk of annoying customers if she ends up quickly raising them again—the manager may want to see how much the recession affects tourism and business travel in that city. In this case, we can think of the cost of changing prices as the cost of determining how the firm should respond to a macroeconomic shock. Finally, information is also costly. Continuously collecting information about market conditions, competitor behaviour, and forecasting the relevant variables is a costly process. Given the expense of information collecting, firms may choose to get the full information and change prices only once a year, for example.

How Long Prices Are Sticky Economic research has shown that most retailers in Western Europe and the United States (no Canadian data are available) change prices just once or twice a year, with firms in the service sector typically changing prices less frequently than manufacturing firms.[3] Wholesale prices are changed more often than retail prices.[4] Economists have also found that a firm is more likely to change prices as a result of shocks to the firm's sector than as a result of shocks to the aggregate economy. For instance, book publishers may adjust prices fairly quickly in response to changes in the cost of paper but respond more slowly to changes in the demand for books that results from the bursting of a housing bubble.

Making the Connection

The Curious Case of the 5-Cent Bottle of Coke

There is price stickiness, and then there is the case of the price of a bottle of Coke. As we have seen, there are reasons firms may not fully adjust the prices of their products to changes in demand and supply in the short run. The period involved, though, is usually a year or two. After that time has passed, firms will typically have fully adjusted their prices. Over a period of decades, most firms experience many shifts in demand and supply. Despite short-run price stickiness, these shifts ought to result in the prices of the firm's products changing many times. Not so with a bottle of Coca-Cola, however. Between 1886 and 1955, the price of a standard, 6.5-ounce glass bottle of Coke remained unchanged, at 5 cents.

During this nearly 70-year period, wars, the Great Depression, the passage and repeal of a ban on selling alcoholic beverages, a tripling of the price of sugar, and changes in the technology of producing soft drinks all occurred, but Coca-Cola held the price of its most important product constant.

Coca-Cola was introduced in 1886 by an Atlanta, Georgia, druggist named John Stith Pemberton. At first, most Coke was sold by the glass at soda fountains, drug stores, and restaurants. Following the introduction of the distinctive 6.5-ounce "hobble skirt" bottle in 1916, bottle sales, particularly through vending machines, became increasingly important.

Daniel Levy and Andrew T. Young of Emory University have provided the most careful account of why Coca-Cola kept the price of its most important product fixed for decades. Levy and Young argue that three main factors account for this extraordinary episode of price rigidity:

1. From 1899 to 1921, the firm was obligated by long-term contracts to provide its bottlers with the syrup that Coca-Cola is made from at a fixed price of $0.92 per gallon.

---

[3]Peter Klenow and Benjamin Malin, "Microeconomic Evidence on Price-Setting," in B. Friedman and M. Woodford, eds., *Handbook of Monetary Economics 3A*, (Elsevier, 2011).

[4]See, for example, David Amirault, Carolyn Kwan, and Gordon Wilkinson, "Survey of Price-Setting Behaviour of Canadian Companies," Bank of Canada Working Paper, 2006-35.

Although Coca-Cola manufactured the syrup, the bottlers that actually produced the soft drink and distributed it for sale were independent businesses. After 1921, the price Coca-Cola charged its bottlers for syrup varied, and this no longer became an important reason for inflexibility in the retail price.

2. Vending machines could accept only a single coin and could not make change. Coca-Cola, therefore, could not adjust the price of a bottle in penny increments.

3. Coca-Cola believed that it was important that consumers be able to buy the signature 6.5-ounce Coke bottle using a single coin. This meant that to raise the price from a nickel, the firm would have to start charging a dime, which would be a 100% increase in price. During the 1950s, Robert Woodruff, who was then president of Coca-Cola, tried to get around this problem by urging newly elected President Eisenhower, who happened to be Woodruff's friend and hunting companion, to have the U.S. Treasury begin issuing a 7.5-cent coin. Eisenhower forwarded the proposal to the Department of the Treasury, but the Treasury did not pursue the idea further.

Ultimately, rising costs and advances in vending machine technology led Coca-Cola to abandon its fixed-price strategy. By 1955, Coke was selling for 5, 6, 7, or even 10 cents in different parts of the country. In 1959, 6.5-ounce bottles of Coke were no longer selling for 5 cents anywhere in the United States.

The saga of the nickel Coke provides an extreme example of why a firm may consider it profitable to hold the price of a product constant, despite large swings in demand and costs.

Sources: Daniel Levy and Andrew T. Young, "'The Real Thing': Nominal Price Rigidity of the Nickel Coke, 1886–1959," *Journal of Money, Credit, and Banking* 36, no. 4 (2004): 765–799; Richard S. Tedlow, *New and Improved: The Story of Mass Marketing in America* (New York: Basic Books, 1990); and E. J. Kahn, Jr., *The Big Drink: The Story of Coca-Cola* (New York: Random House, 1960).

See related Problem 1.7 at the end of the chapter.

Nominal Wage Rigidity Firms are likely to hold their prices constant if the wages they pay are constant. For most firms, wages are their largest cost. Many firms adjust the wages or salaries they pay only once per year. Long-term labour contracts explain some nominal wage stickiness. For example, when a firm negotiates a long-term labour contract with a labour union, the contract fixes the nominal wage for the duration of the contract, which is typically several years. Even if economic conditions change, it is often difficult and costly to renegotiate long-term contracts. In addition to formal contracts, firms often arrive at *implicit contracts* with workers. An implicit contract is not a written, legally binding agreement. Instead, it is an informal arrangement a firm enters into with workers in which the firm refrains from making wage cuts during recessions in return for workers being willing to accept smaller wage increases during expansions. Firms may also refrain from cutting wages during recessions for fear that their best workers will quit to find jobs at other firms once an economic expansion improves conditions in the labour market. Firms also sometimes pay higher-than-equilibrium real wages, known as *efficiency wages*, to motivate workers to be more productive. Efficiency wage considerations can also lead firms to maintain wages unchanged during a recession. All these reasons help to explain why nominal wages are typically sticky in the short run.

What Happens during a Business Cycle?

9.2
Learning Objective
Understand what happens during a business cycle.

Economists think of the business cycle as resulting from macroeconomic shocks that push real GDP away from potential GDP. For example, Canada experienced two large shocks that precipitated the Great Recession: the collapse of exports, and a decline in consumption and investment caused by households' and firms' concerns about the recession in the United

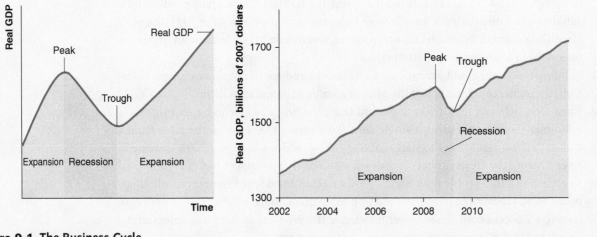

Figure 9.1 The Business Cycle

Panel (a) shows an idealized business cycle, with real GDP increasing smoothly in an expansion to a business cycle peak and then decreasing smoothly in a recession to a business cycle trough, followed by another expansion. The periods of expansion are shown in green, and the period of recession is shown in red. Panel (b) shows the Great Recession in Canada was a severe but brief recession.

Sources: Statistics Canada, CANSIM Table 380-0064; C.D. Howe Institute.

States. As a result of these shocks, the growth rate of real GDP decreased from 1.8% during the first quarter of 2008 to −3.7% during the third quarter of 2009.

Figure 9.1 illustrates the phases of the business cycle. Panel (a) shows an idealized business cycle, with real GDP increasing smoothly in an expansion to a business cycle peak and then decreasing smoothly in a recession to a business cycle trough, followed by another expansion. Panel (b) shows the period before, during, and after the Great Recession. Using the C.D. Howe Business Cycle Council dates, the recession started in October 2008 and ended in May 2009; these dates are marked in Figure 9.1 panel (b). The recession was severe, with output falling for two quarters by almost 4% on a yearly basis. The C.D. Howe Council ranks the recession on par with the previous two recessions (1981–82 and 1990–92); the only recessions that were more severe were before WWII. Despite its severity, the recession was quite short, lasting only three quarters. (The 1981–82 recession was twice as long; the 1990–92 recession was three times longer).

Why do we care about the business cycle? Declining real GDP is always accompanied by declining employment. As people lose jobs, their incomes and standard of living decline. In severe recessions, the long-term unemployed can encounter severe financial hardship, even destitution. Declining GDP also increases business bankruptcies, with some entrepreneurs having a lifetime's investment in a business wiped out in a year or two. Expanding GDP, in contrast, opens up employment opportunities to millions of additional workers and makes it possible for more entrepreneurs to realize the dream of opening a business.

The Changing Severity of the Canadian Business Cycle

One way to gauge the severity of the economic fluctuations caused by a business cycle is to look at annual percentage changes, or growth rates, in real GDP. Figure 9.2 shows the annual growth rates for real GDP between 1870 and 2010. The fluctuations in real GDP were clearly more severe before 1950. In particular, there were 12 years before 1950 during which real GDP declined by 3% or more, but there were none since 1950. The increased stability of real GDP after the early 1980s led some economists to describe the period as the *Great Moderation*.

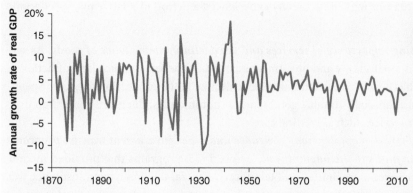

Figure 9.2

Fluctuations in Real GDP, 1870–2010

The annual growth rate of real GDP fluctuated more before 1950 than it has since 1950.

Sources: J. Baldwin and R. Macdonald, 2011, "Natural Resources, the Terms of Trade, and Real Income Growth in Canada: 1870 to 2010," Economic Analysis research paper series, No. 079, Statistics Canada catalogue number 11F0027M, (Ottawa: Ontario, 2011), Statistics Canada, CANSIM Table 380-0064

Table 9.1 shows the dates of the recessions and expansions in Canada. The picture of the Great Moderation is less clear if we look at the length of recessions and expansions. Since the Great Depression (1929–33) the three longest peacetime expansions were from 1992 to 2008, from 1962 to 1974 and from 1982 to 1990. The longest recessions were the 1990–92 and 1981–82 recessions. So, in the past 30 years, the business cycle became longer: both expansions and recessions were longer than before.

The Canadian experience during the Great Recession differs significantly from that of the United States, where it lasted 18 months, making it the longest since the Great Depression. The decline in output was also greater than in Canada. Unlike in the United States, where the Great Recession was much more severe, it appears that Canada may still be in the age of the Great Moderation.

One way to get a better idea of whether the Great Moderation will continue is to look at explanations of the milder fluctuations in real GDP in the past 60 years. Economists have

Table 9.1   Recessions and Expansions in Canada since 1926

Monthly peak		Monthly trough		Recession length (months)	Expansion length (months)
April	1929	February	1933	46	55
November	1937	June	1938	7	110
August	1947	March	1948	7	37
April	1951	December	1951	8	19
July	1953	July	1954	12	32
March	1957	January	1958	10	26
March	1960	March	1961	12	165
December	1974	March	1975	3	58
January	1980	June	1980	5	12
June	1981	October	1982	16	89
March	1990	April	1992	25	198
October	2008	May	2009	7	62 +

Source: Adapted from Philip Cross and Philippe Bergevin, "Turning Points: Business Cycles in Canada since 1926", C.D. Howe Institute Commentary No. 366, October 2012.

offered several reasons why the economy experienced a period of relative macroeconomic stability after 1950:

- ***The increasing importance of services and the declining importance of goods.*** As services, such as medical care and investment advice, have become a much larger fraction of GDP, there has been a corresponding relative decline in the production of goods. Spending on goods, especially durable goods such as automobiles, fluctuates more than does spending on services such as medical care.
- ***The establishment of employment insurance and other government transfer programs that provide funds to the unemployed.*** Before 1935, programs that provided income to the unemployed were limited and temporary. Federal unemployment insurance was introduced in 1940 with the Unemployment Insurance Act, and its coverage was extended over time. Payments to workers losing their jobs in recessions help maintain their income and raise their spending, limiting the decline in consumption and, consequently, decline in output during recessions.
- ***Active fiscal and monetary stabilization policy.*** Before the Great Depression of the 1930s, the prevailing economic thinking was that the *classical* approach. According to classical economists, recessions are temporary thanks to price and wage flexibility. When a recession starts, prices and wages quickly adjust, bringing the recession to an end so there is no role for the government to intervene. The severity of the Great Depression, when unemployment was over 20% and real GDP fell by 30% in many countries, led to the development of Keynesian economics. In the Keynesian view, the adjustment of prices and wages is slow and macroeconomic policy should be used to mitigate business cycles. Following WWII, both fiscal and monetary policies were actively used to combat recession. Many economists believe that these government policies have played a key role in stabilizing the economy. Some economists, however, argue that activist policy has had little effect. This macroeconomic debate is an important one, so we will consider it further in later chapters when we discuss the federal government's monetary and fiscal policies.

Solved Problem 9.1

Dating Canadian Recessions

You may have heard that a recession is defined as two consecutive quarters of declining real GDP. This is a definition often used in the press. In fact, though, as you have seen in the chapter introduction, neither the C.D. Howe Institute Business Cycle Council nor the NBER Business Cycle Dating Committee use this simple definition. In this exercise we compare the dates established by the C.D. Howe and those using the simple definition for the past two recessions. The following table shows the data. Use the simple definition to date the recessions. Why is there a difference between the dates established by C.D. Howe and the dates established using the simple definition?

	C.D. Howe recession dates	Negative GDP growth
1990–92 recession	Q2 1990–Q2 1992	Q4 1989
		Q2 1990–Q1 1991
2008–09 recession	Q4 2008–Q2 2009	Q4 2008–Q2 2009

Source: Statistics Canada, CANSIM, Table 380-0064. The data show quarter over quarter change.

Solving the Problem

Step 1 **Review the chapter material.** The problem asks you to think about dating business cycles, so you may want to review the section "How Do We Know the Economy Is in an Expansion or a Recession?" in the chapter introduction.

Step 2   **Use the simple definition to determine when a recession occurred, and compare the results to the C.D. Howe dates.** The simple definition states that a recession begins with two consecutive negative quarters of real GDP growth. Although output fell in Q4 1989, it increased in the following quarter. So, using the simple definition, the recession at the beginning of 1990s lasted four quarters, from the second quarter of 1990 to the second quarter of 1991. (The economy was still in a recession in the first quarter of 1991 according to the simple rule.) The C.D. Howe also dates the start in the second quarter of 1990 but dates the end in the second quarter of 1992. According to the simple definition the recession lasted one year while, according to the C.D. Howe, it lasted two years.

For the Great Recession, the two definitions coincide, with the start in the last quarter of 2008 and end in the second quarter of 2009.

Step 3   **Explain why there is a difference between the simple definition and the C.D. Howe dates.** As noted in the text, C.D. Howe defines a recession on the basis of length, size, and scope of the decline in output, attaching particular importance to manufacturing, construction, and related industries, while the simple definition looks only at the rate of GDP growth. During the 1990–92 period, output fell (all rates are on a yearly basis) by 0.2% in the fourth quarter of 1989 and increased by 0.9% in the first quarter of 1990 and subsequently was falling for the next four quarters. Both the simple definition and the C.D. Howe dating do not consider the small drop of GDP at the end of 1989 as the start of the recession. They both date the recession to begin in the second quarter of 1990. Between the second quarter of 1991 and the second quarter of 1992, the economy grew at no more than 0.3% per year. This slow growth indicated it was still in a recession.

So, to sum up, both the simple definition and the C.D. Howe dates coincide three times out of four: They provide identical dates for the beginning of both recessions, as well as the end of the Great Recession. Three out of four may not sound too bad, but there is a large difference in the dating of the 1990–92 recession. Economists agree that the recession in early 1990s stretched into 1992.

See related Problem D9.1 at the end of the chapter.

Measuring Business Cycles

Economists typically use the deviation of real GDP from potential GDP as the best measure of the size of the economic fluctuations. For a particular time period, we can write

Real GDP = Potential GDP + Deviation from potential GDP

or

$$Y = Y^p + (Y - Y^p),$$

where Y is real GDP, Y^p, is potential GDP, and $(Y - Y^p)$ is the deviation of real GDP from its potential level.

Because potential GDP grows over time, economists measure economic fluctuations as the percentage deviation of actual real GDP from potential GDP rather than the absolute difference. This percentage deviation of real GDP from potential GDP is called the **output gap**:

$$\text{Output gap} = \frac{(Y - Y^p)}{Y^p} = \tilde{Y}.$$

Output gap The percentage deviation of real GDP from potential GDP.

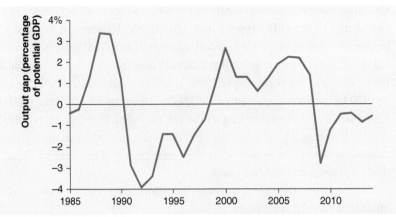

Figure 9.3

**The Output Gap,
1985–2014**

During a recession, real GDP declines below potential GDP, and the output gap becomes negative. Even after an expansion begins and real GDP begins to increase, real GDP typically remains below potential GDP for a considerable time, and the output gap remains negative.

Source: OECD

The output gap, which we denote as $\tilde{Y}$, measures how fully the economy is employing its resources, such as labour, natural resources, and physical and human capital. When the output gap equals zero, the economy is producing at its long-run capacity and so is producing the maximum sustainable level of goods and services. If the output gap is greater than zero, the economy is operating at a level that is greater than it can sustain in the long run. If the output gap is less than zero, the economy is operating below its capacity. For example, in 2009, real GDP was $1539 billion, potential output was $1583 billion, and the output gap was −2.8% or $44 billion. In other words output was $44 billion lower than potential output.

Figure 9.3 shows the output gap for Canada since 1985; the number for 2014 is a projection. During a recession, real GDP declines below potential GDP, and the output gap becomes negative. Even after an expansion starts and real GDP begins to increase, it typically remains below potential GDP for a considerable time, so the output gap remains negative. After the 1990–92 recession, the output gap remained negative until 1999; after the Great Recession, it is expected to remain negative five years after the recession ended. Eventually, as the expansion continues, real GDP should rise above potential GDP, and the output gap should become positive. Note, however, that as the recent experience in Europe shows, an economy may fall into another recession before output reaches full employment. Several European countries experienced "double-dip" recession shortly after the Great Recession ended.

Costs of the Business Cycle

Should we care about the fluctuations in real GDP that occur during the business cycle? As real GDP per capita increases over time, the effects of economic growth should overwhelm the effects of the business cycle on the average person's well-being. Moreover, the business cycle results in real GDP sometimes being below potential GDP, but it also results in periods during which real GDP is above potential GDP. It might seem as if the costs of economic fluctuations will average out across the business cycle. Actually, though, economic research and simple observations of the effects of recessions on workers and firms indicate that economic fluctuations have costs—and the costs can be large. Furthermore, recent research suggests that the business cycle may affect the level of potential GDP.

Economists and policymakers focus on two key costs of the business cycle: the lost income that occurs when real GDP is below potential GDP and the inflation that often develops when the economy is operating above potential GDP. To explain the costs of operating below potential GDP, we focus on labour markets.

Okun's Law and Unemployment When real GDP falls below potential GDP during a recession, firms lay off workers, so the unemployment rate rises, and households earn less

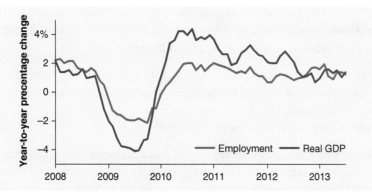

Figure 9.4

Changes in Output and Employment, 2008–13

During the Great Recession, the percentage decline in real GDP in Canada, and the subsequent percentage increase, were bigger than changes in employment.

Sources: Statistics Canada, CANSIM, Tables 379-0031 and 282-0087.

income. The *cyclical unemployment rate* is the difference between the unemployment rate and the natural unemployment rate. The cyclical unemployment rate increases during recessions. As the economy enters an expansion, cyclical unemployment may continue to rise for a period, before falling later in the expansion.

The link between the output gap and cyclical unemployment is summarized by **Okun's law**. Okun's law is the relationship between cyclical unemployment and output gap,

Okun's law A statistical relationship between the cyclical unemployment rate and the output gap.

$$\text{Cyclical unemployment rate} = -h \cdot \text{Output gap}.$$

or

$$u - u^N = -h\left[\frac{Y - Y^p}{Y^p}\right] = -h\tilde{Y}. \tag{9.1}$$

The term in brackets is the output gap, which we denote as $\tilde{Y}$. It is equal to the percentage difference between current output and potential output. When the output gap is equal to zero, i.e., when output is equal to potential output, the unemployment rate is equal to the natural unemployment rate and the cyclical unemployment rate is zero. When output is above potential: $Y > Y^P$, the unemployment rate is lower than the natural rate: $u < u^N$. When output is below potential, $Y < Y^P$, the unemployment rate exceeds the natural rate: $u > u^N$. The Okun's law coefficient, h, shows the effect of a one percentage drop in output on the unemployment rate. The coefficient, which is estimated from the data, varies across countries and across time. For example, for Canada over 1961–2009 the coefficient was 0.38 while for the United States over 1948–2009 it was 0.5.[5] In general, the coefficient is less than one, which means that a 1% change in output relative to potential is related to a less than 1 percentage point change in unemployment. The reason is *labour hoarding*. In recessions, firms do not reduce employment in line with the decline in output. Even if the number of workers they need falls a lot, firms know that the recession will eventually come to an end and they will need more workers. The process of letting workers go and hiring new workers is expensive. Also, workers often have firm-specific knowledge and new hires need to be trained first. For all those reasons, many firms try to minimize the turnover of labour over the business cycle and hoard labour in recessions. As a result employment, and unemployment, vary less than output.

In Figure 9.4 we show the rates of growth of real GDP and employment during and after the Great Recession in Canada. Changes in output are significantly bigger than changes in employment. For example, in mid-2009 output was falling at the yearly rate of 4% while

---

[5]Kimberly Beaton, "Time Variation in Okun's Law: A Canada and U.S. Comparison," Bank of Canada Working Paper 2010-7.

employment was falling at the rate of only 2%. In mid-2010 output growth was 4% per year while employment growth was only 2% per year. The fact that variations in employment are smaller than variations in output indicate labour hoarding.

The Costs of the Business Cycle to Workers The income that unemployed workers lose is one of the most important costs of the business cycle. Although cyclical unemployment falls and household incomes rise during expansions, the costs of the business cycle do not necessarily average out across the cycle for four reasons:

1. A business cycle consists of an expansion and a recession, but recessions do not necessarily have the same magnitude as expansions. As a result, real GDP may be below potential GDP more than half the time. Over the 1985–2012 period, output was below potential exactly half of the time. Note, however, that this period included the longest expansion in Canadian history, from 1992 to 2008.

2. If workers are unemployed for long periods of time, their skills often deteriorate. In the extreme case, this deterioration can be severe enough to make some workers structurally unemployed and increase the natural rate of unemployment. Some economists believe that a prolonged period of unemployment can result in *hysteresis*, which means that, even when output returns to potential, employment does not, and the natural rate of unemployment may increase for a number of years. Hysteresis may have occurred in some Western European countries during the 1980s where an increase in unemployment, initially due to recessions brought on by sharp increases in oil prices, persisted for years. For example, while the unemployment rate in France averaged 3.8% during the 1970s, it averaged 9.0% during the 1980s. Similarly, while the unemployment rate in the United Kingdom averaged 4.4% during the 1970s, it averaged 10.1% during the 1980s. In Canada the unemployment rate, while fluctuating with the business cycle, was increasing in 1980s and 1990s, raising serious concerns. But in 2000s the unemployment rate fell below earlier levels, even taking into account the temporary increase during the Great Recession.

3. Unemployment and lost income resulting from a recession is concentrated among low-income workers. Wages of workers with a lower level of education are affected more by high unemployment than are the wages of workers with a higher level of education. Low-income workers and workers who lack skills do particularly well during periods of low unemployment, such as the mid-2000s, but much more poorly during periods of high unemployment.

4. The negative effects of recessions on workers can last many years. Economist Lisa Kahn of Yale University has studied the effects on workers of graduating from college during a recession. Kahn found that graduating during a recession reduced a worker's wage and job prospects. However, what is surprising is that these effects lasted for up to 15 years.[6] Losing a job is not painful just for new workers. Experienced workers who lose their jobs during a recession have significantly lower incomes over their lifetimes than do workers who lose their jobs during expansions.

Furthermore, while a minority of workers become unemployed during a recession, rising unemployment causes many workers to worry about the safety of their jobs. According to one report, almost half of workers in the United States were concerned about losing their jobs during the Great Recession. Over 70% of people knew someone who lost a job in the previous six months.[7]

---

[6]Lisa Kahn, "The Long-Term Labour Market Consequences of Graduating from College in a Bad Economy," *Labour Economics* 17, no. 2 (2010): 303–316.
[7]"People Fear Losing a Job," CNBC, February 19, 2009.

The Effect of the Business Cycle on Inflation Business cycles typically affect the inflation rate. Inflation usually increases in booms and decreases in recessions. As actual GDP increases relative to potential GDP, resources become fully employed, so it becomes difficult for firms to find idle labour, capital, and natural resources to produce goods and services. As a result, prices of these inputs begin to rise, and firms try to pass along the cost increases to consumers in the form of higher prices, thereby increasing inflation. For the same reason, inflation is lower in recessions since high unemployment moderates wage increases and firms have ample spare capacity. The combination of slow wage growth and spare capacity moderates price increases. So the business cycle increases the variability in inflation. As we discussed in Chapter 4, inflation, especially high and variable inflation, makes the economy less efficient and can discourage capital accumulation. As a result, fluctuations in the inflation rate represent another important cost of the business cycle.

Links between Business Cycles and Growth It is possible that business cycles affect potential GDP and have long-lasting effects on the economy as a whole. The uncertainty associated with business cycles can reduce investment spending, providing one possible link between business cycles and potential GDP. The greater the uncertainty about the future demand for a firm's product, the more difficult it is for the firm to determine whether investment in machinery or a new factory will be profitable. This uncertainty also makes it difficult for the firm to determine the size of the factory to build and the most appropriate technology to use. Because of uncertainty, the firm may choose not to pursue the investment at all. Business cycles, particularly when they are severe, can cause uncertainty about future demand. An economy with more severe business cycles experiences greater uncertainty about future demand, so it may invest less than an economy with milder business cycles.

Gadi Barlevy of the Federal Reserve Bank of Chicago shows that eliminating business cycles would raise the growth rate of per capita consumption by 0.4% per year.[8] While this percentage may seem small, small changes in growth rates become large differences in the standard of living over time due to the power of compounding. So, an increase in the growth rate of this magnitude would have a very large effect on households' well-being in the long run.

Movements of Economic Variables during the Business Cycle

In studying business cycles, economists are interested in movements of economic variables relative to the cycle. An economic variable is a **procyclical variable** if it moves in the same direction as real GDP and other measures of aggregate economic activity: increasing during business cycle expansions and decreasing during recessions. For example, employment, investment spending, and spending on durable goods tend to increase during expansions and decrease during recessions, so these variables are procyclical. An economic variable is a **countercyclical variable** if it moves in the opposite direction to real GDP and other measures of aggregate economic activity: decreasing during expansions and increasing during recessions. For example, the unemployment rate tends to decrease during expansions and increase during recessions, so the unemployment rate is countercyclical.

Economists also study fluctuations in economic variables in order to predict changes in real GDP. No single variable and no set of variables can perfectly predict the next recession. If that had been the case, macroeconomic policy would have been much easier! Rather, economists look at several variables that fairly reliably indicate a future recession or expansion. Such variables are called *leading indicators*. Until 2012 Statistics Canada produced

Procyclical variable An economic variable that moves in the same direction as real GDP—increasing during expansions and decreasing during recessions.

Countercyclical variable An economic variable that moves in the opposite direction to real GDP—decreasing during expansions and increasing during recessions.

---

[8]Gadi Barlevy, "The Cost of Business Cycles Under Endogenous Growth," *American Economic Review* 94, no. 4 (1994): 964–990.

Table 9.2 Leading Indicators

---
1. Average work week hours, manufacturing
2. Housing index
3. U.S. composite leading index
4. Money supply
5. New orders, durable goods
6. Stock price index
7. Retail trade, furniture and appliances
8. Durable goods sales excluding furniture and appliances
9. Shipment to inventory ratio, finished products (ratio)
10. Business and personal services employment
---

an index of leading economic indicators, based on 10 variables that tended to rise and fall before the real GDP and other measures of economic activity did. These variables are listed in Table 9.2. After the discontinuation of the Statistics Canada series, the Macdonald-Laurier Institute, an independent research organization, introduced its Composite Leading Index for Canada. It includes the first six variables in Table 9.2 plus commodity prices, Employment Insurance claims, and the spread between the interest rate for private versus government short-term borrowing.

For example, stock prices tend to peak and then decrease prior to the start of a recession. The TSE/S&P index peaked on June 2, 2008, four months before the Great Recession in Canada started, and reached the bottom on March 2, 2009, two months before it ended. The average work week peaked in August 2007, more than a year before the recession started, and bottomed in April 2009, a month before it ended. The housing index peaked in October 2007 and bottomed in March 2009.[9]

The Global Business Cycle

All countries experience business cycles. Figure 9.5 shows the deviations for potential GDP from 1985 to 2013 for Canada, the Eurozone, Japan, and the United States. As you can see, business cycles are often, but not always, synchronized across countries. All countries experienced expansion in the second half of the 1980s and in the mid-2000s. The Great Recession hit all countries, but the recovery has been slow in the United States, rapid in Canada, and uneven in the Eurozone. On the other hand, Japan experienced a recession in 1998–99 when the other economies were booming. Similarly, the expansion in Japan that started in 1986 continued into 1991, when other economies were already in a recession.

Three key factors explain why business cycles are related across countries. First, countries trade with one another, so a downturn in one country can spread to other countries. The effect, of course, depends on country size: If income falls in Canada, Canadian imports decline but the effect on other countries will not be large. If the United States enters a recession, the impact will be large since the United States is the world's biggest importer. For example, falling incomes in the United States will reduce purchases of lumber or car parts from Canada, electronic equipment from Japan, or wine from France. As a result, real GDP in those countries will decrease as well. The effect of the U.S. business cycle is particularly strong for Canada: Almost three quarters of our exports go to the United States. Second,

---

[9]Statistics Canada, CANSIM Table 377-0003, smoothed data. Another index of leading indicators is produced by the Organisation of Economic Co-operation and Development (OECD) for 33 member countries.

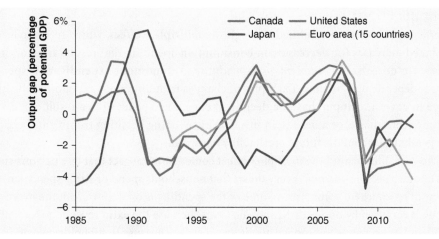

Figure 9.5

The International Business Cycle, 1985–2013

Business cycles are often, but not always, synchronized across countries. In the Great Recession all countries were negatively affected by the worldwide disturbances in financial markets.

Source: Organisation for Economic Co-operation and Development.

shocks, such as the oil price shocks of 1973 and 1990 and the financial market shock of 2008–09, are often global in nature. In such cases, all countries experience a similar shock at the same time, so it is not surprising that business cycles appear to be synchronized across countries. Third, financial linkages, including international businesses (multinational companies), are also an important factor linking business cycles across countries.[10]

Shocks and Business Cycles

9.3
Learning Objective
Explain how economists think about business cycles.

The many markets that make up the economy are constantly buffeted by shocks that affect the consumption and investment decisions of households and firms. Some shocks affect many markets in the economy at once. In the past, various shocks led to a recession. Let us look at some examples.

1973–75: When oil prices spiked in the early 1970s, households faced higher gasoline prices, and firms faced higher fuel costs and higher costs of goods, such as plastics, that are made from oil. Households responded to this shock by reducing consumption spending on products other than gasoline, and firms reduced production as their costs rose. These reductions in spending and increases in production costs contributed to recessions in many countries in 1973–75. As an energy producer, Canada was less affected than other countries that were oil importers.

1990–92: In the United States, Iraq's invasion of Kuwait in August 1990 caused a spike in oil prices and a drop in consumer confidence that, some economists believe, contributed to the 1990–91 recession. In Canada, the 1990–92 recession was caused by the anti-inflationary policy of the Bank of Canada.

2001: The collapse of the dot-com bubble in 2001 dampened consumer spending and investment in the United States, leading to a recession there. The terrorist attacks of September 11, 2001, led to a dramatic decline in consumption for that month in the United States, which worsened the 2001 recession. Canada avoided the recession as it was less affected by both shocks.

2007–09: The collapse of financial markets after the bankruptcy of Lehman Brothers in September 2008 had a worldwide negative effect on advanced economies.

---

[10]Business cycles in developing countries and in emerging economies (for example BRICS—Brazil, Russia, India, China and South Africa) are less synchronized with cycles in developed countries as their financial linkages are weaker and, for many, trade with developed countries is not a large fraction of GDP.

Multiplier Effects

Multiplier effect A series of induced increases (or decreases) in consumption spending that results from an initial increase (or decrease) in autonomous expenditure; this effect amplifies the effect of economic shocks on real GDP.

Autonomous expenditure Spending that is independent of income.

The effects of shocks are amplified through the **multiplier effect**, which refers to a series of induced increases (or decreases) in consumption spending that results from an initial increase (or decrease) in *autonomous expenditure*. **Autonomous expenditure** is spending that is independent of income. Examples of changes in autonomous expenditure include a change in government purchases, a decline in consumer spending as a result of a drop in consumer confidence, or a decline in investment spending resulting from firms becoming more pessimistic about the future profitability of capital.

The basic idea behind the multiplier effect comes from the fact that one person's spending is another person's income. Every dollar that households spend or firms spend generates a dollar of revenues for some firms. Some of the spending is on imports, but the majority of revenue is captured by domestic firms. The firms then use the extra revenue to hire labour, capital, and other inputs to produce goods and services. Because households own all inputs, the extra revenue ultimately goes to households as income. Those households spend part of the increase in income, while using the rest of the increase to pay taxes or to save. This extra spending initiates a second round of spending and income changes, and so on.

We will now develop an example of the multiplier effect. We assume that the tax rate is 25%, households spend $0.80 of each additional dollar of income and save the remaining $0.20, and that a third, or 33.3%, of spending is on imported goods and services.

We start with a shock, such as an optimistic forecast about economic expansion, which increases investor confidence. As a result, there is an increase in spending on capital goods such as buildings or machines by $1 billion. This additional $1 billion in spending generates $1 billion in revenues for firms. Firms hire labour, capital, and natural resources to produce goods and services, so the $1 billion in revenues generates $1 billion in income for households, who own these inputs. (Note that households are the ultimate owners of firms.) We now calculate how much spending on domestic goods and services increases when households receive the $1 billion in extra income. We have to take into account that, when income increases, (a) households pay taxes on the extra income, (b) households save, and (c) some of the spending is on imported goods and services.

(a) When income increases by $1 billion, households pay 25% in extra taxes. So taxes rise by $250 million and disposable income increases by $750 million.
(b) Out of the increase of disposable income by $750 million, households save 20%, or $150 million, and spend the rest. So, after paying taxes and saving, household spending increases by $600 million.
(c) Out of the extra $600 million in spending, a third, or $200 million, is on imported goods and services. So after paying taxes, saving, and purchasing imported goods and services, households increase spending on domestic goods and services by $400 million.

We have established that the initial increase in spending (due to the increased confidence) induces additional spending of $400 million on domestic goods and services. So total spending has so far increased by $1.4 billion. But it is not the end. Just as the initial increase in spending by $1 billion raised incomes of households, so does the extra $400 million of induced spending. Now begins the second round of spending. Just as with the initial increase, firms hire labour, capital, and resources to produce goods and services. The second round of spending increases the income of households by a further $400 million.

We could now guess what happens further in the second round of spending, but let us go through the steps again. Out of the $400 million in income, (a) households pay 25%, or $100 million in taxes, so disposable income increases by $300 million. Of the $300 million of extra disposable income, (b) households save 20%, or $60 million, and increase their spending by

$240 million. Of the $240 million increase in spending, (c) a third, or $80 million, is on imported goods and services and $160 million is on domestic goods and services. So, in the second round of spending, purchases of domestic goods and services increase by $160 million. This starts the third round of spending: Income increases by $160 million; (a) disposable income increases by $120 million (since taxes on $160 million are 25%, or $40 million); (b) spending increases by $96 million (since out of the $120 million of disposable income households save 20% or $24 million); (c) spending on domestic goods and services increases by $64 million (since of the $96 million in spending a third, or $32 million, is on imported goods and services). The extra $64 million in spending on domestic goods and services at the end of the third round starts the next round of spending. And so on. In every consecutive round, the increase in income becomes smaller: It is equal to 0.4 of the increase in the previous round.

We can now calculate the final effect of the initial $1 billion increase in income. Let m denote the proportion of an increase in income that is spent on domestic goods and services. In our example the proportion is 40%. It is the product of the proportion of (a) an increase in income households retain after paying taxes, 75%; (b) the proportion of a change in disposable income spent, 80%; and (c) the proportion of spending that is on domestic goods and services, 66.7%: $m = 75\% \cdot 80\% \cdot 66.7\% = 0.4$. If we add up all rounds, the total increase in income becomes

$$\text{Total income generated} = \$1 \text{ billion} + \$1 \text{ billion} \cdot 40\% + \$1 \text{ billion} \cdot (40\%)^2 + \ldots$$
$$= \$1 \text{ billion} + \$400 \text{ million} + \$160 \text{ million} + \ldots$$
$$= \$1.667 \text{ billion.}$$

The total increase is $1/(1 - m)$ times the initial increase. In our case $m = 0.4$ so the increase is $1 billion $\cdot (1/(1 - 0.4)) = \$1$ billion $\cdot 1.667$. In the appendix we derive the formula for a total increase in income when, in each round, the increase is m times the increase in the previous round.

Because the change in total income equals the change in real GDP, in this example, a $1 billion increase in investment spending results in a $1.667 billion increase in GDP in our example. The fact that the total income generated is greater than the initial change in household spending is the result of the multiplier effect. The **multiplier** is the change in equilibrium GDP divided by the change in autonomous expenditure. In our case the multiplier equals $1.667 billion/$1 billion = 1.667.

Multiplier The change in equilibrium GDP divided by the change in autonomous expenditure.

The multiplier is the same for any change in autonomous expenditure. An increase in government purchases (for example, to stimulate the economy), an increase in autonomous consumption (for example, because consumers become optimistic about the future), or an increase in our exports (for example, because of an increase in demand for Canadian wheat) will all have the same effect on Canadian GDP. We can define the *autonomous expenditure multiplier* as

$$\text{Autonomous expenditure multiplier} = \frac{\Delta \text{GDP}}{\Delta \text{ autonomous expenditure}} = \frac{1}{1 - m}.$$

The effect of a $1 billion tax cut is different, for two reasons. First, to increase GDP, taxes need to fall. Therefore the multiplier for taxes is equal to *minus* the change in income divided by the change in taxes. Second, when taxes are cut by $1 billion, households save a part of the tax cut and spend the rest. If households save 20% of the increase in disposable income, the initial increase in spending is $800 million of which a third, or $267 million, is spent on imported goods and services. So, when taxes are reduced by $1 billion, the initial increase in spending is $533 million. The total increase in income is $533 million · 1.667 = $889 million.

We can summarize our account of economic fluctuations during a business cycle with the following simple schematic:

Shock → Spending response by households and firms → Multiplier effect → Change in real GDP.

Making the Connection

How Big Is the Multiplier? Is it the Same in Recessions and Expansions?

The size of the multiplier is of central interest to policymakers. A large multiplier means government spending has big effects on the economy. A small multiplier, on the other hand, implies that fiscal policy is not effective. Establishing the size of the multiplier turns out to be a complex task, certainly much more complex than in the simplified framework typically used in a first-year course and the slightly more advanced framework we developed.

In a first-year course, the typical setup is of a closed economy, without imports or taxes. The only variable that matters for the multiplier is the marginal propensity to consume (*MPC*). A $1 increase in government purchases generates $1 of additional income, of which the portion equal to *MPC* is spent. The additional spending generates more income, and so on. In each consecutive round the increase in spending is equal to *MPC* times the increase in the previous round. So, ignoring the effect of taxes and imports, the multiplier is equal to $1/(1-MPC)$. Since the MPC can be as high as 0.8, the multiplier can be as high five. This implies that fiscal policy has very powerful effects on output. But, as we have discussed, taxes increase with income, and some of the extra spending is on imports. When we take these two factors into account, multiplier is much smaller, equal to 1.667.

In actual economies, there are other factors reducing the size of the multiplier. An increase in government purchases often *crowds out*, or reduces, consumption, investment, and exports. As we will see in Chapter 11, higher government purchases may lead to higher interest rates. When interest rates increase, households delay consumption, investment falls since the interest rates are a main cost of investment, and the Canadian dollar appreciates, reducing net exports. Given this discussion, it is not surprising that the estimated values of the multiplier are modest. After reviewing the literature Valerie A. Ramey from the University of California, San Diego, concluded that the multiplier is between 0.8 and 1.5. Estimates for Canada usually fall in this range.

The Great Recession increased interest in the multiplier. Many countries responded to the recession by increasing government spending. One possibility considered by economists was that the multiplier is bigger in a weak economy, when unemployment is high and capacity utilization is low. In those circumstances an increase in government purchases does not lead to crowding out of the private sector. Michael T. Owyang from the Federal Reserve Bank of St. Louis and Valerie A. Ramey, and Sarah Zubairy from the Bank of Canada found that, in Canada, the multiplier was 1.6 when unemployment was high and 0.4 when unemployment was low. It seems that fiscal policy is more effective when it is needed!

Sources: Valerie A Ramey. "Can Government Purchases Stimulate the Economy?" *Journal of Economic Literature* 49, no. 3 (2011):, pp. 673–685; Michael T. Owyang, Valerie A. Ramey, and Sarah Zubairy, "Are Government Spending Multipliers Greater During Periods of Slack? Evidence from 20th Century Historical Data," *American Economic Review* 100, no. 3 (2013): 129–134.

A Simple Model of the Business Cycle: Aggregate Demand and Aggregate Supply

To this point in the chapter, we have concentrated on what happens during business cycles and the way in which the effects of shocks are multiplied. In this section, we take a step further by introducing the basic *aggregate demand–aggregate supply model*, or *AD–AS model*, of how the economy adjusts to shocks. Although we present more detailed models in the following chapters, this simple model provides us with the tools for understanding some of the key facts about the business cycle. As we saw at the beginning of the chapter, some economists follow the Keynesian approach, which emphasizes the consequences of short-run wage and price stickiness. Other economists follow the classical approach, which holds that wage and price stickiness is unimportant, and that there are other reasons why output and employment fluctuate in response to shocks. An advantage of the *AD–AS* model is that it can be used to illustrate both approaches.

Aggregate Demand and Aggregate Supply: An Introduction

Figure 9.6 on the next page shows the three components of the *AD–AS* model:

1. The aggregate demand (*AD*) curve
2. The short-run aggregate supply (*SRAS*) curve
3. The long-run aggregate supply (*LRAS*) curve

The Aggregate Demand (AD) Curve The **aggregate demand curve**, which we denote *AD*, shows the relationship between the aggregate price level and the total amount of expenditure on domestically produced goods and services. As the aggregate price level increases, expenditure on domestic goods and services falls. But the reason is different from microeconomics. In microeconomics we look at a single market, and keep everything else constant. So when the price of apples increases, households buy fewer apples as they switch to, for example, pears. The effect on expenditure is small and we neglect it. In macroeconomics, we consider an increase in the price level—in other words, an increase in the prices of all goods. The effect on aggregate expenditure is now large, and so we need to take it into account. For the economy as a whole, as the price level rises, so do the incomes of households and firms. The explanation of why aggregate expenditure falls when the price level increases is therefore different from the microeconomic argument. We provide a more complete discussion in later chapters. Here, we provide three brief reasons for why aggregate demand falls when the price level increases.

Aggregate demand (*AD*) curve A curve that shows the relationship between the aggregate price level and the total amount of expenditure on domestically produced goods and services.

1. *The wealth effect and consumption.* As the price level increases, the *real value* of household wealth declines, making households poorer. As a result, consumption spending falls.
2. *The interest rate effect and investment (and consumption).* A higher price level increases the demand for money, causing an increase in the interest rate (Chapter 3). A higher interest rate reduces firms' spending on investment goods and households' spending on consumer durables, such as cars and appliances, and on new houses.
3. *The international trade effect and net exports.* As higher money demand raises Canadian interest rates. Demand for the Canadian dollar increases, raising the nominal exchange rate (Chapter 5). With higher nominal exchange rate and higher prices, our real exchange rate rises, making Canadian goods more expensive relative to foreign goods and reducing net exports.

The Aggregate Supply Curves We now turn to the description of aggregate supply. An aggregate supply curve shows the macroeconomic relationship between the price level and the amount of goods and services firms are willing to supply. We assume that prices and wages are sticky in the short run, with one exception that we discuss below, and flexible in the long run. Therefore we distinguish between a short-run and long-run aggregate supply curves.

Short-run aggregate supply (*SRAS*) curve
A curve that shows the relationship between the aggregate price level and the quantity of real GDP that firms would like to produce when the aggregate price level and wages are constant.

Long-run aggregate supply (*LRAS*) curve
A curve that shows the relationship between the aggregate price level and the quantity of real GDP that firms produce in the long run when prices and wages are flexible.

The **short-run aggregate supply (*SRAS*) curve** shows the relationship between the aggregate price level and the quantity of real GDP that firms would like to produce in the short run, when the aggregate price level and wages are constant. Earlier in the chapter, we saw that nominal wages and prices are often sticky in the short run. If we assume for simplicity that prices and wages are constant in the short run, then the short-run aggregate supply curve is a horizontal line. Firms are supplying the level of output demanded at current prices, whether it is a high level of output above potential GDP or a low level of output below potential GDP.

The **long-run aggregate supply (*LRAS*) curve** shows the relationship between the aggregate price level and the quantity of real GDP that firms produce in the long run when prices and wages are flexible. As we saw in earlier chapters, potential GDP represents the long-run equilibrium level of output. So, the long-run aggregate supply curve is vertical at potential GDP. Recall that at potential GDP, cyclical unemployment is zero, so potential GDP is also called *full-employment GDP*.

Equilibrium in the Short Run and in the Long Run. Because in the short run and in the long run price and wage behaviour differ, we have two different types of equilibrium. A short-run equilibrium occurs where the aggregate demand curve and the short-run aggregate supply curve intersect. A long-run equilibrium occurs where the three curves (the aggregate demand curve, the short-run aggregate supply curve, and the long-run aggregate supply curve) all intersect at a single point. Figure 9.6 shows the equilibrium at point *A*. It is both a short-run equilibrium, since the *AD* and *SRAS* curves intersect at *A*, and a long-run equilibrium, because all three curves intersect at *A*. Note that every long-run equilibrium is also a short-run equilibrium. The only short-run equilibrium that is also a long-run equilibrium is when the intersection of the *AD* and *SRAS* curves is on the *LRAS* curve, i.e., at the level of output equal to potential output.

We now turn to a discussion of factors that might cause the economy to temporarily move away from its long-run equilibrium. We have seen that macroeconomic shocks cause households and firms to change their behaviour, which changes their expenditures, which in turn causes real GDP to change. We first consider a shock to aggregate demand and then shock to aggregate supply.

Aggregate Demand Shocks and the Business Cycle

An aggregate demand shock causes the aggregate demand curve to shift. The shock to the Canadian economy that started the Great Recession in Canada is an example of the aggregate

Figure 9.6

The Aggregate Demand–Aggregate Supply Model

The aggregate demand (*AD*) curve slopes downward because as the price level increases, aggregate expenditures decreases. The short-run aggregate supply (*SRAS*) curve is horizontal to reflect the view that nominal wages and prices are sticky in the short run. The long-run aggregate supply (*LRAS*) curve is vertical at potential GDP to reflect the view that nominal wages and prices are flexible in the long run. Long-run equilibrium is at point *A* where all three curves intersect.

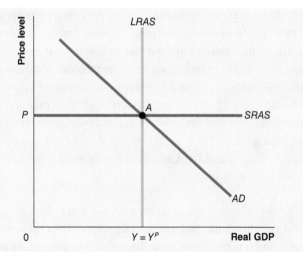

demand shock. The disruptions in the U.S. economy following the collapse of Lehman Brothers in September 2008 undermined the confidence of Canadian households and firms about the future state of the economy in Canada. Households reduced housing purchases, as well as purchases of goods and services, in particular big-ticket durable goods like cars, furniture, and so on. Fearing that their profits may be lower than they had previously believed, firms became less willing to purchase new capital goods and build new factories, so investment spending decreased. As a result, the aggregate demand curve shifted to the left. A shock that reduces expenditure is called a *negative aggregate demand shock*, and a shock that increases expenditure is called a *positive aggregate demand shock*. Figure 9.7 uses the *AD–AS* model to analyze the effect of a negative aggregate demand shock. We first describe the short-run equilibrium, then the path from the short-run to the long-run equilibrium, and then the final, long-run equilibrium.

Short Run When an aggregate demand shock reduces consumption and investment, the aggregate demand curve shifts to the left, from AD_1 to AD_2. The new short-run equilibrium occurs at point *B*, where the new aggregate demand curve intersects the initial short-run aggregate supply curve. At point *B*, real GDP, equal to Y_2, is below potential GDP, equal to Y^P, so the negative aggregate demand shock has caused a recession. Employment and capacity utilization both fall. Unemployment rises and firms have spare production capacity.

From the Short Run to the Long Run The main mechanism that takes the economy from the short run to the long run operates through changes in wages and other costs and their effect on prices. When unemployment is high, wages fall, reducing labour costs. Spare production capacity and competition for sales lead to reduction in other costs of production. As costs fall, firms reduce prices. This process is gradual: The price level falls slowly over time, shifting the short-run aggregate supply curve down, from $SRAS_1$ to $SRAS_2$. The real GDP increases toward potential GDP. The speed of adjustment depends on how fast wages and other costs decline in a recession.

Long Run The recession ends when the price level has fallen from P_1 to P_2 and the economy ends up in long-run equilibrium at point *C*.

Aggregate Supply Shocks and the Business Cycle

A large, widespread **aggregate supply shock** results in a change to firms' costs of production. If a shock causes a large increase in the costs of production, then even in the short run firms

Aggregate supply shock A large, widespread shock that results in a change to firms' costs of production.

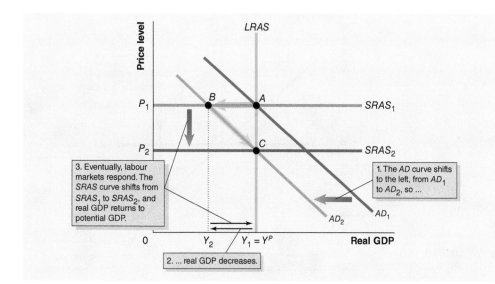

Figure 9.7

Negative Aggregate Demand Shock

A negative aggregate demand shock causes the aggregate demand curve to shift from AD_1 to AD_2. The new short-run equilibrium is at point *B*. The economy falls into a recession. As unemployment and spare production capacity are high, wages and other costs fall, resulting in a gradual decline in the price level. The short-run aggregate supply curve shifts down from $SRAS_1$ to $SRAS_2$, bringing the economy back to long-run equilibrium at point *C*.

will bear the cost of changing prices and increase them. As a result the short-run aggregate supply curve shifts up. For example, if oil prices increase, the cost of producing many goods and services increases. As costs rise, firms will increase their prices and the short-run aggregate supply curve will shift up. Note that only a big, widespread shock to costs becomes a supply shock. If the increase in costs is small, for example if an early frost damages the apple crop, few firms will change prices and the *SRAS* curve will not shift.

A large widespread shock is the one reason prices change even in the short run. Why is that? Recall that the reasons for price stickiness are menu costs, the concern firms have over pricing themselves out of the market, and negative customer reaction. If the shock is large and widespread, the firm knows that it affects other firms and that they will change prices as well. Customers will not get upset because they understand that if costs go up, prices increase as well. Since the costs of price stickiness are small in the face of a widespread supply shock, firms adjust prices even in the short run.

A shock that increases the costs of production is a *negative aggregate supply shock* because it results in lower real GDP and employment. A shock that decreases the costs of production is a *positive aggregate supply shock* because it results in higher real GDP and employment.

Figure 9.8 shows the effect on the economy of an increase in oil prices. To describe what happens, we focus on the initial, short-run effect, the transition from the short run to the long run and the final, long-run effect.

Short Run When oil prices rise, production costs throughout the economy rise and firms raise prices. The short-run aggregate supply curve shifts up from $SRAS_1$ to $SRAS_2$, and the new *short-run* equilibrium is at point B. The increase in oil prices has caused real GDP, Y_2, to fall below potential GDP, Y^P, so the economy is in a recession. Employment and capital utilization both fall. Unemployment rises and firms have spare production capacity.

From the Short Run to the Long Run The decrease in real GDP from Y^P to Y_2 causes the unemployment and spare capacity to rise. As with a negative aggregate demand shock, wages and other production costs fall. As costs fall, firms reduce prices. This process is gradual: The price level falls slowly over time, shifting the short-run aggregate supply curve down, from $SRAS_2$ to $SRAS_1$. The real GDP increases toward potential GDP. The speed of adjustment depends on how fast wages and other costs decline in a recession.

Figure 9.8

Negative Aggregate Supply Shock

Shocks that initially increase the costs of production, such as an increase in oil prices, cause the short-run aggregate supply curve to shift up, and the short-run equilibrium moves from point A to point B. The economy falls into a recession. As unemployment and spare production capacity are high, wages and other costs fall, resulting in a gradual decline in the price level. The short-run aggregate supply curve shifts back down from $SRAS_2$ to $SRAS_1$, bringing the economy back to long-run equilibrium at point A.

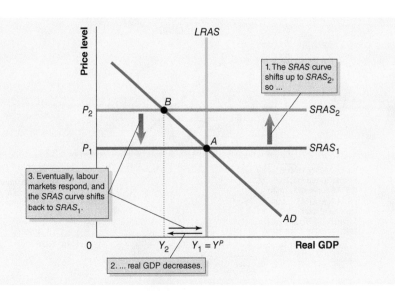

Long Run The recession ends when the price level has fallen from P_2 back to P_1 and the economy is back in long-run equilibrium at point *A*.

Should Policy Try to Offset Shocks?

The aggregate demand–aggregate supply model shows the automatic mechanism that brings the economy back to potential GDP following a shock. The mechanism operates through the decline of wages and production costs when unemployment and spare capacity are high. Following both the aggregate demand shock and the aggregate supply shock, the economy gradually returns to long-run equilibrium, even without any policy intervention. The central question is how long it takes for the automatic mechanism to bring the economy back to potential GDP. Economists are split on this question. Most economists, including new Keynesian economists, believe that the automatic mechanism acts slowly because nominal wages and prices are sticky in the short run. As a result, real GDP can remain below potential and the cyclical unemployment rate can remain positive, for several years following a negative shock. That is why Keynesian economists argue that government should intervene to reduce the severity of business cycles.

The new-classical economists, however, believe that nominal wages and prices respond quickly to shocks, so the automatic mechanism will keep real GDP close to potential GDP most of the time. If, for example, a demand shock reduces potential GDP below the current level of real GDP, nominal wages and prices quickly adjust to bring real GDP to the new level of potential GDP. In later chapters we will discuss the speed of the automatic mechanism, and the case for and against government intervention, in detail.

Key Terms and Problems

Key Terms

Aggregate demand curve (*AD*), p. 283
Aggregate supply shock, p. 285
Autonomous expenditure, p. 280
Classical economics, p. 265
Countercyclical variable, p. 277
Expansion, p. 265

Keynesian economics, p. 265
Long-run aggregate supply (*LRAS*) curve, p. 284
Macroeconomic shock, p. 266
Multiplier, p. 281
Multiplier effect, p. 280
Okun's law, p. 275

Output gap, p. 273
Potential GDP, p. 265
Procyclical variable, p. 277
Recession, p. 265
Short-run aggregate supply (*SRAS*) curve, p. 284

9.1 ## The Short Run and the Long Run in Macroeconomics
Explain the difference between the short run and the long run in macroeconomics.

Review Questions

1.1 What is an expansion? What is a recession?

1.2 What is a macroeconomic shock? How do macroeconomic shocks relate to the business cycle?

1.3 What are sticky prices? What are three key factors that cause price stickiness? What effect might sticky prices have on an economy that has experienced a macroeconomic shock?

Problems and Applications

1.4 Strong labour unions may increase the severity of a business cycle by increasing wage stickiness. Draw a graph of the aggregate labour market in equilibrium. Then assume that the demand for labour decreases due to an economic downturn and that nominal wages and prices are sticky in the short run. Show the effect on the quantity of labour employed and the quantity unemployed.

MyEconLab Visit www.myeconlab.com to complete these exercises online and get instant feedback.

1.5 Consider the following statement: "If all nominal wages and prices adjusted instantly, there would be no business cycle." Do you agree with this statement? Briefly explain.

1.6 What effect would each of the following factors have on the stickiness of nominal wages and prices? Briefly explain whether these factors increase or decrease the severity of the business cycle.

    a. Grocery stores change from stamping individual prices on products to using bar codes to scan prices into a cash register.

    b. The size of the unionized manufacturing sector increases relative to the size of the nonunionized service sector.

    c. More firms move to selling via the internet rather than using printed catalogues.

1.7 [Related to the Making the Connection on page 268] An *Associated Press* article about sticky prices states: "That's what analysts call it when companies slap higher prices on products and keep them there even though the rationale for the price hikes . . . is gone."

    a. Prices for goods such as cereal and toothpaste did not fall during the Great Recession. Why might these prices be sticky?

    b. Prices for goods such as oil and wheat did fall during the Great Recession. Why are these prices different from the prices for goods such as cereal and toothpaste?

Source: Christopher Leonard, "Despite Threat of Recession, 'Sticky Prices' Keep Bills High," Associated Press, October 19, 2008.

1.8 Economist P. Nicholas Rowe of Carleton University notes that one source of sticky prices is what he calls "sticky coordination":

"Each individual firm can adjust its price easily, but one firm's equilibrium price depends on the prices it expects other firms to set. And it is difficult for all firms to coordinate a change in all their prices. Each firm does not know whether the other firms will change their prices, and each waits for the others to go first."

Why would one firm's equilibrium price depend on other firms' prices? How might this dependence lead to price stickiness following a negative demand shock?

Source: P. Nicholas Rowe, "Sticky Prices vs. Sticky Coordination; Inflation vs. NGDP Targeting," Worthwhile Canadian Initiative blog, March 3, 2012.

9.2 **What Happens During a Business Cycle?**
Understand what happens during a business cycle.

Review Questions

2.1 How is the output gap measured?

2.2 Briefly discuss the reasons for macroeconomic stability in Canada after 1950.

2.3 Explain why the costs of the business cycle do not always average out over the cycle.

Problems and Applications

2.4 Suppose that potential GDP in a small country is $10 000 in year 1, and real GDP is also $10 000. Potential GDP grows at a rate of 3% per year. Assume that the Okun's law coefficient is 0.5.

    a. Calculate potential GDP for the next six years.

    b. If real GDP in year 4 is $10 500, what is the output gap?

    c. If real GDP in year 6 is $11 700, what is the output gap?

2.5 Refer to Problem 2.4. Use Okun's law to answer the following questions:

    a. What is the cyclical rate of unemployment in year 1 if real GDP is $10 000?

    b. What is the cyclical rate of unemployment in year 4?

    c. What is the cyclical rate of unemployment in year 6?

2.6 What would each of the following tend to indicate about the state of the economy? That is, in each of these situations, is the economy likely to be headed for a recession, in a recession, headed for an expansion, or in an expansion?

    a. A sharp decline in real GDP

    b. A decrease in international trade

    c. A decrease in the unemployment rate below the natural rate

2.7 Briefly explain whether you agree with the following statement: "Large countries such as the United States or Japan, in which a relatively small portion of GDP comes from international trade, are not likely to be affected by business cycles in other countries."

2.8 In 2009, the unemployment rate in Canada was 8.3%. If the natural rate of unemployment is assumed to be 7%, what was the output gap? Assume that the Okun's law coefficient is 0.38, as estimated in Kimberly Beaton, "Time Variation in Okun's Law: A Canada and U.S. Comparison," Bank of Canada Working Paper 2010-7.

9.3 Shocks and Business Cycles

Explain how economists think about business cycles.

Review Questions

3.1 What is a multiplier effect? Give an example.

3.2 Explain why macroeconomic shocks have a larger effect on real GDP when prices and wages are sticky than when prices and wages are flexible.

Problems and Applications

3.3 The costs of the Japanese earthquake and tsunami of March 2011 include the direct cost of cleanup and additional costs, such as the loss of revenues from seafood harvests, tourism, and related industries. The cost has been estimated at around 6% of Japan's GDP, making it the most expensive natural disaster ever. Using the concept of multipliers, explain how this disaster may affect the Japanese economy as a whole.

Source: "Japan says quake rebuilding to cost as much as 25tn yen," BBC News, March 23, 2011.

3.4 Suppose that the following event had occurred: Because of the severity of the Great Recession, all car companies in Canada had closed.

   a. What would be the direct effect of the failure of the automobile industry?

   b. What other industries are closely connected to the automobile industry? How would these industries have been affected by the failure of the car producers?

   c. Would there have been other multiplier effects? If so, briefly describe them.

9.4 A Simple Model of the Business Cycle: Aggregate Demand and Aggregate Supply

Use the aggregate demand and aggregate supply model to explain the business cycle.

Review Questions

4.1 Explain why the short-run aggregate supply curve is horizontal but the long-run aggregate supply curve is vertical.

4.2 Explain the differences between aggregate demand shocks and aggregate supply shocks.

Problems and Applications

4.3 Draw an aggregate demand–aggregate supply graph to illustrate each of the following scenarios. Make sure to identify the short-run and long-run equilibrium points. Assume that the economy is initially in long-run equilibrium.

   a. The economy experiences a positive aggregate supply shock.

   b. The economy experiences a negative aggregate supply shock.

   c. The economy experiences a positive aggregate demand shock.

   d. The economy experiences a negative aggregate demand shock.

4.4 Suppose that the economy is initially in long-run equilibrium and unexpectedly experiences a large decrease in oil prices. In each part of the problem, draw a graph to illustrate your answer.

   a. What will initially happen to short-run aggregate supply, long-run aggregate supply, and aggregate demand?

   b. What will happen to the price level and real GDP in the short run?

c. What will happen in the long run to short-run aggregate supply, long-run aggregate supply, and aggregate demand?

d. What will happen in the long run to the price level and real GDP?

4.5 Suppose that the economy is initially in long-run equilibrium and unexpectedly experiences a large increase in housing prices. In each part of the problem, draw a graph to illustrate your answer.

a. What will initially happen to short-run aggregate supply, long-run aggregate supply, and aggregate demand?

b. What will initially happen to the price level and real GDP?

c. What will happen in the long run to short-run aggregate supply, long-run aggregate supply, and aggregate demand?

d. What will happen in the long run to the price level and real GDP?

4.6 Explain whether each of the following best represents an aggregate demand shock or an aggregate supply shock and whether the shock is positive or negative.

a. The government unexpectedly doubles military spending due to a war.

b. Households become concerned about whether they will lose their jobs, so they reduce consumption and increase savings.

c. Major technological progress occurs in the market for alternative energy sources.

d. A tsunami wipes out 20% of the manufacturing capacity of an economy.

e. Stock prices unexpectedly increase by 50%.

4.7 In a blog on the *Economist* website, correspondent Matt Yglesias makes the following statement: "[We] need to note that rising oil prices represent both demand shocks and supply shocks to the economy." Explain how increases in oil prices could be considered both a demand shock and a supply shock to an oil-importing economy. Draw a graph illustrating your answer.

Source: Matt Yglesias, "Oil: When the Supply Shocks Are Demand Shocks and the Demand Shocks are Supply Shocks," *Economist*, February 26, 2012.

Data Exercises

D9.1: [Related to the Solved Problem on page. 272] The C.D. Howe website is www.cdhowe.org.

a. Find the C.D. Howe Institute listing of all business cycle peaks and troughs since 1929. Do these data support the claim that the length of recessions has declined over time?

b. Find the C.D. Howe Institute announcement on the Great Recession (2008–09). Which data series does the announcement mention as being relevant to its decision?

D9.2: The Leading Economic Indicator index is published by the Macdonald-Laurier Institute (www.macdonaldlaurier.ca).

a. Go to the Macdonald-Laurier Institute site and find the latest index. What does the most recent value for the index indicate about the state of the economy?

b. Are all components of the index moving in the same direction?

D9.3: The Conference Board (www.conference-board.org) publishes a Leading Economic Indicators (LEI) index.

a. What are the components of the index for India?

b. What does the most recent value indicate? What effect is this value likely to have on Canada?

D9.4: [Spreadsheet exercise] While it is preferable to use quarterly data to follow business cycles, it is often difficult to find consistent data for a broad range of countries. The International Monetary Fund's *World Economic Outlook* (www.imf.org/external/pubs/ft/weo/2012/01/weodata/index.aspx) has annual data on the output gap as a percentage of potential GDP for most countries from 1980 to the present.

a. Choose two countries that you think have interrelated economies (for example, Canada and the United States). Graph the data and calculate the correlation coefficient. How closely correlated are the output gaps for these countries? Do business cycles appear to be related in the two countries?

b. Repeat the steps above for two countries that you think are less likely to be closely related, such as the United States and Chile. Briefly explain how your answers here are different from your answers in part (a).

D9.5: Using data from the Bank of Canada website (www .bankofcanada.ca/rates/interest-rates/canadian-interest-rates), examine the relationship between the slope of the yield curve and recessions. Many people believe that if the slope of the yield curve becomes negative then a recession is likely to start within the next twelve months. Using monthly data, we can measure the slope of the yield curve as the difference between the bank rate and 2-year, 5-year and 10-year Government of Canada bonds. Look for times when the bank rate was higher than any of the bond rates, i.e., the slope of the yield curve was negative.

a. Calculate and graph the slope of the yield curve from January 2005 to the present, comparing the bank rate separately with the 2-, 5-, and 10-year bond rates. How many times does the slope of the yield curve become negative?

b. According to C.D. Howe, the Great Recession in Canada started in October 2008 and ended in May 2009. Has the yield curve slope predicted the recession? When did a negative slope incorrectly predict the Great Recession?

c. Do you think that the slope of the yield curve is a useful predictor of a recession? Briefly explain.

The Formula for the Expenditure Multiplier

We can find the total increase in real GDP resulting from an increase in autonomous expenditure by using the formula for an infinite series. Suppose that there is an initial increase of $1000 in government purchases and that the induced spending on domestic goods and services is $400. In each subsequent round, new spending is 40% of the spending from the previous round. Therefore

$$\text{Total increase in spending} = \$1000 + 0.4 \times \$1000 + 0.4 \cdot (0.4 \cdot \$1000) + \ldots$$
$$= \$1000 + 0.4 \cdot \$1000 + 0.4^2 \cdot \$1000 + 0.4^3 \cdot \$1000 + \ldots$$
$$= (1 + 0.4 + 0.4^2 + 0.4^3 + \ldots) \cdot \$1000.$$

The expression in parentheses is an infinite series and, as derived below, it equals

$$(1 + 0.4 + 0.4^2 + 0.4^3 + \ldots) = 1/(1 - 0.4) = 1.667.$$

Therefore, the total change in real GDP is

$$\text{Total increase in spending} = \text{Total increase in real GDP} = 1.667 \cdot \$1000 = \$1667,$$

where 1.667 is the value of the multiplier.

To derive a general formula for the multiplier, let m represent the fraction of income spent during each round through the circular flow (0.4 in the above example). The infinite sum f in parentheses represents the multiplier:

$$f = (1 + m + m^2 + m^3 + \ldots).$$

To solve for the value of the multiplier, multiply both sides of the equation by m to get

$$mf = (m + m^2 + m^3 + \ldots).$$

Now, subtract mf from f to get

$$f - mf = (1 + m + m^2 + m^3 + \ldots) - (m + m^2 + m^3 + \ldots).$$

Notice that the two infinite sums in bracket are almost identical. The first sum is equal to 1 plus the second sum. So the difference on the right hand side is 1:

$$f - mf = 1.$$

Solving for f we get

$$f = \frac{1}{1 - m}.$$

So, if $m = 0.4$, then $f = 1.667$.

Explaining Aggregate Demand: The *IS–MP* Model

The Great Recession and Policy Response

According to the C.D. Howe Institute, the Great Recession in Canada started in October 2008 and ended in May 2009. As we discussed in the introductory chapter, the Great Recession was not as serious as initially feared. When Lehman Brothers collapsed in September 2008, some economists were concerned about a repeat of the Great Depression of 1929–33, which lasted almost four years in Canada, with unemployment exceeding 20%. In the end, the recession was the worst since 1930s in several countries, in particular in the United States, but nowhere near as serious as the Great Depression. The recovery from the recession, while slow in several European countries, was rapid in North America. One reason the Great Recession was not as severe as feared was that governments and central banks responded with very strong fiscal and monetary policies. The Bank of Canada reduced the target overnight rate to, essentially, zero. In addition it promised to keep interest rates low for an extended period of time—a commitment without precedent. The federal government introduced an expansionary fiscal policy. The figure on the next page shows the deterioration of the Canadian economy and the rapid policy response. Note that, while monetary policy responded quickly to the recession, the response of fiscal policy was slower, reflecting the fact that fiscal policy is subject to significant lags.

The rapid recovery from the Great Recession did not, however, last. After the initial period of rapid output and employment growth the Canadian economy started slowing down, with real GDP growing at, on the average, 2%

Continued on next page

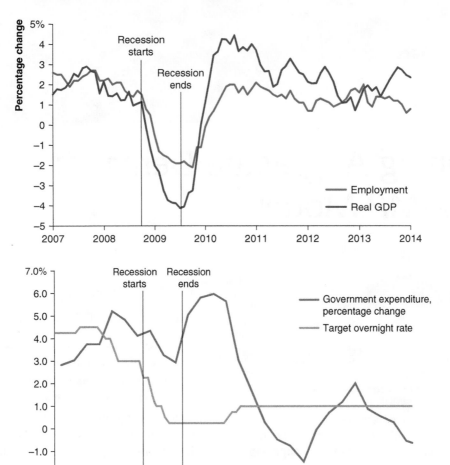

per year in 2011–13, and employment stagnant, as can be seen in the figures. The end of fiscal stimulus, as well as the weakness of the U.S. economy, the sovereign debt crisis in Europe, double-dip recessions in several European countries, and the slowdown in BRIC countries contributed to weak economic growth in Canada. While there was little danger that the economy would fall into another recession, the slow growth was a reason for concern. Should the policymakers intervene again?

There are three competing views on actions policymakers should take. Most economists believe that there is an important difference between the *short run* and the *long run* in macroeconomics. The existence of the business cycle shows that in the short run, real GDP can fall below or rise above potential GDP. As we noted in the previous chapter, British economist John Maynard Keynes began the modern analysis of the short run in macroeconomics. In a famous passage from his 1923 book *A Tract on Monetary Reform*, Keynes argued against focusing on the long run during periods of high unemployment or high inflation.

Keynes's macroeconomic analysis was not universally accepted when he first developed it, and it remains controversial among economists and policymakers today. In particular, some economists argue that the economy typically adjusts smoothly to short-run shocks to the economy. These economists, contrary to Keynes, argue that policymakers would be better off taking measures to promote long-run growth rather than attempting to offset short-run shocks to the economy. In fact, these economists argue that government policies contribute to fluctuations in unemployment and inflation rather than reducing them.

Some economists believe that the role of the fiscal authority and the central bank is to create appropriate conditions for the private economy to grow, through low marginal tax rates and moderate and stable inflation rate. They argue that such policy will lead to sustained long-run growth.

The severity of the Great Recession led governments and central banks around the world to take unprecedented fiscal and monetary actions. Most economists agree that without those actions the Great Recession would have been longer and more severe. Some economists, however, argue that the policies were too stimulative and will lead to high inflation and unsustainable debt. The debate on how best to understand and deal with the business cycle is ongoing. Would a decline in government spending or a decline in exports to Europe push the Canadian economy into recession? These questions are important not just to economists and policymakers but also to the owners and managers of firms and to the millions of workers whose incomes depend on the answers.

Sources: "Turning Points: Business Cycles in Canada since 1926", *C.D. Howe Institute* Commentary 366, October 2012; "Canada 'entering a recession,' central bank slashes key rate to 1.5 per cent," The Canadian Press, December 9, 2008; John Maynard Keynes, *A Tract on Monetary Reform* (London: Macmillan, 1923), p. 80; Statistics Canada, CANSIM, Tables 282-0087, 380-0064, Bank of Canada.

Introduction

In the previous chapter we discussed the basic facts of the business cycle. We saw that the unemployment rate rises and the inflation rate falls during recessions and that the unemployment rate falls and the inflation rate increases during expansions. During the Great Depression of the 1930s, the most severe economic downturn in Canadian history, the unemployment rate rose above 20% and the economy experienced significant *deflation*, or declines in the price level. While the unemployment rate in Canada has never again been as high as 20%, the unemployment rate did rise above 10% during the 1981–82 recession and above 8% during the Great Recession. High rates of unemployment and large declines in GDP can result in severe hardships for many households and can drive firms into bankruptcy.

In the previous chapter, we used the simple *AD–AS model* to help us understand the causes of the business cycle. Although aggregate supply shocks are capable of causing recessions, most economists believe that recessions are caused by aggregate demand shocks. In this chapter, we look more closely at aggregate demand. Our aim is to develop a model that can help to explain changes in the unemployment rate, real GDP, interest rates, and the inflation rate. The *IS–MP model* we develop in this chapter is a short-run model that assumes that the price level is fixed, or, equivalently, that the short-run aggregate supply curve is horizontal. In the next chapter, we complete the model by considering a longer period over which the price level adjusts to changes in aggregate demand.

We begin the chapter by developing the *IS–MP* model. It consists of three curves. The first is the *IS* curve, which shows the all combinations of the real interest rate and output such that the goods market is in equilibrium. The second is the *MP* curve, which represents monetary policy of the central bank when it uses the interest rate to conduct monetary policy. The third is the *Phillips* curve, which represents the short-run relationship between the output gap (or the unemployment rate) and the inflation rate. In this chapter we focus on the *IS* and *MP* curves and leave the Phillips curve to the next chapter. In the next section we develop the *IS* curve. In Section 10.2 we develop the *MP* curve. As the central bank controls the short-term nominal interest rate, we discuss the relationship between the short-term nominal interest rate and the long-term real interest rate, which underlies private expenditure and demand. In the following section we analyze equilibrium in the *IS–MP* model. We discuss how macroeconomic shocks affect the equilibrium and analyze how fiscal and monetary policies can affect the output gap. We then use the *IS–MP* model as an alternative way of deriving the aggregate demand curve that we discussed in the previous chapter. In the appendix we discuss an alternative model, the *IS–LM* model, which is more useful when the central bank uses the money supply to conduct monetary policy. We show that the models are very similar.

10.1
Learning Objective
Explain how the *IS* curve represents the relationship between the real interest rate and aggregate expenditure.

IS–MP model A macro-economic model consisting of an *IS* curve, which represents equilibrium in the goods market; an *MP* curve, which represents monetary policy; and a Phillips curve, which represents the short-run relationship between the output gap and the inflation rate.

IS curve A curve in the *IS–MP* model that shows all combinations of the real interest rate and output such that the goods market is in equilibrium.

MP curve A curve in the *IS–MP* model that represents the Bank of Canada monetary policy.

Phillips curve A curve that represents the short-run relationship between the output gap (or the unemployment rate) and the inflation rate.

The *IS* Curve: The Relationship between the Real Interest Rate and Aggregate Expenditure

Economists' ideas about short-run macroeconomics have evolved over the years since Keynes first studied these issues in the 1930s. The most important of these ideas are captured in the **IS–MP** model, which is a macroeconomic model that economists use to analyze the determinants of real GDP, the inflation rate, the unemployment rate, and the real interest rate. The model is also used to analyze the effects of *monetary* and *fiscal policies*. Economic forecasters who work for manufacturing firms, financial firms, and policymakers typically use macroeconomic models similar to, but of course much more complex than, the *IS–MP* model. A key idea behind the *IS–MP* model is that *changes in aggregate expenditure cause changes in real GDP*.

The *IS–MP* model consists of three parts:

1. The **IS curve**, which represents equilibrium in the market for goods and services.
2. The **MP curve**, which represents Bank of Canada monetary policy.
3. The **Phillips curve**, which represents the short-run relationship between the output gap or the unemployment rate, and the inflation rate.

The interaction of the *IS* curve and the *MP* curve allows us to analyze the effect of monetary policy on equilibrium in the goods market. The *IS* and *MP* curves ultimately determine the position and shape of the aggregate demand curve that we studied in the previous chapter.

The *IS* Curve and Equilibrium in the Goods Market

The *IS* curve shows the combinations of the real interest rate and output such that the goods market is in equilibrium. The name *IS* comes from *I* for investment, and *S* for saving. When the goods market is in equilibrium, aggregate expenditure equals real GDP or investment equals savings.

Economists define *aggregate expenditure* (*AE*), or total spending on real GDP, as the sum of

C = consumption expenditure;

I = investment expenditure on capital goods, such as factories, houses, and machinery, and changes in business inventories;

G = government purchases of goods and services; and

NX = net exports of goods and services.

or

$$AE = C + I + G + NX. \tag{10.1}$$

The *goods market* includes all final goods and services that the economy produces during a particular period of time—in other words, all goods that are included in real GDP. Equilibrium in the goods market occurs when the value of goods and services demanded equals the value of goods and services produced or, in other words, when aggregate expenditure (*AE*) equals real GDP (*Y*):

$$AE = Y. \tag{10.2}$$

Note that decisions to buy goods and services, which add up to aggregate expenditure, are made by millions of households independently from each other. Similarly, decisions to produce, which add up to real GDP, are made by thousands of firms independently from each other. So how does the economy get to equilibrium? It happens thanks to firms' reaction to unplanned inventory changes. Suppose the economy starts in equilibrium but then aggregate expenditure declines so that it is less than real GDP. In that case, total spending (or aggregate expenditure) will be less than total production (or GDP), so some goods that were produced will not be sold, and inventories of unsold goods will unexpectedly increase. For example, if in a particular month, Toyota expects to sell and therefore orders 25 000 cars but sells only 22 500 cars, inventories of cars on the lots of Toyota's dealers will rise by 2500 cars. Notice that, since inventories are counted as part of investment, *actual investment spending* will be greater than *planned investment spending*. This means that there will be *unplanned inventory accumulation*. Firms react to unplanned increase in inventories by reducing output and employment. Real GDP and employment will decline, bringing the economy to equilibrium.

If aggregate expenditure is greater than GDP, total spending will be greater than total production, and firms will sell more goods and services than they had expected to sell. If Toyota expected to sell 25 000 cars but sold 30 000, then inventories will unexpectedly decline by 5000 cars. In this case, because dealers are unexpectedly drawing down inventories, actual investment spending will be less than planned investment spending; there will be *unplanned inventory reduction*. The dealers will be likely to increase their orders from Toyota's factories. Firms react to unplanned inventory reduction by increasing output and employment. Real GDP will increase, bringing the economy to equilibrium.

Only when aggregate expenditure equals GDP will firms sell what they expected to sell. In that case, firms will not experience unexpected changes in their inventories, and they will not have an incentive to increase or decrease production. The goods market will be in equilibrium. Table 10.1 summarizes the relationship between aggregate expenditure and GDP.

To analyze the effect of changes in aggregate expenditure on GDP, we make the simplifying assumption that, of the four components of aggregate expenditure: *C*, *I*, *G*, and *NX*, changes in real GDP affect only consumption. To see why consumption depends on GDP, remember that when we measure the value of total production, we are at the same time measuring the value of total income. Consumption depends on (disposable) income. (Sales taxes and some other relatively minor items cause a difference between the value for GDP and the value for national income. But this difference is not important for our analysis.)

Recall that disposable income, Y^D, equals total income (Y) plus transfer payments (TR) minus taxes (T), or

$$Y^D = Y + TR - T.$$

Households spend more when their current disposable income increases and spend less when their current disposable income decreases. (We provide a more detailed discussion of the determinants of consumption in Chapter 16.) The relationship between current

Table 10.1   The Relationship between Aggregate Expenditure and GDP

If aggregate expenditure is ...	then ...	and ...
less than GDP	inventories rise; there is unplanned inventory accumulation	GDP and employment decrease.
greater than GDP	inventories fall; there is unplanned inventory reduction	GDP and employment increase.
equal to GDP	there are no unplanned changes in inventories	the goods market is in equilibrium.

consumption spending and disposable income is called the *consumption function*. Economists often assume that only part of consumption depends on disposable income:

$$C = C' + (MPC \cdot Y^D), \tag{10.3}$$

The amount by which consumption spending changes as disposable income changes is called the **marginal propensity to consume (MPC)**, which we can write as

Marginal propensity to consume (MPC) The amount by which consumption spending changes when disposable income changes.

$$MPC = \frac{\Delta C}{\Delta Y^D}. \tag{10.4}$$

The *MPC* has a value between 0 and 1. For instance, if the *MPC* is 0.75, then households spend $0.75 of every additional dollar they earn.

If taxes and transfer payments are constant, then a change in disposable income is the same as a change in total income, and we can replace disposable income in equation (10.4) with total income:

$$MPC = \frac{\Delta C}{\Delta Y}. \tag{10.4a}$$

It will be convenient to describe aggregate expenditure as a function of real GDP, rather than of disposable income. We will use the following expression for aggregate expenditure:

$$AE = \overline{C} + (MPC \cdot Y) + \overline{I} + \overline{G} + \overline{NX}. \tag{10.5}$$

where $\overline{C}$ represents autonomous consumption. We use the "bar" designation over C to indicate that this expenditure is autonomous, or independent of changes in income. Since $Y^D = Y - T + TR$, to obtain expression (10.5) we replace C' in equation (10.3) with $\overline{C} = C' - MPC(T - TR)$.

Figure 10.1 panel (a) shows equilibrium in the goods market using a *45°-line diagram*. On the vertical axis, we measure planned aggregate expenditure. On the horizontal axis, we

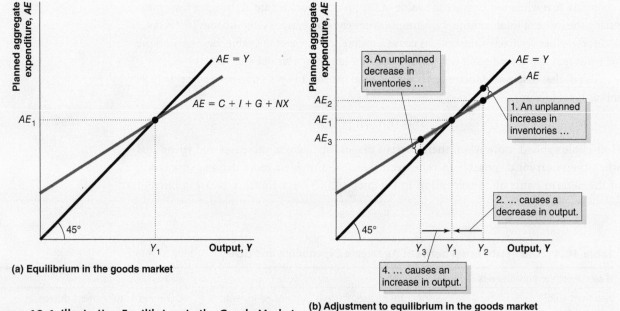

(a) Equilibrium in the goods market

(b) Adjustment to equilibrium in the goods market

Figure 10.1 Illustrating Equilibrium in the Goods Market

Panel (a) shows that equilibrium in the goods market occurs at Y_1, where the AE line crosses the 45° line. In panel (b), if the level of real GDP is initially Y_2, aggregate expenditure is AE_2. Output exceeds aggregate expenditure and there is unexpected inventory accumulation which causes firms to cut production, so the economy will move down the AE line until it reaches equilibrium at Y_1. If real GDP is initially Y_3, aggregate expenditure is AE_3 and there is unexpected fall in inventories, which causes firms to increase production, and so the economy will move up the AE line until it reaches equilibrium at Y_1.

measure real GDP, or real total income, Y. The 45° line represents all points that are equidistant from the two axes. This means that, along the 45° line, aggregate expenditure equals income. Therefore, every potential equilibrium in the goods market must be along the 45° line.

The aggregate expenditure line is upward sloping because, as GDP increases, consumption increases. We find the equilibrium at the point where the aggregate expenditure line crosses the 45° line. Figure 10.1 panel (a) shows that equilibrium in the goods market occurs at Y_1, where the AE line crosses the 45° line. Panel (b) shows why the goods market is not in equilibrium at other levels of real GDP. For example, if real GDP is initially Y_2, aggregate expenditure is AE_2. With real GDP equal Y_2, production exceeds aggregate expenditure and there is an unexpected increase in inventories. Rising inventories cause firms to cut production until the goods market reaches equilibrium at Y_1. If real GDP is initially Y_3, aggregate expenditure is AE_3. With spending greater than production, there is an unexpected decrease in inventories. Falling inventories cause firms to increase production until the goods market reaches equilibrium at Y_1.

The Multiplier Effect

How does a change in aggregate expenditure affect equilibrium real GDP? In the previous chapter we introduced the multiplier (the change in equilibrium GDP divided by the change in autonomous expenditure) and provided an example. We will now analyze the multiplier when equilibrium is determined by the equality between aggregate expenditure and real GDP, at intersection of the AE line and the 45° line. In Figure 10.2, initially equilibrium occurs at point A. Assume that spending on residential construction, a component of I, declines. As a result, the aggregate expenditure line shifts down from AE_1 to AE_2, and the new equilibrium is now at point B. Notice that the initial decrease in investment spending results in a larger decrease in equilibrium real GDP. The decrease in investment spending has had a *multiplied effect* on equilibrium real GDP.

Any decrease in *autonomous expenditure* has the multiplied effect on equilibrium real GDP. In the aggregate expenditure model, investment spending, government spending, and net exports are all assumed to be autonomous expenditures. Consumption has both an autonomous component, which does not depend on the level of GDP, and a

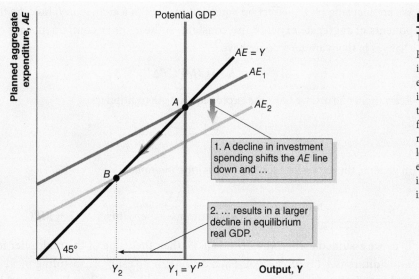

Figure 10.2

The Multiplier Effect

Point A shows the economy initially in equilibrium with real GDP, Y_1, equal to potential GDP, Y^P. Then investment, I, declines. As a result, the aggregate expenditure line shifts from AE_1 to AE_2. Short-run equilibrium is now at point B, with a new level of real GDP, Y_2. The decline in equilibrium GDP is greater than the initial decline in investment spending that caused it.

non-autonomous component that does depend on the level of GDP. For example, if households decide to save more of their incomes—and spend less—at every level of income, there will be an autonomous decrease in consumption spending, and the aggregate expenditure function will shift down. If, however, real GDP decreases and households decrease their consumption spending as indicated by the consumption function, the decrease in consumption spending will be induced rather than autonomous. The result will be a movement along the *AE* curve.

Suppose, for instance, that spending on residential construction declines by $10 billion. Income will also decline by $10 billion, which leads to an *induced* decline in consumption. As spending on residential construction declines, homebuilders cut production, lay off workers, and reduce their demand for construction materials. Falling incomes in the construction industry lead households to reduce their spending on cars, furniture, appliances, and other goods and services. If the *MPC* is 0.75, then an initial $10 billion decline in income results in an induced decline in consumption of $7.5 billion. This $7.5 billion decline in consumption results in a $7.5 billion decline in income because the money is not spent. This reduction in income by $7.5 billion results in a further induced decline in consumption, equal to $0.75 \cdot \$7.5\ \text{billion} = \$5.625\ \text{billion}$. The $5.625 billion decline in consumption reduces income by $5.625 billion and consumption by $0.75 \cdot \$5.625\ \text{billion}$ and so on. As the *MPC* is less than 1, each round of spending decreases will be smaller than the previous round.

The result of the process just described is the *multiplier*, which equals the change in equilibrium GDP divided by the change in autonomous expenditure. We can write the multiplier for a change in investment spending as

$$\text{Multiplier} = \frac{\Delta Y}{\Delta \bar{I}},$$

where we assumed that the autonomous expenditure change is a change in investment. We could use a similar expression for the multiplier resulting from a change in $\overline{C}$, $\overline{G}$, or $\overline{NX}$.

How large is the multiplier? We showed how it can be calculated in the appendix to Chapter 9 by adding up all changes in income. We will now show how to calculate it by using the expression for aggregate expenditure and the equilibrium in the goods market. From the equations (10.2), which shows equilibrium in the goods market, and (10.5) we obtain

$$Y = \overline{C} + (MPC \cdot Y) + \bar{I} + \overline{G} + \overline{NX}.$$

We are focusing on the effect on equilibrium GDP of a change in *I*, holding the other components of aggregate expenditure constant. If these other components are constant, then changes in them are zero, so we have

$$\Delta Y = (MPC \cdot \Delta Y) + \Delta \bar{I}.$$

Rearranging terms, we have the expression for the multiplier

$$\frac{\Delta Y}{\Delta \bar{I}} = \frac{1}{(1 - MPC)}.$$

In general, the expression for the *expenditure multiplier* is

$$\text{Multiplier} = \frac{\Delta Y}{\Delta(\text{Autonomous expenditure})} = \frac{1}{(1 - MPC)}. \tag{10.6}$$

If, as we assumed earlier, the *MPC* is 0.75, then the value of the multiplier for investment expenditure is $1/(1-0.75) = 4$. So, a decline in investment spending of $1 billion would lead to a decline in equilibrium real GDP of $4 billion. When Keynes and his colleagues developed multiplier analysis in the 1930s, they believed that the multiplier might be as large as 10.[1] With a large multiplier, a relatively small decline in investment spending could have led to the large declines in GDP experienced in Canada, the United States, and Europe during the Great Depression. But empirical evidence suggests that the size of the multiplier is unlikely to exceed 2.

Multiplier when Taxes and Imports Depend on Income For simplicity we assumed that only consumption depends on the level of real GDP. With this assumption, out of an extra dollar of income, households spent $$MPC$ and the multiplier was $1/(1 - MPC)$. This is the approach we will use in the rest of the chapter. Here we will return briefly to the case when taxes and imports also depend on the level of real GDP, which we discussed in Chapter 9. When households' income increases by $1, they

- pay $$t$ in taxes and so their disposable income increases by $ $(1 - t)$.
- save part of the increase in disposable income and spend $$MPC (1 - t)$.
- of this spending, the proportion spent on imports is im, so the proportion spent on domestic goods and services is $$MPC(1 - t)(1 - im)$.

So spending on domestic goods and services increases by $m = MPC(1 - t)(1 - im)$ where m denotes, as before, the increase in spending on domestic goods and services. For example if $MPC = 0.75$, $t = 0.2$ and $im = 0.33$, we get $m = 0.75(1 - 0.2)(1 - 0.33) = 0.4$. The multiplier is, therefore, $1/(1 - m) = 1/(1 - 0.4) = 1.67$. So the multiplier is much smaller when the effect of taxes and imports is included. As the size of the multiplier is not crucial below, we will use only the simple case when only consumption depends on income.

The Government Purchases and Tax Multipliers

During a recession, the government can take action to increase real GDP by increasing government purchases or by cutting taxes. For example, an increase in government spending on bridges and highways will have a multiplied effect on equilibrium GDP in the same way that an increase in investment spending would. So, the *government purchases multiplier* is

$$\frac{\Delta Y}{\Delta \overline{G}} = \frac{1}{(1 - MPC)}. \tag{10.6a}$$

Similarly, if the government cuts the personal income tax, disposable income will increase, leading to an increase in consumption. The amount of spending that is subject to the multiplier equals $MPC \times \Delta T$ because households will save part of an increase in disposable income. So, the *tax multiplier* is

$$\text{Tax multiplier} = \frac{\Delta Y}{\Delta \overline{T}} = \frac{-MPC}{(1 - MPC)}. \tag{10.7}$$

Notice that because a *decrease* in taxes *increases* disposable income and real GDP, the tax multiplier is negative. With an MPC of 0.75, the tax multiplier is $-0.75/(1 - 0.75) = -3$. So, while a $1 billion increase in government purchases will increase equilibrium GDP by $4 billion, a $1 billion decrease in taxes will increase equilibrium GDP by $3 billion.

[1]John Maynard Keynes, *The Theory of Employment, Interest, and Money* (London: Macmillan, 1936) p. 51. Because macroeconomic statistics were not yet available in the 1930s, Keynes was unable to provide more than a rough estimate of the multiplier. He did note (p. 56) that Simon Kuznets's early estimates of investment and national income for the United States implied a multiplier of about 2.5. But he thought the value of the marginal propensity to consume used in the calculation was "implausibly low" given the economic conditions in the United States during the 1930s.

Calculating Equilibrium Real GDP

The 45°-line approach is too simplified to address all of the key macroeconomics issues, but it can help us understand the role of aggregate expenditure in determining equilibrium real GDP.

a. Use the following information to calculate equilibrium real GDP. (All values are in billions of dollars.)

Consumption:	$C = \$1.0 + 0.75Y^D$
Investment:	$\bar{I} = \$1.9$
Government purchases:	$\bar{G} = \$2.0$
Net exports:	$\overline{NX} = -\$0.5$
Taxes and transfers:	$\bar{T} = \overline{TR} = 0$

b. Now suppose that all of the information given in part (a) remains the same except that taxes equal $0.5 billion. Calculate equilibrium real GDP.

c. Now suppose that potential GDP equals $17.0 billion. If equilibrium real GDP equals the amount you calculated in part (b), use the value for the government purchases multiplier to calculate how much government purchases would have to change for equilibrium GDP to equal potential GDP (assuming that taxes remain unchanged). Use the value for the tax multiplier to calculate how much the government has to change taxes for equilibrium GDP to equal potential GDP (assuming that government purchases remain unchanged). Use a graph to illustrate your answer.

Solving the Problem

Step 1 **Review the chapter material.** This problem is about determining equilibrium in the 45°-line diagram and the government purchases and tax multipliers, so you may want to review the sections "The *IS* Curve and Equilibrium in the Goods Market," which begins on page 296, and "The Government Purchases and Tax Multipliers," which begins on page 301.

Step 2 **Answer part (a) by solving for equilibrium in the 45°-line model.** We can calculate equilibrium by keeping in mind that $AE = C + I + G + NX$, and that, in equilibrium, $Y = AE$. Also note that because taxes and transfers are zero, real GDP equals disposable income: $Y = Y^D$. We have

$$AE = C + I + G + NX$$
$$= \$1.0 + 0.75Y + \$1.9 + \$2.0 - \$0.5$$
$$= \$4.4 + 0.75Y.$$

In equilibrium, $Y = AE$, so

$$Y = \$4.4 + 0.75Y$$
$$Y - 0.75Y = \$4.4$$
$$Y = \$4.4/(1 - 0.75) = 17.6.$$

Step 3 **Answer part (b) by substituting the values for taxes and transfers into the consumption function and solving again for equilibrium.** Including taxes, the consumption function becomes:

$$C = \$1.0 + 0.75 (Y - \$0.5).$$

So, in equilibrium

$$Y = \$4.4 + 0.75Y - 0.75 \cdot \$0.5$$
$$Y - 0.75Y = 4.025$$
$$Y = \$4.025/(1 - 0.75) = 16.1.$$

Step 4 **Begin answering part (c) by using the values for the government purchases and tax multipliers to calculate the changes necessary in government purchases and taxes.** The value of the government purchases multiplier is

$$\frac{\Delta Y}{\Delta \overline{G}} = \frac{1}{(1 - MPC)} = \frac{1}{(1 - 0.75)} = 4.$$

The necessary change in equilibrium real GDP is $17.0 billion $-$ $16.1 billion $=$ $0.9 billion. Therefore, government purchases need to increase by

$$\Delta G = \frac{\Delta Y}{\text{Multiplier}} = \frac{\$0.9\,\text{billion}}{4} = \$0.225\,\text{billion, or }\$225\,\text{million.}$$

The value of the tax multiplier is

$$\frac{\Delta Y}{\Delta \overline{T}} = \frac{-MPC}{(1 - MPC)} = \frac{-0.75}{(1 - 0.75)} = -3.$$

So, taxes need to be cut by

$$\Delta T = \frac{\Delta Y}{\text{Multiplier}} = \frac{\$0.9\,\text{billion}}{-3} = -\$0.3\,\text{billion, or }\$300\,\text{million.}$$

Notice that because the tax multiplier is smaller (in absolute value) than the government purchases multiplier, the cut in taxes needs to be larger than the increase in government purchases to result in the same increase in equilibrium real GDP.

Step 5 **Finish answering part (c) by drawing a graph that shows the changes in government purchases or taxes necessary for short-run equilibrium to occur at real GDP of $17.0 billion.**

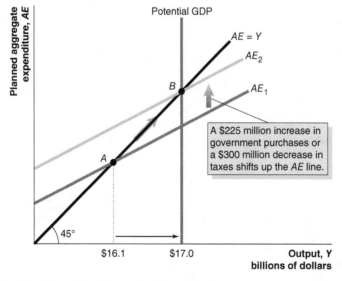

See related Problem 1.9 at the end of the chapter.

Constructing the *IS* Curve

The 45°-line diagram illustrates the important insight that changes in aggregate expenditure cause changes in real GDP. This analysis is incomplete, though, because it does not include the effects of changes in interest rates on spending. To understand how monetary policy and financial markets affect GDP, we need to bring interest rates into the analysis. Changes in the real interest rate affect consumption, investment, and net exports:

- A decrease in the real interest rate increases consumption because it gives consumers an incentive to spend rather than save and reduces their cost of borrowing. We discuss the effect of the real interest rate on consumption in more detail in Chapter 16.
- A decrease in the real interest rate increases investment spending and new house purchases because the real interest rate is an important cost of investment and house ownership.
- A decrease in the domestic real interest rate makes returns on domestic financial assets less attractive to investors relative to the returns on foreign assets, reducing the real exchange rate. The decrease in the real exchange rate increases exports and decreases imports, thereby increasing net exports.

An increase in the real interest rate will have the opposite effect—decreasing consumption, investment, and net exports.

Figure 10.3 panel (a) uses the 45°-line diagram to show the effect of changes in the real interest rate on equilibrium in the goods market. With the real interest rate initially at r_1, the aggregate expenditure line is $AE(r_1)$, and the equilibrium level of real GDP is Y_1 (point A). If the interest falls from r_1 to r_2, the aggregate expenditure line shifts up from $AE(r_1)$ to $AE(r_2)$, and the equilibrium level of real GDP increases from Y_1 to Y_2 (point B).

In panel (b), we use the results from panel (a) to construct the *IS* curve, which shows the combinations of the real interest rate and real GDP for which the goods market is in equilibrium. We know that at every equilibrium point in the 45°-line diagram in panel (a), planned aggregate expenditure equals real GDP. In panel (b) we plot these points on a graph with the real interest rate on the vertical axis and the level of real GDP on the horizontal axis. Points A and B in panel (b) correspond to points A and B in panel (a). The *IS* curve is downward sloping because the lower is the real interest rate the higher is planned aggregate expenditure and the equilibrium level of real GDP.

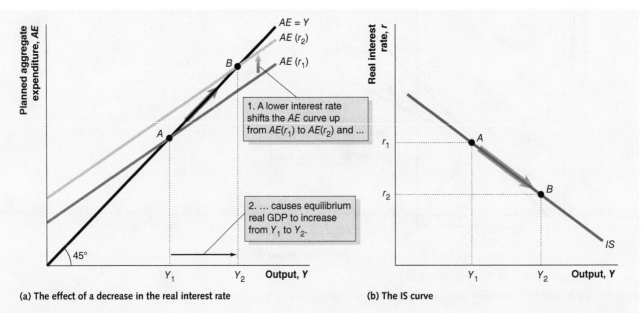

(a) The effect of a decrease in the real interest rate

(b) The IS curve

Figure 10.3 Deriving the *IS* Curve

Panel (a) uses the 45°-line diagram to show the effect of changes in the real interest rate on equilibrium in the goods market. With the real interest rate initially at r_1, the aggregate expenditure line is $AE(r_1)$ and the equilibrium level of real GDP is Y_1 (point A). If the interest rate falls from r_1 to r_2, the aggregate expenditure line shifts up from $AE(r_1)$ to $AE(r_2)$, and the equilibrium level of real GDP increases from Y_1 to Y_2 (point B). In panel (b), we plot the points from panel (a) to form the *IS* curve. The points A and B in panel (b) correspond to the points A and B in panel (a).

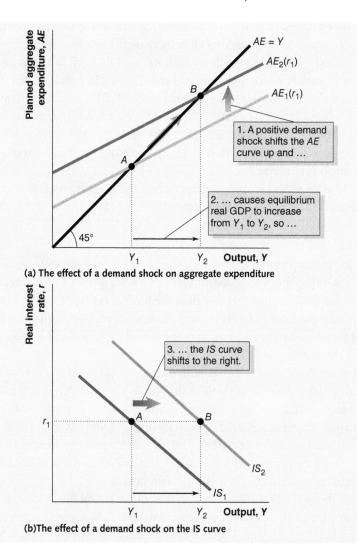

Figure 10.4

A Positive Demand Shock and the *IS* Curve

In panel (a), the positive demand shock shifts up the *AE* curve, and equilibrium moves from point *A* to point *B*.

In panel (b), the *IS* curve shifts to the right, from A to B. Points *A* and *B* represent the same combination of the real interest rate and level of real GDP in both panels.

Shifts of the *IS* Curve

The *IS* curve shows the relationship of changes in the real interest rate and real GDP when the goods market is in equilibrium. To draw the IS curve we hold constant all other factors that might affect the willingness of households, firms, and governments to spend. An increase or a decrease in the real interest rate results in *a movement along the IS curve*. Changing other factors that affect aggregate expenditure will cause a *shift of the IS curve*. These other factors that lead to changes in aggregate expenditure are called *demand shocks*. For example, during the Great Recession Canadian exports fell from $537 billion in 2007 to $446 billion in 2009. This decline in exports was a *negative demand shock* that shifted the *IS* curve to the left. Between 2009 and 2011 exports recovered, increasing to $500 billion in 2011.[2] This increase in exports was a *positive demand shock* that shifted the *IS* curve to the right. Note that the economy can be hit by both positive and negative demand shocks at the same time. Whether the *IS* curve ends up shifting to the right or to the left depends on the relative sizes of the shocks.

Figure 10.4 shows the effect of a positive demand shock on the *IS* curve. In panel (a), we assume that the real interest rate is unchanged at r_1 and the initial aggregate expenditure

---

[2]Statistics Canada, CANSIM Table 380-0064.

curve is AE_1, so equilibrium is at point A with real GDP equal to Y_1. A positive demand shock, such as an increase in net exports or an increase in government purchases, will cause the aggregate expenditure curve to shift up from AE_1 to AE_2. Equilibrium in the goods market now occurs at point B, with a higher level of real GDP, Y_2. In panel (b), equilibrium is initially at point A with a real interest rate of r_1 and real GDP of Y_1. With a constant real interest rate, the positive demand shock moves equilibrium to point B, where real GDP has increased from Y_1 to Y_2, so the *IS* curve has shifted to the right, from IS_1 to IS_2.

A negative demand shock will have the opposite effect on the *IS* curve—shifting the curve to the left. To summarize:

> *If a demand shock increases aggregate expenditure, the IS curve will shift to the right.*
>
> *If a demand shock decreases aggregate expenditure, the IS curve will shift to the left.*

The *IS* Curve and the Output Gap

As we discussed in the previous chapter, economists measure economic fluctuations using the *output gap*, which is the percentage difference between real GDP and potential GDP. So, it is helpful to use the output gap rather than the level of real GDP in the *IS* curve graph. During a recession, the output gap becomes negative when real GDP is below potential GDP. When output increases during an expansion, the output gap eventually becomes positive, as real GDP rises above potential GDP.

We can replace the level of real GDP with the output gap in the *IS* curve graph, with the following qualification: We should think of changes in the real interest rate as affecting the level of investment spending, consumption spending, and net exports *relative to potential GDP*. For instance, when the real interest rate falls and *C, I,* and *NX* increase, the increase in aggregate expenditure will cause real GDP, *Y*, to increase relative to potential GDP, Y^P. In that case, when we graph the *IS* curve with the real interest rate on the vertical axis and the output gap on the horizontal axis, the *IS* curve is still downward sloping.

Figure 10.5 shows the *IS* curve graph with the output gap on the horizontal axis. We use the symbol $\tilde{Y}$ to distinguish the output gap from real GDP, *Y*. As a reference, we have included a vertical line where $Y = Y^P$, which is the point where the output gap is zero. Normally, we

Figure 10.5

The *IS* Curve Using the Output Gap

The graph shows the output gap, rather than the level of real GDP, on the horizontal axis. Values to the left of 0 on the horizontal axis represent negative values for the output gap: periods during which real GDP is below potential GDP. Values to the right of zero on the horizontal axis represent positive values for the output gap: periods during which real GDP is above potential GDP. The vertical line, $Y = Y^P$, is drawn from the point at which the output gap is zero.

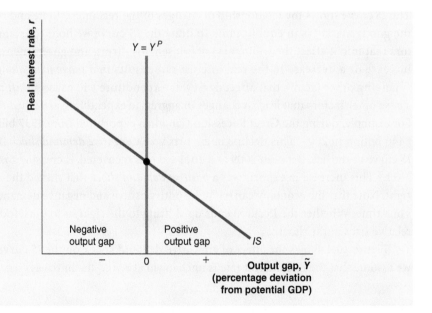

draw graphs with the vertical axis beginning at 0 on the horizontal axis. In this case, though, our graphs are easier to understand if we move the vertical axis to the left, leaving zero in the middle of the horizontal axis. It is important to note that values to the left of zero on the horizontal axis represent negative values for the output gap, and values to the right of zero on the horizontal axis represent positive values for the output gap.

The Monetary Policy Curve: The Relationship between the Central Bank's Target Interest Rate and Output

10.2
Learning Objective
Use the monetary policy, *MP*, curve to show how the interest rate set by the central bank helps to determine the output gap.

The second component of the *IS–MP* model is the *MP* curve, named so for *Monetary Policy*. The Bank of Canada conducts monetary policy by managing the money supply and interest rates. During the past several decades, the Bank of Canada, like most other central banks, has generally focused its monetary policy actions on interest rates. The main problem the Bank of Canada faces in carrying out monetary policy is that it controls a key short-term nominal interest rate, the *overnight rate*, but not the long-term real interest rates. The overnight rate is the interest rate that banks charge each other on short-term loans. The decisions of households and firms about buying houses and investing in new factories, equipment, and office buildings do not depend on the overnight rate but on long-term real interest rates on mortgage loans or on corporate bonds. In this section, we explore the link between the overnight rate that the Bank of Canada controls and the long-term real interest rates that affect aggregate expenditure. After this discussion, we will see that the Bank of Canada *influences* long-term real interest rates, but it does not have complete *control* over them.

The Relationship between the Long-Term Real Interest Rate and the Short-Term Nominal Interest Rate

The relationship between the long-term real interest rate that underlies household and investor decisions and the short-term nominal interest rate that the Bank of Canada controls depends on three factors: the term structure of interest rates, the risk structure of interest rates, and the expected inflation rate.

Recall from Chapter 3 that the *term structure of interest rates* is the relationship among the interest rates on bonds that are otherwise similar but that have different maturities. The interest rate on a long-term bond equals the average of the expected interest rates on short-term bonds plus a *term premium* to compensate lenders for the possibility that interest rates will change while they own the long-term bond. Expectations of a future rise in short-term rates tend to increase current long-term rates. In addition, when interest rates fluctuate, so do the prices of bonds, thereby potentially causing losses to investors in bonds. The *term premium* is the additional interest that investors require in order to buy a long-term bond rather than a comparable sequence of short-term bonds. So the term structure depends on two factors:

1. Investors' expectations of future short-term interest rates, as given by the term structure.
2. The term premium.

Combined, these two factors are called the *term structure effect*, or *TSE*.

The *risk structure of interest rates* shows the relationship among interest rates on bonds that have different characteristics but the same maturity. Bonds differ with respect to *default risk*, which is the risk that a borrower will fail to make payments of interest or principal. The bonds of private corporations have higher interest rates than do comparable bonds issued by the Government of Canada, to compensate investors for the possibility that the corporations might default on the bonds. This extra interest is called a *default-risk premium.* Similarly, households must also pay a default-risk premium when they borrow money because they may default on loans they receive. We denote the default-risk premium as *DP.*

Combining the term structure effect, *TSE,* and the default-risk premium, *DP,* we obtain the relationship between the long-term *nominal* interest rate, i_{LT}, and the short-term *nominal* interest rate, *i*:

$$i_{LT} = i + TSE + DP. \tag{10.8}$$

Finally, we need to consider the link between the long-term *nominal* interest rate and the long-term *real* interest rate. Using the Fisher equation we introduced in Chapter 4, the expected real interest rate is equal to the nominal interest rate minus the expected inflation rate:

$$r_{LT} = i_{LT} - \pi^e.$$

Using this last relationship, we have our final equation for the real interest rate. It equals the short-term nominal interest rate plus the term structure effect, *TSE,* plus the default-risk premium *DP,* minus the expected rate of inflation:

$$r_{LT} = i + TSE + DP - \pi^e. \tag{10.9}$$

The Bank of Canada has good control over the short-term nominal interest rate, *i.* It controls the long-term real interest rate only as long as *term structure effects, the default-risk premium, and the expected inflation rate all remain unchanged.* In practice, the Bank's job can be difficult because events beyond the Bank's control can drive movements in the long-term real interest rate. For example, the Bank of Canada might want to stimulate the economy by lowering the long-term real interest rate. To achieve this goal, the Bank of Canada lowers the short-term nominal interest rate. However, the long-term real interest rate may not decline if (1) lenders, including investors in the bond market, believe that future short-term nominal rates will be higher, (2) lenders require a higher default-risk premium, or (3) lenders lower their expectations of the future inflation rate. These factors may make the Bank's attempts to stimulate the economy ineffective.

The Bank of Canada does have *some* influence over these three factors. For instance, if the Bank of Canada is able to convince lenders that it will keep short-term nominal rates low for an extended period of time (a policy called *forward guidance,* which we will discuss in Chapter 14), then the term structure effect will likely be unchanged. The Bank of Canada may actually bring about a reduction in the default-risk premium if lenders believe that the Bank's expansionary policy will bring the economy out of a recession, thereby reducing the probability that borrowers will default on loans. The effect of Bank of Canada actions on the expected inflation rate can be complex. If the Bank of Canada lowers the short-term nominal interest rate to stimulate the economy, then lenders, households, and firms may believe that increased economic activity will lead to a higher inflation rate. An increase in the expected inflation rate would reinforce the Bank's action by further decreasing the real interest rate. Similarly, if the Bank of Canada increases the short-term nominal interest rate to slow down the economy, the expected inflation rate may fall. A decrease in the expected inflation rate would reinforce the Bank's action by further increasing the real interest rate. This can, however, happen only in the short run. In the long run the *Fisher effect* indicates that increases in expected inflation result in increases in long-term nominal interest rates (Chapter 4): A one-percentage-point increase in the expected inflation rate will result in a one-percentage-point increase in the long-term nominal interest rate, leaving the real interest rate unchanged.

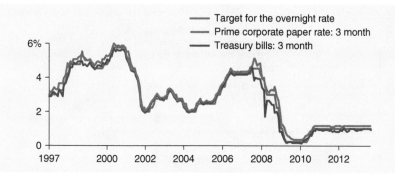

Figure 10.6

Short-Term Nominal Interest Rates Typically Move Together

The target for the overnight rate, the three-month treasury bill rate, and the three-month corporate paper rate all move closely together. The Bank of Canada can therefore be confident that when it takes actions to increase or decrease one short-term rate, other short-term rates will move in the same direction.

Source: Statistics Canada, CANSIM, Table 176-0043.

Deriving the *MP* Curve Using the Money Market Model

The Bank of Canada and other central banks control a specific short-term nominal interest rate and adjust the money supply to achieve this goal. The Bank of Canada explicitly targets the overnight rate, but other short-term interest rates usually move closely with the overnight rate. Figure 10.6 plots three short-term nominal interest rates—the target for the overnight rate, the three-month treasury bill rate, and the three-month corporate paper rate for the years between 1997 and 2013. (Corporations use *corporate paper* to borrow funds for a short period, generally three months or less.) Notice how the rates move very closely together. This shows that the Bank of Canada can be confident that when it takes actions to increase or decrease the overnight rate, other short-term rates will move in the same direction. So which short-term nominal interest rate we focus on is not important.

We can derive the *MP* curve using the money market model (Chapter 3). We assume that the *TSE* and *DP* terms, as well as the expected inflation rate, π^e, are all constant. Given these assumptions, by changing the short-term nominal interest rate, the Bank of Canada can change the long-term real interest rate.

In Figure 10.7, equilibrium is initially at point A in panel (b), with the output gap equal to $\tilde{Y}_1$ and the real interest rate equal to r. Suppose that real GDP increases so that the output

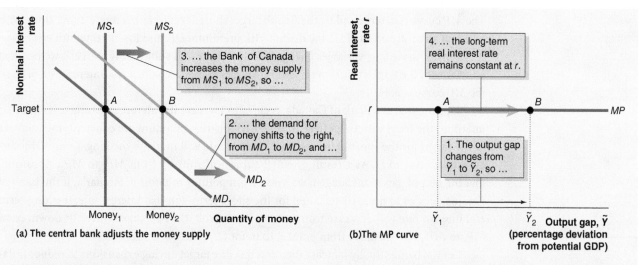

(a) The central bank adjusts the money supply

(b) The MP curve

Figure 10.7 Deriving the *MP* Curve

As the output gap changes from $\tilde{Y}_1$ to $\tilde{Y}_2$ in panel (b), the money demand curve shifts to the right in panel (a). The central bank increases the money supply in panel (a) to keep the short-term nominal interest rate at the target interest rate. Assuming the term structure effect, the default-risk premium, and the expected inflation rate all remaining constant, the long-term real interest rate will also remain constant, and equilibrium moves from point A to point B in both panels.

Figure 10.8

Changes in the Interest Rate Target and the *MP* Curve

When the Bank of Canada increases its target for the short-term nominal interest rate, assuming that expected inflation, the term structure effect, and the default-risk premium are constant, the long-term real interest rate increases, so the *MP* curve shifts up, from MP_1 to MP_2. Conversely, when the Bank of Canada decreases its target for the short-term nominal interest rate, the *MP* curve shifts down, from MP_1 to MP_3.

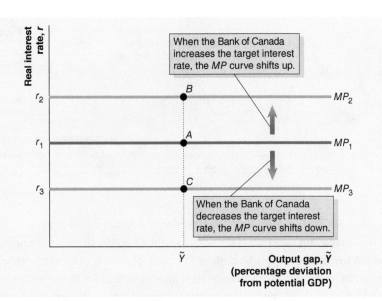

gap changes from $\widetilde{Y}_1$ to $\widetilde{Y}_2$, as shown in panel (b). The increase in real GDP leads households and firms to purchase more goods and services, so the demand for money in panel (a) shifts to the right, from MD_1 to MD_2. If the Bank of Canada keeps the money supply constant, the increase in the demand for money will cause the interest rate to increase. But if the Bank of Canada has a target nominal interest rate, it will increase the money supply to keep the interest rate at the target. As a result, the short-term nominal interest rate remains constant and, assuming the term structure effect, the default-risk premium, and the expected inflation rate all remaining constant, the long-term real interest rate will also remain constant. With the real interest rate constant and the output gap equal $\widetilde{Y}_2$, we move to point *B* in panel (b). The result is that the *MP* curve will be horizontal at the real interest rate, *r*.

Shifts of the *MP* Curve

The *MP* curve is determined by the Bank's target short-term nominal interest rate along with the term structure effect, *TSE*, the default-risk premium, *DP*, and the expected inflation rate, π^e. If any of these four variables change, the *MP* curve will shift. In Figure 10.8, we begin at point *A* with the Bank's initial overnight rate target consistent with a real interest rate of r_1, so the *MP* curve is MP_1[3].

Suppose that the Bank of Canada decides to increase its interest rate target. If expected inflation, the term structure effect, and the default-risk premium are constant, the increase in the target for the short-term nominal interest rate will increase the long-term real interest rate from r_1 to r_2. As a result, the *MP* curve will shift up from MP_1 to MP_2. Assuming that the output gap is unchanged, we move from point *A* to point *B*. Similarly, if the Bank of Canada decides to decrease its target for the short-term nominal interest rate, the long-term real interest rate will decrease from r_1 to r_3. As a result, the *MP* curve will shift down, from MP_1 to MP_3, and we move from point *A* to point *C*.

Central banks usually increase their interest rate target during expansions to reduce inflation. For example, as the Canadian housing market began to overheat in the mid-2000s, the Bank of Canada increased its target overnight rate from 2.00% in September 2004 to 4.50% in

---

[3]In this chapter, we have so far used r_{LT} for the long-term real interest rate. For simplicity, we are dropping the *LT* subscript from *r*. For the remainder of this chapter and in the following chapters, *r* will denote the long-term real interest rate.

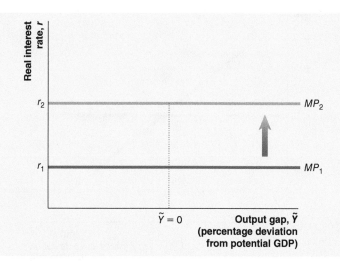

Figure 10.9

Factors that Shift the *MP* Curve Up

If the Bank of Canada increases the short-term nominal interest rate (the overnight rate) (*i* increases), expectations of the future short-term interest rates increase or term premium rise (TSE increases), the default risk premium increases (DP increases), and the expected inflation rate falls (π^e falls), then the MP curve shifts up.

July 2007. Some central banks, for example the Federal Reserve, decrease their target during recessions to help increase output and reduce unemployment. The Bank of Canada, however, has an explicit mandate to control inflation and not real variables. But all roads lead to prices: When the economy is weak, the rate of inflation falls. To prevent inflation from falling too much, the central bank lowers the target rate. If this helps revive the real economy, so much the better. An inflation-targeting central bank would have a problem in a situation when the economy is in a recession but inflation is high. That has not yet happened in Canada since the beginning of inflation targeting, so it is not clear what the Bank of Canada will do in such a situation.

Note that some actions of the Bank of Canada may suggest it does pay attention to real variables. For example, it may reduce interest rates when recession starts but inflation has not fallen yet. This is because, as we discuss in a Chapter 12, monetary policy works with long and variable lags. When a recession begins, the central bank needs to assess for how long it will last, and how far inflation will decrease. Given these forecasts and taking the lags into account, the Bank may choose to lower the target rate as soon as it realizes a recession has started and before inflation starts falling. A casual observer may conclude that the action is aimed at preventing output fall now, but in reality the bank is trying to prevent inflation from declining in the future.

Central bank policy is not the only factor that affects the real interest rate. For instance, increases in the default-risk premium increase the real interest rate in much the same way as does an increase in the target interest rate. The default-risk premium increased after the bankruptcy of Lehman Brothers in September 2008, so real interest rates in financial markets increased, shifting up the *MP* curve.

We summarize the factors affecting the long-term real interest rate and the position of the MP curve in Figure 10.9.

Equilibrium in the *IS–MP* Model

We constructed the *IS* curve to describe how changes in the real interest rate affect equilibrium real GDP. And we constructed the *MP* curve to describe how the Bank of Canada policy, acting through financial markets, determines the real interest rate. Combining the *IS* and *MP* curves allows us to determine short-run macroeconomic equilibrium, under the assumption that the price level remains constant. In this section, we combine the *IS* and *MP* curves to understand how macroeconomic shocks can affect the output gap and how government and central bank policy can respond to the effects of shocks.

10.3
Learning Objective
Use the *IS–MP* model to understand why real GDP fluctuates.

Figure 10.10

Equilibrium in the *IS–MP* Model

The economy is in equilibrium where the *MP* and *IS* curves intersect at point *A*, with real GDP equal to potential GDP, so the output gap equals zero.

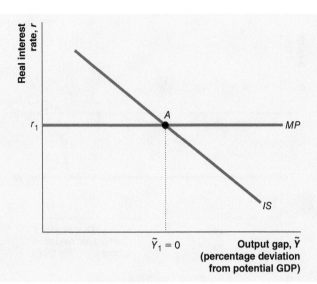

Figure 10.10 shows equilibrium in the *IS–MP* model. For a given *IS* curve, the Bank's choice of the real interest rate determines the equilibrium output gap. If the Bank of Canada sets the real interest rate at r_1, then real GDP equals potential GDP and the output gap, $\tilde{Y}_1$, equals zero. So firms are producing at their normal capacity and there is no cyclical unemployment, leaving the economy at the natural rate of unemployment.

Demand shocks will shift the *IS* curve, which will cause the output gap to change. Changes in the three factors (other than the Bank of Canada policy) affecting the long-term real interest rate (TSE, DP and π^e) will shift the *MP* curve. Fiscal policy (changes in government spending and taxes) shift the *IS* curve and monetary policy (changes in the overnight rate) shift the *MP* curve.

Demand Shocks and Fluctuations in Output

In Section 10.1, we saw how demand shocks affect the *IS* curve. We now explain how these shocks will cause real GDP to fluctuate if the Bank of Canada keeps the overnight rate constant and the other factors affecting the long-term real interest rate do not change. For example, suppose that a collapse in consumer confidence leads households to reduce consumption. This is what happened at the beginning of the Great Recession in Canada. Canadian consumers were concerned about the crisis in the United States and reduced purchases.

Figure 10.11 shows the effect of the decrease in consumer confidence using the *IS–MP* model. Initially, equilibrium is at point *A*, with real GDP equal to potential GDP, so $\tilde{Y}_1 = 0$. As households reduce consumption, the *IS* curve shifts to the left, from IS_1 to IS_2. Assuming that the Bank of Canada does not initially take action to change the interest rate, equilibrium is now at point *B*, with real GDP below potential GDP. In other words, the economy has moved into a recession, with declining levels of output and rising levels of unemployment. A reduction in consumer confidence is just one example of a negative demand shock that shifts the *IS* curve to the left. Any negative demand shock would have a similar effect. Any positive demand shock, such as an increase in investment by firms, would increase aggregate expenditure and shift the *IS* curve to the right.

Monetary Policy and Fluctuations in Output

In the previous section, we saw that a negative demand shock can push the economy into recession when the Bank of Canada keeps the real interest rate unchanged. In practice,

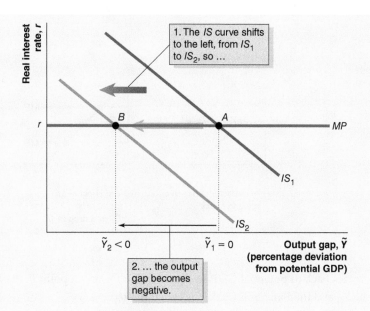

Figure 10.11

A Negative Demand Shock and Equilibrium Real GDP

A negative demand shock shifts the *IS* curve to the left, from IS_1 to IS_2. If the Bank of Canada keeps the real interest rate constant, the output gap becomes negative and equilibrium moves from point *A* to point *B*.

though, if the Bank of Canada recognizes that a negative demand shock has occurred, it will try to offset the effects of the shock by lowering its target for the overnight rate. (We will discuss monetary policy in detail in Chapter 12.)

Figure 10.12 shows the effect of a decrease in the Bank's target interest rate on the output gap. We assume that the economy has been hit by a negative demand shock; therefore we begin in short-run equilibrium at point *A*, with real GDP less than potential GDP. A decrease in the Bank's target for the overnight rate decreases the real interest rate from r_1 to r_2. The *MP* curve shifts down, from MP_1 to MP_2, causing planned aggregate expenditure to increase, so

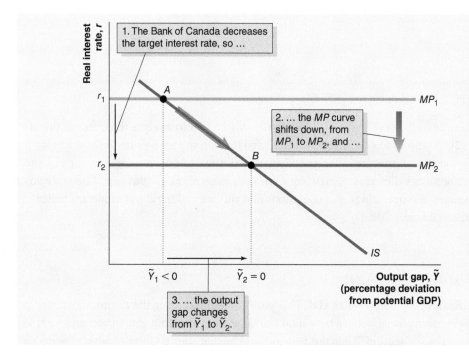

Figure 10.12

The Bank of Canada Ends a Recession

A decrease in the Bank of Canada's target for the overnight rate causes the long-term real interest rate to decrease from r_1 to r_2. As a result, aggregate expenditure increases, causing real GDP to rise back to potential GDP and the output gap to return to zero at $\tilde{Y}_2$. Equilibrium moves from point *A* to point *B*, and the Bank of Canada has ended the recession.

Figure 10.13

Summary of the *IS–MP* Model

A positive demand shock causes the aggregate expenditure to increase at every interest rate and raises the level of output.

If the Bank of Canada increases its target for the short-term nominal interest rate (*i* increases), expectations of the future short-term interest rates increase or the term premium rises (*TSE* increases), the default-risk premium increases (*DP* increases), the expected inflation rate falls (π^e falls), then the *MP* curve shifts up and the equilibrium level of output falls.

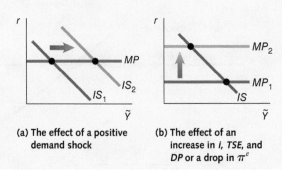

(a) The effect of a positive demand shock

(b) The effect of an increase in *i*, *TSE*, and *DP* or a drop in π^e

real GDP increases back to potential GDP. In the new equilibrium at point *B*, the output gap is again zero at $\tilde{Y}_2$, and the Bank of Canada has ended the recession.

Although the *IS–MP* model used in Figure 10.12 is simplified, it captures how the Bank of Canada responds to a recession—by lowering its target for the overnight rate. The Bank's target for the overnight rate was 4.5% before the Great Recession. To stimulate the economy, the Bank of Canada reduced it to 0.25% by the end of the recession in April 2009 and kept the target rate at a record low levels for more than a year.

Other central banks also use reductions in short-term nominal interest rates to fight recessions. During the early 1990s, Japan experienced the collapse of both real estate and stock prices, and the Japanese economy grew very slowly during the 1990s. In an attempt to increase real GDP, the Bank of Japan lowered its target short-term nominal interest rate in a series of steps to essentially 0% by 1999. In this case, the policy was insufficient to eliminate the output gap. The Japanese economy did not fully recover, and it has experienced sluggish economic growth for nearly 20 years.

Figure 10.13 summarizes the effects of different shocks and changes in policy on real GDP and the real interest rate in the *IS–MP* model.

Solved Problem 10.2

Using the *IS–MP* Model to Analyze the GST Tax Cut

The federal government cut the Goods and Services Tax (GST), from 7% to 6% in July 1, 2006, and to 5% on January 1, 2008. The cut was part of an electoral promise to stimulate the economy, but many economists believed it was not necessary, as the Canadian economy was operating above capacity, with an output gap estimated by the OECD at over +2% of GDP.

Use the *IS–MP* model to analyze the effect of the tax on real GDP and the output gap. Be sure to show any shifts in the *IS* curve and the *MP* curve, as well as the old and new equilibrium values of the output gap. Also state any assumptions that you are making about monetary policy.

Solving the Problem

Step 1   **Review the chapter material.** This problem is about using the *IS* and *MP* curves to determine the effect of a tax cut on real GDP and the output gap, so you may want to review the section "Demand Shocks and Fluctuations in Output," which begins on page 312.

Step 2 **Draw a graph that shows the initial equilibrium.** The problem states that the economy was in good shape with positive output gap at the time of the two cuts to the GST. As a result, we can assume that real GDP exceeded potential GDP.

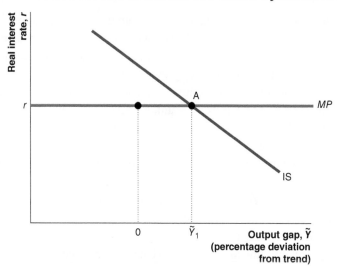

Step 3 **Determine which curve shifts.** A lower GST means that taxed goods and services became cheaper and constitutes positive demand shock. Demand for goods and services increase, raising aggregate expenditure at any given real interest rate. This means the *IS* curve shifts to the right, as shown in Figure 10.13.

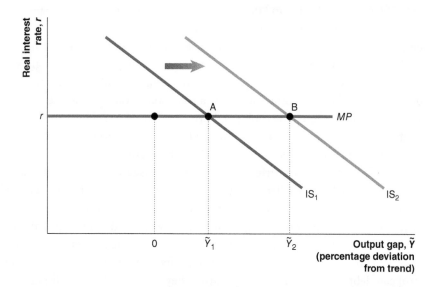

Step 4 **State your assumption about monetary policy, and explain the effect of the act on real GDP and on the output gap.** The simplest assumption is that the Bank of Canada keeps the real interest rate constant. In that case, if the *IS* curve shifts to the right, short-run equilibrium will move from point A to point B in the graph in Step 3. The higher level of consumption causes real GDP to increase relative to potential GDP, so the equilibrium output gap changes from $\tilde{Y}_1 > 0$ to $\tilde{Y}_2 > \tilde{Y}_1 > 0$, i.e. it becomes even more positive.

This analysis indicates that the 2006–08 GST tax cut increased consumption and real GDP. As a result, it made the economic expansion stronger.

See related Problem 3.4 at the end of the chapter.

Making the Connection

Will the European Financial Crisis Cause a Recession in Canada?

By 2012 the Canadian economy had long recovered from the Great Recession, but growth was weak. Many economists and policymakers were concerned that a developing economic crisis in Europe might push Canada back into recession. In Europe, the global recession caused large increases in government spending on unemployment benefits and other transfer payments and also resulted in reductions in tax revenues as incomes and profits declined. Budget deficits soared, particularly in Greece, Ireland, Spain, Portugal, and Italy. Governments financed the resulting budget deficits by selling bonds. By the spring of 2010, many investors had come to doubt the ability of Greece, in particular, to make the interest payments on its bonds. The International Monetary Fund and the European Central Bank made loans to these countries but insisted on *austerity policies*: lower government spending and higher taxes. By 2012, voters in several countries had begun to reject continuing austerity. Investors started to believe that Greece might abandon using the euro and resume using its earlier currency, the drachma. Austerity policies led to a decline in output in many Eurozone countries and resulted in record levels of unemployment, pushing many European countries into another recession.

How did these problems in Europe affect the Canadian economy? As the incomes of Europeans declined, they purchased fewer goods and services from other countries, including from Canada. Holding other factors constant, a decline in Canadian exports to Europe would shift the *IS* curve to the left, reducing real GDP relative to potential GDP. The damage from falling exports was lessened by the fact that three-quarters of our exports go to the United States and only 10% to Europe. So, even a substantial decline in exports to Europe has a relatively small direct effect on Canadian economy. Continued increases in domestic consumption and investment spending also offset the effect of declining exports. But although real GDP in Canada was still increasing through the first half of 2012, growth was slower than it would have been without the decline in exports. In addition, some economists were concerned that the uncertainty caused by a recession in Europe and the possible breakup of the Eurozone might lead households and firms in Canada to cut back on their spending. The result could be a larger shift to the left of the *IS* curve and a decline in real GDP.

Problems in Europe could also affect Canadian economy through the financial system. Financial flows among countries have greatly increased in recent years. As a result, many banks and other financial firms have invested in European sovereign debt or have financial dealings with European banks. Many European banks have suffered losses, and some appeared to be in danger of failing. Policymakers worried that problems at European banks might spill over and cause significant banking losses outside Europe. Few economists were concerned about Canadian banks as our banks had limited exposure to Europe and, as the European debt crisis unfolded fairly slowly, they had had time to sell European sovereign debt as well as some of their holdings with European banks.

As this text book went to press, the European economic crisis had abated. Clearly, though, in an increasingly global economic and financial system, the Bank of Canada and the government had to be prepared to deal with economic developments outside Canada.

Sources: Eric Reguly, "Europe's debt woes could be harbinger," *Globe and Mail*, December 31, 2010; Stephen Fidler, "Crisis Without Borders: Europe's Contagion Woes Illustrate How a Lack of Market Confidence Spreads," *The Wall Street Journal*, November 26, 2010; Jack Ewing, "Euro Zone Economy Skirts Recession," *New York Times*, May 15, 2012; and Corina Ruhe and Angeline Benoit, "Is the Eurozone finally exiting the longest recession in its history?" *The Financial Post*, Aug 30, 2013.

See related Problems 3.5 and D10.2 at the end of the chapter.

IS–MP and Aggregate Demand

We mentioned at the beginning of the chapter that we can use the *IS–MP* model as an alternative way to derive the aggregate demand curve. In the previous chapter, we defined the aggregate demand curve as representing all the equilibrium combinations of real GDP and the price level. We now focus on the output gap so we adjust that definition slightly to say that the aggregate demand curve (*AD*) represents all of the equilibrium combinations of the *output gap* and the price level.

Figure 10.14 illustrates how we can derive the aggregate demand curve from the *IS–MP* model. We consider the effect of a change in the price level on the output gap, keeping everything else (i.e., the term structure effect, the risk premium, and the expected inflation rate) constant. Consider the effect of an increase in the price level on the *IS* curve. In the money market, an increase in the price level causes the demand for money curve to shift to the right, increasing the equilibrium nominal interest rate. Since the expected inflation rate is constant, an increase in the nominal interest rate raises the real interest rate. A higher real interest rate leads to a decline in aggregate expenditure, which causes a movement up along the *IS* curve, resulting in a lower level of real GDP relative to potential GDP. In panel (a) we start in equilibrium at point *A*, with the price level equal to P_1, the interest rate equal to r_1, and the output gap equal to $\tilde{Y}_1$. The increase in the price level from P_1 to P_2 causes a movement along the *IS* curve from point *A* to point *B*. At point *B*, the interest rate is r_2 and the output gap is $\tilde{Y}_2$. So panel (a) shows two pairs of values for the price level and the output gap that represent short-run equilibrium. In panel (b), we plot the corresponding two points in a graph with the price level on the vertical axis and the output gap on the horizontal axis. If we kept varying the price level and plotting the effects on the *IS* curve in panel (a), we would have plotted all the points on the aggregate demand curve (*AD*) in panel (b).

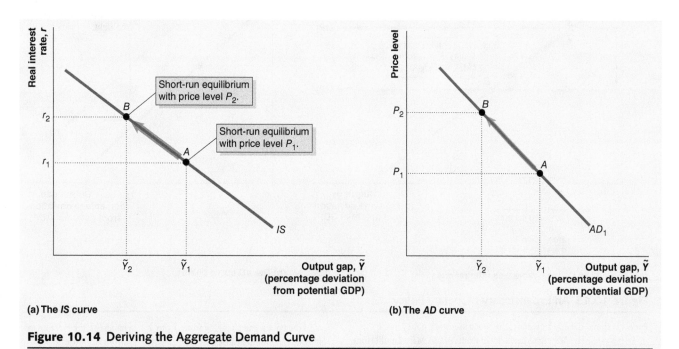

Figure 10.14 Deriving the Aggregate Demand Curve

Panel (a) shows that an increase in the price level from P_1 to P_2 causes a movement along the *IS* curve from point *A* to point *B*. Plotting the equilibrium combinations of the price level and the output gap from panel (a) gives us the aggregate demand curve in panel (b).

The Effect of Fiscal and Monetary Policy on the AD Curve We have shown that an increase in the price level will cause an increase in the interest rate, *provided that the Bank of Canada allows the nominal interest rate to rise.* The Bank of Canada could offset the effects of an increase in the price level on the interest rate by keeping the interest rate constant. We know that demand shocks will cause the *IS* curve to shift. A shift of the *IS* curve represents a change in the level of spending at each interest rate, so a shift of the *IS* curve will cause the *AD* curve to shift in the same direction. For example, a decline in spending on residential construction causes the *IS* curve to shift to the left and, therefore, will also cause the *AD* curve to shift to the left. Similarly, expansionary fiscal policy shifts the *IS* curve to the right, thereby also shifting the *AD* curve to the right.

The effect of monetary policy is a bit more complicated. If the Bank of Canada engages in an expansionary monetary policy by lowering its target interest rate, the *MP* curve will shift down. The lower interest rate results in a movement down the *IS* curve. For a given price level, aggregate expenditure is now higher. This means that the *AD* curve shifts to the right.

Figure 10.15 illustrates the effects of an expansionary monetary policy. In panel (a), an expansionary monetary policy results in the *MP* curve shifting down from MP_1 to MP_2. Equilibrium moves from point *A* to point *B*, with the real interest rate falling from r_1 to r_2 and the output gap changing from $\tilde{Y}_1$ to $\tilde{Y}_2$. In panel (b), equilibrium is initially at point *A*, with a price level of P_1 and an output gap of $\tilde{Y}_1$. The expansionary monetary policy increases aggregate expenditure, which shifts the *AD* curve from AD_1 to AD_2. At point *B*, equilibrium occurs at price level P_1 and output gap $\tilde{Y}_2$.

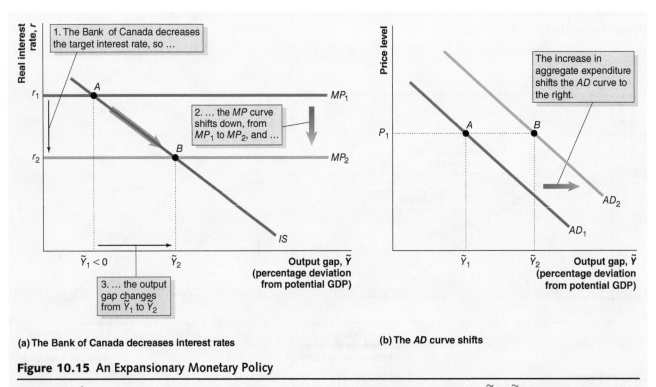

(a) The Bank of Canada decreases interest rates

(b) The *AD* curve shifts

Figure 10.15 An Expansionary Monetary Policy

Panel (a) shows the effect of an expansionary monetary policy in the *IS–MP* model. The *MP* curve shifts down from MP_1 to MP_2. Equilibrium moves from point *A* to point *B*, with the interest rate declining from r_1 to r_2, and the output gap changing from $\tilde{Y}_1$ to $\tilde{Y}_2$. In panel (b), the increase in aggregate expenditure causes the *AD* curve to shift from AD_1 to AD_2. Equilibrium moves from point *A* to point *B*.

In the next chapter, we will complete the *IS–MP* model by incorporating the Phillips curve into the model. The complete *IS–MP* model allows us to determine the equilibrium inflation rate as well as the output gap.

Key Terms and Problems

Key Terms

IS curve, p. 296
IS–MP model, p. 296

Marginal propensity to consume
   (*MPC*), p. 298

MP curve, p. 296
Phillips curve, p. 296

10.1 ### The *IS* Curve: The Relationship between Real Interest Rates and Aggregate Expenditure

Explain how the *IS* curve represents the relationship between the real interest rate and aggregate expenditure.

Review Questions

1.1 What are the components of aggregate expenditure? Explain how equilibrium output is determined in the goods market.

1.2 What is the multiplier effect? What are the formulas for the government purchases and tax multipliers?

1.3 Explain how the *IS* curve represents equilibrium in the goods market. Why is the *IS* curve downward sloping?

1.4. Give an example of a shock that could shift the *IS* curve to the left. Give an example of a shock that could shift the *IS* curve to the right.

Problems and Applications

1.5 Draw a 45°-line diagram and identify the equilibrium level of real GDP. Use your graph to show the effect on equilibrium real GDP of each of the following:

a. Households become more pessimistic about their future incomes and decide to buy fewer new homes.

b. The federal government increases transfer payments without changing taxes.

c. The federal government launches a major program to improve border crossings, including

the Windsor–Detroit bridge, without increasing taxes.

d. Europe enters a severe recession.

1.6 The graph below shows the goods market initially in equilibrium at output Y_1. Then the aggregate expenditure function shifts from AE_1 to AE_2.

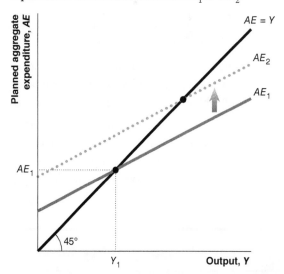

a. Give three examples of events that might have caused this shift in aggregate expenditure.

b. Carefully explain the process by which the economy will adjust to the new equilibrium.

1.7 For each of the following values of the marginal propensity to consume (*MPC*), find the value of the government purchases multiplier and the tax multiplier.

a. *MPC* = 0.80

b. *MPC* = 0.75

c. *MPC* = 0.60

1.8 Suppose that the marginal propensity to consume is 0.80.

a. If the government increases spending by $10 billion, what is the change in equilibrium real GDP?

b. If the government increases taxes by $10 billion, what is the change in equilibrium real GDP?

c. If the government increases spending by $10 billion and, to pay for the extra spending, *at the same time* increases taxes by $10 billion, what is the change in equilibrium real GDP?

1.9 [Related to Solved Problem 10.1 **on page 302**] Consider the following information on an economy. (All values are in billions of dollars.)

Consumption:	$C = \$1.2 + 0.6Y^D$
Investment:	$\bar{I} = \$2.0$
Government purchases:	$\bar{G} = \$2.1$
Net exports:	$\overline{NX} = -\$0.5$
Taxes:	$\bar{T} = 0$

a. Calculate equilibrium real GDP.

b. Now suppose that all the information given in part (a) remains the same except that taxes equal $0.5 billion. Calculate equilibrium real GDP.

c. Now suppose that potential GDP equals $15.0 billion. If equilibrium real GDP equals the amount you calculated in part (b), use the value for the government purchases multiplier

to calculate how much government purchases would have to change for equilibrium GDP to equal potential GDP (assuming that taxes remain unchanged). Use the value for the tax multiplier to calculate how much the government has to change taxes for equilibrium GDP to equal potential GDP (assuming that government purchases remain unchanged). Use a graph to illustrate your answer.

1.10 For each of the following changes, identify (1) whether there is a shift in the *IS* curve or a movement along the curve and (2) if the curve shifts, state the direction in which it shifts.

a. The real interest rate increases.

b. Firms become more pessimistic about the future profitability of investment.

c. Government spending increases.

d. Real GDP falls.

1.11 Briefly explain whether you agree with the following statement: "The *IS* curve slopes downward because a fall in the short-term nominal interest rate increases the money supply and decreases investment spending."

1.12 The government can stimulate the economy by increasing purchases or cutting taxes.

a. Why do most economists believe that the value for the government purchases multiplier is greater than the value for the tax multiplier?

b. If the government was considering a policy of increasing government purchases or cutting taxes in order to increase real GDP, would the relative sizes of the two multipliers be the only factor they should take into account? Briefly explain.

10.2 The Monetary Policy Curve: The Relationship between the Central Bank's Target Interest Rate and Output

Use the monetary policy, *MP*, curve to show how the interest rate set by the central bank helps to determine the output gap.

Review Questions

2.1 Over which interest rates does a central bank have the most control? Briefly explain.

2.2 Briefly explain the effect of each of the following on the long-term real interest rate, assuming everything else is constant:

a. The default-risk premium declines

b. Investors expect future short-term interest rates to rise

c. The expected inflation rate increases

2.3 Briefly explain how we can derive the *MP* curve from the money market model.

2.4 List factors that would cause the *MP* curve to shift up and factors that would cause the *MP* curve to shift down.

Problems and Applications

2.5 Suppose the Bank of Canada increases the target for the overnight rate.

a. Show the effect using a graph for the money market.

b. Show the effect using a graph of the *MP* curve.

2.6 For each of the following changes, identify (1) whether there is a shift in the *MP* curve or a movement along the curve, and (2) if the curve shifts, state the direction in which it shifts.

a. The Bank of Canada decreases the target overnight rate.

b. Real GDP increases.

c. Government purchases increase.

10.3 Equilibrium in the *IS–MP* Model
Use the *IS–MP* model to understand why real GDP fluctuates.

Review Questions

3.1 How does a shift to the right of the *IS* curve affect the output gap and the real interest rate?

3.2 How does a shift up of the *MP* curve affect the output gap and the real interest rate?

3.3 Briefly explain how the *AD* curve can be derived from the *IS–MP* model.

Problems and Applications

3.4 [Related to Solved Problem 10.2 **on page 314**] In the early 1990s, the Japanese economy experienced a number of shocks due to the bursting of bubbles in real estate and the stock market.

a. Use an *IS–MP* graph to show how the shocks affected the economy. Briefly explain what happened to the real interest rate, real GDP, and the output gap.

b. The Bank of Japan responded to the shocks by reducing its target interest rate. Use an *IS–MP* graph to show how this action would affect the output gap.

3.5 [Related to the Making the Connection **on page 316**] In an interview with the *Globe and Mail*, Lucas Papademos, a former prime minister of Greece and a former vice-president of the European Central Bank, stressed that the euro will survive the current crisis.

a. How would countries abandoning the euro be likely to affect Canadian economy?

b. Why might forecasters have trouble estimating the size of these effects on Canadian economy?

Brian Miller, "Why the former Greek prime minister still believes in the euro," *Globe and Mail*, October 8, 2012.

3.6 [Related to the Chapter Opener **on page 293**] In a column in the *New York Times*, the 2013 Nobel Prize winner Robert Shiller of Yale University wrote that the ideas of John Maynard Keynes "enabled us to think of the economy as something that can spontaneously fail, that the government can stimulate to get going again and make everyone better off."

a. What did Shiller mean in saying that the economy can "spontaneously fail"?

b. How can the government stimulate the economy and make everyone better off?

c. Would you expect that the government policies you described in part (b) would make people better off in just the short run or in both the short run and the long run?

Source: Robert J. Shiller, "Making the Most of Our Financial Winter," *New York Times*, October 15, 2011.

3.7 The effectiveness of monetary policy in changing output depends on the slope of the *IS* curve, which in turn depends on the responsiveness of investment and consumption to the real interest rate. The graph below shows two *IS* curves. IS_1 shows the case where households and firms do not increase consumption and investment much in response to lower interest rates; for IS_2, households and firms are more responsive to lower interest rates.

a. Show the effect on the output gap of a decrease in the target overnight rate, given each of the *IS* curves.

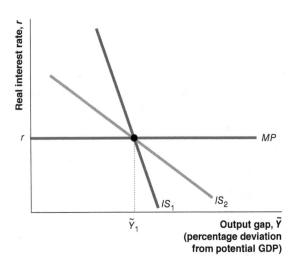

b. Along which *IS* curve is the ability of monetary policy to change real GDP greater? Briefly explain.

Data Exercises

D10.1: Using data from Statistics Canada (www5.statcan .gc.ca/cansim/home-accueil?lang=eng), Table 176-0043, analyze the relationship between the Bank rate and the long-term interest rate. The Bank of Canada and other central banks usually target short-term nominal interest rates. Figure 10.6 showed that there is a close relationship between the Bank's rate and other short-term nominal interest rates in the economy. However, what matters for spending decisions are long-term real interest rates.

a. For 1984 to the present, download monthly data on Bank rate and the Selected Government of Canada benchmark bond yields: long term. Chart the two data series on a graph.

b. Is the relationship between the Bank rate and long-term nominal interest rates as strong as the relationship between the Bank rate and other short-term nominal interest rates? Briefly explain. (Hint: Think of the term structure of interest rates.)

c. Now add the monthly interest rate of the Average residential mortgage lending rate (5-year) to your graph. Is the relationship between the Bank rate and the mortgage rate stronger or weaker than the relationship between the Bank rate and the interest rate on 10-year Selected Government of Canada

benchmark bond yields? Briefly explain. In particular, comment on the behaviour of mortgage interest rates during the Great Recession. (Hint: Think of the risk structure of interest rates.)

D10.2: [Spreadsheet Exercise] **[Related to** Making the Connection **on page 316]** Statistics Canada, in the Canadian International Merchandise Trade Database, provides data on exports of goods to various countries. Statistics Canada also provides data on nominal GDP for Canada.

a. What was the percentage decrease in exports to the United States between 2008 and 2009?

b. Suppose that the autonomous expenditure multiplier is 2. What will be the decrease in GDP for Canada in 2009 as a result of the decrease in trade with the United States?

c. Assume that the government could increase spending at the same time as exports fell. By how much should the government have increased spending to completely offset the effect of exports decline on GDP?

D10.3: Using data from the Bank of Canada website, analyze the default-risk premium. One way to calculate the default-risk premium is to look at the difference between the interest rate on corporate bonds and the interest rate on Canadian government bonds.

a. For 2003 to the present, download monthly data on the interest rate from the Bank of Canada website (www.bankofcanada.ca/rates/interest-rates/lookup-bond-yields) on long-term corporate bonds and the interest rate on long-term Government of Canada benchmark bond yields. Calculate the default-risk premium and plot the data series on a graph.

b. You can find the dates of Canadian recessions from the C.D. Howe Business Cycle Council by searching for "C.D. Howe commentary 366." What happens to the default-risk premium during recessions? Holding everything else constant, what should happen to the *MP* curve during recessions?

c. What would the Bank of Canada have to do to offset the effect of the increase in the default-risk premium on the *MP* curve?

D10.4: Using data from the Bank of Canada (www.bankofcanada.ca/rates/interest-rates/lookup-bond-yields), analyze the long-term real interest rate.

a. Download monthly data for the long-term Government of Canada benchmark bond yields and the long-term real return bonds for the last 10 years. The Fisher relationship tells us that the expected inflation rate is the nominal interest rate minus the real interest rate. Calculate the expected inflation rate over the last ten years using this data.

b. What happened to the inflationary expectations during the Great Recession?

c. What happens to the real interest rate during the Great Recession? Does this suggest that shifts in the *IS* curve or *MP* curve were responsible for the recession? Explain.

IS–LM: An Alternative Short-Run Macroeconomic Model

The *IS–MP* model we developed in this chapter assumes that the Bank of Canada uses a short-term interest rate as an instrument of monetary policy. We presented the *IS–MP* model in the chapter because many central banks today target short-term nominal interest rates. However, central banks may target economic variables other than the short-term nominal interest rate.

In this appendix, we examine the **IS–LM model**, which assumes that the central bank targets the money supply.[5] Whether the Bank of Canada targets interest rates or the money supply, it affects the economy by intervening in the money market. Therefore, the *IS–MP* model and *IS–LM* model are similar. In fact, we can derive the *MP* curve by using the *IS–LM* model, and vice versa. As a result, *you should think of the models as being complementary models rather than competing models.*

As the names suggest, both the *IS–MP* model and *IS–LM* model use the *IS* curve to show the negative relationship between the real interest rate and aggregate expenditure: Households and firms purchase fewer goods and services when interest rates are high, and they purchase more goods and services when interest rates are low. The two models differ in the way they include financial markets. While the *IS–MP* model analyzes the money market using the *MP* curve, which assumes that the Bank of Canada has a short-term nominal interest rate target, the *IS–LM* model analyzes the money market by using the *LM* curve. In the *IS–LM* model the Bank of Canada has a target level of the money stock and allows the interest rate to be determined by market forces. We start the analysis of the IS-LM model by deriving the *LM* curve. The **LM curve** shows the combinations of the interest rate and output that result in equilibrium in the money market.

Asset Market Equilibrium

To simplify, we can think of savers as choosing between two broad categories of assets: money assets, such as chequing accounts and cash, and non-money assets, such as stocks and bonds. The markets for money and non-money assets are in equilibrium when the total quantities demanded equal the total quantities supplied. Therefore, for the economy as a whole, the total demand for money balances, M_d, and non-money assets, N_d, equals total wealth, W, or

$$M_d + N_d = W. \tag{A10.1}$$

[5]*LM* refers to the combinations of r and Y for which the demand for money (L, for demand for liquidity) equals the supply of money (M, for money). *LM* is shorthand for $L = M$.

On the supply side, total wealth, W, equals the sum of the total quantity of money supplied, M_s, and the total quantity of non-money assets supplied, N_s or

$$M_s + N_s = W. \tag{A10.2}$$

In equilibrium, the quantity of an asset demanded equals the quantity of the asset supplied. Combining the equations for the demand and supply for assets, we get

$$M_d + N_d = M_s + N_s. \tag{A10.3}$$

We can combine terms to show the *excess demand* for each type of asset:

$$(M_d - M_s) + (N_d - N_s) = 0, \tag{A10.4}$$

so the excess demand for the different types of assets must sum to zero. Alternatively, we can write this equation as

$$M_d - M_s = N_s - N_d.$$

When the total quantity of money demanded exceeds the quantity supplied, or $M_d > M_s$, there is an excess demand for money. Therefore there is, at the same time, an excess supply of non-money assets: $N_s > N_d$. Similarly, if there is an excess supply of money, there is an excess demand for non-money assets. In equilibrium, asset prices adjust so that there is no excess demand or supply in either market. In other words, the left side and the right side of the equation above must both equal zero. So, the non-money market is in equilibrium if and only if the market for money assets is in equilibrium. This means it is sufficient to consider only the money market equilibrium: Any combination of real GDP and the real interest rate that results in an equilibrium in the money market also results in an equilibrium in the market for non-money assets.

Deriving the *LM* Curve

To derive the *LM* curve, we use a modified version of the money market model from Chapter 3. In that chapter, we used a nominal money demand curve and a nominal money supply curve to determine the short-term nominal interest rate. Because equilibrium in the goods market, as shown by the *IS* curve, depends on the real interest rate, we will make the simplifying assumption that (1) a change in short-term nominal interest rates results in a change in long-term nominal interest rates in the same direction and (2) the expected inflation rate is constant, so that a change in the nominal interest rate is equivalent to a change in the real interest rate. If the conditions (1) and (2) hold, the equilibrium long-term real interest rate is determined in the money market.

We will use the real money supply curve and the real money demand curve to determine the short-term real interest rate. The real money supply is the nominal money supply divided by the aggregate price level, and real money demand is the nominal money demand divided by the aggregate price level. In constructing the *LM* curve, we assume that the central bank keeps the nominal money supply constant. In Figure 10A.1, the economy begins in equilibrium at point *A*. If real GDP increases relative to potential GDP, the output gap changes from $\tilde{Y}_1$ to $\tilde{Y}_2$ and households and firms make more purchases, which shifts the demand for money in panel (a) to the right, from MD_1 to MD_2. The Bank of Canada keeps the real money supply constant, so the equilibrium real interest rate increases from r_1 to r_2. Equilibrium is now at point *B* in both panels. Therefore, as real GDP increases, the interest rate necessary to

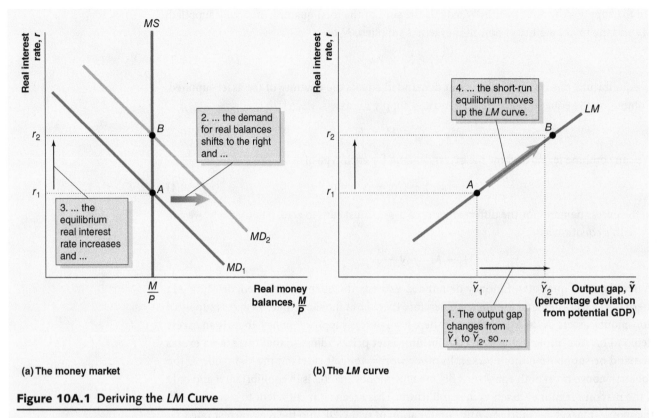

Figure 10A.1 Deriving the *LM* Curve

As real GDP increases relative to potential GDP, the output gap changes from $\tilde{Y}_1$ to $\tilde{Y}_2$ in panel (b), and households purchase more goods and services, so the real money demand curve shifts to the right and the equilibrium real interest rate increases in panel (a). As a result, the real interest rate also increases in panel (b) and the *LM* curve shows a positive relationship between the equilibrium combinations of the output gap and the real interest rate.

keep the money market in equilibrium also increases, and the *LM* curve is upward sloping, as shown in panel (b).

Shifting the *LM* Curve

The *LM* curve shows the combinations of the output gap and the real interest rate that result in equilibrium in the money market. If factors that affect the money market (other than the output gap) change, the *LM* curve will shift. Figure 10A.2 shows the effect of an increase in the money supply, or a decrease in the price level, on the *LM* curve. The economy begins in equilibrium at point *A*, with the output gap equal to $\tilde{Y}_1$ and the real interest rate equal to r_1. In panel (a), suppose that the Bank of Canada decides to increase the nominal money supply. If the price level remains constant, the real money supply increases, so the money supply curve shifts to the right, from MS_1 to MS_2. The equilibrium real interest rate decreases from r_1 to r_2, and equilibrium in the money market is at point *B*. The increase in the real money supply reduces the equilibrium real interest rate from r_1 to r_2. In panel (b), if output remains at $\tilde{Y}_1$ and the equilibrium real interest rate is now r_2, equilibrium is at point *B*. Point *B* is not on the original *LM* curve, so the *LM* curve shifts to the right (or down), from LM_1 to LM_2.

Another factor shifting the LM curve is the price level. The position of the LM curve depends on the real money supply, M^S/P. A decrease in the price level has the same effect as an increase in the money supply: Both raise the real money supply and shift the LM curve to the right, as illustrated in Figure 10A.2.

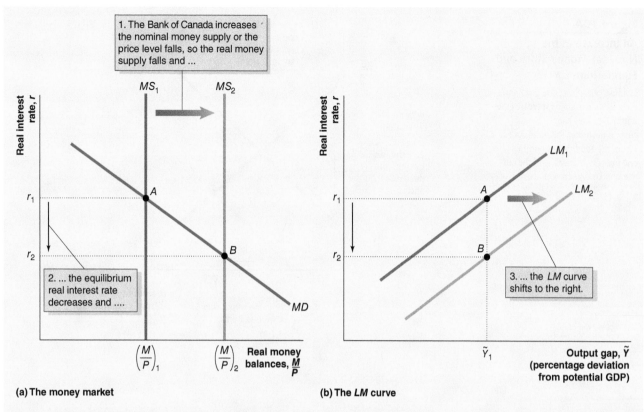

Figure 10A.2 The Effect of an Increase in the Money Supply on the *LM* Curve

In panel (a), the price level is constant. An increase in the nominal money supply shifts the real money supply curve to the right, from MS_1 to MS_2, and

lowers the real interest rate. The real interest rate is now lower for any given level of the output gap, so the *LM* curve shifts to the right in panel (b).

Equilibrium in the *IS–LM* Model

In the *IS–LM* model, the *IS* curve shows the relationship between changes in the real interest rate and the output gap, and the *LM* curve shows the effect of changes in the output gap on the real interest rate. The market for goods and services and the money market are both in equilibrium at the point where the *IS* curve intersects the *LM* curve in Figure 10A.3. For

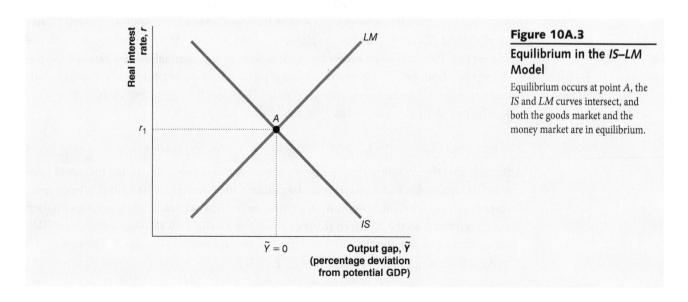

Figure 10A.3

Equilibrium in the *IS–LM* Model

Equilibrium occurs at point *A*, the *IS* and *LM* curves intersect, and both the goods market and the money market are in equilibrium.

Figure 10A.4

An Increase in the Nominal Money Stock and Equilibrium

Holding everything else constant, if the Bank of Canada increases the nominal money supply, the *LM* curve will shift to the right. As a result, the equilibrium nominal and real interest rates fall, and the output gap changes from $\tilde{Y}_1$ to $\tilde{Y}_2$.

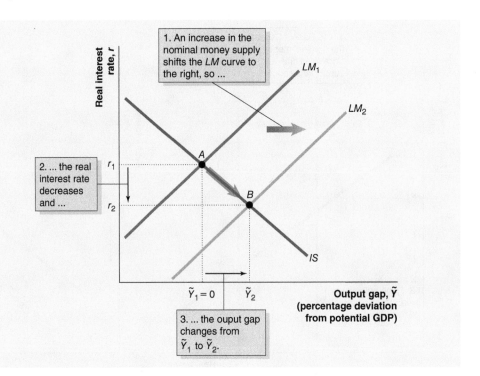

convenience we mark the equilibrium at point *A*, where the real interest rate equals the equilibrium real interest rate and real GDP equals potential GDP, so $\tilde{Y} = 0$. It is possible that in the equilibrium output is different than potential output. In that situation the equilibrium will change over time. We discuss what happens in this situation in the next chapter.

Using Monetary Policy to Increase Output

We derived the *LM* curve by assuming that the Bank of Canada kept the nominal money supply constant. Of course, the Bank of Canada can always change the nominal money supply, and we have already seen that when the nominal money supply increases, the *LM* curve shifts to the right. Figure 10A.4 shows the effect of an increase in the nominal money supply on the equilibrium output gap and the real interest rate. The economy is initially in short-run macroeconomic equilibrium at point *A*. The Bank of Canada increases the nominal money supply, so the *LM* curve shifts to the right, from LM_1 to LM_2. At the initial equilibrium real interest rate, there is now an excess supply of money, so the nominal interest rate and the real interest rate both fall. The lower real interest rate leads to higher consumption and investment, so real GDP increases relative to potential GDP, and the output gap changes from $\tilde{Y}_1$ to $\tilde{Y}_2$. The new short-run macroeconomic equilibrium is at point *B*.

A Positive Demand Shock

Suppose that the economy experiences a positive demand shock due to the increased optimism of households and firms. Figure 10A.5 shows the economy initially in short-run macroeconomic equilibrium at point *A*. A positive demand shock leads to higher consumption and investment, so the *IS* curve shifts to the right, from IS_1 to IS_2. As a result, real GDP increases relative to potential GDP, and the real interest rate also increases. The new short-run macroeconomic equilibrium is at point *B*.

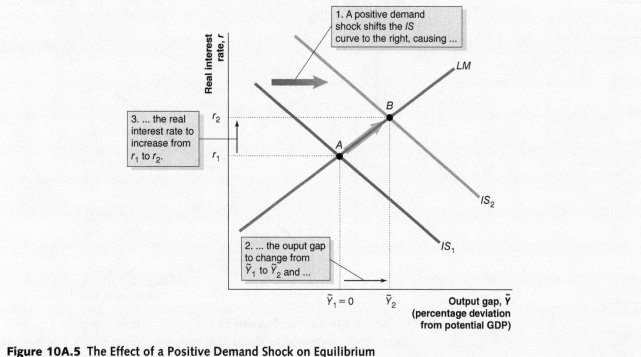

1. A positive demand shock shifts the *IS* curve to the right, causing ...

3. ... the real interest rate to increase from r_1 to r_2.

2. ... the ouput gap to change from $\tilde{Y}_1$ to $\tilde{Y}_2$ and ...

Figure 10A.5 The Effect of a Positive Demand Shock on Equilibrium

Holding everything else constant, a positive demand shock will shift the *IS* curve to the right, so the equilibrium real interest rate increases from r_1 to r_2, and the equilibrium output gap changes from $\tilde{Y}_1$ to $\tilde{Y}_2$.

Solved Problem 10A.1

Monetary Policy during the Great Depression

Nobel Laureate Milton Friedman criticized the Federal Reserve for allowing the money supply to decrease during the Great Depression. The nominal money supply in the United States decreased from $26.2 billion during the third quarter of 1929 to $18.9 billion during the first quarter of 1933—a 27% decrease in just four years. Real interest rates on corporate bonds rose from 6% to about 17%, and real GDP fell by more than 25%. The Canadian economy followed, with equally disastrous results. Real GDP equalled potential GDP at the beginning of the Great Depression, but real GDP may have been as much as 35% below potential GDP during the first quarter of 1933! In Friedman's view, the decrease in the money supply played an important role in the decrease in real GDP during the Great Depression. Is Friedman's view consistent with the *IS–LM* model?

Solving the Problem

Step 1 Review the chapter material. This problem is about applying the *IS-LM* model, so you may want to review the section "Equilibrium in the *IS–LM* Model," which begins on page 327."

Step 2 Draw a graph that shows the initial equilibrium in 1929. Draw the initial equilibrium with the *IS–LM* graph for the year 1929. Because real GDP was equal to potential GDP at the beginning of the Great Depression, make the initial equilibrium occur where the output gap equals zero. The real interest rate was about 6% in

1929, so make the initial equilibrium occur where the real interest rate is 6%. Your graph should look like this:

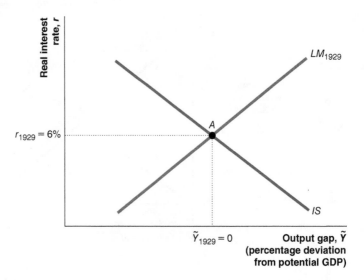

Step 3 **Determine the effect of the decrease in the nominal money supply.** The nominal money supply decreased by about 27% between 1929 and 1933. The nominal money supply is one of the factors that we hold constant when we draw the *LM* curve. Therefore, you should show the effect of the decrease in the money supply by shifting the *LM* curve to the left, from LM_{1929} to LM_{1933}. Label the new equilibrium interest rate r_{1933} and the new equilibrium output gap, $\tilde{Y}_{1933}$. Your graph should look like this:

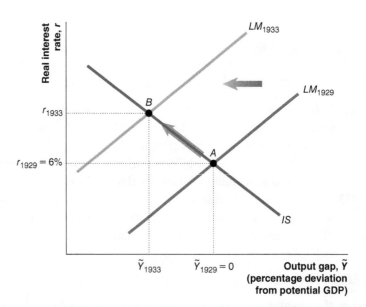

Step 4 **Compare your graph to the actual experience.** Your graph should show that a decrease in the nominal money supply will lead to higher real interest rates and lower real GDP. This is in fact what happened. The real interest rate rose from 6% to about 17%, while the output gap fell from 0% to about −35%. Therefore, the *IS–LM* model is consistent with Milton Friedman's view that the decrease in the nominal money supply contributed to the severity of the Great Depression.

See related Problem 10A.8 at the end of the appendix.

Using the LM Curve to Derive the MP Curve

When the Bank of Canada targets interest rates, it makes sense to use the *MP* curve to represent monetary policy, but when the Bank of Canada targets the money supply, the *LM* curve is more useful to represent monetary policy. Because both the *LM* and *MP* curves are derived from the money market model, the *IS–LM* model is similar to the *IS–MP* model. Holding the expected inflation rate, term structure effects, and the default-risk premium constant, the real interest rate is set by the Bank in the *IS–MP* model. If the Bank of Canada adjusts the money supply to keep the market interest rate at the target interest rate in the *IS–LM* model, then the *IS–LM* and *IS–MP* models are essentially the same model.

Consider the effect of a positive demand shock, as shown in Figure 10A.6. Before the positive demand shock, the economy is in short-run macroeconomic equilibrium at point *A*, where the real interest rate equals the Bank's target real interest rate, r^{target}, and real GDP equals potential GDP. If the Bank of Canada keeps the money supply constant, then the positive demand shock will cause the real interest rate to rise to r_2, which is above the target real interest rate, and the economy will be in short-run macroeconomic equilibrium at point *B*. If, on the other hand, the Bank of Canada targets the real interest rate, the money supply and the *LM* curve must adjust to keep the real interest rate at r^{target}. To maintain the target real interest rate, the Bank of Canada must increase the money supply, shifting the *LM* curve to the right, from LM_1 to LM_2 so that the economy ends up at r^{target}. If the Bank of Canada acts quickly enough, the real interest rate never increases at all, and the economy moves directly from point *A* to point *C*. If we connect those two points, we have a horizontal line at the target real interest rate, which we have previously called the *MP* curve.

We can see that the *LM* and *MP* curves are really not very different. Using the *LM* curve is a convenient way to represent monetary policy when the Bank of Canada targets the money supply. Using the *MP* curve is a convenient way to represent monetary policy when the Bank of Canada targets the interest rate, as it has been doing in recent years.

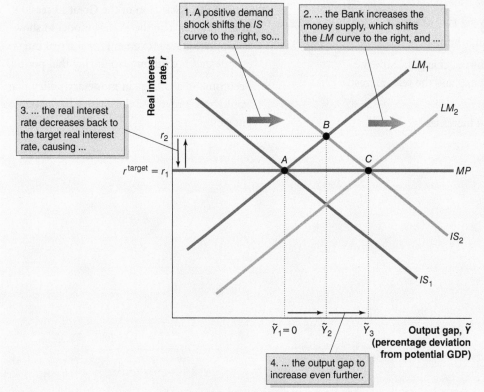

Figure 10A.6

Using the LM Curve to Derive the MP Curve

If the Bank of Canada targets the real interest rate, the money supply and the *LM* curve must adjust to keep the real interest rate equal to the target real interest rate. Therefore, in response to a positive demand shock, the Bank of Canada must increase the money supply, which shifts the *LM* curve to the right and reduces the real interest rate back to the target real interest rate.

Key Terms and Problems

Key Terms

IS–LM model, p. 324
LM curve, p. 324

Review Questions

10A.1: What is the difference between how the *IS–LM* and the *IS–MP* models analyze the money market?

10A.2: How is equilibrium in the money market related to equilibrium in the market for non-money assets?

10A.3: Explain how the *LM* curve represents equilibrium in the money market. How does an increase in the money supply affect the *LM* curve and equilibrium in the *IS–LM* model?

10A.4: How can the *MP* curve be derived from the *IS–LM* model?

Problems and Applications

10A.5: Some time ago, the Bank of Canada targeted the money supply. More recently, the Bank of Canada has targeted the interest rate. Use the money market model to explain why the Bank of Canada cannot target the money supply and the real interest rate at the same time.

10A.6: Draw a graph showing the *IS–LM* model and identify the initial equilibrium.

  a. For each of the following changes, show the effect on the output gap and the real interest rate.

   i. The government increases taxes.

   ii. The Bank of Canada decreases the money supply.

   iii. Consumers experience an increase in wealth due to increases in stock prices.

  b. How would your answers to part (a) be different if you were using the *IS–MP* model?

10A.7: According to an article in *The Economist* magazine the *IS-LM* model's "main virtue is that it brings together both the real and financial parts of the economy." Briefly explain how the *IS-LM* model brings together the real and financial parts of the economy. Why would doing so be a virtue in a macroeconomic model?
Source: "A Working Model," *The Economist*, August 11, 2005.

10A.8: [Related to Solved Problem 10A.1 **on page 329**]

  This appendix demonstrates why the *IS–LM* model accurately represents movements in the real interest rate and the output gap during the Great Depression.

  a. Review the discussion of the Great Recession in the chapter. Use the *IS–LM* model to show the approximate movements of the real interest rate and the output gap during that period.

  b. Recommend a change in monetary policy that would have prevented the change in the output gap.

The *IS–MP* Model: Adding Inflation and the Open Economy

Where's the Inflation?

What if Canada began to experience higher inflation—not the 2% average inflation rate of 2000–14, but 5% or 6%? How would this higher inflation rate affect you? We have seen that the effects of *anticipated* inflation are fairly small (see Chapter 4). If you and your employer both expect 6% inflation, that rate is likely to be reflected in your salary increases. It will also be reflected in the interest rates on your car loan and your student loans. But what if people expect 2% inflation but the inflation rate turns out to actually be 6%? Then the nominal salary your employer agreed to pay you for the year won't keep up with the increase in prices—a loss for you. But you will probably be paying a lower real interest rate on your loans—a gain for you. Unexpected changes in the inflation rate can arbitrarily create winners and losers, which is a key reason that economists, businesses, and policymakers spend considerable time and effort trying to forecast inflation.

But inflation is not easy to forecast. In mid-2009, just as the Great Recession was ending, several economists, in particular in the United States, worried that many countries would soon enter a period of high inflation. Simon Johnson, a former chief economist at the International Monetary Fund, maintained, "The large increase in credit from the Federal Reserve can potentially push up prices. . . . The real danger . . . is that the Fed will lose control over expectations, pushing inflation above 5 percent." Allan Meltzer, an economist at Carnegie Mellon University, worried, "If President Obama and the Fed continue down their current path, we could see a repeat of those dreadful inflationary years [of the 1970s]." What worried these and other economists was that, in responding to the financial crisis and the Great Recession, some central banks

Continued on next page

had greatly increased the monetary base. The monetary base had been increasing at unprecedented pace in the United States and the Eurozone. For example, just prior to the collapse of Lehman Brothers the U.S. monetary base was $850 billion and was increasing at a rate of 2% per year. It then doubled in five months by January 2009, growing around 25% *per month in October and November 2008.* The increases in the money supply were smaller but still substantial. In Canada the problem was not as acute since the Canadian monetary base increased at a slower pace.

Recall that the quantity equation indicates that increases in the money supply should result in increases in the inflation rate. While the correlation between the rate of growth of the money supply and the inflation rate is strong in the long run, it can be weak in the short run. During the years from the beginning of the recession through 2012, the link was quite weak. The adjacent figure shows values for the average annual growth rate of the broad money supply and inflation for Canada, the Eurozone, and the United States. In all cases, the money supply grew much faster than prices. But the forecasts of rapid inflation turned out to be incorrect. By the fall of 2014, the problem politicians were worried about was deflation. In October 2014 prices were falling in Italy, Spain, Sweden, and Switzerland; inflation was only 0.3% in the Eurozone and less than 2% in almost all developed countries.

So the puzzle is why, despite huge increases in high-powered money, inflation did not take off and the fears

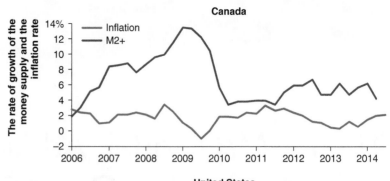

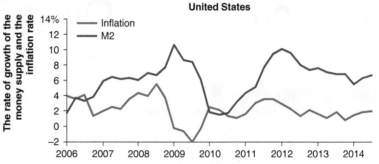

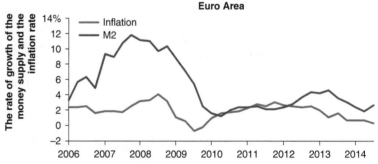

of inflation were replaced by the fears of deflation. To solve the puzzle we need to complete the *IS–MP* model by incorporating the Phillips curve.

See related Problem 1.8 at the end of the chapter.

Sources: Simon Johnson, "Inflation Fears," *New York Times*, May 28, 2009; "Quantitative schemes at the Bank of Canada," *National Post*, www .financialpost.com/story.html?id=fd684b1e-d61f-4525-8549-3a0e0774fd1c&k=57477; Alan H. Meltzer, "Inflation Nation", *New York Times*, May 4, 2009; Bank of Canada; Bank of England; and Federal Reserve.

Introduction

In the previous chapter, we introduced the *IS–MP* model, which allows us to determine the short-run equilibrium of the real interest rate and the output gap. We saw how movements in aggregate expenditure are the key reason real GDP fluctuates relative to potential GDP during the business cycle. In developing the *IS–MP* model, we made the assumption that we were dealing with a short enough period of time that we could consider the price level to be constant. We also did not explicitly take into account the effects of Canada being an open economy. In this chapter, we extend the *IS–MP* model by looking at how changes in the output gap affect the inflation rate and by applying the model to an open economy.

We begin by adding the Phillips curve to the *IS–MP* model. The Phillips curve shows the relationship between the inflation rate and the output gap. We look at the development of the Phillips curve to its current form and the role of expectations in determining the rate of inflation. In Section 11.2 we use our model to analyze two events: the Great Recession and the rapid increase in oil prices in 2007–08. In the last section we extend the *IS–MP* model to the open economy. We determine equilibrium with both flexible and fixed exchange rates, and analyze the effect of monetary policy in both exchange rate regimes.

The *IS–MP* Model and the Phillips Curve

Discovery of the Traditional Phillips Curve Relationship and Initial Interpretation

11.1

Learning Objective

Understand the role of the Phillips curve in the *IS–MP* model.

The traditional Phillips curve, which shows the short-term relationship between the unemployment rate and inflation, is named after the New Zealand economist A. W. H. Phillips. In 1968 Phillips published the first systematic study of the relationship between the state of the economy and the inflation rate.[1] Phillips plotted data on the growth rate of nominal wages and the unemployment rate in the United Kingdom and drew a curve showing their average relationship. The relationship was downward sloping: When the unemployment rate was low, nominal wages increased fast; when the unemployment rate was high, nominal wages increased slowly. Generally, when wages increase, so do prices. So Phillips's results were interpreted as showing a tendency for the inflation rate to increase as the unemployment rate decreases. Since that time, the relationship between the unemployment rate and the inflation rate has been called the *Phillips curve*. The equation for the traditional Phillips curve was

$$\pi_t = A - \alpha u_t.$$

Here π_t denotes the inflation rate at time t, u_t denotes the rate of unemployment; A is a constant; and α (alpha) shows the relationship between unemployment and inflation: A drop in the unemployment rate by 1% is associated with an increase in inflation by α%.

Economists and policymakers initially viewed the traditional Phillips curve as a *structural relationship*. A structural relationship is a relationship that depends on the basic behaviour of households and firms and remains unchanged over long periods. An example of a structural relationship is the demand curve for apples, which is downward sloping. If the Phillips curve is a structural relationship, policymakers faced a trade-off between inflation and unemployment that will not change over time. So the central bank had a choice of high inflation and low unemployment, or low inflation and high unemployment. Economists thought the central bank could *permanently* reduce the unemployment rate by permitting higher inflation rate. Similarly, the central bank could *permanently* reduce the inflation rate if it were willing to accept a higher unemployment rate.

Figure 11.1 shows the traditional Phillips curve. Each point on the curve represents a combination of the inflation rate and the unemployment rate that might be observed in a particular year. The curve in Figure 11.1 is drawn with $A = 8$ and $\alpha = 1$. With these parameters, a 1% decrease in the unemployment is associated with 1% higher inflation. For example, the central bank can choose point A, which represents the combination of a 3% unemployment rate and a 5% inflation rate in one year, or point B, which represents the combination of a 6% unemployment rate and a 2% inflation rate in another year.

The explanation of the traditional Phillips curve relationship was straightforward. When unemployment is low, there is a shortage of workers. In wage negotiations, workers' position is strong and firms' position is weak. So workers manage to negotiate large wage increases.

[1]A. W. H. Phillips, "The Relationship between Unemployment and the Rate of Change of Money Wages in the United Kingdom 1861–1957," *Economica* 25, no. 100 (1958): 283–299.

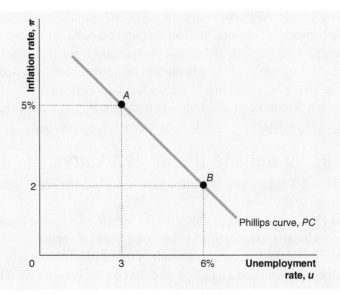

Figure 11.1

The Traditional Phillips Curve

The traditional Phillips curve shows an inverse relationship between the inflation rate and the unemployment rate.

Also, to fill vacancies, firms have to offer higher wages. Wages are a large component of costs and when wages increase fast, so do prices and the inflation rate is high. Conversely, when unemployment is high, there is a shortage of jobs. Workers' position is weak and firms' position is strong. So wage negotiations lead to small wage increases. Also, there are few vacancies and firms can fill them without raising wages much. With moderate wage increases, prices increase little and the inflation rate is low.

Modern Phillips Curve

The Phillips Curve and Expected Inflation The Phillips curve is not, however, a structural relationship. As Nobel Laureates Milton Friedman and Edmund Phelps pointed out in 1968, the relationship depends on the expected inflation rate.[2] They argued that, for any given rate of unemployment, the higher is the expected inflation rate, the higher is actual inflation. To understand the effect of expected inflation on the Phillips curve, consider an economy in which the rate of unemployment is such that the inflation rate is constant. This rate is called the natural unemployment rate; we return to it below. Consider the wage and price setting at Ed's Manufacturing Company. Assume that expected inflation is 2% per year and nominal wages increase by 3% per year, so that the real wage increases by 1% per year. (The real wage may be rising because of rising productivity).

What happens if the expected rate of inflation increases to 5% per year? Workers and Ed's Manufacturing Company care about the real wage, not the nominal wage. The purchasing power of workers' income depends on real wages. For the firm, the real wage is equal to the marginal product of labour. With 5% expected inflation, workers now demand a nominal wage increase of 6%. Ed's Manufacturing will agree, because it will now increase prices by 5%. A wage increase of 6% with a 5% increase in prices means the real wage increases by 1%, just as before. There is nothing unique about Ed's Manufacturing, and so our reasoning applies to other firms as well. So firms increase prices by 5% and the *actual* rate of inflation

---

[2]Milton Friedman, "The Role of Monetary Policy," *American Economic Review* 58, no. 1 (1968): 1–17; Edmund Phelps, "Money–Wage Dynamics and Labor Market Equilibrium," *Journal of Political Economy* 76, no. 4, part 2 (1968): 678–711.

increases, even though the unemployment rate remains unchanged. Note that the increase in actual inflation is the same amount as the increase in expected inflation.

Supply Shocks In the 1970s in most developed countries both the rate of inflation *and* the unemployment rate increased at the same time. In Canada, the average unemployment rate in 1966 was 3.6% and the inflation rate, as measured by changes in the consumer price index (CPI), was 3% in January 1966. By August 1980, the unemployment rate increased to 7.6% and the inflation rate increased to 10.9%. In the United States, in 1966 the unemployment rate was 4% and the inflation rate was 1.9%. By April 1980, the unemployment rate increased to 6.9% and the inflation rate increased to 14.6%. So, in Canada the unemployment rate increased by 4% and the inflation rate increased by 7.9% while the United States the unemployment rate increased by 2.9% and the inflation rate increased by 12.7%. These changes of unemployment and inflation could not be reconciled with the traditional Phillips curve. Economists have concluded that the position of the Phillips curve can shift over time in response to *supply shocks*. A supply shock is a sudden change in supply or in costs that affects prices and the rate of inflation. Examples of negative supply shocks include an increase in the price of oil or a particularly bad crop. When the price of oil increases, the costs of production rise and so firms increase prices at a higher rate. A bad crop increases the cost of food; in both cases the inflation rate increases. An example of a positive supply shock is a rapid increase in productivity. It allows firms to produce the same amount as before with less inputs (or produce a larger amount with the same inputs), reducing production costs. Competition leads to smaller price increases and a reduction in the rate of inflation. The supply shock in 1970s, which resulted in rapid increase in inflation, was the tenfold increase in the price of oil between 1972 and 1981. The resulting increase in production costs led firms to increase prices at a faster rate than in the past, despite the fact that unemployment was increasing.

Friedman's and Phelps's criticism of the theory behind the Phillips curve and the actual experience during the 1970s convinced economists that the Phillips curve did not represent a stable relationship. The position of the Phillips curve depends on two factors: the expected rate of inflation and supply shocks. Once we account for these two factors, the Phillips curve remains a useful tool for explaining the *short-run* trade-off between the unemployment rate and the inflation rate.

The best way to analyze the effect of changes in the unemployment rate on the inflation rate is by looking at the gap between the current unemployment rate and the unemployment rate when the economy is at full employment, or the *natural rate of unemployment*. The gap between the current rate of unemployment and the natural rate equals *cyclical unemployment* because it represents unemployment caused by a business cycle recession. When (a) the current unemployment rate equals the natural rate, (b) expectations of inflation do not change, and (c) there are no supply shocks, the inflation rate typically does not change. When the current unemployment rate is greater than the natural rate, some workers have trouble finding jobs, so wage increases will be limited, as will increases in firms' costs of production. As a result, the inflation rate will be low. When the current unemployment rate is less than the natural rate of unemployment, labour market conditions will be tight, and wages are likely to increase fast, rapidly pushing up firms' costs of production. With costs rising fast, inflation will be high.

We can now write the equation for the modern Phillips curve. There are three changes compared to the traditional version. First, and most important, we include the expected inflation rate. Second, we include (in a very simple way) supply shocks. Third, we write the equation in terms of difference between the unemployment rate and the natural unemployment rate. Taking all these factors into account gives us the following equation for the Phillips curve:

$$\pi_t = \pi_t^e - \alpha(u_t - u^N) - s_t, \tag{11.1}$$

where

π_t = current inflation rate

π_t^e = expected inflation rate

u_t = current unemployment rate

u^N = natural rate of unemployment

s_t = variable that represents the effects of a supply shock. It has a negative value for a negative supply shock, which raises inflation for a given level of unemployment and a positive value for a positive supply shock, which lowers inflation for a given level of unemployment.

α = constant that represents how much the gap between the current rate of unemployment and the natural rate affects the inflation rate.

The coefficient on the expected inflation rate is one: a one percent increase in the expected inflation rate raises the actual inflation rate by one percent. We will call a supply shock negative when it increases the inflation rate, and positive when it reduces the inflation rate. The equation tells us that an increase in expected inflation or a negative supply shock, such as an increase in oil prices, will shift the Phillips curve up, while a decrease in expected inflation or a positive supply shock, such as an increase in the growth rate of productivity, will shift the Phillips curve down.

Figure 11.2 shows the Phillips curve as well as its shifts associated with supply shocks and changes in expected inflation. The position of the Phillips curve is determined by the expected inflation rate and supply shock. As you can see from the Phillips curve equation (11.1), it intersects the vertical line $u = u^N$ at the point where the inflation rate, given by the vertical coordinate, is $\pi_t^e - s_t$. For example, in Figure 11.2 PC_1 is drawn for the case when the expected inflation is 2% and the supply shock is zero. So PC_1 intersects the vertical line $u = u^N$ at the point A, where inflation equals 2%.

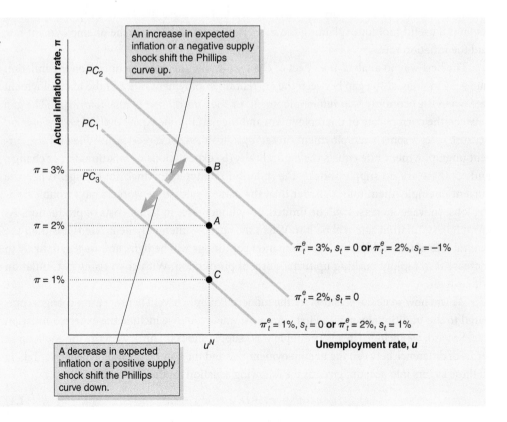

Figure 11.2

Shifts of the Phillips Curve

When unemployment is equal to the natural rate, u^N, the inflation rate is equal to the sum of expected inflation and supply shock. An increase in expected inflation or a negative supply shock shifts the Phillips curve up, so the inflation rate is now higher for any given unemployment rate. A decrease in expected inflation or a positive supply shock shifts the Phillips curve down, so the inflation rate is now lower for any given unemployment rate.

An increase in the expected inflation rate to 3% or a negative supply shock equal −1% (which raises inflation by 1%) shifts the Phillips curve up by 1%, to PC_2. PC_2 intersects the vertical line $u = u^N$ at the point B, where the inflation rate equals 3%. A decrease in the expected inflation rate to 1% or a positive supply shock equal 1% (which lowers inflation by 1%) shifts the Phillips curve down by 1%, to PC_3, which intersects the vertical line $u = u^N$ at the point C, where the inflation rate equals 1%.

What might cause the expected rate of inflation to change? Typically, households and firms adjust their expectations of inflation as they experience persistent rates of actual inflation that are above, or below, the rates they had expected. The experience of the Canadian economy during the 1960s and 1970s provides an example of this point. Inflation during the 1960s averaged about 2% per year but accelerated to 5% per year from 1970 to 1973 and to 8.5% per year from 1974 to 1979. These persistently high rates of inflation led households and firms to revise upward their expectations of inflation, and the Phillips curve shifted up. Notice that once the Phillips curve has shifted up, the economy is worse off. This is because every unemployment rate becomes associated with a higher inflation rate.

The decline in the inflation rate during the 1980s provides an example of how a decrease in expected inflation can lead to lower inflation. In 1981 the Bank of Canada followed the U.S. anti-inflationary policy. When the economy experienced the severe recession of 1981–82, the inflation rate declined sharply from over 12% in 1981 to 4% in 1984. From 1983 to 1986, the inflation rate averaged 4.6% per year, which was less than half of its average value in the previous four years. Accordingly, households and firms lowered their expectations of future inflation, and the Phillips curve shifted down. Notice that once the Phillips curve has shifted down, the economy is better off. This is because every unemployment rate becomes associated with a lower inflation rate.

Okun's Law, the Output Gap, and the Phillips Curve

We will now integrate the Phillips curve into the *IS–MP* model. The Phillips curve shows the short-run relationship between the inflation rate and the unemployment rate. In the *IS–MP* model, however, the variable on the horizontal axis is the output gap: the percentage difference between the level of output and potential output, $\widetilde{Y}_t = (Y_t - Y^P)/Y^P$. We therefore need to develop the short-run relationship between inflation rate and output gap. To do this, we use Okun's law. Recall from Chapter 9 that Okun's law is a relationship between the output gap, $\widetilde{Y}_t$, and the gap between the current and natural rates of unemployment. This gap is equal to cyclical unemployment:

$$u_t - u^N = -h\widetilde{Y}_t, \tag{11.2}$$

where $\widetilde{Y}_t = (Y_t - Y^P)/Y^P$ is the output gap and h shows the effect of a 1% increase in the output gap on the difference between the current rate of unemployment and the natural rate.

According to Okun's law, when the output gap is equal to zero, i.e., when output is equal to potential output, the unemployment rate is equal to the natural unemployment rate and the cyclical unemployment rate is zero. When output is above potential, $Y > Y^P$, then the unemployment rate is lower than the natural rate: $u < u^N$. When output is below potential, $Y < Y^P$, then the unemployment rate exceeds the natural rate: $u > u^N$. If the constant h is, for example, 0.5, it means that when output is 1% below potential, the unemployment rate is 0.5% above the natural unemployment rate.

We can substitute the Okun's law relationship (11.2) into the equation for the Phillips curve (11.1) to obtain the Phillips curve in terms of the output gap:

$$\pi_t = \pi_t^e + \alpha h \widetilde{Y}_t - s_t. \tag{11.3}$$

The coefficient αh in the equation represents the effect of a change in the output gap on the inflation rate. It is the product of the Okun's law coefficient, h, times the constant, α, that represents the effect on the inflation rate of the gap between current rate of unemployment and the natural rate. As before, the term π_t^e shows the effect of the expected inflation rate on the current inflation rate.

The Effect of Demand Shocks on Inflation Inflation often increases during expansions. For example, real GDP was about equal to potential GDP in 1985 but, by 1989, it was 3.3% above potential. The inflation rate increased from 4% in 1985 to 5% in 1989. Similarly, inflation often decreases during recessions, as happened during 1990–92. The output gap was 3.3% in 1989 and −3.9% in 1992, while the inflation rate fell from 5.3% in March 1990 to 1.7% in April 1992. These two experiences illustrate that when real GDP increases relative to potential GDP during economic expansions, the inflation rate typically increases and when real GDP falls relative to potential GDP during recessions, the inflation rate typically decreases.

The Effect of Supply Shocks on Inflation Negative supply shocks raise the inflation rate. Negative supply shocks raise firms' costs of production, which firms typically pass along as increases in the prices of the goods they sell. Through this mechanism, a negative supply shock can increase the inflation rate. For example, in many countries the inflation rate increased in the summer of 2008 due to a boom in oil prices. Similarly, increases in productivity represent positive supply shocks that can reduce firms' costs and decrease the inflation rate. Productivity growth reduces costs per unit of output, so firms can produce more goods and services with the same number of workers. For example, improvements in information technology help firms produce more goods and services without incurring higher costs. Competition among firms ensures that these cost reductions are passed along to consumers in the form of lower prices.

If the recession is caused by a strong negative supply shock, inflation can rise even in a recession. In the United States, the inflation actually increased during the 1973–75, 1980, and 1990–91 recessions. In Canada, however, the inflation rate fell during all post-war recessions with the exception of the mild 1980 recession, when it increased slightly from 9.7% in January to 10% in June.

Stagflation A combination of high inflation and recession or very slow output growth, usually resulting from a supply shock.

An example illustrates the effects of supply shocks. Oil prices tripled in 1973–74. Between 1973 and 1974 in both Canada and the United States the rate of output growth fell while the inflation rate increased. Canada, the United States, and many other countries were experiencing **stagflation**, which is a combination of high inflation and either recession or a very slow output growth. Stagflation is usually the result of a negative supply shock. The tripling of the price of oil during 1973–74 significantly increased firms' costs of production and caused the inflation rate to increase, even though real GDP fell relative to potential GDP.

Rational expectations The assumption that people make forecasts of future values of a variable using all available information and their expectations equal optimal forecasts, given all available information.

Expectations How do households and firms form their expectations of future inflation rates? Many economists assume that people have **rational expectations**. Under the rational expectations assumption, people forecast future values of a variable using all available information, and their expectations are optimal forecasts given the available information. In an economic model, the rational expectation of a variable is equal to the mathematical expected value of the variable. We will return to rational expectations later in the book when we discuss monetary policy in more detail. For now, we will use a simpler concept of **adaptive expectations**, which is the assumption that people make forecasts of future values of a variable using only past values of the variable. Clearly, adaptive expectations are not rational, as they exclude information apart from the past value of the forecasted variable. To see the difference, consider a simple example. In 1988 the new governor of the Bank of Canada, John Crow, announced a change in monetary policy. The new goal of monetary policy became price stability. With adaptive expectations, this announcement was ignored since the past values of inflation were not affected. With rational expectations, this announcement would be taken into account. Its effect on the rational expectation of inflation would depend on how credible the promise is and on many other factors, but in general it would affect expectations.

Adaptive expectations The assumption that people make forecasts of future values of a variable using only past values of the variable.

For our purposes in this chapter, the adaptive expectations assumption is sufficient. It greatly simplifies the analysis and does not affect results. The simplest form of adaptive expectations assumes that people expect that the value of a variable, such as the inflation rate, will be the same this year as it was last year. For example, if the inflation rate in 2013 was 0.9%, with adaptive expectations, households and firms would expect an inflation rate of 0.9% for 2014. An equation for this simplest form of adaptive expectations is

$$\pi_t^e = \pi_{t-1}. \tag{11.4}$$

This equation states that the expected inflation rate for the current year equals the actual inflation rate for the previous year. Using this simple form of adaptive expectations, we can rewrite the Phillips curve as

$$\pi_t = \pi_{t-1} + \alpha h \widetilde{Y}_t - s_t. \tag{11.5}$$

Equilibrium in the *IS–MP* Model with a Phillips Curve

We now characterize the equilibrium in our model. Since the model is short run, it is a short-run equilibrium. The model consists of the *IS–MP* curves and the Phillips curve. In equilibrium three conditions have to be met:

1. The *IS* and *MP* curves intersect at potential output.
2. The inflation rate is constant: $\pi_t = \pi_{t-1}$.
3. The expected inflation rate is equal to the actual inflation rate $\pi_t^e = \pi_t$.

Why do these conditions have to be met in equilibrium? To answer this question we ask what would happen if any one of the conditions is not met. 1) If the *IS* and *MP* curves do not intersect at potential output, inflation will change. 2) If the inflation rate changes so does the expected inflation rate and the Phillips curve will shift. 3) Finally, why should the expected inflation rate equal the actual rate in equilibrium? Consider what will happen if the households and firms expect inflation that is different from the actual inflation rate. As the information about the inflation rate is easily available, households and firms will notice that their expectations are incorrect. They will then change expectations and the Phillips curve will shift. None of these situations would be an equilibrium so, for the economy to be in equilibrium, all three conditions have to be met. Note that, if all three conditions are met, the economy is in equilibrium.

Movement along an Existing Phillips Curve

In Figure 11.3 we draw the Phillips curve using the simple form of adaptive expectations (equation (11.4)). We start in period 1, and assume that there are no supply shocks, so $s_1 = 0$. At point A, real GDP equals potential GDP, so $\widetilde{Y}_1 = 0$. Since the output gap is zero, the inflation rate is constant: $\pi_1 = \pi_0$. As long as the expected inflation rate equals the actual inflation rate: $\pi_1^e = \pi_1$, point A represents the short-run equilibrium.

Now suppose that a positive demand shock, such as an increase in spending on residential construction, causes real GDP to increase above potential GDP and, therefore, the output gap changes from $\widetilde{Y}_1 = 0$ to $\widetilde{Y}_2 > 0$. As firms produce beyond their normal capacity, wages and other production costs rise. Firms pass higher costs on to consumers by increasing prices. In the equation for the Phillips curve, the term $\alpha h \widetilde{Y}_2$ is greater than zero, so in the next period the inflation rate rises from π_1 to π_2 and short-run equilibrium moves from point A to point B. This means we move along the existing Phillips curve up and to the right. Of course, a change in output gap, $\widetilde{Y}$, or in the inflation rate, π, must mean movement along a given Phillips curve since both variables are on an axis in Figure 11.3.

Figure 11.3

An Increase in the Output Gap Increases the Inflation Rate

As real GDP increases relative to potential GDP, firms start to run into capacity constraints, and wages and other production costs increase. Firms pass along the higher costs to consumers in the form of higher prices, so the inflation rate increases and short-run equilibrium moves from point *A* to point *B*.

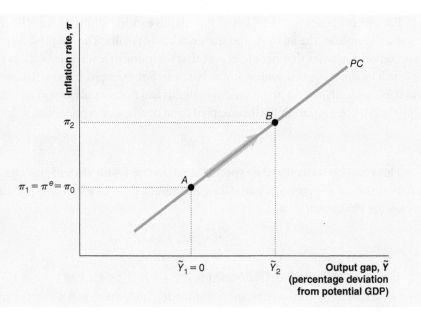

Shifts of the Phillips Curve

Changes in the expected inflation rate, and supply shocks, cause the Phillips curve to shift, as illustrated in Figure 11.4.

We first show the effect of a change in expected inflation on the Phillips curve. In panel (a), the economy is initially at point *A*, where real GDP equals potential GDP, so $\tilde{Y} = 0$ and we assume that there are no supply shocks, so $s_t = 0$. As a result, $\pi_1 = \pi_1^e$. Now suppose that the expected inflation rate decreases so that $\pi_2^e < \pi_1^e$ while the output gap remains equal to 0. In this case, since $\pi_2 = \pi_2^e + \alpha h \tilde{Y}_2 - s_2$, the new inflation rate equals $\pi_2 = \pi_2^e$, and the economy is at point *B*. Point *B* is clearly not on the original Phillips curve, so the Phillips curve must have shifted down, from PC_1 to PC_2.

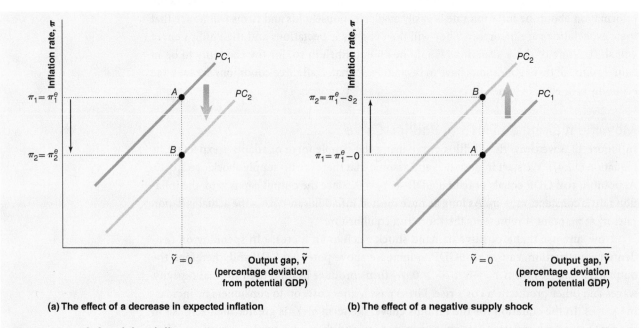

(a) The effect of a decrease in expected inflation

(b) The effect of a negative supply shock

Figure 11.4 Shifts of the Phillips Curve

In panel (a), a decrease in expected inflation shifts the Phillips curve down.

In panel (b), a negative supply shock, such as an increase in the price of oil, shifts the Phillips curve up.

Panel (b) shows the effect of an increase in oil prices that increases the cost per unit of output. The economy starts at point A, where the output gap equals 0. The initial supply shock is zero, so $s_1 = 0$ and $\pi_1 = \pi_1^e - 0$. As a result of the negative supply shock, $s_2 < 0$ and the inflation rate rises to $\pi_2 = \pi_1^e - s_2$. (Recall that because s is preceded by a negative sign in the equation for the Phillips curve, when s takes on a *negative* value, the Phillips curve shifts up.) The economy is now at point B, which is not on the original Phillips curve. The Phillips curve has shifted up, from PC_1 to PC_2.

Making the Connection

Lots of Money but Not Much Inflation Following the Great Recession

We saw in the chapter opener that in 2009, as the recession ended, a number of economists predicted that the inflation rate would increase substantially. A few economists even predicted that several countries might experience one of their worst ever peacetime inflations. This is because, to stimulate the economy, several central banks greatly increased the monetary base. The figure below shows the monetary base in the United States, the United Kingdom, and in Canada since January 2007 (with the value in January 2007 set equal to 100). In the year after the collapse of Lehman Brothers on September 15, 2008, the monetary base in the United States and in the United Kingdom more than doubled. By September 2014 it increased by 400% in the United States and 450% in the United Kingdom. For comparison, the figure also shows money base in Canada, where it increased only 40% over this time. Since the increase in the money supply in Canada was much smaller, the explosion in future inflation was a much smaller concern in Canada than in the United Kingdom and the United States.

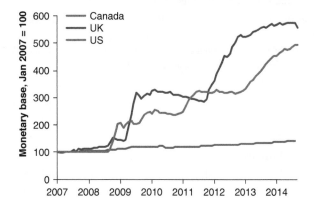

Not surprisingly, many economists were concerned. For instance, in assessing the effects of the Federal Reserve's policies in the United States, Arthur Laffer argued: "To date what's happened is potentially far more inflationary than were the monetary policies of the 1970s, when the prime interest rate peaked at 21.5% and inflation peaked in the low double digits." Clearly, the increase in the monetary base in the United States and in the United Kingdom should, in normal times, lead to runaway inflation. In fact, though, inflation did not increase but rather decreased. Between 2011 and 2014 the monetary base in the United Kingdom almost doubled but the inflation rate declined from 5% to 2%. By September 2014, the inflation rate was 1.7% in the United Kingdom, 1.8% in the United States, and 1.9% in Canada.

Given that the monetary base had soared, why didn't the inflation rate take off as these economists had predicted? The answer is partly that the increases in the monetary base resulted in much smaller-than-expected increases in the money supply. More importantly, though, the recovery from the recession was slow. The United States and the United Kingdom suffered from a large output gap and high rates of unemployment through 2013.

Recall that when the central bank engages in open market operations it purchases financial securities, such as Treasury bills (see Chapter 4). The payment for these securities ends up either as bank reserves or as currency in circulation. The monetary base is the sum of bank reserves plus currency. So if, for example, the central bank purchases $1 billion in Treasury bills, the monetary base will also increase by $1 billion. We can determine the value of the money supply by multiplying the value for the monetary base by the money multiplier (see Chapter 4). When the Great Recession started, in many countries the value of the multiplier decreased greatly, sometimes falling below 1. In effect, the money multiplier had become a money *divisor* so that a $1 billion increase in the monetary base resulted in a less than $1 billion increase in the money supply. The explanation for the decline in the value of the money multiplier is that banks were worried about the creditworthiness of borrowers and deterred by the low interest rates on loans. So, instead of lending the extra funds, they piled up huge reserves while cutting back on their loans.

Still, despite the low value of the money multiplier, if the economy had been in a strong expansion, the increases in the money supply would have been large enough to have eventually resulted in large increases in the inflation rate. But the expansion was weak and the output gap remained large. With real GDP far below potential GDP, there was little pressure for wages and other costs to increase, which helped to keep the inflation rate low. As an article in *The Economist* magazine put it, "On at least some measurements, both inflation and inflation expectations are behaving *exactly* as one would expect given a persistent, large output gap."

The question remained, however, about what would happen to inflation once the economy entered a stronger expansion. The large reserves held by banks had the potential to result in large increases in the money supply once banks resumed lending at more normal levels. Economists disagreed over whether central banks would be able to successfully implement a strategy to reduce the monetary base and avoid triggering inflation, or whether the predictions that inflation would accelerate would eventually prove correct.

Sources: Arthur B. Laffer, "Get Ready for Inflation and Higher Interest Rates," *The Wall Street Journal*, June 11, 2009; "What's Inflation Telling Us About the Output Gap?" *The Economist*, March 20, 2012; and Statistics Canada, CANSIM Table 176-0025, Bank of England, Federal Reserve.

See related Problem 1.9 at the end of the chapter.

Using Monetary Policy to Fight a Recession

In this section, we combine the *IS* and *MP* curves and the Phillips curve to explain how monetary policy responds to demand shocks. Figure 11.5 shows how the Bank of Canada can try to use monetary policy to move the economy back to potential GDP following a negative demand shock.

Suppose that the economy begins in equilibrium at point *A* in panel (a). The economy then experiences a negative demand shock, such as the one that occurred in 2008, when consumer spending in Canada fell as a result of the recession in the United States. Panel (a) shows that the demand shock causes the *IS* curve to shift to the left, from IS_1 to IS_2. Real GDP falls below potential GDP, so the economy is in a recession at point *B*. Panel (b) shows the decrease in real GDP as a movement down the Phillips curve from point *A* to point *B*, which reduces the inflation rate from π_1 to π_2. The Bank of Canada typically fights recessions by lowering its target for the overnight rate. As long as the term structure effect, default-risk premium, and the expected inflation rate do not change (see Chapter 10), this Bank of Canada action lowers the real interest rate, shifting the monetary policy curve down, from MP_1 to MP_2. A lower real interest rate leads to increases in consumption spending, investment spending, and net exports, causing a movement down the *IS* curve from point *B* to point *C* in panel (a). Real GDP returns to its potential level, so the output gap again equals 0.

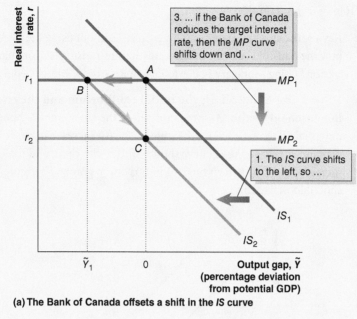

3. ... if the Bank of Canada reduces the target interest rate, then the *MP* curve shifts down and ...

1. The *IS* curve shifts to the left, so ...

(a) The Bank of Canada offsets a shift in the *IS* curve

Figure 11.5

Monetary Policy Responds to a Negative Demand Shock

A negative demand shock leads to lower real GDP and inflation, shown in both panels by movements from point *A* to point *B*. The Bank of Canada responds by decreasing real interest rates, so real GDP and inflation both rise back to their original levels, shown in both panels by movements from point *B* to point *C*. Notice that in the new equilibrium the output gap and the inflation rate have returned to their original values, so point *C* is the same as point *A*.

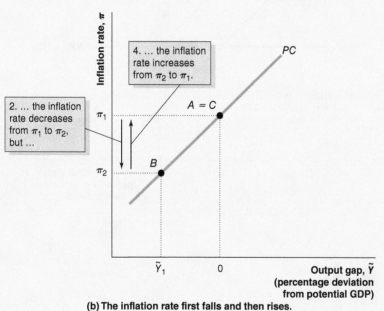

4. ... the inflation rate increases from π_2 to π_1.

2. ... the inflation rate decreases from π_1 to π_2, but ...

(b) The inflation rate first falls and then rises.

In panel (b), the inflation rate rises from π_2 back to π_1 causing a movement back up the Phillips curve from point *B* to point *C*, which is the same as point *A*. Note that, in this discussion, we assume that the expected inflation rate does not change. If it did, the Phillips curve would have shifted. The analysis that takes into account changes in the expected inflation rate would be much more complex.

Solved Problem 11.1

Bank of Canada Policy to Keep Inflation from Increasing

During the expansion of the 2000s, the Canadian economy was strong, unemployment was low, and the stock market was booming, increasing household wealth and the willingness of households to spend. As a result, the Bank of Canada was concerned that inflation would increase.

What policy could the Bank of Canada have pursued to keep the inflation rate from rising? Use the *IS–MP* model to answer this question. Be sure to show any shifts in or movements along the *IS* curve, the *MP* curve, and the Phillips curve.

Solving the Problem

Step 1 **Review the chapter material.** This problem is about using the *IS–MP* model to analyze how the Bank of Canada can keep inflation from rising, so you may want to review the section "Using Monetary Policy to Fight a Recession," which begins on page 344.

Step 2 **Draw a graph that shows the initial equilibrium and the effect of the increase in household wealth.** Assume that before the stock market boom, real GDP equals potential GDP, and the inflation rate is 2%. An increase in consumption is a positive demand shock, so the *IS* curve should shift to the right, and the inflation rate should increase to 4%, as shown by the Phillips curve graph. Therefore, your initial graphs should look like this:

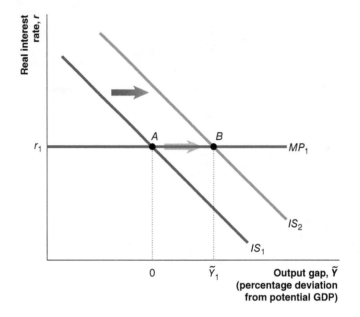

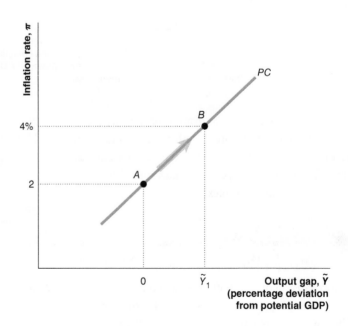

Step 3 **Determine the Bank's response.** How can the Bank of Canada keep the inflation rate from increasing? The Phillips curve shows that the output gap would have to remain equal to 0 to keep the inflation rate at 2%. The Bank of Canada affects the output gap by changing the real interest rate and the position of the *MP* curve. To keep the output gap at 0, the real interest rate would have to increase, so the *MP* curve must shift up. Your graphs should now look like this:

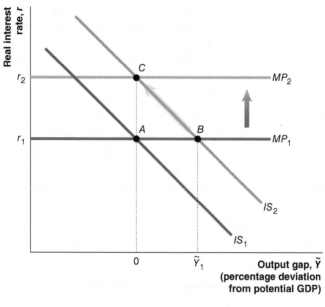

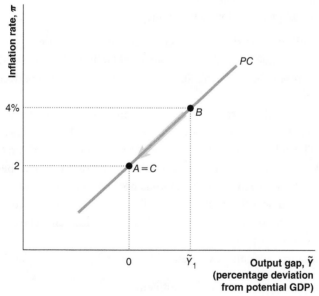

The increase in the interest rate can, in principle, prevent the increase in the inflation rate. In fact, the Bank of Canada increased the bank rate from 2.75% in August 2005 to 4.75% in July 2007. The policy was successful. The inflation rate reached a peak of 3.2% per year in September 2005 and then fell, staying below 2.5% for almost three years.

See related Problem 1.10 at the end of the chapter.

The *IS–MP* Model and the Great Recession

We now turn to the analysis of the performance of the Canadian and the U.S. economies during the Great Recession. We look at both economies because the events in Canada were a direct consequence of what happened in the United States. In principle, there were no internal causes for the recession in Canada. Prior to the recession, the Canadian economy was strong. House price increases were moderate, especially in comparison to the United States, Spain, Ireland, and several other countries, and there was no housing bubble in Canada. Canadian banks' exposure to risky assets was limited. In the absence of negative development abroad, especially in the United States, the Canadian economy would have likely avoided the recession. The recession in Canada was a direct result of economic developments in the United States.

The *IS–MP* model is a useful tool for analyzing short-run fluctuations in the output gap and in the inflation rate. The *IS* curve captures the effect of demand shocks that can temporarily push short-run macroeconomic equilibrium away from a zero output gap. The *MP* curve captures the effects not only of monetary policy, but also the effects of fluctuations in the real interest rate resulting from changes in the default-risk premium, changes in investors' expectations of future interest rates, and changes in the expected inflation rate. Finally, the Phillips curve captures the effect of changes in the output gap on the inflation rate and the effects of supply shocks.

We start with the shocks to the U.S. economy, since they induced shocks in Canada. The U.S. economy experienced the following shocks in the 2007–09 period:

- a financial crisis, which greatly reduced the availability of credit
- the collapse of the housing bubble, which reduced wealth
- a drop in consumption and investment
- a surge in oil prices, followed by a rapid decline

As a result of these shocks, real GDP fell from 0.2% above potential GDP during the second quarter of 2007 to 7.4% below potential GDP during the third quarter of 2009. The inflation rate rose to 3.2% during the third quarter of 2008, before decreasing to −0.4% during the second quarter of 2009.

As we discussed in detail in Chapter 1, financial crisis caused a large decline in the availability of credit that led to a decrease in investment as well as a decrease in purchases of durable goods. The collapse of the housing bubble led to a decline in consumption as it reduced household wealth. During the housing bubble, consumption had been supported by borrowing against the increasing value of housing. Economic uncertainty reduced investment. Construction of new residential housing fell, which contributed to the decline in investment since residential construction is considered part of investment. The changes in oil prices constituted large supply shocks.

The Canadian economy experienced the following shocks in 2008:

- a decline in consumption and investment
- a decline in exports to the United States
- somewhat reduced availability of credit
- a surge in oil prices, followed by a rapid decline

As a result of these shocks, the output gap fell from plus 2.2% in 2007 to minus 2.8% in 2009. The inflation rate rose to 3.4% in September 2008 but then fell to −0.3% in June 2009.

In Canada, there was a negative demand shock caused by the reaction of consumers and investors (those who build new factories or equipment) to the worsening situation in the United States. In addition, as the United States entered a recession, Canadian exports fell. About 75% of our exports, and close to a quarter of Canadian GDP, goes to the United States, so a large decline in the U.S. demand for Canadian goods and services creates a significant negative demand shock in Canada. With the financial crisis in the United States, Canadian financial institutions became more cautious and, for a period of time, credit was more difficult than usual to obtain. The changes in oil prices constituted large supply shocks.

As you can see, the difference between the shocks in Canada and in the United States was that in Canada exports fell more, as a proportion of GDP, and the availability of credit did not fall as much in Canada as in the United States. In addition, there was no housing bubble and housing crash in Canada, and the decline in consumption and investment was, to a large extent, for psychological reasons. The latter allowed the Canadian economy to come out of the recession faster. Once consumers and investors realized that the economic situation in Canada was much better than in the United States, consumption and investment started increasing.

Using the *IS–MP* Model to Analyze the Great Recession

We now turn to the analysis of the Great Recession in Canada and in the United States. Qualitatively, the experience of both countries was similar: output fell and inflation initially increased and then declined. So we will analyze both countries together, pointing out the differences between the experience of the U.S. and Canadian economies. We will discuss the U.S. economy first since this is where the Great Recession originated.

Let us provide a brief overview. The analysis is in two steps. In the first step we consider, for the United States, the effect of the financial crisis, the decline in consumption and investment, and the decline in house prices. The financial crisis made lending more risky, and the default-risk premium increased. The increase in the risk premium shifted the *MP* curve up. The decline in consumption and investment meant a negative demand shock, so the *IS* curve shifted to the left. For Canada we consider the decline in exports, consumption, and investment caused by the recession in the United States. In Canada, exports fell; the increase in default risk was limited; and the decline in consumption and investment was due to households' and investors' concerns, rather than real changes. So the main difference between Canada and the United States was that the upward shift in the *MP* curve in Canada was small; the shift in the *IS* curve was roughly similar in both countries. In the second step we add the supply shock: the increase in the oil prices prior to the recession. This is a negative supply shock that shifts the Phillips curve up and increases the inflation rate. Note that we do not describe the events chronologically. The increase in the price of oil predates the Great Recession, and the drop in the price of oil is the result of the Great Recession. Putting changes in the price of oil at the end of the analysis greatly simplifies it.

Upward Shift of the *MP* Curve The default-risk premium is measured as the difference between the interest rate on AAA (highest rated) corporate bonds and the interest rate on a long-term government bonds. The default-risk premium typically rises during recessions because investors believe that firms are more likely to default on their loans. In a typical recession, though, the increase in the default-risk premium is smaller than the central bank's reduction in short-term interest rates so that overall the long-term real interest rate falls.

But the Great Recession in the United States was anything but typical! In the United States in June 2007, the default-risk premium was 0.65%, which was just below the average of 0.77% over the 1953–2008 period. By March 17, 2008, the day JPMorgan Chase purchased the investment bank Bear Stearns, thereby saving it from bankruptcy, it increased by almost 1.5%. Because investors had become very concerned that firms might default on their bonds, they were unwilling to purchase corporate bonds except at higher interest rates. So the default-risk premium rose, shifting the *MP* curve up. With higher real interest rates, credit became more expensive, reducing investment and credit-financed consumer purchases.

In addition, the disruption in the credit market made banks unwilling to lend even at the higher interest rates. Many firms were simply unable to obtain financing for investment projects. Similarly, it became more difficult for households to obtain credit as banks raised lending standards. The restricted the ability of households to borrow caused consumption and housing sales to decline. So, the financial market shock reduced both consumption and investment.

If financial market turbulence had lasted a brief period, it would probably not have significantly affected investment, because it can take months or longer for firms to plan investment projects or for individuals to purchase a home. However, the default-risk premium continued to rise and in November 2008 was 2% higher than prior to the Great Recession. It remained elevated as late as May 2010. Recall that the position of the *MP* curve depends on the risk premium. When the risk premium increases, the *MP* curve shifts up. Both countries experienced an upward shift in the *MP* curve, but in Canada the shift was smaller.

Leftward Shift of the *IS* Curve Housing prices began to decline in the United States in 2006, as the housing bubble burst. The value of a home is a major component of a household's wealth, and when wealth decreases, so does household consumption. In addition, as housing sales declined, builders cut back on the construction of new homes. The growth rate of residential construction went from 6.2% during 2006 to -22.9% during 2008, and it was still -3.0% in 2010. The rapid decrease in housing prices reduced both consumption and investment. (Recall that residential construction is considered investment.) In Canada, while there was no housing boom and so house prices did not collapse, consumers and investors became concerned with the economic problems in the United States, and both consumption and investment fell.

Figure 11.6 uses the *IS–MP* model to show the effects of the shocks. We use the same figure for both the United States and Canada, since changes are qualitatively the same (meaning that the *MP* and the *IS* curves move in the same direction in both countries) and the differences are only quantitative, i.e. only the magnitude of the shifts differs between the two countries. Panel (a) shows the effect of shocks on the *IS* and *MP*. For simplicity we start at point *A* where the output gap is zero: $\tilde{Y}_t = 0$. The financial crisis increased the default-risk premium, so the *MP* curve shifted up, from MP_1 to MP_2. In the United States the collapse of the housing market and the resulting decline in consumption and investment caused a negative demand shock and the *IS* curve shifted to the left, from IS_1 to IS_2. In Canada, the decline in consumption, investment, and exports to the United States, also caused a negative demand shock, which we mark with the same shift of the *IS* curve to the left, from IS_1 to IS_2. By 2009, the short-run equilibrium was at point *B*, with real GDP below potential GDP and the output gap at $\tilde{Y}_2$. Panel (b) uses the Phillips curve to show the effect of the change in the output gap on the inflation rate in both countries. As the short-run equilibrium moves from point *A* to point *B*, the inflation rate falls from, π_1 to π_2.

Figure 11.6 shows the shifts in the two curves. It applies both to Canada and the United States; the difference is that, were you to graph them separately, the shifts in the *MP* curve in Canada would have been smaller since the increase in the default risk in Canada was smaller than in the United States. The leftward shift in the *IS* curve was roughly similar, but the decline in consumption and investment in Canada happened later. This is because the decline in Canadian consumption and investment was a reaction to events in the United States. As you saw in Chapter 1, Figure 1.14, output in Canada declined about three months later than in the United States.

The *IS–MP* model predicts that, if there had been no supply shock from higher oil prices, the negative demand shock would have reduced real GDP *and* the inflation rate, as shown in panel (b). Our discussion is, however, incomplete. We have yet to consider the effect on the economy of the surge in oil prices during 2008.

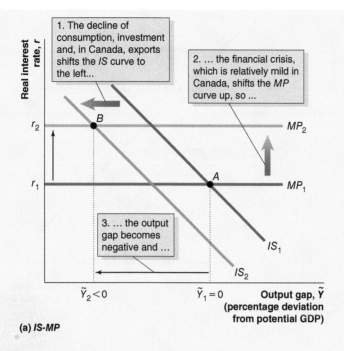

(a) *IS-MP*

Figure 11.6

The Financial and Real Estate Market Shocks and the Canadian and U.S. Economies.

The financial crisis shifts the *MP* curve upward, and the negative demand shock shifts the *IS* curve to the left in panel (a). As a result, the real interest rate increases and the output gap becomes negative in panel (a). If there had been no adverse supply shock, the inflation rate would have decreased, as shown in panel (b). In both panels, short-run equilibrium moves from point *A* to point *B*. Changes in Canada were smaller than in the United States and happened about three months later.

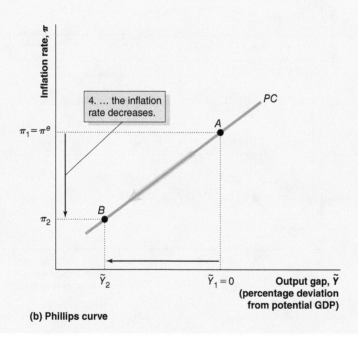

(b) **Phillips curve**

The *IS–MP* Model and the Oil Shock of 2007–08

We now turn to the analysis of the supply shock. The price of oil rose from $56.60 a barrel in March 2007 to a high of $145.66 in July 2008, before decreasing to $30.81 in December 2008. An increase in the price of oil is a negative supply shock, which shifts the Phillips curve up and, all other things being equal, increases the inflation rate.

Figure 11.7 shows the effect of the oil price shock, using the *IS–MP* model. As we just saw, the financial market shock and the housing market crash moved the short-run equilibrium to point *B* in Figure 11.7, so we continue our analysis from point B. Panel (a) reproduces panel (a) in Figure 11.6. The increase in oil prices was a negative supply shock that caused

Figure 11.7

The Oil Price Shock and the Canadian and U.S. Economies

The increase in the price of oil does not shift the curves in panel (a), which is the same as Figure 11.6 panel (a). However, it shifts the Phillips curve up in panel (b), which puts upward pressure on inflation.

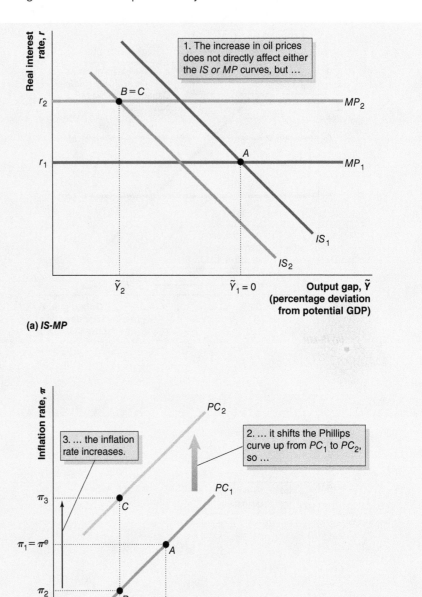

1. The increase in oil prices does not directly affect either the *IS* or *MP* curves, but …

(a) IS-MP

2. … it shifts the Phillips curve up from PC_1 to PC_2, so …

3. … the inflation rate increases.

(b) Phillips curve

the Phillips curve in panel (b) to shift up from PC_1 to PC_2. The inflation rate increased to π_3, output remained at $\tilde{Y}_2$, and short-run equilibrium moved to point *C*. Because the increase in inflation did not cause an additional decline in real GDP, in panel (a) point *C* is also point *B*. As a result of the supply shock, the inflation rate increased. After September 2008, oil prices fell, and the inflation rate declined. These changes can be shown in Figure 11.17 as a downward shift of the Phillips curve.

To summarize, our model is a useful tool for analyzing short-run fluctuations in the output gap and in the inflation rate. The *IS* curve captures the effect of demand shocks that can temporarily push short-run macroeconomic equilibrium away from a zero output gap. The *MP* curve captures the effects not only of monetary policy, but also the effects of fluctuations in the real interest rate resulting from changes in the default-risk premium, changes in investors' expectations of future interest rates, and changes in the expected inflation rate. Finally, the Phillips curve captures the effect of changes in the output gap on the inflation rate and the effects of supply shocks. So far we have only analyzed the demand and supply shocks which led to the Great Recession. We will discuss policy response in Chapters 12 and 13.

The *IS–MP* Model in an Open Economy

In this section we extend our analysis of the *IS–MP* model to the case of an open economy. Doing so is important because Canada is an open economy, with exports and imports amounting to over 30% of GDP, and the flow of trade and financial investments between Canada and other countries has been increasing over time.

11.3
Learning Objective
Understand the *IS–MP* model in an open economy.

To simplify the analysis of the *IS–MP* model in an open economy we make several assumptions. Unless stated otherwise, we will assume that the term structure of interest rates, the default premium, and the expected inflation rates are constant. These assumptions are necessary since the interest rate parity condition (see Chapter 5), which plays the central role in the analysis, involves nominal interest rates and the expected appreciation/ depreciation of the currency, while the *IS–MP* model focuses on the long-term real interest rate. With the expected inflation rate constant, the changes in the real and in the nominal interest rates are the same, and the interest rate parity condition can be expressed in terms of the real interest rate. We also note that foreign real interest rates are not affected by changes in Canada, since Canada is a small, open economy. As usual, we will assume that prices are sticky, so the real exchange rate changes in the same direction as the nominal exchange rate. Finally, we will assume that changes in the real exchange rate affect the current account and net exports in the same direction. Recall that the current account is the sum of net exports and net factor income from abroad. This assumption is justified by the fact that, in Canada and most other countries, net exports are much larger and, usually, more volatile than net factor income.

The *IS-MP* Model with a Flexible Exchange Rate

The details of the open economy version of the *IS–MP* model differ depending on whether the economy has a fixed or flexible exchange rate system. We first consider the case of a flexible exchange rate. This is the case in Canada; apart from the period 1962–71, Canada has had a flexible exchange rate.

The *IS* Curve with a Flexible Exchange Rate

We begin the analysis by re-examining the *IS* curve. The *IS* curve shows the negative relationship between the real interest rate and aggregate expenditure in the goods market. In a closed economy, as the real interest rate increases, the cost of borrowing increases, so households and firms borrow less to finance consumption and investment. In an open economy, changes in the real interest rate affect, in addition, the exchange rate and net exports. In this section, we modify the *IS* curve to take into account the effect of changes in the real interest rate on the exchange rate and net exports.

As we discussed in Chapter 5, the demand for Canadian dollars depends on the expected return on Canadian assets relative to foreign assets. The interest rate parity condition says that the expected returns on Canadian and foreign assets are equal. If the expected return on Canadian assets was higher, both Canadian and foreign investors would buy Canadian assets and sell foreign assets, raising the demand for Canadian dollars so that the Canadian dollar would appreciate relative to foreign currencies. As the appreciation would have little effect on the expected future value of the exchange rate, it will lead to expectations of future depreciations, reducing the expected return on Canadian assets.

354 CHAPTER 11 • The *IS–MP* Model: Adding Inflation and the Open Economy

The interest rate parity condition implies that, if the real interest rate in Canada increases, Canadian and foreign investors will increase their demand for Canadian dollars to buy Canadian financial assets. The higher demand for dollars will increase the nominal exchange rate. Since prices adjust slowly, the real exchange rate will also rise, thereby decreasing foreign demand for our exports and increasing our demand for foreign imports. As a result, a higher Canadian real interest rate would reduce net exports, the current account, and aggregate expenditure. Similarly, a decrease in the Canadian real interest rate would increase net exports, the current account, and aggregate expenditure. Therefore, explicitly incorporating nominal exchange rates and net exports into the model gives us another reason why changes in the real interest rate affect real GDP and the output gap.

We conclude that, in an open economy with flexible exchange rates, changes in the real interest rate have a bigger effect on aggregate expenditure than in a closed economy. Exchange rates and net exports provide a country with an additional channel through which an increase in the real interest rate will lead to lower aggregate expenditure and output and a decrease in the real interest rate will lead to higher aggregate expenditure and output. This means that the *IS* curve in an open economy is flatter than the *IS* curve in a closed economy.

What happens when foreign interest rates change? Since we compare asset returns in Canada and abroad, what matters is not Canadian interest rates but the difference between Canadian and foreign interest rates. So, for a given real interest rate in Canada, if foreign real interest rates increase, foreign investments become more attractive relative to Canadian investments. Canadian and foreign investors will then want to sell Canadian financial assets and purchase foreign financial assets. The demand for Canadian assets will decrease, and the nominal and real exchange rates will fall, raising net exports, the current account, and aggregate expenditure. So, for a given real interest rate in Canada, if the foreign real interest rate increases, the Canadian dollar depreciates, raising net exports, the current account, and aggregate expenditure. This means that the *IS* curve shifts to the right. Similarly, a decrease in foreign real interest rates will cause the Canadian dollar to appreciate, which will decrease net exports and aggregate expenditure in Canada and shift the *IS* curve to the left.

The *MP* Curve and the Net Capital Outflow with a Flexible Exchange Rate

The *MP* curve in the open economy looks the same as the *MP* curve in a closed economy. It is a horizontal line at the level of the long-term real interest rate. Its position depends on the short-term nominal interest rate set by the central bank, the term structure effect, the default premium, and the expected inflation rate. The *MP* curve shifts up if the Bank of Canada increases the policy rate, the term structure effect increases (i.e., the difference between the long-term and the short-term nominal interest rates rises), the default premium increases, or the expected inflation rate falls. With the exception of an increase in the default premium, these changes in the real interest rate make financial investments in Canada more desirable compared to financial investments in other countries. As a result, capital will flow into Canada.

An increase in the default premium, however, does not make Canadian assets more desirable. This is because the decision where to locate financial investments does not depend just on the interest rate, but it depends on the *risk-adjusted* interest rate. If an increase in default premium or in another source of risk is exactly compensated by a higher interest rate, it does not affect the perceived profitability of financial investments in Canada versus abroad. For example, during the Greek debt crisis, the real interest rate on Greek government bonds was up to 20%–30% higher than on German government bonds. Despite the high interest rates on Greek bonds, demand was very limited. The extra interest was required to compensate for the fact that Greek bonds were riskier than German bonds since the Greek government could default on its debts or Greece could leave the Eurozone.

We will define *net capital outflow* as the difference between capital outflow and capital inflow. If we ignore the capital account (which, as you can recall from Chapter 5, is very small), the current account balance has the same value as net capital outflows:

$$CA = NCO. \tag{11.6}$$

where *CA* is the current account balance and *NCO* is net capital outflows. If a country has a current account surplus, capital flows out of the country and the net capital outflow is positive. If a country has a current account deficit, there is a capital inflow into the country and the net capital outflow is negative. For example, Canada ran a current account deficit in 2013, and so net capital outflow was negative, which means capital was flowing into Canada during 2013.

Equilibrium in an Open Economy with a Flexible Exchange Rate

Figure 11.8 shows equilibrium in the *IS–MP* model Panel (a) shows the *IS–MP* equilibrium. It is similar to the equilibrium in the closed economy, but the *IS* is flatter, reflecting the fact that a higher real interest rate reduces net exports. The equilibrium value of the real interest rate determines the current account and net capital outflows. Panel (b) shows a situation in which, in equilibrium, net capital outflows are negative, i.e. there is a current account deficit and a capital inflow.

The *IS–MP* Model with a Fixed Exchange Rate

Since Canada has almost always had flexible exchange rates, we will refer to the country with a fixed exchange rate system as the domestic country, and to its currency as the domestic currency. Under a fixed exchange rate system, the central bank agrees to buy and sell domestic currency at a fixed nominal exchange rate. Let us say the exchange rate is $2 for one unit of the domestic currency. The fixed exchange rate means that (1) no currency trader would sell the domestic currency for less than $2 since he can get two dollars from the central bank for it and (2) no currency trader would pay more than $2 for the currency since they can buy it from the central bank for two dollars. By standing ready to buy and sell the country's currency at the specified exchange rate, the central bank assures the exchange rate remains fixed at $2.

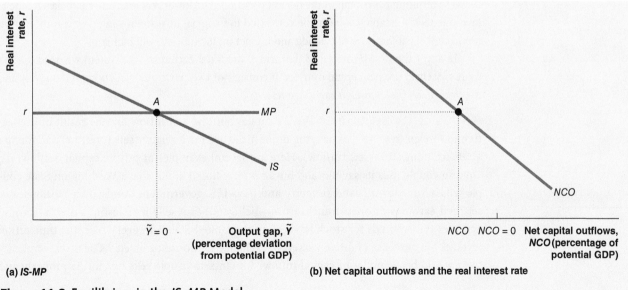

(a) *IS-MP*

(b) Net capital outflows and the real interest rate

Figure 11.8 Equilibrium in the *IS–MP* Model

Equilibrium occurs in panel (a) where the *IS* and *MP* curves intersect.

Panel (b) shows that net capital outflows decrease as the real interest rate increases.

The *IS* Curve with a Fixed Exchange Rate

Under a fixed exchange rate system, changes in the real interest rate do not affect the exchange rate or the current account. But the *IS* curve still slopes downward because a higher real interest rate still reduces consumption and investment. The *IS* curve under a fixed exchange rate system is very similar to the *IS* curve in a closed economy and is flatter than the *IS* curve under a flexible exchange rate system.

With a fixed exchange rate, changes in the exchange rate shift the IS curve. For example, suppose that the government decides to reduce the fixed exchange rate, i.e., devalue the currency. In that case, exports would become cheaper and imports would become more expensive, so net exports and the current account would both increase. At the same level of the real interest rate, aggregate expenditure would be higher. This means that devaluation, through its effect on net exports and the current account, would shift the *IS* curve to the right. Similarly, if the government decides to increase the fixed exchange rate, i.e., revalue the currency, exports would become more expensive, and imports would become cheaper. Net exports would decrease, and the *IS* curve would shift to the left.

The MP Curve and the Net Capital Outflow with a Fixed Exchange Rate

The *MP* curve with fixed exchange rate is the same as the *MP* curve with the flexible exchange rate: It is a horizontal line at the level of the long-term real interest rate. Its position depends on the short-term nominal interest rate set by the central bank, the term structure effect, the default premium, and the expected inflation rate. The *MP* curve shifts up if the Bank of Canada increases the policy rate, the term structure effect increases (i.e., the difference between the long-term and the short-term nominal interest rates rises), the default premium rises, or the expected inflation rate falls. Except from an increase resulting from a rise in the default premium, the higher real interest rate makes financial investments in Canada more desirable compared to financial investments in other countries. As a result, capital will flow into Canada and the net capital outflow will fall. The *MP* curve shifts down if the Bank of Canada reduces the policy rate, the term structure effect falls (i.e., the difference between the long-term and the short-term nominal interest rates becomes smaller), or the expected inflation rate increases. Except from a decrease resulting from a fall in the default premium, the lower real interest rate makes financial investments in Canada less desirable compared to financial investments in other countries. As a result, capital will flow out of Canada and the net capital outflow will increase.

To apply the *IS–MP* model to the case of the fixed exchange rate system we need to look more closely at the net capital outflow. It consists of two parts: *net private capital outflow* and the *change in official foreign exchange reserves*.

Net Private Capital Outflow Private capital outflow and inflow are the result of domestic and foreign investors exchanging domestic assets for foreign assets (outflow) and foreign assets for domestic assets (inflow). Here are several examples of private capital outflow: An Ontario couple uses its savings and buys a winter home in Florida; a Washington State couple sells a Vancouver Island property and buys U.S. government bonds; Tim Hortons uses retained earnings to open franchises in Michigan; Sears sells its flagship store in Toronto and uses the proceeds for stock buyback in the United States. In every case, the transaction involves the purchase of foreign assets in exchange for domestic assets.[3] The reverse transactions would be examples of capital inflow: An Ontario couple sells its Florida property and

---

[3]If foreign assets are purchased with other foreign assets, for example, if the Ontario couple sells a property in Michigan and buys one in Florida at the same price, the capital outflow is zero.

uses the proceeds to buy Canadian stocks and bonds; Target issues new shares in the United States and uses the proceeds to buy Zellers properties in Canada, and so on. *Net private capital outflow* equals the difference between private capital outflow and private capital inflow over some period, for example, a year.

Changes in Official Foreign Exchange Reserves Central banks hold stocks of foreign exchange reserves, often called official foreign exchange reserves or official reserves. The reserves play a central role in the maintenance of the fixed exchange rate. To keep the exchange rate from increasing (appreciating) the central bank must buy foreign currencies in exchange for domestic currencies. As a result, official foreign exchange reserves increase. To keep the exchange rate from depreciating, the central bank must sell foreign currencies in exchange for domestic currency. As a result, official foreign exchange reserves fall. The change in official reserves over some period (for example, a year) is equal to the difference between the level of reserves at the end and at the beginning of the period.

We can express net capital outflow as the sum of net private capital outflow and the change in official foreign exchange reserves:

$$NCO = NCO^P + \Delta R. \tag{11.7}$$

where NCO^P denotes net private capital outflow and ΔR denotes the change in official foreign exchange reserves. Since net capital outflow equals the balance on current account, CA, we obtain the following simple equation for the change in official reserves under fixed exchange rate system:

$$\Delta R = CA - NCO^P. \tag{11.8}$$

To understand this equation, assume that the current account is zero and private capital outflow exceeds inflow so that net private capital outflow is positive. A positive net private capital outflow means that domestic purchases of foreign assets exceed foreign purchases of domestic assets, so foreign currency payments exceed foreign currency receipts. The only way this is possible is when the difference between foreign currency payments and receipts is coming from the central bank's official reserves.

Real Interest Rate, Net Capital Outflow, and Official Foreign Exchange Reserves What is the effect of changes in the real interest rate on net capital outflow and its two components? When the exchange rate is fixed, changes in the real interest rate do not affect the current account balance, so net capital outflow is also unaffected. On the other hand, the net private capital outflow increases as the real interest rate falls. This is because the lower is the real interest rate, the lower is the return on domestic assets relative to foreign assets, so investors sell domestic assets and buy foreign assets, increasing net private capital outflow. Under the fixed exchange rate system, the change in official reserves is the balancing item, equal to the difference between the current account balance and the net private capital outflow. If net private capital outflow is smaller than the current account balance, official reserves increase. If net private capital outflow exceeds the current account balance, official reserves fall.

In Figure 11.9 we show the net private and total capital outflows under a fixed exchange rate system. When the domestic real interest rate equals r_1, net private capital outflow is equal to the current account balance, and official reserves do not change. If the real interest rate is $r_2 > r_1$, net private capital outflow is smaller than the current account balance and, to maintain the fixed exchange rate, the central bank must sell domestic currency on the foreign exchange market and buy foreign currency, so official reserves increase. If the interest rate is $r_3 < r_1$, net private capital outflow exceeds the current account balance and, to maintain the fixed exchange rate, the central bank must sell foreign currency assets and buy domestic currency on the foreign exchange market, so official reserves fall. When the

Figure 11. 9

Net capital outflows and changes in reserves with a fixed exchange rate.

With fixed exchange rates, the central bank must acquire reserves when net private capital outflow is less than the current account balance and it must sell reserves when net private capital outflow exceeds the current account balance. As the real interest rate falls, net private capital outflow increases and the official reserves decline. When the real interest rate approaches $\bar{r}$, a speculative attack begins.

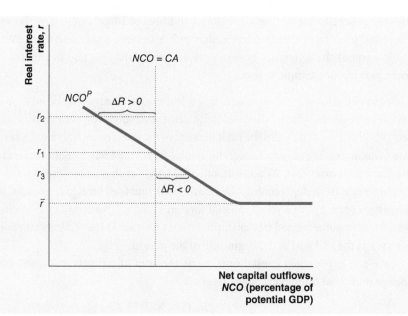

interest rate approaches the lower limit, which we will denote $\bar{r}$, a *speculative attack* begins. Net private capital outflow becomes much larger, official reserves fall rapidly, and the central bank quickly runs out of reserves.

Speculative Attack What happens when the real interest rate approaches $\bar{r}$? As the real interest rate falls, the bank loses foreign exchange reserves more rapidly. With fixed exchange rate and free capital movements, the country is at a risk of a speculative attack. Currency speculators figure out that official reserves are low and start selling the currency short. Short-selling currency involves borrowing the currency and selling it on the foreign exchange market in the expectation that the exchange rate will fall and the currency can be bought back at a lower cost, yielding a profit.

To see how it works, let us use a specific example. In Chapter 5 we described the experience of Mexico with fixed exchange rates. On December 19, 1994, the exchange rate of the peso was 0.28875 U.S. dollar per one peso. Conversely, one dollar cost 3.4632 pesos. A speculator could borrow 3.4632 million pesos and exchange it on the foreign exchange market for $1 million (US$). On December 20 the Mexican peso was devalued and the exchange rate fell to 0.25575 U.S. dollar per one peso. At this rate, the speculator could buy 3.4632 million pesos for $885 713 (US$) and repay the loan. The profit on the transaction would be over $114 000, minus transaction costs, in one day. Of course, the timing of this transaction required a lot of skill, but in late 1994 it was clear that the Bank of Mexico reserves were not sufficient to maintain the fixed exchange rate for a long time. A speculator who, for example, entered a short-sale transaction at the beginning of November would have had to pay a high interest rate on the borrowed peso for two months but would have ended up with substantial profit as well.

Clearly, the possibility of earning an extraordinary return on a well-placed bet on currency movements brings about a lot of speculators. They borrow the domestic currency and sell it on the foreign exchange market so that the net private capital outflow becomes a flood. But the bet on currency devaluation is, like other financial bets, risky. For example, during the Asian financial crisis in 1997, speculators made large profits on Indonesian rupiah and Thai baht, forcing the central banks to abandon the fixed exchange rates. The speculators then turned their attention to Hong Kong. Hong Kong, however, had ample foreign exchange reserves; in addition, China promised to lend its own, even bigger, foreign currency reserves to the Hong Kong Monetary Authority. The combined reserves of Hong

Kong and China were too large, and the speculative attack ended. Speculators incurred interest and transaction costs and lost money.

Equilibrium in an Open Economy with a Fixed Exchange Rate

Figure 11.10 shows equilibrium in the *IS–MP* model under a fixed exchange rate system. Equilibrium occurs at point *A*, where the *IS* and *MP* curves intersect. The *IS–MP* graph in panel (a) determines the equilibrium real interest rate, just as it does under a flexible exchange rate system. The equilibrium real interest rate then determines net capital outflow, NCO^P, and the change in official reserves, ΔR. The change in official reserves is equal to the distance between the net private capital outflow and the current account at the prevailing real interest rate. At a high domestic real interest rate, investors want to purchase domestic financial assets. These purchases increase the demand for the domestic currency, so the central bank acquires foreign exchange reserves as currency traders exchange foreign currency for the domestic currency. Such equilibrium can be maintained for a long time since the central bank can issue domestic currency. At a low domestic real interest rate, investors want to sell domestic financial assets. This is the case shown in panel (b). Sales of domestic assets decrease the demand for the domestic currency, and, to maintain the fixed exchange rate, the central bank must purchase domestic currency on the foreign exchange market, so official reserves decline. An equilibrium with falling official reserves is only temporary, since foreign currency reserves are limited. How long can such equilibrium last? It depends on the speed of reserve loss as well as the initial level of reserves. For example, if the central bank has $10 billion in foreign currency reserves and the net private outflow exceeds the current account balance by $500 million a day, it will take 20 days for the reserves to be exhausted. (Of course, the fixed exchange rate will be devalued or abandoned earlier, as the central bank will not want to completely run out of reserves). Saudi Arabia, which has ample foreign exchange reserves ($700 billion in 2013) could maintain an equilibrium with falling official reserves for a much longer period of time than Benin, which has limited reserves ($700 million in 2013). Lowering the *MP* curve to *MP*min causes a speculative attack and the central bank quickly runs out of reserves.

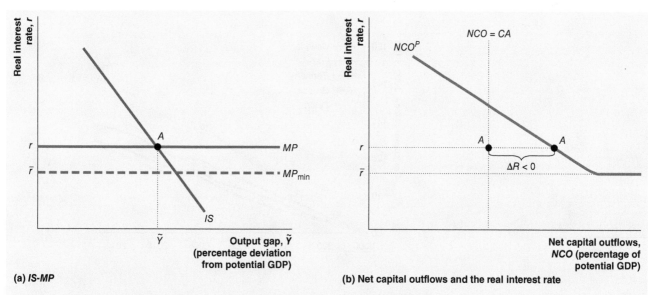

(a) *IS-MP*

(b) Net capital outflows and the real interest rate

Figure 11.10 Equilibrium in the *IS–MP* Model with a Fixed Exchange Rate

Equilibrium occurs in panel (a), where the *IS* and *MP* curves intersect. Panel (b) shows that net capital outflows increase as the real interest rate falls. If the central bank is acquiring foreign exchange reserves, it can maintain the fixed exchange rate system for a long time. An equilibrium in which the central bank loses foreign exchange reserves is only temporary as reserves eventually get exhausted.

We conclude that, with fixed exchange rates, there is a lower limit below which the real interest rate cannot fall. As we will see in the next chapter, this limits the central bank's ability to conduct monetary policy. When the central bank reduces the real interest rate, it suffers an outflow of reserves and eventually has to devalue the currency or switch to a flexible exchange rate.

Making the Connection

Can the Euro Survive?

There are advantages to having a fixed exchange rate. Firms that export find it easier to plan if they know what the foreign currency price of their products will be. In addition, if the exchange rate is fixed, firms can borrow in foreign currencies with less risk. The appeal of fixed exchange rates eventually led the European Union (EU) in 1999 to decide to move to a common currency. In 2002, the euro replaced individual currencies in participating countries. By 2014, 18 members of the EU, including all of the largest economies with the exception of the United Kingdom, had adopted the euro. The European Central Bank assumed responsibility for monetary policy and for issuing currency.

The period from 2001 until the beginning of the global economic downturn at the end of 2007 was one of relative economic stability in most of Europe. With low interest rates, low inflation rates, and expanding employment and production, the advantages of the euro seemed obvious. With the beginning of the financial crisis of 2007, the disadvantages of the euro also began to become obvious. Although the EU had been taking steps to integrate the economies of the member countries, many aspects of these economies, including rates of taxation, extent of unionization, government spending and transfer policies, and so on, remained quite different. One result of these differences among economies was differences in inflation rates. The figure below shows increases in the consumer price level between 2000 and 2013 for France, Germany, Greece, and Spain. Canada is shown for comparison. Prices in Greece and Spain increased much more than in France or Germany.

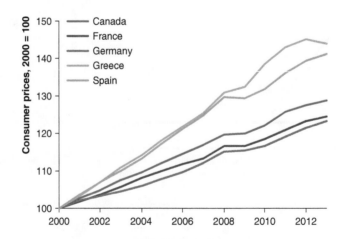

Recall the formula for the real exchange rate:

$$e = E\frac{P}{P*},$$

(11.9)

where

e = real exchange rate
E = nominal exchange rate
P = domestic price level
P^* = foreign price level

Once the euro was introduced, the nominal exchange rate among these countries was fixed, but the real exchange could still change as the price levels in the countries changed. As the figure shows, the price levels in Greece and Spain rose much more than the price levels in France and Germany. As a result, Greece and Spain experienced a sharp increase in their real exchange rate compared to France and Germany. The higher exchange rates reduced Greece's and Spain's net exports and slowed their recovery from the Great Recession. While France and Germany were running current account surpluses, Greece and Spain were running large current account deficits. In fact, these economies were worse off in 2011 than they had been during the worldwide financial crisis a few years earlier. In 2011, the unemployment rate in Spain was 21.6% and in Greece it was 17.3%, while in France it was 9.7% and in Germany it was 6.0%.

If Spain and Greece still had their own currencies, their nominal exchange rates could have declined, thereby increasing their exports and reducing their imports. Iceland, which does not use the euro, experienced a substantial decline in its nominal exchange rate. Partly as a result, the unemployment rate in Iceland in 2011 was only 7.4%.

There were two ways in which, in order to increase competitiveness, Spain and Greece could reduce the prices of their exports and of their domestic goods in competition with foreign imports:

1. *Reduce inflation rates to below those of their major trading partners.* This way of restoring competitiveness was difficult because in 2010 and 2011 the inflation rates in France and Germany were lower than in Greece and Spain. Some economists and policymakers suggested that price levels in Greece and Spain would have to fall—in other words, deflation would have to occur—to restore the competitiveness of their economies. This is sometimes called *internal devaluation* since domestic goods become cheaper than foreign goods without the use of the exchange rate. It was difficult to achieve because, as we have seen, wages and prices tend to exhibit downward rigidity, which means that, in practice, cutting wages and prices is difficult. Attempting to reduce wages and prices led to significant political unrest in both Spain and Greece. An alternative to deflation was for Germany, in particular, to have a significantly higher inflation rate than Spain or Greece. There was little political support for this approach in Germany, however.

2. *Abandon the euro.* If Spain and Greece reverted to using their own currencies, these currencies could depreciate against the euro, boosting exports, reducing imports, and helping to restore competitiveness.

Most economists and policymakers believed that a breakup of the euro—or even the exit of a few countries—would be likely to cause extensive economic disruptions, probably pushing the Eurozone countries into a serious recession. By 2014, it appeared likely that the worst was behind them and both Greece and Spain would continue using the euro.

Sources: David Román, Santiago Perez, and Jonathan House, "Rajoy Upbeat on Aid Plan," *The Wall Street Journal*, June 10, 2012; Charles Forelle and Marcus Walker, "Dithering at the Top Turned EU Crisis to Global Threat," *The Wall Street Journal*, December 29, 2011; Kathleen Madigan, "Forecasters Flying Blind When Predicting Repercussions of Greek Exit," *The Wall Street Journal*, May 25, 2012; "A Central-Bank Failure of Epic Proportions," *The Economist*, June 1, 2012; and Organisation of Economic Development and Cooperation.

See related Problem 3.7 at the end of the chapter.

Key Terms and Problems

Key Terms

Adaptive expectations, p. 340

Rational expectations, p. 340

Stagflation, p. 340

11.1 ### The *IS–MP* Model and the Phillips Curve
Understand the role of the Phillips curve in the *IS–MP* model.

Review Questions

1.1 What is the Phillips curve? Why did economists and policymakers initially believe that the Phillips curve represented a structural relationship in the economy?

1.2 What is the equation for the Phillips curve with the output gap on the horizontal axis? How does a supply shock affect the Phillips curve with the output gap on the horizontal axis?

1.3 What causes a movement along the Phillips curve with the output gap on the horizontal axis? What causes the Phillips curve to shift?

Problems and Applications

1.4 "Supply-side" government policies aim to stimulate productivity through tax cuts and work incentives.

   a. What effect would an increase in productivity have on the Phillips curve? Illustrate your answer with a graph.

   b. What effect would the productivity increase have on the inflation rate, holding other factors constant?

1.5 Suppose that the output gap is zero.

   a. Graph the economy's initial equilibrium using the *IS–MP* model including the Phillips curve.

   b. Now suppose that the government increases spending due to a war. Show the effect on output and inflation, using both the *IS–MP* and Phillips curve graphs.

1.6 Recent evidence suggests that over time the Phillips curve has flattened. An article in *The Economist* states, "A flatter Phillips curve is good news when unemployment is falling. But it also implies bad news if inflation rises significantly."

   a. If firms find it difficult to raise prices, why might the result be a flatter Phillips curve?

   b. How would the effect of a demand shock be different if the Phillips curve is relatively flat than if it is relatively steep?

   c. Why does the article argue that a flatter Phillips curve may be bad news if there is high inflation?
Source: "Curve Ball," *The Economist*, September 28, 2006.

1.7 Expectations of inflation are considered "well anchored" if expectations do not respond to current inflation

   a. What is the benefit of well anchored inflation expectations?

   b. If expectations are adaptive, are they likely to be well anchored? Briefly explain.

1.8 [**Related to the** Chapter Opener **on page 333**] In 2009, Simon Johnson, former chief economist at the International Monetary Fund, believed that Federal Reserve policies might lead to a sharp increase in inflation. He argued:

"The large increase in credit from the Federal Reserve can potentially push up prices, even though unemployment remains relatively high. . . ."

Use the equation for the Phillips curve to explain how it is possible to have a high inflation rate even if the unemployment rate is high.
Source: Simon Johnson, "Inflation Fears," *New York Times*, May 28, 2009.

1.9 [**Related to the** Making the Connection **on page 344**] Following the Great Recession, the very large increases in monetary base in several countries were expected to lead to high inflation.

   a. Did inflation increase?

   b. Explain your answer in (a).

1.10 [**Related to** Solved Problem 11.1 **on page 345**] In 2013, several central banks became concerned about deflation.

   a. Use the *IS–MP* model including the Phillips curve to show how a decrease in aggregate expenditure could cause deflation.

   b. What policies should the central bank pursue to attempt to prevent deflation? Use the *IS–MP* model, including the Phillips curve in your answer.

11.2 The *IS–MP* model and the Great Recession
Use the *IS–MP* model to understand the Great Recession.

Review Questions

2.1 Briefly explain what happened to real GDP and the inflation rate in Canada and in the United States during the Great Recession.

2.2 What were the four shocks that the Canadian economy experienced during the period of 2008–09? Explain how each of these four shocks can be shown in the *IS–MP* model including the Phillips curve.

Problems and Applications

2.3 China experienced many of the negative effects of the 2007–09 recession. Like other countries, China was faced with higher oil prices. Housing prices in China, however, did not fall. China's exports did decline sharply as the recession lowered incomes in China's trading partners. Assume that China was producing at potential GDP prior to the recession. Use the *IS–MP* model including the Phillips curve to show the effects of the recession in China.

2.4 Prior to the Great Recession, China's inflation rate appeared to be increasing.

    a. What would a high and increasing rate of inflation imply about China's output gap?

    b. What would you expect to happen to China's inflation rate as a result of the recession in its major trading partners?

2.5 Consider the following statement: "The event that caused the Great Recession was the failure of Lehman Brothers. If Lehman Brothers had not been allowed to fail, there would have been no effect on the default-risk premium and thus no demand shock." Do you agree with this statement? Briefly explain.

11.3 The *IS–MP* Model in an Open Economy
Understand the *IS–MP* model in an open economy.

Review Questions

3.1 How does the open-economy *IS–MP* model incorporate net exports assuming a flexible exchange rate system? Assuming a fixed exchange rate system?

3.2 What is different about the *MP* curve in a fixed exchange rate system as compared to a flexible exchange rate system?

3.3 Explain how the equilibrium real interest rate, net capital outflows, and the level of net exports are determined in an open economy.

Problems and Applications

3.4 For each of the following cases, use the *IS–MP* model and the *NCO* curve to explain the effect on the output gap, the real interest rate, and net capital flows, assuming that exchange rates are flexible.

    a. Consumers decide to spend more on domestic goods and services and save less.

    b. There is an increase in incomes in the United States, so Canada's net exports increase.

    c. The Bank of Canada reduces the money supply.

    d. Profits from newly built factories in Canada are expected to increase.

3.5 In April 2011, the European Central Bank (ECB) increased its target interest rate, while other major central banks held their target interest rates constant.

    a. What effect would a rise in European interest rates be expected to have on output in Europe? What effect would it have on net capital flows?

    b. How would this rise in European interest rates affect the value of the euro relative to the value of the dollar?

3.6 The Greek unemployment rate rose from 7.5% during the first quarter of 2008 to 28% during the last quarter of 2013. Because Greece uses the euro rather than its own currency, the country is not able to depreciate its currency in an attempt to stimulate the economy.

    a. Suppose in 2008 Greece's output gap was zero. Assume Greece abandoned the euro as its currency and reintroduced its former currency, the drachma, with an exchange rate of 1 euro = 1 drachma. Draw a graph using the *IS–MP* model to show the effect on Greece's output gap and inflation rate if the country then devalued the drachma to 1 euro = 2 drachma.

b. Based on the experience of countries leaving the gold standard and devaluing their currencies during the Great Depression, discuss what you think would be the ultimate effect on the Greek economy of abandoning the euro.

3.7 [Related to the Making the Connection on page 360] A column published in the *New York Times* in 2012

observes that "Greece suffers from a crippling competitiveness gap and is locked into the euro."

a. What is a "competitiveness gap"?

b. Was Greece's competitiveness gap connected to its use of the euro? Briefly explain.

Source: Katrin Bennhold, "What History Can Explain About Greek Crisis," *New York Times*, May 21, 2012.

Data Exercises

D11.1: During the 2007–09 period, shocks affected the United Kingdom much more than Canada. As in the United States, oil prices were high, and housing prices had sharply escalated after 2000. The financial crisis in the United States also affected investment in the United Kingdom, both by limiting credit and increasing risk premiums.

Using data from the St. Louis Federal Reserve (http://research.stlouisfed.org/fred2/) FRED database, examine the behaviour of the U.K. economy since 2007.

a. Download quarterly data for real GDP (GBR-RGDPQDSNAQ) and the GDP deflator (GBRGDPDEFQISMEI) from 2006 to the present. Calculate the growth rate of real GDP as the percentage change from the same quarter in the previous year and calculate the inflation rate as the percentage change in the GDP deflator from the same quarter in the previous year. Download data on the unemployment rate (GBRURHARMMDSMEI) for the same time period.

b. Chart the three data series from 2007 to the present in a graph.

c. How similar is the experience of the United Kingdom to the experience of Canada?

D11.2: [Spreadsheet exercise] Another way of viewing the Phillips curve relationship is to relate the inflation rate to the unemployment rate. Using data from the Bank of Canada and from Statistics Canada, examine the relationship between unemployment and the annual inflation rate.

a. Download monthly data for the unemployment rate from Statistics Canada, Table 282-0087 for both sexes, 15 years and over, and

the CPI inflation rate, Table 326-0020, from 1976 to present.

b. Chart the two data series on a graph. For what periods does there appear to be a clear inverse relationship between the inflation rate and the unemployment rate?

c. Calculate the correlation coefficient for the inflation and unemployment rates for this entire period. Now calculate the correlation coefficient for the periods for which you can identify a distinct inverse relationship.

D11.3: [Spreadsheet exercise] Using data from Statistics Canada, CANSIM Tables 326-0020 and 282-0085, examine the experience of the Canadian economy during the period 1982–2007. The Canadian economy experienced a positive technology shock with the spread of information communication technology and the internet after 1995.

a. Download monthly data on the all items CPI from 1981 to the present. Calculate the inflation rate from 1982 to 2007 as the percentage change in the CPI price index from the same month in the previous year. Download the data on the R4 measure of unemployment for the same period

b. Calculate the average inflation and unemployment rates from 1982 to 1995 and from 1996 to 2007.

c. Are your calculations consistent with a Phillips curve that did not shift between 1982 and 2007?

d. Are your calculations consistent with a positive technology shock? Explain.

e. Can you conclude that the changes between the two periods were caused by a positive supply shock?

Monetary Policy in the Short Run

Learning Objectives

After studying this chapter, you should be able to:

Why Didn't the Federal Reserve and the Bank of Canada Avoid the Great Recession?

After the 1990–92 recession ended in April 1992, the Canadian economy experienced an unprecedented period of growth. The economy grew for over 16 years. The growth came to an end when the Great Recession started in Canada in October 2008, a month after Lehman Brothers collapsed. In contrast, the U.S. economy experienced a brief recession in 2001. During the Great Recession, as unemployment soared and the financial system in the United States and some European countries seemed to teeter on the verge of collapse, many people asked the same question: Why hadn't government policymakers avoided this disaster? Many economists had given the Bank of Canada substantial credit for the good performance of the economy between 1992 and 2008. Why, then, had the Bank of Canada been unable to prevent the recession? To answer the question we need to focus on the events in the United States, since the recession in Canada was caused by the crisis there.

We now have a much better idea how to react to a recession and a financial crisis than we had during the Great Depression, thanks in part to path-breaking work of Milton Friedman and Anna Schwartz. In the early 1960s, Milton Friedman of the University of Chicago and Anna Schwartz of the National Bureau of Economic Research published an influential discussion of the importance of bank panics in their book *A Monetary History of the United States, 1867–1960*. In *A Monetary History* and later writings, Friedman and Schwartz singled out the failure in December 1930 of the Bank of United States, a large private bank located in New York

Continued on next page

City, as being particularly important in explaining the severity of the Great Depression. For Friedman and Schwartz, the failure of the Federal Reserve to stop the bank panics of the early 1930s was the key reason the Great Depression was so severe. In 2002, when Ben Bernanke was a member of the Fed's Board of Governors, but not yet the chair, he told Friedman, "Regarding the Great Depression, you're right, we did it. We're very sorry. But thanks to you, we won't do it again." When the financial crisis started in August 2007, Bernanke's words were put to the test. At that point, Bernanke faced a dilemma similar to the one Federal Reserve officials faced in the 1930s: If the Federal Reserve moved to save failing financial firms, it could reduce the severity of the financial crisis, but it might also increase the extent of *moral hazard* in the financial system by changing the behaviour of the managers of the financial firms. The Federal Reserve was worried that the managers of financial firms might be more likely to make risky investments if they believed that the Federal Reserve would bail them out.

In an attempt to avoid the errors the Federal Reserve committed in the 1930s, the Fed saved Bear Stearns from bankruptcy in March 2008 by arranging for another bank, JPMorgan Chase, to purchase it. Fear of increasing moral hazard, though, contributed to the Fed's decision not to save Lehman Brothers, which failed on September 15, 2008. What the Federal Reserve did not predict was the market panic that followed the collapse of Lehman Brothers. At the beginning of 2014, the Federal Reserve released minutes and transcripts of meetings held during the crisis. They showed that central bank officials were not expecting problems. A *New York Times* summary of the transcripts begins with a revealing sentence: "On the morning after Lehman Brothers filed for bankruptcy in September 2008, most Federal Reserve officials still believed that the American economy was growing, and that it would continue to grow, avoiding a recession." Once Federal Reserve officials realized the severity of the banking panic, they decided to put aside concerns about moral hazard and act aggressively to stabilize the financial system. As some commentators pointed out, there was a silver lining in the Lehman collapse. It scared policymakers into bailing out the insurance giant AIG, which asked for assistance the next day. If Lehman Brothers had been bailed out and AIG not, the crisis would have been incomparably more serious. AIG was about three times bigger than Lehman Brothers, with $2 trillion in assets.

But after the collapse of Lehman Brothers it was too late to avoid the financial panic and the most severe recession in the United States in 70 years, even though the policy actions the Federal Reserve took were very aggressive. So we can conclude that the Federal Reserve did not do too little, but it did it too late.

How about the Bank of Canada? Canada was an innocent bystander. Once there is a recession in the United States, the likelihood of a recession in Canada is high. While Canada managed to avoid the 2001 recession, the U.S. economy decline in the last quarter of 2008 was too big, and the news from the collapsing U.S. economy too scary. Concerned with the recession in the United States, consumers and investors cut spending, and exports fell at an unprecedented pace. The Bank of Canada tried hard: Its policy to stimulate the economy after the collapse of Lehman Brothers became very expansionary. It reduced the target overnight rate, which was 3% in September 2008, to 1% in January 2009 and 0.25% in April 2009. In April 2009 the Bank of Canada introduced a new tool for monetary policy: forward guidance, promising to keep interest rates at the record-low level until mid-2010. But monetary policy has its limits, and the shock to the Canadian economy was simply too big to be offset by monetary policy.

Sources: Milton Friedman and Anna Schwartz, *A Monetary History of the United States, 1867–1960* (Princeton, NJ: Princeton University Press, 1963): 308–313; Friedman quote from Milton Friedman, "Anti-Semitism and the Great Depression," *Newsweek* 84 (November 16, 1974); "The Very Model of a Modern Central Banker," *The Economist*, August 29, 2009; Robert Lavigne, Rhys R. Mendes and Subrata Sarker, "Inflation Targeting : The Recent International Experience," *Bank of Canada Review*, Spring 2012; Binyamin Applebaum, "A Chronicle of Uncertainty, Then Bold Action, in 2008 Fed Transcripts," *New York Times*, February 21, 2014; and Andrew Ross Sorkin, "What Might Have Been, and the Fall of Lehman," *New York Times*, September 9, 2013.

Introduction

Monetary policy refers to the actions the central bank takes to manage interest rates and the money supply to pursue macroeconomic goals. In this chapter, we use the *IS–MP* model to explain how the Bank of Canada can employ monetary policy to help stabilize the economy and the financial system and reduce the severity of economic fluctuations. We will also discuss how in practice it can be difficult for the Bank of Canada and other central banks to implement effective policies.

In this chapter we study the Bank of Canada and monetary policy in the short run. As we discussed in Chapter 4, in the long run, the rate of growth of the money supply affects inflation but does not affect real variables. In the short run, monetary policy has real effects. We begin by describing the structure of the Bank of Canada. In Section 12.2 we discuss the goals of monetary policy. In Canada, it involves keeping inflation close to target. In other countries, monetary policy may involve concerns about unemployment or the state of the economy directly. Bank of Canada's tools are described in Section 12.3. The Bank of Canada announces the target for the overnight rate and manipulates bank reserves so that the overnight rate set by banks is close to the target. The main tool is temporary open market operations: The Bank of Canada buys or sells government bonds with an agreement that these transactions are soon reversed. In Section 12.4 we use the *IS–MP* model to analyze monetary policy. We use the model to study the Great Recession and the preceding boom in oil prices. In Section 12.5 we analyze limitations to monetary policy: the lags in recognizing a recession, the delayed reaction of the economy to interest rate changes and the difficulty in forecasting the future behaviour of the economy. We then discuss arguments for and against central bank independence. The chapter concludes with an analysis of monetary policy in an open economy.

The Bank of Canada

12.1
Learning Objective
Understand the structure of the Bank of Canada.

The Bank of Canada was created by the *Bank of Canada Act* of 1934 and started operating in 1935. Its creation was recommended by a royal commission that was created to analyze the lessons from the Great Depression. Initially a private institution, it was nationalized in 1938 and is now a Crown corporation, fully owned by the federal government. It operates largely independently of the federal government; we discuss the issue of central bank independence later in the chapter. The Bank of Canada has four tasks. It conducts monetary policy, regulates financial institutions, issues paper currency (coins are the responsibility of the Canadian Mint), and provides banking services for the federal government. The Bank also conducts research on monetary policy and related issues and, sometimes, co-operates with foreign central banks.

The ultimate responsibility for the Bank lies with the Board of Directors, which consists of 12 outside directors, the governor, the senior deputy governor, and a deputy minister of finance. The outside directors come from all regions of Canada and variety of backgrounds. The board appoints the governor and the senior deputy governor, with the approval of the federal government, for a period of seven years, i.e., longer than the period between federal elections (which is up to five years). This arrangement reduces the potential influence of the federal government on the Bank of Canada.

Since 1994, the **Governing Council** has been the body responsible for major decisions. The Governing Council consists of the governor, senior deputy governor, and the four deputy governors. It is chaired by the governor. The current governor is Stephen Poloz who, in 2013, succeeded Mark Carney, the governor during the financial crisis.

The most important policy tool used by the Bank of Canada is the target for the **overnight rate**, which we encountered in Chapter 10. The **target for the overnight rate** is set by the Governing Council. Decisions are made eight times a year; meetings are between five weeks and eight weeks apart, but a special meeting can be called under exceptional circumstances. (Indeed, during the Great Recession, the Bank of Canada reduced the target for the overnight rate from 3% to 2.5% on October 8, 2008 and to 2.25% on October 21, 2008. The process of setting the rate starts with economic projections prepared by Bank staff. Using the Bank's model of the Canadian economy, staff analyzes international developments and the current and near-future situation of the Canadian economy. Staff prepares the "base case"

Governing Council The governing board of the Bank of Canada, consisting of the governor, senior deputy governor, and four deputy governors.

Overnight rate The rate at which banks lend and borrow from each other at the end of each day; the basis for other interest rates.

Target for the overnight rate The main policy tool of the Bank of Canada; the interest rate the Bank of Canada would like to see in the overnight market.

projection and makes a recommendation. The recommendation is then discussed by the Governing Council. A few days before the decision is made a meeting is held with all members of the Governing Council, special advisers, chiefs of the Bank's four economics departments, and the heads of the Montreal and Toronto regional offices. The final decision is made by the Governing Council by consensus. It is announced the next day at 9 a.m.[1] Prior to announcement the decision is a closely guarded secret, as it can affect share and bond prices.

12.2
Learning Objective
Describe the goals of monetary policy.

The Goals of Monetary Policy

Most economists and policymakers agree that the overall aim of monetary policy is to advance the economic well-being of the population. Economic well-being arises from the efficient employment of labour and capital in the production of goods and services and the steady growth in output. In addition, stable economic conditions (minimal fluctuations in production and employment and smoothly functioning financial markets) are qualities that enhance economic well-being. While most economists agree on these goals, there are differences in opinion on how the central bank can advance economic well-being. Some central banks do it by maintaining a fixed exchange rate (for example, Hong Kong). A fixed exchange rate facilitates planning and reduces risks for exporters and importers, and so increases international trade. Other central banks have several goals: For example, the goals of the U.S. Federal Reserve are price stability, high employment, and interest rate stability. The goal of the Bank of Canada, as well as several other banks, including the European Central Bank and Bank of England, is price stability. Stable prices, which, in practice, means not zero but low inflation, allow firms to plan for the future in real terms; also, they reduce the costs of inflation that we discussed in Chapter 4. Since the Great Recession, central banks have also been paying more attention to financial market stability.

Price Stability

Inflation, or persistently rising prices, erodes the value of money. Ever since the dramatic rise of inflation during the 1970s, policymakers in most high-income countries have set price stability as a policy goal. In a market economy, in which prices communicate information about costs and demand for goods and services to households and firms, inflation reduces the usefulness of prices as signals for resource allocation. Given uncertainty about future prices, families have trouble deciding how much to save for retirement, and firms hesitate to invest or enter into long-term contracts with suppliers or customers. Fluctuations in inflation can also arbitrarily redistribute income. As we discussed in Chapter 4, lenders suffer losses when inflation is higher than expected and borrowers suffer losses when inflation is lower than expected. For all these reasons the goal of many central banks is price stability. In practice, price stability means that the central bank attempts to achieve low and stable inflation rather than zero inflation. The preferred target for the inflation rate is around 2%: In Canada the goal is inflation between 1% and 3%, preferably close to 2%. The European Central Bank aims for inflation below 2%; Japan and the United Kingdom have 2% inflation targets; in Australia the target is 2%–3%. Since 2012 the Federal Reserve in the United States has considered an inflation rate of 2% consistent with the its mandate of price stability and maximum employment.

Why Don't Central Banks Aim for Zero Inflation? There are four reasons not to aim for zero inflation. First, as we discussed in Chapter 2, the recorded rate of inflation is higher than the actual rate of inflation. There are four reasons for the rate of inflation being biased down (i.e., underestimated): Consumers substitute away from more expensive goods (*the substitution bias*); they switch to discount stores (*the outlet bias*); they benefit from quality improvements; and

---

[1]For more details see www.bankofcanada.ca/about/what-we-do/, on which the description is based.

they benefit from the introduction of new goods. These factors are not completely accounted for in the measurement of inflation. As a result, the actual rate of inflation is lower than the CPI inflation by around 0.5% in Canada and 1% in the United States.[2] Second, if the central bank aimed for zero inflation, the inflation rate would sometimes be negative, and many economists and policymakers believe that a negative inflation rate (deflation) is very detrimental for the economy. Third, the experience of the Great Recession drew attention to another reason not to aim for zero inflation: the *zero lower bound* on nominal interest rates, which we discussed in Chapter 4. A low inflation rate limits the ability of the central bank to stimulate the economy. To see this recall that, from the Fisher equation, the lower is the expected rate of inflation, the lower is the nominal interest rate. If firms and households believe the central bank will achieve the inflation target, then the expected rate of inflation is equal to the inflation target, and so the lower is the target inflation rate, the lower is, all other things equal, the nominal interest rate. For example, if the short-term real interest rate is 1% and the inflation target is 2%, the short-term nominal interest rate is 3%. So, in a recession, the central bank can cut the short-term nominal interest rate by at most 3%, since the nominal interest rate cannot be negative. If the inflation target was set at zero, the central bank could cut the rate by at most 1%.

During the Great Recession, central banks in many countries did reduce the short-term nominal interest rate to near zero. As we mentioned in the chapter introduction, in April 2009 the Bank of Canada reduced its policy rate to 0.25% per year. Some economists suggested that a higher target inflation rate of around 4% should be considered to ameliorate the zero lower bound problem.[3] Increasing the target inflation rate has not been a popular goal, however, and it seems that, at least in the near future, few if any central banks will raise their inflation target.

The final reason for not aiming for zero inflation is the argument that positive inflation "greases the wheels" of the labour market. This is based on a view that workers resist *nominal* wage cuts but tolerate *real* wage cuts. The baseline for wage negotiations between unions and firms is often a wage increase equal to the inflation rate plus the rate of productivity growth, which keeps wages constant in terms of the firm's output. If, for example, the inflation rate is 2% and productivity declines 1% then, to keep wages constant in terms of output, the firm can raise workers' nominal wages by 1%. If the inflation rate is zero and productivity falls by 1%, nominal wages need to be reduced by 1%. While in both situations real wages fall by 1%, workers will resist more the second situation, when nominal wages are reduced. This argument is controversial. Some economists think this is an important problem. Other economists think it is not because, first, workers care about their real wages and not nominal wages and, second, even if workers only cared about nominal wages, firms have many ways to reduce labour costs without cutting nominal wages.

Financial Market Stability

When financial markets and institutions do not effectively match savers and borrowers, the economy is inefficient. Firms with the potential to produce high-quality products and services cannot obtain the financing they need to design, develop, and market these products and services. Savers waste resources looking for satisfactory investments. The stability of financial markets and institutions facilitates the efficient matching of savers and borrowers.

Financial market stability is a goal of monetary policy. Banks and financial institutions are prone to *liquidity problems* because they borrow in the short term—sometimes

---

[2]For details see the Bank of Canada backgrounder "Measurement Bias in the Canadian Consumer Price Index (CPI)" at www.bankofcanada.ca; search for "backgrounders."
[3]Olivier Blanchard, Giovanni Dell'Ariccia, and Paolo Mauro, "Rethinking Macroeconomic Policy," International Monetary Fund, February 12, 2010.

overnight—and use the funds to make long-term investments. Therefore, if a large number of depositors want to withdraw funds, a bank may have trouble meeting demands and face a liquidity crisis (so called because the bank liabilities are more liquid than its assets). In a system without deposit insurance, depositors may worry that unless they are among the first to withdraw their money when their bank encounters trouble, they may not be able to retrieve all of it. If many depositors try to withdraw their funds at the same time, the result is a bank run that may cause the bank to fail. The failure of one bank may lead depositors at other banks to withdraw their money in a process called *contagion*. A *bank panic* starts and many banks may be forced to close. A central bank can aim to head off such a panic by acting as a *lender of last resort* to help troubled banks get through temporary liquidity problems.

The Great Recession and the financial crisis that started when Lehman Brothers collapsed brought financial regulation into the spotlight. The two main issues are the determination of the level of adequate reserves and the regulation of systematically important financial institutions. During the boom prior to the crisis, many financial institutions reduced their reserves to maximize profits. To increase reserves during the crisis, banks reduced lending activity. As loans became more difficult to obtain, investment and consumer purchases of durables fell, increasing the severity of the recession. *Systematically important* institutions are banks and other financial institutions whose failure would lead to large disruptions in the economy. These institutions are sometimes called "too big to fail." In case of difficulty, they are expected to be bailed out by the government. To minimize the likelihood of a bailout, new regulations are being introduced aimed at assuring their stability.

Monetary Policy Tools

(12.3)

Learning Objective

Explain the Bank of Canada's monetary policy tools.

The Target for the Overnight Rate

Central banks conduct monetary policy by controlling a short-term interest rate. In Canada, the most important tool of monetary policy is the overnight rate: the rate that financial institutions use to lend and borrow from each other at the end of the day. Financial institutions enter into overnight lending and borrowing agreements to achieve the desired level of reserves. Hence the overnight rate is affected by the supply and demand for reserves.

How does the Bank of Canada control the overnight rate? Once the target rate is set, the Bank of Canada sets the operating band. The band is 0.5% wide; the target rate is in the middle of the band. The upper end of the band (target +0.25%) is called the bank rate, the lower end of the band (target –0.25%) is simply called bottom of the operating band. The Bank of Canada keeps the actual overnight rate within the operating band by providing backstops at both ends of the band. It stands ready to lend funds overnight at the bank rate, and pays the rate equal to the bottom of the band on deposits. The Bank of Canada can do this essentially without limits. By law it can create funds, in this case bank reserves, so there is no limit to overnight lending. There is a cost to the Bank of Canada accepting reserves and paying the overnight rate but this cost can be covered by its earnings from holding government bonds. In addition, the Bank has control over the amount of deposits, as it can reduce the rate it pays. As a result of the Bank of Canada standing ready to lend and borrow, no bank will borrow from another bank at a rate above the bank rate, and no bank will lend to another at a rate below the bottom of the band; in both cases they would prefer to deal with the Bank of Canada.

What is the effect of control of the overnight rate? Here is the description by the Bank of Canada:

> Changes in the Target for the Overnight Rate influence market interest rates. When the Bank changes the Target for the Overnight Rate (the policy interest rate), this sends a clear signal about the direction in which it wants short-term interest rates to go. Changes in the target

rate usually lead to moves in the prime rate of commercial banks, and also influence other lending rates, including mortgage rates, as well as the interest rate paid on deposits, GICs, and other savings.

When interest rates go down, people and businesses are encouraged to borrow and spend more, boosting the economy. But if the economy grows too fast, it can lead to rising inflation. The Bank will then raise interest rates to slow down borrowing and spending, thus putting a brake on inflation.

The Bank of Canada sets the Target for the Overnight Rate at a level that will keep inflation low, stable, and predictable over the medium term. Low and stable inflation provides a favourable climate for sustainable growth in output, employment, and incomes.[4]

Open Market Operations

The most common tool of monetary policy is open market operations. We describe them here since they are used by many central banks, though not by the Bank of Canada. Open market operations are sales and purchases of government securities by the central bank. They affect the policy rate, i.e., the short-term nominal interest rate that the central bank uses to affect the economy, as well as the level of bank reserves. The central bank can decrease the policy rate and raise bank reserves through an *open market purchase*, and it can increase the policy rate and reduce bank reserves through an *open market sale*. Suppose the central bank wants to reduce the policy rate. To do this, it buys short-term Treasury bills (T-bills). The purchase increases the price of short-term Treasury bills and reduces their interest rate since, as we discussed in Chapter 3, bond prices and interest rates are inversely related. If the T-bills are bought from a bank, its reserves increase by the amount it receives.[5] The policy rate falls since it is always closely related to the interest rate on short-term Treasury bills. Conversely, if the central bank wants to reduce the policy rate, it sells short-term government bonds, reducing their price so that the interest rate on these bonds as well as the policy rate both increase.

The Bank of Canada used to conduct open market operations. Since 1994, the Bank of Canada switched to the so called *repo* and *reverse repo transactions*. In a repo transaction, the Bank of Canada buys government bonds and the seller agrees to repurchase the bonds the next day (or at some predetermined date). In a reverse repo, the Bank of Canada sells bonds and agrees to repurchase them from the buyer the next day (or at some predetermined date). So, essentially, the repo and reverse repo transactions are temporary open market operations. Their advantage over traditional open market operations is that they are easily reversed.

The Bank of Canada uses repo and reverse repo transaction to accomplish two goals: affect the interest rate and affect the level of bank reserves. Interest rate on T-bills is 4% per year and the Bank of Canada wants to lower it to 3%. To do this, it enters in a repo transaction with, for example, CIBC. The Bank of Canada buys T-bills from CIBC, and CIBC agrees to buy the bills back the next day at a rate that works out to 3% per year. This rate is 0.0081% per day (to calculate the daily rate, raise 1.03 to the power of 1/365 and subtract one). In other words, CIBC buys the bonds back the next day for an extra $81 per $1 million. The repo transaction works like an open market purchase which is followed the next day with an open market sale. In effect, CIBC borrows money from the Bank of Canada for one day at 3% per year. The repo transaction raises CIBC's reserves for a day. CIBC agrees to the repo transaction since it allows it to acquire funds at less than 4%. The lower rate allows CIBC to

---

[4]Quoted from http://www.bankofcanada.ca/wp-content/uploads/2010/11/target_overnight_rate_sept2012.pdf.
[5]If the T-bills are bought from non-bank public, the seller receives a payment from the central bank and usually deposits it at a bank, raising the bank's reserves.

reduce the rate it charges on its loans to households and firms. The Bank of Canada repeats the transaction for as long as it wants to keep the interest rate at 3%.

Now assume that the Bank of Canada would like to raise the interest rate to 5%. To do this, it enters in a reverse repo transaction with CIBC. It sells T-bills to CIBC and agrees to buy them back the next day at a rate that works out to 5% per year. This rate is 0.0133% per day, i.e., the Bank of Canada buys back the T-bills the next day for an extra $133 per $1 million. The reverse repo transaction works like an open market sale which is followed the next day with an open market purchase. The reverse repo reduces CIBC's reserves and raises its return on funds, which induces CIBC to raise the rate it charges on its loans to households and firms. The Bank of Canada repeats the transaction for as long as it wants to keep interest rates at 5%.

Shifting of Government Balances between the Bank of Canada and Chartered Banks

Another tool of monetary policy used by the Bank of Canada is manipulation of government balances by the central bank. The Bank of Canada is the federal government banker. It uses this function to move government deposits between itself and chartered banks. When the Bank of Canada moves federal government funds to a bank, it does so by crediting the bank's account at the Bank of Canada and, conversely, when it withdraws government funds, it reduces the balance in the bank's account at the Bank of Canada. Since the balance of the bank's account at the Bank of Canada is part of the bank's reserves, by switching government deposits the Bank of Canada affects the amount of reserves in the banking system.

Lender of Last Resort

One of most important functions of the central bank is its role as the lender of last resort. Consider a bank that is solvent, in the sense that its assets exceed its liabilities, but that has a liquidity crisis. A liquidity crisis can happen when the bank has illiquid assets, for example long-term loans, real estate holdings, etc. Liabilities, in particular chequing accounts, are more liquid: If you have a chequing account, you can withdraw your money at any time. Typically, the amount of withdrawals does not vary over time, and the bank can meet them by holding adequate reserves. In case of a financial disruption, however, many customers may want to withdraw their funds at once. If the bank reserves are insufficient, it can ask the Bank of Canada for a loan. This emergency lending is available as long as the institution is solvent and has the appropriate collateral.

Figure 12.1 shows the reaction of the Bank of Canada at the height of the financial crisis. The Bank of Canada provided liquidity to the financial system, acting like the lender of last

Figure 12.1

Advances and Repo Transactions during the Financial Crisis

During the financial crisis, lending by the Bank of Canada increased from under $0.5 billion to almost $40 billion and remained at a high level for almost two years.

Source: Statistics Canada, CANSIM Table 176-0008.

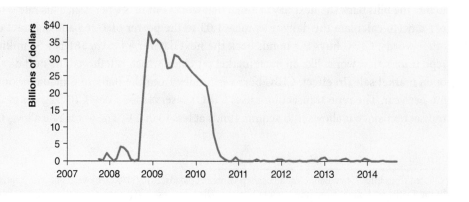

Macro Data: Does the Bank of Canada Manage to Keep the Overnight Rate near the Target?

The Bank of Canada conducts monetary policy by setting the target for the overnight rate. It then carries out the repo and reverse repo transactions each day to keep the overnight rate close to the target rate. Although the Bank of Canada controls the supply of bank reserves, the overnight rate is a market interest rate that is determined by both demand for and supply of reserves. Fluctuations in the demand for bank reserves may cause the overnight rate in the market to deviate from the target. But, as you can see in the figure here, the overnight rate is very close to target. With the exception of a very small difference in 2006 and 2008, it is difficult to spot a difference on the graph. The Bank of Canada is very effective at determining the level of the overnight rate.

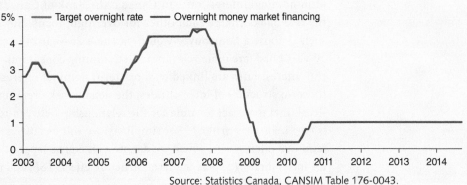

Source: Statistics Canada, CANSIM Table 176-0043.

See related problem D12.1 at the end of the chapter.

resort. Advances and securities purchased under repo agreements rose rapidly in 2008, from around $0.5 billion in September to almost $40 billion in December. They stayed at a very high level for almost two years. As the financial markets stabilized, the value of advances and repos declined over time and fell below $0.5 billion in September 2010.

Reserve Requirements

In many countries, banks are required to hold reserves. Such reserves are called required reserves. They are equal to a certain percentage of various liabilities. Required reserves are usually the highest for chequing accounts, from which funds can be withdrawn at any time, and lower for term deposits, which cannot be immediately withdrawn. The reserve requirement is aimed at forcing banks maintain sufficient funds to meet withdrawals. **Reserve requirements** provide central banks with a monetary policy tool because raising the *required reserve ratio*, or the percentage of chequing account deposits that banks must hold as reserves, reduces the ability of banks to make loans and other investments. Lowering the required reserve ratio increases the ability of banks to make loans and other investments. Changes in reserve requirements are a rarely used policy tool in part because banks find it disruptive to adjust to frequent changes in the required reserve ratio. But some central banks use this policy tool frequently. For example, the People's Bank of China reduced required reserves several times in late 2011 and early 2012 in an effort to stimulate lending and economic activity.

Reserve requirements
Regulations that require banks to hold a fraction of deposits as vault cash or deposits with the central bank.

Reserve requirement were eliminated in Canada in 1994, so Canadian banks are not required to hold any reserves. In practice they do hold reserves, which are called *desired reserves*. Before 1994, Canadian banks almost always held reserves in excess of the required level, and so the Bank of Canada decided there was no need to regulate the level of reserves.

12.4
Learning Objective
Use the *IS–MP* model to understand how monetary policy affects the economy in the short run.

Monetary Policy and the *IS–MP* Model

In this section, we use the *IS–MP* model to analyze monetary policy actions.

Monetary Policy and Aggregate Expenditure

How does monetary policy affect aggregate expenditure? The interest rate on a bond or a loan is the nominal interest rate. As we have seen, central banks control the short-term nominal interest rate. In Canada, the Bank of Canada controls the overnight rate: the rate banks charge each other for overnight loans. But long-term real interest rates, such as those a homebuyer would pay on a 25-year mortgage or a firm would pay on a 10-year bond, are more relevant in determining consumption and investment. Long-term real interest rates are linked to short-term nominal interest rates through three factors: the term structure of interest rates, the default-risk premium, and the expected inflation. Recall that the exact formula for the relationship between real and nominal interest rates is $r = (1 + i)/(1 + \pi^e) - 1$. For simplicity, we will use the approximate formula. The long-term real interest rate, which we denote as r, equals (approximately) the short-term nominal interest rate, i_{ST}, plus the term-structure effect, TSE, and the default-risk premium, DP, minus expected inflation:

$$r = i_{ST} + TSE + DP - \pi^e. \tag{12.1}$$

As Figure 12.2 shows, various interest rates indeed tend to move together. The figure plots the overnight rate, the chartered bank prime business rate (the rate banks charge their best—prime—customers), and the mortgage interest rate. The three rates generally move in the same direction: When the overnight rate increases, so do the long-term nominal interest rates. If the changes in the overnight rate do not affect expected inflation, the real interest rate will also change in the same direction.

We will typically assume that when the central bank changes its target for the short-term nominal interest rate, then the term-structure effect, the default-risk premium, and the expected inflation rate will remain unchanged, and so the long-term real interest rate will change by the same amount.

When the Bank of Canada lowers its target for the overnight rate it is conducting an *expansionary monetary policy*. If the real interest rates decline as a result, it becomes less expensive for households and firms to borrow, and aggregate expenditure increases. When the Bank of Canada raises its target for the overnight rate it is conducting a *contractionary*

Figure 12.2

The Target for the Overnight Rate and Interest Rates on Business Loans and Mortgages

The Bank of Canada controls the overnight rate. The long-term interest rates that households pay to purchase a house or that corporations pay to finance investment generally rise and fall with the overnight rate.

Source: Statistics Canada, CANSIM Table 176-0043.

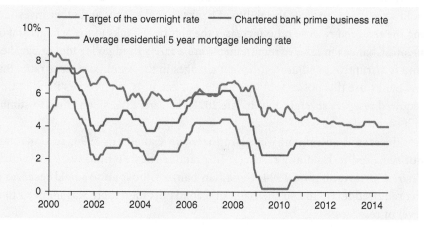

monetary policy. If the real interest rates increase as a result, the cost of borrowing rises and aggregate expenditure falls.

Using Monetary Policy to Fight a Recession

The Bank of Canada goal is to maintain inflation between 1% and 3%; its goal does not include low unemployment, unlike, for example, the U.S. Federal Reserve. Does that mean that the Bank of Canada completely ignores the unemployment rate? The answer is no. Unemployment has an indirect effect on the Bank of Canada policy. It operates through the Phillips curve relationship between unemployment and inflation. If unemployment is high, and output is below potential, inflation falls, leading to lower expected inflation and a further decline in inflation. Since, as we discuss later in the chapter, monetary policy works with a lag, the Bank of Canada reacts to higher unemployment rates with expansionary monetary policy to prevent inflation from falling in the future.

In Figure 12.3, equilibrium is initially at point *A* in panels (a) and (b), with real GDP equal to potential GDP, inflation equal to the target inflation rate, and the expected inflation rate equal to the actual inflation rate. Now assume that the economy experiences a *negative demand shock*, as happened in 2008, when consumer spending fell as a result of the recession in the United States. Panel (a) shows that the demand shock causes the *IS* curve to shift to the left, from IS_1 to IS_2. Real GDP falls below potential GDP, so the output gap becomes negative and the economy enters a recession. In panel (b), a negative output gap pushes short-run equilibrium down the Phillips curve, from point *A* to point *B*, reducing the inflation rate from π_1 to π_2. The Bank of Canada reacts by lowering the target overnight rate, pushing the real interest rate down. As inflation is lower than before, however, the expected inflation rate falls, pushing the real interest rate up (see equation (12.1)). The reduction in the overnight rate needs to be big enough so that the combined result of lower overnight rate and lower expected inflation shifts the monetary policy curve down from MP_1 to MP_2. A lower real interest rate leads to increases in consumption, investment, and net exports, moving short-run equilibrium from point *B* to point *C* on the *IS* curve. Real GDP returns to its potential level, so the output gap is again zero. In panel (b), the inflation rate rises from π_2 back to π_1.

Using Monetary Policy to Fight Inflation

During the economic expansion of the 1980s, the inflation rate increased significantly. In 1987 John Crow, the newly appointed governor of the Bank of Canada, announced that the Bank would reduce the inflation rate. The policy led to a severe recession, but the inflation rate did fall.

Figure 12.4 shows how the Bank of Canada can use monetary policy to reduce the inflation rate and achieve its goal of price stability. Suppose a positive demand shock has pushed real GDP above potential GDP, so that short-run equilibrium is at point *A* in panels (a) and (b). (For simplicity, we do not show the initial shift of the *IS* curve.) At point *A*, the output gap is positive and the inflation rate is greater than expected: $\pi_1 > \pi^e$. To reduce the inflation rate, the Bank of Canada increases the interest rate from r_1 to r_2, causing the *MP* curve to shift up from MP_1 to MP_2. The short-run equilibrium is now at point *B*, and real GDP equals potential GDP, i.e. $\tilde{Y}_2 = 0$. Along the Phillips curve, the output gap changes from $\tilde{Y}_1$ to $\tilde{Y}_2$, so the inflation rate decreases to π_2. At point *B* in panels (a) and (b), both the inflation rate and the output gap have been reduced.

Using Monetary Policy to Deal with a Supply Shock

In the two previous examples, the Bank of Canada used changes in its target interest rate to fully offset the effects on the economy of demand shocks. In theory, when demand shocks

Figure 12.3

Expansionary Monetary Policy

In panel (a), a demand shock causes the *IS* curve to shift to the left, from IS_1 to IS_2. Real GDP falls below potential GDP, so the economy has a negative output gap at $\tilde{Y}_2$ and enters a recession. Panel (b) shows that a negative output gap results in a movement down the Phillips curve, lowering the inflation rate from π_1 to π_2. The Bank of Canada lowers the target overnight rate, and the expected inflation rate falls. The monetary policy curve shifts down from MP_1 to MP_2. Real GDP returns to its potential level, so the output gap is again zero. In panel (b), the inflation rate rises from π_2 back to π_1.

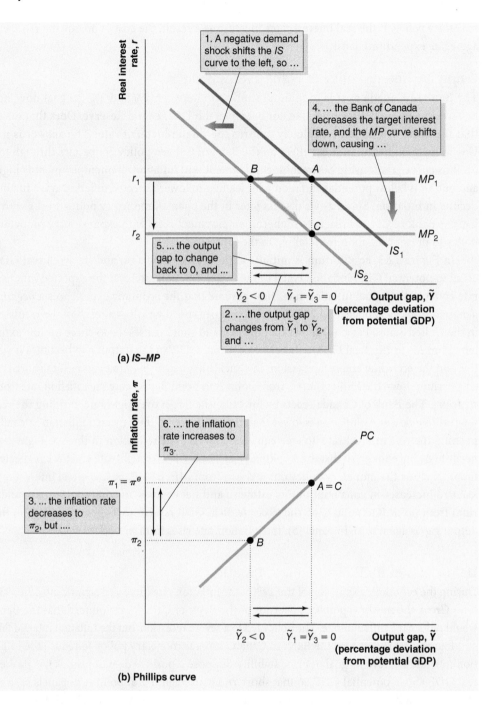

(a) *IS–MP*

(b) Phillips curve

cause the output gap and the inflation rate to fluctuate, it is clear which policy the Bank of Canada should use to achieve its goals. But what should the Bank of Canada do when dealing with a supply shock, such as a significant increase in oil prices? The correct policy for the Bank of Canada to pursue following a supply shock is less clear.

The Canadian economy suffered from a large supply shock in the 1970s, when the price of a barrel of oil nearly tripled from $3.56 per barrel in July 1973 to $11.16 per barrel in October 1974. This increase in oil prices significantly raised the costs of production for many firms. As firms raised prices in response to these higher costs, the inflation rate rose.

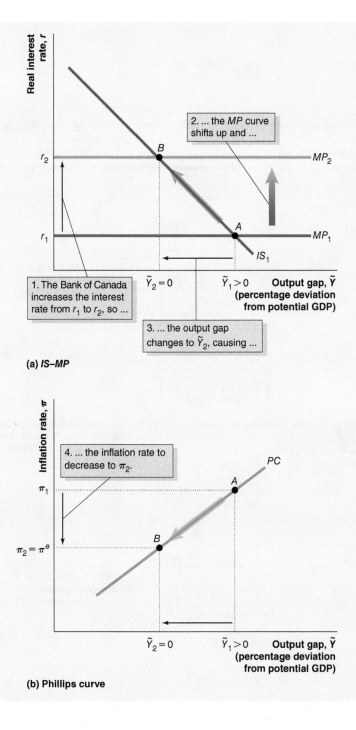

(a) *IS–MP*

2. ... the *MP* curve shifts up and ...

1. The Bank of Canada increases the interest rate from r_1 to r_2, so ...

3. ... the output gap changes to $\tilde{Y}_2$, causing ...

4. ... the inflation rate to decrease to π_2.

(b) Phillips curve

Figure 12.4

Contractionary Monetary Policy

After a positive demand shock, the economy is at point *A* in panels (a) and (b), in which the output gap is positive and inflation is greater than expected. To reduce inflation, the Bank of Canada increases the real interest rate, which shifts up the *MP* curve in panel (a). As a result, the output gap changes from $\tilde{Y}_1$ to $\tilde{Y}_2$. The Phillips curve in panel (b) shows us that the inflation rate will decrease.

Figure 12.5 illustrates the effects of a supply shock. The short-run equilibrium before the supply shock is shown by point *A* in both panels. As panel (b) shows, the supply shock causes the Phillips curve to shift up, from PC_1 to PC_2 as the inflation rate increases for every value of the output gap.

Panel (b) illustrates the dilemma that supply shocks pose for the Bank of Canada. If the Bank of Canada keeps the real interest rate unchanged, then the economy will end up at point *B*, where the inflation rate is higher, undermining the Bank's goal of price stability. The Bank of Canada could attempt to maintain the inflation rate at its initial level by raising the target

Figure 12.5

Monetary Policy and an Increase in Oil Prices

After an increase in oil prices, the economy's equilibrium is at point B in panels (a) and (b), with inflation exceeding the expected inflation rate. The Bank of Canada faces a choice. It can reduce inflation toward the original level by raising the target overnight rate so that the real interest rate rises. This would shift the economy's short-run equilibrium to point C in panels (a) and (b), at the cost of lower real GDP. Alternatively, the Bank of Canada can keep interest rates constant, so the economy's equilibrium remains at point B in panels (a) and (b), but this action leaves the economy with a higher inflation rate.

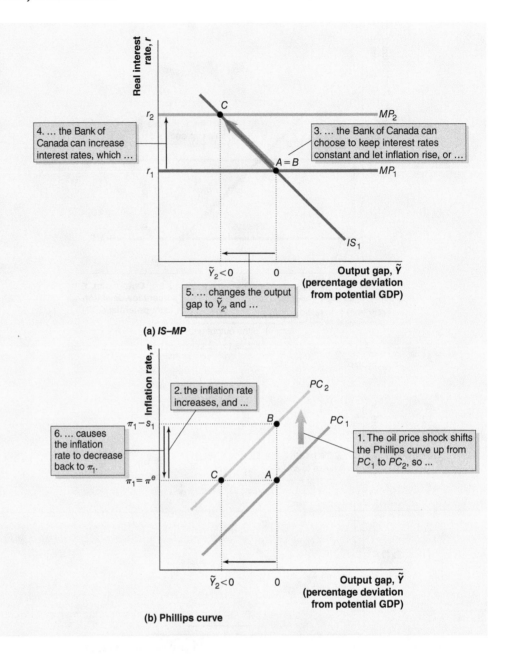

4. ... the Bank of Canada can increase interest rates, which ...

3. ... the Bank of Canada can choose to keep interest rates constant and let inflation rise, or ...

5. ... changes the output gap to $\tilde{Y}_2$, and ...

(a) IS–MP

2. the inflation rate increases, and ...

6. ... causes the inflation rate to decrease back to π_1.

1. The oil price shock shifts the Phillips curve up from PC_1 to PC_2, so ...

(b) Phillips curve

overnight rate so that the real interest rate increases from r_1 to r_2. But, as shown in panel (a), the higher interest rate would result in a movement along the IS curve from point A to point C, as consumption and investment decline. At point C, real GDP falls below potential GDP, so the output gap is negative. The Bank of Canada has succeeded in keeping the inflation rate constant at point C in panel (b) but at the cost of lower output.

The reaction of the Bank of Canada to supply shocks changed over time. In the 1970s, following the tripling of oil prices, the Bank of Canada was concerned about output and unemployment and allowed inflation to increase. As a result, the recession in Canada was mild, but inflation increased above 10%. Many countries followed the same route. The experience of the 1970s changed the thinking about inflation. Faced with high inflation, the Bank of Canada introduced an anti-inflationary policy in 1981–82, and again in

1990–92. In both cases the Bank policy caused recessions but reduced the inflation rate. Nowadays the Bank of Canada focuses on the inflation rate and is not directly concerned with the level of employment.

Solved Problem 12.1

Did the Federal Reserve Make the Great Depression Worse?

The Great Depression, which lasted from 1929 to 1933, was the most severe economic contraction that Canada and the United States have ever experienced. Economists debate whether the U.S. Federal Reserve made the Great Depression worse. (The Bank of Canada was created after the Great Depression, in 1935.) During the first years of the Great Depression in the early 1930s, the Federal Reserve thought that its monetary policy was expansionary because interest rates were low and stable. For example, the *nominal* interest rate on the safest corporate bonds varied from 4.4% to 5.4%. The Fed thought that these low interest rates represented an expansionary policy, so that there was no need to change policy.

Because the United States experienced deflation during these years, however, the *real* interest rate on the safest corporate bonds increased from 4.8% in October 1929, when the stock market crashed, to 15.8% in May 1932! Use the *IS–MP* model to show the effect of a monetary policy that allowed the real interest rate to increase from 4.8% to 15.8%.

Solving the Problem

Step 1   **Review the chapter material.** The problem asks you to explain the effect of the Fed's allowing real interest rates to increase, so you may want to review the section "Monetary Policy and Aggregate Expenditure," which begins on page 374.

Step 2   **Draw the relevant *IS–MP* and Phillips curve graphs.** The Federal Reserve did not target interest rates during the Great Depression as it does today. In fact, the failure of Fed policymakers to understand the distinction between nominal and real interest rates played an important role in the monetary policy failures that worsened the Great Depression. To show the effect of the Fed's action—or inaction!—draw *IS–MP* and Phillips curve graphs with the initial *MP* curve at 4.8%. Label the initial equilibrium as point *A*. The Fed allowed the real interest rate to increase to 15.8%, so draw a second *MP* curve, at a real interest rate of 15.8%. Short-run equilibrium is now at point *B*. As real GDP falls relative to potential GDP and the output gap becomes negative, short-run equilibrium on the Phillips curve moves from point *A* to point *B*, and the inflation rate becomes negative. Your graphs should look like the ones on the next page.

Step 3   **Discuss the effects of a rising real interest rate on the economy.** If the Fed's policy made the Great Depression worse, the increase in the real interest rate would have led to lower real GDP. In fact, real GDP did fall. The increase in the real interest rate made it more expensive for households and firms to borrow to finance consumption and investment, so aggregate expenditure decreased and real GDP fell between 1929 and 1932. The Phillips curve in panel (b) in Step 2 shows that as real GDP declined far below potential GDP, the economy experienced deflation, or a falling price level.

As Milton Friedman argued, the Fed's policies were at least partly responsible for the severity of the Great Depression. Friedman emphasized the Fed's failure to stop the bank panics and the decline in the money supply, but the Fed's failure to distinguish real interest rates from nominal interest rates was also a serious policy mistake. The Federal Reserve's lessons from the Great Depression allowed it to reduce the impact of the financial panic that followed the collapse of Lehman Brothers.

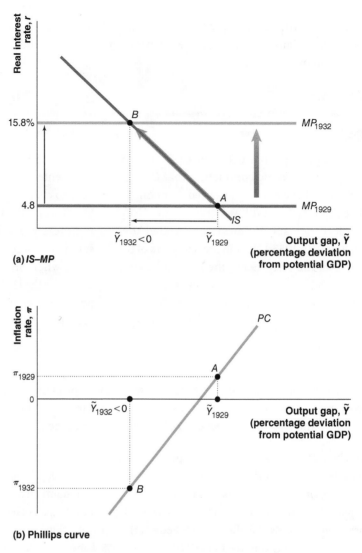

(a) IS–MP

(b) Phillips curve

See related Problems 4.4 and 4.5 at the end of the chapter.

The Liquidity Trap and the Zero Lower Bound on Nominal Interest Rates

So far we discussed the main tool of monetary policy in many countries: the short-term nominal interest rate (the target for the overnight rate in Canada). Sometimes, however, the central bank may not be able to stimulate the economy by lowering the short-term nominal interest rate. To lower the rate, the central bank buys short-term Treasury bills, increasing their price and lowering their interest rate. Recall, from Chapter 3, that short-term Treasury bills are a bit different from long-term bonds. They do not directly pay interest, but instead sell at a discount. The difference between the face value and the purchase price is the return to the holder; it determines the interest rate. The higher is the purchase price, the lower is the return and so the lower is the interest rate. To calculate the interest rate on a Treasury bill, take the difference between face value and purchase price and divide by the *purchase price*. For example, a three-month T-bill with a face value of $100 000, bought for $99 500, yields a return of $500 on $99 500 invested over a quarter of a year. The interest earned is $(100 000 − $99 500)/$99 500 = 0.5025% per quarter. The interest rate per year, assuming the money is reinvested each quarter, is $(1 + 0.5025\%)^4 − 1 = 2.0253\%$. (This is the exact calculation of the interest rate. You may be tempted to calculate the interest rate as 2%, using the approximate calculation 2% = 4 × ($100 000 − $99 500)/$100 000. The difference is small, less than 0.03%, but since the amount of T-bills is in billions of dollars, it should not be neglected.)

If the Bank of Canada's wants to reduce the interest rate, it can raise the price of the T-bill from $99 500 to, for example, $99 800. The interest rate then falls to 0.2004% per quarter or 0.8041% per year. The return seems paltry but, on December 31, 2013, the interest rate on three-month T-bills was 0.89%, which means that the price of a $100 000 T-bill was $99 779.

The decision whether to hold T-bills instead of cash involves a trade-off between interest earned and the loss of liquidity. Financial institutions and households hold Treasury bills, rather than cash, in order to earn interest. On the other hand, cash is more liquid than T-bills since, when funds are needed, T-bills need to be sold first. The *liquidity trap*, hypothesized by John Maynard Keynes, is a situation in which the interest rate is so low that the benefit from holding liquid funds (cash) offsets interest earnings on bonds. In a liquidity trap the central bank cannot push short-term nominal interest rates down. This is easiest to see with an example. Assume that financial institutions and households can earn $200 on $99 800 by holding T-bills for a quarter, and that the value of liquidity of $99 800 in cash is also equal to $200. This means they are indifferent between holding T-bills and cash. In this situation, when the Bank of Canada buys T-bills, the price remains at $99 800 and the interest rate does not fall. Because the interest rate is "trapped" at a low level, Keynes called this phenomenon the *liquidity trap*.

Economists have debated whether the liquidity trap is just a theoretical curiosity or a real phenomenon. But the inability to stimulate the economy by lowering the short-term interest rate became a big obstacle to monetary policy in the Great Recession since the nominal interest rate cannot be negative. A negative nominal interest rate means that the *lender* is paying the *borrower* to borrow the lender's money. Under normal circumstances, that is not going to happen since the lender can, instead, keep funds in cash. The interest rate on cash is zero: If you put $100 in a safety deposit box, at any time you can withdraw $100.

In order to stimulate the economy, several central banks reduced the short-term policy rate essentially to zero. As a consequence, they could not reduce them further. The inability of the central bank to reduce interest rates to negative values is referred to as the **zero lower bound** problem, which we briefly discussed in Chapter 4. When the policy rates fall to zero, the central bank cannot decrease real interest rates by decreasing nominal interest rates. For example, in July 2012, the policy rates were 0.05% in Japan, 0.125% in the United States, and 0.2% in Denmark. Clearly, there was little room for the central banks to reduce interest rates further.

Zero lower bound The inability of the central bank to reduce nominal interest rates below zero.

Making the Connection

Can Nominal Interest Rates Be Negative?

A negative nominal interest rate means, at a personal level, that if you lend someone $100, in the future you will receive less than $100. You will not do it since you can put the cash under the mattress or in a safety deposit box. Similarly, a negative nominal interest rate between financial institutions would mean that one bank would be willing to *pay* another bank to borrow its reserves. For example, CIBC would pay TD a fee for holding its funds overnight. This is an event that is about as likely as CIBC paying you to take out a car loan or a student loan. Neither is going to happen. But, under extraordinary circumstances, nominal interest rates have been negative. At times, government bond yields were negative in the United States, Germany, Switzerland, and Japan. For example, in August 2011, Swiss six-month bonds paid a negative 1% (on a yearly basis). This means that investors were willing to pay 1 005 000 CHF (Swiss francs) for a government bond with face value of 1 000 000 CHF maturing in six months.

Why is that? Under conditions of extreme uncertainty, financial institutions and very rich individuals may not be able to find a safe way to save their funds. It is difficult to convert $1 billion of assets into cash and put the money under the mattress or in a safety deposit box. So it may be cheaper to buy safe government bonds even if the nominal interest rate is negative.

There is another reason for negative nominal interest rate, related to exchange rate policy. In July 2012 the Danish central bank reduced the deposit rate (the rate it pays banks on reserves) to –0.2%. This means that a bank that would keep $1 000 000 in reserves at the central bank would receive, after a year, $998 000. The reason for this odd situation was the Danish exchange rate policy. Denmark did not join the Eurozone but chose to have an exchange rate that could move no more than 2.5% relative to the euro. With much better prospects for the Danish economy than for the Eurozone, interest rates in Denmark were lower than in the Eurozone countries. When the European Central Bank lowered its policy rate, the Danish central bank needed to do the same to prevent appreciation of the Danish currency.

Note, however, that, as we mentioned in Chapter 4, the real interest rate can be negative. The main reason people save is for retirement. When other ways of saving are risky, many savers accept nominal interest rates lower than the rate of inflation in exchange for safety of their savings.

Source: Flemming Emil Hansen, "Denmark Moves to Drop Deposit Rate Below Zero," *The Wall Street Journal*, July 5, 2012.

See related Problem 5.5 at the end of the chapter.

New Monetary Policy Tools in Response to the Great Recession

When the central bank cannot reduce the policy rate any more, what can it do? Recall that, to stimulate the economy, the central bank needs to lower the long-term real interest rate. The equation (12.1) $r = i_{ST} + TSE + DP - \pi^e$ suggests that there are three additional ways to do it:

- reduce the term-structure effect, *TSE*, i.e., flatten the yield curve
- reduce the default premium, *DP*
- *increase* the expected inflation rate, π^e

Before we turn to discussing the three alternatives, we describe how monetary policy may affect credit markets in ways that are independent of the interest rate.

Credit Channels The term *credit channels* refers to the ways monetary policy increases the availability of credit without affecting the policy rate. These channels exist due to *asymmetric information* in the financial system. Asymmetric information occurs when one party in an economic transaction has better information than the other party. The *bank lending channel* of monetary policy emphasizes the behaviour of borrowers who depend on bank loans. Firms have better information about their true financial condition than do potential investors who might be willing to buy their stocks or bonds. Some firms, such as Bombardier or Tim Hortons, are so large and well known that most of the information investors need is publicly available, and the firms can borrow directly from financial markets by selling corporate bonds. However, most firms are not well known, and investors are not willing to buy their bonds. These firms are forced to rely on banks and other financial intermediaries for loans. Banks develop specialized knowledge about firms. For example, a local bank may have made loans to a neighbourhood bakery or beauty salon over a period of years, so the bank knows the owner's history of repaying loans and the owner's general creditworthiness. Many households also rely on banks to finance consumption and investment, by borrowing money to buy cars and homes.

The *bank lending channel* operates through the effect of changes in bank reserves on lending activity. When the Bank of Canada purchases government securities, bank reserves increase. Banks can use the increased reserves to make new loans. If they do, borrowing from banks increases, so consumption and investment increase. The increase in spending leads firms to increase output. An open market sale of government securities would have the opposite effect: The sale of government securities to banks reduces reserves and leads banks to decrease lending. As a result, some households and firms will not be able to obtain loans, so consumption and investment will decrease. The decrease in spending leads firms to decrease output. Notice, though, that the bank lending channel operates regardless of the short-term nominal interest rate. The bank lending channel provides one way in which monetary policy may still be effective even when short-term nominal interest rates equal zero.

The *balance sheet channel* provides an alternative way for monetary policy to affect households and firms that are dependent on banks for loans. Banks often require firms and households to post collateral for a loan. The more collateral that a firm has, the easier it is for the firm to get a loan because the loan becomes less risky for the bank. The same is also true of households that borrow to finance consumption or the purchase of a house. Expansionary monetary policy will often increase stock prices and the value of other assets. An increase in asset values can increase the net worth of firms and the wealth of households, providing them with more collateral to use for loans. As a result, expansionary monetary policy may increase the amount of lending and, therefore, consumption and investment—even if interest rates do not change.

During the Great Recession, however, the bank lending and the balance sheet channels did not provide sufficient stimulus, forcing central banks to introduce new tools of monetary policy to reduce the long-term real interest rates. These tools are called **unconventional monetary policy**.

Reducing the Difference between the Long-Term and the Short-Term Interest Rates Several new tools were aimed at decreasing the *TSE* term by reducing the difference between long-term and short-term nominal interest rates. These included *quantitative easing, operation twist,* and *forward guidance.*

Quantitative Easing When interest rates on short-term securities are close to zero and further purchases by the central bank do not affect interest rates, the bank can try to stimulate the economy by buying long-term securities. Such policy is called **quantitative easing.**

Quantitative easing reduces the long-term interest rates relative to short-term rates. The term structure of interest rates becomes flatter, and the term-structure effect, *TSE*, falls. This means that, for a given policy rate *i*, the *MP* curve shifts down. In practice, the market for long-term government bonds is usually very large, and so even large purchases of long-term securities have only limited effect on long-term interest rates. Therefore, it is unclear whether quantitative easing has a significant effect on real GDP and employment.

Quantitative easing was used extensively by the central banks in the U.S., the U.K., and in Japan. By December 2008, the Federal Reserve had driven the target for the federal funds rate nearly to zero, but the financial crisis and the economic recession were getting worse. These continuing problems led the Federal Reserve to take the unusual step of buying more than $1.7 trillion in mortgage-backed securities and longer-term Treasury bills during 2009 and early 2010. The Fed's objective was to reduce the interest rates on mortgages and on 10-year Treasury bills. By buying large amounts of Treasury bills and mortgage-backed securities, the Federal Reserve would increase the demand for them, forcing up their prices and reducing their interest rate. Lower interest rates on mortgage-backed securities would translate into lower interest rates on mortgages, helping to increase sales of new homes. The Fed's purchases of mortgage-backed securities also helped to reduce the default-risk premium on mortgages. Because the Fed was buying mortgage-backed securities, banks could pass the risk of default to the Fed, and mortgages became less risky for banks.

The interest rate on the 10-year Treasury bill plays a particularly important role in the financial system because it is a benchmark default-free interest rate. A lower interest rate on 10-year Treasury bills can help to lower interest rates on corporate bonds, thereby increasing investment spending. In November 2010, the Federal Reserve announced a second round of quantitative easing (dubbed QE2). With QE2, the Federal Reserve bought an additional

Unconventional monetary policy New tools used by central banks to stimulate the economy at the zero lower bound.

Quantitative easing A central bank policy that attempts to stimulate the economy by buying long-term securities.

$600 billion in long-term Treasury bills through June 2011. In September 2012, the Federal Reserve announced a third round of quantitative easing (QE3), focused on purchases of mortgage-backed securities. The Federal Reserve pledged to buy $85 billion of securities a month and continue QE3 until growth in real GDP and employment returned to more normal levels. (The QE3 program ended in the Fall of 2014 as the U.S. economy improved.)

Why did central banks not buy long-term securities before? Because these securities are risky and central banks have very little capital. For example, in October 2013 the Bank of Canada had $435 million in equity and over $90 billion in assets, i.e., a leverage of over 200. So even minimal losses on risky securities would wipe out the entire capital of a central bank, making it insolvent in the accounting sense. Of course, the central bank cannot go bankrupt. It can receive funds from the government and, at a pinch, print money to meet its obligations. But a situation in which the central bank makes losses on its assets would not be welcome and so, under normal circumstances, central banks restrict their holdings to riskless short-term government bonds.

Figure 12.6 shows the effects of the Fed's policies during the financial crisis of 2007–09 and the period immediately following on the value of assets on the *Fed's balance sheet*. The turmoil following the collapse of Lehman Brothers on September 15, 2008, led to a dramatic change in Federal Reserve policy. The Fed's assets exploded from $927 billion before the Lehman Brothers bankruptcy to $2.2 trillion on November 12, 2008. They continued to increase, reaching over $4 trillion in the last quarter of 2014. Central bank assets in Canada, Japan and the Eurozone countries also rose, but the increase was much smaller. Between the first quarter of 2007 and the last quarter of 2013, the assets of the Federal Reserve increased by 350%; the increase was less than 100% in the other central banks shown in Figure 12.6.

The Bank of Japan tried using quantitative easing as the Japanese economy struggled through a decade of extremely slow economic growth throughout the 1990s. During 2001–06, the Bank of Japan set targets for the volume of bank reserves and purchased long-term government securities until reserves hit the target level. At one point, the Bank of Japan set a target of 30–35 trillion yen for bank reserves when the required level of bank reserves was just 6 trillion yen. In the Fall of 2014 the Bank of Japan announced it will by buying $700 billion a year of securities. Economists still debate whether the Bank of Japan's quantitative easing helped the economy, but the Japanese economy has yet to return to the growth rates it experienced prior to the 1990s.

Quantitative easing has a drawback: By increasing bank reserves and the monetary base, it has the potential to significantly increase inflation. Although critics of the quantitative easing were concerned that inflation would increase as early as 2009, in fact, inflation remained at low levels and, by 2013, policymakers started worrying about inflation being *too low*, rather than too high. The low rate of inflation since the Great Recession, despite the very

Figure 12.6

Central Bank Assets in Canada, Japan, the United States, and the European Central Bank

After the collapse of Lehman Brothers, the Federal Reserve assets increased over fourfold. The increases in asset holdings of other central banks were much smaller.

Source: The International Monetary Fund.

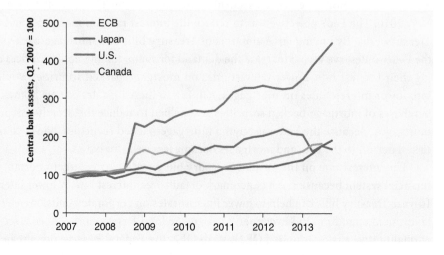

expansionary monetary policy, has been seen by many economists as an indication of the severity of the recession and the weakness of the subsequent recovery.

Operation Twist In September 2011, the Federal Reserve announced that it would purchase $400 billion of long-term securities while also selling $400 billion of short-term securities. The financial press referred to this policy as *Operation Twist*. The policy's name reflects its goal of twisting the yield curve by increasing short-term interest rates and lowering long-term interest rates. In effect, Operation Twist would reduce the term premium in the term-structure effect. Because Operation Twist attempted to directly reduce long-term interest rates through bond purchases, it was similar in its effects to quantitative easing. By selling $400 billion of short-term bonds at the same time that it bought $400 billion of long-term securities, the Federal Reserve did not increase the monetary base or the threat of future inflation. Most economists believe that Operation Twist had only modest success in increasing real GDP and employment.

Forward Guidance Another type of unconventional monetary policy is forward guidance. **Forward guidance** is a central bank's commitment about future behaviour of the policy rate. It was pioneered by the Bank of Canada in April 2009, when the target for the overnight rate has been cut to 0.25%. As the policy rate could not be decreased further, the Bank of Canada issued a conditional promise to keep the interest rates low until mid-2010. Since then conditional guidance has been adopted by the Federal Reserve and the Bank of England. The promise to keep the interest rates low can be made conditional on the state of the economy. For example, in August 2013 the Bank of England announced that it would not increase the policy rate until the unemployment rate falls below 7%. In June 2014 the U.S. Federal Reserve announced that its decision to change the policy rate will depend on the progress toward its goals of maximum employment and 2% inflation and is unlikely to happen "for a considerable time."

Forward guidance flattens the yield curve, reducing the *TSE* term in equation (12.1). Recall that long-term interest rates depend on the average of short-term interest rates. When short-term interest rates are unusually low, households and firms expect them to increase and the term structure is very steep (see Chapter 3). In other words, expectations of an increase in interest rates raise the long-term interest rate. When the central bank provides forward guidance, i.e., promises to keep the policy rate low for an extended period of time, it offsets the expectations of an increase in interest rates in the future. In addition, forward guidance helps firms to plan for the future. Long-term projects become less risky if firms know interest rates will remain low for an extended period of time. So at a given long-term real interest rate, firms undertake more investment projects.

Reducing the Default Premium Can the central bank reduce the default premium? Yes, it can do it indirectly, by stabilizing the economy. When the economy improves, there is lower risk that firms or individuals will default on loans. The decline in the default premium is an additional benefit of stabilizing the economy. The central bank can also reduce the default premium by guaranteeing private loans, for example through an implicit promise to bail out **systemically important financial institutions**. But such action raises the risk of moral hazard, which we discussed before. Financial investments are inherently risky, and it is possible for financial institutions to earn huge profits. It is often the case, however, that the larger the potential profits, the larger the potential losses. Ordinarily, managers of financial institutions have a strong financial incentive to carefully balance potential reward against risk. Sometimes, however, a financial institution becomes so large that its failure would damage the financial system and, potentially, the broader economy. If the government adopts a **too-big-to-fail policy**, it does not allow large financial firms, often called systemically important financial institutions, to fail for fear of damaging the financial system. This is because one of the goals of monetary policy is financial market stability. As a result, many central banks provide support to systemically important financial

Forward guidance The central bank's commitment about future behaviour of the policy rate, an unconventional monetary policy.

Systemically important financial institution A bank, investment bank, insurance company, or another financial institution whose failure may lead to a financial crisis.

Too-big-to-fail policy A policy in which the government does not allow large financial firms to fail for fear of damaging the financial system.

institutions during a crisis, saving them from collapse and achieving financial stability in the short run. In the Great Recession, financial institutions receiving government or central bank help included Bank of America and Citigroup in the United States; Lloyds and the Royal Bank of Scotland in the United Kingdom; Commerzbank, Hypo Real Estate, and many other banks in Germany; ING and ABN Amro in the Netherlands; Fortis in Belgium; and the three largest banks in Ireland. But the expectation of government support during a crisis changes the attitude to risk at those firms. The riskier are a financial firm's activities, the greater are the potential benefits and losses. The expectation of government help in case of problems puts a floor under the size of the possible losses but they also may increase *moral hazard*. Recall that moral hazard involves actions taken by participants in a transaction that make other participants in the transaction worse off. In this case, moral hazard leads to large financial institutions taking on too much risk, which could destabilize the financial system in the long run.

Increasing the Expected Inflation Rate Finally, the central bank can lower the long-term real interest rate by *increasing* the expected rate of inflation. For a given policy rate, if the term-structure effect and default premium do not change, the higher is the expected inflation rate, the lower is the real interest rate (see equation 12.1). Central banks are reluctant to do that because they are afraid that higher inflation expectations will become entrenched, shifting the Phillips curve up and raising the inflation rate. But if the expected interest rate is unusually low, raising it becomes a feasible option. This is what happened in Japan in 2013. Japan has, for a long time, had inflation close to zero. By making a promise to raise the inflation rate to around 2%, the Bank of Japan tried to raise the expected inflation rate and reduce the real interest rate. At the time of writing, it seems that the policy was successful. As the inflation rate in many countries has fallen well below 2%, other central banks can try the same route, by promising to aggressively raise the inflation rate back to 2%.

The Limitations of Monetary Policy

12.5
Learning Objective
Explain the challenges in using monetary policy effectively.

Our discussion thus far may make it seem easy for central banks to eliminate economic fluctuations and achieve price stability and high employment following a demand or a supply shock. In fact, though, central banks face several important challenges to implementing policy successfully.

The ability to quickly recognize the need for a change in monetary policy is a key to its success. If the central bank is late in recognizing that inflation rate is increasing or a recession has begun, it may not be able to implement a new policy soon enough to avoid a significant increase in inflation or a significant recession. In fact, particularly when dealing with temporary shocks, if the central bank implements a policy too late, it may actually destabilize the economy.

Policy Lags

In this section, we discuss *policy lags*: the time between the shock and the effect of the central bank policy. There are three sources of lags. First, it takes some time for the central bank to recognize that a shock has occurred (*recognition lag*). Second, after the central bank realizes that a shock has occurred, it takes time to decide on an appropriate policy (*implementation lag*). Finally, it takes time for the new policy to actually affect inflation, real GDP, and employment (*impact lag*). Due to *lags* between the time a shock occurs and the time the effects of the policy change occur, monetary policy cannot immediately offset the effects of shocks.

A **recognition lag** is the period of time between when a shock occurs and when policymakers recognize that the shock has affected the economy. Economic data become available to policymakers with a delay of up to several months. It takes up to three months (a quarter) for all the relevant data to be provided by the statistical office. In addition, in many countries initial estimates of economic variables, such as employment and real GDP, are often inaccurate and are subsequently revised. In Canada data revisions are small but the delay is large as Statistics Canada puts greater focus on the accuracy of the data than on how fast they are

Recognition lag The period of time between when a shock occurs and when policymakers recognize that the shock has affected the economy.

available. In contrast, in the United States there is greater focus on speed, and economic data are available with smaller delay, but are often substantially revised.

Even when a shock occurs, it is difficult to know if a shock has had a large effect on the economy. This uncertainty makes it difficult for policymakers to know if a shock requires a policy response. For example, in 2000, stock markets around the world declined. NASDAQ (a U.S. stock index based largely on high-tech companies) peaked on March 10, 2000, and then rapidly declined as the dot-com bubble burst. The TSE index lost 15% of its value between March 20, 2000, and April 10, 2000. A destruction in stock market wealth could potentially lead to a recession. However, it was not initially clear that the U.S. economy would enter a recession after the dot-com bubble burst. In fact, on May 16, 2000, the Federal Reserve actually increased interest rates from 6.0% to 6.5% even though the NASDAQ had decreased by 26.4% because it was still worried that inflation was accelerating. In the end, while there was a recession in the United States in 2001, the Canadian economy continued to grow.

An **implementation lag** is the period of time between when policymakers recognize that a shock has occurred and when they adjust policy to the shock. Implementation lags exist because, once the central bank recognizes that a shock has occurred, it still takes time to determine whether and how to respond. For monetary policy, implementation lags are short. For example, Bank of Canada started reducing the target for the overnight rate three weeks after the collapse of Lehman Brothers.

An **impact lag** is the period of time between a policy change and the effect of that policy change on real GDP, employment, inflation, and other economic variables. Nobel Laureate Milton Friedman famously described the lags for monetary policy as "long and variable," which means that it can take months or years for changes in monetary policy to affect real GDP and inflation and that the lags vary based on historical circumstances. When the central bank reduces the policy rate, the long-term real interest rates that affect corporate and household behaviour decline with some delay. Then it takes time for firms to identify newly profitable investment projects, obtain loans from banks or borrow by selling corporate bonds, and start spending the borrowed funds. Similarly, it takes time for families to respond to lower mortgage interest rates by buying houses. As a result, the full effect of a change in monetary policy is typically spread out over several years.

Implementation lag The period of time between when policymakers recognize that a shock has occurred and when they adjust policy to the shock.

Impact lag The period of time between a policy change and the effect of that policy change.

Economic Forecasts

Because it can take a long time for the effect of a change in monetary policy to affect real GDP, central banks do not respond to the current state of the economy. Instead, they respond to the state of the economy they think will exist in the future, when the policy change actually affects the economy. For example, following the collapse of Lehman Brothers, the Bank of Canada started cutting the target for the overnight rate on October 8, 2008 (from 3% to 2.5%). At that time it was not yet apparent how serious the crisis was. As, over time, new information made clear the seriousness of the crisis, the policy rate was cut five more times, reaching 0.25% in April 2009. Given the impact lags associated with monetary policy, the full effect of the rate cuts on real GDP was likely to be spread out over several years. In making the cuts, the Bank of Canada was thinking about the economy's future performance.

For a central bank to succeed in reducing the severity of business cycles, it must often act *before* the size of a shock is apparent in the economic data. So, good policy requires good economic forecasts based on models that describe accurately how the economy functions. Unfortunately, economic forecasts and models can be unreliable because the factors determining real GDP can change quickly. Shocks, by their nature, are unpredictable. For example, the forecasts of most economists made at the end of 2006 and the beginning of 2007 did not anticipate the severity of the economic slowdown that began in the United States in December 2007. Only after financial market conditions began to deteriorate rapidly did economists significantly reduce their forecasts of GDP growth in 2008 and 2009.

Model Uncertainty

An issue related to difficulty in economic forecasting is model uncertainty. Even if the Bank of Canada is convinced that the economy will enter a recession or that inflation will accelerate next year, it still faces problems in implementing monetary policy. Why? Economic models are just approximations of how the world works. As a result, economists do not know precisely how any given event will change real GDP and inflation, how a change in the target short-term nominal interest rate will affect the long-term real interest rate, how much consumption and investment will respond to changes in the long-term real interest rate, how much real GDP will respond to the changes in consumption and investment, or how much inflation will respond to changes in real GDP.

Economic models are not sophisticated enough to tell us precisely the effect of an event on aggregate expenditure. For example, we know that consumption responds to changes in wealth, so a reduction in real estate values should reduce consumption. The key question for central bankers is, By how much? Various studies provide estimates of consumption reduction to be in the range of 2% to 20% of the wealth decline. The high estimate is an order of magnitude (ten times) larger than the low estimate, so it is difficult for the Bank of Canada to know exactly the size of the consumption decline when house prices fall. In addition, changes in the policy rate do not necessarily lead to identical changes in the long-term real interest rates. There is only a *tendency* for long-term rates to decrease as the policy rate is cut. Figure 12.2 on page 374 shows that the interest rates are related but that the relationship is not perfect. As a result, the Bank of Canada does not know for certain by how much a given change in the policy rate will reduce the long-term real interest rate, nor does it know by how much the long-term real rates should be reduced. Finally, economic models cannot tell us exactly how much inflation will respond to changes in real GDP, or the output gap.

Consequences of Policy Limitations

Policy lags and the inherent uncertainty of economic forecasts mean that policymakers may make mistakes. Figure 12.7 provides an example of a poorly timed monetary policy. The economy starts at point C in panels (a) and (b). Suppose that stock market wealth falls by 10% on a single day. Based on its models and economic forecasts, the central bank believes the result will be reduced consumption, leading to a recession. Therefore, the central bank believes that short-run equilibrium will occur at point A in panels (a) and (b).

At point A, real GDP is below potential GDP, so $\widetilde{Y}_1 < 0$ and cyclical unemployment is positive. In response, the central bank decreases the target interest rate to increase consumption, investment, and net exports and shift short-run equilibrium to point B. If the policy is well-timed and the IS curve remains at IS_1 then when the central bank reduces interest rates, real GDP increases relative to potential GDP and the output gap moves to $\widetilde{Y}_2$, i.e., it returns to zero. The change in the output gap causes the inflation rate to increase to π_2. Short-run equilibrium is now at point B, and the recession has ended. What happens when the policy is not well-timed? Since lags for monetary policy are long and variable, it takes time for the monetary policy to have full effect on the economy. So it is possible that, by the time monetary policy takes effect, the stock market has already recovered, and by the time real GDP begins responding to the policy, the IS curve has shifted back to IS_2 and the short-run equilibrium is at point C. The recession is over *before* the change in policy affects real GDP. Therefore, the change in policy will move the short-run equilibrium to point D in panel (a), where $\widetilde{Y}_4 > 0$. With the output gap equal to $\widetilde{Y}_4$, the inflation rate increases to π_4 and short-run equilibrium is now at point D in panel (b). In this case, monetary policy has pushed real GDP beyond potential GDP, causing the inflation rate to increase.

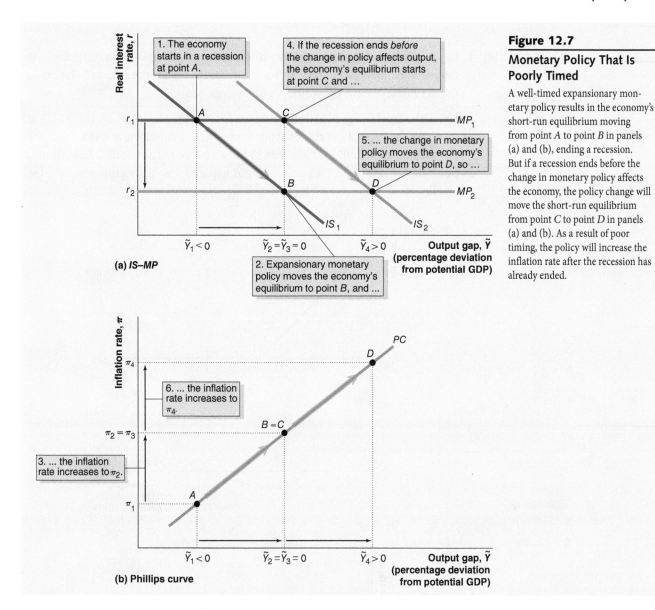

(a) *IS–MP*

1. The economy starts in a recession at point *A*.

4. If the recession ends *before* the change in policy affects output, the economy's equilibrium starts at point *C* and ...

5. ... the change in monetary policy moves the economy's equilibrium to point *D*, so ...

2. Expansionary monetary policy moves the economy's equilibrium to point *B*, and ...

6. ... the inflation rate increases to π_4.

3. ... the inflation rate increases to π_2.

(b) Phillips curve

Figure 12.7

Monetary Policy That Is Poorly Timed

A well-timed expansionary monetary policy results in the economy's short-run equilibrium moving from point *A* to point *B* in panels (a) and (b), ending a recession. But if a recession ends before the change in monetary policy affects the economy, the policy change will move the short-run equilibrium from point *C* to point *D* in panels (a) and (b). As a result of poor timing, the policy will increase the inflation rate after the recession has already ended.

Solved Problem 12.2

Did the Federal Reserve Help Cause the 2001 Recession in the United States?

In the third quarter of 1998 real GDP in the United States was 1.1% greater than potential GDP. Because of rapid growth it rose to 3.5% above potential GDP by the second quarter of 2000. With real GDP above potential GDP, the inflation rate began to increase. The U.S. inflation rate increased from 1.4% during September 1998 to 3.7% during June 2000. The Federal Reserve responded by increasing the policy rate (the target federal funds rate) from 5.0% in September 1998 to 6.5% in May 2000. The last increase in the target rate came after the dot-com bubble burst and all major stock indexes started to

decline rapidly. By March 2001, the U.S. economy had entered a recession. The terrorist attacks on September 11, 2001, led households and firms to reduce consumption and investment, and worsened the recession. The recession was short, ending in November 2001, but the U.S. economy recovered slowly, and real GDP was 1.9% below potential GDP as late as the first quarter of 2003. Did the Federal Reserve's decision to increase the policy rate contribute to the recession and the slow recovery? Use the *IS–MP* model to show the effect of the U.S. central bank's policy.

Solving the Problem

Step 1 **Review the chapter material.** The problem asks you to explain the difficulty in the timing of the monetary policy, so you may want to review the section "The Limitations of Monetary Policy," which begins on page 386.

Step 2 **Draw the initial equilibrium using an *IS–MP* graph.** Draw an initial *IS–MP* graph for the second quarter of 2000. In your graph equilibrium real GDP should exceed potential GDP by 3.5%. Your Phillips curve graph should show an inflation rate for 2000 of 3.7% and an output gap of 3.5%. Your graphs should look like these:

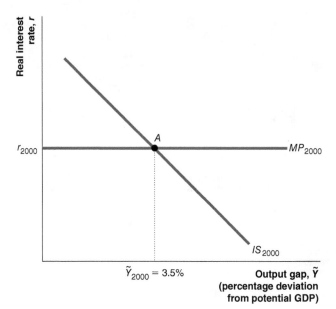

(a) *IS–MP*

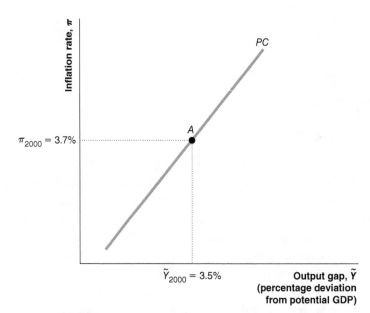

(b) Phillips curve

Step 3 **Show the effect of the increase in interest rates.** The Federal Reserve increased the policy rate, which should increase long-term real interest rates. Assume that the central bank knows exactly how much to increase interest rates to move real GDP to potential GDP. Therefore, you should shift the *MP* curve up on the *IS–MP* graph, and you should show the short-run equilibrium moving down the Phillips curve so that the output gap falls to zero. Your graphs should now look like these:

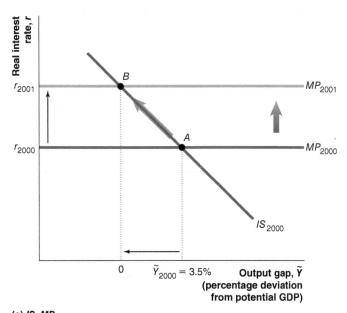

(a) *IS–MP*

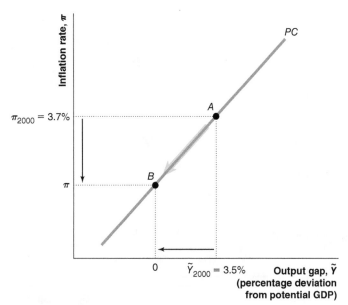

(b) Phillips curve

Step 4 **Show the effect of the collapse in stock prices and the terrorist attacks.** A stock market collapse such as the one that occurred in 2000 reduces household wealth, which reduces consumption. The stock market collapse also increases uncertainty about the future, leading firms to reduce investment spending and leading households to further reduce consumption. The terrorist attacks also increased uncertainty, leading firms and households to reduce expenditures on goods and services. Show the effect of the decrease in aggregate expenditure by shifting the *IS* curve to the left in the *IS–MP* graph and by moving the short-run equilibrium further down the Phillips curve. Your graphs should look like these:

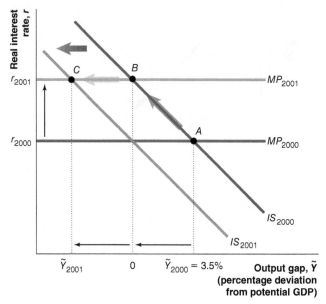

(a) *IS–MP*

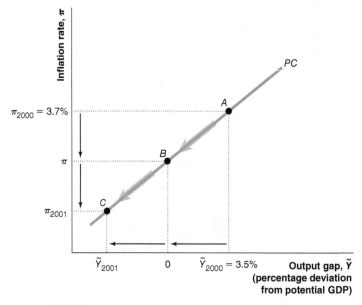

(b) Phillips curve

The Federal Reserve did not predict the collapse of the stock market; obviously, it could not predict the terrorist attacks. Therefore, it based its policy decisions in 2000 on where it *thought* the *IS* curve would be. The U.S. central bank may have anticipated that the *IS* curve would remain at IS_{2000} but, as a result of the unanticipated events, the actual *IS* curve has shifted left, to IS_{2001}. As a result, the decision to increase the policy rate during 2000 may have contributed to the 2001 recession and to the slow recovery.

See related Problem 5.3 at the end of the chapter.

Central Bank Independence

12.6

Learning Objective

Evaluate the arguments for and against central bank independence.

Governments create central banks, and governments also appoint the heads of central banks. This process does not necessarily mean, however, that governments control the decisions of central bankers. When a central bank is independent, its board and the head of the bank are selected by the government, but they are appointed for several years, usually longer than the government term in office. An independent central bank manages monetary policy without interference from the elected officials.

What are the benefits of an independent central bank? First, it is not subject to the political cycle. A government may be tempted to stimulate the economy before the election, creating a boom and reducing the unemployment rate. An independent central bank, with a governor whose term ends after the next election, would be more resistant to political pressures. Second, an independent central bank cannot be ordered to finance government spending. A central bank that is subject to government control may be used to finance government spending, sometimes with catastrophic results. An example is the last note issued by the central bank of Zimbabwe, with a denomination of $100 trillion Zimbabwean dollars (shown in Chapter 1). This is the result of the central bank of Zimbabwe being under control of the government and buying government bonds by printing larger and larger quantities of money.

The Independence of the Bank of Canada

Is the Bank of Canada independent? Surprisingly, this question is difficult to answer. The federal government influences the Bank of Canada by appointing its governor. The governor of the Bank of Canada is appointed for a period of seven years, while the maximum period between federal elections is five years. This means that a newly elected government is usually not able to appoint a new governor (unless an election and end of governor's term coincide). The government does get involved with setting the goals of monetary policy. Inflation targets are jointly set by the Minister of Finance and the governor. But the government does not interfere in how the policy is conducted. The deputy minister of finance sits on the policy-making body but is a non-voting member.

The uncertainty about Bank of Canada independence is due to a peculiar nature of the main mechanism, called *the directive*. It was introduced in early 1960s, following a conflict between the governor of the Bank at the time (James Coyne) and the government. The directive clarifies the relationship between the government and the bank. The government, as an elected body, is superior. In case of a fundamental disagreement on monetary policy, the Minister of Finance can issue a directive, which will be announced in official government records. The governor will have to follow the directive and, as is understood, will resign. The directive provides a mechanism for the government to gets its way. But the mechanism is blunt. An official announcement of a conflict, followed by resignation of the governor, may undermine the confidence in government and upset financial markets. Such a blunt mechanism is not likely to be misused.

In fact, the directive has never been used. There are two potential explanations. The governor of the Bank of Canada may be afraid of being replaced and would not risk a public disagreement. In case of a fundamental disagreement, following behind-the-scenes talks the governor does what he is ordered to do. If this is the case, the bank is not independent.

An alternative explanation why the directive has never been used is that Finance Ministers would not risk political fallout from a governor's resignation. In behind-the-scenes talks they press the governor but, ultimately, give up if the governor stands his ground. If that is the case, the bank is de facto independent.

The Case for Central Bank Independence The main argument for central bank independence is that monetary policy—which affects inflation, interest rates, exchange rates, and economic growth—is too important and technical for politicians to determine. Because of the frequency of elections, politicians may be concerned with the short-term benefits of policies, without regard for the policies' potential long-term costs. In particular, the short-term desire of politicians to be re-elected may clash with the country's long-term interest in low inflation. The public may well prefer that the experts at the central bank, rather than politicians, make monetary policy decisions.

Another argument for central bank independence is that complete control of the central bank by elected officials increases the likelihood of fluctuations in the money supply caused by political pressure. For example, particularly just before an election, those officials might pressure the central bank to assist the government's borrowing efforts by buying government bonds, which would increase the money supply and temporarily increase real GDP and employment, but at the risk of increasing the variability of inflation.

The Case Against Central Bank Independence The importance of monetary policy for the economy is also the main argument against central bank independence. Supporters of reducing the central bank's independence argue that in a democracy, public policy should be conducted by elected officials. Because the public holds elected officials responsible for monetary policy problems, some analysts advocate giving those officials more control over it. While some economists argue that monetary policy is too technical for elected officials to understand, other economists argue that elected officials have experience dealing with equally complex tasks, such as fiscal policy, national security, and foreign affairs. In addition, critics of central bank independence argue that placing the central bank under the control of elected officials could confer benefits by coordinating monetary and fiscal policies.

Those in favour of greater government control argue that the central bank has not always used its independence well. For example, critics note that the Federal Reserve's concern about inflation contributed to its failure to assist the banking system during the Great Depression. The Bank of Canada's efforts to reduce inflation led to two recessions in early and late 1980s. So central bank independence is by no means a guarantee of sound monetary policy. However, research on central bank independence indicates that the more independent the central bank, the better the economy's performance. Alberto Alesina and Lawrence Summers, economists at Harvard University, examined the relationship between central bank independence and macroeconomic performance for 16 high-income countries from 1955 to 1988. Figure 12.8 shows their findings on the relationship between central bank independence and average inflation rates. Alesina and Summers measured central bank independence using an index ranging from 1 (minimum independence) to 4 (maximum independence). Their results show that the more independent the central bank,

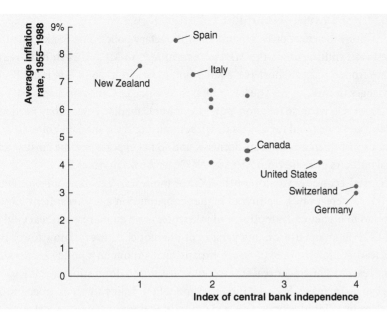

Figure 12.8

Central Bank Independence and the Average Inflation Rate

For 16 high-income countries, the greater the degree of central bank independence from the rest of the government, the lower the inflation rate.

Source: Alberto Alesina and Lawrence Summers, "Central Bank Independence and Macroeconomic Performance: Some Comparative Evidence," *Journal of Money, Credit, and Banking*, May 1993, Vol. 25, No. 2, pp. 151–162. Copyright © 1993. Reproduced with permission of Blackwell Publishing Ltd.

the lower the average inflation rate. During this period, New Zealand's central bank was least independent, and the inflation rate averaged 7.6%. In contrast, the central banks of Germany and Switzerland were the most independent and experienced average inflation rates of about 3%. This result is consistent with the view that independent central banks resist political pressure to stimulate the economy in the short run at the cost of higher inflation in the long run. Alesina and Summers also found that central bank independence reduces the volatility of both the inflation rate and the real interest rate. More stable prices and real interest rates make it easier for households and firms to make long-term plans such as saving for retirement or deciding to build a new factory. Therefore, central bank independence improves the performance of the economy. The benefits of improved economic performance, however, must be weighed against the cost of having monetary policy conducted by a central bank that is not directly responsible to the voters.

Monetary Policy in an Open Economy

12.7
Learning Objective
Explain how monetary policy operates in an open economy.

Canada is an open economy and has extensive foreign trade and financial links with other countries. To this point, we have not considered in detail international trade and international monetary flows when discussing monetary policy. We have also not taken into account exchange rate policies. A country can either allow the exchange rate for its currency to float, so the exchange rate changes from day to day, or a country can try to fix the exchange rate at some level. As it turns out, the decision to either fix the exchange rate or let it float can help determine the effectiveness of monetary policy. The discussion of the monetary policy with flexible and fixed exchange rates closely follows the discussion in the previous chapter.

In the discussion of monetary policy in this chapter we focus on an expansionary monetary policy. We start with a situation in which the economy was previously in long-run equilibrium but a shock resulted in output falling below the full employment level of output, creating a negative output gap. The task of the monetary policy is then to increase the level of output to close the output gap.

Monetary Policy with Flexible Exchange Rates

Figure 12.9 shows the effect of an expansionary monetary policy. The Bank of Canada reduces the interest rate, shifting down the MP curve from MP_1 to MP_2. This shift decreases the real interest rate, from r_1 to r_2, so short-run equilibrium moves from point A to point B, and the output gap changes from $\tilde{Y}_1$ to $\tilde{Y}_2$. The lower interest rate makes Canadian assets less attractive, so their purchases fall. Because investors purchase fewer Canadian assets, they need fewer Canadian dollars, so the demand for dollars decreases, causing the Canadian dollar to depreciate in value. Our exports increase, imports decrease, and so net exports and the current account rise. Net capital outflows increase from NCO_1 to NCO_2, as shown in panel (b).

In a closed-economy version of the IS–MP model, an expansionary monetary policy would reduce interest rates, leading to higher consumption and investment. Lower interest rates still lead to higher consumption and investment and an increase in real GDP relative to potential GDP in an open-economy version of the model. However, now lower real interest rates also lead to higher net exports, so expansionary monetary policy increases real GDP for a third reason: The lower real interest rates cause the domestic currency to depreciate, and net exports increase. We conclude that monetary policy in an open economy is more effective than in a closed economy. A reduction in real interest rates, apart from increasing consumption and investment, leads to the depreciation of the currency and an increase in net exports.

Monetary Policy with a Fixed Exchange Rate

Fixed exchange rate systems pose a challenge for governments. Central banks have an unlimited ability to create their own currency, so they have no difficulty maintaining a fixed

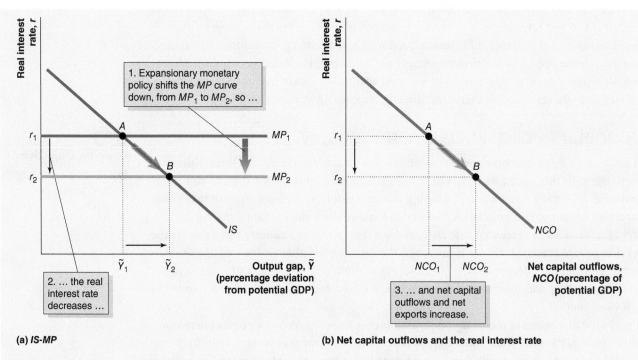

(a) IS-MP

(b) Net capital outflows and the real interest rate

Figure 12.9 An Expansionary Monetary Policy with a Flexible Exchange Rates

An expansionary monetary policy decreases the real interest rate in panel (a). The decrease in the real interest rate causes the exchange rate to depreciate, so net capital outflows increase in panel (b). In both panels, equilibrium moves from point A to point B.

exchange rate system when they need to sell the domestic currency in exchange for a foreign currency, for example, selling yuan in exchange for dollars. Things are quite different when a central bank needs to sell foreign currency in exchange for domestic currency. As the central bank has only limited reserves of foreign currencies, it may eventually run out of reserves and no longer be able to maintain the fixed exchange rate. It may then have to *devalue* the currency or abandon the fixed exchange rate and switch to a flexible exchange rate. We described these problems in more detail in Chapter 5, where we discussed the case of China managing the pressure on the yuan to appreciate and the case of Mexico managing the pressure on the peso to depreciate. Recall that, faced with the loss of reserves during the 1994 crisis, the central bank of Mexico initially devalued the peso and then switched to a flexible exchange rate.

Expansionary Monetary Policy Figure 12.10 shows the effect of an expansionary monetary policy with a fixed exchange rate. The initial equilibrium is at point A in both panels. In panel (a) at point A there is a negative output gap. In panel (b) net private capital outflow is equal to the current account balance, so official reserves do not change. As long as the initial real interest rate is greater than $\bar{r}$, the central bank can increase real GDP with an expansionary monetary policy that shifts the MP curve down, from MP_1 to MP_2. The expansionary monetary policy has the usual effect: The output gap changes from $\widetilde{Y}_1$ to $\widetilde{Y}_2$ in panel (a). In panel (b) net private capital outflow increases above the current account balance and, to maintain the fixed exchange rate, the central bank must buy the domestic currency on the foreign-exchange market. The central bank loses reserves, so such policy cannot be run indefinitely. The central bank cannot reduce the real interest rate below the lower bound, $\bar{r}$, as it would trigger a speculative attack. A fixed exchange rate clearly puts severe limits on the ability of conventional monetary policy to stimulate the economy: The lower is the real interest rate relative to the world real interest rate, the faster official reserves are exhausted and the sooner the fixed exchange needs to be abandoned or devalued.

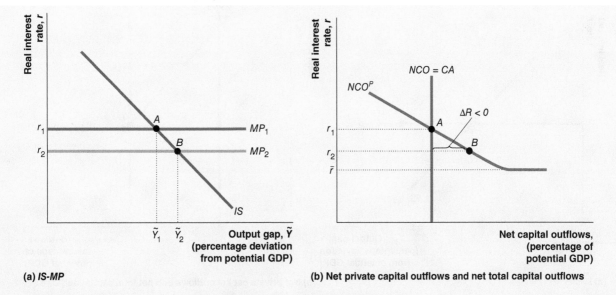

(a) *IS-MP*

(b) Net private capital outflows and net total capital outflows

Figure 12.10 An Expansionary Monetary Policy with a Fixed Exchange Rate

With fixed exchange rates, an expansionary monetary policy shifts the *MP* curve down, raising output relative to potential output. To maintain the fixed exchange rate, the central bank loses reserves. In both panels, monetary policy results in short-run equilibrium moving from point *A* to point *B*. The central bank cannot shift the *MP* curve below the lower bound of $\bar{r}$ in panel (b) for a significant amount of time while maintaining the fixed exchange rate.

Devaluation. If a country operates under a fixed exchange rate system, policymakers have an additional way to affect economic activity. The government can decide to maintain a fixed exchange rate system but with a devalued currency. If the government devalues the currency there is a one-time decrease in the nominal exchange rate and, with prices adjusting slowly, a one-time decrease in the real exchange rate. The decrease in the real exchange rate will make exports of goods and services cheaper and imports more expensive, so the current account balance will increase.

Figure 12.11 illustrates a successful devaluation. Initially, the equilibrium is shown at points denoted A, with output gap equal $\tilde{Y}_1$ in panel (a) and reserves falling by the distance AA in panel (b). The net private capital outflow line is NCO_1^p so that the current interest rate is close to the rate that would trigger currency speculation. A currency crisis is looming. To avoid the crisis the central bank could increase the real interest rates by shifting the MP curve up, but such contractionary monetary policy would reduce output. Currency devaluation offers an alternative policy. It makes exports cheaper and imports more expensive and so raises aggregate expenditure at every level of the real interest rate. This implies that the IS curve shifts right, from IS_1 to IS_2 in panel (a), raising the level of output. The new equilibrium is shown at points denoted B. The current account increases and the net capital outflow line shifts to the right, from NCO_1 and NCO_2 in panel (b), so that, without a change in the real interest rate, the current account balance now equals the net private capital outflow and the central bank no longer loses reserves. As a result, speculators give up. The net private capital outflow becomes NCO_2^p and the interest rate that would cause a speculative attack is now lower than before.

Of course, not every devaluation is so simple or so successful. The devaluation in Mexico in December 1994, which we discussed in Chapter 5, happened much too late, and the speculative attack continued, resulting in Mexico abandoning the fixed exchange rate and Mexican

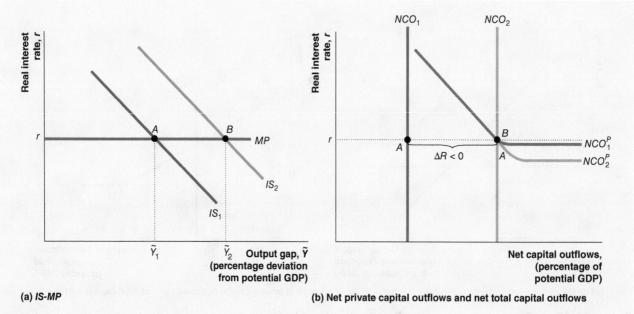

(a) *IS-MP*

(b) Net private capital outflows and net total capital outflows

Figure 12.11 A Currency Devaluation

A currency devaluation increases net exports, so the *IS* curve shifts to the right from IS_1 to IS_2 in panel (a) and the net capital outflow line shifts to the right in panel (b). In both panels, equilibrium moves from point A to point B. The central bank now gains reserves and the speculators go away, ending the crisis.

peso depreciating further. Also, a typical defense in a currency crisis combines devaluation with an increase in the real interest rate. The increase in the real interest rate makes domestic assets more attractive and reduces net private capital outflow, helping to increase central bank reserves.

The Policy Trilemma for Economic Policy

Our discussion of macroeconomic theory and the real-world experience of many countries shows that a country cannot achieve all three of the following policy goals:

1. Exchange rate stability
2. Monetary policy independence
3. Free capital flows

We consider why each of these goals is desirable and then explore why they cannot be simultaneously attained.

Exchange Rate Stability Exchange rate stability is desirable because it reduces the uncertainty of buying, selling, and investing across borders. For example, if a Mexican firm knows that the exchange rate between the Canadian dollar and the Mexican peso will always be 12.8 pesos per dollar, then it is easier for the firm to know whether it will be profitable to build a factory to export goods to Canada. Uncertainty about the exchange rate makes the firm less likely to invest. Uncertainty about exchange rates also means that Canadian investors will be less willing to purchase Mexican assets, such as stocks and bonds, due to the risk that the exchange rate will change and reduce the rate of return on the investment. Remember that the nominal exchange rate is a price, so the benefits of nominal exchange rate stability are similar to the benefits of general price stability (see Chapter 4). As with stability in other prices, stable nominal exchange rates make it easier for households and firms to plan.

Monetary Policy Independence Monetary policy independence means the ability of the central bank to use monetary policy to achieve macroeconomic objectives such as stable prices and high employment, without regard to movements in exchange rates. If monetary policy can respond to demand and supply shocks, then it is possible for monetary policy to reduce the severity of business cycles.

The Bank of Canada is free to adjust monetary policy to pursue macroeconomic objectives because Canada has a flexible exchange rate. In contrast, countries with fixed exchange rates and free capital flows must adjust the interest rate to maintain their fixed exchange rate, so they cannot also adjust interest rates to achieve price stability or high employment.

Free Capital Flows The free flow of capital across borders is a desirable policy goal. One way for a country to finance gross private investment is through capital flows from abroad. These flows can also finance government budget deficits so that the deficits do not crowd out domestic private investment.

While access to capital flows seems desirable, some countries believe that large capital flows make economic activity more volatile. For example, a large increase in capital outflows will reduce the demand for the domestic currency and lead to a rapid depreciation of the currency. The rapid depreciation of the currency can make critical imports, such as food and fuel, more expensive for households and firms. As a result, some countries impose *capital controls*, which are legal limits or restrictions on the flow of financial capital into and out of a country. Capital controls can limit the excessive swings in the nominal exchange rate by limiting the ability of capital to flow into and out of a country. In the extreme, capital controls may prohibit international transactions in assets such as stocks and bonds, or the controls may require official government permission to engage in these international transactions. In 1990s, developing countries such as Brazil (1993–97), Chile (1991–98), Colombia (1993–98), Malaysia (1998–99), and Thailand (1995–97) have all used capital controls to restrict short-term capital flows into and out of their countries. Capital controls have an important drawback, however. If foreign firms believe that they will have difficulty exchanging local currency for foreign currency, they may be reluctant to invest in the country. Particularly for developing countries, foreign direct investment and foreign portfolio investment may be indispensable for economic growth.

The Policy Trilemma for Economic Policy The hypothesis that it is impossible for a country to have exchange rate stability, monetary policy independence, and free capital flows at the same time is called the **policy trilemma**. This hypothesis is based on the work of the Canadian Nobel Laureate Robert Mundell and Marcus Fleming. The hypothesis says that it is possible to achieve at most two of the policy goals at the same time. Therefore, policymakers must choose which goal they do not wish to pursue. Figure 12.12 shows the policy trilemma. Each side of the triangle indicates one of the desirable policy goals, and each corner indicates the result of the unattainable policy goal.

The lower left of the triangle indicates that, if policymakers choose to allow free capital flows and have an independent monetary policy, they must let the exchange rate float. Canada currently allows free flow of capital, and the Bank of Canada is free to use monetary policy to pursue macroeconomic objectives such as low inflation. As a consequence, Canada must let the Canadian dollar float in foreign-exchange markets. Why? Changes in the nominal exchange rate depend not only on domestic monetary policy but also on monetary policy in other countries. If, for example, foreign interest rates fall, Canadian assets will become relatively more attractive and the Canadian dollar will appreciate. If the Bank of Canada wanted to prevent the appreciation, it would have to lower its policy rate, giving up monetary independence. Alternatively, appreciation could be prevented by

Policy trilemma The hypothesis that it is impossible for a country to have exchange rate stability, monetary policy independence, and free capital flows at the same time.

Figure 12.12

The Policy Trilemma

It is impossible for a country to achieve the goals of exchange rate stability, monetary policy independence, and free capital flows at the same time. At most, a country can achieve two of the three goals, and there is no clear consensus on which two are the best to pursue.

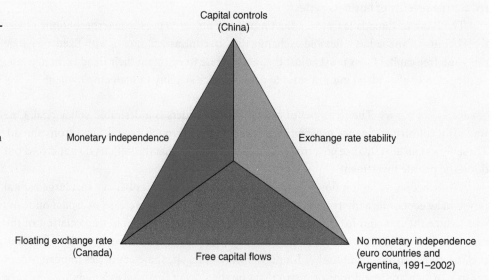

capital controls, which would mean the elimination of free capital flows. So to maintain free capital flow and monetary independence, the Bank of Canada must adopt flexible exchange rates.

The lower-right point of the triangle indicates that if policymakers choose to allow free capital flows and have exchange rate stability, they must give up monetary policy independence. Argentina from 1991 to 2002 maintained a currency board that exchanged Argentine pesos for U.S. dollars at the rate of one peso per dollar. Argentina also allowed free capital flows across its borders, so it could not use monetary policy to respond to macroeconomic shocks. Why? Consider what would happen if the Federal Reserve increased interest rates in the United States. The increase would make U.S. assets more attractive relative to Argentine assets, so investors would sell Argentine assets to purchase U.S. assets. This shift would decrease the demand for Argentine pesos, so the peso would depreciate below the official exchange rate. To maintain the official exchange rate of $1 per peso, the Argentine currency board would have to use dollars to purchase pesos. Consequently, the supply of pesos in the foreign-exchange market would fall, so the peso would appreciate back to $1 per peso. Alternatively, Argentina could increase interest rates along with the United States to prevent Argentinian assets from becoming unattractive. Either way, if a country such as Argentina wants to keep a fixed exchange rate in addition to free capital flows, the country must use monetary policy to maintain the official exchange rate rather than to stabilize the domestic economy.

The top of the triangle indicates that, if policymakers choose monetary policy independence and a stable exchange rate, they must restrict the flow of capital. China maintains an independent monetary policy and has essentially fixed the value of the yuan (the official name of the Chinese currency is renmimbi, but yuan is more often used) against a market basket of foreign currencies, so it has had to restrict capital flows. Why? If China allowed free capital flows, and interest rates outside of China fell, the demand for Chinese assets would increase, raising the demand for its currency. This increase in the demand for yuan would cause an appreciation of the yuan. To maintain a constant value of the yuan, China needs to restrict capital flows so that the demand for yuan does not rise. Alternatively, the Chinese central bank could lower interest rates in line with the decline abroad, preventing Chinese assets from becoming more attractive. The Bank of China could also maintain a constant value of the yuan by selling yuan in the foreign currency markets, giving up control of the money supply. Either way, it would have to use monetary policy to keep the value of the yuan constant, and so would not be able to conduct an independent monetary policy.

Key Terms and Problems

Key Terms

Forward guidance, p. 385	Quantitative easing, p. 383	Too-big-to-fail policy, p. 385
Governing council, p. 367	Recognition lag, p. 386	Unconventional monetary policy,
Impact lag, p. 387	Reserve requirements, p. 373	p. 383
Implementation lag, p. 387	Systematically important financial	Zero lower bound, p. 381
Overnight rate, p. 367	institution, p. 385	
Policy trilemma, p. 400	Target for the overnight rate, p. 367	

The Bank of Canada
Understand the structure of the Bank of Canada.

Review Questions

1.1 What is the Governing Council, and why is it important?

1.2 What is the membership of the Governing Council?

Problems and Applications

1.3 Why is the term of the Bank of Canada governor long?

1.4 Consider the following statement: "Because the governor of the Bank of Canada is appointed by the federal government, the government controls the Bank." Briefly explain whether you agree with this statement.

The Goals of Monetary Policy
Describe the goals of monetary policy.

Review Questions

2.1 What are the primary goals of a central bank?

2.2 What is the goal of the Bank of Canada?

Problems and Applications

2.3 Central banks view price stability as keeping the inflation rate at 2%. Why don't they target a 0% rate of inflation?

2.4 Consider the following statement: "On average, rates of unemployment in Europe are higher than rates of unemployment in Canada. Thus, the Bank of Canada must be doing a good job of maintaining high employment." Briefly explain whether you agree with this statement.

2.5. Most economists estimate that the natural rate of unemployment is between 6% and 7%. However, some evidence suggests that the natural rate of unemployment may have increased after the recession of 2008–09. If the Bank of Canada believed that the natural rate of unemployment was lower than it actually is, what would be the consequences for the economy?

2.6. When financial markets do not function well, savers and investors waste resources, and the economy is less efficient.

    a. How might problems in financial markets affect employment and economic growth?

    b. Some people argue that the Bank of Canada should not interfere in financial markets. Why is maintaining the stability of financial markets important to the Bank's other goals?

Monetary Policy Tools
Explain the Bank of Canada's monetary policy tools.

Review Questions

3.1 Explain how the Bank of Canada uses repo and reverse repo transactions to affect the level of bank reserves. What is the advantage of repos over open market operations?

3.2 Why is it important to have a central bank to act as a lender of last resort?

Problems and Applications

3.3 Briefly explain how the Bank of Canada can reduce the overnight rate.

3.4 Why is the overnight rate considered important if no households or firms (other than banks) can borrow or lend at this rate?

12.4 **Monetary Policy and the *IS–MP* Model**
Use the *IS–MP* model to understand how monetary policy affects the economy in the short run.

Review Questions

4.1 How can monetary policy affect aggregate expenditure? How can the Bank of Canada use monetary policy to fight a recession? How can the Bank of Canada use monetary policy to fight inflation?

4.2 What is quantitative easing, and under what circumstances would a central bank use it to stimulate the economy?

4.3 What is *Operation Twist*? Why did the Federal Reserve pursue this policy beginning in 2011?

Problems and Applications

4.4 [Related to Solved Problem 12.1 **on page 379**] In 2005–06, the Bank of Canada increased the target for the overnight rate repeatedly, partly because it believed that the economy was overheating and that inflation would increase. The following graph shows the position of the economy prior to the Bank's actions:

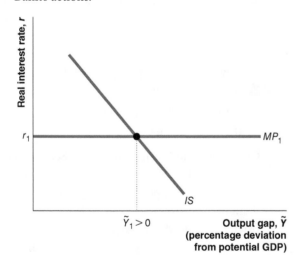

a. Carefully explain in words how the Bank's actions would be expected to affect the economy.

b. Show the effect of the Bank's actions on the *IS–MP* graph including the Phillips curve.

4.5 [Related to Solved Problem 12.1 **on page 379**] To fight the Great Recession, the Bank of Canada reduced the target for the overnight rate.

a. Draw an *IS–MP* graph to show the position of the economy in late 2008.

b. What actions would you expect the Bank of Canada to have taken in this situation?

c. Use your *IS–MP* graph from part (a) to show the effect of the Bank's actions.

4.6 During the 1990s, changes in technology lowered production costs. Use the *IS–MP* model, including the Phillips curve, to analyze the situations described below.

a. Suppose the Bank of Canada does not change the real interest rate following this positive supply shock. What will happen to the inflation rate?

b. Draw a graph to show what actions the Bank of Canada can take if it decides to keep the inflation rate constant.

4.7 Suppose that rather than expectations being strictly adaptive, increases in the money supply cause the expected inflation rate to increase immediately.

a. In this case, when the Bank of Canada increases the money supply, what happens to long-term real interest rates?

b. How does the link between money supply increases and expected inflation change the Bank of Canada's ability to affect the economy through the interest rate channel?

4.8 During the 2007–09 financial crisis, banks faced liquidity problems, in part due to the illiquidity of some of their assets. These problems made some banks reluctant to lend, making it difficult for households and firms to borrow funds, which in turn caused economic activity to decline.

a. Explain how the central bank can use the bank lending channel and the balance sheet channel to solve this problem.

b. Stock markets reached a bottom in March 2009 and then increased rapidly. Assume that it was the result of stimulative monetary policy. How do higher share prices help firms borrow?

4.9 Consider the following statement: "If the short-term nominal interest rate is zero, monetary policy can have no further expansionary effect on the economy." Briefly explain whether you agree with this statement.

4.10 In early 2011, unrest in the Middle East caused a sharp increase in the price of oil. Suppose that the economy was below potential GDP prior to the oil shock, as shown at point *A* on the following Phillips curve graph:

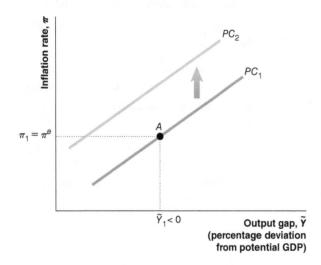

a. If the Bank of Canada keeps the real interest rate constant, show on the graph a possible short-run equilibrium inflation rate and output gap.

b. If the Bank of Canada acts to keep the inflation rate constant, use the Phillips curve to show the new short-run equilibrium.

4.11 The Bank of Canada policy rate fell as low as 0.25% and could not be lowered further. Additional easing did not appear possible.

a. What is the Bank of Canada's "policy rate"?

b. What is "additional easing"?

12.5 The Limitations of Monetary Policy
Explain the challenges in using monetary policy effectively.

Review Questions

5.1 What are the lags associated with monetary policy? How long are these lags?

5.2 Briefly discuss why timing is important when conducting monetary policy, and how poorly timed monetary policy can negatively affect the economy.

Problems and Applications

5.3 [Related to Solved Problem 12.5 on page 390] The initial recovery from the 2001 recession in the United States was very slow. As a result, the Federal Reserve reduced the policy rate to just 1% in 2003 and kept it there for a full year. Some economists argue that the low policy rate kept mortgage rates too low for too long and helped cause housing prices to rise. The rise in housing prices in 2001–06 was a key factor in setting the stage for the financial crisis of 2007–09.

a. Why might the Federal Reserve have kept interest rates too low for too long? Frame your answer in terms of policy lags and the uncertainty of modelling.

b. Illustrate your answer by drawing an *IS–MP* graph, including the Phillips curve.

5.4 Consider the following statement. "Because economic models cannot precisely predict the effect of policy changes, policymakers should not use them to make predictions about the economy." Briefly explain whether you agree with this statement.

5.5 [Related to the Making the Connection on page 381] Some analysts claim that many wealthy depositors prefer maintaining accounts with large "too-big-to-fail" banks, even if they could earn higher interest rates from smaller banks.

a. Briefly explain why these depositors use this strategy.

b. Are there any negative consequences for the efficiency of the economy from depositors following this strategy? Briefly explain.

12.6 Central Bank Independence

Evaluate the arguments for and against central bank independence.

Review Questions

6.1 What does it mean to describe a central bank as independent? Why might independence be desirable?

6.2. Describe the relationship between central bank independence and inflation rates. What are the reasons for this relationship?

6.3 Explain how the importance of monetary policy can be the main argument both for *and* against central bank independence.

Problems and Applications

6.4 In 2010, the European Central Bank (ECB) purchased bonds issued by Greece and other Eurozone economies with excessive government debt. This bailout raised a number of concerns, as discussed in the *Economist*: "Even as the bank's dealers were pushing cash into the bond markets of selected euro-zone countries, its president . . . was trying to reassure Germans that the ECB had not lost . . . its independence."

   a. What risks would be created by a loss of ECB independence?

   b. Does it matter what people in Germany think of ECB independence?

   Source: "After the Fall," *The Economist*, May 10, 2010.

6.5 It is frequently said that people "vote with their pocketbooks."

   a. What monetary policies would a government that was solely interested in re-election wish to pursue?

   b. What risks for the economy would such monetary policies present?

12.7 Monetary Policy in an Open Economy

Explain how monetary policy operates in an open economy.

Review Questions

7.1 How do imports and exports relate to the *IS* curve under a flexible exchange rate system? Under a fixed exchange rate system?

7.2 What are the effects on interest rates and real GDP of expansionary monetary policy in an open economy with flexible exchange rates? With fixed exchange rates?

7.3 What is the policy trilemma?

Problems and Applications

7.4 The International Monetary Fund (IMF) makes loans to countries that are running out of reserves of foreign currency.

   a. How would a loan of foreign currency help a country maintain a fixed exchange rate?

   b. The IMF makes loans only when it believes that currency problems are temporary. Why would a country have temporary currency problems? What must happen to the exchange rate if these problems persist rather than being temporary?

7.5 A currency devaluation can stimulate economic activity in the short run.

   a. Draw an *IS–MP* graph to show the effect of a currency devaluation.

   b. Why don't countries with fixed exchange rates use devaluation more often as a policy tool?

7.6 China has used a fixed exchange rate to keep the value of its currency below its market level.

   a. Why is it easier for a country to undervalue a currency than to overvalue it?

   b. How does China's exchange rate policy affect its purchase of other countries' securities?

   c. What is likely to happen to China's imports, exports, and purchases of other countries' securities if the exchange rate is allowed to float?

7.7 Because the Bank of Canada is not constrained by a fixed exchange rate, it is free to set monetary policy without concerns about the effect on the value of the dollar.

a. How would the Bank's actions during the 2007–09 financial crisis have been constrained if the exchange rate had been fixed?

b. The Canadian dollar actually depreciated in terms of the U.S. dollar at some points during the Great Recession. Is this increase the result you would have expected? If not, how can you explain this increase?

7.8 Suppose that a country has a fixed exchange rate and no capital controls. Due to a political crisis, projections for economic growth in coming years are revised sharply downward. As a result of the new projections, savers wish to purchase financial assets in other countries.

a. What is the likely effect of having savers purchase foreign assets on the ability of the country to maintain its exchange rate?

b. How would the situation be different if there were a flexible exchange rate?

7.9 Capital flows can cause problems for exchange rate stability. So, why do most countries allow the free movement of capital?

Data Exercises

D12.1: [Related to the Macro Data feature **on page 373**]

The *Macro Data* box shows the relationship between the effective overnight rate and the target rate. Using data from Statistics Canada (http://www5.statcan.gc.ca/cansim), analyze the relationship between the overnight rate and the Bank of Canada's target for the overnight rate.

a. Obtain daily data since December 16, 2008, for both rates.

b. Has the Bank of Canada been able to keep the overnight rate close to the target? Explain.

D12.2: Go to the Web site of the Bank of England, www.bankofengland.co.uk. The interactive database for the Bank of England has a section entitled *Monetary financial institutions' balance sheets, income and expenditure*. That section has data on the Bank of England's balance sheet. What happened to the bank's balance sheet since 2007? How do these changes compare to the changes in the Federal Reserve's balance sheet?

D12.3: Using data from Statistics Canada (http://www5.statcan.gc.ca/cansim), analyze the relationship between the bank rate and the five-year mortgage rate.

a. Find the most recent values and values from two years earlier from CANSIM Table 176-0043.

b. Using the data you found in part (a), describe what has happened to the relationship between the short rates and the long rates over the past two years.

Fiscal Policy in the Short Run

Learning Objectives

After studying this chapter, you should be able to:

13.1 Explain the goals and tools of fiscal policy (pages 409–413)

13.2 Distinguish between automatic stabilizers and discretionary fiscal policy and understand how the budget deficit is measured (pages 413–416)

13.3 Use the *IS–MP* model to understand how fiscal policy affects the economy in the short run (pages 416–426)

13.4 Use the *IS–MP* model to explain the challenges of using fiscal policy effectively (pages 426–429)

13.5 Explain how fiscal policy operates in an open economy (pages 429–431)

How Canada Eliminated the Deficit

The figure on the next page tells the story. It shows the changes in debt-to-GDP ratio in G7 countries between 1978 and 2015. (The numbers for 2014 and 2015 are forecasts. For visual clarity, the values for Japan are shown only until 2001. Afterward they increased above 150% of GDP.) In 1978, the debt to GDP ratio was around 30% in France, 40% in Japan and in the United States, 50% in Canada and in the United Kingdom and 90% in Italy. The numbers for Germany are available only from 1991, after unification. What followed was 16 years of continuous deficits in Canada. Canadian debt-to-GDP ratio rose faster than in any other G7 country and reached 100% in 1993. The Canadian dollar got a nickname "the Northern peso," and at the beginning of 1995 the *Wall Street Journal* called Canada "a honorary member of the Third World."

The *Wall Street Journal's* criticism was late. The rising debt was a problem politicians had already recognized. In November 1993 the government of Jean Chrétien took office after an election in which it promised to reduce the deficit, from 8.6% of GDP at the time to 3% of GDP in three years. The government succeeded: By 1996 the deficit fell to 2.7% and, in 1997, Canada had the first surplus since 1969. The vertical line in the figure marks 1996 – the year fiscal situation started to turn around. The subsequent improvement was remarkable. Ten more consecutive years of budget surplus followed. Canada was the only country in G7 that reduced its debt-to-GDP ratio between 1997 and 2013, with the debt-to-GDP ratio in 2013 the second lowest among G7 countries.

Continued on next page

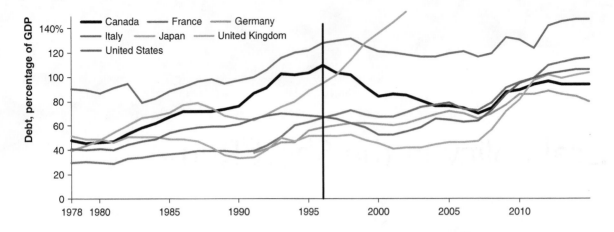

How did this remarkable turnaround come about? Concerns about the deficit began in the early 1980s, but in 1981–82 Canada went through a severe recession and the federal government decided to stimulate the economy. When the government of Brian Mulroney took office in 1984 it undertook a fiscal review aimed at reducing the deficit. The recommendations from the review were only partially implemented. The result was a lower deficit, but the problem of excessive government spending relative to revenue was not solved. Repeated attempts to improve the fiscal situation were interrupted by the 1990–92 recession, which was more severe than the 1981–82 recession. Government revenues fell and transfers increased. Combined with high interest rates on government debt, the deficit and debt grew rapidly.

By 1993 the situation became so dire that, in the federal election, all parties promised a reduction in deficit. The new government set up a Program Review that analyzed all government programs carefully. Government departments participated in the review and proposed reductions. The involvement of government bureaucracy was aimed at securing its willingness to participate in spending cuts. Rather than impose across-the-board cuts (as, for example, occurred in the United States with the budget sequestration of 2013), spending reductions were carefully calculated. The more important spending was considered, the lower the reduction was. In the end, the budget of the Indian and Northern Affairs Department was actually increased, and budgets of all other government departments were cut, by amounts that varied from minimum reductions for the Departments of Health and of Justice to over 60% in the budget of Regional Agencies. The program was spearheaded by the Finance Minister Paul Martin and the Governor of the Bank of Canada, Gordon Thiessen. Canada was also a little bit lucky since the U.S. economy was booming and exports increased, which partially offset the negative effects of the policy on output and employment. As a result of these cuts, federal government spending declined by 4% of GDP between 1995 and 1999.

The successful elimination of deficits provided several lessons. First, it can be done. Second, it has to be done in a comprehensive way, with full involvement of government departments rather than imposed by the Ministry of Finance. Third, the most important factor is political will. The need for political will means that it is easier to reduce large deficits than small ones. This is because, as long as the deficit is not perceived as a serious problem, political commitment to reduce it is insufficient. Only when deficits become large, do both politicians and the general public become convinced of the need to improve the fiscal situation. Until this happens, plans to reduce the deficit are not fully implemented and so are unsuccessful. Finally, the last lesson is that the public attitude to deficits and debt can change. While in the past large deficits were accepted, there is now a clear preference for a balanced federal budget.

Sources: "Bankrupt Canada?" *The Wall Street Journal*, January 12, 1995; Phred Dvorak, "Emerging from the Shadow," *The Wall Street Journal*, November 30, 2010; and Jocelyne Bourgon, "Program Review: The Government of Canada's Experience Eliminating the Deficit, 1994–1999: A Canadian Case Study," Centre for International Governance Innovation (CIGI), September 10, 2009; OECD Economic Outlook 95 database.

Introduction

In this chapter, we study fiscal policy and use the *IS–MP* model to explain how it affects the economy in the short run. Fiscal policy refers to changes the federal government makes in taxes, purchases of goods and services, and transfer payments that are intended to achieve macroeconomic policy objectives. As we will see, fiscal policy can encounter problems in achieving its goals. We begin by describing the goals and tools of fiscal policy. In Section 13.2 we discuss automatic stabilizers, which are taxes, transfer payments, or government expenditures that automatically increase or decrease along with the business cycle, and discretionary fiscal policy, which involves deliberate changes in taxes, transfer payments, or government purchases to achieve macroeconomic policy objectives. In Section 13.3 we use the *IS–MP* model to describe how fiscal policy operates and discuss its limitations. In Section 13.4 we analyze the fiscal expenditure multiplier and ask when it is large and, in particular, what size it is in a recession. We use the *IS–MP* model to discuss effective applications of fiscal policy. In the last section we analyze the operation of fiscal policy in an open economy.

The Goals and Tools of Fiscal Policy

Who Conducts Fiscal Policy?

What is fiscal policy? It involves changes in expenditure and taxation by the federal government aimed at affecting the entire economy. Apart from the federal government, provincial and local governments also have responsibility for taxing and spending. Economists typically use the term *fiscal policy* to refer only to the actions of the federal government. Provincial and local governments sometimes change their taxing and spending policies to aid their local economies, but these are not considered fiscal policy actions because they are not intended to affect the national economy. Note that not all of federal government decisions about taxes and spending are fiscal policy actions. Some of these decisions are not intended to achieve macroeconomic policy goals. For example, introducing tax breaks for renewable energy production is an environmental policy, not a fiscal policy. Similarly, aid to Syrian refugees is a part of foreign policy, not fiscal policy. For changes in taxes of spending to be considered fiscal policy, the main reason for their introduction must be to affect the national economy.

In Canada, the federal budget is proposed by the Finance Minister to the House of Commons for approval in February or March every year. The work on the budget is a year-round process that starts with estimates of spending by federal government departments (national defence, foreign affairs, etc.). An initial budget is prepared by the Treasury Board; the final budget is determined by the cabinet. The importance of the budget is underscored by the fact that a House of Commons vote on the budget is, at the same time, a vote of confidence: If the budget does not pass, the government will resign.

The goal of fiscal policy is to reduce the severity of economic fluctuations. Typically, in Canada and most other countries, fiscal policy focuses on employment and production and leaves price stability to the central bank.

Traditional Tools of Fiscal Policy

Fiscal policy can affect the economy in the short run by changing aggregate expenditure. In the sections that follow, we discuss three fiscal policy tools that affect real GDP:

1. Government purchases
2. Taxes
3. Transfer payments

13.1
Learning Objective
Explain the goals and tools of fiscal policy.

Government Purchases The federal government purchases goods, such as computers or aircraft carriers, and purchases services, such as those provided by ambassadors or RCMP officers. Governments have traditionally used spending on infrastructure projects to try to stimulate the economy during a recession. For example, the Japanese government during the 1990s and the U.S. and Chinese governments during 2009 and 2010 spent hundreds of billions of dollars on building and repairing domestic infrastructure, including roads, the rail network, and bridges. While building and repairing infrastructure may be valuable in its own right, the specific reason the Chinese, Japanese, and U.S. governments increased infrastructure spending was to provide a stimulus to the economy in the short run. Holding all else constant, an increase in government purchases, G, will increase aggregate expenditure, AE. The increase in aggregate expenditure means that firms sell more goods and services, which leads them to expand production, increasing real GDP. To summarize, we would expect

An increase in government purchases → An increase in aggregate expenditures → *An increase* in real GDP and employment.

Taxes Governments obtain tax revenue from many different sources. They include *personal income tax*, *corporate income tax*, *payroll tax*, *consumption tax*, and various special taxes.

Economists divide taxes into *direct* and *indirect taxes*. Direct taxes are taxes imposed on factors of production: labour, capital, and land. They include personal and corporate income taxes, payroll taxes, and taxes paid by unincorporated businesses. Direct taxes are typically paid by individuals or institutions on which the tax is imposed. Indirect taxes include sales taxes, value-added taxes, and excise taxes. Indirect taxes are typically collected for the government by an intermediary, usually the seller. An example of an indirect tax is a consumption tax, which is imposed at the time of a purchase. It introduces a wedge between the price paid by the buyer and the amount kept by the seller: When you pay $113 for a coat in Ontario, the seller transfers $13 to the government and keeps $100. This means that the value of expenditure ($113) differs from the value of production ($100).

Consumption tax systems vary across countries. Some countries have a sales tax: a tax imposed on the final sale only. Unlike in Canada, in most countries the sales tax is included in the posted price so if the price tag is 100, you pay 100. Canada and a vast majority of countries have a *value-added tax* (VAT), called the Goods and Services Tax (GST) or Harmonized Sales Tax (HST)[1] in Canada. The federal government also imposes special taxes, called *excise* taxes, such as on gasoline. It also receives revenue from import tariffs. VAT is paid on the difference between the revenue from sales and cost of supplies and other inputs. Recall that this difference is equal to value added. For example, assume that Petra's Bakery sells bread for $1000, and buys flour for $700 from Jean's Mills, which in turn pays $500 for grain from Marianne's Farms. Then Petra's Bakery pays the VAT on the $300 value added by the company ($1000–$700); Jean's Mill's pays VAT on the $200 value added by the company ($700–$500) and so on. Many governments have been increasing their reliance on consumption taxes, but in Canada the GST was reduced from 7% to 5% in two steps in 2006 and 2008.

Changes in taxes affect the consumption and investment components of aggregate expenditure, as we discuss next.

Consumption Changes in taxes on personal income affect disposable income, which equals national income plus transfer payments minus personal tax payments. Households either spend their disposable income or save it. If income taxes increase, then, holding all else

---

[1]GST is the federal tax. HST is a combined federal and provincial tax, used in Ontario and Atlantic Canada

constant, disposable income decreases, so household spending and saving both decrease. As a result, consumption, *C*, and aggregate expenditure, *AE*, decrease, which reduces spending on goods and services, leading firms to decrease production and employment. Similarly, a decrease in taxes will increase consumption and aggregate expenditure, leading firms to increase production and employment. To summarize, holding all else constant, we would expect

> *An increase in personal income taxes* → A decrease in disposable income → A decrease in consumption → A decrease in aggregate expenditure → *A decrease* in real GDP and employment.

The GST, VAT, and sales taxes also affect consumption. An increase in these taxes makes goods and services more expensive by raising the after-tax prices, so households reduce their consumption. As a result, consumption and aggregate expenditure decrease, which leads firms to decrease production and employment. Holding all else constant, we would expect

> *An increase in consumption taxes* → An increase in after-tax prices of consumption goods → A decrease in consumption → A decrease in aggregate expenditure → *A decrease* in real GDP and employment.

Investment An increase in corporate income taxes reduces the after-tax profitability of investment projects. So, an increase in corporate income tax rates will cause firms to abandon their least profitable investment projects, reducing spending on new plant and equipment. As a result, investment and aggregate expenditure decrease. This decrease in aggregate expenditure reduces firms' sales, leading them to reduce production and employment. Holding all else constant, we would expect

> *An increase in corporate income taxes* → A decrease in the after-tax profitability of investment projects → A decrease in investment → *A decrease* in aggregate expenditure → *A decrease* in real GDP and employment.

Transfer Payments *Transfer payments*, such as employment insurance, are payments by the government to individuals for which the individuals do not provide a good or service in return. An increase in transfer payments will increase disposable income and lead to more spending on goods and services. As a result, consumption and aggregate expenditure increase, leading firms to increase production and employment. Holding all else constant, we would expect

> An increase in transfer payments → An increase in disposable income → An increase in consumption → An increase in aggregate expenditure → *An increase* in real GDP and employment.

Expansionary Policy and Contractionary Policy Economists distinguish between *expansionary fiscal policy* and *contractionary fiscal policy*. Expansionary fiscal policy is intended to increase real GDP and employment by increasing aggregate expenditure. Expansionary fiscal policy actions include increases in government purchases, reductions in taxes, and increases in transfer payments. Contractionary fiscal policy is intended to reduce aggregate expenditure to reduce the threat of inflation. Contractionary fiscal policy actions include decreases in government purchases, increases in taxes, and reductions in transfer payments.

> ### Making the Connection
>
> ## Banking Crises and the Severity of the Great Recession
>
> Policymakers, economists, and corporate CEOs were surprised by the severity of the Great Recession in the United States. A key reason for the surprise was that the country had not experienced a financial crisis since the 1930s, and so economists did not expect how serious the effect of the financial crisis on the economy could be. The Great Recession was the first since the 1930s to be accompanied by a banking crisis. Both the Great Depression and the Great Recession were severe. Was their severity the result of the accompanying bank crises? More generally, do recessions accompanied by banking crises tend to be more severe than recessions that do not involve banking crises?
>
> Carmen Reinhart and Kenneth Rogoff of Harvard University have gathered data on recessions and banking crises in a number of countries in an attempt to answer this question. The table below shows the average change in key economic variables during the period following a banking crisis. For the United States it is the Great Depression; for other countries, including Japan, Norway, Korea, and Sweden, financial crises were in the post–World War II era. The table shows that for these countries, on average, the recessions following bank crises were quite severe. Unemployment rates increased by 7 percentage points—for example, from 5% to 12%. Unemployment continued to increase for nearly five years after a crisis had begun. Real GDP per capita also declined sharply, and the average length of a recession following a banking crisis has been nearly two years. Adjusted for inflation, stock prices following a banking crisis dropped by more than half, and housing prices dropped by more than one-third. Government debt soared by 86%. The increased public debt was partly the result of increased government spending, including spending to bail out failed financial institutions. But most of the increased debt was the result of government budget deficits resulting from sharp declines in tax revenues as incomes and profits fell as a result of the recession.
>
> | Economic variable | Average change | Average duration of change (years) | Number of countries involved |
> |---|---|---|---|
> | Unemployment rate | +7 percentage points | 4.8 | 14 |
> | Real GDP per capita | −9.3% | 1.9 | 14 |
> | Real stock prices | −55.9% | 3.4 | 22 |
> | Real house prices | −35.5% | 6.0 | 21 |
> | Real government debt | +86.0% | 3.0 | 13 |
>
> The table below shows some key indicators for the Great Recession (2008–09 for Canada and 2007–09 for the United States) compared with other recessions in Canada and the United States after the World War II:
>
> | | | Duration (months) | Decline in real GDP | Peak unemployment rate |
> |---|---|---|---|---|
> | Canada | Postwar average | 16.6 | −1.9% | 6.9% |
> | | 2008–09 recession | 7 | −4.2% | 8.3% |
> | United States | Postwar average | 10.4 | −1.7% | 7.6% |
> | | 2007–09 recession | 18.0 | −4.1% | 10.0% |
>
> Note: In this table, the duration of recessions is based on C.D. Howe and the National Bureau of Economic Research (NBER) business cycle dates for Canada and the United States, respectively.

Consistent with Reinhart's and Rogoff's findings that recessions that follow banking crises tend to be unusually severe, the Great Recession was the most severe in the United States since the Great Depression of the 1930s. In Canada, the recession was also serious, with a big drop in output and high unemployment, but it was almost 10 months shorter than the postwar average. The peak unemployment rate in Canada was higher in the 1981–82 and 1990–92 recessions than in the Great Recession. This is consistent with Reinhart's and Rogoff's findings, since there was no banking crisis in Canada.

Sources: The first table is adapted from data in Carmen M. Reinhart and Kenneth S. Rogoff, *This Time Is Different: Eight Centuries of Financial Folly*, Princeton, NJ: Princeton University Press, 2009, Figures 14.1–14.5; the second table uses data from the Statistics Canada and U.S. Bureau of Economic Analysis.

See related Problem 1.8 at the end of the chapter.

Budget Deficits, Discretionary Fiscal Policy, and Automatic Stabilizers

Some changes in government spending and taxes occur due to the effects of existing laws, and some changes occur because the government decides to change current laws to achieve its macroeconomic policy objectives. In this section, we distinguish between these two types of fiscal policies.

Discretionary Fiscal Policy and Automatic Stabilizers

Discretionary fiscal policy involves deliberate changes in taxes, transfer payments, or government purchases to achieve macroeconomic policy objectives. The extraordinary stimulus introduced by Canada and many other countries during the latest recession is an example of discretionary fiscal policy.

Some types of government spending and taxes automatically respond to changes in output and employment. **Automatic stabilizers** refer to taxes, transfer payments, or government expenditures that automatically increase or decrease along with the business cycle. Unexpected events—"shocks"—accentuated by the multiplier effect lead to fluctuations in real GDP. Automatic stabilizers help reduce the severity of these fluctuations by reducing the size of the multiplier. Consider the case of employment insurance, a government program that replaces a portion of the lost wages of recently unemployed workers. Without this insurance, the disposable income of a worker who loses her job may drop to zero. She would have to pay for food, clothing, and rent by drawing on savings or by borrowing. As a result, she would likely significantly decrease consumption. With employment insurance, the unemployed worker's disposable income would decline, but not all the way to zero. Because consumption would not fall by as much as it would without employment insurance, the size of the multiplier effect is reduced, as is the total effect on real GDP of any initial decrease in aggregate expenditure.

The income tax and the transfer payments systems act as an automatic stabilizers. During a recession, as unemployment rises, household incomes fall, causing personal income taxes to automatically fall. Similarly, as profits decline during a recession, corporate income tax falls, and so after-tax profits fall less than profits before tax. In both cases the effect is similar to a tax cut. In addition, as the number of people who are unemployed or on welfare rises, transfer payments increase. As a result, disposable income and consumption, as well as investment, decrease less than they otherwise would have. During an economic expansion, as households' incomes and firms' profits rise, so do personal and corporate income taxes. The number of people receiving unemployment benefits and welfare falls. As a result, disposable income and consumption, as well as investment, increase less than they otherwise would have.

13.2

Learning Objective

Distinguish between automatic stabilizers and discretionary fiscal policy and understand how the budget deficit is measured.

Discretionary fiscal policy
Government policy that involves deliberate changes in taxes, transfer payments, or government purchases to achieve macroeconomic policy objectives.

Automatic stabilizers
Taxes, transfer payments, or government expendit that automatically increase or decrease along with the business cycle.

Figure 13.1

The Federal Budget Surplus and Deficit, 1966/7–2013/4

The federal government has run a deficit since 1966 except for 1969/70 and 1997/8–2007/8 fiscal years.

Source: Federal Department of Finance Fiscal Reference Tables, October 2014.

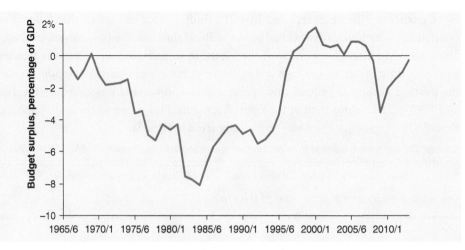

Budget deficit The situation in which the government's expenditure is greater than its tax revenue.

Budget surplus The situation in which the government's expenditure is less than its tax revenue.

Cyclically adjusted (structural) budget deficit or surplus The deficit or surplus in the federal government's budget if real GDP equalled potential GDP; also called the full-employment budget deficit or surplus.

The Budget Deficit and the Budget Surplus

The budget shows the relationship between the federal government's expenditure—including both federal government purchases of goods and services and transfer payments—and its tax revenue. If the federal government's expenditure is greater than its tax revenue, there is a **budget deficit**. If the federal government's expenditure is less than its tax revenue, there is a **budget surplus**.

As with other macroeconomic variables, it is useful to consider the size of the surplus or deficit relative to the size of the overall economy. Figure 13.1 shows the federal government surpluses and deficits for fiscal years (April 1 to March 31) since 1966/7. Over the almost 50 years since 1966, the federal government had a deficit for 38 years and a surplus for only 12 years: in 1969/70 and from 1997/8 to 2007/8. In general, there is nothing wrong with the budget being in a deficit. The federal government finances a lot of long-term projects, for example, defence, national parks, office construction, etc. These projects are similar to investments in the sense that the cost is paid up front and they provide future benefits. It makes sense that they are paid for with borrowed money (i.e., deficits), which are repaid by future users through taxes. In general, economists consider a deficit up to 3% of GDP acceptable. In addition, as we discuss below, the government may run deficits during a recession when revenue is low and expenditure high.

Looking at the budget deficit in isolation can provide a misleading picture of discretionary fiscal policy, because through automatic stabilizers the deficit rises and falls with the business cycle even if the government does not undertake any action. Automatic stabilizers, including the tax systems, the employment insurance systems, and the programs to provide income to low-income households, vary from country to country, so their effect over the business cycle also varies from country to country. In general, policies in Europe and in Canada provide more of an automatic fiscal stimulus than do those in the United States or Japan. As the global economy experienced a recession during 2008 and 2009, the spending increases and tax reductions due to automatic stabilizers increased by 1.6% of potential GDP in the United States, 1.8% in Japan, 2.7% in France and Germany, 2.9% in the United Kingdom, and 3.0% in Canada.

We can think of the government's actual budget deficit in any particular year as resulting from two factors: discretionary fiscal policy and the response of automatic stabilizers to the state of the economy. To focus on that part of the budget deficit that is due to discretionary fiscal policy, economists often use the **cyclically adjusted budget deficit or surplus**, also called **structural deficit or surplus**, which measures what the deficit or surplus in the federal government's budget would be if real GDP equalled potential GDP. (Economists sometimes

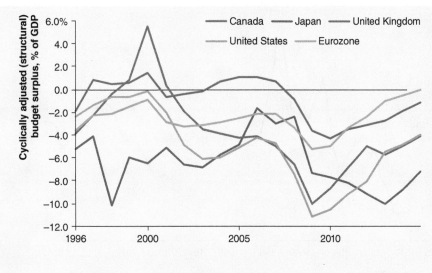

Figure 13.2

Cyclically adjusted (structural) budget surplus or deficit for Canada Japan, the United Kingdom, the United States, and the Eurozone, 1996–2013.

The United States and the United Kingdom used discretionary fiscal policy to a greater extent during the 2007–09 financial crisis than did Canada, Japan, or the Eurozone countries. As a result, the United States and the United Kingdom experienced a much larger increase in their cyclically adjusted budget deficits and, in 2009, had cyclically adjusted deficits exceeding 10% of potential GDP.

Source: Organisation for Economic Co-operation and Development

call the cyclically adjusted budget deficit the *full-employment budget deficit* because it is the budget deficit that would exist if there was full employment.) In other words,

Budget deficit = Cyclically adjusted budget deficit + Effect of automatic stabilizers.

Because the cyclically adjusted budget deficit removes the effects of automatic stabilizers, and therefore also the effect of economic fluctuations on the budget deficit, the cyclically adjusted budget deficit tells us whether discretionary fiscal policy is expansionary or contractionary. If the government is running a cyclically adjusted budget deficit, discretionary fiscal policy is expansionary because it would increase aggregate expenditure when output is equal to potential output. If the government is running a cyclically adjusted budget surplus, discretionary fiscal policy is contractionary because it would decrease aggregate expenditure when output is equal to potential output.

Figure 13.2 shows the cyclically adjusted budget deficits for Canada, Japan, the United Kingdom, the United States, and the Eurozone, such as France and Germany, from 1996 to 2013. A positive number indicates a cyclically adjusted budget surplus, so discretionary fiscal policy is contractionary. A negative number indicates a cyclically adjusted budget deficit, so discretionary fiscal policy is expansionary. Each country experienced an increase in its cyclically adjusted budget deficit during the 2007–09 period. Figure 13.2 shows that all countries had large cyclically adjusted budget deficits during the Great Recession, which means that their fiscal response to the recession was stronger than required by the actual fall in output. Note also that, in 2007, Canada's fiscal position was much better than that of the other countries. Canada had a cyclically adjusted surplus of 0.7% of GDP while the other countries had cyclically adjusted deficits, ranging from 2.2% in the Eurozone to around 5% in the United States and the United Kingdom. The large initial deficits and very expansionary fiscal policies in the U.S and United Kingdom resulted in cyclically adjusted deficits exceeding 10% of potential GDP in 2009.

The Deficit and the Debt

Every time the federal government runs a budget deficit, it has to borrow funds from investors by selling T-bills and bonds. For simplicity, we will refer to all these securities as "government bonds." When the federal government runs a budget surplus, it pays off some existing bonds. As a result of federal budget deficits the total amount of government bonds has grown

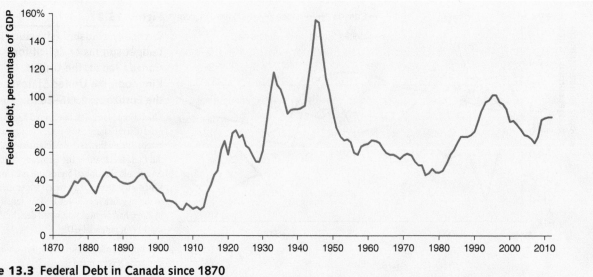

Figure 13.3 Federal Debt in Canada since 1870

The federal debt increased during the two world wars, the Great Depression, and from 1976 to 1996. Federal surpluses between 1997 and 2007 reduced the debt-to-GDP ratio from over 100% to 67%.

Source: The International Monetary Fund, Historical Public Debt Database

Gross federal debt The total dollar value of government bonds outstanding plus superannuation (pensions) owed by the federal government as an employer to its employees plus accounts and interest payable.

over the years. The total value of federal government bonds outstanding is referred to as the *federal debt* or, sometimes, as the *national debt*. **Gross federal debt** is the total dollar value of government bonds outstanding plus superannuation (pensions) owed by the federal government as an employer to its employees plus accounts and interest payable. Each year that the federal budget is in deficit the federal government debt grows. Each year that the federal budget is in surplus, the debt shrinks.

Figure 13.3 shows the gross federal debt in Canada as a percentage of GDP since 1870. Over the long run, the federal debt has increased during wars, during the Great Depression, and during the 20 years between 1976–96. The last period involved the largest increase in federal debt in peacetime, from just over 40% of GDP in 1976 to over 100% of GDP in 1996. A series of surpluses between 1997 and 2007 brought the debt-to-GDP ratio down to 67% of GDP. The last period shows the accumulation of debt due to the last recession.

13.3
Learning Objective
Use the *IS–MP* model to understand how fiscal policy affects the economy in the short run.

The Short-Run Effects of Fiscal Policy

We will now use the *IS–MP* model to analyze the effects of fiscal policy. There are two separate issues we will investigate. The first is the effect of fiscal policy on real GDP and inflation. The second is the effect of fiscal policy on potential GDP. Fiscal policy may affect potential GDP by changing the incentives of households and firms to save and invest.

Fiscal Policy and the *IS* Curve

Governments can use fiscal policy to reduce the severity of economic fluctuations. Some governments, including Canada and many countries in Western Europe, have relied more on automatic stabilizers, while other governments, such as the United States and Japan, have relied more on discretionary fiscal policy. Table 13.1 shows changes in discretionary fiscal policy (i.e., changes in cyclically adjusted deficit) and changes in automatic stabilizers during the Great Recession.

Fiscal policy affects aggregate expenditure, which causes the *IS* curve to shift. All else being equal, an increase in government purchases causes aggregate expenditure to increase,

Table 13.1 Fiscal Policy in Advanced Economies, 2008–2009

	Change in the cyclically adjusted budget deficit (as a percentage of potential GDP)	Change in automatic stabilizers (as a percentage of potential GDP)	Change in the budget deficit (as a percentage of potential GDP)
Canada	−1.8	−3.0	−4.8
Euro countries	−1.5	−2.7	−4.1
Japan	−2.8	−1.8	−4.6
United States	−3.1	−1.6	−4.7

Note: Negative numbers indicate that the budget deficit became larger, and so fiscal stimulus increased.

Sources: Organisation for Economic Co-operation and Development and authors' calculations.

and firms respond by increasing output and employment. Graphically, we can show an increase in government purchases as a shift of the *IS* curve to the right. An increase in taxes will shift the *IS* curve to the left, while an increase in transfer payments will shift the *IS* curve to the right. Figure 13.4 summarizes the relationship between fiscal policy and real GDP.

Using Discretionary Fiscal Policy to Fight a Recession

In response to the Great Recession governments in many countries introduced expansionary fiscal policies. In Canada, tax reductions and increased expenditure programs aimed at stimulating the economy amounted to $64 billion, almost all in the 2009–11 fiscal years. In the United States, fiscal stimulus was $787 billion; in China it was $586 billion. We will now use the *IS–MP* model to analyze the effects of these policies.

The fiscal stimulus packages increased aggregate expenditure, shifting the *IS* curve to the right. Figure 13.5 shows how discretionary fiscal policy can help end a recession. We show the effect of an increase in government purchases, decrease in taxes, or an increase in transfer payments. We assume that the economy is already in a recession caused by, for example, a drop in exports. (For simplicity we do not show the effect of the recession, which involved movement from *B* to *A* in both panels.) The short-run equilibrium is at point *A*, where $\widetilde{Y} < 0$. Real GDP is less than its potential level, so cyclical unemployment is greater than zero.

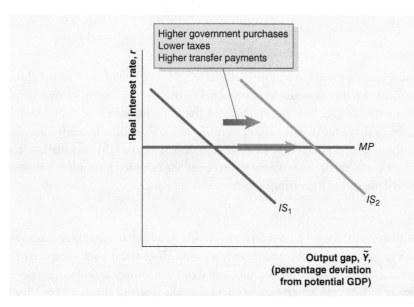

Figure 13.4

Fiscal Policy Tools and the *IS* curve

If government purchases increase, taxes fall or transfer payments increase, then the *IS* curve shifts to the right.

Figure 13.5

Discretionary Fiscal Policy to End a Recession

Increases in government purchases and transfer payments or decreases in taxes raise aggregate expenditure and shift the *IS* curve to the right, from IS_1 to IS_2, as shown in panel (a). As a result, real GDP again equals potential GDP, ending the recession and increasing the inflation rate from π_1 to π_2 which was its value before the recession, as shown in panel (b). In both panels, short-run equilibrium moves from point *A* to point *B*.

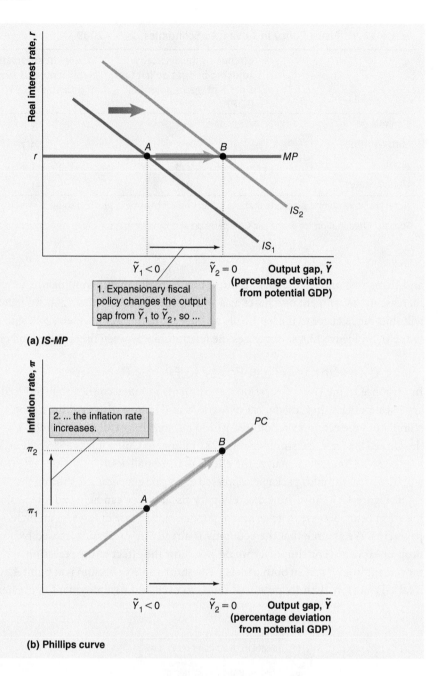

1. Expansionary fiscal policy changes the output gap from $\tilde{Y}_1$ to $\tilde{Y}_2$, so ...

(a) IS-MP

2. ... the inflation rate increases.

(b) Phillips curve

Because the economy is in a recession and real GDP is less than potential GDP, in panel (b) the inflation rate, π_1, is less than it would be at potential GDP.

When government purchases increase, taxes fall, or transfers rise as a result of discretionary fiscal policy, the *IS* curve shifts to the right, from IS_1 to IS_2. Real GDP increases back to potential GDP, so the output gap changes from $\tilde{Y}_1$ to $\tilde{Y}_2 = 0$, and in panel (b) the inflation rate increases to π_2. Short-run equilibrium is now at point *B*, and the recession has ended. The government has achieved the goal of increasing output back to potential.

Automatic Stabilizers

We can also use the *IS–MP* model to analyze the effects of automatic stabilizers on the economy. Because of automatic stabilizers, there is an immediate fiscal policy response to a decline in aggregate expenditure, even without any new fiscal policy actions. This automatic fiscal response reduces the adverse consequences of the demand shock, so any given

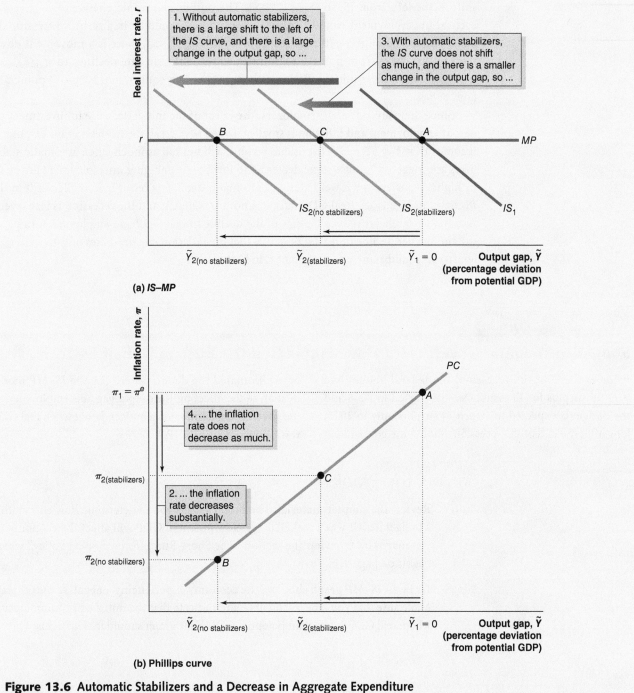

1. Without automatic stabilizers, there is a large shift to the left of the *IS* curve, and there is a large change in the output gap, so ...

3. With automatic stabilizers, the *IS* curve does not shift as much, and there is a smaller change in the output gap, so ...

(a) IS–MP

4. ... the inflation rate does not decrease as much.

2. ... the inflation rate decreases substantially.

(b) Phillips curve

Figure 13.6 Automatic Stabilizers and a Decrease in Aggregate Expenditure

Automatic stabilizers reduce the size of the multiplier. As a result, a shock such as an increase in uncertainty has a smaller effect on real GDP and the output gap. Without automatic stabilizers, the *IS* curve shifts to $IS_{2(\text{no stabilizers})}$ and the output gap moves to $\tilde{Y}_{2(\text{no stabilizers})}$. With automatic stabilizers, though, the *IS* curve shifts only to $IS_{2(\text{stabilizers})}$, so real GDP declines by less and the output gap moves only to $\tilde{Y}_{2(\text{stabilizers})}$ in panel (a), and the inflation rate only decreases to $\pi_{2(\text{stabilizers})}$ in panel (b).

decrease in aggregate expenditure has a smaller effect on real GDP and employment. Figure 13.6 shows the automatic stabilizers at work in response to, for example, an increase in economic uncertainty that leads to reduced investment.

In panel (a), the initial short-run equilibrium is at point *A*, with real GDP equal to potential GDP. Suppose that uncertainty about the future state of the economy increases, causing investment to decrease. If there were no automatic stabilizers, the *IS* curve would shift to the left, from IS_1 to $IS_{2(\text{no stabilizers})}$. The output gap would change to $\tilde{Y}_{2(\text{no stabilizers})}$, cyclical unemployment would rise, and the economy would be in a serious recession. In panel (b), as the output gap changes from $\tilde{Y}_1$ to $\tilde{Y}_{2(\text{no stabilizers})}$, there is a movement down the Phillips curve from point A to point B, so the inflation rate declines to $\pi_{2(\text{no stabilizers})}$, which is less than the initial inflation rate, π_1. Short-run equilibrium is now at point B in both panels.

Since there are automatic stabilizers, the effect of the initial decrease in investment on output, employment and inflation is smaller. To see why, recall the expression for disposable income: $Y^D = Y + TR - T$. Disposable income will not fall as much when automatic stabilizers are triggered because some decreases in income from higher unemployment are offset by higher transfers and lower taxes. So, automatic stabilizers result in a smaller shift in the IS curve, to $IS_{2(\text{stabilizers})}$. Real GDP falls, but not by as much, and the recession is less severe. Automatic stabilizers reduce the size of the decline in real GDP and employment. In panel (b), the smaller decline in real GDP means that the inflation rate decreases only to $\pi_{2(\text{stabilizers})}$. Short-run equilibrium is now at point C in both panels.

Should the Federal Government Have Eliminated the Budget Deficit Faster?

Prior to the 2008–09 recession, the federal budget had been in surplus for 11 years. Deficits started in 2008 and the budget is expected to return to surplus only in 2015, long after the end of the recession. Should the government have eliminated the deficit faster? Use the IS–MP model to analyze the effect on the output gap and employment if the government eliminated a budget deficit when real GDP was below potential GDP.

Solving the Problem

Step 1 **Review the chapter material.** The problem asks you to determine how eliminating a budget deficit when real GDP is below potential GDP will affect the economy, so you may want to review the section "The Short-Run Effects of Fiscal Policy," which begins on page 416.

Step 2 **Draw an IS–MP graph showing the economy experiencing a negative output gap.** Make sure that you label each curve and indicate that the initial equilibrium occurs where real GDP is less than potential GDP. Your graph should look like this:

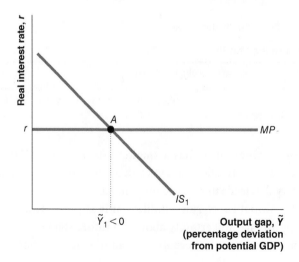

Step 3 **Determine the effect on the *IS* curve of eliminating the budget deficit.** To eliminate the budget deficit, the government must decrease government purchases, decrease transfer payments, increase taxes, or some combination of the three. Decreasing government purchases reduces aggregate expenditure, all else being equal. Decreasing transfer payments reduces disposable income, which leads households to consume less, so aggregate expenditure decreases. If the government increases taxes on households, then disposable income decreases, so consumption and aggregate expenditure will decrease. If the government increases taxes on firms, then investment is less profitable, and investment and aggregate expenditure decrease. This reasoning suggests that regardless of how the government decides to eliminate the budget deficit, aggregate expenditure decreases. So, eliminating the budget deficit will cause the *IS* curve to shift to the left.

Step 4 **Add the new *IS* curve to your *IS–MP*.** The size of the output gap has increased, so real GDP is now further away from potential GDP:

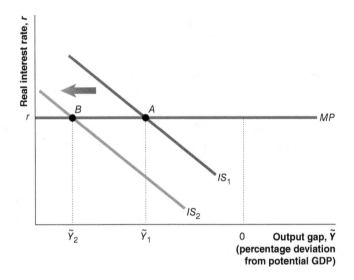

This analysis shows that eliminating a budget deficit when the economy is below potential GDP may reduce further real GDP and employment. For example, in Japan in 1997, the government increased the national sales tax to balance the budget, after which real GDP decreased by 2.0% in 1998 and 0.1% in 1999. Perhaps most dramatically, since 2010 Greece has been reducing spending and increasing taxes in a recessionary economy. The restrictive fiscal policy was mandated as a condition of receiving loans from the Eurozone countries and the International Monetary Fund. As a result, Greece has gone through a prolonged and extremely difficult recession, similar in its severity to the Great Depression: Output fell by 20% and unemployment exceeded 27%.

Nevertheless, sometimes reducing the budget deficit is necessary during recessions, especially for developing countries such as Mexico or Thailand. These economies do not have a long track record of sound fiscal policies, so they are often unable to borrow in international financial markets during recessions because investors fear that the countries may default on their debts. To maintain access to international financial markets, the countries may be forced to reduce their budget deficits even during a recession. Some economists believe that in the future even high-income countries may face limits on their ability to borrow. The willingness of investors to lend depends on investors' confidence that a country will repay the loans as promised. Once that confidence disappears, it can become very difficult for a country to borrow. Indeed, in recent years several Eurozone countries, including Greece, were unable to borrow in the market and had to bailed out by other Eurozone nations. This event became known as the European or sovereign debt crisis.

See related Problem 3.5 at the end of the chapter.

Conceptually, using fiscal policy to reduce the severity of economic fluctuations is straightforward: The government uses fiscal policy to offset the effect of an increase or a decrease in aggregate expenditure by adjusting government purchases of goods and services, transfer payments, and taxes. In practice, implementing a successful fiscal policy may be difficult for many of the same reasons that monetary policy is difficult to implement. We discuss these difficulties in the next section.

Personal Income Tax Rates and the Multiplier

In Chapters 9 and 10 we analyzed the multiplier when households paid taxes that are independent of income and when taxes are proportional to income. Taxes that increase with income are an example of automatic stabilizers. The effect of a change in autonomous expenditure depends on the *marginal income tax rate*: the tax rate paid on the last dollar earned. When taxes are independent of the level of income, the marginal tax rate is zero. Such taxes are often called *poll taxes*. Under a poll tax, the value of the revenue is equal to the number of people, determined by a poll (an old English word for census) of the population, times the amount of tax. Such taxes were popular in the past but are now rare. This is because poll taxes are seen as unfair since the poor and the rich pay the same amount of tax. One example is the so-called Community Charge, proposed by the government of Margaret Thatcher in the United Kingdom in 1990. The opposition to the tax led to riots in London and the eventual resignation of Ms. Thatcher. The poll tax was eliminated by the next government.

Modern personal tax systems involve tax rates that increase with the level of income. For example, in 2014 the federal income tax in Canada had five tax brackets, with different tax rates. The tax brackets change each year because they are indexed to inflation, so for simplicity we have rounded the numbers. The first $10 000 of income in a year is tax free (i.e., the rate is zero). The tax rate is 15% on income between $10 000 and $55 000; 22% on income between $55 000 and $100 000, 26% on income between $100 000 and $150 000, and 29% on income over $150 000. For our discussion here what matters is the marginal tax rate: the rate one pays on an extra dollar of income. For example, someone making $56 000 pays a marginal tax rate of 22% while someone making $156 000 per year pays a marginal tax rate of 29%.

Why does the marginal tax rate affect the size of the multiplier? This is because it affects the amount that households spend out of an extra dollar of income. Using the Canadian tax information above would be complicated, so to simplify the discussion we will assume that there is only one tax rate. This is similar to the situation in Russia, where personal income is taxed at the flat rate of 13%.[2] Let t denote the single marginal tax rate. So if total income is Y, disposable income is given by

$$Y^D = (1 - t)Y.$$

---

[2]Actually, there are two tax rates in Russia. Up to a certain amount, income is tax free, i.e., the marginal tax rate is zero. All other income is taxed at the rate of 13%.

An increase in income by a dollar raises disposable income by $(1 - t)$. Households increase their spending by the amount equal to MPC times the change in disposable income. So, if income increases by \$1, household spending increases by $(1 - t)MPC$. The higher is the marginal tax rate t, the lower is the extra amount spent.

In the appendix to Chapter 9 we derived the value of the expenditure multiplier. We found that, if the amount of extra spending is equal to m times the increase in income, the multiplier is equal to $1/(1 - m)$. When taxes are proportional to income we have $m = (1 - t)MPC$. Taking account of the income tax reduces the value of the multiplier, and so income taxes act as an automatic stabilizer. When, for example, a wave of optimism raises investment by $\Delta \bar{I}$, the eventual increase in income is

$$\Delta Y = \frac{\Delta \bar{I}}{1 - (1 - t)MPC}. \tag{13.1}$$

Imports also act as a stabilizer. When disposable income increases, spending rises by the marginal propensity to consume times the increase in income. But spending on domestic goods and services rises less, since a part of the spending increase is on imports. We again denote the proportion of spending that is on imported goods and services as im, so the proportion of spending on domestic goods and services is $(1 - im)$. Let income increase by \$1. We can now calculate the increase in spending on domestic goods and services when income increases by \$1:

- disposable income increases by $(1 - t)$
- consumption increases by $(1 - t)MPC$
- spending on domestic goods and services increases by $(1 - t)MPC(1 - im)$

Putting it all together we get $m = (1 - t) MPC (1 - im)$ and the change in income, when, for example, a wave of optimism raises investment by $\Delta \bar{I}$:

$$\Delta Y = \frac{\Delta \bar{I}}{1 - [(1 - t)MPC(1 - im)]}. \tag{13.2}$$

Using the example from Chapter 10, when the tax rate $t = 0.25$, the marginal propensity to consume $MPC = 0.8$, and the proportion of all spending that is on imports is $im = 0.33$, we get

$$\Delta Y = \frac{\Delta \bar{I}}{1 - [(1 - 0.25)0.8(1 - 0.33)]} = \frac{\Delta \bar{I}}{0.6} = 1.67\Delta \bar{I}.$$

Other automatic stabilizers, such as employment insurance (EI), similarly affect the value of the multiplier. With employment insurance, rising real GDP and employment will cause a less-than-proportional increase in disposable income because rising employment means a lower level of employment insurance payments. This is equivalent to a higher value of t since, we can interpret t as the effect on disposable income from a \$1 increase in income. For example assume that the tax rate is 0.25 and employment insurance payments fall by \$0.05 for a \$1 increase in income. So when income increases by \$1, disposable income increases by \$0.70 since households pay an extra 25 cents in taxes and lose 5 cents in EI payments. Incorporating this into our example, with $MPC = 0.8$, and $im = 0.33$ we obtain $m = 0.7 \cdot 0.8 \cdot 0.67 = 0.3752$, and so the multiplier is 1.6.

Our example was for a change in autonomous investment, but the formulas are equally valid for autonomous changes in government purchases, consumption, and net exports.

Solved Problem 13.2

Calculating Equilibrium Real GDP and the Expenditure Multiplier with Income Taxes

Assume that the Bank of Canada is keeping the real interest rate constant. Use the following data to calculate the equilibrium level of real GDP and the value of the investment expenditure multiplier:

$$C = \overline{C} + MPC(1 - t)Y = \$1.0 \ trillion + 0.8(1 - 0.20)Y$$
$$\overline{I} = \$1.6 \text{ trillion}$$
$$\overline{G} = \$1.3 \text{ trillion}$$
$$\overline{NX} = -\$0.4 \text{ trillion}$$

Solving the Problem

Step 1 **Review the chapter material.** The problem asks you to calculate equilibrium real GDP and the value of the expenditure multiplier, so you may want to review the discussion of the multiplier in Section 9.3 "Shocks and Business Cycles," which begins on page 279 as well as the section "Personal Income Tax Rates and the Multiplier," which begins on page 422.

Step 2 **Use the data to calculate equilibrium real GDP.** We know that in equilibrium, aggregate expenditure equals real GDP. The expression for aggregate expenditure is

$$AE = \overline{C} + MPC(1 - t)Y + \overline{I} + \overline{G} + \overline{NX}.$$

So, in equilibrium

$$Y = AE = \overline{C} + MPC(1 - t)Y + \overline{I} + \overline{G} + \overline{NX}.$$

Substituting the values above gives us

$$Y = \$1.0 \text{ trillion} + 0.80(1 - 0.20)Y + \$1.6 \text{ trillion} + \$1.3 \text{ trillion}$$
$$- \$0.40 \text{ trillion}$$
$$Y = 0.64Y + \$3.5 \text{ trillion}$$
$$0.36 \ Y = \$3.5 \text{ trillion}$$
$$Y = \frac{\$3.5 \text{ trillion}}{0.36} = \$9.7 \text{ trillion}.$$

Step 3 **Calculate the value of the multiplier from the data given.** The expression for the investment expenditure multiplier is

$$\frac{\Delta Y}{\Delta \overline{I}} = \frac{1}{1 - (1 - t)MPC}.$$

With $MPC = 0.80$ and $t = 0.20$, the value of the multiplier is

$$\frac{\Delta Y}{\Delta \overline{I}} = \frac{1}{1 - (1 - 0.20)0.80} = \frac{1}{1 - (0.80)0.80} = \frac{1}{1 - 0.64} = \frac{1}{0.36} = 2.8.$$

See related Problem 3.8 at the end of the chapter.

The Effects of Changes in Tax Rates on Potential GDP

So far, we have concentrated on the effect of fiscal policy on aggregate expenditure. But changes in marginal tax rates may also have important effects on potential GDP. Potential GDP is determined by the quantity of labour, the quantity of capital goods, and the overall level of efficiency in the economy. To the extent that marginal tax rates affect these three factors, changes in marginal tax rates will cause changes in potential GDP.

The difference between the before-tax and after-tax return to an economic activity is known as the **tax wedge**. Suppose you are paid a wage of $20 per hour. If your marginal income tax rate is 25%, then for every additional hour you work, your after-tax wage is $15, and the tax wedge is $5. The higher is the marginal tax rate, the lower is the after-tax wage and so the lower is the labour supply (see Chapter 6). A reduction the marginal tax rate on income results in a larger quantity of labour supplied because the after-tax wage would be higher. Similarly, a reduction in the tax rate increases the after-tax return to saving, causing an increase in the supply of loanable funds, a lower equilibrium real interest rate, and an increase in investment. In general, economists believe that the smaller the tax wedge for any economic activity—working, saving, investing, or starting a business—the more of that economic activity will occur.

We can look briefly at the effects on potential GDP of cutting each of the following taxes:

- *Personal income tax.* Reducing the marginal tax rates on personal income will reduce the tax wedge workers face, thereby increasing the quantity of labour supplied. The increase in the labour supplied will increase potential GDP. Many small businesses are *sole proprietorships*, whose profits are taxed at the personal income tax rates. So cutting the personal income tax rates also raises the return to entrepreneurship, encouraging the opening of new businesses. Most household saving is also taxed at the personal income tax rates. Reducing marginal income tax rates increases the return to saving resulting in more funds available for investment. As the economy accumulates more capital goods, potential GDP will increase.

- *Corporate income tax.* The federal government taxes the profits earned by corporations under the corporate income tax. In 2014, the federal corporate tax rate was 15%. Cutting this tax rate would encourage investment by increasing the return corporations receive from new investments in equipment, factories, and office buildings. Because innovations are often embodied in new investment goods, cutting the corporate income tax rate can potentially increase the pace of technological change and the overall level of efficiency in the economy. Increased capital and increased efficiency will increase potential GDP.

- *Taxes on dividends and capital gains.* Corporations distribute some of their profits to shareholders in the form of payments known as *dividends*. A *capital gain* is the change in the price of an asset, such as a share of stock. Rising profits usually result in rising stock prices and capital gains to shareholders. Individuals pay taxes on both dividends and capital gains (although the tax on capital gains is paid only when the capital gain is realized, i.e., when the shares are sold). Lowering the tax rates on dividends and capital gains increases the return to saving, thereby increasing saving and investment. So, all else being equal, decreasing taxes on capital gains and dividends leads to a larger capital stock and increases potential GDP.

The increases in potential GDP due to the increases in capital, labour, and the overall level of efficiency are sometimes called the *supply-side effects* of fiscal policy. Most economists would agree that there is a supply-side effect from reducing taxes, but the magnitude of the effect is the subject of considerable debate. For example, some economists argue that the increase in the quantity of labour supplied following a tax cut will be limited because many people work a number of hours set by their employers and lack the opportunity to work additional hours. Similarly, some economists believe that tax changes have only a small effect on saving and investment. In this view, saving and investment are affected much more by changes

Tax wedge The difference between the before-tax and after-tax return to an economic activity.

in income or changes in expectations of the future profitability of new investment due to technological change or improving macroeconomic conditions than they are by tax changes.

The Limitations of Fiscal Policy

13.4
Learning Objective
Use the *IS–MP* model to explain the challenges of using fiscal policy effectively.

Fiscal policy, like monetary policy, faces many challenges in attempting to reduce the severity of business cycles. For a fiscal policy to be implemented successfully, the federal government must quickly recognize that a recession has started, draw up spending plans, and have them approved by the parliament. If the government is late to respond, the policy may not be of much help. In fact, if the government responds slowly enough, policy may actually destabilize the economy by increasing aggregate expenditure when a recovery is well underway.

Policy Lags

We have seen that three policy lags make it difficult for monetary policy to reduce the severity of economic fluctuations. These lags are the *recognition, response,* and *impact* lags. The fiscal authorities have access to the same information as do monetary policymakers, so the *recognition lag* for both monetary and fiscal policy is typically several months.

The *response lag* is different for automatic stabilizers than for discretionary fiscal policy. Many automatic stabilizers respond immediately to changes in economic conditions. There are some exceptions. As demand falls, it takes some time for firms to decide to reduce their workforce. Workers who lost jobs do not receive employment insurance immediately but must wait for a two-week period. But these lags are small and, in general, automatic stabilizers have a shorter response lag than monetary policy. On the other hand, the response lag for discretionary fiscal policy is usually much longer than for monetary policy. This is because discretionary fiscal policy requires deciding what changes should be made to government expenditure, transfers, and taxes. Changing government expenditure is a complex process. Projects that can be started quickly (the so-called "shovel-ready projects") need to be identified. Typically, discretionary fiscal policy changes have to be approved by the parliament so a detailed proposal needs to be put forward by the government; parliamentary approval may take a significant amount of time. In contrast, changes in monetary policy can be made at a single meeting of the policymaking body. The response lag for discretionary fiscal policy can be several months or longer.

The *impact lag* for fiscal policy can last from several months to several years. The government can often quickly adjust taxes and transfer payments, and these changes result in immediate changes in disposable income. However, there is no guarantee that after a tax cut households will immediately use their extra disposable income to consume more goods and services; they may maintain old spending patterns and change their spending slowly over time. Similarly, an increase in taxes or a reduction in transfer payments immediately reduces disposable income, but households may take some time to reduce their spending. If the government cuts tax rates on corporate profits, it takes time for firms to evaluate and pursue new investment projects. An increase in corporate profit tax does not initially have a big effect on investment, as firms are likely to complete existing investment projects. Therefore, the impact lags for discretionary changes to taxes and transfer programs can be long. The impact lag for government purchases can also be long because even after the government authorizes new expenditures on, say, roads and bridges, it takes time to plan new projects. Also, spending is spread over time as the projects are implemented and completed.

A good example of the lags associated with discretionary fiscal policy is the expansionary fiscal policy adopted by the Canadian government during the latest recession. Of the $64 billion of fiscal stimulus, 52% was in the fiscal year 2009–10, 42% in 2010–11, and 5% in 2011–12. According to C.D. Howe, the recession ended in May 2009. Since the fiscal year starts at the

Table 13.2 Estimates of the Multiplier from Various Academic and Government Sources

Economist or Organization	Type of Multiplier	Estimated Size of Multiplier
Christina Romer and David Romer, University of California, Berkeley	Tax	2–3
Robert J. Barro, Harvard University, and Charles J. Redlick, Bain Capital, LLC	Tax	1.1
Sarah Zubairy, Bank of Canada	Government purchases	1.07
Tommaso Monacelli, Roberto Perotti, and Antonella Trigari, Universita Bocconi	Government purchases	1.2 (after 1 year) 1.5 (after 2 years)
Ethan Ilzetzki, London School of Economics, and Enrique G. Mendoza and Carlos A. Vegh, University of Maryland	Government purchases	0.8

Sources: Tommaso Monacelli, Roberto Perotti, and Antonella Trigari, "Unemployment Fiscal Multipliers," *Journal of Monetary Economics* 57, no. 5 (2010): 531–553; Ethan Ilzetzki, Enrique G. Mendoza, and Carlos A. Vegh, "How Big (Small?) Are Fiscal Multipliers?" *Journal of Monetary Economics* 60, no.2 (2013): 239–254; Sarah Zubairy, "On Fiscal Multipliers: Estimates From a Medium Scale DSGE Model", *International Economic Review* 55, no. 1 (2014): 239–254; Robert J. Barro and Charles J. Redlick, "Macroeconomic Effects from Government Purchases and Taxes," *Quarterly Journal of Economics* 126, no 1 (2011): 51–102; and Christina Romer and David Romer, "The Macroeconomic Effects of Tax Changes: Estimates Based on a New Measure of Fiscal Shocks," *American Economic Review* 100, no. 3 (2010): 763–801.

beginning of April, almost all of stimulus took place after the recession had ended. So the main effect of the fiscal stimulus was to improve the recovery after the recession.

The Uncertainty of Economic Models

We have seen that economic models do not provide exact estimates of how real GDP, employment, or inflation will respond to changes in policy. Such uncertainty makes fiscal policy challenging because fiscal authorities do not know exactly how much a change in government purchases or taxes will affect output or inflation. Recent debates about fiscal policy have centred on the magnitude of the multipliers for changes in government purchases and taxes.

As Table 13.2 shows, estimates of the size of the multiplier vary. It is not even clear whether tax cuts or spending increases have a larger effect on GDP. The uncertainty over the magnitude of the multipliers made it difficult for economists to provide policymakers with clear advice.

Crowding Out and Forward-Looking Households

Two phenomena help explain why the multiplier may not be large (and possibly even less than one): crowding out and the forward-looking behaviour of households and firms. Recall that *crowding out* is a reduction in private investment caused by government budget deficits. The government running a deficit affects the ability of households and firms to borrow. For example, suppose the government borrows $10 billion to spend on infrastructure projects. A $10 billion increase in government purchases will reduce national saving by $10 billion. If the central bank does not change short-term interest rates, the term premium effect will increase, raising long-term real interest rate. This is because government borrowing will reduce the availability of funds for long-term bonds, increasing their price. When the long-term real interest rates increase, firms find it more expensive to borrow to finance investment, so investment decreases. As a result of crowding out, aggregate expenditure increases by less than $10 billion. If the budget deficit crowds out, say, $3 billion of private investment, aggregate expenditure increases by $7 billion (the $10 billion increase in government purchases minus the $3 billion decrease in private investment). The exact degree of crowding out depends on how much real interest rates increase and how sensitive investment is to real interest rate. The sensitivity of investment to the real interest rate is the amount of investment reduction for a 1% increase in the real interest rate. The bigger is the increase in the real interest rate, and the higher is the sensitivity of investment to the real interest rate, the bigger is the crowding out effect. Higher real interest rates may also encourage households to save rather than consume, so consumption may also decrease.

Forward-Looking Households Most economists believe that households and firms are forward looking in the sense that they care about the future when they make decisions about how much to consume and invest. Households need to save for future spending on things such as cars, homes, and retirement. So households care not only about taxes this year but also about taxes in the future. Similarly, the profits earned from investing in factories and other capital goods are earned for many years into the future, so firms care about taxes in the future.

When the government borrows to run a budget deficit, it must pay back the loans at some point in the future, which will require higher taxes. As households and firms anticipate paying higher taxes in the future, they may reduce consumption and investment today. Consider the following simple example. Andrei's income is the same as in the previous year but his taxes are reduced by $1000. His disposable income is therefore $1000 higher than in the previous year. How much extra should he spend? If he is forward looking, he realizes that sometime in the future the government will have to raise his taxes to repay the debt. It makes sense for him to save a large part of the increase to be able to pay the higher tax in the future. Similarly, assume that the government announces an increase in spending of $1000. Since Andrei expects his taxes will rise in the future to pay for the spending increase, he reduces consumption today and increases his savings to be able to pay higher taxes in the future.

Robert Barro of Harvard University calls the idea that households save a large portion of a tax cut *Ricardian equivalence* because it was first discussed in the early nineteenth century by British economist David Ricardo. In an extreme case, Ricardian equivalence reduces to zero the multiplier effect of increases in government spending or cuts in taxes. For example, assume that the interest rate is zero; Andrei's taxes are cut by $1000; and the government will repay the debt next year, when the recession ends. In this case Andrei knows that next year his taxes will increase by $1000. It makes sense for him to save the entire $1000 and use it to pay higher taxes in the future. In this extreme case the multiplier would be zero: A tax cut will have no effect on consumption spending. Most economists doubt that Ricardian equivalence reduces multipliers to zero, but opinions differ over how important Ricardian equivalence is.

When Will Fiscal Multipliers Be Large?

Economists have identified two situations in which expenditure and tax multipliers are likely to be large. First, multipliers for expansionary fiscal policy are likely to be large during severe recessions when there are substantial unemployed resources in the economy. The multiplier story depends on the ability of firms to use additional revenue to hire resources, such as labour, to produce more goods and services. For example, if the government spends an additional $10 billion on building roads, firms hire $10 billion of labour, materials, and equipment to build the roads. Imagine what would happen if all workers were already employed at the time the government increases expenditures by $10 billion. To produce the $10 billion in roads, firms would have to hire workers away from other firms that produce other goods and services. The result would be an additional $10 billion of roads but $10 billion less of private goods and services, so real GDP would not increase. If the economy is already at full employment, the likely effect of an expansionary fiscal policy would be to increase nominal wages and prices but there would be a limited increase in output. So, the further away from full employment the economy is, the larger the multiplier is likely to be.[3]

---

[3]See, for example, J. Bradford Delong and Lawrence H. Summers, "Fiscal Policy in a Depressed Economy," *Brookings Papers on Economic Activity* (Spring 2012): 233–274.

Second, the central bank may reduce the policy rate to keep the long-term real interest rates constant. Then the multipliers for fiscal policy are more likely to be large. Crowding out occurs when government borrowing increases the real interest rate that firms must pay when borrowing to finance investment. So, if monetary policy keeps real interest rates from rising, the multiplier will be larger.

Moral Hazard

Fiscal policy, like monetary policy, creates moral hazard because it can insulate households and firms from the consequences of poor decisions, making such decisions more likely. Poor decisions by households and firms can make economic fluctuations more severe.

During the Great Recession many governments bailed out some large banks and industrial firms. A bailout involves a government providing funds for failing firms. Fiscal authorities decide whether a firm should be prevented from failing, so bailouts are part of fiscal policy. For example, the federal governments of Canada and the United States, as well as the government of Ontario, provided equity financing to Chrysler and General Motors in 2009. Many banks were bailed out in the United States and in Europe. Governments prevented these companies from bankruptcy out of fear that, given their size, their collapse would greatly disrupt the economy, as happened when Lehman Brothers was allowed to fail. The bailed-out companies and other large firms may conclude that, in the future, the governments will not let them go bankrupt. As a result, they have less incentive to avoid risky investments. If their investments work out well, the firms get to keep the profits, but if the investments fail, taxpayers may protect them from bankruptcy.

Various steps were undertaken to reduce moral hazard. They involved a reduction of shareholder ownership. As part of the bailout, government would take on equity position in the firm, becoming its partial owner. (When governments became partial owners of General Motors through their financial aid, many commentators started calling the company Government Motors.) Other measures involved suspension of dividends and limits on executive compensation. The idea was to make the shareholders and executives bear some of the cost of the poor performance of their companies. Whether these measures effectively reduced moral hazard will not likely be known until the next crisis: Few, if any, large firms have failed or required a bailout since the Great Recession.

Moral hazard also occurs in the case of employment insurance. As an unemployed person is receiving employment insurance payments, he may have less incentive to find a job. It certainly does happen: It is not uncommon for the unemployed to start a new job only when their benefits expire. But the advantages of providing the unemployed with income outweigh, in the view of politicians and general population, the risks of moral hazard.

Fiscal Policy in an Open Economy

In Chapter 12 we found that taking into account the effect of international trade, international financial flows, and exchange rate policies changes our analysis of monetary policy. In this section we find that the same is true of fiscal policy.

Fiscal Policy with Floating Exchange Rates

As we will see, a floating exchange rate reduces the effectiveness of fiscal policy. Figure 13.7 panel (a) shows the effect of an increase in government purchases that shifts the *IS* curve to the right, from IS_1 to IS_2. The increase puts upward pressure on inflation. Typically, the Bank of Canada responds to an increase in the inflation rate by shifting up the *MP* curve from MP_1 to MP_2, which increases the real interest rate from r_1 to r_2. Short-run equilibrium moves from point *A* to point *B*. The higher real interest rate makes investment in Canada more attractive,

13.5
Learning Objective
Explain how fiscal policy operates in an open economy.

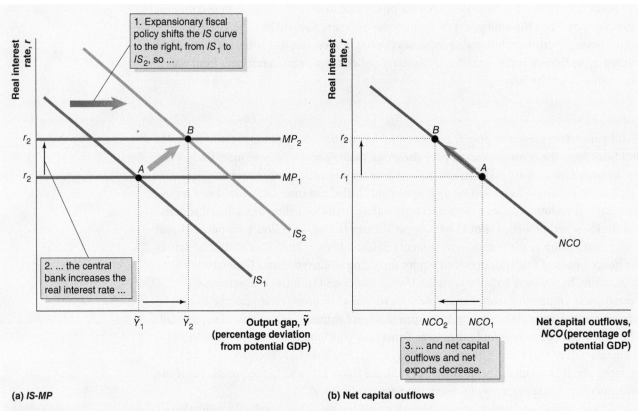

Figure 13.7 An Expansionary Fiscal Policy with Floating Exchange Rates

Panel (a) shows that under a floating exchange rate system, an increase in government purchases typically leads the Bank of Canada to shift up the *MP* curve from MP_1 to MP_2. Short-run equilibrium moves from point *A* to point *B*.

In panel (b), the increase in the real interest rate causes the exchange rate to appreciate, so net capital outflows and net exports decrease. Short-run equilibrium moves from point *A* to point *B*.

so investors purchase more Canadian assets and net capital outflows decrease from NCO_1 to NCO_2, as shown in panel (b). To purchase Canadian assets, investors need Canadian dollars, so the demand for dollars increases, causing the Canadian dollar to appreciate in value. When the Canadian dollar appreciates, our exports become more expensive and our imports become cheaper, reducing net exports.

In the closed-economy version of the *IS–MP* model, a higher real interest rate reduces private consumption and investment. The open-economy version of the *IS–MP* model shows that expansionary fiscal policy will also reduce net exports due to the appreciation of the domestic currency. Therefore, fiscal policy is less effective at increasing real GDP in an open economy with a floating exchange rate than in a closed economy.

Fiscal Policy with a Fixed Exchange Rate

With a fixed exchange rate, an expansionary fiscal policy is more effective than with a flexible exchange rate. To see this consider, for example, Saudi Arabia. If the government of Saudi Arabia decides to pursue an expansionary fiscal policy, the result will be both an increase in real GDP and a higher inflation rate. If Saudi Arabia had a flexible exchange rate, the Saudi central bank would respond to the higher inflation rate by increasing the policy rate so as to raise the real interest rate, as the Bank of Canada did in our earlier example. However, increasing the real interest rate would cause the Saudi riyal to appreciate, which would violate the Saudi central bank's commitment to a fixed exchange rate. To prevent the riyal from appreciating, the Saudi central bank will have to act to keep the real interest rate constant. In terms of Figure 13.7, panel (a), the *MP* curve does not shift up. As a result, consumption and investment does not decline and expansionary fiscal policy is more effective than it would be under a floating exchange rate.

Key Terms and Problems

Key Terms

Automatic stabilizers, p. 413

Budget deficit, p. 414

Budget surplus, p. 414

Cyclically adjusted (structural) budget deficit or surplus, p. 414

Discretionary fiscal policy, p. 413

Gross federal debt, p. 416

Tax wedge, p. 425

13.1 **The Goals and Tools of Fiscal Policy**
Explain the goals and tools of fiscal policy.

Review Questions

1.1 What is fiscal policy? Who is responsible for conducting fiscal policy?

1.2 What are the goals of fiscal policy? What tools have policymakers traditionally used to achieve these goals?

1.3 Describe how changes in personal income taxes, corporate income taxes, and transfer payments affect real GDP and employment.

Problems and Applications

1.4 For each of the following situations, choose a fiscal policy and explain how it could be used to correct the economic problem.

  a. Real GDP is above potential GDP after a stock market boom.

  b. The economy is in a recession due to a decline in spending on residential construction.

1.5 Consumption taxes (mostly the value-added tax) are much higher in European countries than in Canada.

  a. If Canada were to reduce income taxes and increase the GST, briefly explain what the effects would be on consumption and investment.

  b. Would you expect a consumption tax to have a different effect on consumer savings than would an income tax? Briefly explain.

1.6 In the United Kingdom, gross debt as a percentage of GDP rose from 43% in 2007 to over 98% in mid-2011. A primary reason for the large increase in the debt was the Great Recession and the subsequent slow recovery.

  a. What fiscal policies could the government of the United Kingdom use to reduce the national debt?

  b. What effect would these policies have on the economy of the United Kingdom?

1.7 Consider the following statement: "Monetary policy and fiscal policy are really the same thing because they both can involve the buying and selling of government bonds." Briefly explain whether you agree with this statement.

1.8 [Related to the Making the Connection on page 412] One reason it was difficult to predict the severity of the Great Recession is that most economists did not anticipate the financial crisis.

  a. What might the failure to anticipate the recession imply about the effectiveness of fiscal policy in preventing or reducing the severity of the recession?

  b. What fiscal policies might have been implemented earlier if economists had more accurately predicted the severity of the recession?

MyEconLab   Visit **www.myeconlab.com** to complete these exercises online and get instant feedback.

13.2 Budget Deficits, Discretionary Fiscal Policy, and Automatic Stabilizers

Distinguish between automatic stabilizers and discretionary fiscal policy and understand how the budget deficit is measured.

Review Questions

2.1 How is discretionary fiscal policy different from automatic stabilizers? List examples of both discretionary fiscal policy and automatic stabilizers during the Great Recession.

2.2 What is a cyclically adjusted budget deficit or surplus? How is it used to determine whether fiscal policy is expansionary or contractionary?

2.3 Describe the difference between a federal budget surplus, a federal budget deficit, and the national debt. Briefly describe trends in the federal budget surplus and deficit, and the federal debt since1981.

Problems and Applications

2.4 Briefly explain whether each of the following is (1) an example of a discretionary fiscal policy, (2) an example of an automatic stabilizer, or (3) not a fiscal policy.

a. The federal government increases spending on rebuilding highways

b. The Bank of Canada sells government bonds

c. The total the federal government pays out for employment insurance increases during a recession

d. Personal income revenues decline during a recession

e. The federal government changes the required gasoline mileage for new cars

f. Income tax rates increase by 5%

2.5 According to the chapter, contractionary fiscal policy is rarely used. But between 1997 and 2007 the federal government ran a surplus. Does this surplus imply that fiscal policy in this period was contractionary? Briefly explain.

2.6 Most of the programs that we think of as automatic stabilizers did not exist in 1929. Suppose that the automatic stabilizers had existed in 1929. Briefly explain the effect these stabilizers would have had on the severity of the Great Depression.

13.3 The Short-Run Effects of Fiscal Policy

Use the *IS–MP* model to understand how fiscal policy affects the economy in the short run.

Review Questions

3.1 How are changes in discretionary fiscal policy shown in the *IS–MP* model? Include the Phillips curve in your discussion.

3.2 How are automatic stabilizers shown in the *IS–MP* model? Include the Phillips curve in your discussion.

3.3 How does a change in the personal income tax rate affect the multiplier? How does a change in the size of the multiplier affect the economy?

3.4 Explain how cuts in personal income taxes, corporate income taxes, and taxes on dividends and capital gains affect potential GDP.

Problems and Applications

3.5 [Related to Solved Problem 13.1 on page 420] The adjacent graph illustrates an economy that is experiencing inflation. In order to prevent the inflation rate from increasing, the government introduces a surtax on personal and corporate income. Use the graph to illustrate the effect of the surcharge on the economy. Explain the likely effect of the surcharge on the Phillips curve and the output gap.

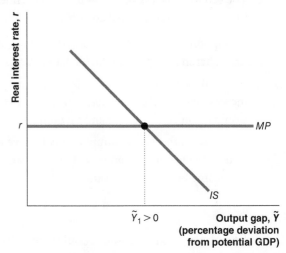

3.6 From 1991 to 2000, the Japanese economy grew so slowly that those years have become known as the "Lost Decade." Nevertheless, the Japanese government increased the national sales tax in 1997 because it had become concerned about its budget deficit. As a result, real GDP decreased by 2.0% in 1998 and 0.1% in 1999. The graph below shows short-run equilibrium in the Japanese economy in 1997 prior to the sales tax increase. The graph assumes that growth had been slow but not negative, so the economy was at or near full employment.

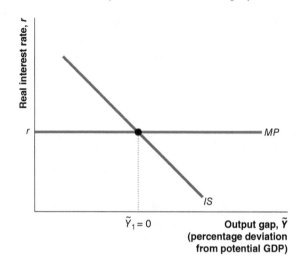

a. Show the effect of the sales tax on the *IS–MP* graph and describe any change that would take place on the Phillips curve.

b. If the primary goal of the government is full employment, was increasing the national sales tax in 1997 a wise policy? Briefly explain.

3.7 Consider the following statement: "Because automatic stabilizers are built into the economy, there is no need for discretionary fiscal policy." Do you agree with this statement? Briefly explain.

3.8 [Related to Solved Problem 13.2 **on page 424**] An economy can be described by the following data:

$$C = \overline{C} + MPC(1 - t)Y = \$1.0 \text{ million}$$
$$+ 0.758(1 - 0.25)Y$$
$$\overline{I} = \$2.0 \text{ million}$$
$$\overline{G} = \$3.0 \text{ million}$$
$$\overline{NX} = \$0.5 \text{ million}$$

a. Calculate the equilibrium level of real GDP.

b. Suppose that the government increases purchases by $1 million. Calculate the change in real GDP.

c. What is the value of the multiplier?

3.9 An economy has a marginal propensity to consume of 0.90. The tax rate is 0.10.

a. What is the value of the multiplier?

b. What would the value of the multiplier be if the tax rate increased to 0.15?

c. Suppose that the government increases purchases by $2 billion in (a) and (b). What is the change in real GDP in each case?

d. How do changes in the tax rate affect the amount by which equilibrium real GDP changes as government purchases change?

3.10 For each of the following, describe the change in consumption, investment, and aggregate expenditure, and explain what happens to the *IS* curve and the Phillips curve.

a. The government increases infrastructure spending on roads and bridges by 25%.

b. The government cuts the corporate tax rate in half.

c. Payroll taxes are increased on workers who earn over $100 000.

d. Personal income tax rates are reduced for anyone earning less than $40 000.

13.4 **The Limitations of Fiscal Policy**
Use the *IS–MP* model to explain the challenges of using fiscal policy effectively.

Review Questions

4.1 How are lags different for fiscal policy than for monetary policy? How are they the same?

4.2 How does the accuracy of economic forecasts present a problem for fiscal policy? How do the uncertainties involved in policymaking limit the use of fiscal policy?

4.3 Explain the effect of crowding out and forward-looking households on the size of the multiplier.

4.4 Why is the multiplier likely to be large during a severe recession or when the Bank of Canada keeps real interest rates constant?

Problems and Applications

4.5 In a typical recession, monetary policy is usually changed faster than fiscal policy. Comment on the length of fiscal and monetary policy lags and why it takes less time to change monetary than fiscal policy.

4.6 In order to stimulate the economy, the government starts running a large budget deficit.

    a. If households are forward looking, what effect will increased budget deficits have on their spending and saving choices?

    b. Discuss the relevance of these spending and saving choices for the effectiveness of fiscal policy.

4.7 The size of the expenditure multiplier varies depending on economic conditions and the conduct of monetary policy. Suppose that the government decides to spend an extra $10 billion on infrastructure projects and that the central bank targets an inflation rate of 2%. In addition, assume that the central bank always adjusts policy to hit this target. Use the *IS–MP* diagram and the Phillips curve to explain the effect of the increase in government spending on the economy.

Fiscal Policy in an Open Economy
Explain how fiscal policy operates in an open economy.

Review Questions

5.1 Briefly explain whether fiscal policy is more or less effective in an open economy with a floating exchange rate than in a closed economy.

5.2 Briefly explain whether fiscal policy is more or less effective in an open economy with a fixed exchange rate than in a closed economy.

Problems and Applications

5.3 What is the difference between the effectiveness of fiscal policy in a small economy, such as Canada, and in a closed economy? Briefly explain.

5.4 In July 2012, the government of newly elected French president François Hollande announced that it would sharply increase taxes to try to close a government budget deficit. Use the *IS–MP* model to analyze the effect of this tax increase on the output gap and the inflation rate, assuming that the real interest rate remains unchanged. Is the effect of the tax increase greater if you assume that France is a closed economy or an open economy? Briefly explain.

Source: "François Hollande's Fiscal Puzzle," *The Economist*, July 7, 2012.

Data Exercises

D13.1: [Spreadsheet exercise] The International Monetary Fund publishes the World Economic Outlook. Go to www.imf.org and look at the most recent version available. Look at the data for the cyclically adjusted budget deficit (which the World Economic Outlook calls "General Government Structural Balance") for Brazil, China, France, and Germany from 2000 to 2017. Use the series for the cyclically adjusted budget deficit that is measured as a percentage of potential GDP.

    a. Download the data and plot the data in a graph. Which country relied the most on discretionary fiscal policy in response to the financial crisis of 2008 and 2009?

    b. How do these countries' discretionary fiscal policies compare to the countries in Table 13.1 on page 417?

    c. From 2012 to 2017, which of these four countries is expected to have the most expansionary discretionary fiscal policy? Briefly explain.

D13.2: Using data from Statistics Canada, analyze the relationship between government spending, tax revenue, and the business cycle.

    a. Download quarterly data from 1979 to the present for federal government consumption expenditures and gross investment, federal government current receipts, nominal GDP, and the GDP deflator.

b. Calculate real GDP, real federal consumption expenditures and investment, and real federal current receipts. Calculate the annual growth rate for each of these series as the percentage change from the same quarter in the previous year.

c. Calculate the correlation between the growth rate of real GDP and the growth rate of real federal consumption expenditures and investment. Calculate the correlation between the growth rate of real GDP and real federal current receipts.

d. One way to measure the business cycle is to look at the growth rate of real GDP. Based on the correlations you previously calculated, has Canadian fiscal policy made the business cycle more severe or less severe? Briefly explain.

D13.3: The International Monetary Fund publishes the World Economic Outlook. Go to www.imf.org and look at the most recent version available. Look at the data on the forecasted output gap for Canada, Japan, the United Kingdom, and the United States for 2012 to 2017.

a. Based on these data, design a fiscal policy for each year that would make the output gap equal to zero.

b. Describe at least two problems that these countries would have in implementing your suggested policies.

D13.4: [Spreadsheet exercise] The International Monetary Fund publishes the World Economic Outlook. Go to www.imf.org and look at the most recent version available. Look at the data for cyclically adjusted budget deficit (which the World Economic Outlook calls "General Government Structural Balance") and output gap from 1980 to 2011 for France and the United Kingdom. Use the series for the cyclically adjusted budget deficit that is measured as a percentage of potential GDP.

a. If these countries used discretionary fiscal policy to try to stabilize the economy (that is, to keep the output gap close to zero), then what should be the correlation between the cyclically adjusted budget deficit and the output gap?

b. Plot the output gap and the cyclically adjusted budget deficit for France on the same graph. Does the correlation between the two series look as if it is positive or negative? Repeat your analysis for the United Kingdom.

c. Calculate the correlation between the output gap and the cyclically adjusted budget deficit for France. Is the correlation consistent with a discretionary fiscal policy that stabilizes the economy? Repeat your analysis for the United Kingdom.

Aggregate Demand, Aggregate Supply, and Monetary Policy

Did Central Banks Create and Kill the Great Moderation?

The key short-run macroeconomic problem is the business cycle. Economists believe that business cycles make households and firms worse off. If macroeconomic policy can reduce the severity of business cycles, people will find jobs more easily, entrepreneurs will have an easier time starting new businesses, and households will not have to worry about high inflation rates eroding the value of their savings.

Unfortunately, macroeconomic policy has often failed to reach its objectives. Sometimes monetary and fiscal policy have actually made macroeconomic conditions worse rather than better. A number of policy mistakes contributed to the Great Depression. Most economists believe that restrictive monetary policy made the Great Depression longer and deeper than it would otherwise have been. In addition, some economists believe fiscal policy mistakes during this period also made the Great Depression worse.

Many economists have also criticized macroeconomic policy during the 1970s. Until the 1970s, Canada had experienced high inflation rates only during wartime, but by 1973, the inflation rate soared to 9% and in 1974 reached almost 15%. The inflation rate declined a bit during the next few years, only to rise above 10% in 1979. Between 1974 and 1981 the average inflation rate was almost 10%, the highest since the early 1950s. These high inflation rates imposed serious costs on many households and firms. Workers whose nominal wages did not keep pace with these high inflation rates suffered large declines in real wages. Bondholders, people

Continued on next page

receiving fixed-dollar pensions, and banks that had made fixed-interest-rate loans all suffered losses. Most economists believe that monetary policy could have been used more skillfully to keep inflation from reaching such high levels. Between 1975 and 1980 the average unemployment rate was almost 8%, higher than in any year since 1946. This combination of high inflation and high unemployment, dubbed *stagflation*, left much of the general public wondering whether policymakers knew what they were doing.

After the early 1980s, however, the performance of the economy improved, and so did the reputation of the Bank of Canada. In 1981–82 the Bank of Canada raised interest rates to reduce inflation. This anti-inflationary policy resulted in the 1981–82 recession. Following the end of the 1981–82 recession, Canada experienced 89 months of economic expansion, ending with the 1990–92 recession, which was caused by another round of anti-inflationary policy by the Bank of Canada. After that recession ended, Canada experienced an unprecedented 198 months of economic expansion. In other words, over the 26 years between October 1982 and October 2008, there was one recession that lasted 25 months, and two expansions that lasted 287 months. Over the same period the United States experienced a long period of economic expansion interrupted by two relatively mild recessions of 1990–91 and in 2001. The inflation rate was also well under control, averaging just 2.9% in Canada and 2.6% in the United

States between 1983 and December 2008. This 26-year run of long expansions with few recessions (one in Canada, two in the United States) and low inflation was arguably the longest period of macroeconomic stability in Canada and in the United States. The period was a sufficiently sharp break with the past that economists James Stock of Harvard University and Mark Watson of Princeton University named it the "Great Moderation." Many economists attributed the Great Moderation to better macroeconomic policies, especially to the focus of the Bank of Canada and the Federal Reserve on low and stable inflation. The Great Moderation ended abruptly in the United States in 2007 and in Canada in 2008. As we discussed in earlier chapters, the Great Recession was the worst in the United States since the Great Depression of the 1930s. Many economists blame the Federal Reserve for planting the seeds of the Great Recession by keeping interest rates too low for too long and creating the housing bubble that, when it burst, started the Great Recession. Canada was a bystander: There was no housing bubble in Canada in the 2000s, and the recession in 2008–09 was severe but brief. So the question economists are asking is: Has the Great Moderation ended?

As we have already seen, explaining business cycles is not an easy task. In this chapter, we will look more closely at monetary policy, with the aim of being better able to evaluate the role of central banks in the Great Moderation and in the Great Recession.

Sources: C.D. Howe Institute, U.S. Bureau of Economic Analysis; U.S. Bureau of Labor Statistics; and James Stock and Mark Watson, "Has the Business Cycle Changed and Why?" *NBER Macroeconomics Annual*, 2002, pp. 159–218.

Introduction

We used the aggregate demand and aggregate supply model to illustrate changes in real GDP and the price level during the business cycle (Chapter 9). Our initial discussion illustrated the aggregate demand and aggregate supply model using a graph with real GDP on the horizontal axis and the price level on the vertical axis. Now that we have explored the *IS–MP* model, including the Phillips curve, we can present a more complete version of the aggregate demand and aggregate supply (*AD–AS*) model using graphs with the output gap on the horizontal axis and the inflation rate on the vertical axis. This approach makes it easier to use the model to analyze the business cycle and macroeconomic policies. The *AD–AS* model completes our discussion of business cycles.

We begin by introducing the central bank reaction function. It shows how the central bank reacts to deviations of inflation from its inflation target. When output is above target, the central bank raises the real interest rate; when output is below target, the central bank reduces the real interest rate. We then use the reaction function together with the IS curve to obtain the aggregate demand curve: the relationship between inflation and aggregate expenditure. In Section 14.2 we describe the aggregate supply curve, which is essentially the same as the Phillips curve. In Section 14.3 we use the aggregate demand-aggregate supply model to analyze the economy. The last two sections discuss the importance of expectations and the use of rules or discretion in monetary policy.

Aggregate Demand Revisited

We begin building the model by developing the *aggregate demand (AD) curve*, which shows the relationship between the inflation rate and aggregate expenditure on goods and services by households, firms, and the government. The *AD* curve is based on the *IS–MP* model. Recall that, in the *IS–MP* model, the central bank chooses the nominal interest rate in order to set the real interest rate so that output is equal to potential output. The *IS* curve shows the relationship between the real interest rate and the level of aggregate expenditure on goods and services. The MP curve is a line that is horizontal at the current level of the real interest rate. Equilibrium in the model is at the intersection of the *IS* and *MP* curves. Whenever output differs from potential, the central bank would adjust the short-term nominal interest rate. The relationship between the short-term nominal interest rate, which the central bank controls, and the long-term real interest rate, which affects aggregate expenditure, depends on the term-structure effect (TSE), the default-risk premium (DP), and the expected inflation rate. For simplicity we assume that the term-structure effect and the default-risk premium are constant. This means that, for a given expected inflation, the central bank can set the level of the long-term real interest rate. In the description of the model we will simply say that the real interest rate depends on the nominal interest rate set by the central bank and on the expected rate of inflation. You should remember that for this to be true, TSE and DP need to be constant.

The *IS–MP* model is a static model. It allows us to determine the real interest rate that is needed to equate output with potential output, but does not describe the adjustment process. The aggregate demand–aggregate supply model we analyze in this chapter is a dynamic model. It shows the interrelationship between the state of the economy and actions of the central bank. It will allow us to determine what happens after a shock (the short-run equilibrium), how the economy changes over time (the adjustment process), and the final situation (the long-run equilibrium).

We begin constructing the aggregate demand and aggregate supply model by noting that one of the main goals of central banks is price stability. To achieve this goal, the central bank often sets an inflation target. When inflation is greater than the target rate, the central bank increases real interest rates to reduce aggregate expenditure and real GDP, which in turn reduces the inflation rate. When inflation is less than the target rate, the central bank reduces the real interest rate to increase aggregate expenditure and real GDP, which in turn raises the inflation rate.

Central bank reaction function A rule or formula that a central bank uses to set interest rates in response to changing economic conditions.

We can think of the central bank's response to changes in inflation as a **central bank reaction function**, which is a rule or formula that a central bank uses to set interest rates in response to changing economic conditions. The rule is simple: If inflation is above target, the central bank attempts to slow down the economy by raising the *real* interest rate; if inflation rate is below target, the central bank attempts to stimulate the economy by lowering the *real* interest rate. We stress the fact that it is the real interest rate that the central bank needs to change to affect the economy. The central bank reaction function is shown in Figure 14.1. When the inflation rate is equal to target, $\pi = \pi_{\text{Target}}$, the central bank sets the real interest rate equal to r_1. The reaction function slopes upward because the central bank increases the real interest rate as the inflation rate rises, and reduces the real interest rate as the inflation rate falls.

There are two key components of the reaction function: the target inflation rate and the slope of the reaction function. The target inflation rate is the inflation rate that the central bank wants to achieve in the long run. The slope of the reaction function indicates how

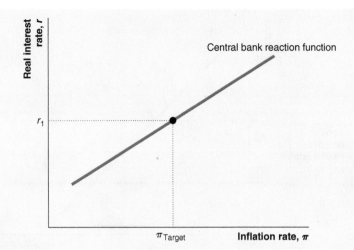

Figure 14.1

The Central Bank Reaction Function

The reaction function slopes upward, indicating that the central bank increases the real interest rate as the inflation rate rises, and decreases the real interest rate as the inflation rate falls.

much the central bank responds to short-run differences between the actual inflation rate and the target inflation rate: The steeper the reaction function, the more the central bank increases the real interest rate in response to the current inflation rate being above the target inflation rate and the more the central bank decreases the real interest rate in response to the actual inflation rate being below the target inflation rate. The flatter the reaction function, the smaller the changes the central bank makes in the real interest rate in response to differences between the actual inflation rate and the target inflation rate. In other words, if the reaction function is steep, the central bank responds more aggressively to differences between the actual inflation rate and the target inflation rate than if the reaction function is flat.

We can write the central bank's reaction function as

$$r = r_1 + b\,(\pi - \pi_{Target}). \qquad (14.1)$$

In this equation r_1 is the real interest rate the central bank sets when the inflation rate is equal to target and b is a coefficient that shows how aggressively the central bank responds to changes in inflation. The coefficient b is positive since, when inflation exceeds target, the central bank increases the real interest rate. A large value of b means that the central bank reacts very aggressively to inflation by raising the real interest rate a lot when inflation is above target and lowering it a lot when inflation is below target.

The reaction function described in Figure 14.1 and in equation (14.1) simplifies the actual policy situation that central banks face. For one thing, central banks often have goals beyond just price stability. The Federal Reserve in the United States, for example, is tasked, in addition to price stability, with achieving high employment and financial market stability. Also, as we discussed in Chapter 12, monetary policy works with long and variable lags, and so the interest rate decision takes into account not only the current but also the future expected inflation rates. We consider more complicated reaction functions later in this chapter.

The Aggregate Demand Curve

The reaction function shows how the central bank adjusts the real interest rate in response to changes in the inflation rate. Changes in the real interest rate, in turn, affect aggregate expenditure. Raising the real interest rate makes it more costly for households and firms to borrow to finance consumption and investment. A higher real interest rate also increases the exchange rate between the Canadian dollar and foreign currencies, which reduces net exports. Because aggregate expenditure and real GDP decrease as the real interest rate increases, there is a negative relationship between the real interest rate and the quantity of real GDP demanded by households and firms.

Figure 14.2

Deriving the Aggregate Demand Curve

The aggregate demand curve shows the relationship between the inflation rate and aggregate expenditure, which operates through the central bank reaction function. An increase in the inflation rate from π_1 to π_2 in panel (b) causes the central bank to increase the real interest rate, so the MP curve shifts from MP_1 to MP_2, causing a movement along the IS curve from point A to point B in panel (a). Consumption, investment, and net exports all decline, which reduces aggregate expenditure. As a result, the output gap changes from $\tilde{Y}_1$ to $\tilde{Y}_2$ and, in panel (b), short-run equilibrium moves from point A to point B on the AD curve.

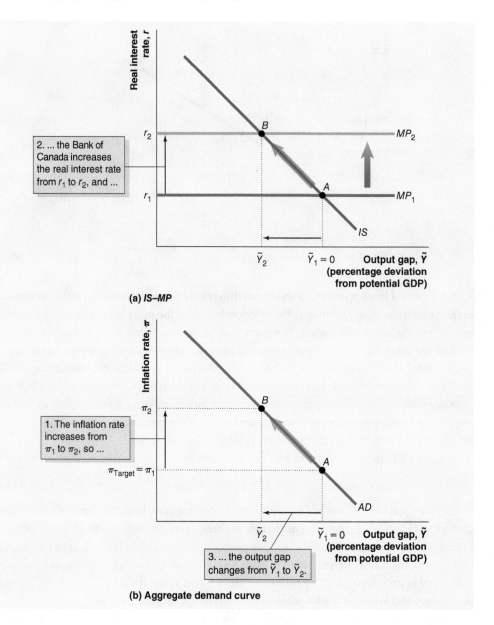

(a) *IS–MP*

(b) **Aggregate demand curve**

Deriving the Aggregate Demand Curve In Figure 14.2 we derive the aggregate demand (AD) curve. We will draw it as a straight line so we only need to specify two points. One of the points is point A in both panels, with the real interest rate equal to r_1, real GDP equal to potential GDP so the output gap equals zero at $\tilde{Y}_1$, and the inflation rate, π_1, equal to the central bank's target rate, π_{Target}. Now suppose that the inflation rate increases from π_1 to π_2, i.e., above the central bank's target rate. The reaction function tells us that, in response, the central bank raises the real interest rate so the MP curve shifts up to MP_2. As a result, aggregate expenditure falls below potential GDP and the output gap is now $\tilde{Y}_2 < 0$. The new equilibrium combination of inflation and real GDP is π_2 and $\tilde{Y}_2$, so short-run equilibrium is now at point B in both panels. Drawing a line connecting points A and B gives us the aggregate demand curve.

Slope of the Aggregate Demand Curve Why is the aggregate demand curve negatively sloped? An increase in the inflation rate leads the central bank to increase the real interest rate, which lowers aggregate expenditure. The slope of the reaction function affects the slope of the AD curve. The steeper is the reaction function (the bigger is b), the flatter is the AD

curve. The explanation is as follows. We consider an increase in inflation by 1% and ask how big is the resulting decrease in aggregate expenditure. Consider first the case of a central bank that focuses on price stability and reacts aggressively when inflation differs from target (i.e., the coefficient b is large). So, the central bank raises the real interest rate a lot. This means that the reaction function is steep. As a consequence of a big increase in the real interest rate, expenditure falls a lot. So, in the AD graph, a 1% increase in the inflation rate has a big effect on aggregate expenditure and the AD curve is flat. Conversely, if the central bank is not very sensitive to changes in the inflation rate (the coefficient b is small), it will increase the real interest rate little. As a consequence of a small increase in the real interest rate, aggregate expenditure falls little. So, in the AD graph, a 1% increase in the inflation rate has a small effect on aggregate expenditure and the AD curve is steep.

How the IS and AD Differ An important point to remember is how the IS and AD curves differ. Both show the relationship with the aggregate expenditure, but with respect to different variables. The IS curve shows the relationship between the real interest rate and aggregate expenditure, while the AD curve shows the relationship between the inflation rate and aggregate expenditure. The IS curve is a building block of the AD curve. The AD curve is obtained from the IS curve and the central bank's reaction function. The IS curve shows that a higher real interest rate lowers aggregate expenditure. The central bank's reaction function links the real interest rate and inflation. The higher is the inflation rate, the higher is the real interest rate set by the central bank. The higher is the real interest rate the lower is (by the IS curve) aggregate expenditure.

Shifts of the Aggregate Demand Curve

Anything That Shifts the IS curve Shifts the AD Curve The AD curve tells us what happens to the quantity of real GDP demanded relative to potential GDP if the inflation rate increases, *holding everything else constant*. Therefore, a change in the inflation rate causes a *movement along* a particular AD curve. If a factor that would affect the demand for goods and services other than the inflation rate changes, the AD curve will *shift*.

As the AD curve is derived from the IS curve, anything that causes the IS curve to shift will cause the AD curve to shift. Factors that cause the IS curve to shift are changes in autonomous consumption, taxes and transfer payments, investment, government purchases of goods and services, and changes in net exports. For example, if the government increases spending on infrastructure projects, such as highways and bridges, both the IS curve and the AD curve will shift to the right.

Figure 14.3 shows the effect of an increase in government purchases on the AD curve. In panel (b), the short-run equilibrium is initially at point A, with the inflation rate π and the output gap $\tilde{Y}_1$. When government purchases increase, the IS curve in panel (a) shifts to the right, from IS_1 to IS_2. At the original real interest rate, short-run equilibrium is now at point B, and the output gap equals Y_2. At the initial inflation rate π_1, the new output gap is $\tilde{Y}_2$. Short-run equilibrium is at point B in panel (b), which is to the right of the original AD curve. Therefore, the AD curve has shifted to the right, from AD_1 to AD_2.

A Change in the Inflation Target A change in the central bank's inflation target will also shift the AD curve. Figure 14.4 shows the effect of an increase in the inflation target. Initially, both the target inflation rate and the actual inflation rate equal 2%, so the central bank has no reason to change the real interest rate, and the equilibrium is at the point A in both panels. Now suppose that the actual inflation rate remains at 2%, but the central bank increases the target inflation rate to 3%. The actual inflation rate is now 1% below the target inflation rate, so, at the current inflation rate, the central bank will reduce the real interest rate to increase aggregate expenditure. The MP curve shifts down from MP_1 to

Figure 14.3

An Increase in Government Purchases Shifts the Aggregate Demand Curve

An increase in government purchases increases aggregate expenditure, so the IS curve shifts to the right, from IS_1 to IS_2. As a result, the AD curve also shifts to the right, from AD_1 to AD_2. Any increase in autonomous spending that causes the IS curve to shift to the right in panel (a) will also cause the AD curve to shift to the right in panel (b). Similarly, any decrease in autonomous spending that causes the IS curve to shift to the left will also cause the AD curve to shift to the left.

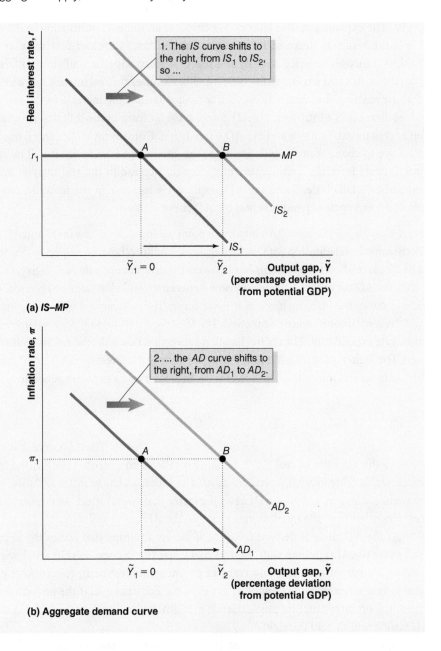

1. The IS curve shifts to the right, from IS_1 to IS_2, so ...

2. ... the AD curve shifts to the right, from AD_1 to AD_2.

(a) IS–MP

(b) Aggregate demand curve

MP_2. The increase in aggregate expenditure will shift the AD curve to the right. The new equilibrium is at point B.

A good example of a change in an inflation target is Japan in 2013. The Japanese economy has experienced slow growth since the crash in 1989. Real GDP in Japan grew at an average annual rate of 4.5% from 1970 to 1991, but it has grown at a rate of less than 1.5% per year since then. Not surprisingly, slow growth has led to low inflation rates. The annual inflation rate in Japan from 1991 to 2011 averaged just 0.2%, and the economy experienced deflation during nine of those years. Some economists have argued that the Bank of Japan should not have allowed the inflation rate to fall so low. In January 2013 the new government of Shinzo Abe convinced the Bank of Japan to adopt an inflation target of 2%. The goal of adopting the target was, first of all, to avoid deflation and, more importantly, to stimulate the economy with expansionary monetary policy. This argument is consistent with our discussion of the AD curve. By increasing the target inflation rate the Bank of Japan hoped to increase the expected inflation rate. With the Bank of Japan keeping the nominal interest rate constant, the real interest rate would fall. (Recall that the real interest rate is approximately

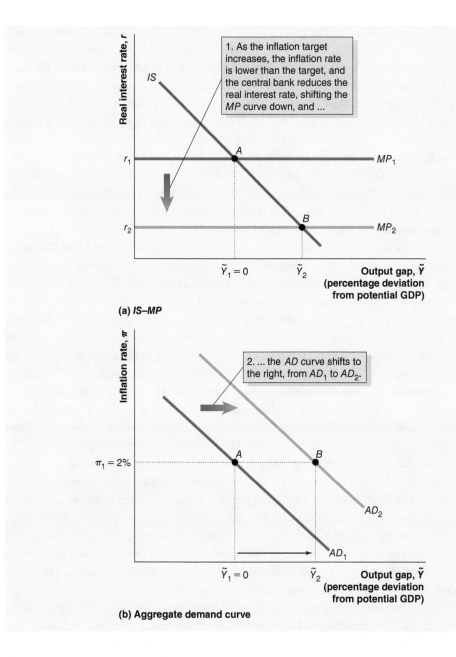

1. As the inflation target increases, the inflation rate is lower than the target, and the central bank reduces the real interest rate, shifting the *MP* curve down, and ...

(a) *IS–MP*

2. ... the *AD* curve shifts to the right, from AD_1 to AD_2.

(b) Aggregate demand curve

Figure 14.4

An Increase in the Inflation Target Shifts the Aggregate Demand Curve

An increase in the inflation rate puts the current inflation below the new target, so the central bank reduces the real interest rate. The *MP* curve shifts down and the aggregate demand curve shifts to the right.

equal to the difference between the nominal interest rate and the *expected* rate of inflation.) As a consequence aggregate expenditure and output would both increase. At the time of writing the policy appears to have been a partial success. By the end of 2014 the inflation rate increased to 3%; the core inflation rate, which excludes prices of food and energy, was the highest in 15 years. In 2013 the Japanese economic growth was 2.4% but, in the fall of 2014, real GDP started falling.

When Are Shifts to the Aggregate Demand Curve Permanent? In Figure 14.3 on page 442, we used the example of an increase in government purchases to demonstrate a shift to the right of the *AD* curve. This shift is not permanent, and the *AD* curve will eventually shift to the left, from AD_2 to AD_1. Why? We know that in long-run equilibrium, aggregate expenditure, real GDP, and potential GDP are all equal. Therefore, aggregate expenditure cannot exceed potential GDP in long-run equilibrium. If point *A* in Figure 14.3 is the long-run equilibrium, then aggregate expenditure equals potential GDP at point *A*, and aggregate expenditure is 100% of potential GDP. Suppose that government purchases are initially 20% of potential GDP, so consumption, investment, and net exports are 80% (= 100% − 20%)

of potential GDP. If government purchases increase from 20% to 25% of potential GDP, and all other expenditures are initially constant, then aggregate expenditure is now 105% (= 25% + 80%) of potential GDP. Both the *IS* curve and the *AD* curve shift to the right, and real GDP increases, but this higher real GDP is not a long-run equilibrium because aggregate expenditure cannot remain equal to 105% of potential GDP indefinitely.

There are two ways in which real GDP can return to potential GDP. First, if the increase in government purchases is temporary, government purchases decline back to 20% of potential GDP. The temporary surge in government purchases during wars is an example of a temporary shift in the *AD* curve. In such cases, aggregate expenditure declines to 100% of potential GDP when government purchases decrease. Second, if the increase in government purchases to 25% of potential GDP is permanent, as with a permanent increase in spending on education or highways and bridges, then the sum of consumption, investment, and net exports must decrease to 75% of potential GDP. Our discussion of the loanable funds model (see Chapter 5) suggests a mechanism by which this decrease in consumption, investment, and net exports can take place. If the government permanently spends more, and finances this spending through budget deficits, real interest rates will increase, which will cause investment, consumption, and net exports to fall. If the government chooses to finance the increase in government purchases by raising taxes, consumption and investment will decrease. Either way, expenditure by the private sector, as a proportion of potential GDP, will decrease in the long run to offset the effect of the increase in government purchases. We reach the same conclusion if consumption, investment, or net exports initially increase to cause the *AD* curve to shift to the right. A permanent increase in one component of aggregate expenditure as a share of potential GDP means that one, or some combination, of the other three components of aggregate expenditure must decrease. When this decrease occurs, the *AD* curve shifts back to the left. Therefore, we can conclude that when the economy starts at equilibrium with real GDP equal to potential GDP, changes in autonomous expenditure cause temporary shifts to the *AD* curve.

In contrast to changes in autonomous expenditure, changes in the inflation target cause the *AD* curve to shift permanently. When the central bank announces a higher inflation target, it is announcing that it will accept a higher rate of inflation for any given level of the output gap. For example, when the output gap is zero, the central bank is willing to accept an inflation rate of 3% rather than 2%. This result also holds for all other values of the output gap, so the shift in the *AD* curve is permanent.

When we discuss the complete aggregate demand and aggregate supply model in Section 14.3, it will be important to keep these two results in mind: *Shifts in the IS curve temporarily shift the AD curve, but changes to the reaction function permanently shift the AD curve.* Knowing the difference between permanent and temporary shifts in the *AD* curve helps in understanding how the economy adjusts toward long-run equilibrium. It is also important to note that while the *AD* curve may shift permanently, in the long run, real GDP will always return to its potential level. We will explore why this is the case in the next section.

Aggregate Supply and the Phillips Curve

Aggregate supply (AS) curve A curve that shows the total quantity of output, or real GDP, that firms are willing and able to supply at a given inflation rate.

We now consider the **aggregate supply (AS) curve**, which shows the total quantity of output, or real GDP, that firms are willing and able to supply at a given inflation rate. This definition of the *AS* curve is similar to the definition of the Phillips curve because, in fact, the two curves are the same.[1]

14.2

Learning Objective

Explain the relationship between aggregate supply and the Phillips curve.

---

[1]Why two names for the same curve? The traditional name for a curve that relates the inflation rate to the output gap (or to the unemployment rate) is the Phillips curve, which was first derived in the 1950s by the New Zealand economist A. W. H. Phillips. We could have continued to use that name in this chapter, but in the context of a model that includes aggregate demand, it is less confusing to call the curve an aggregate supply curve.

As we saw when we first discussed the Phillips curve (see Chapter 11), there are three sources of inflationary pressure in the short run: changes in the expected inflation rate, demand shocks, and supply shocks. The expected inflation rate is important because firms set their prices based on the prices they expect their competitors to charge and the prices they expect to pay their suppliers and employees. If firms expect inflation to increase, they will increase the prices they charge for a given level of the output gap. Inflation can increase following a demand shock that causes real GDP to increase relative to potential GDP because firms experience capacity constraints as raw materials and labour become harder to find at existing prices. Inflation can also occur as a result of a supply shock when, for instance, the price of a key input, such as oil, unexpectedly rises, and firms pass along some of the price increase to the consumers of final goods and services. An increase in the inflation rate as a result of a supply shock tends to be temporary. For example, a 10% increase in oil prices will increase the inflation rate for a time. But once the economy adjusts to the higher price of oil, the inflation rate will return to its previous level unless oil prices increase again.

Making the Connection

Cigarette Smuggling and the Inflation Rate

In the early 1990s the price difference between cigarettes in the United States and in Canada was large. The result was massive smuggling of cigarettes. Sales of cigarettes in Canada fell significantly, but Canadian exports of cigarettes to the United States increased by about 1000%. It was clear that the exported cigarettes were then smuggled back to Canada. To combat smuggling, the federal government and several provincial governments reduced excise taxes on cigarettes. As a result, prices of cigarettes fell by as much as 50%, reducing smuggling incentives. Below is the plot of the inflation rate over the period February 1993 to February 1996. Even though the price of cigarettes fell only in February 1994, inflation was lower for a year. Furthermore, even though nothing as dramatic happened in February 1995, the inflation rate jumped from 0.6% per year to 1.9% per year. How can we explain this seemingly odd behaviour of the inflation rate?

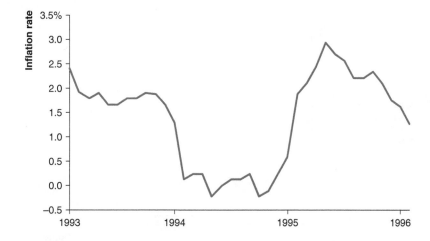

At that time, the weight of cigarettes in the CPI was 2% (i.e., 2% of consumer spending was on cigarettes). As a result of the cigarette tax reduction, prices of cigarettes fell by about 50%. The effect on the CPI inflation rate of the decline in cigarette prices was 2% $\times$ (-50%) = -1%. In fact, the inflation rate fell from 1.3% in January 1994 to 0.1% in February 1994, so the decline in cigarette prices explains almost all of the decline in the inflation rate in February 1994. To understand the rest of the period consider a simple example in which all other components of inflation are ignored. Assume that the price level is constant until January 1994, falls by 1% in February 1994, and remains constant afterwards. We want to know what the effect of this one-time change in the price level would be.

To answer this question, you need to know how the inflation rate is calculated. If we would like to calculate the monthly inflation rate, we would take the price level in a given month, divided by the price level in the previous month, minus 1. Such inflation is called month-on-month inflation rate. Month-on-month inflation rates are, however, very volatile, and so economists prefer a year-on-year inflation rate. It is calculated as the price level in a given month, divided by the price level a year earlier, minus 1. Let the price level be 100 until January 1994, fall to 99 in February 1994, and equal to 99 afterward. So the year-on-year inflation rate in January 1994 and earlier is $100/100 - 1 = 0\%$. In February 1994 the inflation rate is $99/100 - 1 = -1\%$, i.e., it falls by 1%. In every month up to and including January 1995 the inflation rate is the same: $99/100 - 1 = -1\%$. In February 1995 the inflation rate becomes $99/99 - 1 = 0\%$, i.e., it increases by 1%. It remains equal to 1% afterward. This information is summarized in the table below.

	Jan 1994 and earlier	Feb 1994–Jan 1995	Feb 1995 and later
Price level	100	99	99
Inflation rate	0%	−1%	0%

So even though the price level falls in one month only, the year-over-year inflation rate falls for one year. This is, indeed, what happened in Canada in 1994–95.

Source: Statistics Canada, CANSIM Table 326-0020.

Figure 14.5 shows the aggregate supply curve. Short-run equilibrium is initially at point A, with the inflation rate, π_1, equal to the expected inflation rate, π^e, and real GDP equal to potential GDP. If short-run equilibrium moves from point A to point B, real GDP increases relative to potential GDP, so the output gap changes from $\widetilde{Y}_1$ to $\widetilde{Y}_2$, and the inflation rate rises

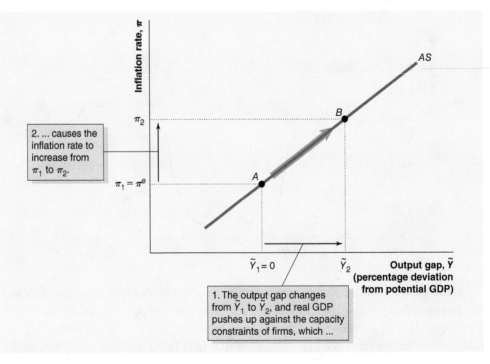

Figure 14.5

The Aggregate Supply Curve

The aggregate supply curve is drawn assuming that the expected inflation rate is constant. As aggregate expenditure increases and the output gap changes from $\widetilde{Y}_1 = 0$ to $\widetilde{Y}_2 > 0$, real GDP pushes up against the capacity constraints of firms. In response, some firms increase prices; the inflation rate increases from π_1 to π_2; and short-run equilibrium moves from point A to point B on the AS curve.

2. ... causes the inflation rate to increase from π_1 to π_2.

1. The output gap changes from $\widetilde{Y}_1$ to $\widetilde{Y}_2$, and real GDP pushes up against the capacity constraints of firms, which ...

from π_1 to π_2. Notice that a change in the output gap causes a *movement along* an aggregate supply curve from point A to point B.

Because the aggregate supply curve is the same as the Phillips curve, we can use the equation for the Phillips curve to represent the aggregate supply curve:

$$\pi_t = \pi_t^e + b\widetilde{Y}_t - s_t, \tag{14.2}$$

where π_t is current inflation rate, π_t^e is the expected inflation rate, $\widetilde{Y}_t$ is the output gap, b is the sensitivity of the inflation rate to changes in the output gap, and s_t is the effect of supply shocks.

The supply shock in the equation of the aggregate supply curve, equation (14.2), has a negative sign because we call a supply shock negative when it increases prices. An example is a large increase in the price of oil. A positive supply shock, such as an increase in productivity, decreases the inflation rate. The parameter b is positive, since the inflation rate increases as real GDP and the output gap increase.

It is important to note that a change in the output gap or in the inflation rate is a *movement along* a given aggregate supply curve, as shown in Figure 14.5. Recall from "Avoiding a Common Mistake," in Chapter 3, page 72, that a change in the variable that is on either axis is a movement along the curve, not a shift of the curve.

The Position of the *AS* Curve The equation of the *AS* curve shows how to find the position of the curve. If there is no supply shock, the *AS* curve goes through the point where the output gap is zero and inflation is equal to expected inflation. So, in Figure 14.5, the *AS* curve goes through point A.

Adaptive Expectations In this section, we assume that expectations are adaptive in the sense that households and firms expect that the inflation rate from the previous period will persist into the future. The expected inflation rate in the current year equals the actual inflation rate in the previous year: For example, if the inflation rate in 2013 is 2%, the expected inflation rate for 2014 will also be 2%. But if the inflation rate rises to 4% in 2014, the expected inflation rate for 2015 will also rise to 4%. The assumption about expectations allows us to describe the adjustment of the economy following a shock.

Shifts in the Aggregate Supply Curve

There are two reasons for the aggregate supply curve to shift: a change in the expected inflation rate and a supply shock. A decrease in expected inflation shifts the aggregate supply curve down, as shown in Figure 14.6. A decrease in costs of production, resulting from a positive supply shock, has the same effect. The experience of the Canadian economy during the 1981–82 recession provides an example of a downward shift of the aggregate supply curve. Recall that the recession was caused by the Bank of Canada restrictive monetary policy aimed at reducing inflation. The inflation rate fell from a peak of 12.9% in July 1981 to 5.4% two years later. Figure 14.6 shows the effect of a decrease in expected inflation on the aggregate supply curve.

From the equation for the aggregate supply curve: $\pi_t = \pi_t^e + b\widetilde{Y}_t - s_t$, we can see that, if the supply shock is equal to zero, $s_t = 0$, and the output gap is zero, $\widetilde{Y}_1 = 0$, the inflation rate is equal to the expected inflation rate. So, when expected inflation falls from π_1^e to π_2^e then, for an output gap equal to zero, the aggregate supply curve shifts down from point A to point B. Notice that, on the new aggregate supply curve, inflation is now lower for any given level of the output gap. Similarly, if the output gap is zero, a positive supply shock, for example, due to fast productivity growth, reduces the inflation rate and so shifts the *AS* curve down.

Figure 14.6

A Decrease in Inflationary Expectations or a Positive Supply Shock and the Aggregate Supply Curve

If the expected inflation rate decreases or there is a positive supply shock, the aggregate supply curve shifts down.

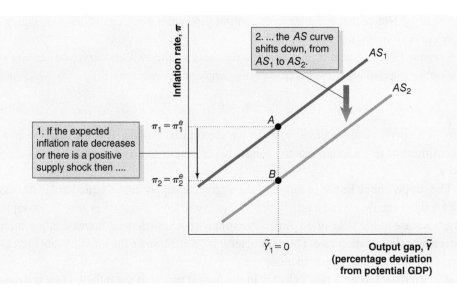

The Aggregate Demand and Aggregate Supply Model

14.3

Learning Objective

Use the aggregate demand and aggregate supply model to analyze macroeconomic conditions.

Aggregate demand and aggregate supply (AD–AS) model A model that explains short-run fluctuations in the output gap and the inflation rate.

The **aggregate demand and aggregate supply (AD–AS) model** explains short-run fluctuations in the output gap and in the inflation rate. Before we analyze the model, let us summarize its two main elements, the aggregate demand (*AD*) and the aggregate supply (*AS*) curves.

The *AD* curve shows the relationship between aggregate expenditure and the rate of inflation. This relationship is based on the central bank reaction function. The central bank has a target for the inflation rate. If inflation moves above target, the central bank raises the real interest rate to slow down the economy, and aggregate expenditure decreases *along* the *AD* curve. If inflation moves below target, the central bank lowers the real interest rate to stimulate the economy, and aggregate expenditure increases *along* the *AD* curve. The *AD* curve *shifts* to the right if (a) aggregate expenditure increases *at a given inflation rate*, (for example, when government purchases rise or when the central bank reduces the real interest rate), or (b) if the central bank raises inflation target. If the central bank reacts aggressively to inflation departing from target, by changing the real interest rate a lot, the aggregate demand curve is flat.

The *AS* curve shows the amount firms are willing to supply at a given inflation rate. It is the same as the Phillips curve. To find the position of the *AS* curve, remember that, if there are no supply shocks, the *AS* curve goes through at point at which the output gap is zero and inflation is equal to expected inflation. The *AS* curve shifts down if the expected inflation rate falls or if there is a positive supply shock (i.e., costs of production fall at all level of output, such as a rapid technological progress or a decline in the price of oil).

To explore the model, we first discuss how long-run equilibrium is determined and then analyze what factors cause the equilibrium to change and how the economy moves to the new equilibrium.

Equilibrium in the AD–AS Model

The long-run equilibrium in the *AD–AS* model is characterized by three conditions—one for the real GDP and two for the inflation rate. The economy is in long-run equilibrium if and only if

1. Real GDP equals potential GDP: $\tilde{Y} = 0$.
2. The inflation rate equals the central bank's target inflation rate: $\pi = \pi_{Target}$.
3. The inflation rate equals the expected inflation rate: $\pi = \pi^e$.

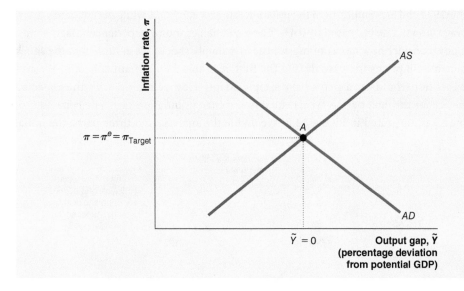

Figure 14.7

Equilibrium in the Aggregate Demand and Aggregate Supply Model

Point A represents a long-run equilibrium because real GDP equals potential GDP, the inflation rate equals the target inflation rate and the inflation rate equals the expected inflation rate.

If the economy is in long-run equilibrium, the three conditions must be met. First, as we know from earlier analysis, in the long run output has to be equal to potential output. Second, if the inflation rate is different from target inflation rate, the central bank will change real interest rates and the level of output will change. So, in the long-run equilibrium, the inflation rate has to be equal to the target level. Third, if the inflation rate is different from the expected inflation rate, households and firms will realize the error they are making and their expected inflation rate will change, shifting the aggregate supply curve.

Conversely, if all those conditions are met, the economy is in long-run equilibrium. First, we know that if the output gap is zero, the output side of the economy is in equilibrium. Second, if inflation is equal to target and output is equal to potential, the central bank does not engage in active policy to change inflation or output. Third, if inflation is constant and equal to its expected level, inflation expectations will not change.

In Figure 14.7 long-run equilibrium in the *AD–AS* model is at point A, where the aggregate demand and aggregate supply curves intersect. Point A is a long-run equilibrium because (1) real GDP equals potential GDP, so the output gap is zero, (2) the inflation rate equals the target inflation rate, and (3) the inflation rate equals the expected inflation rate.

We will now use the *AD–AS* model to explain how the output gap and the inflation rate respond to shocks such as an increase in oil prices, a change in the central bank reaction function, or a collapse in stock prices. To accomplish this goal, we discuss how the economy responds to shifts in the aggregate supply curve and the aggregate demand curve.

The Effects of a Supply Shock

Oil price increases can play an important role in causing *stagflation*, a shorthand for stagnation and inflation, which is a period of both high inflation and recession, usually resulting from a supply shock. The classic case of stagflation is the severe 1973–75 global recession. The world economy experienced an oil shock in late 1973, after the Organization of the Petroleum Exporting Countries (OPEC) imposed an oil embargo in response to Western support of Israel in the 1973 Arab–Israeli War. The price of a barrel of oil rose from US$4.31 during December 1973 to US$10.11 during January 1974—a 135% increase in just one month! Such a large increase in the price of a key-input-generated inflation in many countries as firms passed their increased costs to consumers in the form of higher prices for final goods and services. In Canada, June 1974 prices of energy were 21% higher than a year earlier. Between

September1974 and September 1975 the inflation rate exceeded 11% while output barely grew: The average growth rate increased by 0.4%. The Canadian economy experienced stagnation.

We now consider how an economy adjusts to a supply shock. We assume that the shock is permanent: Oil prices increase during the first year and then remain constant. We also assume that households and firms have simple adaptive expectations, with the expected inflation rate for the next period (year) equal to the current inflation rate. The behaviour of the economy is illustrated in Figure 14.8. We divide the analysis into three parts: the initial

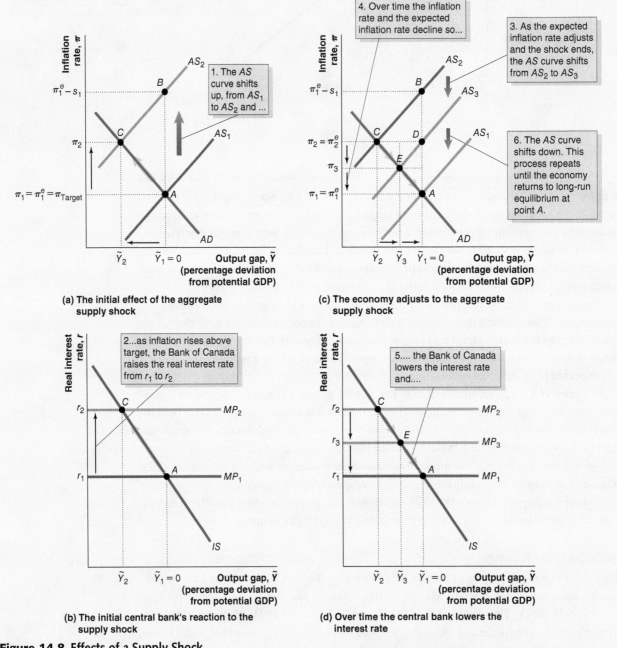

Figure 14.8 Effects of a Supply Shock

In panel (a), a supply shock causes the AS curve to shift up, from AS_1 to AS_2. As the inflation rate increases above target, the central bank raises the real interest rate in panel (b) from r_1 to r_2 and the new short-run equilibrium is at point C.

Panels (c) and (d) show the adjustment to long-run equilibrium. After oil prices have increased, the shock returns to zero and the AS curve shifts

down from AS_2 to AS_3, moving the short-run equilibrium from point C to point E. Inflation falls and the central bank reduces the real interest rate part way toward r_1. Over time, the expected inflation rate and the actual inflation rate decrease, the central bank continues to reduce the real interest rate back toward r_1, the AS curve shifts from AS_3 toward AS_1, moving short-run equilibrium from point E back to point A.

short-run equilibrium following the shock, the adjustment process, and the final, long-run equilibrium. To simplify analysis we start at a long-run equilibrium at point A, where real GDP equals potential GDP; the inflation rate is equal to the target inflation rate and the inflation rate equals the expected inflation rate.

Overview To facilitate the analysis of the adjustment process, we start with its overview. As we are considering a supply shock, the aggregate demand curve does not shift. All the changes come from the shifts in the aggregate supply curve, and movements along the aggregate demand curve. So we need to keep track of the position of the aggregate supply curve. The easiest way to find it is to look at the vertical line at full employment, where $\widetilde{Y}_1 = 0$. The equation of the aggregate supply curve is $\pi_t = \pi_t^e + b\widetilde{Y}_t - s_t$. When $\widetilde{Y}_1 = 0$, this simplifies to $\pi_t = \pi_t^e - s_t$. The aggregate supply curve goes through the point where $\widetilde{Y}_1 = 0$ and $\pi_t = \pi_t^e - s_t$. So, to find the position of the aggregate supply curve, for each period we need to determine the current inflation rate, which is equal to the sum of the expected inflation rate and the current shock. As we will see, the expected inflation rate will change every period until the new equilibrium is reached. On the other hand, as the shock is permanent, we add it only in the initial period, denoted as period 1. This is because the price of oil stays constant at the new level and there are no further shocks. If the increase in the price of oil was temporary, we would consider two shocks: a negative shock when the price of oil increases, and a positive shock when oil prices fall back to the original level.

Initial, Short-Run Equilibrium Following a Negative Supply Shock The increase in the price of oil is a negative supply shock of size equal to $(-s_1)$, with $s_1 < 0$ since the shock is negative. The results of the shock are shown in panels (a) and (b). The aggregate supply curve shifts up, from AS_1 to AS_2. How big is the shift? The old aggregate supply curve, AS_1, goes through the point where $\widetilde{Y}_1 = 0$ and $\pi_1 = \pi_1^e$. The new aggregate supply curve, AS_2, goes through the point where $\widetilde{Y}_1 = 0$ and $\pi_1 = \pi_1^e - s_1$. This means that the vertical shift of the AS curve is equal to minus the size of the shock, $(-s_1)$.

Once we established the new position of the aggregate supply curve, we can determine the initial, short-run equilibrium. If the central bank did nothing, the inflation rate would have increased to $\pi_1^e - s_1$. However, the inflation rate has increased and is so is now above the target inflation rate. So the central bank acts in accord with its reaction function, raising the real interest rate from r_1 to r_2 in panel (a). The increase in the real interest rate reduces consumption, investment, and net exports. The initial short-run equilibrium is at point C where the new aggregate supply curve, AS_2, intersects the aggregate demand curve. The inflation rate is π_2 and output gap is $\widetilde{Y}_2 < 0$. The intervention of the central bank increased the real interest rate and reduced aggregate expenditure *along* the AD curve. In addition the inflation rate did not increase all the way to $\pi_1^e - s_1$.

To summarize, the initial supply shock results in higher inflation. The central bank increases the real interest rate, and the level of output falls.

The Adjustment Process Adjustment to new long-run equilibrium is illustrated in panels (c) and (d). We now consider the adjustment process in the second period. We are assuming that households and firms have adaptive expectations, so the expected inflation rate is equal to the current inflation rate: $\pi_2^e = \pi_2$. This means expected inflation has increased from π_1^e to π_2^e. Note that π_2^e denotes the expectations in period two about the inflation rate in period three. Oil prices no longer change, so the shock is now equal to zero, $s_2 = 0$, and so the sum of expected inflation and supply shock in period 2 is equal to $\pi_2^e + 0$. This means that the AS curve goes through the point D, where $\widetilde{Y}_1 = 0$ and inflation is π_2^e. The aggregate supply curve has shifted down to AS_3.

The new short-run equilibrium is therefore at point E, where the aggregate supply curve, AS_3, intersects the aggregate demand curve, AD. Inflation falls to π_3. Since the inflation rate falls, the central bank reduces the real interest rate from r_2 to r_3, as shown in panel (c). With a lower real interest rate than at the end of the initial period, aggregate expenditure starts increasing and the economy moves *along* the *AD curve* from point *C* to point *E*.

What happens in subsequent periods? As the inflation rate declines, the expected inflation rate falls, shifting the *AS* curve down. The actual inflation rate declines, allowing the central bank to reduce the real interest rate further toward the initial value. As the real interest rate declines, aggregate expenditure increases and the economy moves along the *AD* curve. This adjustment process continues until eventually the economy is back at long-run equilibrium at point *A*.

To summarize, during the adjustment process the inflation rate falls, the central bank reduces the real interest rate, and the level of output increases.

Long-Run Equilibrium As long as inflation exceeds target inflation, the central bank keeps the real interest rate above the original equilibrium value, and the level of output is lower than potential. Over time the inflation rate falls. The adjustment ends when the economy returns to the original equilibrium at point *A*. We can see from Figure 14.8 that the initial effect of a supply shock is both higher inflation and lower real GDP relative to potential GDP. Note that the Bank of Canada increases interest rates in a recession. This is a problem unique to supply shocks and comes from the fact that the Bank of Canada concentrates on the inflation rate rather than on output.

In other words, our model predicts that an increase in oil prices can cause periods of stagflation similar to the 1973–75 recession. There is an important difference, however, between the model and what happened in 1970s. At the time of the oil shocks in 1970s central banks did not raise real interest rates, as they focused more on the level of output. Their policy resulted in a smaller reduction of output (or, in some cases, output actually slowly increased) but a much higher rate of inflation. The improvement in output was only temporary: In early 1980s, with inflation in double digits, central banks raised interest rates, causing a recession but bringing the inflation down. The experience of that period led to changes in monetary policy, which is now conducted as our model describes.

Macro Data: Are Oil Supply Shocks Really That Important?

Athanasios Orphanides of the Massachusetts Institute of Technology argues that, in the past, poor policy decisions due to measurement problems have caused inflation rates to increase. Policymakers receive economic data with a lag, and the initial estimates for key variables such as inflation and the output gap are often incorrect. Orphanides looked at the data available to policymakers *at the time they made their decisions* and found that they underestimated how much inflation was increasing and overestimated the level of potential GDP, which caused them to believe that real GDP was further from potential GDP than it actually was. As a result, monetary policy turned out to be more expansionary than it would have been had the U.S. Federal Reserve had more accurate data.

In another study, Christiane Baumeister from the Bank of Canada, Gert Peersman from the University of Ghent, and Ine Van Robays from the European Central Bank found that the effect of higher oil prices varies across countries. Inflation increases in oil-importing counties, but the size of the increase depends on how much wages rise.

In oil-exporting countries, for example, in Canada, the effect of higher oil prices on inflation is smaller. They suggest this is because when oil prices increase, oil-exporting countries experience a currency appreciation, which reduces prices of imported goods.

We discuss the possibility that monetary policy caused the poor economic performance during the 1970s in greater detail in the next section. While most economists continue to believe that an oil price shock was the main reason for the stagflation of the mid-1970s, the effect of oil price shocks on the economy remains an active area of macroeconomic research.

Sources: Athanasios Orphanides, "The Quest for Prosperity Without Inflation," *Journal of Monetary Economics* 50, no. 3 (2003): 633–663; and Christiane Baumeister, Gert Peersman, and Ine Van Robays, "The Economic Consequences of Oil Shocks: Differences across Countries and Time," in R. Fry, C. Jones, and C. Kent eds., *Inflation in an Era of Relative Price Shocks* (Sydney: Reserve Bank of Australia, 2010) 91–137.

See related Problem 3.8 at the end of the chapter.

Changes in the Target Inflation Rate

Following the Great Recession, expansionary monetary policy in many countries hit a limit: The policy rates, which are usually the very short-term nominal interest rates, fell essentially to zero. Nominal interest rates cannot fall below zero since a negative nominal interest rate would mean that, when a loan is repaid, the lender would get *less* money than the original value of the loan. Lenders would not agree to such terms since they can hold cash instead. In November 2014, the policy rate of the Bank of Canada (the target for the overnight rate) was 1%, leaving some possibility for further reductions. But the policy rate of the European Central Bank was 0.25%. It was between 0 and 0.25% in the United States, 0.1% in Japan, and 0.5% in the United Kingdom. Clearly, several central banks could no longer reduce their policy rate. The inability of a central bank to lower interest rates to negative values is called the *zero lower bound* constraint. In Chapter 12 we discussed several policies central banks used when facing the zero lower bound constraint. In that case, other channels of monetary policy may still operate, such as quantitative easing or forward guidance. Changing the target inflation rate provides another possible channel through which the central bank can affect real GDP and employment when facing a zero lower bound constraint. For example, as we discussed earlier in the chapter, in 2013 the Bank of Japan raised its inflation target to 2% in order to stimulate the economy and raise both inflation and expected inflation to the new target.

We can use the *AD–AS* model to explain how changing the target inflation rate can provide the central bank with another way to affect the economy when facing a zero lower bound constraint. Recall that the expression for the (expected) real interest rate is $r = i - \pi^e$. So, The real interest rate can become negative if the expected inflation rate is greater than the nominal interest rate. For example, suppose that the nominal interest rate is 0.25%, and expected inflation and target inflation both equal 2%. In this case, the real interest rate is -1.75% ($= 0.25\% - 2\%$). If the central bank announces that it has increased the target inflation rate to 4% and households and firms believe it will meet its target, the real interest rate will decrease to -3.75% ($= 0.25\% - 4\%$). Therefore, the announcement of a higher inflation target decreases the expected real interest rate. The lower real interest rate will increase consumption, investment, and net exports, resulting in an increase in real GDP and employment.

The effect of a change in the inflation target is shown in Figure 14.9. As before, we start in long-run equilibrium at point *A* where (1) real GDP equals potential GDP, (2) the inflation rate is equal to the target inflation rate, and (3) the inflation rate equals the expected inflation rate. Now suppose that the central bank increases the target inflation rate from π_{Target} to π'_{Target}.

Initial, Short-Run Equilibrium following the Increase in the Target Inflation Rate Since initially the inflation rate, π_1, was equal to the old target, denoted π_{Target}, it is now lower than the new target: $\pi_1 < \pi'_{\text{Target}}$. To hit the new higher target inflation rate, the central bank decreases the real interest rate *without* a change in the inflation rate. The lower real interest rate causes consumption, investment, and net exports to rise. At the given inflation rate aggregate expenditure is higher, so the *AD* curve shifts to the right, from AD_1 to AD_2, and real GDP increases, causing the output gap to become positive, equal to $\tilde{Y}_2$. Short-run equilibrium is now at point *B*, with inflation equal to π_2.

The Adjustment Process Note that point *B* is not a long-run equilibrium, because real GDP is above potential GDP and the inflation rate, π_2, is greater than the expected inflation rate, π_1^e, but lower than the new target inflation rate, π'_{Target}. Because expectations are adaptive, the expected inflation rate will increase, and the *AS* curve will shift up. More precisely, in the next period the expected inflation rate increases to π_2, so the *AS* curve shifts up from AS_1 to AS_2.

How can we determine the size of the shift? As the expected inflation rate is now π_2 and there are no supply shocks, the new supply curve AS_2 intersects the vertical line $\tilde{Y}_1 = 0$ at the inflation rate equal to π_2. The economy moves to point *C*.

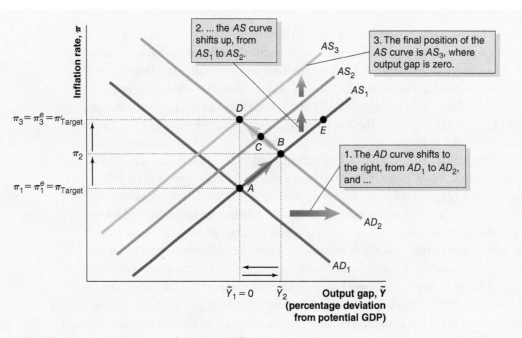

Figure 14.9 The Effects of an Increase in the Target Inflation Rate

From an initial long-run equilibrium at point A, the central bank raises the target inflation. To bring inflation to the new target it lowers the real interest rate. This increases investment, consumption, and net exports, which shifts the AD curve to the right, from AD_1 to AD_2. The economy moves to a new short-run equilibrium at point B and the inflation rate increases, raising the expected inflation rate. Higher expected inflation rate causes the AS curve to shift up, from AS_1 to AS_2. The process continues as long as the inflation rate is below the new target. The economy returns to long-run equilibrium at point D, with real GDP equal to potential GDP. At point D, the inflation rate equals the new, higher target inflation rate. There is a temporary boom. In the long run, the inflation rate is higher, equal to the new target, and there is no change in the unemployment rate.

When the expected inflation rate increases, the actual inflation rate increases as well. The central bank therefore raises the real interest rate, reducing consumption, investment, and net exports so that the output gap falls and the economy moves *along* the new AD curve. The process continues as long as the output gap is positive and inflation is below the new target.

Long-Run Equilibrium The new long-run equilibrium is at point D, where the output gap is zero and the inflation rate equals both the expected inflation rate and the new target inflation rate. In the long run inflation is higher than before, but output and unemployment return to original values. An increase in the inflation target leads to a temporary boom.

In this description we assume that the initial reduction in the real interest rate raised the inflation rate but not all the way to the new target. What would happen if the central bank wanted to raise the inflation rate to the new target right away? It could accomplish it by a bigger reduction in the real interest rate so that the new AD curve, AD_2, intersects the original AS curve, AS_1, at point E, where inflation is equal to the new target. What would happen then? As the inflation rate increases, the expected inflation rate increases and the AS curve will shift up. As a result, the inflation rate will overshoot the target inflation rate.

Figure 14.9 shows that a central bank can temporarily increase real GDP and decrease the unemployment rate by announcing a higher inflation target. The model makes another important point: In the short run, the central bank can achieve a higher level of real GDP and a lower unemployment rate by tolerating a higher inflation rate. However, once the expected inflation rate adjusts, real GDP will return to potential GDP, and the unemployment rate will increase back to its initial level. As a result, *there is no trade-off between the inflation rate and the unemployment rate in the long run. In fact, even to achieve a temporarily higher level of real GDP and a lower unemployment rate, a central bank has to accept a permanently higher inflation rate.*

Many central banks have either a formal or informal inflation target of about 2% because the costs of inflation are thought to be relatively small when the inflation rate is low and stable. However the zero lower bound problem led some economists to advocate an increase in the target inflation rate above 2%. We have already seen that a higher inflation target can temporarily increase real GDP and employment.

More recently, Olivier Blanchard, Giovanni Dell'Ariccia, and Paolo Mauro, economists at the International Monetary Fund (IMF), have argued that central banks around the world should permanently increase the target inflation rate from 2% to 4%.[2] Blanchard, Dell'Ariccia, and Mauro believe that the costs of inflation are still low when the inflation rate is 4%. With a higher expected inflation rate, however, central banks can cut real interest rates more before the nominal interest rate reaches zero and the central banks are forced to resort to nontraditional monetary policy tools such as quantitative easing. Most central bankers disagree with Blanchard, Dell'Ariccia, and Mauro's argument for permanently higher inflation rates. For example, former Federal Reserve Chairman Ben Bernanke and former European Central Bank President Jean-Claude Trichet have suggested that a higher inflation target would be counterproductive because higher inflation rates tend to be more volatile. When the volatility of the inflation rate increases, it becomes harder to predict, so it is more likely that fluctuations in the inflation rate will cause arbitrary redistributions in wealth. The fact that economists raised the possibility of raising the inflation target above 2% indicates how the Great Recession has forced economists to rethink their policy advice. At the time of writing, no central bank has raised its inflation target.

Temporary Changes in Aggregate Expenditure

In the mid-1990s, innovations in information and communications technology, such as the development of the World Wide Web and the rapid decline in the prices of personal computers, encouraged optimism about the future profits of technology and internet-based firms. Investors rushed to purchase the stocks of firms such as Amazon, Nortel, or Yahoo. At its peak in September 2000, the value of Nortel shares was $400 billion, (equivalent to almost $525 billion in 2013 dollars) or over a third of the capitalization of the Toronto Stock Exchange. This period became known as the *dot-com bubble*. Unfortunately for investors, the expected profits from many technology and internet firms failed to materialize, and in 2000, investors fled these stocks, causing their prices to collapse. Within two years Nortel shares lost 99% of their value. The tech-heavy NASDAQ stock market fell over 75%; the Dow Jones and the TSX fell 40%. The $400 billion decline in Nortel stock alone was equal equivalent to around 35% of Canadian GDP (as a large portion of Nortel shares was held by foreigners, the decline in Canadian wealth was smaller than $400 billion but still significant). The fall in stock prices had two important effects on the economy: It reduced household wealth, which led households to reduce consumption, and it increased uncertainty about the future, which decreased firms' willingness to invest and further decreased the willingness of households to consume. The effect was much bigger in the United States than in Canada and, while Canada avoided a recession, the decrease in investment and the slowdown in consumption growth contributed to the recession in the United States that began in March 2001.

In Figure 14.10, we use the *AD–AS* model to show the effect of a temporary negative demand shock such as a stock market crash, which makes households poorer and reduces consumption. A reduction in government expenditure, for example, implementing austerity programs introduced after the Great Recession in many European countries to reduce the

[2]Olivier Blanchard, Giovanni Dell'Ariccia, and Paolo Mauro, "Rethinking Macroeconomic Policy," *Journal of Money, Credit, and Banking* 42, no. S1(2010): 199–215.

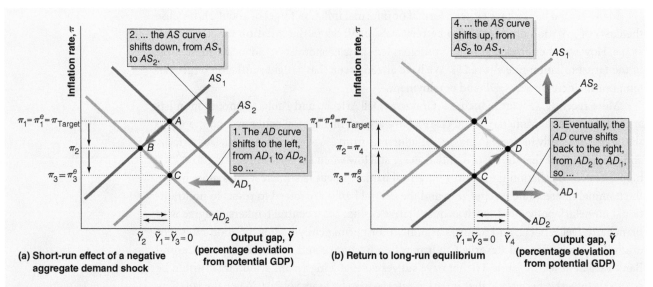

Figure 14.10 Short-Run and Long-Run Effects of a Negative Demand Shock

Panel (a) shows the effect of a negative demand shock, which temporarily shifts the AD curve to the left, from AD_1 to AD_2. Expected inflation decreases, the AS curve shifts down, from AS_1 to AS_2, and equilibrium moves from point B to point C. Adjustment to the new equilibrium is shown in panel (b). As the inflation rate is below target, the central bank reduces the real interest rate, raising consumption, investment, and net exports. In addition, when the shock passes the AD curve shifts back to the right, from AD_2 to AD_1. Equilibrium moves to point D. Expected inflation adjusts, causing the AS curve to shift up, from AS_2 to AS_1. Equilibrium is now at point A, which is the long-run equilibrium. A temporary negative demand shock causes a pattern of recession, followed by expansion.

large deficits, will have the same effect. As usual we start at long-run equilibrium where (1) the output gap is zero, (2) the inflation rate is equal to the target inflation rate, and (3) the inflation rate is equal to the expected inflation rate.

Initial, Short-Run Equilibrium following a Negative Aggregate Expenditure Shock We start in a long-run equilibrium at point A. The collapse in stock prices reduces consumption and shifts the AD curve to the left, from AD_1 to AD_2. So, in (a), equilibrium moves from point A to point B. The economy enters a recession, with real GDP declining, as the output gap moves from $\widetilde{Y}_1$ to $\widetilde{Y}_2$. At point B, the actual inflation rate, π_2, at the intersection of the AS curve and the new AD curve, is less than the expected inflation rate, π_1^e.

The Adjustment Process Because we assume that expectations are adaptive. As the inflation rate has fallen, the expected inflation rate will decrease, and the AS curve will shift down, from AS_1 to AS_2. The new short-run equilibrium is at point C.

Point C is not, however, a long-run equilibrium because the inflation rate is now less than the central bank's target inflation rate. Therefore the central bank reduces the real interest rate, raising consumption, investment, and net exports. The AD curve shifts to the right, as stock prices recover and uncertainty declines. Short-run equilibrium moves to point D in panel (b). Real GDP increases, moving the output gap from $\widetilde{Y}_3$ to $\widetilde{Y}_4$. In other words, the economy experiences an expansion as it recovers from the recession caused by the demand shock. But the actual inflation rate, π_4, is greater than the expected inflation rate, π_3^e, so because expectations are assumed to be adaptive, the expected inflation rate increases, and the AS curve shifts up.

Long-Run Equilibrium The adjustment process continues until the economy returns to the original equilibrium at point A, where the output gap equals zero and the inflation rate, the expected inflation rate, and the target inflation rate are all equal. The collapse in stock prices causes a recession, but the model shows that the economy will eventually adjust, leading to an expansion that restores long-run equilibrium at potential GDP, with inflation equal to the inflation target.

We can conclude that demand shocks *temporarily* change real GDP and the output gap. As the central bank reacts to the recession and the drop in inflation by lowering the real interest rate, the recession is followed by a boom. Eventually, though, the economy adjusts to move real GDP back to potential GDP, so the output gap returns to zero, and the inflation rate returns to the target inflation rate.

Rational Expectations and Policy Ineffectiveness

14.4

Learning Objective

Discuss the implications of rational expectations for macroeconomic policymaking.

In Section 14.3 we saw that, by increasing its target for the inflation rate, the central bank can cause real GDP to increase temporarily above its potential level. In arriving at this result, though, we assumed that expectations are adaptive. In our example, expected inflation always lagged behind actual inflation, and expectations caught up with actual inflation only when real GDP equalled potential GDP. But is the assumption of adaptive expectations correct or sensible?

The assumption of adaptive expectations has two fundamental flaws. The first is that, under some circumstances households and firms make systematic errors. The second flaw is that adaptive expectations use only past values of inflation to predict inflation about the future. To see the problem of systematic errors, consider a situation in which the inflation rate increases every year by 1%. In 2011 it is 1%, in 2012 it is 2%, for 2013 it is 3%, and so on. With adaptive expectations, the expected inflation rate for 2012 is the inflation rate in 2011, i.e., 1%, but the actual inflation rate is 2%. The expected inflation rate for 2013 is the inflation rate in 2012, i.e., 2%, but the actual inflation rate is 3%, and so on. It is easy to see that, with adaptive expectations, every year the actual inflation rate is 1% higher than the expected inflation rate for that year. If we stick to adaptive expectations, households and firms will never realize they are making a systematic error by underestimating inflation by 1% every year. But, sooner or later, households and firms will notice this—after all, as the saying goes, you can only fool all the people some of the time—and the expected inflation rate will change accordingly. When this happens, the expected inflation rate will be equal to the previous year's rate plus the correction for the systematic error. This means that the adaptive expectations formula is incomplete. This result does not depend on the particular type of adaptive expectations we assume: All forms of adaptive expectations based on past inflation rates lead, under some circumstances, to systematic errors.

The second problem with adaptive expectations is that they are based only on past values of inflation and ignore all other information, even information that is clearly relevant. Consider a simple example to show the costs a firm may incur from using adaptive expectations. Suppose that the Bank of Canada has a target inflation rate of 2%; it always hits its target for inflation; and inflation has been 2% for several years. Furthermore, assume that Apple sets the price of a basic model for the iPad at $500 and wants to keep the *real* price of the iPad constant in order to maximize profits. That is, the firm wants to increase the price of its product at the same rate as the inflation rate. In 2014, the price of the iPad is $500, and inflation in 2013 is 2%—so the firm expects that inflation will be 2% in 2014.

Based on expected inflation of 2%, Apple should set the price in 2014 at $510. Now suppose that the Bank of Canada announces on January 1, 2014, that it will increase its target for inflation to 4%. If it successfully increases the inflation rate to 4%, Apple's actual profit-maximizing price turns out to be $520. If Apple has adaptive expectations, however, it will, set its price too low—at $510—and it will not maximize profits. Apple would make a costly pricing mistake by ignoring the Bank of Canada's announcement that it intended to increase the target inflation rate.

This example is extreme as it is fairly obvious that, given the past success of the Bank of Canada in setting the inflation rate, Apple should take the announcement into account. But there are many situations when changes are more subtle yet should be taken into account by firms and households in forming expectations. Recall that the inflation target in Canada is established jointly by the federal government and the Bank of Canada and set for a period of five years. The current target of 2% will be in place until the end of 2016. If, in the next federal election, the party in power changes, it may be reasonable to contemplate a change in the inflation target and, consequently, a change in inflation. The point is that it makes sense that households and firms will use all information available to them in order to avoid making inaccurate predictions of inflation.

Rational expectations is the hypothesis that people make forecasts of future values of a variable using all available information and do not make systematic errors. In our previous example, if Apple has rational expectations, it will take into account the Bank of Canada's announcement of a new, higher target for the inflation rate and set the price of the iPad at $520. Rational expectations are consistent with profit maximization, while adaptive expectations may not be. As a result, many economists believe that rational expectations may better describe the way households and firms form expectations than do adaptive expectations. As we discuss next, the assumption of rational expectations leads to a surprising conclusion about the effectiveness of monetary policy.

Rational Expectations and Anticipated Policy Changes

Central bank credibility
The degree to which households and firms believe the central bank's announcements about future policy.

Suppose that the central bank announces that it will permanently increase its target inflation rate and that households and firms believe the announcement. That is, there is strong **central bank credibility**, which is the degree to which households and firms believe the central bank's announcements about future policy. Because the policy is announced and credible, we can say that the change represents an *anticipated policy* change. With adaptive expectations, expectations of inflation adjust slowly because the actual inflation rate has to change before the expected inflation rate changes. But with rational expectations, expectations of inflation adjust immediately.

Refer to Figure 14.9 on page 454 to see why this difference is important when discussing monetary policy. Assuming rational expectations, the increase in the inflation target still shifts the *AD* curve to the right. But because rational individuals take into account all available information, the expected inflation rate increases the moment the central bank announces a higher inflation target. The aggregate supply curve *immediately* shifts from AS_1 to AS_3, and equilibrium immediately moves from point *A* to point *D*. As a result, the inflation rate immediately increases from π_1 to π_3. In contrast to the result when expectations are adaptive, the economy never experiences a temporary expansion. Therefore, a central bank cannot achieve a temporary increase in real GDP, even if it is willing to tolerate permanently higher inflation. *We can conclude that there is no trade-off between inflation and unemployment, even in the short run, when expectations are rational and policy changes are anticipated.*

This surprising result is called the *policy ineffectiveness proposition* and was developed by Robert Lucas of the University of Chicago, Thomas Sargent of New York University, and Neil Wallace of Pennsylvania State University.[3] According to this proposition, households

---

[3]Robert Lucas, "Some International Evidence on Real GDP-Inflation Tradeoffs," *American Economic Review* 63, no. 3(1973): 326–324; and Thomas Sargent and Neil Wallace, "Rational Expectations and the Theory of Economic Policy," *Journal of Monetary Economics* 2, no. 2 (1976): 169–183.

and firms use all available information, including information about monetary policy rules, to form expectations of the inflation rate. When expected inflation increases, households and firms immediately adjust expectations and nominal prices. For example, if the Bank of Canada announces a 4% inflation target, Apple will increase the nominal price of the iPad by 4%, to $520. As a result, the real price of the iPad will remain unchanged, so monetary policy has no effect on the real price of the iPad. Therefore, the Bank of Canada's announced change in the inflation target will not have any effect on the quantity of iPads sold. What is true of Apple's iPad is also true of all other goods and services, so an announced change in the inflation target will not affect real GDP, assuming that there is no cost to adjusting wages and prices.

The policy ineffectiveness proposition led many economists to conclude that because households and firms take into account changes in central bank policy when forming their expectations of inflation, announced and credible monetary policy do not affect real GDP and employment.

Rational Expectations and Unanticipated Policy Changes

Rational expectations do not imply that all changes in monetary policy are ineffective. For the policy ineffectiveness result to hold, policy changes must be anticipated and credible. If a policy change is a surprise, firms and households will not change their expectations. If the policy change is not completely credible, i.e., if households and firms have doubts whether the central bank will actually follow through and change the policy, they will not respond completely to the announcement of the policy change. In these cases, the aggregate supply curve in Figure 14.9 on page 454 will not shift immediately; the short-run equilibrium will move to point *B*; and the economy will experience an expansion. If the policy change is unannounced or not credible, then the change in the policy has the same result on the economy as it does when we assume that households and firms have adaptive expectations.

Rational Expectations and Demand Shocks

If expectations are rational, then any anticipated demand shock should affect only the inflation rate. However, to the extent that households and firms do not anticipate the shock or do not understand how the shock will affect the economy, demand shocks can still affect real GDP. For example, if the decrease in stock prices we discussed in Figure 14.10 on page 456 had been expected, firms would have expected a lower inflation rate and changed their pricing decisions accordingly. The aggregate supply curve would have immediately adjusted; real GDP would never have decreased; the output gap would have remained zero; and the unemployment rate would never have increased. If households and firms have rational expectations, there is no trade-off between inflation and unemployment in either the short run or the long run when events such as a change in policy or a decrease in asset prices are anticipated. If a demand shock is unanticipated, however, then there is a trade-off between inflation and unemployment in the short run, although not in the long run.

Are Anticipated and Credible Policy Changes Actually Ineffective?

The assumption of rational expectations is compelling to many economists because it is consistent with the view that households and firms act systematically to achieve their goals: maximizing utility in the case of households, and maximizing profit in the case of firms. But not all economists accept rational expectations or the policy ineffectiveness proposition. Many economists argue that even if expectations are rational, changes in policy can affect real GDP even if the changes are both anticipated and credible. For the policy ineffectiveness proposition to hold, firms must change prices in response to a change in expected inflation. But we know that it can be costly for firms to change prices and wages. If the cost of changing prices is high enough, Apple, for instance, may not adjust the price of its iPads even when its expectations of the inflation rate change. When prices and wages are sticky, real GDP and employment may increase even when households and firms have rational expectations.

Some economists also question whether the assumption of rational expectations is realistic. Rational expectations imply that households and firms know how the economy operates, that they have all the relevant information, and that they know how to use that information to make predictions about inflation and other economic variables. Critics of the rational expectations assumption argue that households and firms typically lack the technical sophistication and time to completely analyze all relevant information. Given these constraints, households and firms may disregard information and make decisions according to simple rules of thumb that require less time and effort. For instance, firms may use adaptive expectations and expect the following year's inflation rate to be the same as the current year's inflation rate. Moreover, as we saw when discussing the limitations of monetary and fiscal policy, there is a great deal of uncertainty over the values for key economic parameters, such as the marginal propensity to consume or the multiplier, so it is unlikely that households and firms are using a macroeconomic model capable of yielding optimal forecasts.

The evidence on whether anticipated changes in monetary policy can affect real GDP is mixed. Thomas Sargent of New York University argued that the hyperinflation in Germany at the end of World War I ended when the government announced a credible commitment to a lower inflation rate. If expectations of inflation were adaptive, then ending the hyperinflation would have required a severe recession. Germany did not experience a severe recession as the hyperinflation ended, which Sargent interpreted as evidence in favour of the rational expectations assumption.

Sargent's research provides some evidence in favour of the policy ineffectiveness proposition. Other studies, however, find that anticipated monetary policy does affect real GDP.[4] As a result, many economists take the view that anticipated changes in monetary policy do affect real GDP, although by less than do unanticipated changes in policy. These economists argue that households and firms take actions to offset the effects of changes in monetary policy, but because they are not able to calculate exactly what the effects of the changes will be on monetary policy and because it is costly to change prices and wages, real GDP and employment respond to anticipated changes in policy. Clearly, in conducting monetary policy, the Bank of Canada assumes that changes in policy affect real GDP and employment.

Economists continue to research how households and firms form their expectations of inflation and the extent to which the assumption of rational expectations matches actual behaviour.

14.5
Learning Objective
Discuss the pros and cons of the central bank's operating under policy rules rather than using discretionary policy.

Monetary Policy: Rules versus Discretion

Central banks are responsible for keeping inflation low and stable, but they are not always successful. The annual inflation rate in Canada measured by the CPI rose steadily from the early 1960s through 1980. To reduce inflation, the Bank of Canada increased interest rates to over 20% in mid-1981, which led to the severe recession of 1981–82. Our discussion of rational expectations and the evidence cited by Thomas Sargent and other economists suggests that reducing inflation rates does not have to be so costly. If the central bank convinces households and firms that the inflation rate will be lower, and the expected inflation rate falls, the inflation will decline without causing a recession. In practice, however, expectations

---

[4]Two classic studies that find that anticipated changes in policy can affect output are Frederic S. Mishkin, "Does Anticipated Monetary Policy Matter? An Econometric Investigation," *Journal of Political Economy* 90, no. 1 (1982): 22–51; and Robert J. Gordon, "Price Inertia and Policy Effectiveness in the United States, 1890–1980," *Journal of Political Economy* 90, no. 6 (1982): 1087–1117.

adjust slowly, and disinflation does lead to a recession. In 1988 John Crow, the new Governor of the Bank of Canada, made it perfectly clear that he was intending to reduce inflation. Nonetheless, the anti-inflationary policy, often called "the Crow disinflation," resulted in the severe recession of 1990–92. This suggests that households and firms did not have entirely rational expectations and/or they did not believe the governor's announcement.

Reducing inflation in 1990–92 was costly because the Bank of Canada pursued a **discretionary policy**, which means that it conducted monetary policy in whatever way it believed would achieve its goals at the moment. In other words, when the economic situation changes, a central bank following a discretionary policy adjusts its policy as needed. As inflation reached record levels in 1970s and the Bank of Canada's attempts to reduce the inflation rate were unsuccessful, the credibility of its policies was undermined.

An alternative to using discretionary policy is a **monetary rule**, which is a commitment by the central bank to follow specific and publicly announced guidelines for monetary policy.

Monetary Policy Rules

Monetary policy rules can take many forms. Some rules place severe restrictions on the central bank's ability to conduct monetary policy, while other rules are more guidelines for good policy than they are formal rules. Below we provide some examples of monetary policy rules.

Money Growth Rule Nobel Laureate Milton Friedman proposed that the central bank follow a policy rule such that the nominal money supply would grow at a constant rate, regardless of economic conditions.[5] Friedman's proposal, which was based on his belief in the importance of the quantity theory of money as a guide to policy, was a central idea in *monetarism*. Friedman and other monetarists argued that because the effects of monetary policy were powerful, but the lags with which it affected the economy were "long and variable," the central bank would be likely to destabilize the economy if it did not follow a *money growth rule*. Recall that, according to the quantity theory of money, the rate of inflation plus the rate of growth of output is equal to the rate of growth of the money supply plus the rate of change of velocity. If velocity is stable (i.e., the rate of growth of velocity is zero), setting the growth rate of the money supply equal to the long-run growth rate of real GDP would result in a stable price level. Monetarist arguments led the Bank of Canada to attempt to control inflation through the control of the rate of growth of the money supply. But, as we discussed in Chapter 4, financial innovation and changes in the velocity of money made the approach unsuccessful and led the Bank of Canada to abandon that approach.

Fixed Exchange Rate A fixed exchange rate system is an example of a monetary policy rule where the central bank maintains a specific value for the exchange rate of the domestic currency in terms of another country's currency or a basket of currencies from various countries. The gold standard was a special case of a fixed exchange rate where the central bank committed to maintaining a specific price of gold. The gold standard was widely adopted during the nineteenth and early twentieth centuries. Under a fixed exchange rate, the rule is strict in the sense that the central bank cannot undertake any discretionary actions.

Inflation Targeting An inflation target is an example of a more flexible policy rule. Under inflation targeting, the goal of the central bank is to keep inflation within some bounds, for example, between 1% and 3%, as is the case in Canada, or below but close to 2%, as is the case with the European Central Bank. In addition, departures from the goal do not have to be immediately corrected. This leaves some flexibility for the central bank to follow other policy goals on a temporary basis.

Discretionary policy
Policy conducted in whatever way is believed at the moment best to achieve goals.

Monetary rule A commitment by the central bank to follow specific and publicly announced guidelines for monetary policy.

---

[5]Milton Friedman, *A Program for Monetary Stability* (New York: Fordham University Press, 1960).

Taylor rule A monetary policy guideline developed by economist John Taylor for determining the target for the short-term *nominal* policy rate.

Taylor Rule John Taylor of Stanford University has suggested that a central bank that focuses not only on inflation but also on the rate of unemployment, or on another variable related to the state of the economy, follows the so-called **Taylor rule**.[6] The general equation representing the Taylor rule is

$$i_{\text{Target}} = r^* + \pi_t + g\left(\pi_t - \pi_{\text{Target}}\right) + h\widetilde{Y}_t, \tag{14.3}$$

where i_{Target} is the target for the short-term nominal interest rate, r^* is the long-run equilibrium real interest rate target, π_t is the current inflation rate, and π_{Target} is the target inflation rate. The coefficient g shows how much the policy rate (target for overnight rate in Canada, federal funds rate in the United States) responds to a deviation of inflation from its target and the coefficient, and h shows how much the policy rate responds to the output gap.

The Taylor rule differs from our earlier central bank reaction function because, with the Taylor rule, the central bank responds not only to changes in the inflation rate relative to the inflation target (the third term in equation 14.3), but also to changes in the level of output relative to potential output (the last term in equation 14.3). The central bank reaction function we used to derive the AD curve was a special case of the Taylor rule, with the coefficient h equal to zero. A central bank using the Taylor rule is directly concerned with the output gap. So the Taylor rule is particularly suitable to study the behaviour of the U.S. Federal Reserve, which operates under the dual mandate of controlling both inflation and unemployment. It is less suitable to study the behaviour of the Bank of Canada, which has an explicit inflation target and is not tasked with keeping output near potential. Note, however, that even with a pure inflation target, the Bank of Canada reacts to changes in output. Recall that monetary policy works with significant lags. If output falls below potential, the Bank of Canada knows that, in the future, inflation will fall below target. To prevent this, it reduces interest rates.

Taylor found that his rule did a good job of predicting the behaviour of the U.S. Federal Reserve with the following simple parameters:

$$i_{\text{Target}} = 2\% + \pi_t + 0.5(\pi_t - 2\%) + 0.5\widetilde{Y}_t. \tag{14.4}$$

In other words, the Taylor rule does a good job when it assumes that the Federal Reserve weighs inflation and the output gap as equally important, the target inflation rate is 2%, and the long-run equilibrium real federal funds rate is 2%. Figure 14.11 shows the actual federal funds rate and the level of the federal funds rate that would have occurred if the Federal Reserve had strictly followed the Taylor rule. Because the two lines are close together during most years, the Taylor rule does a reasonable job of explaining Federal Reserve policy.

There are, however, some periods when the lines diverge significantly. During the late 1960s and early to mid-1970s, the federal funds rate predicted from the Taylor rule was consistently above the actual federal funds rate. This gap is consistent with the view of most economists that in the face of a worsening inflation rate during those years, the Federal Reserve should have raised the target for the federal funds rate more than it did; in other words, monetary policy was too expansionary. The Federal Reserve also kept the target federal funds rate at levels well below those indicated by the Taylor rule during the recovery from the 2001 recession in the United States. Some economists and policymakers have argued that, by keeping the target federal funds at a very low level for an extended period, the Fed helped fuel the

---

[6]Taylor's original discussion of the rule appeared in John Taylor, "Discretion Versus Policy Rules in Practice," *Carnegie-Rochester Conference Series on Public Policy* 39, no. 1 (1993): 195–214.

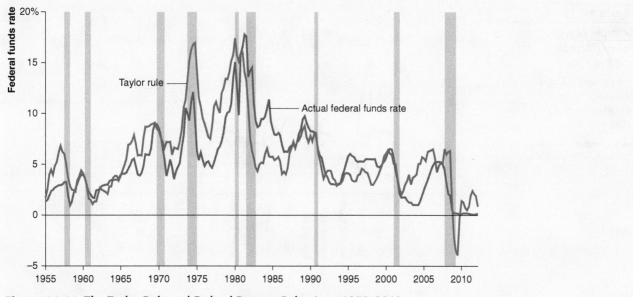

Figure 14.11 The Taylor Rule and Federal Reserve Behaviour, 1955–2012

The Taylor rule does a good job of predicting the nominal federal funds rate from the mid-1980s to the end of the 2001 recession. Shaded areas represent recessions, as determined by the National Bureau of Economic Research.

Sources: U.S. Bureau of Economic Analysis; U.S. Congressional Budget Office; Federal Reserve System; National Bureau of Economic Analysis; and authors' calculations.

housing boom of the mid-2000s. The argument is that a low federal funds rate contributed to low mortgage interest rates, thereby encouraging the housing boom. Finally, notice that the Taylor rule indicates that the federal funds rate should have been negative throughout 2009. This result is another indication of the severity of the Great Recession in the United States. As the federal funds rate, which is a nominal interest rate, cannot be negative, the Taylor rule shows that the Federal Reserve indeed faced the zero lower bound constraint, and it helps to explain why it resorted to nontraditional monetary policy tools such as quantitative easing.

The Taylor Rule and the Real Interest Rate

What does the Taylor rule imply for the setting of the nominal interest rate? To see this, we can simplify the rule with the parameters obtained by Taylor:

$$i_{\text{Target}} = 2\% + \pi_t + 0.5(\pi_t - 2\%) + 0.5\widetilde{Y}_t = 1\% + 1.5\pi_t + 0.5\widetilde{Y}_t. \qquad (14.5)$$

According to the Taylor rule, the central bank should increase the policy rate by 1.5 percentage points for each 1-percentage-point increase in inflation. This observation is important because the Fisher relationship tells us that the real interest rate equals the nominal interest rate minus the inflation rate. If inflation increases by one percentage point, then the target nominal federal funds rate will increase by 1.5 percentage points, so the real interest rate will increase by 0.5 percentage point. The result is that a higher inflation rate results in a higher real interest rate. The higher real interest rate reduces consumption and investment, which slows the growth of real GDP and lowers the inflation rate. By following this rule, monetary policy helps keep the inflation rate stable.

The Case for Discretion

Economists who believe that policymakers should be allowed discretion argue that simple rules such as the Taylor rule or Friedman's constant money growth rate rule cannot accommodate new and unexpected events. So policymakers must be free to use all available

Figure 14.12

Example of a Discretionary Policy (October 7, 1987 = 100)

Both the Bank of Canada and the Federal Reserve lowered interest rates when the stock market crashed in October 1987.

Sources: Statistics Canada, CANSIM Tables 176-0078 and 176-0042.

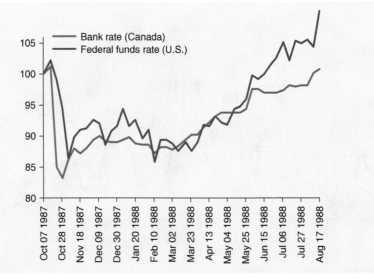

information in setting monetary policy and not just the information incorporated in a simple rule. For example, when the inflation rate exceeded 3% in late 2002 and at the beginning of 2003, the Bank of Canada did not increase the interest rates as it expected the increase in inflation to be temporary. Similarly, when the stock markets crashed in October 1987, the Bank of Canada, as well as the Federal Reserve, lowered interest rates, as shown in Figure 14.12. The interest rate cuts sent a signal to households and firms that central banks were determined to prevent the stock market crash from harming the economy. Had the Bank of Canada been following rules, it would have been unable to change interest rates. Advocates of discretion argue that the stock market crash was a unique event that no rule could have accounted for, so the proper policy response required central banks to use discretion.

In addition, rules often assume that key economic values are constant, when they often are not. For example, financial innovation and financial crises change the value of velocity in the quantity equation and the value of the money multiplier. So, as we learned, following the Friedman rule of constant money growth may destabilize the economy. With respect to the Taylor rule, it is possible that the equilibrium real interest rate changes over time in response to technological change and other factors that affect the economy's long-run equilibrium. In those circumstances, strict adherence to the Taylor rule could potentially increase fluctuations in unemployment and inflation.

The Case for Rules

Economists who believe that policymakers should follow a monetary policy rule argue that the period between the mid-1960s and 1970s, when inflation rose steadily, shows the problems associated with discretionary policy. As we discussed earlier, during this period the Bank of Canada policy was not effective and the Bank lost credibility with the general public. Some economists also argue that a policy rule avoids the **time-inconsistency problem**, which is the tendency of policymakers to announce one policy in order to change the expectations of households and firms, and then to follow another policy after households and firms have made economic decisions based on the announced policy. For example, a central bank may announce a target inflation rate of 2% for the next year to get households and firms to make decisions about nominal prices, nominal wages, and nominal interest rates based on an expectation of 2% inflation. Then the central bank could actually increase the target inflation rate to 4%, which would lower real wages and real interest rates, resulting in increased aggregate expenditure and real GDP.

Time-inconsistency problem The tendency of policymakers to announce one policy in advance in order to change the expectations of households and firms, and then to follow another policy after households and firms have made economic decisions based on the announced policy.

Nobel Laureates Finn Kydland of the University of California, Santa Barbara, and Edward Prescott of Arizona State University have analyzed the time-inconsistency problem that central banks face.[7] Policymakers have an incentive to promise low inflation in order to reduce the expected inflation rate. A lower expected inflation rate results in a lower actual inflation rate as households and firms build the lower expected inflation rate into their pricing decisions. Once households and firms have made their pricing decisions, there is a trade-off between inflation and real GDP: If the inflation rate increases, real wages and real interest rates fall and output rises. The central bank has an incentive to exploit that trade-off by lowering interest rates to increase real GDP and employment. But this involves fooling households and firms: The central bank promises a low inflation rate but breaks its promise. If the central bank breaks its promises repeatedly, it will lose credibility. But the time-inconsistency problem is more fundamental. Households and firms are not so easily fooled, because they understand that the central bank has an incentive to break a promise to achieve low inflation. As a result, households and firms will expect the central bank to break its promise and will not believe its announcements. This means that the expected inflation rate and, therefore, the actual inflation rate will remain high. This means that a central bank that follows discretionary policy cannot reduce inflation expectations by promising to reduce inflation and must raise interest rates. Many economists believe that the time-inconsistency problem explains the poor economic performance of the mid-1960s to the early 1980s.

Advocates of rules argue that following a monetary policy rule provides the central bank with credibility because it is easier for individuals and firms to verify whether it is behaving as promised. Once the central bank achieves credibility, the expected inflation rate will fall; households and firms will build the lower expected inflation rate into their pricing decisions; and inflation will decrease.

Following a rule can also reduce uncertainty about monetary policy and improve economic performance in two other ways. First, when households and firms know how the central bank will respond to changes in the economy, they can more easily plan for the future. Second, rules provide discipline for the central bank, so that it does not constantly switch from trying to fight inflation to trying to keep the output gap close to zero. Uncertainty will still exist with rules because no one can predict all the shocks, but following a policy rule does eliminate the uncertainty that discretionary monetary policy might create.

Making the Connection

Central Banks around the World Try Inflation Targeting

Since 1989, when the Reserve Bank of New Zealand became the first central bank to adopt an explicit inflation target (Canada was the second country to introduce inflation targets, in 1991), the number of central banks doing so has grown to around 40, including high-income economies such as the United Kingdom and the United States and emerging markets such as Colombia, Hungary, and South Africa. Inflation targeting usually involves an explicit statement that the central bank will pursue price stability as its sole or primary objective, along with an explicit target inflation rate, usually between 1% and 3%. Sometimes penalties for missing the target rate are also involved. For example, the head of New Zealand's central bank can be fired for not meeting the inflation target.

An explicit inflation target acts as a rule to constrain the discretion of the central bank and provide it with credibility as an inflation fighter. Therefore, having an explicit inflation

---

[7]Finn Kydland and Edward Prescott, "Rules Rather Than Discretion: The Inconsistency of Optimal Plans," *Journal of Political Economy* 85, no. 3 (1977): 473–491.

target may be a way to reduce the time-inconsistency problem. The central bank does retain some discretion in pursuing goals other than price stability because most countries allow the central bank to keep inflation within a specified range. For example, the central bank can increase inflation to the higher end of the range to stimulate the economy, if necessary.

The reason that countries adopt inflation targets is to bring down the inflation rate, but has it worked? In general, the evidence is positive. Since the introduction of inflation targeting in Canada over 20 years ago, inflation has been low and much more stable than in the past. A recent study by economists at the IMF found that the surge in oil prices during 2008 caused a smaller increase in the inflation rate in countries that had explicit inflation targets. This connection provides some evidence that explicit inflation targets may help keep actual and expected inflation rates low and stable. Carl Walsh and other authors found that, in general, inflation targeting countries performed better during the Great Recession.

Inflation targeting is not, however, universally supported. Jeffrey Frankel, an economist at Harvard University's Kennedy School of Government, questioned the usefulness of inflation targeting because countries that had adopted targeting were not immune to the collapse of asset prices in 2008. Some economists have argued that by fixing the central bank's focus on inflation, an inflation target may cause the central bank to be less concerned with rising unemployment. Some critics argued that the European Central Bank failed to take actions to reduce unemployment during and after the 2007–09 recession because it was focused too closely on inflation.

Sources: Karl Habermeier, *et al.*, "Inflation Pressures and Monetary Policy Options in Emerging and Developing Countries: A Cross Regional Perspective," International Monetary Fund working paper 09/1, January 2009; Irineu de Carvalho Filho, "28 Months Later: How Inflation Targeters Outperformed Their Peers in the Great Recession," *B.E. Journal of Macroeconomics*, 2011; Carl E. Walsh, "Inflation Targeting: What Have We Learned,"*International Finance*, Summer 2009, pp. 195–233; Angelo Melino, "Inflation Targeting: A Canadian Perspective," *International Journal of Central Banking*, Summer 2012, pp. 105–131; and Jeffrey Frankel, "The Death of Inflation Targeting," *Project Syndicate*, May 16, 2012.

See related Problem 5.4 at the end of the chapter.

Key Terms and Problems

Key Terms

Aggregate demand and aggregate supply (*AD–AS*) model, p. 448

Aggregate supply (*AS*) curve, p. 444

Central bank credibility, p. 458

Central bank reaction function, p. 438

Discretionary policy, p. 461

Monetary rule, p. 461

Taylor rule, p. 462

Time-inconsistency problem, p. 464

14.1 Aggregate Demand Revisited
Understand how aggregate demand is determined.

Review Questions

1.1 What is a central bank reaction function? What are its key components? What does the slope of the reaction function indicate?

1.2 What is the aggregate demand curve? Explain how the aggregate demand curve is derived using the *IS–MP* model and the central bank reaction function.

1.3 What factors shift the aggregate demand curve?

Problems and Applications

1.4 In January 2012, the Federal Reserve changed its policy of implicitly targeting inflation to setting an explicit inflation target of 2%. According to a *Reuters* article, "Skeptics, particularly among congressional Democrats, have in the past worried that an explicit inflation target would relegate the full employment goal to the back burner." Why might setting an explicit inflation target conflict with a goal of full employment?

Source: Jonathan Spicer, "In Historic Shift, Fed Sets Inflation Target," *Reuters*, January 25, 2012.

1.5 Briefly explain whether you agree with the following statement: "Until the Bank of Canada set an explicit inflation target, it did not have a reaction function."

1.6 For each of the following scenarios, state the short-run effect on the *AD* curve.

a. There is an increase in government purchases.

b. Costs of production increase.

c. Investors become more pessimistic.

d. The central bank becomes less tolerant of deviations in inflation from the target rate.

e. The price level increases.

f. The target inflation rate increases.

14.2 **Aggregate Supply and the Phillips Curve**
Explain the relationship between aggregate supply and the Phillips curve.

Review Questions

2.1 What is the aggregate supply curve? Explain how the aggregate supply curve is related to the Phillips curve.

2.2 What demand factors contribute to inflation? What cost factors contribute to inflation? How do these factors relate to the aggregate supply curve?

2.3 Explain what factors cause the aggregate supply curve to shift.

Problems and Applications

2.4 For each of the following scenarios, state the short-run effect on the *AS* curve.

a. An increase in government spending causes aggregate expenditure and real GDP to increase.

b. Nominal wages increase rapidly.

c. Lower inflation is expected in the future.

d. A change in technology lowers the costs of production.

2.5 Write two equations for the *AS* curve. In both cases, assume that expectations are adaptive and that the effect of supply shocks is zero. For the first equation, assume that the inflation rate is very sensitive to changes in the output gap. For the second equation, assume that it is not. Graph your two curves.

2.6 Briefly explain whether you agree with the following statement: "The supply shock inflation parameter, *s*, must always be positive because supply shocks always increase production costs."

14.3 **The Aggregate Demand and Aggregate Supply Model**
Use the aggregate demand and aggregate supply model to analyze macroeconomic conditions.

Review Questions

3.1 What are the long-run equilibrium conditions in the *AD–AS* model? What is the relationship between the *AD–AS* model and the *IS–MP* model?

3.2 What is stagflation, and how does it occur? How does the economy readjust to long-run equilibrium after a period of stagflation, assuming that the central bank does not change its reaction function?

3.3 Using the *AD–AS* model, briefly explain how the economy responds differently to demand shocks and to changes in the central bank reaction function.

Problems and Applications

3.4 Draw a graph of the *AD–AS* model. Label the curves and axes carefully. Then show the effects of the following:

a. a positive demand shock

b. a positive supply shock

How are the effects of these changes on the output gap different from the effects on inflation? If you observed an increase in real GDP so the output gap moved to a value greater than zero, how could you tell whether *AD* or *AS* had shifted?

 MyEconLab   Visit **www.myeconlab.com** to complete these exercises online and get instant feedback.

3.5   The slope of the aggregate supply curve will vary based on the sensitivity of inflation to the output gap. The following graph shows a curve that is sensitive to inflation changes (AS_1) and a curve that is less sensitive (AS_2):

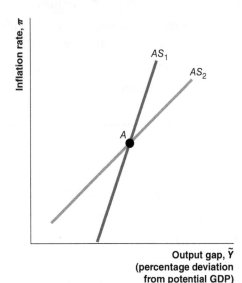

a. Draw an *AD* curve and assume that the equilibrium point represents the long-run equilibrium point. For simplicity, have the *AD* curve intersect the *AS* curves at point *A*.

b. Suppose that a housing boom takes place. Show the effect on *AD* and explain how the short-run changes in inflation and the output gap are different in the two cases.

3.6   Analyze a decrease in expected inflation and Bank of Canada reaction.

a. Assume that households and firms now expect that inflation will be considerably lower next period (i.e., they recognize the threat of deflation). Use the *AD–AS* model to show the short-run effect of this change.

b. What will the Bank of Canada have to do to increase inflation to the original level? Carefully analyze using the *AD–AS* model.

3.7   In 1981–82, contractionary monetary policy was successfully used to reduce the rate of inflation in Canada. More recently, expansionary policy has been less successful in helping the economy to recover quickly from the last recession. Why was monetary policy more effective in reducing the rate of inflation in the early 1980s than it was in stimulating the economy after 2008?

3.8   **[Related to the** Macro Data feature **on page 452]** Real oil prices decreased significantly during the 1990s. The following graph shows the initial equilibrium at point *A* and the shift in aggregate supply due to lower oil prices:

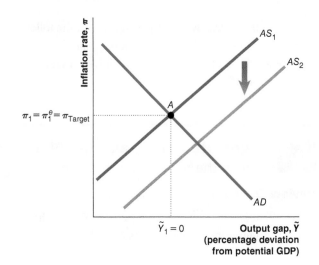

a. Identify the new equilibrium output gap and inflation rate.

b. Assuming that monetary policy does not change, show on the graph how the economy will adjust to the new long-run equilibrium.

3.9   Assume that the central bank has an inflation target of 2% and always adjusts monetary policy to keep the inflation rate at 2%. Now assume that the government announces an expansionary fiscal policy of more spending on infrastructure projects and lower taxes. Given the central bank's monetary policy, will this fiscal policy have any effect on the output gap and inflation? Briefly explain.

3.0   In early 2010, consumer prices in the United Kingdom rose above 3%, even though the economy was growing slowly. An article in the *Economist* commented: "This may not be stagflation, 1970s-style; rather it is slumpflation, given that the economy is bumping along the bottom of the biggest hole dug in GDP since the Second World War."

a. What does the article mean by "slumpflation"?

b. Why would we not expect to see rising inflation during a time of slow economic growth?

c. The article also stated that the inflation rate was expected to decline. Explain this expectation using the *AD–AS* model.

Source: "Storm Before the Calm," *Economist*, February 11, 2010.

3.11 During the financial crisis, the Bank of Canada developed a number of new policy tools to stimulate the economy. However, the Bank never indicated that it was willing to allow the inflation rate to rise above its inflation target of 2%.

    a. What would be the effect on the output gap and the inflation rate of the Bank of Canada indicating it is willing to increase its target inflation rate?

    b. In August 2013 Mark Carney, the new Governor of the Bank of England (and a former Governor of the Bank of Canada) announced that interest rates will remain low until unemployment falls below 7%. Do you think such promise, called "forward guidance" helps monetary policy in stimulating the economy? Explain.

Source: "Mark Carney adjusts Bank interest rate policy," BBC News, February 12, 2014.

Rational Expectations and Policy Ineffectiveness
Discuss the implications of rational expectations for macroeconomic policymaking.

Review Questions

4.1 What are rational expectations? What is the difference between adaptive expectations and rational expectations?

4.2 How might rational expectations make monetary policy ineffective?

4.3 Explain why monetary policy might be effective if expectations are rational but a change in policy is a surprise.

4.4 If expectations are rational, explain how anticipated and unanticipated demand shocks will affect real GDP.

4.5 Are there reasons to doubt the policy ineffectiveness proposition? Briefly explain.

Problems and Applications

4.6 Suppose that inflation has increased at an annual rate of 2% for several years. Also assume that the central bank's target inflation rate is 2%.

    a. If sellers all charge $100 for their products and expectations are adaptive, what price will they charge next year, assuming that the relative demand for their products is unchanged?

    b. Suppose that the central bank now announces that its target inflation rate has increased to 5%, and the actual inflation rate also becomes 5%. What price should sellers charge to keep real prices constant? What price will they actually charge if expectations are adaptive?

    c. If expectations are adaptive, what will be the consequences for the economy as a result of the situation described in part (b)?

4.7 In Problem 4.6, answer parts (b) and (c) again, assuming that expectations are rational rather than adaptive.

4.8 Brazil experienced high inflation in the late 1980s and early 1990s. To bring prices under control, the country changed its currency to a new currency unit, the real. Explain why Brazil might use a strategy of introducing a new currency in order to lower the inflation rate.

4.9 Briefly explain whether you agree with the following statement: "Rational expectations assumes that all people are completely rational, and because this probably is not true, this theory doesn't help us to evaluate the effectiveness of monetary policy."

4.10 Briefly explain whether you agree with the following statement: "Currently, interest rates are very low. Because everyone knows that the central bank will raise rates at some point, raising rates will have no effect on real GDP or employment when it happens."

4.11 Deflation can be as great a problem for economies as inflation. An article in the *Financial Times* reported that there is a serious risk of deflation in the Eurozone.

    a. Why might falling prices cause problems for an economy?

    b. Most central banks in high-income countries have been credibly committed to low inflation rates for some time, and the European Central Bank has an inflation target of just under 2%. Why might this commitment make the task of preventing deflation more difficult?

Source: Wolfgang Münchau, "Europe cannot afford to ignore its deflation problem," *Financial Times*, February 23, 2014.

Monetary Policy: Rules versus Discretion

14.5 Discuss the pros and cons of the central bank's operating under policy rules rather than using discretionary policy.

Review Questions

5.1 Explain the difference between a rules strategy and discretionary policy. What are the primary arguments in favour of a rules approach and of a discretionary approach when conducting monetary policy?

5.2 What is the Taylor rule? How might deviations from the Taylor rule have contributed to the 2007–2009 Great Recession in the United States?

Problems and Applications

5.3 If central banks follow the Taylor rule, how does the real interest rate change during the business cycle?

5.4 [Related to the Making the Connection on page 465] Some central banks have explicit inflation targets, while others have implicit targets.

   a. In the context of topics discussed in this section, what is the advantage of having an explicit target?

   b. What is the advantage of having an implicit target or no target at all?

5.5 [Related to the Chapter Opener on page 436] Explain how central banks may have created the Great Moderation. In what way may the U.S. Federal Reserve have contributed to the end of the Great Moderation?

5.6 A very simple monetary rule might be, "Increase the money supply at the rate of growth of real GDP."

   a. What would be the advantages of this monetary rule? What would be the problems?

   b. What if the rule said, "Increase the money supply at the rate of growth of real GDP plus 2%." Now what would be the advantages and problems?

   c. What if the rule said, "Increase the money supply at the rate of growth of real GDP plus 2%

plus one-half of the output gap." Now what would be the advantages and problems?

5.7 Briefly explain whether you agree with the following statement: "Because the business cycle is unpredictable and real-time data are usually unobtainable, monetary policy rules probably won't be successful."

5.8 Both Alan Greenspan and Ben Bernanke have claimed that monetary policy was not responsible for the housing bubble. Instead, they blame a change in the relationship between short-term interest rates and long-term mortgage rates. An article in the *Economist* that summarizes their positions states part of the Greenspan explanation as follows: "The rise in desired global saving relative to desired investment caused a global decline in long-term rates, which became delinked from the short-term rates that central bankers control." How would the delinking of short- and long-term rates create a problem for monetary policy and policy rules?

Source: "It Wasn't Us," *The Economist*, March 18, 2010.

5.9 A column in the *Economist* magazine argues that

   Central banks should focus their efforts on measures of demand—nominal GDP, nominal income, nominal spending—rather than measures of inflation. If nominal GDP is at a level that's inconsistent with full employment, demand is too low and the central bank should do more.

   a. In what ways is a central bank targeting nominal GDP different from a central bank targeting the inflation rate?

   b. If a central bank is targeting nominal GDP, what actions would it take to "do more" if the economy was not at full employment?

Source: "Rethinking Macro," *The Economist*, July 26, 2012.

Data Exercises

D14.1: [Spreadsheet exercise] Using data from the St. Louis Federal Reserve (FRED) (http://research.stlouisfed.org/fred2/), examine the effect on the Brazilian inflation rate of the introduction of the real on July 1, 1994.

a. Download quarterly data on the consumer price index (BRACPIALLQINMEI) from January 1980 to the present. Calculate the inflation rate as the percentage change from the same quarter in the previous year. Plot the data on a graph.

b. Describe the differences in the inflation rate before and after July 1, 1994.

c. Calculate the mean and standard deviation of the inflation rate before and after July 1, 1994.

d. Are your results in parts (b) and (c) consistent with the view that the introduction of the real reduced the inflation rate and made the inflation rate less volatile? Briefly explain.

D14.2: The growth rate of real GDP is an alternative to the output gap as a measure of the business cycle. Using data from Statistics Canada CANSIM database (http://www5.statcan.gc.ca/cansim/a01?lang=eng/), analyze the sources of business cycles in Canada.

a. Download the data for GDP at market prices, in chained 2007 dollars (Table 380-0064) and the implicit price deflator, GDP at market prices (Table 380-0066).

b. Plot the growth rate of real GDP and the inflation rate on the same graph.

c. You can find the dates of recessions on the internet. (Search for "C.D. Howe Recession dates.") Based on these data, which recessions do you think were caused primarily by aggregate demand shocks, and which recessions were caused primarily by aggregate supply shocks? Briefly explain.

Fiscal Policy and the Government Budget in the Long Run

Drowning in a Sea of Debt?

Most people have debt: They owe money on student loans, car loans, or mortgage loans. What about the debt that the government has, in effect, taken out in their name? In 2013 the net federal debt in Canada was $20 000 per person. At some point, will the government raise your taxes to help pay off the national debt? If so, should you change your spending and saving behaviour now to prepare for the possibility of paying higher taxes in the future?

Most high-income countries, including Canada, the majority of Eurozone countries, Japan, the United Kingdom, and the United States, suffer from rising national debts. National debts are increasing because many countries are currently running large deficits and are likely to continue to do so for years into the future. The current deficits are largely the result of the lower tax revenues and higher government spending associated with the slow recovery from the Great Recession. In the future, rising expenses on public health care and public pensions may lead to large increases in national debt.

Economists often measure budget deficits as a fraction of GDP. For reasons we will discuss in this chapter, when the deficit rises above about 3% of GDP, it reaches levels that governments find difficult to sustain in the long run. In Canada, the federal government's budget deficit averaged 2.3% of GDP from 1981 to 2012. The budget, which fell into deficit in the latest recession, is expected to return to surplus in 2015 and, according to the Ministry of Finance long-run forecasts, will remain in surplus in the future. If these predictions turn out to be correct, the debt-to-GDP ratio in Canada will decline over time. The situation of other countries is, however, more difficult. For OECD countries, the deficit was 5.3% of GDP in 2012 and

Continued on next page

was expected to fall below 3% in 2015. In 2012 the deficit was 8.6% of GDP in Japan, 8.1% in the United States, and 7.4% in the United Kingdom. In all three countries, it was not expected to fall below 3% before 2016. These levels of deficit were unprecedented in peacetime; they were previously seen only during major wars such as World War I and World War II.

High deficits have contributed to long-term fiscal problems for many countries. The gross debt of countries in the OECD was over 110% of GDP in 2013 and was not expected to fall in the following two years. Out of the G7 countries, the debt-to-GDP ratio was below 100% of GDP in 2013 only in Germany and in Canada; it was expected to increase further in the other five countries (France, Italy, Japan, United Kingdom and the United States) by 2015.

What happened? The large debts were the result of the Great Recession. Governments used aggressive expansionary fiscal policies at the same time as automatic stabilizers led to large increases of spending over revenue. The figure on the right shows the *change* in the gross debt-to-GDP ratio between 2007 and 2010, as well as between 2007 and 2015, in several countries and for the OECD as a whole. (The numbers for 2015 are projections.) We can think of the increase between 2007 and 2010 as the direct effect of automatic stabilizers and expansionary fiscal policies during the Great Recession. In Canada, debt increased by 19% of GDP, from 70% in 2007 to 89% of GDP in 2010. Among G7 countries, the increase in debt varied from 15% of GDP in Italy to 40% of GDP in the United Kingdom. We included Ireland and Sweden in the figure as examples of extreme changes. In Ireland, the debt-to-GDP ratio increased by 60% between 2007 and 2010; it was the result of the decision by the Irish government to bail out its

banks, resulting in an unprecedented deficit of over 30% of GDP in 2010. On the other hand, in Sweden the debt-to-GDP ratio was unaffected by the Great Recession.

As the figure below illustrates, the fiscal deterioration did not end in 2010. Between 2010 and 2015 the debt-to-GDP ratio is expected to increase in all countries except in Germany; the expected increase varies between 7% of GDP in Canada and 42% in Japan. The overall increase between 2007 and 2015 in G7 countries varies between 16% in Germany and 73% in Japan. In Ireland, the expected increase in the debt-to-GDP ratio between 2007 and 2015 is an astounding 100% of GDP. In contrast, the ratio in Sweden is expected barely to change.

With aging populations and rising health care and pension costs, countries face hard choices: Governments

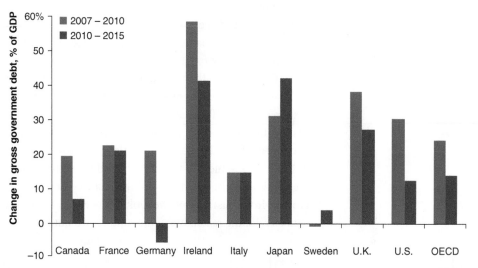

must choose among (1) reducing health care and pension benefits for the elderly, (2) reducing other spending, and (3) raising taxes to levels that might significantly reduce economic efficiency. The deterioration of the fiscal position in the Great Recession and its aftermath makes those choices much more difficult. How governments choose to deal with these looming fiscal problems will have important consequences for the future of their economies.

Sources: Mary Anastasia O'Grady, "How Canada Saved Its Bacon," *Wall Street Journal*, September 26, 2012; Statistics Canada; and Economic Outlook, Organisation for Economic Co-operation and Development (OECD).

See related Problem 3.4 at the end of the chapter.

Introduction

The Bank of Canada uses monetary policy to pursue macroeconomic policy goals (see Chapter 12). In the long run, monetary policy affects only nominal variables such as the inflation rate and leaves real variables such as output and employment unchanged. By the *long run*, we mean a period of time sufficiently long so that nominal wages and prices are flexible and real GDP equals potential GDP. The government also uses fiscal policy, such as changes in taxes and government purchases, to achieve macroeconomic goals in the short run (see Chapter 13). In this chapter, we analyze how fiscal policy affects real variables in the long run. We focus on the federal government's long-run fiscal policy, which determines deficits and debt. In principle there is nothing wrong with a government having a deficit and debt. Just as you may borrow to study, it makes perfect sense for the government to pay for education with borrowed money. When the government spends money on education now, it obtains return in the future. Better educated workers are more productive, earn more, and pay higher taxes. In general, anything that requires an up-front payment and provides additional government revenue or services in the future can reasonably be financed with debt. On the other hand, government should not be borrowing to pay for current expenses. And just like you, it needs to make sure that the burden of the debt is not excessive and it can make interest payments.

We begin the chapter by analyzing the government budget constraint. The federal government must pay for its spending by raising revenue, printing money, or borrowing. We study the history of the federal debt in Canada and the main ways it raises revenue as well as the major categories of government expenditure. In Section 15.2 we introduce the concept of sustainable debt. If the ratio of debt to GDP is constant or decreasing over time, the policy is sustainable in the sense that it can be continued indefinitely. On the other hand if the ratio of debt to GDP is increasing over time, the government must, eventually, reduce spending or increase revenue. We look at the condition under which debt is sustainable: It depends on the relationship between the real interest rate on government debt and the rate of economic growth. In the last section we look at the effects of deficits in the long run. We ask whether deficits raise the real interest rates and crowd out private spending.

15.1
Learning Objective
Discuss basic facts about Canada's fiscal situation.

Debt and Deficits in Historical Perspective

To provide context for understanding how fiscal policy affects an economy in the long run, it is important to first review some historical facts and key definitions. Gross federal debt is equal to the total dollar value of government bonds outstanding plus superannuation (pensions) owed by the federal government as an employer to its employees plus accounts and interest payable. Federal debt has tended to increase during wars and decrease during times of peace. The notable exceptions include the Great Depression, the 1980s, and the Great Recession. Before we can analyze the key issues connected with the federal debt, though, we need to understand the government's budget constraint, which spells out how governments finance their spending.

The Government Budget Constraint

Households face a budget constraint because the total amount that a household spends cannot exceed its income plus the amount it can borrow. The government faces a similar budget constraint. On the spending side, the government purchases goods and services (G), makes transfer payments (TR) to households, and makes interest payments on existing debt. We typically write the government budget constraint over a period of a year. If i is the average nominal interest rate on existing government bonds (B), then the interest payments in year t are $i_t B_{t-1}$, where t denotes the current year and $t-1$ denotes the previous year. For example, the value of interest payments on government debt in 2014 is the product of the average interest rate on government debt in 2014 times the amount of debt outstanding at the end of 2013. On the sources of funds side, the government receives tax revenue (T), issues new government bonds ($\Delta B_t = B_t - B_{t-1}$), or increases the monetary base ($\Delta MB_t = MB_t - MB_{t-1}$). In other words, the government must pay for its spending through taxes, borrowing, or creating money by increasing the monetary base.[1] Increasing the monetary base provides the government with *seigniorage*.

The government's budget equates spending to available funds:

$$G_t + TR_t + i_t B_{t-1} = T_t + \Delta B_t + \Delta MB_t. \tag{15.1}$$

The terms on the left of the equation represent the *uses* of government funds, and the terms on the right side represent the *sources* of government funds. In equation (15.1) all variables are flow variables: They are measured *per unit of time*. Note that the amount of bonds outstanding, B_t, or the monetary base, MB_t, are stocks: They are measured at *a moment of time*. The two related terms in equation (15.1) are the change in bonds outstanding, ΔB_t, and monetary base, ΔMB_t, over a period of one year. These changes are measured per unit of time and so they are flows.

If we move taxes to the left side, we have

$$(G_t + TR_t + i_t B_{t-1}) - T_t = \Delta B_t + \Delta MB_t. \tag{15.2}$$

The left side of the equation is the *budget deficit*, which is the difference between government expenditure and tax revenue.[2] The right side of equation (15.2) tells us that the budget deficit is financed by issuing new government securities and seigniorage.

A useful concept is that of **primary budget deficit (PD)**. It is equal to government purchases of goods and services plus transfer payments minus tax revenue:

$$PD_t = G_t + TR_t - T_t. \tag{15.3}$$

Primary budget deficit (*PD*) Government purchases of goods and services plus transfer payments minus tax revenue.

The primary budget deficit excludes the interest payments on government debt. It summarizes the current government operations. We can rewrite the equation for the budget deficit as

$$PD_t + i_t B_{t-1} = \Delta B_t + \Delta MB_t. \tag{15.4}$$

For example, in 2012, federal government expenditure on goods and services plus transfer payments was $271 billion, and revenue was $253 billion, so the budget deficit was $18 billion. The government made interest payments of $27 billion, which means that there was a primary surplus of $9 billion. As you can see, the total deficit and the primary deficit can provide a different picture of government finances. Figure 15.1 shows the total deficit and the primary budget deficit, as well as debt payments, as a percentage of GDP in Canada from 1981 to 2012. The total budget deficit and primary budget deficit track each other fairly well over time. For the past 30 years Canada had primary surplus, except for the years 1982–86 and 2009–11. On the other hand, the total budget had a surplus only for the period 1997–2007.

Interest payments on debt show the benefits of surpluses and low interest rates. The large deficits in 1980s resulted in interest payments increasing as proportion of GDP. Interest payments reached a peak of 5.6% of GDP in 1990 and then fell almost continuously. The

---

[1]Money is created by the central bank and, in most countries, the government does not control changes in the monetary base, but it receives the central bank's profits. In that case ΔM is, from the point of view of the government budget, exogenous.

[2]In this chapter, we will use the convention that a positive number represents a budget deficit and a negative number represents a budget surplus. This convention is different from the one we used in earlier chapters, where a negative number was a budget deficit and a positive number was a surplus. We make this change in order to make the algebra easier to follow.

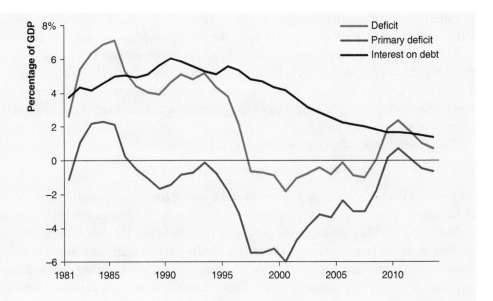

Figure 15.1

The Budget Deficit, Primary Budget Deficit, and Interest Payments on Debt, 1980–2013

Because interest payments are always positive, the primary budget deficit is always less than the total budget deficit. The primary budget deficit was negative, and therefore in surplus, between 1987 and 2008 and since 2012. The budget was in surplus between 1997 and 2007. Interest on debt as a percentage of GDP reached a peak in 1990 and has been declining every year since 1995.

Sources: Statistics Canada, CANSIM Tables 380-0080 and 380-0063.

combination of a reduction in debt and a large reduction in interest rates on government debt reduced interest payments on debt to 1.5% of GDP in 2012. Between 1995 and 2012 interest payments fell by 4.1% of GDP—more than total government purchases of goods and services. Without the decline in interest payments, the deficit in 2012 would have been 5.1% of GDP.

The Relationship between the Deficit and the National Debt

The debt is the total value of government bonds outstanding, B_t. Putting aside changes in the monetary base, which in Canada are small, the budget deficit is the yearly flow of new government bonds, ΔB. The value of bonds outstanding increases when the government runs a budget deficit and decreases when the government runs a budget surplus.

We can think about the debt and the deficit in terms of a bathtub analogy. Debt is the level of water in a bathtub; government expenditure is the water flowing in; and revenue is the water flowing out. Note that the value of the debt, like the amount of water in the tub, is a stock variable, measured *at a moment of time* while government expenditure and revenue, like the flow into and out of bathtub, are flow variables, *measured per unit of time*. During years that expenditures are greater than tax revenue, the government runs a budget deficit and more water flows into the bathtub than flows out, so the stock of government bonds and the federal debt increases. During years that expenditures are less than tax revenue, the government runs a budget surplus and more water flows out of the bathtub than flows in, so the stock of government bonds and the federal debt decreases.

Whether we focus on the deficit, the debt, or both depends on the question we are asking. If we want to know the effect of fiscal policy on the ability of households and firms to borrow to finance consumption and investment when the economy is at potential GDP, we should look to the yearly budget deficit. Remember that if the government increases its budget deficit, it reduces the pool of national saving available to households and firms to finance consumption and investment. If we want to know whether the government's fiscal policy is sustainable, we need to focus on both the debt and the deficit. There is a limit to how much financial markets will lend to governments, so the debt-to-GDP ratio cannot increase forever. **Sustainable fiscal policy** is when the debt-to-GDP ratio is constant or decreasing, and **unsustainable fiscal policy** is when the debt-to-GDP ratio is increasing. A fiscal policy that

Sustainable fiscal policy A situation in which the debt-to-GDP ratio is constant or decreasing.

Unsustainable fiscal policy A situation in which the debt-to-GDP ratio is increasing.

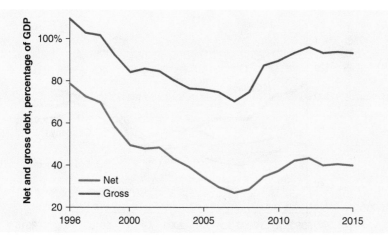

Figure 15.2

Gross and Net Federal Debt in Canada, 1996–2015

Debt is calculated as the ratio of fiscal year debt to calendar year GDP. The numbers for 2014–15 are projections.

Source: Organisation for Economic Co-operation and Development.

results in an increasing debt-to-GDP ratio must eventually change so that the ratio either remains constant or begins to decrease.

Gross and Net Federal Debt

Figure 15.2 shows gross federal debt and net federal debt. *Gross federal debt* is the total dollar value of government bonds outstanding plus superannuation owed by the federal government as an employer to its employees plus accounts and interest payable. It may also include the debt of state-owned enterprises; for example, in Japan it includes the debt of Japan Railways. **Net federal debt** is the dollar value of gross federal debt minus government financial assets. Such assets include currency and deposits, accounts receivable, reserves, and other financial assets. Net federal debt provides a complete picture of assets and liabilities, but it is not very useful for economic analysis. The federal government assets arise, to a large extent, from current government operations, and so the government cannot use them to pay off the debt. Therefore, economists usually focus on gross, rather than net, debt.

Net federal debt The dollar value of gross federal debt minus government financial assets.

The Debt-to-GDP Ratio

In this chapter, we emphasize the debt-to-GDP ratio rather than the dollar value of the debt. The debt-to-GDP ratio does a better job of measuring whether fiscal policy is sustainable. The federal government obtains most of its revenues through taxes, and GDP represents the income potentially available to be taxed. Thinking about the debt of an individual helps us understand why it makes sense to measure debt relative to a nation's income. Is $1 million a high level of debt? It depends. If your income is $50 000 per year, then $1 million in debt is extremely high. However, if you are a rich entrepreneur who earns $50 million per year, then $1 million is a low level of debt. It makes sense to measure debt relative to income because income represents your ability to make interest payments or repay the debt.

Figure 15.3 shows the gross debt of the federal government of Canada and of the central governments of the other G7 countries since 1981. Data for 2014–15 are projections. For clarity, we cut off the figure at 150% of GDP so the data for Japan end in 2002. (Since then Japan's debt-to-GDP ratio increased to well over 200%.) Among the remaining countries the debt-to-GDP ratio in 2013 varied between 86% in Germany and 146% in Italy. Debt-to-GDP ratio in Canada was the second lowest (94% of GDP). Debts in G7 countries are large compared to other OECD countries: in half of them, the ratio is lower than in Germany. The differences within the OECD are substantial: the debt-to-GDP ratio varies from 13% in Estonia to over 200% in Japan.

Figure 15.3

Government Debt for G7 Countries, 1996–2015

The debt in Canada is below average for countries in the Organisation for Economic Co-operation and Development. Canada is the only G7 country with current debt lower than in 1996. Data for 2014–15 are projections.

Source: Organisation for Economic Co-operation and Development.

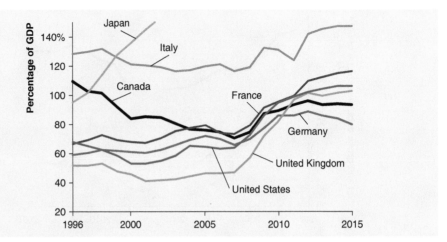

As can be seen in Figure 15.3, between 1996 and 2013 the debt-to-GDP ratio increased in all countries except for Canada. The increase varied between 17% in Italy and an astounding 130% in Japan. In contrast, the debt-to-GDP ratio in Canada fell by 16%. This is the result of the deficit reduction policy in mid 1990s that we discussed before.

We can divide the period between 1996 and 2013 into two sub-periods: before and after the Great Recession. Between 1996 and 2007 the debt to GDP ratio increased by 67% in Japan, fell by 40% in Canada, and changed little (by less than 7%) in the remaining countries. Since 2008 debt increased significantly in all countries: The increase in the debt-to-GDP ratio was around 20% in Germany and Canada, 30% in Italy, 40% in France and the United States 50% in the United Kingdom and 60% in Japan. By historical standards, currents debts are unprecedented in peacetime. Because the population is aging in most OECD countries, government expenditures on programs for the elderly, including health care and pensions, will likely cause the debt-to-GDP ratio to increase in the future. Germany and Canada appear to be in better position than other countries to face future fiscal challenges.

Composition of Federal Government Revenue

To understand the fiscal challenges Canada faces, it is helpful to first understand the composition of federal government revenue and expenditure and how the composition has changed over time.

Federal Government Revenue   As mentioned earlier, the federal government obtains most of its revenue through taxes:

- *Individual income taxes* are taxes that households pay on their wage and non-wage income.
- *Corporate income taxes* are taxes that corporations pay on their profits.
- *Social insurance contributions* are the contributions to Canada and Quebec Pension Plans and to employment insurance premiums. They are often called *payroll taxes* since they are paid at the same time as wages and salaries.
- *The Goods and Services Tax* (GST) is an indirect tax paid at each stage of production.

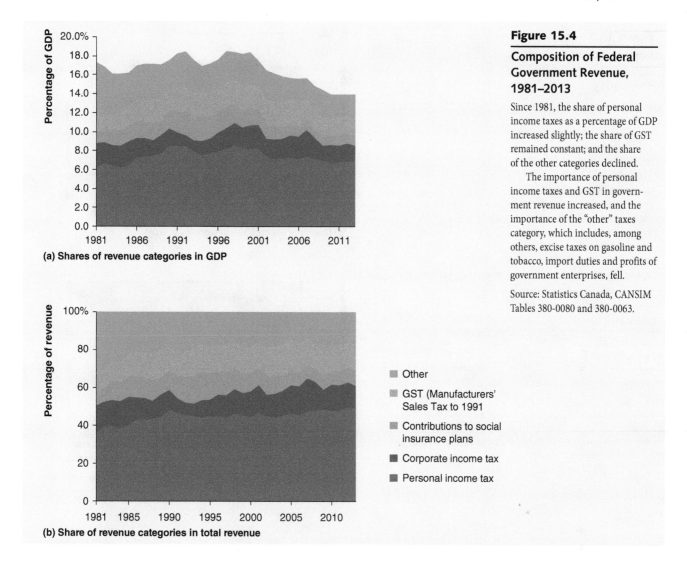

Figure 15.4

Composition of Federal Government Revenue, 1981–2013

Since 1981, the share of personal income taxes as a percentage of GDP increased slightly; the share of GST remained constant; and the share of the other categories declined.

The importance of personal income taxes and GST in government revenue increased, and the importance of the "other" taxes category, which includes, among others, excise taxes on gasoline and tobacco, import duties and profits of government enterprises, fell.

Source: Statistics Canada, CANSIM Tables 380-0080 and 380-0063.

Figure 15.4 shows that since 1981, total federal revenue has averaged about 17% of GDP. Federal revenue as a share of GDP was increasing until 1997. In 1997 the federal budget had the first surplus in many years, and revenue as a share of GDP started falling. Just before the Great Recession, 2007, it was 15.7% of GDP. Between 2008 and 2010 it declined rapidly, reaching 14% of GDP, and then stabilized.

The relative importance of the four categories of revenue has changed over the years. Since federal revenue as a percentage of GDP changed significantly over time, we first look at the share of revenue categories in GDP and then at the share of the revenue categories in federal revenue. Panel (a) shows the revenue categories as percentage of GDP between 1981 and 2013. The share of the personal income tax increased slightly, from 6.3% of GDP in 1981 to 6.9% of GDP in 2013; the share of GST remained almost unchanged while the share of "other" revenues (which include, among others, excise taxes on gasoline and tobacco, import duties, as well as profits of government enterprises) fell by over 3% of GDP. Overall, the decline in tax burden as proportion of GDP was mostly due to a decline in the "other" category.

Panel (b) shows revenue categories as proportion of all revenues. The importance of the revenue categories in total revenue fluctuates year-to-year, reflecting the effects of the

Figure 15.5

Composition of Federal Government Expenditure, 1981–2013

As a percentage of GDP, transfers to other governments and old age security were stable between 1981 and 2013, while the share of the other categories of expenditure fell. The decline in interest payments was particularly significant. The share in federal government spending of interest and employment insurance payments fell, while the share of spending on old age security and transfers to governments increased.

Source: Statistics Canada, CANSIM Tables 380-0080 and 380-0063.

■ Other
■ Goods and services
■ Employment insurance benefits
■ Old age security
■ Transfers to other governments
■ Interest on debt

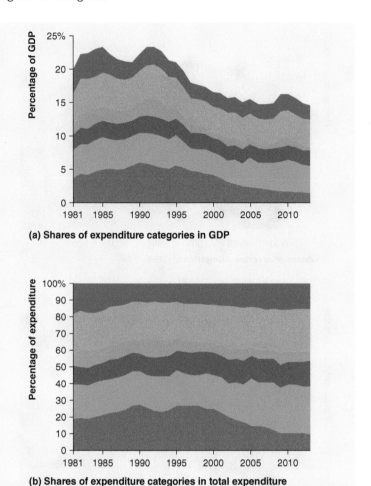

(a) Shares of expenditure categories in GDP

(b) Shares of expenditure categories in total expenditure

business cycle and changes in tax laws. There is a long-term trend: Personal income tax has become a much more important source of revenue. It was 36% of federal revenue in 1981 and increased to almost 50% of federal revenue in 2013. The GST also became a more important source of revenue, increasing from 10% to 13%. The share of the "other" category in total revenues declined significantly, from 31% to 17% of all revenues.

Seigniorage Tax revenue is by far the most important source of revenue for the federal government, but the government also obtains revenue from seigniorage. When the Bank of Canada increases the monetary base it makes a profit which is, at the end of the fiscal year, transferred to the federal government. For governments in high-income countries, seigniorage is usually not an important source of revenue; in Canada it averaged around 1% of federal revenue and 0.2% of GDP from 1981 to 2008.

Composition of Federal Government Expenditure

We now turn to the analysis of federal government expenditure, shown in Figure 15.5. Panel (a) shows the shares of various components of expenditure as a percentage of GDP. Total expenditure was increasing until 1992, with a peak of over 23% of GDP. It then fell continuously until 2007, when it reached 14.7% of GDP. As a result of automatic stabilizers and discretionary fiscal policy during the Great Recession, the expenditure increased by

1.6% of GDP until 2009, but by 2012 it had returned to the pre-recession share. Over the past 30 years transfers to other levels of government and old age security payments remained stable while the other categories of expenditure declined. The biggest decline was in the interest on debt, from a peak of 6.1% of GDP in 1990 to 1.4% of GDP in 2013. The decline was the result of surpluses between 1997 and 2007 and the large decline in interest rates. The reduction in debt interest as a result of surpluses is often called *the fiscal dividend*. The fiscal dividend arises because, after debt has fallen, lower interest on debt allows the federal government to redirect funds toward current expenditures without raising taxes. It is worth noting that the reduction in interest on debt between 1990 and 2013 was greater than total federal spending on goods and services in 2013.

Panel (b) shows the share of various categories in federal spending. The biggest change in the composition of government expenditure was interest on debt, which declined from a high of 28% of all spending in 1997 to 9% in 2013. Employment insurance benefits share of federal spending increased following the 1981–82, 1990–92 and 2008–09 recessions. The increase in the Great Recession was smaller than during the previous two recessions. The benefits have been on a downward trend since 1993. Old age security payments and transfers to other level of governments were the two categories of expenditure with increased share in federal spending.

The Sustainability of Fiscal Policy

15.2
Learning Objective
Explain when fiscal policy is sustainable and when it is not sustainable.

The federal government ran budget deficits before 1997 and again from 2009 on. As the economy returns to full employment, the size of the deficit will shrink. The 2014 Federal Budget predicts a return to surplus in 2015. Longer term, though, as the population of Canada gets older and as medical costs are likely to rise faster than the inflation rate, the federal government will spend increasing amounts on health care and old age security. In this section, we examine whether the federal government's fiscal policy is sustainable.

Expressing the Deficit as a Percentage of GDP

We start by recalling equation (15.4): $PD_t + i_tB_{t-1} = \Delta B_t + \Delta MB_t$. In this equation PD_t is the primary deficit and i_tB_{t-1} is the value of nominal interest payments on government bonds. Their sum, $PD_t + i_tB_{t-1}$, is equal to total deficit and shows the amount of funds the government needs. The right side, $\Delta B_t + \Delta MB_t$, is the total amount of new bonds (borrowing) and new cash issued by the government. This equation is in nominal terms: PD_t is the nominal primary deficit, B is the nominal value of government bonds, and MB is the nominal value of the money supply. Rearranging terms, we obtain the equation for the change in government borrowing: $\Delta B_t = PD_t + i_tB_{t-1} - \Delta MB_t$.

As we argued before, it is useful to measure debt and deficit as percentage of GDP. Dividing the change in borrowing by nominal GDP, which is equal to P_tY_t, we obtain

$$\frac{\Delta B_t}{P_tY_t} = \frac{PD_t}{P_tY_t} + i_t\frac{B_{t-1}}{P_tY_t} - \frac{\Delta MB_t}{P_tY_t}. \tag{15.5}$$

This equation is equivalent to

$$\Delta\left(\frac{B_t}{P_tY_t}\right) = \frac{PD_t}{P_tY_t} + [i_t - (\pi_t + g_t)]\frac{B_{t-1}}{P_{t-1}Y_{t-1}} - \frac{\Delta MB_t}{P_tY_t}, \tag{15.6}$$

where π_t is the inflation rate and g is the growth rate of real GDP. The somewhat tedious derivation of equation (15.6) is in Online Appendix 15.A. To avoid confusion, note that the left-hand side terms in equations (15.5) and (15.6) are different. The term in equation (15.5), $\frac{\Delta B_t}{P_t Y_t} = \frac{B_t - B_{t-1}}{P_t Y_t} = \left(\frac{B_t}{P_t Y_t}\right) - \left(\frac{B_{t-1}}{P_t Y_t}\right)$, is equal to the *increase in bonds outstanding as a proportion of current* GDP, while the term in equation (15.6), $\Delta\left(\frac{B_t}{P_t Y_t}\right) = \left(\frac{B_t}{P_t Y_t}\right) - \left(\frac{B_{t-1}}{P_{t-1} Y_{t-1}}\right)$ is equal to the *change in the debt-to-GDP ratio.*[3]

The debt-to-GDP ratio is stable when the change in the debt-to-GDP ratio, which is the expression on the left side of equation (15.6), equals zero. Equation (15.6) shows the factors affecting the change in the debt-to-GDP ratio. A higher primary deficit or a smaller increase in the money base raises the debt-to-GDP ratio. The intuition for the term $[i_t - (\pi_t + g_t)]\frac{B_{t-1}}{P_{t-1} Y_{t-1}}$ is that the higher the nominal interest rate, the larger the interest payments the government must make during the year, which increases the debt-to-GDP ratio. On the other hand, nominal GDP growth will reduce the debt-to-GDP ratio. The formula for the term, which is crucial for our considerations, can be explained using *Useful Math 4.2* equations for the rate of growth of a ratio and a product. The middle term shows the effects of the past debt-to-GDP ratio on current borrowing. When the government pays the interest on bonds at the nominal rate, i_t, the percentage change in the amount of bonds (not counting the current deficit or surplus) is i_t, so the numerator of the middle term grows at the rate of i_t. Nominal GDP equals $P_t Y_t$. Recall that the growth rate of a product is equal to the sum of the rates of growth of the factors. So the percentage change of the denominator equals the inflation rate plus the growth rate of real GDP, or $\pi_t + g_t$. The percentage change of the ratio is the difference between the percentage change of the numerator and the denominator, so the amount of real bonds last year grows at the rate $i_t - (\pi_t + g_t)$.

The Solow growth model (see Chapter 8) tells us that, in the long run, the growth rate of real GDP equals the growth rate of the labour force plus the rate of technological change. So, if either the growth rate of the labour force or the rate of technological change increases, the debt-to-GDP ratio will decrease.

The effect of an increase in the growth rate of the money supply is more difficult to analyze because the inflation rate also affects the nominal interest rate. When the nominal interest rate is constant, an increase in the growth rate of the money supply increases the inflation rate and reduces the debt-to-GDP ratio. This means that an unexpected increase in the rate of growth of money supply will decrease the debt-to-GDP ratio. Such unexpected increase in money printing is called the monetization of debt. Many countries have tried this in the past. However, when the money supply continues to increase faster and higher inflation persist, the expected rate of inflation will increase and, as the Fisher effect tells us, the nominal interest rate will increase. That increase in the nominal interest rate will, in turn, raise the debt-to-GDP ratio. Therefore, the net effect of an increase in the growth rate of the money supply is ambiguous and may be zero. This observation raises an important point: *It is difficult to finance budget deficits simply by printing more money, because nominal interest rates adjust upward, causing interest payments to also increase.* This effect is one explanation for the unsustainable hyperinflation in Germany from 1922 to 1923, discussed in Chapter 4.

---

[3]The difference is in the left-hand side of equations (15.5) and (15.6). The term on the left hand side of equation (15.5), $\frac{\Delta B_t}{P_t Y_t}$ is equal to the real value of bonds this year minus B_{t-1} divided by *current GDP*, $P_t Y_t$. The term on the left hand side of equation (15.6), $\Delta\left(\frac{B_t}{P_t Y_t}\right)$ is equal to the real value of bonds this year minus B_{t-1} divided by *last year's* GDP, $P_{t-1} Y_{t-1}$.

The European Debt Crisis: PIGS and FANGs

During the Great Recession government revenues in most countries fell and transfer payments increased. In addition, several countries raised their spending to stimulate the economy. As a result, the countries started running large deficits and, as you could see from Figure 15.3, the debt-to-GDP ratio increased a lot. Investors in several countries became concerned with the possibility of *sovereign default* (the government not being able to repay its debt). In the spring of 2010, many investors became reluctant to buy Greek government bonds because they were afraid that the government might default on the bonds. Greece could still borrow in international markets but at interest rates that would have made it impossible for Greece to pay the interest on borrowing. If the Greek government could not sell new bonds, the left-hand side term in the government budget constraint equation (15.6) would become zero. Because Greece uses the euro as its currency, the European Central Bank, rather than the central bank of Greece, controls the Greek monetary base. Greece does not have the option of expanding the monetary base to finance a budget deficit, and ΔMB is outside its control. Accordingly, the Greek government faced the hard choice of either defaulting on the interest payments due on its debt or dramatically reducing its primary budget deficit. To help prevent a default, the Eurozone countries and the International Monetary Fund (IMF) put together a bailout package of €110 billion. To receive these funds, the Greek government had to agree to increase taxes and cut spending. Essentially, other Eurozone countries lent funds to Greece at acceptable interest rates, on the conditions that Greece reform its economy, achieve a primary surplus, and, by 2020, reach a sustainable fiscal position. European countries and the IMF also created a €750 billion fund to help other European governments that might have difficulty financing their debts. The goal of the fund was to reassure investors that no country using the euro would default on its debt.

The sovereign debt crisis that started with Greece during the spring of 2010 spread to Ireland during the fall. Ireland had kept government spending under control, but the collapse of its real estate market greatly weakened Irish banks. In an attempt to calm financial markets and assure the public, the Irish government guaranteed the debt of Irish banks. As a result, the Irish government's budget deficit exploded, as we described earlier in the chapter. Ireland eventually had to accept a bailout of €85 billion from other Eurozone countries and the IMF in November 2010. In the spring of 2011, Portugal's high level of debt forced it to seek a bailout from other Eurozone countries and the IMF.

To make matters worse, the same concerns that forced a bailout of the Irish government led to problems in Spain. The economies of Greece, Ireland, and Portugal were small—total GDP of these three countries was about half of Spanish GDP. Although Spain's sovereign debt burden was much less than that of Greece, by 2012 regional Spanish banks were in a very difficult situation, and the Spanish government did not have sufficient funds to bail them out. In June 2012 the Spanish government received a loan from other Eurozone countries to be used to prevent a banking crisis in Spain.

The countries that required bailouts were jointly called PIGS, for Portugal, Ireland, Greece, and Spain. The acronym PIIGS was also sometimes used, with the second "I" denoting Italy, another highly indebted economy. The problems of the PIGS countries began when the introduction of the euro allowed them to borrow at lower interest rates and they ran expansionary fiscal policies, paying little attention to deficits. In addition, labour costs in the PIGS countries increased rapidly, undermining their competitiveness with other Eurozone countries, in particular with Finland, Austria, the Netherlands, and Germany, which we will call FANG countries. When the Great Recession started, the fiscal position of PIGS countries deteriorated rapidly. By 2012, with the exception of Spain, their debt-to-GDP ratio exceeded

100%. The ratio is expected to continue increasing in all PIGS countries so that, by 2015, their average debt-to-GDP ratio is expected to be 142%. While the fiscal position of FANG countries also deteriorated, the increase in the debt-to-GDP ratio was much smaller.

The figure below shows the increase in debt-to-GDP ratio between 2007 and 2012. The contrast between PIGS countries and FANG countries is striking. The second figure below shows the evolution of the debt-to-GDP ratio. While in 2007 Ireland had lower debt than all of the FANG countries and Spain's debt-to-GDP ratio was higher only than Finland's, by 2012 all PIGS countries had significantly higher debt-to-GDP ratios than any of the FANGs.

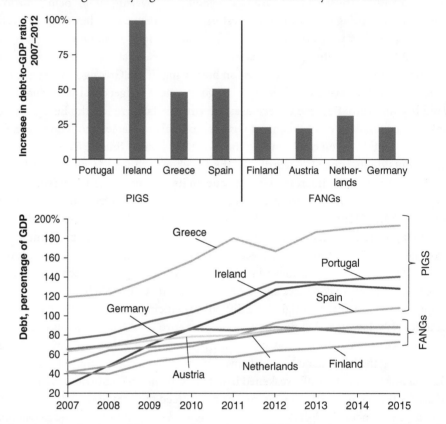

Before the introduction of the euro, when prices in PIGS countries increased faster, they allowed their currencies to depreciate relative to the currencies of strong European economies, restoring competitiveness. With a common currency, however, that is no longer possible. To restore competitiveness, PIGS countries need to reduce their inflation rates below that of FANG countries. This is, however, difficult when inflation in Germany is only 1%. The only solution is a painful austerity process of cutting government expenditure and reducing wages. The result is a recession and high unemployment: In Greece and Spain, which were the most affected, unemployment at the beginning of 2014 was over 25%, and youth unemployment approached 60%!

The debt crisis has forced many countries to re-evaluate the wisdom of having budget deficits in good times. The fiscal conditions of admission to the euro, agreed upon in the Maastricht Treaty that created the euro, was that the deficit not exceed 3% of GDP and debt not exceed 60% of GDP. These conditions were not strictly enforced in the past. The Euro-zone may be stricter to enforce these conditions in the future.

Sources: Jack Ewing, "The Euro Zone Crisis: A Primer," *New York Times*, May 22, 2012; "Saving the Euro: Ireland's Woes Are Largely of Its Own Making but German Bungling Has Made Matters Worse," *Economist*, November 18, 2010; "No Easy Exit," *Economist*, December 4, 2010; Stephen Castle, "Economic Divisions in Euro Zone Are Seen as Threat," *New York Times*, November 30, 2010; and Organisation for Economic Co-operation and Development. Data for 2014–15 are projections.

See related Problem 2.4 at the end of the chapter.

When Is Fiscal Policy Sustainable?

We now ask under what conditions fiscal situation is sustainable, which we define as a situation when the debt-to-GDP ratio is constant or decreasing. To do this we simplify the term in square brackets in equation (15.6). Recall that the real interest rate, r, equals the nominal interest rate minus the inflation rate. We can use this relationship to eliminate the nominal interest rate and the inflation rate from the government budget constraint and rewrite the equation as

$$\Delta\left(\frac{B_t}{P_tY_t}\right) = \frac{PD_t}{P_tY_t} + (r_t - g_t)\frac{B_{t-1}}{P_{t-1}Y_{t-1}} - \frac{\Delta MB_t}{P_tY_t}. \tag{15.7}$$

We start with a simple case when both seigniorage revenue and the government's primary deficit are zero. With these simplifications equation (15.7) becomes

$$\Delta\left(\frac{B_t}{P_tY_t}\right) = (r_t - g_t)\frac{B_{t-1}}{P_{t-1}Y_{t-1}}. \tag{15.8}$$

This equation shows that the change in the debt-to-GDP ratio depends only on the real interest rate and the growth rate of real GDP. If the real interest rate is greater than the growth rate of real GDP, i.e., if $r_t > g_t$, then $\Delta\left(\frac{B_t}{P_tY_t}\right) > 0$, i.e., the debt-to-GDP ratio will increase even if the government has a primary deficit of zero. In this case, the government is forced to run a primary surplus just to prevent the debt-to-GDP ratio from rising to higher and higher levels. However, if $r_t < g_t$, then $\Delta\left(\frac{B_t}{P_tY_t}\right) < 0$, i.e., the debt-to-GDP ratio will decrease. In this case, it is possible to have a primary deficit greater than zero and still have a sustainable fiscal policy.

To see what equation (15.7) means, let us use the data for Canada in 2012.[4] To calculate the real interest rate on government debt, we would need to know the structure of debt (how much of the debt is in T-bills, 1-year bonds, 2-year bonds, etc.). That is difficult, so we will, instead, use the real interest rate on long-term government bonds. There are two ways to obtain the real interest rate. The Bank of Canada provides data on long-term real return bonds. In 2012 it was 0.42%. We can also use the nominal interest rate on long-term bonds and the inflation rate. In 2012 the nominal interest rate on 10-year Government of Canada bonds was 1.85%, and the inflation rate for the GDP deflator was 1.4%. Both calculations indicate that the real interest rate was around 0.4%. The real GDP growth rate was 1.7%; gross debt in 2011 was 83.5% of GDP (we use debt from 2011 since equation (15.7) uses the previous year's debt-to-GDP ratio); and seigniorage was around 0.1% of GDP.

What is the level of primary deficit that Canada could have in 2012 while having sustainable fiscal policy? Since sustainable fiscal policy means falling or constant debt-to-GDP ratio, we equate left side of the equation (15.7) to zero. Using our data we have

$$0 = \frac{PD_{2012}}{P_{2012}Y_{2012}} + (0.4\% - 1.7\%) \times 83.5\% - 0.1\% = -1.1\% - 0.1\% = -1.2\%.$$

So in 2012 Canada could have a primary deficit as high as 1.2% of GDP and maintain constant debt-to-GDP ratio. However, the primary deficit in Canada was 2.6%, and so the debt-to-GDP ratio increased.

---

[4]We use data from the Bank of Canada, Statistics Canada, and OECD.

Can Japan Grow Its Way Out of Debt?

In Japan, the government debt reached 219% of GDP in 2012. Since 1990, economic growth in Japan has averaged just 0.7% per year, and the inflation rate (calculated as the growth rate of the GDP deflator) has averaged −0.7%. The Ministry of Finance reported that the average nominal interest rate that the government paid to borrow for 10 years was 1.2%. Given this information, was Japanese fiscal policy sustainable? If not, what would the primary budget deficit have to be to make fiscal policy sustainable?

Solving the Problem

Step 1 **Review the chapter material.** The problem asks you to determine whether fiscal policy is sustainable, so you may want to review the section "When Is Fiscal Policy Sustainable?" which begins on page 485.

Step 2 **Determine whether Japanese fiscal policy is sustainable.** To determine whether the debt is sustainable, you have to compare the real interest rate with the growth rate of real GDP. You know that the growth rate of real GDP was just 0.7%. You also know that the nominal interest rate was 1.2% and that the inflation rate was −0.7%. Using the definition of the real interest rate, you can calculate the real interest rate as

$$r = 1.2\% - (-0.7\%) = 1.9\%.$$

Because

$$r > g,$$

Japan's debt was not sustainable, so even if the Japanese government had a primary deficit of zero, the debt-to-GDP ratio would continue to increase.

Step 3 **Determine the primary deficit necessary to make the debt stable.** You can use equation (15.7) for the government budget constraint from page 485:

$$\Delta\left(\frac{B_t}{P_t Y_t}\right) = \frac{PD_t}{P_t Y_t} + (r_t - g)\frac{B_{t-1}}{P_{t-1}Y_{t-1}} - \frac{\Delta MB_t}{P_t Y_t}.$$

Seigniorage is usually small, so you can rewrite the preceding equation without seigniorage:

$$\Delta\left(\frac{B_t}{P_t Y_t}\right) = \frac{PD_t}{P_t Y_t} + (r_t - g)\frac{B_{t-1}}{P_{t-1}Y_{t-1}}.$$

The real interest rate was 1.9%, or 0.019, and the growth rate of real GDP has averaged 0.7%, or 0.007, so plugging these values into the preceding equation, you get

$$\Delta\left(\frac{B_t}{P_t Y_t}\right) = \frac{PD_t}{P_t Y_t} + (0.019 - 0.007)\frac{B_{t-1}}{P_{t-1}Y_{t-1}}.$$

In 2012, the debt-to-GDP ratio was 219%, or 2.19, so you should plug this value in for the lagged debt-to-GDP ratio. Because the debt-to-GDP ratio is sustainable when the ratio is constant, you should plug in a value of 0 for the change in the debt-to-GDP ratio on the left side:

$$0 = \frac{PD_t}{P_t Y_t} + (0.019 - 0.007)2.19.$$

We can solve for the primary deficit:

$$\frac{PD_t}{P_t Y_t} = -0.026, \text{ or } 2.6\%.$$

A negative number means that the Japanese government would have to run a primary *surplus* of 2.6% of GDP to make the debt sustainable. However, Japan actually had a primary *deficit* of 8.8% in 2013, so Japan's debt is not sustainable. Unless Japan significantly increases its growth rate in the near future, it will not be able to grow its way out of the debt. Due to the slow growth of real GDP, moving to a sustainable fiscal policy will require Japan to run a primary surplus by increasing taxes and cutting spending.

See related Problem 2.7 at the end of the chapter.

The Effects of Budget Deficits in the Long Run

In earlier chapters we discussed the short-run effects of fiscal policy. In this section, we shift the focus to the long-run effects of fiscal policy.

15.3

Learning Objective
Understand how fiscal policy affects the economy in the long run.

The Budget Deficit and Crowding Out
The national income identities are useful because they must hold, given the definition of the variables (see Chapter 2). So the identities act as constraints. Recall the following identity:

$$Y = C + I + G + NX.$$

As we show in Online Appendix 15.B, we can modify the preceding equation to become

$$[(G + TR) - T] = S_{\text{Household}} - I - NX, \tag{15.9}$$

where TR denotes transfers, $S_{\text{Household}} = Y + TR - T - C$, and budget deficit $= [(G + TR) - T]$ $= -S_{\text{Government}}$. This equation tells us that the government's budget deficit, $(G + TR) - T$, is equal to private savings minus private investment minus net exports. The relationship between net exports and government deficits seems strange, but a trade deficit means that financial capital from abroad flows into the country. So, for a given level of private savings and investment, an increase in government deficit means that the trade deficit must increase and more capital must flow into the country. In effect, the country is borrowing from abroad to finance its budget deficit.

Suppose the government decides to decrease income taxes by $1 billion. To keep the deficit from increasing, the government could (1) reduce purchases by $1 billion, (2) reduce transfer payments by $1 billion, or (3) increase other taxes by $1 billion. If the government does not change policy, the budget deficit will increase by $1 billion. The government will have to issue $1 billion in new bonds, which requires the private sector to adjust. One possibility is that households may increase savings by $1 billion to purchase the new bonds. In this case, domestic households could reduce consumption by $1 billion. In effect, domestic households finance the higher deficit by cutting their own consumption. This has been the case in Japan, where large household savings financed government deficits. Alternatively, firms and households could decrease investment by $1 billion. This decline is called *crowding out*, a reduction in private investment caused by government budget deficits. Finally, the trade deficit could increase by $1 billion. The increased trade deficit is the equivalent of foreign governments and individuals purchasing $1 billion in new government bonds. In that case, the international indebtedness of the government increases.

The Conventional View: Crowding Out Private Investment

The conventional view among economists is that persistent budget deficits lead to higher real interest rates and crowd out private investment. If the government borrows $1 billion, that is $1 billion that households and firms cannot borrow to finance private investment. In other words, national savings have decreased. Because there are now fewer funds available for the private sector to borrow, competition among borrowers causes the real interest rate to increase. The higher real interest rate increases the cost of borrowing to finance investment, so investment spending decreases.

With a lower level of spending on new capital goods such as factories and computers, the private capital stock grows more slowly. As a result, the private capital stock in the future is not as large as it otherwise would have been. Therefore, the conventional view suggests that persistent budget deficits lead to a higher real interest rate, a smaller capital stock, and a lower level of potential GDP in the long run. This analysis implies that there are significant long-run costs to running persistent budget deficits. We have to bear in mind, however, that budget deficits may finance investments in roads, bridges, and education, all of which may help increase economic growth. In addition, budget deficits might help stimulate the economy and reduce unemployment in the short run if the economy is below potential GDP. Policymakers have to balance the costs and benefits of budget deficits.

Ricardian Equivalence

Most economists agree that if government expenditure increases, national saving will decrease. The effect of tax cuts on national saving is subject to more debate, however. Robert Barro of Harvard University began the modern debate over the effects of tax cuts by reviving an argument he attributed to David Ricardo, the great nineteenth-century British economist.

Ricardian equivalence
The theory that forward-looking households fully anticipate the future taxes required to pay off government debt, so that reductions in lump-sum taxes have no effect on the economy.

Following Barro's argument, **Ricardian equivalence** is the theory that forward-looking households fully anticipate the future taxes required to pay off government debt and care only about lifetime disposable income. It was discussed briefly in Chapter 13; we return to it here in more detail. The surprising implication of Ricardian equivalence is that a reduction in lump-sum taxes has no effect on the economy.[5] *Lump-sum* taxes are taxes that are independent of the level of income. They do not have the distortionary effects on the decisions to save, invest, and work that changes in marginal tax rates do. If households consider lifetime disposable income, and not just current disposable income, when making consumption decisions, they will increase consumption only when lifetime disposable income increases and reduce consumption only when lifetime disposable income decreases.

Consider the effects of a $1 billion tax cut. To keep the analysis simple, let's just consider the situation over two years when the new debt must be paid off in the second year. Also assume that the government can borrow at an interest rate of 0%. This year, the government announces that it will cut taxes by $1 billion. Because the government must pay off the debt next year, it must raise taxes by $1 billion next year. Therefore, the decision by the government to cut taxes today by $1 billion is also a decision to increase taxes next year by $1 billion.

If households are forward looking in their consumption decisions, they recognize that their disposable income increases this year by $1 billion but then decreases next year by

---

[5]David Ricardo actually considered but rejected the idea of Ricardian equivalence. Harvard economist Robert Barro is the most famous modern proponent of Ricardian equivalence. When Barro formulated the argument, he credited Ricardo for first mentioning the idea, and so the view has become known as Ricardian equivalence. See Robert J. Barro, "Are Government Bonds Net Wealth?" *Journal of Political Economy* 82, no. 6, (1974): 1095–1117.

Macro Data: Do Government Deficits Increase Real Interest Rates?

The conventional view predicts that government budget deficits lead to higher real interest rates. What is the evidence to support this prediction? Economists William Gale of the Brookings Institution and Peter Orszag, former director of the U.S. Office of Management and Budget, conducted a study in which they found relatively large effects of fiscal policy on long-term real interest rates. Gale and Orszag found that each one percentage points increase in the deficit relative to GDP raises long-term real interest rates by 0.25 to 0.35 percentage point. They also found that the increase is between 0.40 and 0.70 percentage points when the primary budget deficit increases by one percentage point of GDP.

Studies using the debt-to-GDP ratio as the measure of fiscal policy, rather than the deficit-to-GDP ratio, often find smaller effects of fiscal policy on real interest rates. Economists Eric Engen of the Board of Governors of the Federal Reserve System and Glenn Hubbard of Columbia University examined the effect of government debt on real interest rates and investment. They found that a one-percentage-point increase in the debt-to-GDP ratio increases long-term real interest rates by about 0.03 percentage point, which is a relatively small amount. The Congressional Budget Office in the United States estimates that gross federal debt held by the public will increase by 25% of GDP between 2011 and 2022. This is a 25 percentage point increase in the debt-to-GDP ratio in just 10 years. The study by Engen and Hubbard suggests that the forecasted increase in the debt-to-GDP ratio will increase long-term real interest rates 0.75 percentage point over what they otherwise would have been. The higher real interest rates should lead to lower investment.

Unlike the United States, Canada is a small open economy, and changes in Canadian deficit or debt should have limited effect on Canadian interest rates. Canadian interest rates depend on world interest rates, and deficits in Canada are unlikely to affect world interest rates. Economist Pierre Siklos of Wilfrid Laurier University did not find any effect of deficits in Canada on Canadian interest rates. On the other hand, Robert Ford and Douglas Laxton of the International Monetary Fund found that changes in world public debt had a significant effect on real interest rate in Canada.

Economists have found a variety of estimates of the effects of fiscal policy on long-term real interest rates. The differences arise because some studies focus on the federal debt, others focus on deficits, and the definitions of *debt* and *deficit* can vary from study to study. In addition, the statistical techniques that economists use can also vary from study to study. As a result, the estimated magnitude of the effect of fiscal policy on long-term real interest rates varies. However, most studies support the conventional view that fiscal policy affects these rates.

Sources: William Gale and Peter Orszag, "Budget Deficits, National Savings, and Interest Rates," *Brookings Panel on Economic Activity* 2004, no. 2 (2004): 101–187; and Eric Engen and R. Glenn Hubbard, "Federal Government Debt and Interest Rates," in Mark Gertler and Kenneth Rogoff, eds., *National Bureau of Economic Research Macroeconomics Annual* (Cambridge, MA: MIT Press, 2004): 83–160; Pierre Siklos, "The Deficit—Interest Rate Link: Empirical Evidence for Canada," *Applied Economics* 20 (1988): 1563–1577; Robert Ford and Douglas Laxton, "World Public Debt and Real Interest Rates," *Oxford Review of Economic Policy* 15, no. 2 (1999): 77–94

See related Problem 3.8 at the end of the chapter.

$1 billion. There is no change in lifetime disposable income for households, so there is no change in consumption. If consumption does not change, how do households alter their behaviour in response to the $1 billion tax cut? They save the entire $1 billion increase in their current disposable income. Ricardian equivalence implies that households use the extra disposable income from the tax cut to purchase government bonds this year and use the revenues from the maturing bonds next year to pay for the higher taxes.

Many economists are skeptical that Ricardian equivalence accurately describes the behaviour of households. First, Ricardian equivalence assumes that households are forward looking in an extreme sense. In the previous example, we assumed that the relevant time frame was just two years. In reality, the government could cut taxes today and then not raise taxes to pay for the debt for 10 or more years. When the tax increase is in the distant future, households may not realize that their taxes will increase, so they may think that their lifetime disposable income has increased. As a result, they may increase consumption. Possibly the tax increase is not even in the current household's lifetime but instead occurs during their children's or grandchildren's lifetimes. In this case, the tax cut increases lifetime disposable income for existing households, so current consumption will increase, unless current households take into account the future incomes of their children and grandchildren. Of course, the tax increase in the future reduces lifetime disposable income of future households, but those households do not yet exist, so they cannot reduce consumption in the present.

Second, for Ricardian equivalence to hold, financial markets must work well enough that households can borrow or save as much as they would like at current interest rates. Suppose the government announces a tax increase this year of $1 billion and a corresponding tax cut of $1 billion next year. Lifetime disposable income has not changed, but current disposable income has decreased by $1 billion. According to Ricardian equivalence, consumption will not change because households can borrow to compensate for the drop in disposable income this year. But if some households are not able to borrow enough to keep consumption constant—perhaps because they lack acceptable collateral to get a loan—the tax increase will cause consumption to decrease.

Third, Ricardian equivalence applies only to lump-sum taxes, while tax changes typically involve changes in tax rates. As Barro acknowledges, changes in tax rates may affect household behaviour by, for example, affecting the decision of individuals to supply labour. As a result, a tax increase today may reduce the quantity of labour supplied and reduce real GDP today. Taxes on capital income will affect the accumulation of the capital stock, which will also affect real GDP. So tax changes that affect the behaviour of households and firms may affect real GDP and consumption.

Key Terms and Problems

Key Terms

Net federal debt, p. 477
Primary budget deficit (*PD*), p. 475

Ricardian equivalence, p. 488
Sustainable fiscal policy, p. 476

Unsustainable fiscal policy, p. 476

 15.1

Debt and Deficits in Historical Perspective
Discuss basic facts about Canada's fiscal situation.

Review Questions

1.1 What is the difference between gross debt and net debt?

1.2 Why is debt usually measured using the debt-to-GDP ratio rather than the absolute amount of debt? How is the debt-to-GDP ratio used to determine whether a fiscal policy is sustainable?

1.3 What is the difference between the budget deficit and the primary budget deficit? Use the government's budget constraint to express the relationship between the budget deficit and the primary budget deficit algebraically.

Problems and Applications

1.4 Gross debt was around 85% of GDP at the end of 2012. Historically, interest rates on government

bonds have been considerably higher than they were in 2012. Assume, for simplicity, that the government pays the same interest rate on all outstanding debt. What is the approximate annual interest payment if the debt is 85% of GDP and the interest rate is

a. 0.5%?

b. 3%?

c. 5%?

1.5 Briefly explain whether you agree with the following statement: "Because the government can always print more money, the size of the budget deficit doesn't matter."

1.6 What were the benefits of the elimination of deficits in 1990s?

15.2 The Sustainability of Fiscal Policy
Explain when fiscal policy is sustainable and when it is not sustainable.

Review Questions

2.1 What does it mean to say that fiscal policy is either sustainable or unsustainable? What are the consequences for a country of having a fiscal policy that is unsustainable?

2.2 Identify each term in the following equation:

$$\Delta\left(\frac{B_t}{P_t Y_t}\right) = \frac{PD_t}{P_t Y_t} + (r_t - g_t)\frac{B_{t-1}}{P_{t-1} Y_{t-1}} - \frac{\Delta MB_t}{P_t Y_t}.$$

How can this equation be used to determine whether a country's debt is sustainable? In your analysis, assume that seigniorage and the government's primary deficit are both zero.

Problems and Applications

2.3 For each of the following scenarios, explain the effect on the debt-to-GDP ratio.

  a. The growth rate of the labour force decreases.

  b. The nominal interest rate on existing bonds increases.

  c. The monetary base increases, which causes the rate of inflation to rise.

  d. The monetary base decreases, but there is no change in the rate of inflation.

2.4 [Related to the Making the Connection **on page 482**] In July 2012, the Greek finance minister announced that the country's 2012 deficit would be 5.4% of GDP, down from 9% in 2011, and primary public expenditure would decline by more than €2.7 billion from the previous year. Aside from spending cuts, does Greece have any other alternatives for reducing its deficit? Briefly explain.

Source: "Greece Budget 2012," http://finance.mapsofworld.com/budget/greece/.

2.5 Briefly explain whether you agree with the following statement: "The only way for a country with a budget deficit to have sustainable fiscal policy in the long run is to cut government spending."

2.6 In 2012, interest rates in the United States remained at historically low levels, and the Fed indicated that it would not increase its target for the federal funds rate until at least mid-2015. A July 2012 article in the *New York Times* reported, "[Federal Reserve Chairman] Bernanke told Congress that . . . he and other Fed officials had concluded that the central bank needed to expand its stimulus campaign unless the nation's economy showed signs of improvement, including job growth." How is a monetary policy of maintaining low interest rates likely to affect the sustainability of fiscal policy?

Source: Binyamin Appelbaum, "Fed Leaning Closer to New Stimulus if No Growth Is Seen," *New York Times*, July 24, 2012.

2.7 [Related to Solved Problem 15.1 **on page 486**] The sustainability of fiscal policy is partly a function of the growth rate of GDP. Some economists have forecast that Japan's growth rate may decrease below the current 10-year average of 0.7%.

  a. If the growth rate of GDP fell to –0.5%, how would this affect the sustainability of Japan's fiscal policy?

  b. Based on the growth rate in part (a) and using the other values from Solved Problem 15.1, calculate the level of the primary deficit required to make Japan's fiscal policy sustainable.

2.8 Suppose that a country has a debt-to-GDP ratio of 64%. Its growth rate of real GDP is 3%. Assume that seigniorage is zero and the real interest rate is 2%. What primary deficit as a percentage of GDP would be required to make fiscal policy sustainable?

15.3 The Effects of Budget Deficits in the Long Run
Understand how fiscal policy affects the economy in the long run.

Review Questions

3.1 Briefly describe the ways to finance a government budget deficit.

3.2 Explain what effects a government budget deficit and a surplus have on long-term real interest rates, the capital stock, labour productivity, and potential GDP.

3.3 Explain Ricardian equivalence. Why are some economists skeptical about the validity of Ricardian equivalence?

Problems and Applications

3.4 [Related to the Chapter Opener on page 472] The chapter opener suggests that deficits are generally a problem for many countries. Based on the discussion in Section 15.3, are there circumstances in which it might be possible that deficits could increase productivity and long-run growth?

3.5 Use the following equation to demonstrate how an increase in the budget deficit must increase the trade deficit if neither consumption nor investment changes:

$$[(G + TR) - T] = S_{Household} - I - NX.$$

What must happen if there is an increase in the budget deficit in a closed economy?

3.6 In January 2008 the GST was reduced by 1%.

a. Assume that the tax cuts were lump-sum tax cuts. If Ricardian equivalence holds, what should have been the effect of the GST cut?

b. The GST reduction changed prices of goods and services subject to the tax. How does this fact change your answer to part (a)?

3.7 In March 2012, Spain announced budget cuts of €27 billion, in an effort to reduce its budget deficit. A *CNN* article quotes Treasury Minister Cristobal Montoro: "We are in a critical situation. This is the most austere budget in our democracy." The budget proposal included spending cuts for government agencies, infrastructure, defence, and education, as well as reduced aid for immigrants. The proposal also included increases in business taxes and a salary freeze and extended work hours for civil servants.

a. What is the likely effect of these actions on savings, investment, and the real interest rate?

b. In what ways are the short-run and long-run effects of this deficit reduction likely to differ?

Source: Al Goodman, "Spain Announces 27 Billion Euros in Budget Cuts," *CNN*, March 30, 2012.

3.8 [Related to the Macro Data feature on page 489] Studies have shown a link between rising debt-to-GDP ratios and real interest rates. Investment is not the only category of spending that might be sensitive to interest rates.

a. How might consumption be affected by rising interest rates due to a government deficit? Will all types of consumption be affected equally?

b. Do the data presented suggest that rising interest rates are currently a significant concern in the Canada?

Data Exercises

D15.1: [Spreadsheet exercise] Countries in the Eurozone are required to place limits on the debt and budget deficits of the national government. Deficits are required to be less than 3% of GDP, and government debt is required to be less than 60% of GDP. The International Monetary Fund's World Economic Outlook database provides data on government deficits and debt that will allow you to determine how well governments meet both of these criteria. The data are available at http://www.imf.org/external/pubs/ft/weo/2014/01/weodata/index.aspx. This report is regularly updated, so you can also search for "World Economic Outlook."

a. For France, Germany, Greece, Italy, and Spain, download annual data for the 2011 to 2017 period on "General government net lending/borrowing" as a percentage of GDP to use as a measure of the budget deficit. Note that the values for later years are forecasted values and that negative values indicate a budget deficit. Calculate the average forecasted budget deficit from 2012 to 2017.

b. Repeat part (a) for government debt using "General government gross debt."

c. How will fiscal policy have to change for these countries to meet the requirements for remaining in the Eurozone?

d. What would be the short-run effect of these policy changes on the Eurozone economy? What would be the short-run effect on the Canadian economy?

D15.2: [Spreadsheet exercise] The International Monetary Fund's World Economic Outlook database provides annual data on government debt and deficit for the United Kingdom from 1980 to the present. The data are available at www.imf.org/external/pubs/ft/weo/2014/01/weodata/index.aspx.

a. Download the data for "General government net lending/borrowing" as a measure of the budget deficit. Note that a negative number indicates a budget deficit. In addition, download the data for "General government gross debt" as a percentage of GDP as a measure of government debt.

b. Graph the data. How do the debt and deficit data compare to the values for the United States discussed in the chapter?

D15.3: [Spreadsheet exercise] The International Monetary Fund's World Economic Outlook database contains data on government debt for many of the countries in the world. The data are available at www.imf.org/external/pubs/ft/weo/2014/01/weodata/index.aspx.

a. Download data for "General government gross debt" as a percentage of GDP as a measure of government debt for the current year.

b. Calculate the mean and standard deviation for government debt for all of the countries in the database. Is Canada's government debt above or below the average? Is it above or below the median?

c. What does your answer to part (b) tell you about Canada's government's fiscal situation compared to other countries? Explain.

d. The International Monetary Fund also provides forecasts of government debt in the future. Pick the year furthest into the future and repeat parts (b) and (c).

D15.4: [Spreadsheet exercise] The International Monetary Fund's World Economic Outlook database contains data on government spending and taxes. The data are available at www.imf.org/external/pubs/ft/weo/2014/01/weodata/index.aspx. Canada is frequently described as having lower levels of government spending and taxes compared to countries in Western Europe, but higher than the United States and Japan.

a. For the sub-category of countries that the International Monetary Fund describes as "Major advanced economies (G7)" download annual data on "General government revenue" and "General government total expenditure" both measured as a percentage of GDP from 2001 to the present.

b. Plot the revenue data on a graph. How does Canada compare to the countries from Western Europe? How does it compare to the United States and to Japan?

c. Repeat part (b) for total expenditure.

Consumption and Investment

Learning Objectives

After studying this chapter, you should be able to:

16.1 Discuss the macroeconomic implications of microeconomic decision making by households and firms (pages 495–496)

16.2 Explain the determinants of personal consumption (pages 496–508)

16.3 Explain the determinants of private investment (pages 508–516)

Are All Tax Cuts Created Equal?

Suppose you read that to increase growth in real GDP and reduce unemployment, the federal government enacted a tax cut. Your employer tells you to expect an extra $80 per month in your paycheque. What will you do with the money? Spend all of it? Save all of it? Spend some and save some? Will your decision depend on whether the tax cut will last just one year or is a permanent change in the tax laws?

How consumers respond to a tax cut clearly affects how much the tax cut will increase aggregate expenditure. In particular, most economists believe that whether a tax cut is *temporary* or *permanent* affects consumers' decisions about how much of a tax cut they will spend. Why is that? Consider an example of a lucky lottery winner, Serena. She tells you she just won a lottery and this year she will have an extra $100 000. She asks you by how much you think she will increase her consumption this year. To answer the question, you need to know where she won the lottery since she divides her time between Canada and the United States and may have won a lottery in either country. If she won a Canadian lottery, she gets $100 000 up front and nothing later. If she won a U.S. lottery, she will be likely getting $100 000 a year for 20 years. Obviously, winning the U.S. lottery will have a bigger effect on her spending. With the Canadian lottery, she gets nothing in the future, so she may choose to save a significant part of her winnings. With the U.S. lottery she does not need to save much as she can count on receiving another $100 000 the next year, and the year after that, and so on.

Winning a lottery or getting a tax cut raises disposable income. A Canadian lottery win is like a temporary tax cut (admittedly, a big tax cut in our example). A U.S. lottery

Continued on next page

win is like a permanent tax cut. People are likely to save less, and spend more, out of a permanent increase in disposable income than out of a temporary increase.

So, we can conclude that policymakers should rely on permanent tax cuts rather than temporary tax cuts to stimulate the economy. But permanent tax cuts will result in continuing budget deficits unless the tax cuts are offset by spending decreases. Indeed, following the second GST tax cut in January 2008 and the Great Recession, the federal budget fell into deficit in 2009. While the deficit was unavoidable given the need to stimulate the economy, it would have been smaller had the GST tax rate not been reduced. Shortly after the tax cut, "the former governor of

the Bank of Canada, David Dodge, called for the federal government to restore at least one percentage point to the GST when the economy begins recovering from its swoon: otherwise, he suggested, the country is headed toward a pit of debt." (*Maclean's*)

The response of households and firms to changes in taxes play an important role in formulating economic policy. In this chapter, we look more closely at how households and firms make their decisions about consumption and investment. Doing so will help us to better predict the effectiveness of different fiscal policy actions.

See related Problem 2.8 at the end of the chapter.

Sources: Phil Demont, "Ottawa's GST cut hiked deficit by as much as $10B[illion]", June 19, 2009, *CBC News*; Charlie Gillis, "GST cuts, harmonization and other blessings in disguise," *Maclean's*, March 30, 2009.

Introduction

The consumption and investment behaviour of households and firms is important in explaining how the economy responds both to shocks—unexpected events that have an effect on an important sector of the economy or on the economy as a whole—and to macroeconomic policy. In this chapter, we look more closely at the determinants of consumption and investment to better understand how shocks and policy affect economic activity.

We start by analyzing consumption and investment choices of households and firms over time and discussing similarities and differences between spending decisions of consumers and firms. In Section 16.2 we analyze determinants of consumption and the phenomenon of consumption smoothing. We discuss two theories of consumption smoothing: the permanent-income hypothesis of Milton Friedman and the life-cycle hypothesis of Franco Modigliani. Both theories imply that consumption depends on the lifetime income and responds more to permanent than to temporary changes in income. We analyze the effect on savings of changes in the real interest rate and of government incentives. We consider liquidity constraints, precautionary savings, and government policy to promote savings. In the last section we consider factors affecting investment. We look at the effect of changes in the marginal product of capital, the real interest rate, and depreciation rate. We also discuss several related theories: Tobin's q, the accelerator model, and investment irreversibility.

The Macroeconomic Implications of Microeconomic Decision Making: Intertemporal Choice

16.1

Learning Objective

Discuss the macroeconomic implications of microeconomic decision making by households and firms.

The key decisions that affect GDP are made at the microeconomic level—that is, by households and firms. For example, the decision of a household in Ontario to save for retirement rather than purchase a car or the decision of Magna to begin building a new factory in Quebec now rather than wait until next year will, by themselves, not have a large effect on GDP. However, the combined decisions of *all* households and firms are critically important for the economy.

Households and Firms Are Forward Looking

Economists assume that households and firms share two important characteristics: First, they act rationally to meet their objectives. Economists assume that the objective of households is to maximize *utility*, or well-being, and that the objective of firms is to maximize profits. Second, they are *forward looking*—that is, they take into account the future when making decisions. The decision of a household to consume or save today is really a decision about when to consume, because saving today makes it possible to consume in the future. Households save to accumulate assets necessary to purchase a house, pay for college or university, or pay for consumption during retirement. To prepare for retirement, most households save part of their current income by purchasing stocks, mutual funds, or other financial assets. What we expect to happen in the future affects our decisions today. For example, suppose you conclude that the value of your house will increase more rapidly than you had previously expected. As a result, you will need to save less out of your current income for retirement and can consume more today. We conclude that expectations about the future affect consumption decisions today.

Expectations about the future are also critical for investment decisions by firms. Capital goods, such as factories, last many years, so a firm must consider the profits to be earned from a factory in the future when deciding whether to invest. If, for example, Magna thought that demand for cars was going to decrease in the future, it would be less likely to build a factory today. So, expectations about future profitability affect the level of investment today.

Factors That Determine Consumption

16.2

Learning Objective

Explain the determinants of personal consumption.

In this section, we discuss the determinants of consumption and explain why consumption is relatively smooth over time.

Consumption and GDP

Figure 16.1 shows that, while household consumption averages 61.5% of GDP for all countries for which the World Bank has data, this percentage varies significantly across countries. Household consumption averages nearly 80% of GDP in low-income countries but about 60% in high- and middle-income countries. Consumption is a particularly high portion of GDP in the United States (72%) and a strikingly small portion of GDP in China (34%). In Canada and in India it is close to the world average.

Some types of consumption are more volatile than others. Figure 16.2 shows the growth rates of expenditure in Canada on durable consumption goods, nondurable consumption goods, and services. The figure shows that expenditure on durable consumption goods, such as cars and furniture, is quite volatile, but expenditure on nondurable goods, such as food, and on services, such as health care, varies much less over time. Expenditure on durable goods almost always decreases significantly during recessions, while expenditure on services decreases little or even increases. For example, during the Great Recession, expenditure on durable goods declined by over 7%, on nondurable goods by 1.5%, and on services by only 0.25%. Why are households more willing to delay purchases of new cars and other durable

Figure 16.1

Consumption Around the World, 2012

For most countries, consumption is the largest component of GDP. The share of consumption in Canadian GDP is close to the world average of 60%. Consumption is a larger fraction of GDP in the United States than in most other high-income countries. Consumption is only a third of China's GDP.

Source: The World Bank, *World Development Indicators*.

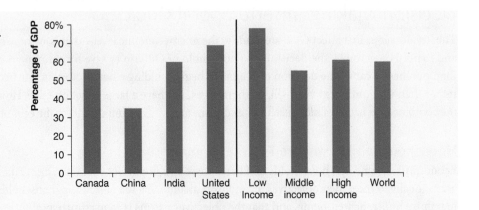

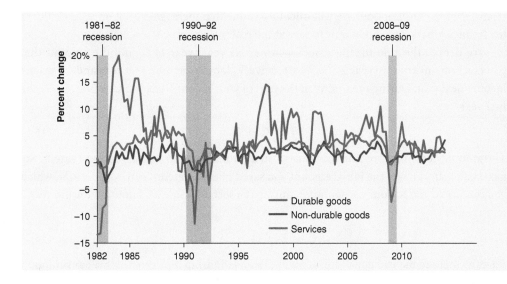

Figure 16.2

Growth Rates in Real Expenditure on Durable Goods, Nondurable Goods, and Services, 1990–2014

Expenditure on durable consumption goods is much more volatile than expenditure on nondurable goods and services. Shaded areas indicate recessions.

Source: Statistics Canada, CANSIM Table 380-0084

goods than health care and other services? To answer this, we need to consider how households determine consumption over time.

Consumption Smoothing

Empirical studies of consumption provide evidence of **consumption smoothing**: a tendency of households to consume an equal amount over time. It is a consequence of the **decreasing marginal utility of consumption**. The marginal utility of consumption is the benefit a person obtains from another unit of consumption. Evidence suggests that, for most people and for most goods and services, marginal utility is decreasing in the amount of consumption: Each additional unit provides less benefit than the previous unit. For example a second meal in a week in a good restaurant generates less benefit than the first; a third pair of jeans generates less benefit than the second pair, etc.

Consumption smoothing is the consequence of decreasing marginal utility of consumption applied to consumption choice over time. Consider the consumption choice of Lucrezia, whose parents set up a university fund for her. For simplicity assume the interest rate is zero. At the beginning of her studies Lucrezia receives $60 000 that she can spend however she wants over the four years she will be in school. How would she choose to spend her funds? She considers spending $30 000 in the first year and $10 000 per year afterwards and asks herself if she could divide the money better. She contemplates moving $1000 from the first year to the second. It is clear that the shift of spending from the first to the second year makes her better off. The loss of utility in the first year, when her planned consumption is high ($30 000) will be less than the gain in the second year, when her planned consumption is low ($10 000). Continuing this reasoning she concludes that it would be optimal for her to distribute her consumption evenly, spending $15 000 every year for the four years of her studies.

If you have already studied utility maximization in your microeconomics course, you know that our example is very simple and the full analysis of consumption choice over time involves real interest rates, time preference, uncertainty, and other issues. The simple example is sufficient for our purpose, which is to indicate that when households allocate consumption over time they tend to choose a roughly constant level of consumption over time.

The Intertemporal Budget Constraint

We now consider a simple model of consumption in which there are just two time periods (the current year and next year, or the working period and retirement) and there is no government, so we can ignore taxes and transfer payments. The only reason you would save is to

Consumption smoothing A tendency of households to consume an equal amount over time.

Decreasing marginal utility of consumption The property that each additional unit of consumption yields less extra satisfaction (utility) than the previous unit of consumption.

finance future consumption. We will initially assume that there is no limit on your ability to use financial markets to borrow or to save at the real interest rate, r.

We denote the amount that you consume this year (year 1) C_1 and the amount that you consume next year (year 2) C_2. You receive Y_1 labour income this year and Y_2 labour income next year. During the first year, the part of your income that you save is S_1. So, in the first year

$$Y_1 = C_1 + S_1. \tag{16.1}$$

The amount that you save this year earns you a return equal to the real interest rate, r. So, next year, you will have the initial amount you saved plus the interest earned, $(1 + r)S_1$, which you can use to add to your consumption during the second year. Consumption during year 2 is, therefore

$$C_2 = Y_2 + (1 + r)S_1. \tag{16.2}$$

We can combine the two equations to obtain the relationship between lifetime consumption and lifetime income:[1]

$$C_1 + \frac{C_2}{1 + r} = Y_1 + \frac{Y_2}{1 + r}. \tag{16.3}$$

Intertemporal budget constraint A budget constraint that applies to consumption and income in more than one time period; it shows how much a household can consume, given lifetime income.

The expression on the left hand side is the *present value* of consumption. We obtain the present value by adding to current consumption the value of future consumption divided by $(1 + r)$. The present value tells you how much money you need today to be able to buy C_1 this year and C_2 next year. To buy C_1 this year you need to have C_1 today. To buy C_2 next year you need $C_2/(1 + r)$ today. This amount, saved in a bank, will earn interest and, in real terms, a year from now you will receive the amount you saved, $C_2/(1 + r)$, multiplied by one plus the real interest rate: $[C_2/(1 + r)] \cdot (1 + r) = C_2$. Similarly, the expression on the right-hand side is the *present value* of income. Our equation says that, over your (two-period) lifetime, the present value of your consumption is equal to the present value of your income. It is called the **intertemporal budget constraint** because it applies to consumption and income in more than one time period. Although in our simple model, "lifetime" is just two years, we could use the same reasoning to expand the model to more periods.[2]

---

[1]Here is how we arrived at this equation: If we substitute the expression for saving in period 1, $S_1 = Y_1 - C_1$, into the expression for consumption in period 2, $C_2 = Y_2 + (1 + r)S_1$, we obtain

$$C_2 = Y_2 + (1 + r)(Y_1 - C_1).$$

Dividing each side of the equation by $(1 + r)$ produces

$$\frac{C_2}{(1 + r)} = \frac{Y_2}{(1 + r)} + (Y_1 - C_1).$$

Rearranging terms to put consumption on the left side and income on the right side yields the equation in the text:

$$C_1 + \frac{C_2}{1 + r} = Y_1 + \frac{Y_2}{1 + r}.$$

This is the household's intertemporal budget constraint.

[2]When we consider many periods, the present value of consumption is $C_1 + \frac{C_2}{(1 + r)} + \frac{C_3}{(1 + r)^2} + \ldots$, and similarly for the present value of income. This is because, to obtain C_3 of consumption two periods from now, you need to save $\frac{C_3}{(1 + r)^2}$ now, and so on.

To understand the intertemporal budget constraint, assume for simplicity that the real interest rate is zero. In that case, the sum of your consumption in both years equals the sum of your income from both years. If you prefer to perfectly smooth consumption—that is, have equal consumption in both years—you will choose $C_1 = C_2$. Suppose you work during the first year, and your income is $Y_1 = \$60\ 000$. You retire during the second year, so income in that year is zero, $Y_2 = 0$. To be able to consume during retirement, you will save \$30 000 during the first year and purchase assets such as stocks or bonds, and then you will sell those assets during the second year to finance your consumption. If, instead, your income were zero during the first year while you were going to school, and \$60 000 in the second year when you worked, you would borrow \$30 000 in financial markets during the first year to finance consumption during that period and then repay the loan in the second period.

Two Theories of Consumption Smoothing

We can use this simple model to show the effect of changes in income on consumption. Nobel Laureate Milton Friedman developed the **permanent-income hypothesis** to explain consumption smoothing.[3] Friedman argued that income can be divided into **permanent income**—what you normally expect to receive each year—and **transitory income**—what you normally expect to receive only once. According to this hypothesis, household consumption depends on permanent income, and households use financial markets to save and borrow to smooth consumption in response to fluctuations in transitory income. You can think of permanent income as average lifetime income and transitory income as a temporary deviation from the lifetime average.

Household income is the sum of permanent income, $Y^{\text{Permanent}}$, and transitory income, $Y^{\text{Transitory}}$:

$$Y = Y^{\text{Permanent}} + Y^{\text{Transitory}}.$$

Milton Friedman argued that the level of consumption depends primarily on the level of permanent income:

$$C = aY^{\text{Permanent}},$$

where a is a constant and represents the fraction of permanent income that households consume. Friedman argued that if someone experienced an unexpected windfall, such as winning a Canadian lottery or receiving a temporary tax cut, the person would view most of that change in income as transitory. As a result, the person would save most of it and increase consumption only a little this year. Similarly, if someone experienced an unexpected job loss, the person's income would fall temporarily, meaning that transitory income would be negative. In this case, the person would borrow to keep consumption at the typical level. In contrast, if the person received a permanent increase in income due to unexpectedly obtaining a better job, her consumption would increase significantly. Similarly, if she accepted a job at a lower salary, the person's permanent income would fall, and her consumption would fall a lot. We can conclude that *consumption responds more to changes in permanent income than to changes in transitory income.*

An alternative explanation of consumption smoothing was developed by another Nobel Laureate, Franco Modigliani. He developed the **life-cycle hypothesis**, according to which households borrow and save to transfer funds from high-income periods, such as their working years, to low-income periods, such as their retirement years or periods of unemployment. For example, to maintain consumption during retirement, you have to save during your working years. When you retire and no longer receive a salary, you can use the income from your stocks, bonds, and other assets or sell your assets to finance consumption. You are

Permanent-income hypothesis The hypothesis that household consumption depends on permanent income and that households use financial markets to save and borrow to smooth consumption in response to fluctuations in transitory income.

Permanent income Income that households normally expect to receive each year.

Transitory income Income that households do not expect to receive each year.

Life-cycle hypothesis The theory that households use financial markets to borrow and save to transfer funds from high-income periods, such as working years, to low-income periods, such as retirement years or periods of unemployment.

---

[3]Milton Friedman, *A Theory of the Consumption Function*, Princeton, NJ: Princeton University Press, 1957.

Figure 16.3

Consumption, Income, and Saving over the Life Cycle

If you plan to keep consumption constant over your life cycle, you will borrow when you are young and your income is low, accumulate assets during peak earning years, and then sell off assets during retirement, when your income is low.

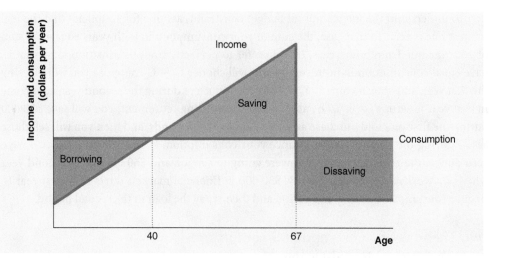

saving during the part of your life cycle when your income is high in order to transfer funds to the part of your life cycle when your income is low. In other words, *the goal of saving is to provide for future consumption.*

Figure 16.3 provides an example of the life-cycle hypothesis that shows how you can smooth your consumption so that it is constant each year. Initially, your income is low, so you borrow to finance consumption. As income rises, you borrow less. After age 40, your income is greater than consumption, so you pay off the debts acquired during earlier years and begin to save for retirement. After retirement at age 67, your income falls below consumption, so you sell off assets accumulated during your working years to finance consumption.

If you completely smooth consumption so that it is the same during each year of your life, then your consumption equals the sum of your initial wealth and your lifetime income divided by the number of years you expect to live (assuming again that the real interest is zero). For example, if you earn Y each year and expect to work for B years, your lifetime income is BY. If you expect to live for N years, then your consumption is

$$C = \frac{\text{Wealth} + BY}{N}.$$

This expression is equivalent to

$$C = \left(\frac{1}{N}\right)\text{Wealth} + \left(\frac{B}{N}\right)Y, \tag{16.4}$$

where: $1/N$ is the amount by which spending increases when wealth increases by \$1. $1/N$ is the *marginal propensity to consume out of wealth*. B/N is the amount by which spending increases if income increases by \$1 every year (i.e., permanently), i.e., B/N is the familiar marginal propensity to consume, *MPC* (although it should be called more precisely the marginal propensity to consume out of permanent income).

If an increase in income is transitory, then consumption will increase much less than in the case of a permanent increase. People use wealth to finance consumption, and if you expect to live 50 more years, the *marginal propensity to consume out of wealth* equals $1 \div 50 = 0.02$, so you will consume \$2 per year for each additional \$100 in wealth.

Do households really smooth consumption? Our discussion indicates that households should smooth consumption if they are maximizing utility. And many economists have found strong evidence in favour of consumption smoothing for aggregate consumption.[4] We can conclude that consumption smoothing is a powerful force that affects a large portion of consumer expenditure.

Figure 16.2 on page 497 suggests that households more completely smooth expenditure on services and nondurable goods than on durable goods. Durable goods, such as cars, last many years. Households have significant flexibility about when to replace them. If you experience an unexpected decrease in income due to a job loss during a recession, you are likely to continue driving your current car rather than buy a new one. So, expenditures on durable goods fall during a recession, as households respond to temporarily low income by delaying these purchases. In contrast, nondurable goods, such as food and clothing, are consumed or wear out and must be purchased more frequently. Services, such as health care, are consumed the moment they are purchased, so people have to purchase a service when they need it. Therefore, expenditure on nondurable goods and on services tends not to decrease as much during recessions. For these reasons, expenditure on durable goods is more volatile than expenditure on nondurable goods and on services.

Permanent versus Transitory Changes in Income

The permanent-income hypothesis and the life-cycle hypothesis imply that households will smooth consumption over time. As a result, permanent changes in income will have much larger effects on consumption than will transitory or one-time changes in income. We can illustrate this point using the life-cycle hypothesis. Suppose that you are currently 20 years old, your wealth is zero, you will work for 40 years at a constant salary of $50 000, and you expect to live to age 70. The real interest rate is zero. Your lifetime income is $50 000 · 40 years = $2 000 000, so your consumption is

$$C = \left(\frac{1}{50}\right)0 + \left(\frac{40}{50}\right)\$50\ 000 = \frac{\$2\ 000\ 000}{50} = \$40\ 000.$$

Therefore, each year you will consume $40 000 and save $10 000. Now suppose that you experience a transitory increase in your income to $60 000 during your first year of work. Your lifetime income is now ($50 000 · 39 years) + ($60 000 · 1 year) = $2.01 million, and you still expect to live to age 70, so

$$C = 0 + \frac{\$2\ 010\ 000}{50} = \$40\ 200.$$

If you completely smooth consumption, then you consume only $200 per year out of the $10 000 transitory income. Your marginal propensity to consume out of transitory income is

$$MPC^{\text{Transitory}} = \frac{\Delta C}{\Delta Y} = \frac{\$200}{\$10\ 000} = 0.02.$$

The *MPC* out of transitory changes in income is low because you smooth the $10 000 increase in income over the 50 additional years you expect to live.

The situation is quite different if your salary permanently increases to $60 000 per year, starting with your first year of work. In this case, your lifetime income is now $60 000 · 40 years = $2.4 million, so

$$C = 0 + \frac{\$2\ 400\ 000}{50} = \$48\ 000.$$

[4]A classic article is Robert E. Hall, "Intertemporal Substitution in Consumption," *Journal of Political Economy* 96, no. 2 (1988): 339–357.

Your consumption increases by $8000 per year when the change in income is permanent. As a result, the *MPC* is

$$MPC^{\text{Permanent}} = \frac{\Delta C}{\Delta Y} = \frac{\$8\,000}{\$10\,000} = 0.80.$$

The *MPC* is much larger for permanent changes in income. As we will see in the next section, policymakers who want to use changes in taxes to increase consumption should take into account that the *MPC* for permanent income changes is higher than the *MPC* for transitory income changes.

Consumption and the Real Interest Rate

Households use financial markets to smooth consumption by borrowing and saving, and the real interest rate plays an important role in these decisions. A change in the real interest rate has both a *substitution effect* and an *income effect*. We explain them in turn, using a simple two-period model.

The real interest rate is the relative price at which an individual trades off current consumption for future consumption. We need to do all calculations in real terms, so we will analyze an example in terms of beer. Assume beer costs $1 per bottle, the inflation rate is 2%, and the nominal interest rate is 6%. You save $100 and deposit it in a bank. To do this, you need to reduce your consumption by 100 beers. The next year you receive $106 from the bank (since the nominal interest rate is 6%). Beer now costs $1.02 (since the inflation rate is 2%). For $106 you can buy approximately 104 beers. This means that you saved 100 beers and a year later you got 104 beers, i.e., the real interest rate was 4%. When the real interest rate is 4%, for 100 beers today you get 104 beers in a year. This means that the relative price of beer today in terms of beer in one year is 1.04: You have to give up 1.04 beers next year to get one beer today. You can think of the relative price the same way as you think of a nominal price: If the price of beer is $1.04, you need to give up 1.04 dollars to get one beer. In the relative price you replace dollars with bottles of beer received in a year.

If the real interest rate is 8%, then for 100 beers today you will receive 108 beers in a year, which means that the relative price of beer today in terms of beer in one year is 1.08. A higher real interest rate increases the price of today's beer in terms of next year's beer: Today's beer becomes more expensive, which is equivalent to next year's beer becoming cheaper. Households respond to the increase in the relative price by reducing current consumption and increasing future consumption. This mechanism is called *the substitution effect*.

There is also an *income effect* associated with a change in the real interest rate. The income effect looks at the change in savings and consumption as a higher interest rate affects the interest earnings of savers and borrowers. Consider, for example two friends, Edmund and Daniel. There are two periods; they work in the first and are retired in the second. Edmund and Daniel just went to their financial adviser to make plans for retirement. They both learned they will need the equivalent of 1 000 000 bottles of green tea to retire. Edmund has assets worth 500 000 bottles of tea, and Daniel has debt equivalent to 500 000 bottles of tea. The real interest rate is zero. So Edmund plans to save the equivalent of 500 000 bottles from the income he will earn during his working period while Daniel plans to save the equivalent of 1 500 000 bottles.

While they are talking to the adviser, however, the real interest rate increases to 100% between now and when they retire. What is the effect of the increase in the real interest rate on their saving and consumption plans? Edmund's assets will now grow to the equivalent of 1 000 000 bottles by the time he retires. This means he does not have to save any more. For Edmund, who is a saver, this means higher consumption. Daniel, on the other hand, must now save more. His debt will grow to the equivalent of 1 000 000 bottles by the time he retires, so he needs to save 2 000 000 bottles to pay off his debt and have funds for retirement.

Table 16.1   The Effect of the Real Interest Rate on Consumption

	Lender	Borrower
Substitution effect	Negative	Negative
Income effect	Positive	Negative
Net effect	Ambiguous	Negative

For Daniel, who was a borrower, this means a lower consumption. We conclude that the income effect of a higher interest rate increases consumption of savers and reduces consumption of borrowers.

Table 16.1 summarizes the effect of an increase in the real interest rate on consumption. The substitution effect is negative for all households because an increase in the real interest rate leads to a decrease in current consumption. The income effect is positive for lenders and negative for borrowers. An increase in the real interest rate will therefore definitely decrease current consumption for households that are borrowers because both the income and substitution effects are negative. The effect on lenders is ambiguous because the income and substitution effects move in opposite directions.

Whether an increase in the real interest rate increases or decreases current consumption depends partly on whether there are more net borrowers or more net lenders in the economy, and we cannot answer this question with theory alone. Empirical evidence suggests that the substitution effect dominates and an increase in the real interest rates reduces consumption and increases savings. We will therefore assume that an increase in the real interest rate will increase saving and decrease current consumption for both lenders and borrowers.

Liquidity Constraints

So far, we assumed that households can borrow without problems if they prefer to consume more than their income. But, as any student knows, the assumption of unlimited access to credit is not accurate. In reality, many households, in particular those of young people who have not yet worked for a long time, find it difficult to obtain credit. Even if the bank knows that, in the future, income will be sufficient to pay off the loan, it is not likely to extend credit. The reason is the lack of credit history, as well as a lack of collateral (an asset that the bank can take over in case of loan default). We call the inability to borrow to achieve the desired level of consumption **liquidity constraints**.

Liquidity constraints are something you are painfully aware of (even if you did not know the term economists use). The term liquidity constraints comes from the fact that people often have asset that will provide income in the future, but these assets are not liquid: They cannot be used for current consumption. For a student, this asset is human capital: University graduates earn more than high school graduates. So your degree will allow you to have high income in the future. But it is not liquid: You cannot sell it nor used it as collateral. A bank that accepts a house as collateral knows it can sell it when the loan is non-performing. It would not be able to sell your human capital since the bank knows it will not be able to force you to work.

In the presence of liquidity constraints, temporary increases in income may have big effects on consumption. Assume, for example, that you expect to study for a year, earn $50 000 for 40 years and live in retirement for another 10 years. Your income while studying is $20 000 and the real interest rate and inflation are both zero. So your lifetime income is $20 000 + 40 · $50 000 = $2 020 000. You expect to live 51 years (one as a student, 40 working and 10 retired). So you would like to consume $2 020 000/51 = $39 608 a year. This will provide you with a constant stream of consumption. But, because of liquidity constraints, you are unable

Liquidity constraints
The inability to borrow to achieve the desired level of consumption.

to borrow. So, during your studies, you can consume only the $20 000 you earn. When you graduate, your spending will be $40 000 = $2 000 000/50 every year afterward.

Now assume that this year you win $10 000 in a lottery. How will you spend it? As you planned to consume $20 000 this year and $40 000 every subsequent year, you will spend the extra funds this year and consume $30 000 when you are studying and $40 000 afterward. The increase in your funds is temporary, but your marginal propensity to consume is 1. On the other hand if you win the $10 000 when you start working, to smooth consumption you will be spending an extra $200 a year when you graduate and your marginal propensity to consume will be 0.02. The difference is that during your studies you are liquidity constrained and would like to consume more but cannot borrow. When you are working you do not have liquidity constraints, and you spread the temporary increase in income over your lifetime.

How Policy Affects Consumption

Government policy affects consumption by altering disposable income today and in the future. Recall that *disposable income* is total income plus transfer payments minus taxes:

$$Y^D = Y + TR - T.$$

To see how government policy can affect consumption, consider another example in which you are 20 years old, your wealth is 0, you plan to work for 40 years earning $50 000 per year, and expect to live until age 70. If you pay $10 000 per year in taxes and receive no transfer payments, your disposable income is just $40 000 per year, and your lifetime disposable income is $1 600 000. Therefore, your consumption is

$$C = \left(\frac{1}{N}\right)\text{Wealth} + \left(\frac{B}{N}\right)Y^D = \left(\frac{1}{N}\right)0 + \left(\frac{40}{50}\right)\$40\,000 = \frac{\$1\,600\,000}{50} = \$32\,000.$$

If your disposable income is $40 000 per year and you consume $32 000 per year, then you are saving $8000 per year. When taxes are $0 you consume $40 000 and save $10 000 per year. An increase in taxes causes both consumption and saving to decrease. A permanent increase in taxes from $0 to $10 000 reduced consumption by $8000. In the language of the permanent-income hypothesis, the tax increase represents a decrease in permanent income, so consumption responds significantly. In Solved Problem 16.1, we ask you to determine the effect of a temporary tax cut. Given what you already know about the permanent-income hypothesis, you should be able to predict that the effect of temporary tax cuts is relatively modest.

Summary We can now summarize the effect of various changes on consumption:

- *a one-time, temporary increase in disposable income* increases consumption a little because households smooth the one-time increase in income over their lifetimes.
- *a permanent increase in disposable income* increases consumption a lot (more than in the case of a temporary increase) because households experience a large increase in lifetime income.
- *an increase in the real interest rate* has both substitution and income effects on consumption. The substitution effect lowers consumption since current consumption becomes relatively more expensive. The income effect increases the consumption of savers and lowers the consumption of borrowers.
- *an increase in wealth* raises consumption. Households will consume an equal part of their wealth during each time period.
- *liquidity constraints* raise the marginal propensity to consume.

Solved Problem 16.1

Effects of a Temporary Tax Cut on Consumption

In order to stimulate the economy the government temporarily reduces taxes. Would a temporary tax cut have a large effect on consumption? We can gain some insight by continuing with our previous example in which you are 20 years old, you plan to work for 40 years at an after-tax salary of $40 000, and you expect to live to age 70. Assume that your initial wealth is zero. Now suppose the government gives you a one-time tax cut of $1000 during your first year of work. Predict the effect of the tax rebate on your consumption.

Solving the Problem

Step 1 **Review the chapter material.** The problem asks you to use the theory of consumption to determine the effect of a one-time tax rebate on consumption, so you may want to review the section "Factors That Determine Consumption," which begins on page 496.

Step 2 **Determine the effect on your lifetime disposable income**. Your lifetime disposable income is now

$$\$40\ 000 \cdot 39\ \text{years} + \$41\ 000 \cdot 1\ \text{year} = \$1\ 601\ 000.$$

Step 3 **Show the effect of the tax cut if you smooth consumption.** If you smooth consumption completely, then you have the following:

$$C = \left(\frac{1}{N}\right)\text{Wealth} + \left(\frac{B}{N}\right)Y^D = \frac{\$1\ 601\ 000}{50} = \$32\ 020.$$

Step 4 **Compare your new level of consumption to your initial level of consumption.** Before the one-time tax rebate, you consumed $32 000 and saved $8000 during the first year. Now you consume $32 020 and save $8980 during the first year because you smooth the $1000 tax rebate over the entire 50 more years that you expect to live. In subsequent years you continue to consume $32 020 and save only $7980. A one-time tax rebate is a transitory increase in disposable income. Given our discussion of the permanent-income hypothesis and consumption smoothing, it should come as no surprise that a one-time tax rebate has a small effect on consumption.

See related Problems 2.6 and 2.9 at the end of the chapter.

Precautionary Saving

So far, we have assumed that households know their future disposable income with certainty. In fact, of course, households do not know the future and may adjust consumption and saving to protect themselves from unexpected events. **Precautionary saving** is the extra saving by households to protect themselves from unexpected decreases in future income due to job loss, illness, or disability. In this case, saving acts as insurance against unexpected declines in income. For example, if the economy enters a recession and households believe that the probability of a job loss has increased, they are likely to increase precautionary saving and reduce consumption.

One way to think of precautionary saving is to view households as having a desired level of wealth. When wealth is above the desired level, households draw down their assets to finance consumption. In contrast, if wealth is below the desired level, households save to

Precautionary saving
Extra saving by households to protect themselves from unexpected decreases in future income due to job loss, illness, or disability.

reach their desired level of wealth. For example, suppose that James makes $1000 per month and wants to have six months' worth of income, i.e., $6000, saved and invested in the stock market. If stock prices unexpectedly rise and his stock market wealth becomes equal to seven months' of disposable income, James will increase spending until his wealth decreases to six months' of disposable income. If an unexpected event decreases his wealth, then James is likely to decrease consumption to rebuild his wealth.

The theory of precautionary savings emphasizes the importance of future events in determining the level of consumption and saving. An increase in uncertainty about the future will increase the desired level of wealth and lead to lower consumption until households have accumulated sufficient funds. A decrease in uncertainty about the future will reduce the desired level of wealth and will allow households to increase spending. Since uncertainty increases in recessions and falls in expansions (for example, the uncertainty about keeping or losing a job), precautionary savings reduce consumption in recessions and raise it in expansions, exacerbating economic fluctuations.

Making the Connection

Record Household Debt in Canada

Following the Great Recession the Canadian economy improved faster than the U.S. economy. In particular, Canadian households were much less adversely affected by the recession than U.S. households. With central banks maintaining the policy of low interest rates and households feeling optimistic about the future, Canadian households started taking on large debts. This behaviour of Canadian consumers differed from that of consumers elsewhere. While the Great Recession led to more cautious spending in many countries, Canadian consumers continued to borrow and spend, despite an economy that was not particularly strong. The expansion of consumption spending was, in part, driven by house prices. The figure below shows house prices in Canada since 1981. Following the previous two recessions, in 1981–82 and 1989–91, house prices stabilized for several years. During the Great Recession house prices fell a little but quickly resumed their upward trend.

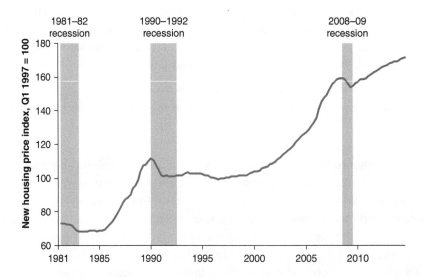

As you recall from our discussion of the Great Recession in Chapter 1, the end of the U.S. boom in house prices was the main reason for the recession. As house prices increase, households feel wealthier and, in line with the life-cycle and permanent-income hypotheses, raise their spending. For households that do not move, the gains in the value of the house are paper, unrealized gains. To raise consumption, they need to borrow. The boom in consumption, caused in part by the increase in the price of housing, led to record debt.

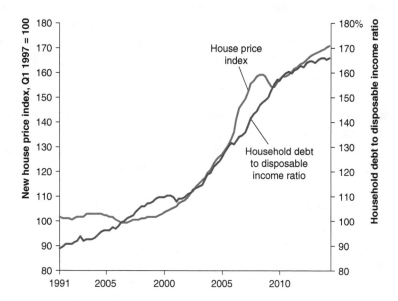

Household debt in Canada, which exceeded 165% of household disposable income in 2013, became a serious concern of macroeconomic policy. To slow down the housing boom, the federal government tightened mortgage rules several times, with limited effect. The governor of the Bank of Canada at the time, Mark Carney, had made housing prices a concern for monetary policy, repeatedly warning against rising levels of household debt. At the time of writing, house prices in Canada continued to rise and, according to *the Economist*, houses in Canada were among the most overvalued in advanced economies. It is not clear how the circle of rising house prices, leading to higher consumption and, in turn, leading to higher house prices will end.

Sources: Gregg Quinn, "Canadians turns deaf ear to Carney's warnings as household debt hits fresh record at 165%," *Bloomberg News*, March 15, 2013; and "Moody Mark, Sunny Stephen," *The Economist*, September 28, 2013; Statistics Canada, CANSIM Tables 327-0046 and 378-0123.

Tax Incentives and Saving

When households save, they are interested in the *after-tax real interest rate*. For any given real interest rate, taxes on income earned from saving reduce the after-tax real interest rate and so reduce the incentive to save.

Two important programs reduce taxes on saving, thereby increasing the after-tax real interest rate. First, Registered Retirement Saving Plans (RRSPs) defer taxes to retirement. Contributions to RRSPs are deducted from taxable income, and earnings in RRSP plans are sheltered from tax. Income taxes are paid when the funds are withdrawn at retirement. Tax-free Savings Accounts (TFSAs) allow earnings to accumulate tax-free, but funds contributed to the accounts are after-tax funds. Both types of accounts increase the after-tax real interest rate on savings.

Glenn Hubbard of Columbia University and Jonathan Skinner of Dartmouth College have surveyed studies of the corresponding U.S. plans, called IRAs and 401(k).[5] They note

---

[5]Glenn Hubbard and Jonathan Skinner, "Assessing the Effectiveness of Saving Incentives," *Journal of Economic Perspectives* 10, no. 4 (1996): 73–90.

that part of the problem with assessing the effectiveness of these plans in increasing saving is determining whether they result in net new saving or just cause households to switch savings from financial assets without tax incentives, such as savings accounts in banks, to the tax-promoted accounts. In addition, if the tax incentives are financed through government budget deficits, then government saving decreases by $1 for every $1 of tax reduction on household saving. After weighing the evidence, Hubbard and Skinner conclude that the plans do increase national saving. They argue that in the long run, IRAs increase the private capital stock by $5 for each $1 reduction in government tax revenue, and 401(k) plans increase the private capital stock by $17 for each $1 reduction in government tax revenue. These effects of tax incentives are large and suggest that government programs designed to increase saving can lead to a significant increase in the capital stock. Growth models suggest that an increase in the capital stock will increase labour productivity and the standard of living.

Factors That Determine Private Investment

16.3

Learning Objective

Explain the determinants of private investment.

We now turn to factors that determine investment. In this section, we focus on the determinants of investment in new plant and equipment.

Figure 16.4 shows gross capital formation (a measure of investment) as a percentage of GDP. It varies between 20% of GDP for high-income countries and 30% for middle-income countries. Low- and middle-income countries invest a larger share of GDP than high-income countries. In Canada, investment as a share of GDP was close to world average. China and India invest a lot. Comparing Figure 16.4 with Figure 16.1, you can see the striking contrast between the world's two largest economies. In the United States, consumption is almost five times larger than investment: Consumption share of GDP is 69% and investment share is 19%. In China, consumption is much smaller than investment: Consumption share of GDP is 35% and investment share is 49%.

Compared with consumption, investment is much more volatile and it therefore may contribute significantly to the business cycle. Figure 16.5 shows the rate of growth of investment and consumption in Canada between 1982 and 2014. The standard deviation of the rate of growth of consumption over 1982–2013 was 1.75% while the standard deviation of investment was 7.3%, i.e., it was over four times higher. As investment was, on the average, a third of consumption but four times more volatile; investment actually contributed more volatility than consumption to business cycle in Canada over this period.

The Investment Decisions of Firms

To analyze the investment decisions of firms we begin by analyzing the amount of capital that firms would like to have: the desired capital stock. Then we look at how firms adjust their capital over time toward the desired level.

Figure 16.4

Gross Capital Formation around the World, 2013

Low- and middle-income countries invest a larger share of GDP than high-income countries. In Canada, the share of investment in GDP is close to the world average of around 20%. In China, investment as a share of GDP is more than double world average. (Data for United States, Low and High Income countries and World, 2012.)

Source: The World Bank, *World Development Indicators*.

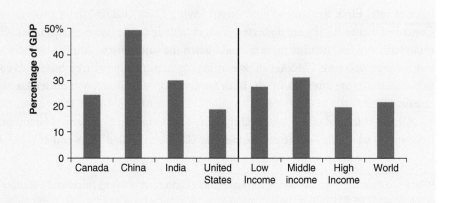

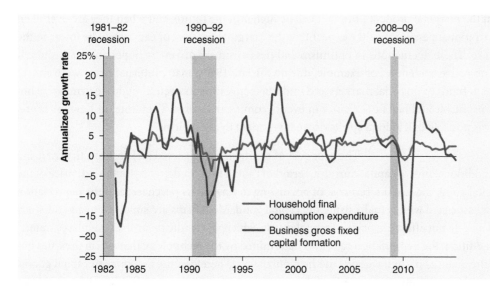

Figure 16.5

Growth Rates for Real Personal Consumption and Real Gross Private Investment, 1982–2014

The growth rate of gross private investment is much more volatile than the growth rate of personal consumption. Investment has always decreased significantly during recessions.

Source: Statistics Canada, CANSIM Table 380-0084.

The **desired capital stock** is the level of the capital stock that maximizes a firm's profits. Firms determine their desired capital stock by comparing the benefits and costs of purchasing additional capital goods. The benefit is the profit firms earn from selling the goods and services that the additional capital goods produce. There are three types of costs associated with purchasing capital: (1) the price of capital goods, (2) the cost of depreciation, and (3) the interest payments to finance the purchase of capital goods. In addition, tax policy affects both after-tax profits through the corporate income tax and the cost of capital. For instance, the tax system allows firms to deduct interest payments and the depreciation of capital goods from their profits before paying taxes, which helps reduce the cost of capital and encourage greater investment.

We now discuss the firm's purchasing decisions in greater detail so that we can analyze the determinants of the desired capital stock.

The Marginal Product of Capital The *marginal product of capital (MPK)* is the extra output a firm receives from adding one more unit of capital, holding all other inputs and efficiency constant. The marginal product of capital decreases as the capital stock increases due to the principle of diminishing marginal returns. This principle states that, holding everything else constant, as firms employ additional capital, the extra output from each additional unit of capital decreases. This means that the line showing the marginal product of capital as a function of the capital stock is downward sloping.

What matters to a firm is not the expected marginal product in any one year but the expected marginal product over the entire life of the capital goods, which we will denote MPK^e. If Magna is considering building another assembly plant in Canada that will last 30 years, it must consider costs and benefits not only this year but also for the next 29 years. For example, Magna must consider what will happen to the demand for automobiles if the world price of crude oil changes. It must also try to anticipate the effects of government policies, such as those to limit carbon emissions, that might raise its production costs. Because Magna is interested in its after-tax profit, it also has to anticipate the taxes that it will have to pay in the future.

We have emphasized how firms respond rationally to changes in their expectations of future profits. Taking a different approach, John Maynard Keynes argued in *The General Theory of Employment, Interest, and Money* that firms are sometimes overtaken by periods of irrational pessimism or irrational optimism known as **animal spirits** that affect their investment behaviour. We can think of animal spirits as causing sudden changes in the expected marginal product of capital. When firms are overtaken by irrational optimism, they expect

Desired capital stock The level of the capital stock that maximizes a firm's profits.

Animal spirits Periods of irrational pessimism and optimism that affect the investment behaviour of firms.

that the marginal product of capital will be higher in the future, and when they are overtaken by irrational pessimism, they expect that the marginal product of capital will be lower in the future. These fluctuations in optimism and pessimism are driven by hopes and fears and not by objective evidence. For example, during the late 1990s, many internet firms were able to obtain funds in financial markets and undertake investments even though the firms were not yet profitable and had little chance of ever becoming profitable. Therefore, in Keynes's sense, it was possible that animal spirits drove investment by these firms.

User cost of capital The expected real cost to a firm of using an additional unit of capital during a period of time.

The User Cost of Capital The **user cost of capital** is the expected real cost to a firm of using an additional unit of capital during a period of time. This cost depends on the real price of the capital good, the real interest cost of borrowing to finance its purchase, and the depreciation cost associated with actually using the capital good. Most firms are small relative to the market and do not affect the price of capital goods, which we denote p_k, or the real interest rate, r. In addition, the depreciation rate, d, is determined by the technology that a firm uses and not by the quantity of capital goods the firm purchases. Therefore, the real price of capital goods, the real interest rate, and the rate of depreciation are constants that a firm can take as given.

The interest cost to a firm equals rp_k and represents the cost of borrowing funds to purchase a capital good. Even if a firm does not borrow to purchase the capital good, it still incurs this cost because the firm could have loaned the funds to other firms or households and received interest income. So, in this case the interest cost is the opportunity cost of the interest that has not been earned. The depreciation cost equals dp_k and represents the cost of capital wearing out or becoming obsolete. The user cost of capital is the sum of these two costs:

$$\text{user cost of capital} = rp_k + dp_k = (r + d)p_k. \tag{16.5}$$

Corporate Taxes After-tax profits, rather than before-tax profits, affect a firm's decision making. For example, if the corporate income tax rate is 30%, a firm retains 70% of its before-tax profits. We can think of corporate taxes as reducing the expected marginal product of capital. If the corporate income tax rate is t, then the firm gets to keep $(1 - t)$ of the output from each unit of capital. If $t = 0.30$, the firm gets to keep $(1 - 0.30) = 0.70$ of output. When accounting for taxes, the expected marginal product of capital is $(1 - t)MPK^e$.

The Desired Capital Stock A firm maximizes profits when the expected marginal product of capital equals the user cost of capital. The expected marginal product of capital is $(1 - t)MPK_e$; the user cost of capital is $(r + d)p_k$. So the equation for the desired capital stock becomes

$$(1 - t)MPK^e = (r + d)p_k. \tag{16.6}$$

Rearranging terms, this expression becomes

$$MPK^e = \frac{(r + d)p_k}{(1 - t)}, \tag{16.7}$$

Tax-adjusted user cost of capital (*uc*) The after-tax expected real cost to a firm of purchasing and using an additional unit of capital during a period of time.

where the term on the right-hand side is the **tax-adjusted user cost of capital**, which is the after-tax expected real cost to a firm of purchasing and using an additional unit of capital during a period of time:

$$uc = \frac{(r + d)p_k}{(1 - t)},$$

The desired capital stock (K^*) is the level of the capital stock that maximizes profits. Figure 16.6 shows that the desired capital stock for an individual firm occurs at the

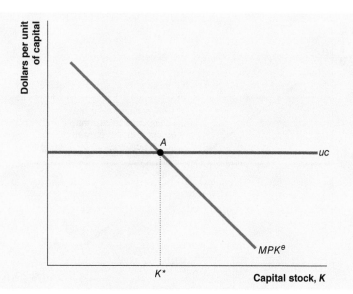

Figure 16.6

The Desired Capital Stock

The desired capital stock for an individual firm occurs at point A where the tax-adjusted user cost of capital (uc) equals the expected marginal product of capital (MPK^e). The expected marginal product of capital curve slopes downward due to diminishing marginal returns.

intersection of the expected marginal product of capital curve and the tax-adjusted user cost of capital curve, uc. The user cost of capital curve is a horizontal line because it is independent of the level of the capital stock. The expected marginal product of capital curve slopes downward due to diminishing marginal returns.

Figure 16.7 shows the effect of a decrease in the expected marginal product of capital. If a firm expects that the demand for its product will decrease in the future, the expected marginal product of capital curve will shift to the left, and the desired capital stock will decrease from K_1^* to K_2^*.

Changes in the tax-adjusted user cost of capital also cause the desired capital stock to change. Figure 16.8 on page 512 shows that an increase in the real interest rate increases the (tax-adjusted) user cost of capital, so the user cost of capital curve shifts up. As a result, the desired capital stock decreases. An increase in the depreciation rate, the real price of capital or in the corporate tax rate would also increase the (tax-adjusted) user cost of capital and reduce the desired capital stock.

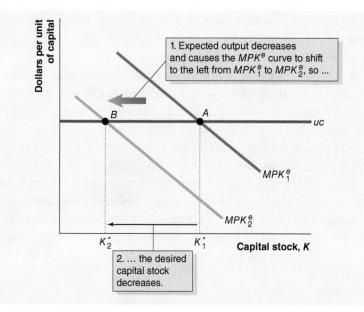

Figure 16.7

A Decrease in the Expected Marginal Product of Capital and the Desired Capital Stock

If a firm expects consumer demand for its product to decrease in the future, the MPK^e curve will shift to the left and the desired capital stock decreases from K_1^* to K_2^*.

Figure 16.8

An Increase in the User Cost of Capital and the Desired Capital Stock

An increase in the real interest rate increases the tax-adjusted user cost of capital, so the user cost of capital curve shifts up from uc_1 to uc_2, and the desired capital stock decreases from K_1^* to K_2^*. An increase in the user cost of capital due to an increase in the price of capital, the depreciation rate, or an increase in the corporate tax rate would have the same effect on the desired capital stock.

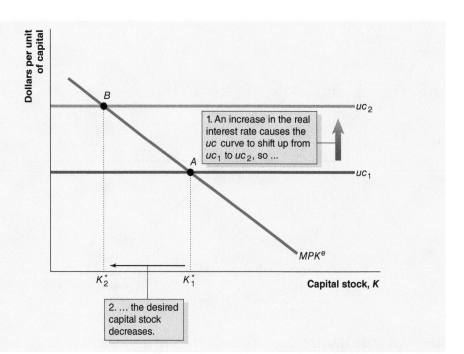

1. An increase in the real interest rate causes the uc curve to shift up from uc_1 to uc_2, so ...

2. ... the desired capital stock decreases.

Making the Connection

From Transitory Tax Cuts to Tax Reform

In late 1990s many governments and business people were concerned about the ability of computers to handle the change of date from 1999 to 2000. When computer systems were first designed in 1960s and 1970s, programmers did not expect the systems to be still in use in 1999. To save memory, which was expensive at the time, they did not include the ability to handle dates over 1999. The potential large-scale failure of computer systems around the world (dubbed the Y2K problem) led to a big effort to update software and hardware. To induce the replacement of old computers, the allowable depreciation of computers bought in 1999 to replace older computers was increased from 33% to 100%. Our discussion suggests that by decreasing the tax-adjusted user cost of capital, this policy increased the desired capital stock. Indeed, many firms replaced their hardware, and the Y2K problem did not lead to large-scale computer failures.

This change in the tax code is an example of a temporary tax change. In order to stimulate an activity, or an industry, special laws are introduced on a temporary basis. Such laws have effects also beyond the particular industry, as increased investment raises incomes of people working in the industry and spill over to other industries.

A drawback of temporary tax cuts is that they increase the complexity of the tax code and make firms uncertain about future tax policy. The problem is particularly large in the United States, where the tax system is very complex. Many economists and business leaders believe that the level of uncertainty and complexity associated with all these temporary provisions discourages firms from hiring and investing. In fact, Jeffrey Owens, who heads the tax division for the Organisation for Economic Co-operation and Development, points out that very few countries have temporary tax provisions similar to those that the United States has enacted or extended.

In recent years the Canadian government adopted a long-term approach of reducing corporate income tax rates. The reductions began in 2008 and reduced the federal general, manufacturing, and production tax rates from 22.2% in 2007 to 15% in 2013.

Sources: "Y2K fears will help boost economy, says bank", *CBC News*, December 11, 1998; John McKinnon, Gary Fields, and Laura Saunders, "Transitory Tax Code Puts Nation in a Lasting Bind," *Wall Street Journal*, December 15, 2010; Daniel Trotta and Kristina Cooke, "Businesses Say Demand, Not Tax Cuts, Drives Growth," www.cnbc.com, December 16, 2010; and "Canadian business tax rate among world's lowest", *CBC News*, December 3, 2012.

From the Desired Capital Stock to Investment

Adjusting its capital stock requires a firm to purchase new capital or sell unwanted capital and to also spend time determining which capital goods to purchase or sell. Firms adjust their capital stock slowly in response to shocks to protect themselves from the negative consequences of building a factory that is too big or building too many factories or too many assembly lines. Also, investment projects take time: Once a company makes a decision to build a new factory, it takes several years to obtain the required permits and finish construction.

Uncertainty about future events is another reason for the slow adjustment of capital stock toward the desired level. Unexpected events that affect the desired capital stock occur frequently. Some events—such as the discovery of a new technology—indicate that future profits will increase, thereby increasing the desired capital stock. Other events—such as a large tax increase—indicate that future profits will decrease, thereby decreasing the desired capital stock. Because of this uncertainty, firms slowly adjust the capital stock as they acquire new information about changes in technology, taxes, and other relevant factors. We can capture the behaviour of firms by assuming that when there is a gap between the desired and actual capital stock, $(K^* - K_{t-1})$, the firm eliminates a constant fraction, z, of that gap each period, through investment:

$$I_t = z(K^* - K_{t-1}) + dK_{t-1}, \tag{16.8}$$

where $0 < z < 1$. If z is 0.10, then firms eliminate 10% of the gap between the actual and the desired capital stock each year; if z is 0.20, then firms eliminate 20% of the gap, and so on. This equation tells us that firms set gross investment, or investment before taking into account depreciation, equal to a level high enough to replace the depreciated capital stock, dK_{t-1}, plus a constant fraction of the gap between the desired capital stock next year and this year's capital stock. Any shock that causes the desired capital stock to increase also causes gross investment to increase. For example, an increase in expected profits in the future will increase the desired capital stock. As a result, firms will increase investment as they slowly try to accumulate more capital goods or increase factory size.

Solved Problem 16.2

Depreciation, Taxes, and Investment Spending

In 1999, special changes in the corporate tax law allowed firms to deduct the full value of computer hardware from profits to avoid the potential failures caused by the Y2K problem. What effect should the change have had on the desired capital stock and on investment in 1999? Draw a graph and illustrate your answer. Should the change have stimulated the economy in 1999?

Solving the Problem

Step 1 **Review the chapter material.** The problem asks you to use the theory of investment to determine the effect of a change in the tax treatment of depreciation, so you may want to review the section "Factors That Determine Private Investment," which begins on page 508.

Step 2 **Determine the effect on the desired capital stock, and draw a graph to illustrate your answer.** Allowing firms to deduct 100% of investment spending from taxable income reduced the tax rate on investment projects for the year 1999 from t_1 to t_2. As a result, the tax-adjusted user cost of capital in 1999 decreased from uc_1 to uc_2. Your graph should show that the tax-adjusted user cost of capital shifts down and that the desired capital stock increases:

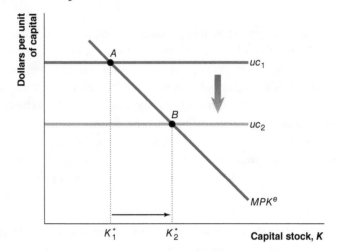

Step 3 **Explain whether this tax provision helped to stimulate the economy.** The equation for investment on page 513 tells us how investment spending is related to the desired capital stock:

$$I_t = z(K_t^* - K_{t-1}) + dK_{t-1}.$$

The increase in the desired capital stock means that the gap between the desired capital stock and the previous period's capital stock, $(K_t^* - K_{t-1})$, has increased. As a result, firms will increase investment spending today in order to increase the capital stock toward the desired level.

The model for investment spending tells us that increasing the amount of investment that firms can deduct from taxable income should lead to an increase in investment spending. Increased investment should have resulted in increased output and employment in 1999. But allowing firms to increase the amount of investment that is deductible from taxable income will also increase the government's budget deficit. Policymakers weigh any short-run benefits from a change in tax laws against the long-run costs. Furthermore, a temporary tax incentive leads to a reallocation of investment over time: The number of computers purchased by businesses in 2000 was lower than it would have been in the absence of the temporary incentive.

See related Problems 3.8 at the end of the chapter.

Tobin's *q*: Another Framework for Explaining Investment

Tobin's *q* The ratio of the market value of a firm to the replacement cost of its capital.

Nobel Laureate James Tobin of Yale University developed a theory that linked the level of investment to the stock market.[6] **Tobin's *q*** is the ratio of the market value of a firm to the replacement cost of its capital:

$$q = \frac{\text{Market value of the firm}}{\text{Replacement cost capital}}.$$

(16.9)

---

[6]James Tobin, "A General Equilibrium Approach to Monetary Theory," *Journal of Money, Credit, and Banking* 1, no. 1 (1969): 15–29.

In this equation, the market value of the firm equals the price per share of the firm's stock multiplied by the number of shares of stock. For example, Apple Inc. had about 6 billion shares outstanding, and it traded for about $115 per share in November 2014, so the market value of Apple was approximately $115 × 6 billion = $690 billion. The replacement cost of capital equals what it would cost to purchase the firm's current stock of capital goods. If Apple owns a building that would cost $100 million to build, then the replacement cost for the building is $100 million. Apple's capital stock was worth about $90 billion, so calculating Tobin's q, we get $690 billion/$90 billion = 7.7. That is, the market valued Apple's capital as being almost eight times more than it would cost Apple to purchase the capital.

A firm's *q value* is a signal from participants in financial markets about whether it is profitable for the firm to acquire more capital goods and use them to expand production. If the value of Tobin's q is greater than 1, the market value of a firm is greater than the cost to the firm of acquiring capital. So, you would expect to see the firm increase its capital stock when Tobin's q is greater than 1. In our example, Tobin's q is 7.7 for Apple, so the market is sending a very strong signal to Apple to invest in more capital goods. Similarly, if Tobin's q is less than 1, the market value of the firm is less than its replacement cost, so the signal from financial markets is that the firm should decrease its capital stock. Therefore, you would expect investment to decrease at a firm with a Tobin's q of less than 1.

The Tobin's q model links investment to fluctuations in stock prices. If expected future profits increase, the price of a share of stock will increase, raising the market value of the firm and Tobin's q. As a result, the firm may increase investment. The emphasis that the Tobin's q model places on expected future profitability is very similar to the emphasis on the expected marginal product of capital in our earlier discussion.

Stock prices are volatile because expectations about future profitability of firms are also volatile. When expectations about future profits decrease substantially, there is a decrease in Tobin's q, which can cause firms to decrease investment. Similarly, when expectations about future profits increase, there is an increase in Tobin's q, and in the level of investment. So, if investors' expectations of the future profitability of firms are volatile, investment will also be volatile, as Figure 16.5 on page 509 shows.

Credit Rationing and the Financial Accelerator

The model of investment assumes that firms undertake all profitable investment opportunities. If a firm has enough funds on hand, it pays for an investment project with those resources. Otherwise, the firm borrows the funds. But just as financial markets do not work perfectly for households, financial markets do not work perfectly for firms. Asymmetric information exists, so some firms may not be able to borrow the funds to finance all profitable investment projects. These firms are credit rationed.

Credit rationing exists because banks and other lenders cannot perfectly observe the financial condition of firms or the willingness of firms to repay loans. To avoid making loans to firms that cannot repay them, banks require firms to post collateral. During recessions, the value of collateral and corporate profits decreases, so firms have more difficulty financing new investment projects. In addition, banks often tighten their lending requirements. The presence of credit rationing suggests that investment depends on the state of the economy. Ben Bernanke, Mark Gertler, and Simon Gilchrist call the dependence of investment on the state of the economy the *financial accelerator*.[7]

---

[7]Ben Bernanke, Mark Gertler, and Simon Gilchrist, "The Financial Accelerator and the Flight to Quality," *Review of Economics and Statistics* 78, no. 1 (1996): 1–15.

Because financing constraints become more binding during recessions, the financial accelerator can worsen economic downturns. As a result, the financial accelerator provides an additional explanation for why investment is as volatile as shown in Figure 16.5 on page 509.

Uncertainty and Irreversible Investment

Ben Bernanke, the former chair of the U.S. Federal Reserve, has argued that some of the volatility of investment comes from investment projects being irreversible.[8] That is, once an investment project is finished, it is hard for a firm to use the fixed capital for another activity. For example, if Magna builds an automobile factory in Ontario, Magna or another firm would have difficultly using that factory to produce other goods. In addition to the irreversible nature of most investment projects, useful information about the profitability of an investment project arrives over time. If the market for automobiles collapses after Magna builds a factory, then the value of the factory will decline sharply.

Magna does not have to build the factory today; it has the option of waiting until it has acquired more useful information about the profitability of the factory. But the sooner Magna builds the factory, the sooner the factory will start producing parts for automobiles and potentially start adding to the firm's profits. Firms trade off the benefit of receiving profits earlier by starting an investment project today against the benefit of waiting to acquire more information, thereby potentially avoiding losses if the economy enters a recession.

Suppose there is an increase in uncertainty about the future price of output, the future price of inputs, future interest rates, or regulation. In that case, the value to firms of waiting to acquire additional information also increases, and current investment is likely to decrease. When aggregate shocks such as oil price increases, changes in monetary policy, or changes in housing prices occur, the value of waiting to obtain more information increases. As a result, some firms may postpone investment projects, thereby magnifying the initial effect of the shock. The fact that investments are irreversible and can be delayed makes investment more volatile.

---

[8]Ben Bernanke, "Irreversibility, Uncertainty, and Cyclical Investment," *Quarterly Journal of Economics* 98, no. 1 (1983): 85–106.

Key Terms and Problems

Key Terms

Animal spirits, p. 509

Consumption Smoothing, p. 497

Decreasing marginal utility of consumption, p. 497

Desired capital stock, p. 509

Intertemporal budget constraint, p. 498

Life-cycle hypothesis, p. 499

Liquidity constraints, p. 503

Permanent income, p. 499

Permanent-income hypothesis, p. 499

Precautionary saving, p. 505

Tax-adjusted user cost of capital, *uc*, p. 510

Tobin's *q*, p. 514

Transitory income, p. 499

User cost of capital, p. 510

16.1 **The Macroeconomic Implications of Microeconomic Decision Making: Intertemporal Choice**

Discuss the macroeconomic implications of microeconomic decision making by households and firms.

Review Questions

1.1 Explain what economists mean when they characterize households and firms as forward looking.

1.2 Describe the relative volatility of investment and consumption.

Problems and Applications

1.3 Loose lending standards in the years before the Great Recession allowed some risky borrowers to obtain loans. What would you expect to happen to lending standards in the wake of the Great Recession, and how might this affect consumers' ability to allocate spending over time?

1.4 Briefly explain whether you agree with the following statement: "A firm would never increase investment during a recession if its sales are currently very low."

 16.2 **Factors That Determine Consumption**

Explain the determinants of personal consumption.

Review Questions

2.1 Write the equation for the intertemporal budget constraint. How does the intertemporal budget constraint change when there are taxes? Why might the intertemporal consumption choices of credit-rationed households be inefficient?

2.2 Explain Milton Friedman's permanent-income hypothesis and Franco Modigliani's life-cycle hypothesis. How are these hypotheses similar to one another, and how are they different?

2.3 Describe the income and substitution effects of a rise in the real interest rate.

2.4 Briefly explain why the marginal propensity to consume out of transitory income is different from the marginal propensity to consume out of permanent income.

Problems and Applications

2.5 For each of the following scenarios, explain the expected effect on consumption.

a. Housing prices rise.

b. The government increases personal income taxes.

c. Uncertainty about the economy causes the desired level of saving to increase.

d. A tax cut that was expected to be temporary becomes permanent.

2.6 [Related to Solved Problem 16.1 **on page 505**] Suppose that you expect to work for another 50 years and then live 20 years in retirement. You have no wealth, and there are no taxes. You want to smooth consumption over your lifetime, and you will earn $75 000 per year.

a. Calculate consumption in each period.

b. Now assume that you unexpectedly receive an inheritance of $500 000. How will your consumption change?

c. The government decides to tax you $15 000 per year. What is your new level of consumption? [Assume that you still receive the inheritance in part (b).]

d. How would your consumption change if the government cut taxes this year from $15 000 to $10 000, but taxes next year and in the future return to $15 000 per year? [Assume that you still receive the inheritance in part (b).]

2.7 Some economists advocate a change from an income tax to a consumption tax, such as the HST. A consumption tax makes consumption more expensive and so encourages households to save. How would such a change, all other things being equal, affect each of the following?

a. Current consumption

b. Current saving

MyEconLab Visit **www.myeconlab.com** to complete these exercises online and get instant feedback.

c. Capital formation

d. Future GDP

2.8 [Related to the Chapter Opener **on page 494**] In January 2008 the GST was reduced from 6% to 5%. The tax cut was expected to stimulate the economy in 2008.

    a. Is it possible that expectations of the tax cut can decrease consumption spending in 2007?

    b. What was the effect, in your view, of the expected change in the GST on consumer savings in 2007 and in 2008?

2.9 [Related to Solved Problem 16.1 **on page 505**] Suppose you are currently 25 years old, your wealth is zero, you will retire at age 55, after working at a constant salary of $150 000, and you expect to live to age 85. Use the life-cycle hypothesis to answer the following questions. Assume that you completely smooth consumption.

a. What is your lifetime income?

b. What is your yearly consumption?

Now assume that you receive a one-time signing bonus of $30 000 when you first accept your job.

c. What is your lifetime income?

d. What is your yearly consumption?

e. What is the *MPC* out of the transitory increase in your income?

Now assume that the signing bonus specified above is a yearly bonus that you will receive each year you are employed.

f. What is your lifetime income?

g. What is your yearly consumption?

h. What is the *MPC* out of the permanent yearly increase in your income?

Factors That Determine Private Investment

Explain the determinants of private investment.

Review Questions

3.1 How does a firm decide on its desired level of capital?

3.2 How do corporate taxes affect the desired level of the capital stock? Explain how the desired level of the capital stock determines the level of investment.

3.3 What is Tobin's *q*, and how does it link financial markets to investment?

3.4 Explain how credit rationing and the financial accelerator can account for the volatility of investment.

Problems and Applications

3.5 For each of the following scenarios, use a graph to show how the firm's desired capital stock is likely to change.

    a. Technological change increases the productivity of capital.

    b. The Bank of Canada decreases interest rates, while the inflation rate is unchanged.

    c. The real price of capital goods decreases.

d. The economy is expected to remain in recession for several years.

3.6 Suppose that the real interest rate is 5%, the depreciation rate is 8%, the real price of capital is $10, and the tax rate is 10%.

    a. Calculate the tax-adjusted user cost of capital.

    b. Calculate the tax-adjusted user cost of capital if the depreciation rate increases to 10%.

    c. Return to the original depreciation rate of 8% and calculate the tax-adjusted user cost of capital if the tax rate falls to 6%.

3.7 In 2009, the stock market value of most firms was lower than it was in 2006.

    a. Why would the market value of most firms have fallen?

    b. The growth rate of non-residential investment steadily fell from 4.0% in the first quarter of 2008 to −19% in the second quarter of 2009. Is this decline consistent with Tobin's *q* model of investment? Briefly explain.

3.8 **[Related to** Solved Problem 16.2 **on page 513]** The following graph shows the marginal product of capital and the (tax-adjusted) user cost of capital. Assume that the economy is currently at point *A*, with the capital stock equal to K_1^*

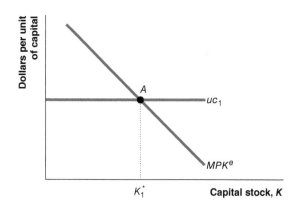

a. All other things being equal, how would you expect Bank of Canada policy that increases the money supply to change the (tax-adjusted) user cost of capital? What effect would you expect this change in the (tax-adjusted) user cost of capital to have on investment and the capital stock in the short run? Show your answer on the graph.

b. Now return to the original graph and suppose that there is an improvement in technology that makes capital more productive. How would the productivity increase change investment and the capital stock in the short run? Show your answer on the graph.

3.9 John Maynard Keynes described firms as having "animal spirits," meaning that they often make decisions based on emotion as much as on more objective factors.

a. How might animal spirits explain the volatility of investment relative to consumption?

b. Are consumers also sometimes motivated by emotion? If so, why isn't consumption more volatile?

Data Exercises

D16.1: Using the St. Louis Federal Reserve Bank's FRED database (http://research.stlouisfed.org/fred2/), examine the differences in consumption behaviour between the United Kingdom and the United States.

a. Download annual data from 1955 to the present on nominal private final consumption expenditure in the United Kingdom (GBRPFCEADSMEI) and the United States (USAPFCEADSMEI). For the same time period, download annual data on nominal GDP for the United Kingdom (GBRGDPNADSMEI) and the United States (USAGDPNADSMEI).

b. Calculate consumption's share of GDP for both the United Kingdom and the United States. Plot the two series on a graph.

c. What differences and similarities do you see in the two data series?

D16.2: [Spreadsheet exercise] For Canada, the chapter showed that consumption is less volatile than GDP but that investment is more volatile than GDP. Using the St. Louis Federal Reserve Bank's FRED database (http://research.stlouisfed.org/fred2/), examine the behaviour of consumption and investment spending in Japan.

a. For 1994 to the present, download quarterly data on real private final consumption (JPNPFCEQDSNAQ), real gross fixed capital formation (JPNGFCFQDSNAQ), and real GDP (JPNRGDPQDSNAQ) for Japan.

b. Calculate the compound annual growth rate for each quarter for all three data series. Economists often use the standard deviation as a measure of volatility. Calculate the standard deviation for all three series of growth rates.

c. Is consumption more or less volatile than GDP? Is this result consistent with consumption smoothing? Explain. Is investment more or less volatile than GDP?

d. The growth rate of real GDP is one measure of the business cycle. Is the behaviour of consumption and investment over the business cycle similar or different from Canada. Briefly explain.

D16.3: Both the permanent-income hypothesis and the life-cycle hypothesis predict that consumption is less volatile than income. Using Statistics Canada (http://www5.statcan.gc.ca/cansim/home-accueil?lang=eng) data, CANSIM Table 380-0064, evaluate this prediction for Canada.

a. Download quarterly data for Household final consumption expenditure and Gross domestic product at market prices from 1981 to the present and calculate the compound average annual growth rates for both data series.

b. Economists often measure the volatility of a data series using the standard deviation. Calculate the standard deviation of both consumption and GDP.

c. Are the results in part (b) consistent with the permanent-income hypothesis and the life-cycle hypothesis? Briefly explain.

Glossary

Adaptive expectations: The assumption that people make forecasts of future values of a variable using only past values of the variable. *(p. 340)*

Adjustable rate mortgage (ARM) A mortgage in which the initial interest rate (called the teaser rate) is low. After a few years the rate is increased upwards, to a significantly higher level. *(p. 27)*

Adverse selection A situation in which one party to a transaction takes advantage of knowing more than the other party. *(p. 79)*

Aggregate demand (*AD*) curve A curve that shows the relationship between the aggregate price level and the total amount of expenditure on domestically produced goods and services. *(p. 283)*

Aggregate demand and aggregate supply (*AD–AS*) model A model that explains short-run fluctuations in the output gap and the inflation rate. *(p. 448)*

Aggregate production function An equation that shows the relationship between the inputs employed by firms and the maximum output firms can produce with those inputs. *(p. 206)*

Aggregate supply (*AS*) curve A curve that shows the total quantity of output, or real GDP, that firms are willing and able to supply at a given inflation rate. *(p. 444)*

Aggregate supply shock A large, widespread shock that results in a change to firms' costs of production. *(p. 285)*

Animal spirits Periods of irrational pessimism and optimism that affect the investment behaviour of firms. *(p. 509)*

Arbitrage Taking advantage of price differences across markets by buying a product in one market and reselling it in another market at a higher price. *(p. 163)*

Asset Anything of value owned by a person or a firm. *(p. 71)*

Asymmetric information A situation in which one party to an economic transaction has better information than does the other party. *(p. 79)*

Automatic stabilizers Taxes, transfer payments, or government expenditures that automatically increase or decrease along with the business cycle. *(p. 413)*

Autonomous expenditure Spending that is independent of income. *(p. 280)*

Balance of payments A record of a country's trade with other countries in goods, services, and assets. *(p. 146)*

Balanced growth A situation in which the capital–labour ratio and real GDP per worker grow at the same constant rate. *(p. 245)*

Bank panic A situation in which many banks simultaneously experience rapid deposit withdrawals. *(p. 84)*

Bank run A situation in which depositors who have lost confidence in a bank simultaneously withdraw their money. *(p. 83)*

Barter Direct exchange of one good or service for another. *(p. 105)*

Bond A financial security issued by a corporation or government that represents a promise to repay a fixed amount of funds with interest. *(p. 71)*

Budget deficit The situation in which the government's expenditure is greater than its tax revenue. *(p. 414)*

Budget surplus The situation in which the government's expenditure is less than its tax revenue. *(p. 414)*

Business cycle Alternating periods of economic expansion and economic recession. *(p. 2)*

Capital accumulation The change in the capital stock over time. *(p. 231)*

Capital goods Machines, machine tools, factories, and office buildings that are used to produce other goods and services. *(p. 44)*

Capital–labour ratio The dollar value of capital goods per unit of labour; measured as the dollar value of capital divided by the total number of workers. *(p. 217)*

Central bank credibility The degree to which households and firms believe the central bank's announcements about future policy. *(p. 458)*

Central bank reaction function A rule or formula that a central bank uses to set interest rates in response to changing economic conditions. *(p. 438)*

Classical dichotomy The assertion that in the long run, *nominal* variables (such as the money supply or the price level), do not affect *real* variables (such as the levels of employment or real GDP). *(p. 104)*

Classical economics The perspective that business cycles can be explained using equilibrium analysis. *(p. 265)*

Closed economy An economy in which households, firms, and governments do not borrow, lend, or trade internationally. *(p. 144)*

Cobb–Douglas production function A widely used macroeconomic production function that takes the form $Y = AK^\alpha L^{1-\alpha}$. *(p. 206)*

Commodity money A good used as money that has value independent of its use as money. *(p. 106)*

Constant returns to scale A property of a production function such that if all inputs increase by the same percentage, *z*, real GDP increases by the same percentage. *(p. 207)*

Consumer price index (CPI) An average of the prices of the goods and services purchased by consumers. *(p. 54)*

Consumption The purchase of new goods and services by households. *(p. 48)*

Consumption smoothing A tendency of households to consume an equal amount over time. *(p. 497)*

Contagion The process of spreading the financial panic affecting a small number of institutions to other financial institutions and to the entire financial system. *(p. 84)*

Core inflation A measure of consumer price inflation used by the Bank of Canada, which excludes the most volatile CPI components. *(p. 57)*

Countercyclical variable An economic variable that moves in the opposite direction to real GDP—decreasing during expansions and increasing during recessions. *(p. 277)*

Crowding out The reduction in private investment that results from an increase in government purchases. *(p. 171)*

Currency appreciation An increase in the market value of one country's currency relative to another country's currency when the exchange rate is not fixed. *(p. 149)*

Currency depreciation A decrease in the market value of one country's currency relative to another country's currency, when the exchange rate is not fixed. *(p. 149)*

Currency devaluation A decrease in the market value of one country's currency relative to another country's currency when the exchange rate is fixed. *(p. 159)*

Currency overvaluation (undervaluation) Overvaluation (undervaluation) is a situation in which, at the current exchange rate, the real exchange rate is higher (lower) than one. *(p. 160)*

Currency revaluation An increase in the market value of one country's currency relative to another country's currency when the exchange rate is fixed. *(p. 159)*

Current account The part of the balance of payments that records a country's net exports, net investment income, and net transfers. *(p. 146)*

Cyclical unemployment Unemployment caused by the business cycle, measured as the difference between the actual rate of unemployment and the natural rate of unemployment. *(p. 192)*

Cyclically adjusted (structural) budget deficit or surplus The deficit or surplus in the federal government's budget if real GDP equaled potential GDP; also called the full-employment budget deficit or surplus. *(p. 414)*

Decreasing marginal utility of consumption The property that each additional unit of consumption yields less extra satisfaction than the previous unit of consumption. *(p. 497)*

Default risk The risk that the borrower will default on the bond. *(p. 94)*

Deflation A sustained decrease in the price level. *(p. 9)*

Deleveraging The reduction of leverage. For financial institutions it is achieved by reducing lending; for households it is achieved by reducing spending and repaying loans. *(p. 31)*

Depreciation rate The rate at which the capital stock declines due to either capital goods becoming worn out by use or becoming obsolete. *(p. 232)*

Desired capital stock The level of the capital stock that maximizes a firm's profits. *(p. 509)*

Desired reserves The reserves a bank would like to hold. *(p. 115)*

Diminishing marginal product Each additional unit of input (capital or labour) raises output by less than the previous unit. *(p. 208)*

Discretionary fiscal policy Government policy that involves deliberate changes in taxes, transfer payments, or government purchases to achieve macroeconomic policy objectives. *(p. 413)*

Discretionary policy Policy conducted in whatever way is believed at the moment best to achieve goals. *(p. 461)*

Disposable income National income plus transfer payments minus personal tax payments. *(p. 50)*

Efficiency wage A higher-than-market wage that a firm pays to motivate workers to be more productive and to increase profits. *(p. 197)*

Employment insurance (EI) A government program that allows workers to receive benefits for a period of time when they are unemployed. *(p. 190)*

Endogenous growth theory A theory of economic growth that tries to explain the growth rate of technological change. *(p. 248)*

Endogenous variable A variable that is explained by an economic model. *(p. 16)*

Exchange rate system An agreement among countries about how exchange rates should be determined. *(p. 153)*

Exogenous variable A variable that is taken as given and is not explained by an economic model. *(p. 16)*

Expansion The period of a business cycle during which real GDP and employment are increasing. *(p. 265)*

Factors of production Capital, labour, and land used to produce goods and services. *(p. 44)*

Fiat money Money, such as paper currency, that has no value apart from its use as money. *(p. 108)*

Final goods and services Goods and services that are produced for purchase by the ultimate user and not used as input for the production of other goods. *(p. 43)*

Financial account The part of the balance of payments that records purchases of assets a country has made abroad and foreign purchases of assets in the country. *(p. 146)*

Financial asset A financial claim on someone to pay you money. *(p. 71)*

Financial crisis A significant disruption in the flow of funds from lenders to borrowers. *(p. 11)*

Financial intermediary A firm, such as a commercial bank, that borrows funds from savers and lends them to borrowers. *(p. 72)*

Financial market A place or channel for buying or selling stocks, bonds, or other financial securities. *(p. 71)*

Financial securities Tradeable financial assets that can be bought and sold. *(p. 71)*

Financial system The financial intermediaries and financial markets that together facilitate the flow of funds from lenders to borrowers. *(p. 71)*

Fiscal policy Changes in government taxes and purchases that are intended to achieve macroeconomic policy objectives. *(p. 11)*

Fisher effect The assertion by Irving Fisher that the nominal interest rate rises or falls point-for-point with changes in the expected inflation rate. *(p. 126)*

Fisher equation The equation stating that the nominal interest rate is the sum of the expected real interest rate and the expected inflation rate. *(p. 126)*

Fixed exchange rate system A system in which exchange rates are set at levels determined and maintained by government or central bank. *(p. 153)*

Floating exchange rate system A system in which the foreign-exchange value of currency is determined in the foreign exchange market. *(p. 153)*

Foreign direct investment Investment into production or firms by foreigners, either by setting up or expanding firms, or by purchasing companies. *(p. 147)*

Foreign portfolio investment The purchase of financial assets such as stocks or bonds by foreigners. *(p. 147)*

Forward exchange rate The exchange rate used to exchange currencies in the future. *(p. 149)*

Forward guidance The central bank's commitment about future behaviour of the policy rate, an unconventional monetary policy. *(p. 385)*

Frictional unemployment Short-term unemployment that arises from the process of matching the job skills of workers to the requirements of jobs. *(p. 190)*

GDP deflator A measure of the price level, calculated by dividing nominal GDP by real GDP and multiplying by 100. *(p. 52)*

Governing Council The governing board of the Bank of Canada, consisting of the governor, senior deputy governor, and four deputy governors. *(p. 367)*

Government expenditures The sum of government purchases, transfer payments, and interest payments on government debt. *(p. 49)*

Government purchases Spending by federal, provincial, and local governments on newly produced goods and services. *(p. 49)*

Great Recession The recession that started in the U.S. in 2007 and spread around the world. Also called the Global Financial Crisis. The most severe recession in many countries since the Great Depression (1929–1933). *(p. 1)*

Gross domestic product (GDP) The market value of all final goods and services produced in a country during a period of time, usually a year. *(p. 43)*

Gross federal debt The total dollar value of government bonds outstanding plus superannuation (pensions) owed by the federal government as an employer to its employees plus accounts and interest payable. *(p. 416)*

Gross national product (GNP) The value of final goods and services produced by residents of a country, even if the production takes place outside that country. *(p. 44)*

Human capital The accumulated knowledge and skills that workers acquire from education and training or from life experiences. *(p. 219)*

Impact lag The period of time between a policy change and the effect of that policy change. *(p. 387)*

Implementation lag The period of time between when policymakers recognize that a shock has occurred and when they adjust policy to the shock. *(p. 387)*

Indexation Increasing dollar values to protect their purchasing power against inflation. *(p. 54)*

Inflation rate The percentage increase in the price level from one year to the next. *(p. 9)*

Inflation tax The loss of purchasing power of money due to inflation. *(p. 129)*

Insolvency The situation in which the value of a bank's or another firm's assets declines to less than the value of its liabilities, leaving it with negative net worth. *(p. 84)*

Interest parity condition The proposition that differences in interest rates on similar bonds in different countries reflect investors' expectations of future changes in exchange rates. *(p. 166)*

Interest rate The cost of borrowing funds, usually expressed as a percentage of the amount borrowed. *(p. 58)*

Interest-rate risk The risk that the price of a financial asset will fluctuate in response to changes in market interest rates. *(p. 95)*

Intertemporal budget constraint A budget constraint that applies to consumption and income in more than one time period; it shows how much a household can consume, given lifetime income. *(p. 498)*

Investment Spending by firms on new factories, office buildings, machinery, and net additions to inventories, plus spending by households and firms on new houses. *(p. 48)*

IS curve A curve in the *IS–MP* model that shows the combinations of the real interest rate and aggregate output that represent equilibrium in the market for goods and services. *(p. 296)*

IS–LM model A macroeconomic model which assumes that the central bank targets the money supply. *(p. 324)*

IS–MP model A macroeconomic model consisting of an *IS* curve, which represents equilibrium in the goods market; an *MP* curve, which represents monetary policy; and a Phillips curve, which represents the short-run relationship between the output gap and the inflation rate. *(p. 296)*

Job-finding rate The percentage of unemployed workers who find a job in a given period. *(p. 192)*

Job-separation rate The percentage of employed workers who separate from a job (lose it or quit) in a given period. *(p. 193)*

Keynesian economics The perspective that business cycles represent disequilibrium or non-market-clearing behaviour. *(p. 265)*

Labour force The sum of employed and unemployed workers in the economy. *(p. 7)*

Labour force participation rate The proportion of people 15 years old and over who are in the labour force. *(p. 61)*

Labour productivity The quantity of goods and services that can be produced by one worker or by one hour of work. *(p. 3)*

Labour-augmenting technological change Improvements in economic efficiency that increase the productivity of labour but that do not directly make capital goods more efficient. *(p. 242)*

Law of one price The notion that identical products should sell for the same price everywhere, including in different countries, as long as they are freely tradeable. *(p. 163)*

Leverage A measure of how much debt an investor takes on when making an investment. *(p. 27)*

Life-cycle hypothesis The theory that households use financial markets to borrow and save to transfer funds from high-income periods, such as working years, to low-income periods, such as retirement years or periods of unemployment. *(p. 499)*

Liquidity The ease of selling an asset without affecting its price. *(p. 94)*

Liquidity constraints The inability to borrow to achieve the desired level of consumption. *(p. 503)*

Liquidity of an asset The ease of using the asset as payment in a transaction. *(p. 105)*

LM curve A curve that shows the combinations of the real interest rate and output that result in equilibrium in the money market. *(p. 324)*

Long-run aggregate supply (LRAS) curve A curve that shows the relationship between the aggregate price level and the quantity of real GDP that firms produce in the long run when prices and wages are flexible. *(p. 284)*

Long-run economic growth The process by which increasing productivity raises the average standard of living. *(p. 3)*

M1+ A narrow measure of the money supply. Currency outside banks plus chequable deposits at chartered banks and other financial institutions. *(p. 112)*

M2+ A broad measure of the money supply. M1+ plus non-chequable and personal term deposits at chartered banks and other financial institutions. *(p. 112)*

Macroeconomic shock An exogenous, positive or negative event that has a significant effect on an important sector of the economy or on the economy as a whole. *(p. 266)*

Macroeconomics The study of the economy as a whole, including topics such as inflation, unemployment, and economic growth. *(p. 2)*

Managed floating exchange rate system A system in which private buyers and sellers in the foreign exchange market determine the value of currencies most of the time, with occasional central bank intervention. *(p. 154)*

Marginal product of capital (*MPK*) The extra output a firm receives from adding one more unit of capital, holding all other inputs and efficiency constant. *(p. 208)*

Marginal product of labour (*MPL*) The extra output a firm receives from adding one more unit of labour, holding all other inputs and efficiency constant. *(p. 182)*

Marginal propensity to consume (*MPC*) The amount by which consumption spending changes when disposable income changes. *(p. 298)*

Medium of exchange Something that is generally accepted as payment for goods and services; a function of money. *(p. 109)*

Menu costs The costs to firms of changing prices due to reprinting price lists, informing customers, and angering customers; costs related to expected inflation. *(p. 128)*

Microeconomics The study of how households and firms make choices, how they interact in markets, and how the government attempts to influence their choices. *(p. 2)*

Minimum wage A legal minimum hourly wage rate that employers are required to pay employees. *(p. 198)*

Monetary aggregates Broad measures combining, on the basis of liquidity, assets that can be used in exchange. *(p. 112)*

Monetary base (or high-powered money) The sum of currency in circulation and bank reserves. *(p. 115)*

Monetary policy The actions that central banks take to manage the money supply and interest rates that are intended to achieve macroeconomic policy objectives. *(p. 11)*

Monetary rule A commitment by the central bank to follow specific and publicly announced guidelines for monetary policy. *(p. 461)*

Money multiplier A number that indicates how much the money supply increases when the monetary base increases by $1. *(p. 116)*

Money supply The quantity of assets available to households and firms to conduct transactions. *(p. 104)*

Moral hazard A situation when, after entering into a transaction, one party takes actions that make the other party to the transaction worse off. *(p. 19)*

***MP* curve** A curve in the *IS–MP* model that represents the Bank of Canada monetary policy. *(p. 296)*

Multilateral exchange rate An index in which the value of the currency is measured against the average of the country's main trading partners. *(p. 150)*

Multiplier The change in equilibrium GDP divided by the change in autonomous expenditure. *(p. 281)*

Multiplier effect A series of induced increases (or decreases) in consumption spending that results from an initial increase (or decrease) in autonomous expenditure; this effect amplifies the effect of economic shocks on real GDP. *(p. 280)*

National income accounting The rules used in calculating GDP and related measures of total production and total income. *(p. 43)*

Natural rate of unemployment The normal rate of unemployment, consisting of frictional unemployment plus structural unemployment. *(p. 192)*

Net exports The value of all exports minus the value of all imports. *(p. 49)*

Net federal debt The dollar value of gross federal debt minus government financial assets. *(p. 477)*

Nominal exchange rate The price of one country's currency in terms of another country's currency. *(p. 148)*

Nominal GDP The value of final goods and services calculated using current-year prices. *(p. 50)*

Nominal interest rate The interest rate in terms of money. *(p. 58)*

Nominal variables Variables measured in terms of money. *(p. 104)*

Normative analysis Analysis concerned with what ought to be. *(p. 17)*

Okun's law A statistical relationship between the cyclical unemployment rate and the output gap. *(p. 275)*

Open economy An economy in which households, firms, and governments borrow, lend, and trade internationally. *(p. 144)*

Open market operations The central bank's purchases and sales of securities, usually short-term government bonds, in financial markets. *(p. 115)*

Output gap The percentage deviation of real GDP from potential GDP. *(p. 273)*

Overnight rate The rate at which banks lend and borrow from each other at the end of each day; the basis for other interest rates. *(p. 367)*

Permanent income Income that households normally expect to receive each year. *(p. 499)*

Permanent-income hypothesis The hypothesis that household consumption depends on permanent income and that households use financial markets to save and borrow to smooth consumption in response to fluctuations in transitory income. *(p. 499)*

Phillips curve A curve that represents the short-run relationship between the output gap (or the unemployment rate) and the inflation rate. *(p. 296)*

Policy trilemma The hypothesis that it is impossible for a country to have exchange rate stability, monetary policy independence, and free capital flows at the same time. *(p. 400)*

Positive analysis Analysis concerned with what is. *(p. 17)*

Potential GDP The level of real GDP attained when firms are producing at capacity and labour is fully employed. *(p. 265)*

Precautionary saving Extra saving by households to protect themselves from unexpected decreases in future income due to job loss, illness, or disability. *(p. 505)*

Present value The value today of funds that will be received in the future. *(p. 89)*

Primary budget deficit (*PD*) Government purchases of goods and services plus transfer payments minus tax revenue. *(p. 475)*

Procyclical variable An economic variable that moves in the same direction as real GDP—increasing during expansions and decreasing during recessions. *(p. 277)*

Profit Total revenue minus total cost. *(p. 212)*

Purchasing power parity (PPP) The theory that, in the long run, nominal exchange rates adjust to equalize the purchasing power of different currencies. *(p. 164)*

Quantitative easing A central bank policy that attempts to stimulate the economy by buying long-term securities. *(p. 383)*

Quantity equation (or equation of exchange) An identity that states that the money supply multiplied by the velocity of money equals the price level multiplied by real GDP. *(p. 118)*

Quantity theory of money A theory about the connection between money and prices that assumes that the velocity of money is constant. *(p. 120)*

Rational expectations The assumption that people make forecasts of future values of a variable using all available information and their expectations equal optimal forecasts, given all available information. *(p. 340)*

Real exchange rate The rate at which goods and services in one country can be exchanged for goods and services in another country. *(p. 151)*

Real gross domestic product (GDP) The value of final goods and services produced during one year, adjusted for changes in the price level. *(p. 4)*

Real interest rate The interest rate in terms of goods and services; the nominal interest rate adjusted for the effects of inflation. *(p. 58)*

Real variables Variables measured in terms of goods and services. *(p. 104)*

Recession The period of a business cycle during which real GDP and employment are decreasing. *(p. 265)*

Recognition lag The period of time between when a shock occurs and when policymakers recognize that the shock has affected the economy. *(p. 387)*

Reserve requirements Regulations that require banks to hold a fraction of deposits as vault cash or deposits with the central bank. *(p. 373)*

Ricardian equivalence The theory that forward-looking households fully anticipate the future taxes required to pay off government debt, so that reductions in lump-sum taxes have no effect on the economy. *(p. 488)*

Risk The chance that the value of a financial security will change relative to what you expect. *(p. 77)*

Risk structure of interest rates The relationship among interest rates on bonds that have different characteristics but the same maturity. *(p. 93)*

Securitization The process of converting loans, and other financial assets that are not tradeable, into securities. *(p. 26)*

Seigniorage The profit from issuing money. *(p. 108)*

Shoe-leather costs The costs of inflation to households and firms from holding less money and making more frequent trips to the bank; costs related to expected inflation. *(p. 128)*

Short-run aggregate supply (SRAS) curve A curve that shows the relationship between the aggregate price level and the quantity of real GDP that firms would like to produce when the aggregate price level and wages are constant. *(p. 284)*

Solow growth model A model that explains how the long-run growth rate of the economy depends on saving, population growth, and technological change. *(p. 231)*

Spot exchange rate The current price of one country's currency for another currency, for immediate exchange. *(p. 149)*

Stagflation A combination of high inflation and recession or very slow output growth, usually resulting from a supply shock. *(p. 340)*

Steady state A long-run equilibrium in the Solow growth model. *(p. 233)*

Stock A financial security that represents a legal claim to a share in the profits and assets of a firm. *(p. 71)*

Store of value The accumulation of wealth by holding dollars or other assets that can be used to buy goods and services in the future; a function of money. *(p. 109)*

Structural unemployment Unemployment that arises from a persistent mismatch between the job skills or attributes of workers and the requirements of jobs. *(p. 191)*

Subprime mortgage A mortgage provided to a borrower with poor credit rating due to past credit problems, short employment history, or personal bankruptcy. *(p. 27)*

Sustainable fiscal policy A situation in which the debt-to-GDP ratio is constant or decreasing. *(p. 476)*

Systemically important financial institution A bank, investment bank, insurance company, or another financial institution whose failure may lead to a financial crisis. *(p. 386)*

Target for the overnight rate The main policy tool of the Bank of Canada; the interest rate the Bank of Canada would like to see in the overnight market. *(p. 367)*

Tax wedge The difference between the before-tax and after-tax return to an economic activity. *(p. 425)*

Tax-adjusted user cost of capital The after-tax expected real cost to a firm of purchasing and using an additional unit of capital during a period of time. *(p. 510)*

Taylor rule A monetary policy guideline developed by economist John Taylor for determining the target for the short-term *nominal* policy rate. *(p. 462)*

Term premium The additional interest investors require in order to be willing to buy a long-term bond rather than a comparable sequence of short-term bonds. *(p. 95)*

Term structure of interest rates The relationship among the interest rates bonds of different maturities that are otherwise similar. *(p. 93)*

Time value of money The way the value of a payment changes depending on when the payment is received. *(p. 90)*

Time-inconsistency problem The tendency of policymakers to announce one policy in advance in order to change the expectations of households and firms, and then to follow another policy after households and firms have made economic decisions based on the announced policy. *(p. 464)*

Tobin's q The ratio of the market value of a firm to the replacement cost of its capital. *(p. 514)*

Too-big-to-fail policy A policy in which the government does not allow large financial firms to fail for fear of damaging the financial system. *(p. 386)*

Total factor productivity (*TFP*) An index of the overall level of efficiency of transforming capital and labour into real GDP. *(p. 210)*

Transaction costs The costs in time or other resources of making a trade or an exchange. *(p. 105)*

Transfer payments Transfer payments by the federal government to individuals for which the government does not receive a good or service in return. *(p. 49)*

Transitory income Income that households do not expect to receive each year. *(p. 499)*

Unconventional monetary policy New tools used by central banks to stimulate the economy at the zero lower bound. *(p. 383)*

Unemployment rate The percentage of the labour force that is unemployed. *(p. 7)*

Unit of account A way of measuring value in an economy in terms of money; a function of money. *(p. 111)*

Unsustainable fiscal policy A situation in which the debt-to-GDP ratio is increasing. *(p. 477)*

User cost of capital The expected real cost to a firm of using an additional unit of capital during a period of time. *(p. 510)*

Value added The difference between the value of production and costs of supplies. *(p. 45)*

Velocity of money The average number of times that each dollar in the money supply is used to purchase goods or services in a given period. *(p. 118)*

Yield curve A curve that shows interest rate on bonds of different maturities that are otherwise similar. *(p. 93)*

Zero lower bound The inability of the central bank to reduce nominal interest rates below zero. *(p. 381)*

Index

Note: Page numbers with *f* indicate figures; those with *n* indicate notes.

Key Symbols and Abbreviations

π_t: Current inflation rate

π_t^e: Expected inflation rate

π_{Target}: Inflation target

α: Capital's share in national income

$1 - \alpha$: Labour's share in national income

A: Index of how efficiently the economy transforms capital and labour into real GDP; total factor productivity

AD: Aggregate demand curve

AE: Aggregate expenditure

AS: Aggregate supply curve

B: Government bonds

C: Personal consumption expenditures

C: Currency in circulation

CA: Current account balance

CPI: Consumer price index

D: Chequing account deposits

d: Depreciation rate

DP: Default-risk premium

$E_t = $ Nominal exchange rate today

$E_{t+1}^e = $ Expected future exchange rate

f: Rate of job finding

G: Government purchases of goods and services

g_y: Growth rate of real GDP

I: Investment or gross private domestic investment

i: Nominal interest rate

i: Investment per worker

i_D: Domestic interest rate

i_F: Foreign interest rate

i_{LT}: Long-term nominal interest rate

im: the proportion of spending on imports

IS curve: Curve that shows the combinations of the real interest rate and aggregate output that represent equilibrium in the goods market

i_{Target}: Target for the short-term nominal interest rate

K: Quantity of capital goods available to firms, or the capital stock

k: Capital per worker, or the capital–labour ratio

$k^\star$: Steady-state capital–labour ratio

L: Quantity of labour

LM curve: Curve that shows the combinations of the real interest rate and aggregate output that represent equilibrium in the money market

M: Money supply

MB: Monetary base

m: Money multiplier

$M1+$: A narrow measure of the money supply

$M2+$: A broad measure of the money supply

M: Sum of currency in circulation, C, and chequing account deposits, D

MP curve: Monetary policy curve

MPC: Marginal propensity to consume

MPK: Marginal product of capital

MPL: Marginal product of labour

n: Labour force growth rate

NCO: Net capital outflows

NCO^P: Net private capita outflows

NX: Net exports of goods and services

P: Price level

PD: Primary budget deficit

r: Real interest rate

r: Real rental price of capital

r_{LT}: Long-term real interest rate

$r^\star$: Long-run equilibrium real interest rate

rr_D: Required reserve ratio

R: Nominal rental cost of capital

R: Desired bank reserves

s: Rate of job separation

s: Saving rate

S_{Foreign}: Saving from the foreign sector

$S_{\text{Government}}$: Saving from the government

$S_{\text{Household}}$: Saving from households

s_t: Effects of a supply shock

T: Taxes

TR: Transfer payments

TSE: Term structure effect

uN: Natural rate of unemployment

u_t: Current rate of unemployment

W: Nominal wage

w: Real wage

Y: Real GDP; also national income and total income

y: Real GDP per worker

$\tilde{Y}$: Output gap

Y^D: Disposable income

Y^P: Potential GDP

Equations